BUSINESS
A Changing World

SIXTH CANADIAN EDITION

O.C. Ferrell
University of New Mexico—Albuquerqu

Geoffrey A. Hirt
DePaul University

Linda Ferrell
University of New Mexico—Albuquerque

Suzanne Iskander
Humber ITAL

Peter Mombourquette
Mount Saint Vincent University

KERENSA CLARKE

McGraw
Hill
Education

BUSINESS: A CHANGING WORLD
Sixth Canadian Edition

ISBN-13: 978-1-25-910267-7
ISBN-10: 1-25-910267-X

1 2 3 4 5 6 7 8 9 0 TCP 1 9 8 7

Printed and bound in Canada.

Care has been taken to trace ownership of copyright material contained in this text; however, the publisher will welcome any information that enables them to rectify any reference or credit for subsequent editions.

Portfolio and Program Manager: *Karen Fozard*
Group Product Manager: *Kim Brewster*
Marketing Manager: *Cathie Lefebvre*
Product Developers: *Lindsay MacDonald & Rachel Wing*
Senior Product Team Associate: *Stephanie Giles*
Supervising Editors: *Shannon Martin & Jessica Barnoski*
Photo/Permissions Editor: *Monika Schurmann*
Copy Editor: *Mike Kelly*
Plant Production Coordinator: *Sarah Strynatka*
Manufacturing Production Coordinator: *Emily Hickey*
Cover Design: *Katherine Strain*
Cover Image: *ra2 studio/Adobe Stock Image*
eBook Interior Design: *MPS Limited*
Print Interior Design: *Dave Murphy*
Composition & Page Layout: *MPS Limited*
Printer: *Transcontinental Printing Group*

DEDICATION

To SPG – S.I.

To the memory of Autumn Lea Mombourquette – P.M.

O.C. Ferrell

O.C. Ferrell is professor of management and Creative Enterprise Scholar in the Anderson School of Management, University of New Mexico. He recently served as the Bill Daniels Distinguished Professor of Business Ethics at the University of Wyoming, and the chair of the department of marketing and the Ehrhardt, Keefe, Steiner, and Hottman P. C. Professor of Business Administration at Colorado State University. He also has held faculty positions at the University of Memphis, the University of Tampa, Texas A&M University, Illinois State University, and Southern Illinois University, as well as visiting positions at Queen's University (Ontario, Canada), University of Michigan (Ann Arbor), University of Wisconsin (Madison), and University of Hannover (Germany). He has served as a faculty member for the master's degree program in marketing at Thammasat University (Bangkok, Thailand). Dr. Ferrell received his B.A. and M.B.A. from Florida State University and his Ph.D. from Louisiana State University. His teaching and research interests include business ethics, corporate citizenship, and marketing.

Dr. Ferrell is widely recognized as a leading teacher and scholar in business. His articles have appeared in leading journals and trade publications. In addition to *Business: A Changing World*, he has two other textbooks, *Marketing: Concepts and Strategies* and *Business Ethics: Ethical Decision Making and Cases*, that are market leaders in their respective areas. He also has co-authored other textbooks for marketing, management, business and society, and other business courses, as well as a trade book on business ethics. He chaired the American Marketing Association (AMA) ethics committee that developed its current code of ethics. He was the vice president of marketing education and president of the Academic Council for the AMA. Currently he is vice president of publications for the Academy of Marketing Science.

Dr. Ferrell's major focus is teaching and preparing learning material for students. He has taught the introduction to business course using this textbook. This gives him the opportunity to develop, improve, and test the book and ancillary materials on a first-hand basis. He has travelled extensively to work with students and understands the needs of instructors of introductory business courses. He lives in Albuquerque, New Mexico, and enjoys skiing, golf, and international travel.

Geoffrey A. Hirt

Geoffrey A. Hirt is currently professor of finance at DePaul University and a Mesirow Financial Fellow. From 1987 to 1997 he was chairman of the finance department at DePaul University. He teaches investments, corporate finance, and strategic planning. He developed and was director of DePaul's M.B.A. program in Hong Kong and has taught in Poland, Germany, Thailand, and Hong Kong. He received his Ph.D. in Finance from the University of Illinois at Champaign–Urbana, his M.B.A. from Miami University of Ohio, and his B.A. from Ohio-Wesleyan University. Dr. Hirt has directed the Chartered Financial Analysts Study program for the Investment Analysts Society of Chicago since 1987.

Dr. Hirt has published several books, including *Foundations of Financial Management* published by McGraw-Hill/Irwin. Now in its 13th edition, this book is used at more than 600 colleges and universities worldwide. It has been used in more than 31 countries and has been translated into more than 10 different languages. Additionally, Dr. Hirt is well known for his text, *Fundamentals of Investment Management*, also published by McGraw-Hill/Irwin, and now in its ninth edition. He plays tennis and golf, is a music lover, and enjoys travelling with his wife, Linda.

Linda Ferrell

Dr. Linda Ferrell is associate professor and Creative Enterprise Scholar in the Anderson School of Management at the University of New Mexico. She completed her Ph.D. in business administration, with a concentration in management, at the University of Memphis. She has taught at the University of Tampa, Colorado State University, University of Northern Colorado, University of

Memphis, and the University of Wyoming. She also team teaches a class at Thammasat University in Bangkok, Thailand, as well as an online business ethics certificate course through the University of New Mexico.

Her work experience as an account executive for McDonald's and Pizza Hut's advertising agencies supports her teaching of advertising, marketing management, marketing ethics, and marketing principles. She has published in the *Journal of Public Policy and Marketing, Journal of Business Research, Journal of Business Ethics, Journal of Marketing Education, Marketing Education Review, Journal of Teaching Business Ethics,* and *Case Research Journal,* and is co-author of *Business Ethics: Ethical Decision Making and Cases* (Seventh Edition) and *Business and Society* (Third Edition). She is the ethics content expert for the AACSB Ethics Education Resource Center and was co-chair of the 2005 AACSB Teaching Business Ethics Conference in Boulder, Colorado.

Dr. Ferrell is the vice president of programs for the Academy of Marketing Science, vice president of development for the Society for Marketing Advances, and a past president for the Marketing Management Association. She is a member of the college advisory board for Petco Vector. She frequently speaks to organizations on teaching business ethics, including the Direct Selling Education Foundation's training programs and AACSB International Conferences. She has served as an expert witness in cases related to advertising, business ethics, and consumer protection.

Suzanne Iskander

Suzanne S. Iskander is professor, finance and economics, at The Business School, Humber ITAL. Suzanne taught the undergraduate Introduction to Business course at the University of Guelph-Humber for many years, and using her skills as teacher, trainer, and coach, teaches finance and economics courses in both the Humber degree and diploma programs. At Humber, she currently serves as Program Coordinator for three programs, and has served as chair, Academic Council; as chair, the Sustainability Conference; and as a member of various committees, including Degree Council, Academic Framework Committee, Economics Conference Committee, Showcase Committee, Program Advisory Committee, and the Business School Scholarly and Professional Society. She participated in the Moshi-Humber Curriculum Development Workshop in Tanzania and has volunteered with DECA to enhance the business skills and education of students in Canada.

Suzanne holds an MBA from Schulich School of Business, is a holder of the Chartered Financial Analyst (CFA) designation, and has completed all qualifying exams for the Chartered Market Technician (CMT) designation. Suzanne has co-authored the Canadian editions of *Business, A Changing World,* and the *Study Guide and Workbook for Money, Banking, and Financial Markets,* and has served as contributor and subject-matter expert for numerous publications. Her previous experience in business and in the financial services industry include the position of vice president, trading for an international financial institution. To those who know her, Suzanne is a Bruce Trail hiker and a nature photographer.

Peter Mombourquette

Peter S. Mombourquette is an associate professor and chair of the department of Business and Tourism and Hospitality Management at Mount Saint Vincent University, where he teaches introduction to business, strategic management, and entrepreneurship and small business. In addition to teaching and research, Peter founded and manages the Entrepreneurship Skills Program (ESP), a highly intensive, multi-disciplinary entrepreneurship program aimed at encouraging entrepreneurship propensity among university graduates. Peter has also founded and chairs the highly successful Social Enterprise for a Day (SE4D) conference where students and community leaders learn about social enterprise and start and run social ventures. Over Peter's time as chair of the department, he has worked with his colleagues in creating an engaging environment for students and provided them with an opportunity to give back to society while learning about career opportunities. Peter has worked collaboratively to create a highly successful Learning Passport program for students, an annual Career Week, a job clubs, a mentorship program with community leaders, an annual Social Enterprise Study Tour, a quarterly newsletter, an annual sustainable business tour, and so forth. Peter was recognized for his efforts by Mount Saint Vincent University when he received the Innovative Teaching Award. Peter has also been nominated on two separate occasions by Mount Saint Vincent University for the Atlantic Canadian Leadership Award in teaching.

Peter has completed his D.B.A. from the University of Southern Queensland and previous to that he graduated with an M.B.A. from Saint Mary's University, a B.Ed. from Saint Francis Xavier University, and a B.A. from Cape Breton University. His research interests include human resource practices in small firms, teaching methodologies, student engagement, and Internet use by small and medium-sized businesses. He has published and/or presented over 45 pieces of scholarly work, co-authored seven books, and been a keynote speaker at a number of conferences. At Mount Saint Vincent University he serves on the team that is managing the implementation of the university's strategic plan, is a member of the University's Senate, chairs the Senate Committee on Teaching and Learning, is a member of the University Curriculum Planning Committee, and sits on the Pension Governance Board, the University Investment Committee, and several other boards and committees. Peter currently resides in Halifax with his wife, Amanda, and they have had the immense pleasure of having four children, their wonderful son, Jack; a beautiful baby girl, Autumn, who tragically passed away shortly before her first birthday; a young girl, April Autumn; and a baby boy, Will.

BRIEF CONTENTS

CONTENTS

PART 5
Marketing: Developing Relationships

Welcome

This new edition reflects many dynamic changes in the business environment related to how managers make decisions. It is important for students to understand how the functional areas of business have to be coordinated as the economy, technology, global competition, and consumer decision making continue to evolve. All of these changes are presented in concepts that entry-level students can understand. Our book contains all of the essentials that most students should learn in a semester. *Business: A Changing World* has, since its inception, been a concise presentation of the essential material needed to teach an introduction to business course. From our experience in teaching the course, we know that the most effective way to engage a student is by making business exciting, relevant, and current. Our teachable, from-the-ground-up approach involves a variety of media, application exercises, and subject matter, including up-to-date content supplements, boxed examples, video cases, PowerPoint presentations, and testing materials that work for entry-level business students. We have worked hard to make sure that the content of this edition is as up to date as possible in order to best reflect today's dynamic world of business. We cover major changes in our economy related to sustainability, digital marketing, and social networking.

The Sixth Canadian Edition

The Sixth Canadian Edition represents one of our most thorough revisions. This is because so many recent events and changes in the environment relate to the foundational concepts in business. Economic and financial instability have resulted in an economy sometimes called the "New Normal." This means that an introduction to business textbook has to provide adequate coverage of these changes as they relate to traditional business concepts. Businesses must adapt to be successful. Therefore, we have listened to your feedback and incorporated needed changes in content, boxes, opening and closing cases, team exercises, and other features.

In this edition we expand on our chapter on digital marketing and social networking in business, a dynamic area that continues to change the face of business. Entrepreneurs and small businesses have to be able to increase sales and reduce costs by using social networking to communicate and develop relationships with customers.

While the title of our book remains *Business: A Changing World*, we could have changed the title to *Business: A Green World*. Throughout the book, we recognize the importance of sustainability and "green" business. By using the philosophy "Reduce, reuse, and recycle," we believe every business can be more profitable and contribute to a better world through green initiatives. There are new "Going Green" boxes that cover these environmental changes. Our "Entrepreneurship in Action" boxes also discuss many innovations and opportunities to use green business for success. We have been careful to continue our coverage of global business, ethics and social responsibility, and information technology as it relates to the foundations important in an introduction to business course. Our co-author team has a diversity of expertise in these important areas.

The foundational areas of introduction to business, entrepreneurship, small business management, marketing, accounting, and finance have been completely revised. Examples have been provided to which students can easily relate. An understanding of core functional areas of business is presented so that students get a holistic view of the world of business. Box examples related to "Responding to Business Challenges," "Entrepreneurship in Action," and "Going Green" help provide real-world examples in these areas.

Our goal is to make sure that the content and teaching package for this book are of the highest quality possible. We wish to seize this opportunity to gain your trust, and we appreciate feedback to help us continually improve these materials. We hope that the real beneficiary of all of our work will be well-informed students who appreciate the role of business in society and take advantage of the opportunity to play a significant role in improving our world. As students understand how our free enterprise system operates and how we fit into the global competitive environment, they will develop the foundation for creating their own success and improving our quality of life.

Chapter-by-Chapter Changes

Chapter 1

- New Destination CEO profile on Sylvian Toutant of Davids Tea with discussion questions
- New boxed features: Consider the Following, Entrepreneurship in Action, Going Green
- Updated Team Exercise
- Updated content in "So You Want a Job in the Business World" box at the end of the chapter to offer valuable advice on a wide spectrum of business career choices
- Inclusion of numerous new examples in the text
- Expanded discussions on the Canadian economy
- Expanded discussion on the role of entrepreneurship in Canada including profiles of young entrepreneurs
- New closing case: "Apple Stores: The Future of Retail?"

Chapter 2

- Updated CEO profile on Russell Girling of TransCanada Corporation with new discussion questions
- Inclusion of multiple new in-chapter discussion cases on relevant topics to encourage student participation. Cases include "The Case of Valeant Pharmaceuticals"; "The Case of Uber in Canada"; "Is Facebook Acting Ethically by Making Billions off Your Personal Information?"; "Fracking for Natural Gas: Clean Energy Solution or Environmental Catastrophe?"; "Are Social Media Sites Fair Game for Employers?".
- Updates to content in in-chapter cases including "When Is Organic Really Organic?"; "Is Helping People Download Music and Videos Wrong?"; "Canada, the Counterfeiters' Safe Haven"; and "Are Energy Drinks Safe?"
- Updated boxed features: Going Green, Responding to Business Challenges
- Updated Team Exercise
- Updated content in "So You Want a Job in Business Ethics and Social Responsibility" box at the end of the chapter to offer valuable advice on a wide spectrum of business career choices
- Updated closing case: "Social Media and Privacy"

Chapter 3

- New Destination CEO profile on Marc Kielburger of Free the Children, with new discussion questions
- New boxed features: Consider the Following
- Updated Team Exercise
- Updated content in "So You Want a Job in Global Business" box at the end of the chapter to offer valuable advice on a wide spectrum of business career choices
- Expanded information on the relation of Canada to the global economy
- Updated information on the European financial crisis
- New closing case: "P&G Steps Up Its International Expansion"

Chapter 4

- Updated CEO profile on Heather Reisman of Chapters-Indigo, with new discussion questions
- New boxed features: Going Green, Entrepreneurship in Action, Responding to Business Challenges
- Updated Team Exercise
- Updated content in "So You Want to Start a Business" box at the end of the chapter to offer valuable advice on a wide spectrum of business career choices

- New information on IPOs, including Shopify, Spin Master, and Facebook
- New information on joint ventures, including information on Tim Hortons and Cold Stone Creamery
- Expanded discussion on mergers and acquisitions including information on Burger King and Tim Hortons, Royal Bank, TD Canada Trust, and the Bank of Nova Scotia making significant acquisitions
- New information on the role of government approval and regulations in approving acquisitions with discussion on Bell Canada's purchase of Astral Media and the purchase of Rona by Lowe's
- Updated closing case: "Canadian Acquisitions—Not as Easy as They Once Were," which discusses acquisitions in the oilsands

Chapter 5

- Updated Destination CEO profile on Kevin O'Leary of O'Leary Funds and *Dragons' Den*, with new discussion questions
- Updated boxed features: Going Green, Entrepreneurship in Action, Responding to Business Challenges
- Updated Team Exercise
- Inclusion of numerous examples of young entrepreneurs who started digital and/or social enterprises
- Updated information on advantages and disadvantages of entrepreneurship
- Numerous new examples on social media
- Expanded discussion on raising money to start a business, including a new in-chapter case on crowdfunding and peer-to-peer lending in Canada
- Updated closing case: "Finding a Niche in the Golf Apparel Business"

Chapter 6

- New Destination CEO profile on Sheryl Sandberg of Facebook, with new discussion questions
- New boxed features: Going Green, Entrepreneurship in Action, Responding to Business Challenges
- Update Team Exercise
- Updated content in "So You Want to be a Manager: What Kind?" box at the end of the chapter to offer valuable advice on a wide spectrum of business career choices
- New information on the role of vision statements, mission statements, and value in an organization
- Enhanced information pertaining to leadership
- Updated closing case: "Lululemon Practises Crisis Management and Perhaps Marketing All at the Same Time"

Chapter 7

- Updated Destination CEO profile on Galen Weston of Loblaw, with new discussion questions
- New boxed features: Going Green, Entrepreneurship in Action, Consider the Following, Responding to Business Challenges
- Updated Team Exercise
- Updated content in "So You Want in Global Business: Managing Organizational Culture, Teamwork, and Communication" box at the end of the chapter to offer valuable advice on a wide spectrum of business career choices
- New closing case: "Keurig Green Mountain Empowers Employees"

Chapter 8

- New CEO profile on Gerald Schwartz of Onex, with new discussion questions
- New boxed features: Going Green, Entrepreneurship in Action, Responding to Business Challenges
- New section on sustainability and manufacturing

- Updated Team Exercise
- Updated content in "So You Want a Job in Operations Management" box at the end of the chapter to offer valuable advice on a wide spectrum of business career choices
- New closing case: "Taco Bell Masters the Drive-Thru"

Chapter 9

- New CEO profile on Deborah Gillis of Catalyst, with new discussion questions
- New boxed features: Going Green, Responding to Business Challenges
- Updated Team Exercise
- Updated content in "So You Want Think You May be Good at Motivating a Workforce" box at the end of the chapter to offer valuable advice on a wide spectrum of business career choices
- Updated closing case: "Is It Possible Your Dog Could Increase Business Productivity?"

Chapter 10

- Updated Destination CEO profile on Jack Welch of GE, with new discussion questions
- New Going Green boxed feature
- Updated Team Exercise
- Updated content in "So You Want to Work in Human Resources" box at the end of the chapter to offer valuable advice on a wide spectrum of business career choices
- New closing case: "Recruiters Embrace Non-traditional Recruitment Methods"

Chapter 11

- Updated Destination CEO profile on Ronnen Harary and Anton Rabie of Spin Master Toys, with new discussion questions
- New and updated boxed features: Going Green, Entrepreneurship in Action, Responding to Business Challenges
- Updated information on the marketing concept and the need by consumers to be heard and engaged
- Introduction of the social media era
- Increased emphasis on the impact of social media and digital marketing
- New information on the marketing mix, including new trends emerging in pricing and place/location strategies
- New in-chapter case on market segmentation using fantasy sports and new media as the major examples
- Updated in-chapter case on the role of Yelp in business in Canada
- Updated Team Exercise
- Updated closing case: "New 'Places' Have Emerged to Sell Wedding Gowns and Rings—Helping Couples Lower Wedding Costs"

Chapter 12

- New Destination CEO profile Tobias Lütke and his company Shopify, with new discussion questions
- New and updated boxed features: Going Green, Entrepreneurship in Action
- Updated and enhanced information on pricing
- New information on the emerging trend of content marketing, including an in-chapter case on Red Bull
- Updated case on Tim Hortons increasing its cup size to make more money
- New and greatly enhanced information on the promotional mix, including in-depth coverage of digital media and social media, including new examples of Canadian companies using Facebook, LinkedIn, Pinterest, Instagram, Tumblr, Twitter, and so forth
- New material on mobile marketing
- Updated in-chapter case: "Lululemon's Unconventional Marketing"
- Updated Team Exercise
- Updated closing case: "Finding the Real Green Products"

Chapter 13

- Updated Destination CEO profile on Arlene Dickinson of Venture Communications, with new discussion questions
- New and updated boxed features: Going Green, Entrepreneurship in Action, Responding to Business Challenges
- Increased emphasis on mobile marketing, including numerous Canadian examples
- Updated and detailed discussion of digital marketing
- Updated discussion on social networking and social media
- Updated discussion on the impact of digital marketing
- New information on the legal and social issues of digital marketing
- Updated in-chapter case on Canadian company Mobovivo, the first company to produce video for iPods
- Enhanced in-chapter cases on topics such as mobile apps and Pinterest
- New Team Exercise
- New closing case: "Should Employees Use Social Media Sites at Work?"

Chapter 14

- Updated Destination CEO profile on Jack Dorsey of Twitter and Square, with new discussion questions
- New boxed features: Going Green, Entrepreneurship in Action
- Updated information on the financial information and ratios of Tim Hortons
- Significant updates to industry analysis section
- New information about accounting standards and principles
- Updated Team Exercise
- Updated content in "So You Want to be an Accountant" box at the end of the chapter to offer valuable advice on a wide spectrum of business career choices
- New closing case: "Web Retailers and Sales Tax"

Chapter 15

- New Destination CEO profile on Stephen Poloz of the Bank of Canada, with new discussion questions
- New boxed features: Going Green, Entrepreneurship in Action
- Updated Team Exercise
- Updated content in "So You're Interested in Financial Systems or Banking" box at the end of the chapter to offer valuable advice on a wide spectrum of business career choices
- Updated closing case: "Are Credit Unions a Better Deal Than Banks?"

Chapter 16

- New Destination CEO profile on Prem Watsa of Fairfax, with new discussion questions
- New boxed features: Entrepreneurship in Action, Going Green
- Expanded coverage concerning capital budgeting
- Updated Team Exercise
- Updated content in "So You Want to Work in Financial Management or Securities" box at the end of the chapter to offer valuable advice on a wide spectrum of business career choices
- Updated closing case: "Hershey Foods: Melts in Your Mouth and May Melt Your Heart"

Created from the Ground Up

Business: A Changing World was built from the ground up—that is, developed and written expressly for faculty and students who value a brief, flexible, and affordable textbook with the most up-to-date coverage available. With market-leading teaching support and fresh content and examples, *Business: A Changing World* offers just the right mix of currency, flexibility, and value that you need. What sets this book by Ferrell/Hirt/Ferrell/Iskander/Mombourquette apart from the competition is an unrivalled mixture of current content, topical depth, and the best teaching support around.

The Freshest Topics and Examples

Business: A Changing World reflects the very latest developments in the business world, from the growth of outsourcing to Asia and Southeast Asia to Toyota's business strategy. In addition, ethics continues to be a key issue, and the authors use pedagogical boxes throughout to encourage discussion about ethical conduct in business.

Just Enough of a Good Thing

It's easy for students taking their first steps into business to become overwhelmed. *Business: A Changing World* carefully builds just the right mix of coverage and application to give students a firm grounding in business principles. Instead of sprinting through the semester to get everything in, the authors allow for time to explore topics and incorporate other activities that are important to teachers and students.

Teaching Assistance That Makes a Difference

The first—and often most serious—hurdle in teaching is engaging students' interest, making them understand how textbook material plays a very real role in real business activities. The instructor's material for *Business: A Changing World* is full of helpful resources, including detailed teaching notes and additional material in the Instructor's Manual. The Instructor's Manual contains a matrix to help teachers decide which exercise to use with which chapter.

There's much more to *Business: A Changing World*, and much more it can do for the introduction to business course. To learn about this book's great pedagogical features and top-notch ancillaries, keep reading.

Getting a Handle on Business

Business: A Changing World's pedagogy helps students get the most out of their reading, from Learning Objectives at the beginning of each chapter to the Learning Objectives Summary at the end of each chapter.

Learning Objectives

These appear at the beginning of each chapter to provide goals for students to reach in their reading. The objectives are then used in the **Learning Objectives Summary** at the end of each chapter, and help the students gauge whether they've learned and retained the material.

LEARNING OBJECTIVES

After reading this chapter, you will be able to:

LO1 Define basic concepts such as business, product, and profit.

LO2 Identify the main participants and activities of business and explain why studying business is important.

LO3 Define economics and compare the four types of economic systems.

LO4 Describe the role of supply, demand, and competition in a free-enterprise system.

LO5 Specify why and how the health of the economy is measured.

LO6 Trace the evolution of the Canadian economy and discuss the role of the entrepreneur in the economy.

DESTINATION CEO

Sylvain Toutant knows beverages, having worked most recently as president of coffee distributor Keurig Canada. Prior to that, he was chief operating officer of coffee distributor Van Houtte and CEO of Quebec's liquor board. Since he joined Davids Tea in 2014, he has taken the company public. Shares of the company now trade on the Nasdaq stock market.

Davids Tea was founded by David Segal, a 28-year-old tea-loving entrepreneur, and his cousin Herschel Segal, a Canadian retail pioneer. What did they have in common? A vision: great tea, a friendly environment, and a colourful, modern store. It seemed like a simple idea, but they couldn't find anyone else that was doing it. So they decided to take matters into their own hands. With David's energy and enthusiasm and Herschel's know-how, it was the perfect balance of youth and experience.

Walk into a Davids Tea today and you can choose from over 150 types of tea, including exclusive blends, limited-edition seasonal collections, traditional straight teas, and exotic infusions from around the globe. Not to mention the largest collection of organic teas and infusions in North America.

Toutant says that tea is a big market that is growing and is very popular with millennials. In the competitive landscape, he states that tea is an evolving category and much of the tea purchased in North America is purchased in a grocery store. Specialty tea retailers compete with each other, and as tea becomes more popular, it's helping Davids Tea to carve out its own place. The company has a different approach to tea: to make tea fun and accessible. The store designs are young, open, and very design-focused. The company has continued its expansion in the United States. In 2014, the company had 130 stores in Canada and 24 in the United States.

So, why tea? The company says because it's healthy, delicious, and fun, and it brings people together, all over the world. Also because it's the second-most popular drink on the planet, second only to water. And in case you wanted to know, Toutant starts his day with his favourite tea blend: Jumpy Monkey—"roasted peaberry coffee beans with Argentine maté, and laced with almonds, white chocolate and other roasted barks and roots."[1]

Introduction

We begin our study of business by examining the fundamentals of business and economics in this chapter. First, we introduce the nature of business, including its goals, activities, and participants. Next, we describe the basics of economics and apply them to the Canadian economy. Finally, we establish a framework for studying business in this text.

Destination CEO

Each chapter opens with an introduction to a key leader in industry, by detailing each leader's personal journey, how they got to the top, and what it took to stay there.

Pedagogical Boxes

An important feature of the book is the **Consider the Following** pedagogical boxes demonstrating real-world examples to drive home the applied lessons to students. These features provide an excellent vehicle for stimulating class discussions.

Consider the Following: Why Study Business?

Studying business can help you develop skills and acquire knowledge to prepare for your future career, regardless of whether you plan to work for a multinational firm, start your own business, work for a government agency, or manage or volunteer at a non-profit organization. The field of business offers a variety of interesting and challenging career opportunities throughout the world, such as human resources management, information technology, finance, production and operations, wholesaling and retailing, and many more.

Studying business can also help you better understand the many business activities that are necessary to provide satisfying goods and services—and that these activities carry a price tag. For example, if you pay to download a song, about half of the price goes toward activities related to distribution and the studio's expenses and profit margins and only a small portion goes to the artist. Most businesses charge a reasonable price for their products to ensure that they cover their production costs, pay their employees, provide their owners with a return on their investment, and perhaps give something back to their local communities. For example, the Royal Bank of Canada (RBC) is

actively involved in supporting scholarships for university students, developing programs to help the mentally challenged, and supporting emerging artists.[9] Canadian Jeff Skoll, former president and first employee of eBay, has donated approximately $1 billion to the Skoll Foundation, an organization he founded to support a sustainable world. Skoll's foundation invests heavily in "social entrepreneurs," who can be defined as people who are using entrepreneurial skills such as creativity and risk taking to solve some of society's problems. Thus, learning about business can help you become a well-informed consumer and member of society.

Business activities help generate the profits that are essential not only to individual businesses and local economies but also to the health of the global economy. Without profits, businesses find it difficult, if not impossible, to buy more raw materials, hire more employees, attract more capital, and create additional products that in turn make more profits and fuel the world economy. Understanding how our free-enterprise economic system allocates resources and provides incentives for industry and the workplace is important to everyone.

The **Responding to Business Challenges** boxes illustrate how businesses overcome tough challenges, and many also highlight the importance of ethical conduct and how unethical conduct hurts investors, customers, and indeed the entire business world.

The **Entrepreneurship in Action** boxes spotlight successful entrepreneurs and the challenges they have faced on the road to success.

The **Going Green** boxes show how issues of sustainability affect all levels of domestic business, and these boxes encourage students to keep their eyes on how "business as usual" now includes an environmentally responsible element.

End-of-Chapter Material

The end-of-chapter material provides a great opportunity to reinforce and expand upon the chapter content.

Key Terms Important terms, highlighted in bold face throughout the text with an accompanying definition on the page, are listed in alphabetical order for ease of reference.

KEY TERMS

budget deficit
budget surplus
business
capitalism, or free enterprise
communism
competition
demand
depression
economic contraction
economic expansion
economic system
economics
equilibrium price
entrepreneur
financial resources
free-market system
gross domestic product (GDP)

human resources
inflation
mixed economies
monopolistic competition
monopoly
natural resources
non-profit organizations
oligopoly
products
profit
pure competition
recession
socialism
stakeholders
supply
unemployment

SO YOU WANT A JOB *in Business Ethics and Social Responsibility*

In the words of Kermit the Frog, "It's not easy being green." It may not be easy, but green business opportunities abound. A popular catch phrase, "Green is the new black," indicates how fashionable green business is becoming. Consumers are more in tune with and concerned about green products, policies, and behaviours by companies than ever before. Companies are looking for new hires to help them see their business creatively and bring insights to all aspects of business operations. The American Solar Energy Society estimates that the number of green jobs could rise to 40 million in North America by 2030. Green business strategies not only give a firm a commercial advantage in the marketplace, but help lead the way toward a greener world. The fight to reduce our carbon footprint in an attempt to reverse climate change has opened up opportunities for renewable energy, recycling, conservation, and increasing overall efficiency in the way resources are used. New businesses that focus on hydro, wind, and solar power are on the rise and will need talented businesspeople to lead them. Carbon emissions trading is gaining popularity as large corporations and individuals alike seek to decrease their footprints. A job in this growing field

could be similar to that of a stock trader, or you could lead the search for carbon-efficient companies in which to invest.

In the ethics arena, current trends in business governance strongly support the development of ethics and compliance departments to help guide organizational integrity. This alone is a billion-dollar business, and there are jobs in developing organizational ethics programs, developing company policies, and training employees and management. An entry-level position might be as a communication specialist or trainer for programs in a business ethics department. Eventually there's an opportunity to become an ethics officer with typical responsibilities of meeting with employees, the board of directors, and top management to discuss and advise on ethics issues in the industry; developing and distributing a code of ethics; creating and maintaining an anonymous, confidential service to answer questions about ethical issues; taking actions on possible ethics code violations; and reviewing and modifying the code of ethics of the organization.

There are also opportunities to support initiatives that help companies relate social responsibility

So You Want a Job This end-of-chapter feature offers valuable advice on a wide spectrum of business career choices.

Build Your Business Plan This end-of-chapter feature (along with Appendix A, **Business Plan Development**) helps students through the development of their business plan by relating the steps to the content of each chapter. Additional information and resources can be found in the Instructor's Manual.

BUILD YOUR BUSINESS PLAN

Business Ethics and Social Responsibility

Think about which industry you are considering competing in with your product/service. Are there any kind of questionable practices in the way the product has been traditionally sold? Produced? Advertised? Have there been any recent accusations regarding safety within the industry? What about any environmental concerns?

For example, if you are thinking of opening a lawn care business, you need to consider what possible effects the chemicals you are using will have on the client and the environment. You have a responsibility not to threaten your customers' health or safety. You also have the social responsibility to let the community know of any damaging effect you may be directly or indirectly responsible for.

Market Leading Technology

Learn without Limits

McGraw-Hill Connect® is an award-winning digital teaching and learning platform that gives students the means to better connect with their coursework, with their instructors, and with the important concepts that they will need to know for success now and in the future. With Connect, instructors can take advantage of McGraw-Hill's trusted content to seamlessly deliver assignments, quizzes, and tests online. McGraw-Hill Connect is a learning platform that continually adapts to each student, delivering precisely what they need, when they need it, so class time is more engaging and effective. Connect makes teaching and learning personal, easy, and proven.

Connect Key Features

SmartBook®   As the first and only adaptive reading experience, SmartBook is changing the way students read and learn. SmartBook creates a personalized reading experience by highlighting the most important concepts a student needs to learn at that moment in time. As a student engages with SmartBook, the reading experience continuously adapts by highlighting content based on what each student knows and doesn't know. This ensures that he or she is focused on the content needed to close specific knowledge gaps, while it simultaneously promotes long-term learning.

Connect Insight®   Connect Insight is Connect's new one-of-a-kind visual analytics dashboard—now available for instructors—that provides at-a-glance information regarding student performance, which is immediately actionable. By presenting assignment, assessment, and topical performance results together with a time metric that is easily visible for aggregate or individual results, Connect Insight gives instructors the ability to take a just-in-time approach to teaching and learning, which was never before available. Connect Insight presents data that helps instructors improve class performance in a way that is efficient and effective.

Simple Assignment Management   With Connect, creating assignments is easier than ever, so instructors can spend more time teaching and less time managing.

- Assign SmartBook learning modules.
- Edit existing questions and create your own questions.
- Draw from a variety of text specific questions, resources, and test bank material to assign online.
- Streamline lesson planning, student progress reporting, and assignment grading to make classroom management more efficient than ever.

Smart Grading   When it comes to studying, time is precious. Connect helps students learn more efficiently by providing feedback and practice material when they need it, where they need it.

- Automatically score assignments, giving students immediate feedback on their work and comparisons with correct answers.
- Access and review each response; manually change grades or leave comments for students to review.
- Track individual student performance—by question, by assignment, or in relation to the class overall—with detailed grade reports.
- Reinforce classroom concepts with practice tests and instant quizzes.
- Integrate grade reports easily with Learning Management Systems including Blackboard, D2L, and Moodle.

Instructor Library   The Connect Instructor Library is a repository for additional resources to improve student engagement in and out of the class. It provides all the critical resources instructors need to build their course.

- Access instructor resources.
- View assignments and resources created for past sections.
- Post your own resources for students to use.

Instructors' Resources

Business: A Changing World, Sixth Canadian Edition, offers a complete, integrated supplements package for instructors to address all your needs.

- **Instructor's Manual:** The Instructor's Manual, prepared by the Canadian text authors, Suzanne Iskander and Peter Mombourquette, accurately represents the text's content and supports instructors' needs. Each chapter includes the learning objectives, the glossary of key terms, a chapter synopsis, a complete lecture outline, and solutions to the end-of-chapter discussion questions.

- **EZ Test Computerized Test Bank:** This flexible and easy-to-use electronic testing program allows instructors to create tests from book-specific items. Created by Sandra Wellman, Seneca College, the test bank has undergone a rigorous auditing and revision process for the Sixth Canadian Edition. It contains a broad selection of multiple choice, true/false, and essay questions, and instructors may add their own questions as well. Each question identifies the relevant page reference and difficulty level. Multiple versions of the test can be created and printed.

- **PowerPoint™ Presentations:** Prepared by Peter Mombourquette of Mount Saint Vincent University, these robust presentations offer high-quality visuals from the text and highlight key concepts from each chapter to bring key business concepts to life.

Business Plan Pro

The Business Plan Pro is available as a bundled option that includes more than 250 sample business plans and 400 case studies to give you a wide variety of examples as you create your own plan. It helps you set up your business by answering questions that help the software customize your plan. Then you enter your financial data to generate financial worksheets and statements.

Superior Learning Solutions and Support

The McGraw-Hill Education team is ready to help instructors assess and integrate any of our products, technology, and services into your course for optimal teaching and learning performance. Whether it's helping your students improve their grades, or putting your entire course online, the McGraw-Hill Education team is here to help you do it. Contact your Learning Solutions Consultant today to learn how to maximize all of McGraw-Hill Education's resources.

For more information please visit us online: www.mheducation.ca/he/solutions.

Acknowledgements

The Sixth Canadian Edition of *Business: A Changing World* would not have been possible without the commitment, dedication, and patience of our excellent task masters and guides at McGraw-Hill Ryerson: Kim Brewster, group product manager; Lindsay MacDonald and Rachel Wing, product developers; Shannon Martin and Jessica Barnoski, supervising editors; Sarah Strynatka, production coordinator; Monika Schurmann, photo/permissions editor; and Mike Kelly, copy editor.

Many others have assisted us with their helpful comments, recommendations, and support throughout this and previous editions. We'd like to express our thanks to the following reviewers who were among the instructors who reviewed previous editions:

Glen Kobussen, St. Peter's College—University of Saskatchewan
Kayrod Niamir, Dawson College
Dustin Quirk, Red Deer College
Frank Saccucci, MacEwan University
Brian Turford, Fanshawe College

—*Suzanne Iskander and Peter Mombourquette*

The Dynamics of Business and Economics

LEARNING OBJECTIVES

After reading this chapter, you will be able to:

LO1 Define basic concepts such as business, product, and profit.

LO2 Identify the main participants and activities of business and explain why studying business is important.

LO3 Define economics and compare the four types of economic systems.

LO4 Describe the role of supply, demand, and competition in a free-enterprise system.

LO5 Specify why and how the health of the economy is measured.

LO6 Trace the evolution of the Canadian economy and discuss the role of the entrepreneur in the economy.

DESTINATION CEO

Sylvain Toutant knows beverages, having worked most recently as president of coffee distributor Keurig Canada. Prior to that, he was chief operating officer of coffee distributor Van Houtte and CEO of Quebec's liquor board. Since he joined Davids Tea in 2014, he has taken the company public. Shares of the company now trade on the Nasdaq stock market.

Davids Tea was founded by David Segal, a 28-year-old tea-loving entrepreneur, and his cousin Herschel Segal, a Canadian retail pioneer. What did they have in common? A vision: great tea, a friendly environment, and a colourful, modern store. It seemed like a simple idea, but they couldn't find anyone else that was doing it. So they decided to take matters into their own hands. With David's energy and enthusiasm and Herschel's know-how, it was the perfect balance of youth and experience.

Walk into a Davids Tea today and you can choose from over 150 types of tea, including exclusive blends, limited-edition seasonal collections, traditional straight teas, and exotic infusions from around the globe. Not to mention the largest collection of organic teas and infusions in North America.

Toutant says that tea is a big market that is growing and is very popular with millennials. In the competitive landscape, he states that tea is an evolving category and much of the tea purchased in North America is purchased in a grocery store. Specialty tea retailers compete with each other, and as tea becomes more popular, it's helping Davids Tea to carve out its own place. The company has a different approach to tea: to make tea fun and accessible. The store designs are young, open, and very design-focused. The company has continued its expansion in the United States. In 2014, the company had 130 stores in Canada and 24 in the United States.

So, why tea? The company says because it's healthy, delicious, and fun, and it brings people together, all over the world. Also because it's the second-most popular drink on the planet, second only to water. And in case you wanted to know, Toutant starts his day with his favourite tea blend: Jumpy Monkey—"roasted peaberry coffee beans with Argentine maté, and laced with almonds, white chocolate and other roasted barks and roots."[1]

Introduction

We begin our study of business by examining the fundamentals of business and economics in this chapter. First, we introduce the nature of business, including its goals, activities, and participants. Next, we describe the basics of economics and apply them to the Canadian economy. Finally, we establish a framework for studying business in this text.

The Nature of Business

A **business** tries to earn a profit by providing products that satisfy people's needs. The outcomes of its efforts are **products** that have both tangible and intangible characteristics that provide satisfaction and benefits. When you purchase a product, you are buying the benefits and satisfaction you think the product will provide. A Subway sandwich, for example, may be purchased to satisfy hunger; a Porsche Cayenne sport utility vehicle, to satisfy the need for transportation and the desire to present a certain image.

Most people associate the word *product* with tangible goods—an automobile, computer, phone, coat, or some other tangible item. However, a product can also be a service, which results when people or machines provide or process something of value to customers. Dry cleaning, a check-up by a doctor, a performance by a hockey player—these are examples of services. Some services, such as Flickr, an online photo management and sharing application, do not charge a fee for use but obtain revenue from ads on their sites. A product can also be an idea. Consultants and attorneys, for example, generate ideas for solving problems.

business individuals or organizations who try to earn a profit by providing products that satisfy people's needs

products goods or services with tangible and intangible characteristics that provide satisfaction and benefits

profit the difference between what it costs to make and sell a product and what a customer pays for it

non-profit organizations organizations that may provide goods or services but do not have the fundamental purpose of earning profits

The Goal of Business

The primary goal of all businesses is to earn a **profit**, the difference between what it costs to make and sell a product and what a customer pays for it. If a company spends $8.00 to manufacture, finance, promote, and distribute a product that it sells for $10.00, the business earns a profit of $2.00 on each product sold. Businesses have the right to keep and use their profits as they choose—within legal limits—because profit is the reward for the risks they take in providing products. Earning profits contributes to society by providing employment, which in turn provides money that is reinvested in the economy. In addition, profits must be earned in a responsible manner. Not all organizations are businesses. **Non-profit organizations**, such as the Canadian Red Cross, Special Olympics, and other charities and social causes, do not have the fundamental purpose of earning profits, although they may provide goods or services and engage in fundraising.

© McGraw–Hill Education/Mark Dierker, photographer

Seventh Generation is a leading brand of environmentally friendly household products. Its Natural 4X Laundry Detergent is packed in a bottle made from 100 percent recycled fibre.

To earn a profit, a person or organization needs management skills to plan, organize, and control the activities of the business and to find and develop employees so that it can make products consumers will buy. A business also needs marketing expertise to learn what products consumers need and want and to develop, manufacture, price, promote, and distribute those products. Additionally, a business needs financial resources and skills to fund, maintain, and expand its operations. Other challenges for businesspeople include abiding by laws and government regulations; acting in an ethical and socially responsible manner; and adapting to economic, technological, political, and social changes. Even non-profit organizations engage in management, marketing, and finance activities to help reach their goals.

To achieve and maintain profitability, businesses have found that they must produce quality products, operate efficiently, and be socially responsible and ethical in dealing with customers, employees, investors, government regulators, the community, and society. Because these groups have a stake in the success and outcomes of a business, they are sometimes called **stakeholders**. Many businesses, for example, are concerned with how stakeholders view the impact that a business's waste has on the environment. Concerns about landfills becoming high-tech graveyards plague many electronics firms. Best Buy offers recycling of electronics at all of its stores. The stores take cellphones, wide-screen TVs, and most other electronic products in their green program, regardless of where they were purchased. Other businesses are concerned about the quality of life in the communities in which they operate. For example, Starbucks Canada launched the "Opportunity Youth" program by committing to hire 10 percent of its workforce from among disadvantaged young people.[2] Petro-Canada sponsors "Stay in School" and "Future Leaders" programs aimed at Aboriginal communities. Other companies are concerned with social responsibility in times of natural disasters. After the devastating earthquake in Nepal in 2015, phone companies, including Wind Mobile, Fido, and Rogers, waived fees for long-distance calls to the Himalayan country. Other companies, such as Home Depot, have a long history of supporting natural disaster victims, relief efforts, and recovery.

The People and Activities of Business

LO2 Identify the main participants and activities of business and explain why studying business is important.

Figure 1.1 shows the people and activities involved in business. At the centre of the figure are owners, employees, and customers; the outer circle includes the primary business activities—management, marketing, and finance. Owners have to put up resources—money or credit—to start a business. Employees are responsible for the work that goes on within a business. Owners can manage the business themselves or hire employees to accomplish this task. The president of Shoppers Drug Mart, Mike Motz, does not own Shoppers, but is an employee who is responsible for managing all the other employees in a way that earns a profit for investors, who are the real owners. Finally, and most importantly, a business's major role is to satisfy the customers who buy its goods or services. Note also that people and forces beyond an organization's control—such as legal and regulatory forces, the economy, competition,

technology, and ethical and social concerns—all have an impact on the daily operations of businesses. You will learn more about these participants in business activities throughout this book. Next, we will examine the major activities of business.

Management. Notice in Figure 1.1 that management and employees are in the same segment of the circle. This is because management involves coordinating employees' actions to achieve the firm's goals, organizing people to work efficiently, and motivating them to achieve the business's goals. Geoff Molson, chairman of Molson Coors and the owner, president, and CEO of the Montreal Canadiens hockey team, recognizes the importance of management to company success. He sees his job as one that supports the role of the CEO. He believes that good strategy drives shareholder value, but that the execution of the strategy is really in the hands of management.[3] Management is also concerned with acquiring, developing, and using resources (including people) effectively and efficiently. Campbell's Soup enlists its workers to help squeeze more efficiency out of its plants. Operating efficiency comes from saving time, money, and effort.[4]

Production and manufacturing is another element of management. At Campbell's Soup, for example, a 20-person work team was created to determine how best to cut costs in some plants. In essence, managers plan, organize, staff, and control the tasks required to carry out the work of the company or non-profit organization. We take a closer look at management activities in Parts 3 and 4 of this text.

Figure 1.1 Overview of the Business World

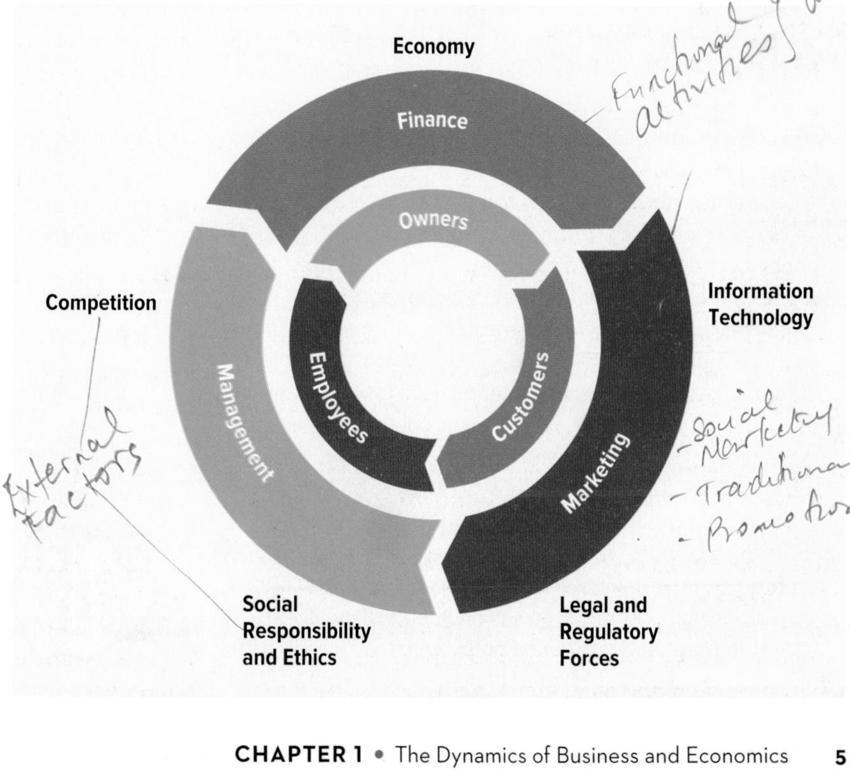

© Helen Sessions/Alamy Stock Photo

One of the most successful marketing efforts in Canada is Tim Hortons' "Roll Up the Rim to Win."

> "Managers plan, organize, staff, and control the tasks required to carry out the work of the company or non-profit organization."

Marketing. Marketing and consumers are in the same segment of Figure 1.1 because the focus of all marketing activities is satisfying customers. Marketing includes all the activities designed to provide goods and services that satisfy consumers' needs and wants. Marketers gather information and conduct research to determine what customers want. Using information gathered from marketing research, marketers plan and develop products and make decisions about how much to charge for their products and when and where to make them available. In response to an American campaign against childhood obesity, Walmart announced that it would lower the sugars, fats, and salts in its products over a five-year period. Such a response could be a smart move on Walmart's part because marketing research shows that consumers are becoming more health-conscious.[5] PepsiCo, for example, has expanded into healthier products such as Tropicana and oatmeal. CEO Indra Nooyi anticipates that healthy products will make up 30 percent of the company's product portfolio by the next decade.[6] Marketers use promotion—advertising, personal selling, sales promotion (coupons, games, sweepstakes, movie tie-ins), and publicity—to communicate the benefits and advantages of their products to consumers and increase sales. Non-profit organizations also use promotion. One of the best-known Canadian marketing initiatives of all time is Tim Hortons' "Roll Up the Rim to Win" campaign. The simple idea was developed by Tim Hortons executive Ron Buist, who says the idea was developed as a way to gain even more marketing leverage (strength) from its paper cup and to increase sales.[7] We will examine marketing activities in Part 5 of this text.

GOING GREEN | Municipal Governments Set the Standard for Green Living

Imagine if every major city reduced its greenhouse gas emissions to 80 percent of its 1990 levels within the next decade. This is the goal Toronto set forth in its Climate Action Plan. Toronto is one of 58 cities worldwide that are part of the Large Cities Climate Leadership Group (C40). Members include cities from capitalistic countries (New York City and Vancouver), socialistic countries (Paris and Stockholm), and communistic countries (Beijing and Ho Chi Minh City).

Governments intervene in the economy through regulations designed to promote competition and protect consumers, employees, and the environment. As the C40 cities demonstrate, many local governments are taking measures that surpass national regulations. Smaller regions such as municipalities can pass legislation more quickly, whereas passing federal legislation can take months or years. This is even harder in capitalistic countries where the government has less power than in socialistic and communistic nations. The green actions taken by C40 cities thus take on even greater importance.

The C40 cities are taking different steps to reduce their environmental impact. Some are passing regulations to limit certain business and consumer activities. Other moves impose fewer burdens on businesses. Toronto, for instance, has a progressive strategy to re-naturalize the mouth of the Don River and comprehensive plans for sustainable community design and flood protection. The City of Vancouver introduced an ambitious plan to become the greenest city in the world by 2020. This Greenest City 2020 Action Plan (GCAP) serves as a guide for Vancouver to achieve targets in 10 goal areas—ranging from climate leadership to zero waste and even local food. If these cities succeed in their goals, they will have a significant impact on sustainability, especially considering that they currently produce 10 percent of the world's carbon emissions.[8]

DISCUSSION QUESTIONS

1. Why might it take longer to pass sustainability laws in capitalistic nations than in socialistic or communistic nations?

2. What are some of the impacts such goals might have on business?

3. Why are such different cities agreeing to set GHG goals?

Studying business can help you develop skills and acquire knowledge to prepare for your future career, regardless of whether you plan to work for a multinational firm, start your own business, work for a government agency, or manage or volunteer at a non-profit organization. The field of business offers a variety of interesting and challenging career opportunities throughout the world, such as human resources management, information technology, finance, production and operations, wholesaling and retailing, and many more.

Studying business can also help you better understand the many business activities that are necessary to provide satisfying goods and services—and that these activities carry a price tag. For example, if you pay to download a song, about half of the price goes toward activities related to distribution and the studio's expenses and profit margins and only a small portion goes to the artist. Most businesses charge a reasonable price for their products to ensure that they cover their production costs, pay their employees, provide their owners with a return on their investment, and perhaps give something back to their local communities. For example, the Royal Bank of Canada (RBC) is

actively involved in supporting scholarships for university students, developing programs to help the mentally challenged, and supporting emerging artists.[9] Canadian Jeff Skoll, former president and first employee of eBay, has donated approximately $1 billion to the Skoll Foundation, an organization he founded to support a sustainable world. Skoll's foundation invests heavily in "social entrepreneurs," who can be defined as people who are using entrepreneurial skills such as creativity and risk taking to solve some of society's problems. Thus, learning about business can help you become a well-informed consumer and member of society.

Business activities help generate the profits that are essential not only to individual businesses and local economies but also to the health of the global economy. Without profits, businesses find it difficult, if not impossible, to buy more raw materials, hire more employees, attract more capital, and create additional products that in turn make more profits and fuel the world economy. Understanding how our free-enterprise economic system allocates resources and provides incentives for industry and the workplace is important to everyone.

Finance. Owners and finance are in the same part of Figure 1.1 because, although management and marketing have to deal with financial considerations, it is the primary responsibility of the owners to provide financial resources for the operation of the business. Moreover, the owners have the most to lose if the business fails to make a profit. Finance refers to all activities concerned with obtaining money and using it effectively. People who work as accountants, stockbrokers, investment advisors, or bankers are all part of the financial world. Owners sometimes have to borrow money from banks to get started or attract additional investors who become partners or stockholders. Owners of small businesses in particular often rely on bank loans for funding. Part 6 of this text discusses financial management.

The Economic Foundations of Business

LO3 Define economics and compare the four types of economic systems.

To continue our introduction to business, it is useful to explore the economic environment in which business is conducted. In this section, we examine economic systems,

the free-enterprise system, the concepts of supply and demand, and the role of competition. These concepts play important roles in determining how businesses operate in a particular society.

Economics is the study of how resources are distributed for the production of goods and services within a social system. The Canadian economy has many of the resources needed for the successful production of goods and services. You are already familiar with the types of resources available. Land, forests, minerals, water, and other things that are not made by people are **natural resources**. Canada has an abundance of natural resources, including vast supplies of fresh water, large areas of forest, nickel, copper, uranium, and large deposits of oil and natural gas. **Human resources**, or labour, refer to the physical and mental abilities that people use to produce goods and services. Some Canadian companies have had challenges finding enough workers in recent years, as the baby boomers,

> **economics** the study of how resources are distributed for the production of goods and services within a social system
>
> **natural resources** land, forests, minerals, water, and other things that are not made by people
>
> **human resources** the physical and mental abilities that people use to produce goods and services; also called labour

© Davewebbphoto/Dreamstime.com

Canada's abundant natural resources include vast quantities of oil.

Economic Systems

An **economic system** describes how a particular society distributes its resources to produce goods and services. A central issue of economics is how to fulfill an unlimited demand for goods and services in a world with a limited supply of resources. Different economic systems attempt to resolve this central issue in numerous ways, as we shall see.

> **economic system** a description of how a particular society distributes its resources to produce goods and services

Although economic systems handle the distribution of resources in different ways, all economic systems must address three important issues:

1. What goods and services, and how much of each, will satisfy consumers' needs?

2. How will goods and services be produced, who will produce them, and with what resources will they be produced?

3. How are the goods and services to be distributed to consumers?

who make up roughly one-third of Canada's population, retire. **Financial resources**, or capital, are the funds used to acquire the natural and human resources needed to provide products. Canadian companies are able to readily access capital. Because natural, human, and financial resources are used to produce goods and services, they are sometimes called *factors of production*. The firm can also have intangible resources such as a good reputation for quality products or being socially responsible. The goal is to turn the factors of production and intangible resources into a competitive advantage.

> **financial resources** the funds used to acquire the natural and human resources needed to provide products; also called capital

Communism, socialism, and capitalism, the basic economic systems found in the world today (Table 1.1), have fundamental differences in the way they address these issues. The factors of production in command economies are controlled by government planning. In many cases, the government owns or controls the production of goods and services. Communism and socialism are, therefore, considered command economies.

Table 1.1 Comparisons of Communism, Socialism, and Capitalism

	Communism	Socialism	Capitalism
Business ownership	Most businesses are owned and operated by the government. *eg Cuba*	The government owns and operates major industries; individuals own small businesses. *Sweeden Denmark*	Individuals own and operate all businesses. *eg US*
Competition	None. The government owns and operates everything.	Restricted in major industries; encouraged in small business.	Encouraged by market forces and government regulations.
Profits	Excess income goes to the government.	Profits earned by small businesses may be reinvested in the business; profits from government-owned industries go to the government.	Individuals are free to keep profits and use them as they wish.
Product availability and price	Consumers have a limited choice of goods and services; prices are usually high.	Consumers have some choice of goods and services; prices are determined by supply and demand.	Consumers have a wide choice of goods and services; prices are determined by supply and demand.
Employment options	Little choice in choosing a career; most people work for government-owned industries or farms.	Some choice of careers; many people work in government jobs.	Unlimited choice of careers.

Source: Based on "Gross Domestic Product or Expenditure, 1930–2002," *InfoPlease* (n.d.), www.infoplease.com/ipa/A0104575.html (accessed February 16, 2004).

Canada — is a mixed economy -

Communism. Karl Marx (1818–1883) first described **communism** as a society in which the people, without regard to class, own all the nation's resources. In his ideal political-economic system, everyone contributes according to ability and receives benefits according to need. In a communist economy, the people (through the government) own and operate all businesses and factors of production. Central government planning determines what goods and services satisfy citizens' needs, how the goods and services are produced, and how they are distributed. However, no true communist economy exists today that satisfies Marx's ideal.

communism first described by Karl Marx as a society in which the people, without regard to class, own all the nation's resources

socialism an economic system in which the government owns and operates basic industries but individuals own most businesses

On paper, communism appears to be efficient and equitable, producing less of a gap between rich and poor. In practice, however, communist economies have been marked by low standards of living, critical shortages of consumer goods, high prices, and little freedom. Russia, Poland, Hungary, and other Eastern European nations have turned away from communism and toward economic systems governed by supply and demand rather than by central planning. However, their experiments with alternative economic systems have been fraught with difficulty and hardship. Cuba continues to apply communist principles to its economy, but is also experiencing economic and political change and appears more open to free enterprise now. Similarly, China has become the first communist country to make strong economic gains by adopting capitalist approaches to business. The Chinese state is the largest shareholder among China's largest companies and influences thousands of other businesses. Economic prosperity has advanced in China with the government claiming to ensure market openness, equality, and fairness.[10]

Socialism. Closely related to communism is **socialism**, an economic system in which the government owns and operates basic industries—postal service, telephone, utilities, transportation, health care, banking, and some manufacturing—but individuals own most businesses. Central planning determines what basic goods and services are produced, how they are produced, and how they are distributed. Individuals and small businesses provide other goods and services based on consumer demand and the availability of resources. As with communism, citizens are dependent on the government for many goods and services.

Most socialist nations, such as Sweden, India, and Israel, are democratic and recognize basic individual freedoms. Citizens can vote for political offices, but central government planners usually make decisions about what is best for the nation. People are free to go into the occupation of their choice, but they often work in government-operated organizations. Socialists believe their system permits a higher standard of living than other economic systems, but the difference often applies to the nation as a whole rather than to its individual citizens. Socialist economies profess egalitarianism—equal distribution of income and social services. They believe their economies are more stable than those of other nations. Although this may be true, taxes and unemployment are generally higher in socialist countries. Perhaps as a result, many socialist countries are also experiencing economic difficulties.

Capitalism. **Capitalism, or free enterprise**, is an economic system in which individuals own and operate the majority of businesses that provide goods and services. Competition, supply, and demand determine which goods and services are produced, how they are produced, and how they are distributed. Canada, the United States, Japan, and Australia are examples of economic systems based on capitalism.

capitalism, or free enterprise an economic system in which individuals own and operate the majority of businesses that provide goods and services

free-market system pure capitalism, in which all economic decisions are made without government intervention

mixed economies economies made up of elements from more than one economic system

There are two forms of capitalism: pure capitalism and modified capitalism. In pure capitalism, also called a **free-market system**, all economic decisions are made without government intervention. This economic system was first described by Adam Smith in *The Wealth of Nations* (1776). Smith, often called the father of capitalism, believed that the "invisible hand of competition" best regulates the economy. He argued that competition should determine what goods and services people need. Smith's system is also called *laissez-faire* ("let it be") *capitalism* because the government does not interfere in business.

"Demand is the number of goods and services that consumers are willing to buy at different prices at a specific time."

Modified capitalism differs from pure capitalism in that the government intervenes and regulates business to some extent. One of the ways in which the Canadian government regulates business is through laws. Laws such as the Privacy Act in Canada, which protects consumers' private information, illustrate the importance of the government's role in the economy.

Mixed Economies. No country practises a pure form of communism, socialism, or capitalism, although most tend to favour one system over the others. Most nations operate as **mixed economies**, which have elements from more than one economic system. In Canada, most businesses are owned and operated by private individuals, yet a number of government-owned businesses or Crown corporations exist, including the Canada Post Corporation, the Bank of Canada, and the Canadian Dairy Commission. While Canada's economy can still be classified as a mixed economy, the trend in recent years is toward a more capitalist system. Many Canadian Crown corporations have been taken private, where the government sells its stake in the business and allows private citizens to manage the company. For example, over the last number of years, Canadian National Railway, Petro-Canada, and NS Power have all been converted to private enterprises. The trend toward greater capitalism has been aided in Canada by deregulation, which is a reduction in the number of laws and rules that govern the economy. In Great Britain and Mexico, the governments are attempting to sell many state-run businesses to private individuals and companies. In Germany, the Deutsche Post is privatized and trades on the stock market. In once-communist Russia, Hungary, Poland, and other Eastern European nations, capitalist ideas have been implemented, including private ownership of businesses.

Countries such as China and Russia have used state capitalism to advance the economy. State capitalism tries to integrate the powers of the state with the advantages of capitalism. It is led by the government but uses capitalistic tools such as listing state-owned companies on the stock market and embracing globalization.[11] State capitalism includes some of the world's largest companies such as Russia's Gazprom, which is the largest natural gas company. China's ability to make huge investments to the point of creating entirely new industries puts many private industries at a disadvantage.[12]

The Free-Enterprise System

Many economies—including those of Canada, the United States, and Japan—are based on free enterprise, and many communist and socialist countries, such as China, are applying more principles of free enterprise to their own economic systems. Free enterprise provides an opportunity for a business to succeed or fail on the basis of market demand. In a free-enterprise system, companies that can efficiently manufacture and sell products that consumers desire will probably succeed. Inefficient businesses and those that sell products that do not offer needed benefits will likely fail as consumers take their business to firms that have more competitive products.

A number of basic individual and business rights must exist for free enterprise to work. These rights are the goals of many countries that have recently embraced free enterprise.

1. Individuals must have the right to own property and to pass this property on to their heirs. This right motivates people to work hard and save to buy property.

2. Individuals and businesses must have the right to earn profits and to use the profits as they wish, within the constraints of their society's laws and values.

3. Individuals and businesses must have the right to make decisions that determine the way the business operates. Although there is government regulation, the philosophy in countries like Canada and Australia is to permit maximum freedom within a set of rules of fairness.

4. Individuals must have the right to choose what career to pursue, where to live, what goods and services to purchase, and more. Businesses must have the right to choose where to locate, what goods and services to produce, what resources to use in the production process, and so on.

Without these rights, businesses cannot function effectively because they are not motivated to succeed. Thus, these rights make possible the open exchange of goods and services. In the countries that favour free enterprise, such as Canada, citizens have the freedom to make many decisions about the employment they choose and create their own productivity systems. Many entrepreneurs are more productive in free-enterprise societies because personal and financial incentives are available that can aid in entrepreneurial success. For many entrepreneurs, their work becomes a part of their system of goals, values, and lifestyle. Consider the panelists ("dragons") on the CBC program *Dragons' Den*. Panelists on *Dragons' Den* give entrepreneurs a chance to receive funding to realize their dreams by deciding whether to invest in their projects. They include Jim Treliving, who built the Boston Pizza franchise in Canada; Michele Romanow, founder of Buytopia.ca; and Joe Mimran, who founded the clothing brands Joe Fresh, Club Monaco, and Pink Tartan.[13]

© CBC

CBC's *Dragons' Den* allows potential entrepreneurs to receive funding for their businesses, but only if they receive approval from the panel of "dragons," self-made millionaires who choose whether to fund the projects.

The Forces of Supply and Demand

> **LO4** Describe the role of supply, demand, and competition in a free-enterprise system.

In Canada and in other free-enterprise systems, the distribution of resources and products is determined by supply and demand. **Demand** is the number of goods and services that consumers are willing to buy at different prices at a specific time. From your own experience, you probably recognize that consumers are usually willing to buy more of an item as its price falls because they want to save money. Consider handmade rugs, for example. Consumers may be willing to buy six rugs at $350 each, four at $500 each, or only two at $650 each. The relationship between the price and the number of rugs consumers are willing to buy can be shown graphically, with a *demand curve* (see Figure 1.2).

demand the number of goods and services that consumers are willing to buy at different prices at a specific time

supply the number of products—goods and services—that businesses are willing to sell at different prices at a specific time

equilibrium price the price at which the number of products that businesses are willing to supply equals the amount of products that consumers are willing to buy at a specific point in time

Supply is the number of products that businesses are willing to sell at different prices at a specific time. In general, because the potential for profits is higher, businesses are willing to supply more of a good or service at higher prices. For example, a company that sells rugs may be willing to sell six at $650 each, four at $500 each, or just two at $350 each. The relationship between the price of rugs and the quantity the company is willing to supply can be shown graphically with a *supply curve* (see Figure 1.2).

In Figure 1.2, the supply and demand curves intersect at the point where supply and demand are equal. The price at which the number of products that businesses are willing to supply equals the amount of products that consumers are willing to buy at a specific point in time is the **equilibrium price**. In our rug example, the company is willing to supply four rugs at $500 each, and consumers are willing to buy four rugs at $500 each. Therefore, $500 is the equilibrium price for a rug at that point in time, and most rug companies will price their rugs at $500. As you might imagine, a business that charges more than $500 (or whatever the current equilibrium price is) for its rugs will not sell many and might not earn a profit. On the other hand, a business that charges less than $500 accepts a lower profit per rug than could be made at the equilibrium price.

"Competition, the rivalry among businesses for consumers' dollars, is another vital element in free enterprise."

If the cost of making rugs goes up, businesses will not offer as many at the old price. Changing the price alters the supply curve, and a new equilibrium price results. This is an ongoing process, with supply and demand constantly changing in response to changes in economic conditions, availability of resources, and degree of competition. For example, the price of oil can change rapidly and has been between $35 and $145 a barrel over the last five years. Prices for goods and services vary according to these changes in supply and demand. This concept is the force that drives the distribution of resources (goods and services, labour, and money) in a free-enterprise economy.

Critics of supply and demand say the system does not distribute resources equally. The forces of supply and demand prevent participation in the market by sellers who have to sell at higher prices (because their costs are high) and buyers who cannot afford to buy goods at the equilibrium price. According to critics, the wealthy can afford to buy more than they need, but the poor are unable to buy enough of what they need to survive.

The Nature of Competition

Competition, the rivalry among businesses for consumers' dollars, is another vital element in free enterprise. According

competition the rivalry among businesses for consumers' dollars

Figure 1.2 Equilibrium Price of Handmade Rugs

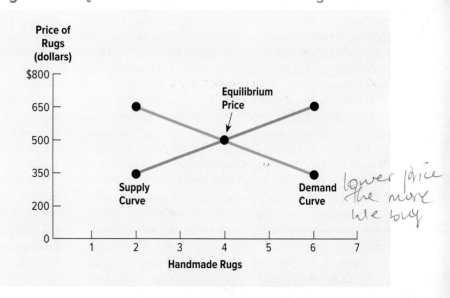

handwritten note: lower price the more we buy

to Adam Smith, competition fosters efficiency and low prices by forcing producers to offer the best products at the most reasonable price; those who fail to do so are not able to stay in business. Thus, competition should improve the quality of the goods and services available or reduce prices. For example, thanks to smart design and excellent timing, Apple dominates the market for downloadable music with its iTunes online service, iPod MP3 player, and iPhone. However, many companies have set their sights on capturing some of the firm's market share with new products of their own. Therefore, Apple must constantly seek to remain competitive by creating new innovations to maintain its market share—and sometimes capture market share from other companies. The iPad device combines the features of the smartphone and the laptop into one product. The iPad also contains an interface that allows users to read books and take pictures, which will capture some of the e-reader market dominated by Amazon's Kindle Fire.[14]

Within a free-enterprise system, there are four types of competitive environments: pure competition, monopolistic competition, oligopoly, and monopoly. *all for the price Tron can get.*

© PhotoLink/Getty Images

With the decline in lobster prices, many fishermen have decided to cut out the middleman and sell directly to consumers. What do you think are the pros and cons of such an approach? *can't distinguish among themselves.*

pure competition the market structure that exists when there are many small businesses selling one standardized product

monopolistic competition the market structure that exists when there are fewer businesses than in a pure-competition environment and the differences among the goods they sell are small

Pure competition exists when there are many small businesses selling one standardized product, such as agricultural commodities like wheat, corn, and cotton. No one business sells enough of the product to influence the product's price. And because there is no difference in the products, prices are determined solely by the forces of supply and demand. For example, Atlantic Canadian lobster prices are set by the forces of supply and demand. In recent years, demand has slowed as people are less likely to spend large amounts of money on premium seafood during periods of economic uncertainty. The low prices have forced some fishermen out of business. Other fishermen have taken a more entrepreneurial route and have started to sell directly to the consumer and eliminated the middleman to maximize their earnings. *can distinguish themselves.*

Monopolistic competition exists when there are fewer businesses than in a pure-competition environment and the differences among the goods they sell are small. Aspirin, soft drinks, and vacuum cleaners are examples of such goods. These products differ slightly in packaging, warranty, name, and other characteristics, but all satisfy the same consumer need. Businesses have some power over the price they charge in monopolistic competition because they can make consumers aware of product differences through advertising. Dyson, for example, attempts to differentiate its vacuum cleaners through product design, quality, and advertising. Consumers

many competitors / still able to differentiate themselves.

value some features more than others and are often willing to pay higher prices for a product with the features they want. Advil is a non-prescription pain reliever that contains ibuprofen instead of aspirin. Consumers who cannot take aspirin or who believe ibuprofen is a more effective pain reliever may not mind paying a little extra for the ibuprofen in Advil.

An **oligopoly** exists when there are very few businesses selling a product. In an oligopoly, individual businesses have control over their products' price because each business supplies a large portion of the products sold in the marketplace. Nonetheless, the prices charged by different firms stay fairly close because a price cut or increase by one company will trigger a similar response from another company. In the airline industry, for example, when one airline cuts fares to boost sales, other airlines quickly follow with rate decreases to remain competitive. This commonly occurs in the Canadian air travel business, which is dominated by Air Canada and WestJet. As soon as one airline drops its prices the other quickly follows. The same thing usually occurs when one of the airlines raises its prices. Oligopolies exist when it is expensive for new firms to enter the marketplace. Not just anyone can acquire enough financial capital to build an automobile production facility or purchase enough airplanes and related resources to build an airline. *Price makers.*

When there is one business providing a product in a given market, a **monopoly** exists. Utility companies that supply electricity, natural gas, and water are monopolies. The government permits such monopolies because the cost of creating the good or supplying the service is so great that new producers cannot compete for sales. Government-granted monopolies are subject to government-regulated prices.

oligopoly the market structure that exists when there are very few businesses selling a product *eg Canada airline industries - WestJet & Air Canada*

monopoly the market structure that exists when there is only one business providing a product in a given market

Some monopolies exist because of technological developments that are protected by patent laws. Patent laws grant the developer of new technology a period of time (usually 20 years) during which no other producer can use the same technology without the agreement of the original developer. Canada granted the first national patent in 1869, and now its patent office receives hundreds of thousands of patent applications a year. It is estimated that China will soon overtake other countries in patent filings.[15] This monopoly allows the developer to recover research, development, and production expenses and to earn a reasonable profit. Examples of this type of monopoly include the drug release process developed by Biovail, a Canadian pharmaceutical company that now operates as Valeant Pharmaceuticals International, Inc. after it purchased the company in 2010 and opted to assume its name. The patented drug release system allows for a gradual release of drugs into a patient's body. Other examples include the dry-copier process developed by Xerox. Xerox's patents have expired, however, and many imitators have forced market prices to decline.

Economic Cycles and Productivity

LO5 Specify why and how the health of the economy is measured.

Expansion and Contraction. Economies are not stagnant; they expand and contract. **Economic expansion** occurs when an economy is growing and people are spending more money. Their purchases stimulate the production of goods and services, which in turn stimulates employment. The standard of living rises because more people are employed and have money to spend. Rapid expansions of the economy, however, may result in **inflation,** a continuing rise in prices. Inflation can be harmful if individuals' incomes do not increase at the same pace as rising prices, reducing their buying power. Zimbabwe suffered from hyperinflation so severe that its inflation percentage rate rose into the hundreds of millions. With the elimination of the Zimbabwean dollar and certain price controls, the inflation rate began to decrease, but not before the country's economy was virtually decimated.[16]

Economic contraction occurs when spending declines. Businesses cut back on production and lay off workers, and the economy as a whole slows down. Contractions of the economy lead to **recession**— a decline in production, employment, and income. Recessions are often characterized by rising levels of **unemployment**, which is measured as the percentage of the population that wants to work but is unable to find jobs. Figure 1.3 shows the overall unemployment rate in the civilian labour force from 2010 to 2015. Rising unemployment levels tend to stifle demand for goods and services, which can have the effect of forcing prices downward, a condition known as *deflation.* Canada has experienced numerous recessions, including 1990–1992, 2001–2003, and 2008–2009. A severe recession may turn into a **depression,** in which unemployment is very high, consumer spending is low, and business output is sharply reduced, such as occurred in Canada and the United States in the early 1930s. The most recent global recession is often called the Great Recession because it was the longest and most severe economic decline since the Great Depression.

Economies expand and contract in response to changes in consumer, business, and government spending. War also can affect an economy, sometimes stimulating it (as in Canada during World Wars I and II) and sometimes stifling it (as in the

economic expansion the situation that occurs when an economy is growing and people are spending more money; their purchases stimulate the production of goods and services, which in turn stimulates employment

inflation a condition characterized by a continuing rise in prices

economic contraction a slowdown of the economy characterized by a decline in spending and during which businesses cut back on production and lay off workers

recession a decline in production, employment, and income

unemployment the condition in which a percentage of the population wants to work but is unable to find jobs

depression a condition of the economy in which unemployment is very high, consumer spending is low, and business output is sharply reduced

Figure 1.3 Unemployment Rate in Canada, 2010–2015

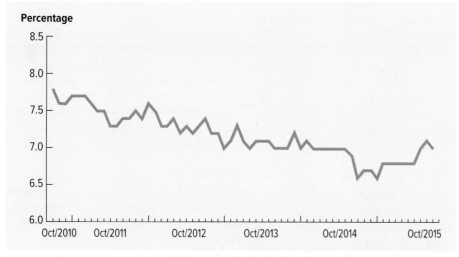

Percentage

Source: Statistics Canada. 2015. "Labour Force Survey, October 2015 (chart). Statistics Canada CANSIM 282-0087. Released: 2015-11-06. http://www.statcan.gc.ca/daily-quotidien/151106/dq151106a-eng.htm (accessed November 17, 2015).

Table 1.2 Economic Indicators of Different Countries

Country	GDP (in billions of dollars)	GDP per Capita	Unemployment Rate (%)	Inflation Rate (%)
Argentina	$972	$22,600	7.60	27.60
Australia	1,489	65,400	6.20	1.50
Brazil	3,192	15,600	6.40	9.00
Canada	1,632	45,600	6.90	1.10
China	19,390	14,100	4.20	1.40
France	2,647	41,200	9.90	0.10
Germany	3,841	46,900	4.80	0.10
India	7,965	6,200	7.10	4.90
Israel	282	33,700	5.60	-0.60
Japan	4,830	38,100	3.30	0.80
Mexico	2,227	15,100	4.50	2.70
Russia	3,718	25,400	5.40	15.50
South Africa	724	13,200	25.90	4.60
United Kingdom	2,679	41,200	5.40	0.10
United States	17,950	55,800	5.20	0.10

Source: *CIA—The World Factbook*, https://www.cia.gov/library/publications/the-world-factbook/rankorder/rankorderguide.html (accessed July 29, 2016).

United States during the Persian Gulf and Iraq wars). Although fluctuations in the economy are inevitable, and to a certain extent predictable, their effects—inflation and unemployment—disrupt lives and thus governments try to minimize them.

Measuring the Economy. Countries measure the state of their economies to determine whether they are expanding or contracting and whether corrective action is necessary to minimize the fluctuations. One commonly used measure is **gross domestic product (GDP)**—the sum of all goods and services produced in a country during a year. GDP measures only those goods and services made within a country and, therefore, does not include profits from companies' overseas operations; it does include profits earned by foreign companies within the country being measured. However, it does not take into account the concept of GDP in relation to population (GDP per capita). Table 1.2 compares a number of economic statistics for a sampling of countries.

Another important indicator of a nation's economic health is the relationship between its spending and income (from taxes). When a nation spends less than it takes in from taxes it has a **budget surplus**, and when it spends more than it takes in from taxes, it has a **budget deficit**.

In recent years, Canada has been fiscally conservative, but in 2016, it moved out of surplus to a planned cumulative deficit of $119 billion over the next decade. Deficits are especially worrisome because, to reduce the debt to a manageable level, the government either has to increase its revenues (raise taxes) or reduce spending on social, defense, and legal programs, neither of which is politically popular. The national debt figure changes daily and can be seen at the Canadian Taxpayers Federation website (www.taxpayer.com). Table 1.3 describes some of the other ways we evaluate our nation's economy.

gross domestic product (GDP) the sum of all goods and services produced in a country during a year

budget surplus the condition in which a nation spends less than it takes in from taxes

budget deficit the condition in which a nation spends more than it takes in from taxes

Table 1.3 How Do We Evaluate Our Nation's Economy?

Unit of Measure	Description
Trade balance	The difference between our exports and our imports. If the balance is positive, as it has been for much of the last 10 years, it is called a trade surplus. Recently, the balance has been negative; when this occurs it is called a trade deficit and is generally viewed as unhealthy for our economy.
Consumer price index	Measures changes in prices of goods and services purchased for consumption by typical urban households.
Per capita income	Indicates the income level of "average" Canadians. Useful in determining how much "average" consumers spend and how much money Canadians are earning.
Unemployment rate	Indicates how many working age Canadians are not working who otherwise want to work.
Inflation	Monitors price increases in consumer goods and services over specified periods of time. Used to determine if costs of goods and services are exceeding worker compensation over time.
Worker productivity	The amount of goods and services produced for each hour worked.

The Canadian Economy

As we said previously, Canada is a mixed economy based on free enterprise. The answers to the three basic economic issues are determined primarily by competition and the forces of supply and demand, although the federal government does intervene in economic decisions to a certain extent. To understand the current state of the Canadian economy and its effect on business practices, it is helpful to examine its history and the roles of the entrepreneur and the government.

A Brief History of the Canadian Economy

LO6 Trace the evolution of the Canadian economy and discuss the role of the entrepreneur in the economy.

The Early Economy. Before the colonization of North America, Native Americans lived as hunter/gatherers and farmers, with some trade among tribes. The first European settlements on the east coast of what was to become Canada came because of the fishing industry. The settlers operated primarily as an agricultural economy. Abundant natural resources nourished industries such as farming, fishing, shipping, and the fur trade. The fur trade was also important to Canada's early development as it began in the sixteenth century and remained a major industry for almost 300 years. The first major business competitors in Canada were the North West Trading Company and the Hudson Bay Company, which remained active in the fur trade until the 1980s.[18]

DID YOU KNOW?

61% of adult women work outside the home.[17]

The Industrial Revolution. The nineteenth century and the Industrial Revolution brought the development of new technology and factories. The factory brought together all the resources needed to make a product—materials, machines, and workers. Work in factories became specialized as workers focused on one or two tasks. As work became more efficient, productivity increased, making more goods available at lower prices. Industrialization mostly occurred in Central Canada. Due to the size of the country, its relatively small population, and the richness of its resources, most Canadians continued to work in primary industries.[19]

The government of the day established the Canadian Pacific Railway and linked the country coast to coast. Railroads brought major changes, allowing farmers to send their surplus crops and goods all over the nation for barter or for sale. Factories began to spring up along the railways to manufacture farm equipment and a variety of other goods to be shipped by rail.

The Manufacturing and Marketing Economies. Industrialization brought increased prosperity, and many Canadians found jobs in the *manufacturing economy*—one devoted to manufacturing goods and providing services rather than producing agricultural products. The assembly line was applied to more industries, increasing the variety of goods available to the consumer. Businesses became more concerned with the needs of the consumer and entered the *marketing economy*. Expensive goods such as cars and appliances could be purchased on a time-payment plan. Companies conducted research to find out what products consumers needed and wanted. Advertising made consumers aware of differences in products and prices.

Because these developments occurred in a free-enterprise system, consumers determined what goods and services were produced. They did this by purchasing the products they liked at prices they were willing to pay. Canada prospered, and Canadian citizens had one of the highest standards of living in the world.

The Service and New Digital Economy. After World War II, with the increased standard of living, Canadians had more money and more time. They began to pay others to perform services that made their lives easier. Beginning in the 1960s, more and more women entered the workforce. The profile of the family changed: Today there are more single-parent families and individuals living alone, and in two-parent families, both parents often work. One result of this trend is that time-pressed Canadians are increasingly paying others to do tasks they used to do at home, like cooking, laundry, landscaping, and child care. These trends have gradually changed Canada to a *service economy*—one devoted to the production of services that make life easier for busy consumers. Service industries such as restaurants, banking, medicines, child care, auto repair, leisure-related industries, and even education are growing rapidly and employ over 75 percent of Canadians. These trends continue with advanced technology contributing to new service products based on technology and digital media that provide smartphones, social networking, and virtual worlds. Table 1.4 provides evidence that the new digital economy is changing how we use information and the service industry. More about the Internet, business, and new online social media can be found in Chapter 13.[20]

Table 1.4 Popular Internet Activities

Activity Internet Users Performing	Each Activity (%)
Send or read e-mail	92
Use a search engine	92
Get news online	76
Buy a product online	71
Visit social network sites	65

Source: The Pew Research Center's Internet & American Life Project tracking surveys, 2002-2011, http://pewinternet.org.

Alex MacLean

Founded: 2013

The Business: East Coast Lifestyle

Success: Alex MacLean, a student at Acadia University, launched East Coast Lifestyle, a line of casual clothing with a stylized anchor logo, while still at university. The business, which is only a few years old, has sold more than 250,000 units through its website.

MacLean, from Halifax, said he borrowed $800 from his father to buy 30 hoodies as part of a marketing class assignment after he came up with the concept of using the words "East Coast Lifestyle" in a logo. Within weeks, ECL became a staple on social media with thousands of photos of East Coasters showcasing their pride from all around the world. The hype continued to escalate as pictures of celebrities representing their coast made their way to social media.

His success is a reminder that strategies taught in business schools, such as social media marketing and social entrepreneurship can both quickly pay off. His professor teaches a systematic approach known as the "lean start-up model," where the goal is to try out business ideas quickly and cheaply with a "minimally viable product."[21]

© East Coast Lifestyle

Clothing is big business for university student Alex MacLean. The entrepreneur was named Enactus Canada's Student Entrepreneur National Champion in the spring of 2014.

The Role of the Entrepreneur

An **entrepreneur** is an individual who risks his or her wealth, time, and effort to develop for profit a product or service that he or she can sell. For example, Ryan Holmes of Vancouver, British Columbia, founded www.HootSuite.com in 2008 with the idea that marketers should be able to manage multiple social media campaigns from one central website. The company currently has 10 million users and is the world's most widely used social relationship platform.[22] While Holmes has been quite successful, he did

entrepreneur an individual who risks his or her wealth, time, and effort to develop for profit an innovative product or way of doing something

take on the risks of entrepreneurship, including investing his money and time with no guarantee of success. We will learn more about starting a new business in Chapter 5.

The free-enterprise system provides the conditions necessary for entrepreneurs to succeed. In the past, entrepreneurs were often inventors who brought all the factors of production together to produce a new product. Joseph-Armand Bombardier, who invented the snowmobile, and Alexander Graham Bell, who invented the telephone, are early Canadian entrepreneurs. Other entrepreneurs have succeeded by offering consumers both services and products. For example, the Irving Group based in New Brunswick retails gasoline, sells hardware supplies, owns sports teams, manufactures products such as paper and tissue, and is heavily invested in the oil and gas business.[23] Garfield Weston Ltd., which was started in the late nineteenth century, now controls a great deal of the retail food business in Canada through its controlling interest in Loblaws.[24] Although these entrepreneurs were born in another century, their legacy to the Canadian economy lives on in the companies they started, many of which still operate today.

Entrepreneurs are constantly changing business practices with new technology and innovative management techniques. Bill Gates, for example, built Microsoft, a software company whose products include Word and Windows, into a multibillion-dollar enterprise. Frederick Smith had an idea to deliver packages overnight, and now his FedEx Company plays an important role in getting documents and packages delivered all over the world for businesses and individuals. Steve Jobs co-founded Apple and turned the company into a successful consumer electronics firm that revolutionized many different industries, with products such as the iPod, the iPhone, Mac computers, and the iPad. The company went from near bankruptcy in the 1990s to become one of the most valuable brands in the entire world. We will examine the importance of entrepreneurship further in Chapter 5.

The Role of Government in the Canadian Economy

The Canadian economic system is best described as a mixed economy because entrepreneurs and citizens control many of the factors of production and own the majority of businesses, but the government is still active in the economic system through its ownership of Crown corporations and the regulations it maintains to preserve competition and protect consumers and employees. Federal and provincial governments intervene in the economy with laws and regulations designed to promote competition and to protect consumers, employees, and the environment. Many of these laws are discussed in Appendix A.

Additionally, government agencies such as Industry Canada and the Department of Finance measure the health of the economy (GDP, productivity, etc.). Furthermore, the government—through the Bank of Canada, tax policy, and, when necessary, spending—takes steps to minimize the disruptive effects of economic fluctuations, and reduce unemployment. When the economy is contracting and unemployment is rising, the federal government tries to spur growth so that consumers will spend more money and businesses will hire more employees. To accomplish this, it may, through the Bank of Canada, reduce interest rates or increase its own spending for goods and services. When the economy expands so fast that inflation results, the government may intervene to reduce inflation by slowing down economic growth. This can be accomplished by raising interest rates to discourage spending by businesses and consumers. Techniques used to control the economy are discussed in Chapter 14.

The Role of Ethics and Social Responsibility in Business

In the past few years, you may have read about a number of ethical issues at several well-known corporations, including Enron, Maple Leaf, and SNC-Lavalin. In many cases, misconduct by individuals within these firms had an adverse effect on current and retired employees, investors, and others associated with these firms. In some cases, individuals went to jail for their actions. For example, former SNC-Lavalin CEO Pierre Duhaime was arrested by the RCMP after it was revealed that $56 million was unaccounted for and appears to have been illegally paid to commercial agents. Top executives like Enron's Jeffrey Skilling received long prison sentences for their roles in corporate misconduct. These scandals undermined public confidence in the free-enterprise system and sparked a new debate about ethics in business. Business ethics generally refer to the standards and principles used by society to define appropriate and inappropriate conduct in the workplace. In many cases, these standards have been codified as laws prohibiting actions deemed unacceptable.

Society is increasingly demanding that businesspeople behave ethically and socially responsibly toward not only their customers but also their employees, investors,

---

Consider the Following: Demand Eclipses Supply: Bluefin Tuna

Bluefin tuna is immensely popular among sushi lovers, creating a high demand for the fish. Supply, on the other hand, is another matter. The bluefin population is being reduced through global overfishing and pollution. The Center for Biological Diversity requested endangered species status for the bluefin, fearing current fishing practices might bring about extinction. The U.S. government declined the request. It argued that scientists need time to assess the current status of bluefin thanks, in part, to the impact on its spawning grounds from the BP Deepwater Horizon oil spill. It did, however, place the fish on its watch list.

Most scientists, environmentalists, and lawmakers agree that the bluefin population has significantly declined, but many feel an international agreement on how best to preserve the population is preferable to a moratorium on fishing it. This assumes that fishermen will comply with regulations. Many fishermen currently fish more than the legal quota, with some fishing 100 percent illegally. Reduced supply and steady demand are driving up the price of bluefin, making it a desirable catch. One fish brought in $396,000. Mitsubishi Corporation (the largest bluefin purchaser globally) has stored a large amount of frozen bluefin in defence of extinction. Unless there is an effective way to police fishing and preserve habitats, the bluefin may ultimately need official protection.[25]

DISCUSSION QUESTIONS

1. Why is the price of bluefin tuna skyrocketing?

2. What are the ethical issues involved in selling bluefin tuna?

3. Why might the United States be reluctant to place the bluefin tuna on the endangered species list? What are some of the consequences of acting too slowly or too quickly in their assessment?

government regulators, communities, and the natural environment. No area is more debated as online privacy. Software, music, and film executives want to defend their intellectual property. On the other hand, companies such as Google are concerned that strict laws would stifle innovation and enable censorship.[26] When actions are heavily criticized, a balance is usually required to support and protect various stakeholders.

While one view is that ethics and social responsibility are a good supplement to business activities, there is an alternative viewpoint. Research has shown that ethical behaviour can not only enhance a company's reputation but can also drive profits.[27] The ethical and socially responsible conduct of companies such as Whole Foods, Starbucks, and the hotel chain Marriott provides evidence that good ethics is good business. There is growing recognition that the long-term value of conducting business in an ethical and socially responsible manner that considers the interests of all stakeholders creates superior financial performance.[28]

To promote socially responsible and ethical behaviour while achieving organizational goals, businesses can monitor changes and trends in society's values. Businesses should determine what society wants and attempt to predict the long-term effects of their decisions. While it requires an effort to address the interests of all stakeholders, businesses can prioritize and attempt to balance conflicting demands. The goal is to develop a solid reputation of trust and avoid misconduct to develop effective workplace ethics.

Figure 1.4 The Organization of This Book

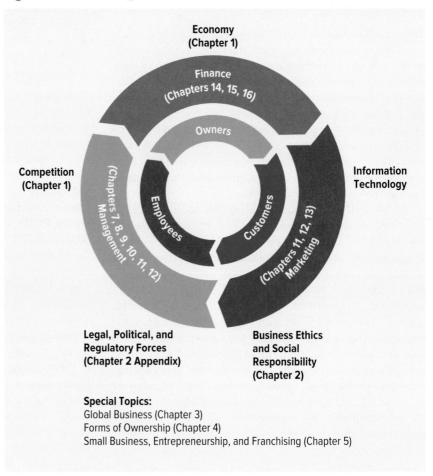

Economy (Chapter 1)

Finance (Chapters 14, 15, 16)

Owners

Competition (Chapter 1)

(Chapters 7, 8, 9, 10, 11, 12) Management

Employees

Customers

(Chapters 11, 12, 13) Marketing

Information Technology

Legal, Political, and Regulatory Forces (Chapter 2 Appendix)

Business Ethics and Social Responsibility (Chapter 2)

Special Topics:
Global Business (Chapter 3)
Forms of Ownership (Chapter 4)
Small Business, Entrepreneurship, and Franchising (Chapter 5)

Can You Learn Business in a Classroom?

Obviously, the answer is yes, or there would be no purpose for this textbook! To be successful in business, you need knowledge, skills, experience, and good judgment. The topics covered in this chapter and throughout this book provide some of the knowledge you need to understand the world of business. The opening vignette at the beginning of each chapter, boxes and examples within each chapter, and the case at the end of each chapter describe experiences to help you develop good business judgment. However, good judgment is based on knowledge and experience plus personal insight and understanding. Therefore, you need more courses in business, along with some practical experience in the business world, to help you develop the special insight necessary to put your personal stamp on knowledge as you apply it. The challenge in business is in the area of judgment, and judgment does not develop from memorizing an introductory business textbook. If you are observant in your daily experiences as an employee, as a student, and as a consumer, you will improve your ability to make good business judgments.

"Business ethics generally refers to the standards and principles used by society to define appropriate and inappropriate conduct in the workplace."

Figure 1.4 is an overview of how the chapters in this book are linked together and how the chapters relate to the participants, the activities, and the environmental factors found in the business world. The topics presented in the chapters that follow are those that will give you the best opportunity to begin the process of understanding the world of business.

TEAM EXERCISE

Major economic systems, including capitalism, socialism, and communism, as well as mixed economies, were discussed in this chapter. Assuming that you want an economic system that is best for the majority, not just a few members of society, defend one of the economic systems as the best system. Form groups and try to reach agreement on one economic system. Defend why you supported the system you advanced.

LEARNING OBJECTIVES SUMMARY

LO1 Define basic concepts such as business, product, and profit.

A business is an organization or individual that seeks a profit by providing products that satisfy people's needs. A product is a good or service with tangible and intangible characteristics that provide satisfaction and benefits. Profit is the difference between what it costs to make and sell a product and what a customer pays for it.

LO2 Identify the main participants and activities of business, and explain why studying business is important.

The three main participants in business are owners, employees, and customers, but others—government regulators, suppliers, social groups, etc.—are also important. Management involves planning, organizing, and controlling the tasks required to carry out the work of the company. Marketing refers to those activities—research, product development, promotion, pricing, and distribution—designed to provide goods and services that satisfy customers. Finance refers to activities concerned with funding a business and using its funds effectively. Studying business can help you prepare for a career and become a better consumer.

LO3 Define economics and compare the four types of economic systems.

Economics is the study of how resources are distributed for the production of goods and services within a social system; an economic system describes how a particular society distributes its resources. Communism is an economic system in which the people, without regard to class, own all the nation's resources. In a socialist system, the government owns and operates basic industries, but individuals own most businesses. Under capitalism, individuals own and operate the majority of businesses that provide goods and services. Mixed economies have elements from more than one economic system; most countries have mixed economies.

LO4 Describe the role of supply, demand, and competition in a free-enterprise system.

In a free-enterprise system, individuals own and operate the majority of businesses, and the distribution of resources is determined by competition, supply, and demand. Demand is the number of goods and services that consumers are willing to buy at different prices at a specific time. Supply is the number of goods or services that businesses are willing to sell at different prices at a specific time. The price at which the supply of a product equals demand at a specific point in time is the equilibrium price. Competition is the rivalry among businesses to convince consumers to buy goods or services. Four types of competitive environments are pure competition, monopolistic competition, oligopoly, and monopoly. These economic concepts determine how businesses may operate in a particular society and, often, how much they can charge for their products.

LO5 Specify why and how the health of the economy is measured.

A country measures the state of its economy to determine whether it is expanding or contracting and whether the country needs to take steps to minimize fluctuations. Commonly used measures include the gross domestic product (GDP), budget deficits/surpluses, the trade balance, the consumer price index, per capita income unemployment rate, inflation, and worker productivity.

LO6 Trace the evolution of the Canadian economy, and discuss the role of the entrepreneur in the economy.

The Canadian economy has evolved through several stages: the early economy, the Industrial Revolution, the manufacturing economy, the marketing economy, and the service and new digital economy of today. Entrepreneurs play an important role because they risk their time, wealth, and efforts to develop new goods, services, and ideas that fuel the growth of the Canadian economy.

budget deficit
budget surplus
business
capitalism, or free enterprise
communism
competition
demand
depression
economic contraction
economic expansion
economic system
economics
equilibrium price
entrepreneur
financial resources
free-market system
gross domestic product (GDP)

human resources
inflation
mixed economies
monopolistic competition
monopoly
natural resources
non-profit organizations
oligopoly
products
profit
pure competition
recession
socialism
stakeholders
supply
unemployment

DESTINATION CEO DISCUSSION QUESTIONS

1. How do you think Sylvain Toutant's experience at Keurig and Van Houtte has helped him at Davids Tea?

2. What do you think of Davids Tea's marketing strategy of making tea fun and accessible? Is the store design what customers are looking for?

3. If large competitors continue to enter the marketplace selling similar products at lower prices, will Davids Tea continue to be as successful as it is today? Will it be able to sell exotic blends tea at high prices when other retailers are selling similar items for a lower price?

4. Do you think customers, or frequent steepers as the company calls members, will continue to pay a premium for teas to be part of the Davids Tea experience?

SO YOU WANT A JOB *in the Business World*

When most people think of a career in business, they see themselves entering the door to large companies and multinationals that they read about in the news and that are discussed in class. Most jobs are not with large corporations but instead are in small companies, non-profit organizations, and government, or are self-employed positions. Small businesses account for more than 98 percent of all firms in Canada and play a large role in net job creation, creating 78 percent of all private jobs from 2002 to 2012. There are nearly 1.1 million small businesses, which employ 99 or fewer workers. With the rise of services in the economy, there are jobs available in industries such as health care, finance, education, hospitality, entertainment, and transportation. The world is changing quickly, and large corporations replace the equivalent of their entire workforce every four years.

The fast pace of technology today means that you have to be prepared to take advantage of emerging job opportunities and markets. You must also become adaptive and recognize that business is becoming more global, with job opportunities around the world. If you want to obtain such a job, you shouldn't miss a chance to spend some time overseas. To get you started on the path to thinking about job opportunities, consider all of the changes in business today that might affect your possible long-term track and that could bring you lots of success. You may want to stay completely out of large organizations and corporations and put yourself in a position for an entrepreneurial role as a self-employed contractor or small-business owner. However, there are many who feel that experience in larger businesses is helpful to your success later as an entrepreneur.

You're on the road to learning the key knowledge, skills, and trends that you can use to be a star in business. Business's impact on our society, especially in the area of sustainability and improvement of the environment, is a growing challenge and opportunity. Green businesses and green jobs in the business world are provided to give you a glimpse at the possibilities. Along the way, we will introduce you to some specific careers and offer advice on developing your own job opportunities. Research indicates that you won't be that happy with your job unless you enjoy your work and feel that it has a purpose. Since you spend most of your waking hours every day at work, you need to seriously think about what is important to you in a job.[29]

BUILD YOUR BUSINESS PLAN

The Dynamics of Business and Economics

Have you ever thought about owning your business? If you have, how did your idea come about? Is it your experience with this particular field? Or might it be an idea that evolved from your desires for a particular product or service not being offered in your community. For example, perhaps you and your friends have yearned for a place to go have coffee, relax, and talk. Now is an opportunity to create the café bar you have been thinking of!

Whether you consider yourself a visionary or a practical thinker, think about your community. What needs are not being met? While it is tempting to suggest a new restaurant (maybe near campus), easier-to-implement business plans can range from a lawn care business or a designated driver business, to a placement service agency for teenagers.

Once you have an idea for a business plan, think about how profitable this idea might be. Is there sufficient demand for this business? How large is the market for this particular business? What about competitors? How many are there?

To learn about your industry you should do a thorough search of your initial ideas of a product/service on the Internet.

CASE | Apple Stores: The Future of Retail?

In 2011, Apple surpassed Google as the most valuable global brand at more than $153 billion. Much of Apple's success can be attributed to its innovative products such as the iPad. However, Apple has also made a profound mark in the world of retailing. Its stores, which were first opened in 2001, are the fastest growing retail stores in history. An obvious draw is store design—modern and spacious, creating a relaxed, low-pressure atmosphere. The stores are like showrooms that allow customers to test products and take educational classes.

To truly understand Apple's retail success, it is important to look beneath the surface. According to Forbes contributor Steve Denning, two keys to Apple's success are delight the customer and avoid selling. Apple focuses extensively on meeting customer needs and wants. This focus significantly alters employee behaviour and complements the avoid selling mantra. Rather than pushing products on consumers, Apple store employees are asked to listen and assist. Employees have been trained to speak with customers within two minutes of them entering the store. Apple executives are also constantly looking for new innovative ways to enhance customer service. The company recently began installing iPad stations equipped with a customer service app designed to answer customer questions. If the customer requires additional assistance, he or she can press a help button on the app.

Apple has been so successful in the retail arena that other stores are looking to adopt its retail strategies. Microsoft and Sony have opened their own stores, and other industries are using Apple products to enhance their businesses. Apple's blend of exceptional products, appealing stores, and knowledgeable and dedicated employees creates a top-notch customer experience and is having enormous repercussions for the retail industry as a whole.[30]

DISCUSSION QUESTIONS

1. Why is Apple having such a profound impact on the retail store experience?

2. How is Apple integrating its products into the retail store experience?

3. Describe Apple's approach to customer service.

Russell K. Girling is past co-chair of the United Way Campaign, director of the Willow Park Charity Golf Classic, and a winner of Canada's Top 40 Under 40 award. To many in the business community, Girling is a respected CEO with a proven track record.

To others, Russell Girling is public enemy number one. Girling's company, TransCanada Corporation, is the firm trying to build the controversial Keystone XL project, which will transport oil from Canada's oil sands in Alberta to Steele City, Nebraska. While Phases I and II of the Keystone Project have been built and Phase III has been approved, it is the controversial fourth phase that has been getting all the attention. For example, Global Exchange, an environmental group supporting a sustainable earth, has Girling's company on the list of the worst "Corporate Human Rights Violators,"[1] while Greenpeace Canada describes the project as " … an act of aggression to the plants, wildlife, and people who live in its path."[2]

Girling admits to being a bit surprised by the opposition and the negative impact on the proposed project. Critics of how Girling has handled the approval say he underestimated the opposition. Girling counters the critics and opponents of the pipeline stating, "There is literally two-and-a-half million (miles) of pipeline traversing the ground. You would think, based on the arguments coming up, that this was the first pipeline that has ever been built and that we have to start from scratch. We have been at this for more than 100 years."[3] Girling's arguments have been focused consistently on facts, but some business pundits think the company hasn't been able to sell the project because of its reliance on repeating facts and not connecting with people, especially Nebraskans.

The original proposed pipeline was to travel through Sand Hills, a large wetland, and Ogallala Aquifer, one of the largest sources of fresh water in the world. The aquifer provides drinking water for eight states and supports a $20 billion agricultural industry. When TransCanada was presented with opposition about the pipeline going through these environmentally sensitive areas, it opted to offer no alternative route. Instead, the company repeated facts about the safety of the pipeline and argued no other feasible route existed. This lack of flexibility seemed to galvanize opposition, including from editors of *The New York Times*, who argued that the pipeline could damage the environment if an oil spill occurred and that oil coming from Alberta's oil sands produces roughly 12 percent more greenhouse gas than conventional production.

Girling's response was to change the route of the pipeline away from the two environmentally sensitive areas cited above and to continue to argue for the merits of the Keystone Project, which include the creation of thousands of jobs and millions, if not billions, in economic spinoffs. Girling further says the U.S. needs access to Canadian oil and getting oil from a friendly North American company is better than alternatives. Girling states, "Importing oil from a friendly, stable, reliable neighbour that shares the interests and values of the United States with respect to environmental management and safety of workers is far better than importing from other jurisdictions around the world that don't share those same values.… The U.S. needs 10 million barrels a day of imported oil and the debate over the proposed pipeline is not a debate of oil versus alternative energy. This is a debate about whether you want to get your oil from Canada or Venezuela or Nigeria."[4]

© AP Photo/Nati Harnik/CP Images

Determining what is ethical is often difficult. Both advocates and opponents of the Keystone XL and Energy East Pipeline no doubt feel they are acting ethically while their opposition is acting unethically.

Changing the route led to an approval from the Nebraska state government, but President Obama opted to reject the deal in late 2015, citing the deal was not in the best interest of America.[5] Girling, who was disappointed but not surprised by the decision, offered, "Today, misplaced symbolism was chosen over merit and science—rhetoric won out over reason."[6]

Most environmentalists and oil analysts believe this is not the end of Keystone XL but more of a time out. President Obama, who is almost at the end of his term, believes that the fight against climate change will be a big part of his legacy and rejecting the deal was an important step in defining his presidency. Once Obama's term is over, most pundits believe TransCanada will re-apply for the project, perhaps with a different name.[7] In fact, most oil analysts believe the chances of the project still being built are roughly 50-50.[8]

In the meantime, TransCanada seems willing to pursue another controversial pipeline known as Energy East. The pipeline, if built, would run approximately 4,600 km, cost roughly $12 billion to construct, and bring oil from Alberta and Saskatchewan directly to refineries in Saint John, New Brunswick. The pipeline would be the longest in North America, and special interest groups are already lining up to either support or stop the project.[9] Only time will tell if either of the pipelines are built, but the controversial projects are great examples how people see ethics differently. Proponents of pipelines consistently argue they will create jobs and much-needed government revenue, and that the construction of the pipelines is ethical and

socially responsible; opponents talk about the negative impact that oil and the potential for oil spills has on the environment, and that stopping the construction of these pipelines is ethical and socially responsible.

Introduction

Auto manufacturers that make hybrid cars have taken on the challenge of positively contributing to society through their business activities. At the other extreme, wrongdoing by some businesses has focused public attention and government involvement to encourage more acceptable business conduct. Almost any business decision may be judged as right or wrong, ethical or unethical, depending on who is doing the judging. For example, the Keystone XL and Energy East projects, which we discussed in the opening Destination CEO profile, has many proponents and opponents. Canadians in favour of the projects argue that Canada's oil sands industry needs the pipelines to ship oil to refineries. They state that Alberta's oil currently sells at a discount because there is a lack of means to transport the oil to refineries, and as a result, tax dollars and jobs are being lost. If the pipelines are approved, Canadian companies will be able to get more money for their oil, resulting in more jobs and additional tax dollars. These tax dollars support health care, scientific research, education, and a number of positive initiatives. Many politicians, including Prime Minister Justin Trudeau have supported the projects. In addition, many labour groups support the proposed pipelines for the thousands of jobs it will create, and shareholders favour the deals as they will lead to further profits for the company. Opponents of the deals, including many people in the general public and some politicians, say the oil sands produce more greenhouse gas than traditional oil production and should be discouraged, not encouraged. Furthermore, with any pipeline there is a danger of a spill that can harm the environment.

Another example of a business proposal that attracted both supporters and detractors is BlackBerry, which urged the government to stop the sale of Nortel Networks' assets to foreign companies. BlackBerry argued that technology developed in Canada should stay in Canada and that the government had a moral and ethical duty to intervene. Shareholders and creditors, on the other hand, wanted

the assets sold to the highest bidder regardless of the buyer's location. The Canadian government opted not to interfere with the sale, which resulted in many of Nortel's prized assets being bought by Ericsson, the Swedish telecommunications manufacturer.[10]

In this chapter, we take a look at the role of ethics and social responsibility in business decision making. First we define business ethics and examine why it is important to understand the role of ethics in business. Next we explore a number of business ethics issues to help you learn to recognize such issues when they arise. Finally, we consider steps businesses can take to improve ethical behaviour in their organizations. The second half of the chapter focuses on social responsibility. We survey some important responsibility issues and detail how companies have responded to them.

Business Ethics and Social Responsibility

LO1 Define business ethics and social responsibility, and examine their importance.

In this chapter, we define **business ethics** as the principles and standards that determine acceptable conduct in business organizations. The acceptability of behaviour in business is determined by customers, competitors, government regulators, interest groups, and the public, as well as each individual's personal moral principles and values. Readers should realize that determining ethical behaviour is not as easy as one may think and often depends on which stakeholder group an individual belongs to. Reconsider the Keystone XL and Energy East projects that were discussed above. Advocates of the pipelines, including the management of the company, shareholders, and some people in the public including the government, likely believe their arguments are ethical. People opposing the pipelines, including some government officials both in Canada and the U.S., environmental groups, and some labour unions, have stated that approving the pipelines would constitute unethical behaviour. You may also want to consider the situation with General Motors (GM), Ford, and Chrysler, which all maintain manufacturing facilities in Canada. During the 2008–2010 recession, these companies laid off thousands of workers and essentially tore up contracts that they had negotiated with their employees, claiming that this was the only way to ensure that any manufacturing jobs were left in the local economies.[11] GM went a step further and entered into bankruptcy protection in the

business ethics principles and standards that determine acceptable conduct in business

© Frui/Dreamstime.com

Facebook has millions of active users and has become an important business tool for networking, marketing, sourcing suppliers, finding employers and employees, and much more—but the site has led to some ethical dilemmas, especially with regards to privacy.

United States, enabling the company to avoid paying some creditors, to pass off some expenses to government, and essentially to destroy any shareholder value. Ford opted not to enter into bankruptcy protection but did receive some government support. During the recession, the companies continued to manufacture cars, offered consumers better warranties, and attempted to introduce more environmentally friendly automobiles to the marketplace, including the GM Volt which may be the most environmentally friendly car in the world. If you worked for these companies in the past couple of years, would you consider them ethical? As a consumer, would your opinions differ those of the from employees? One of the reasons Ford avoided bankruptcy was its ability to drastically reduce wages, thus allowing its shareholders to avoid losing everything they had invested. Would shareholders and employees have a different opinion of Ford? Another interesting ethical dilemma is any action that has a perceived negative environmental impact, such as tree-cutting by the Irving Group's forestry division. While one may presume that the cutting of trees is unethical behaviour, the Irving Group is the largest private planter of trees in the country. Does knowing this affect your opinion of the company and its business practices?

At other times, determining ethical behaviour is much easier. For example, Quebec police have charged Pierre Duhaime, former CEO of SNC-Lavalin, along with other high-ranking executives of the company, with fraud.. The police allege that Duhaime and others paid a $22.5 million bribe to ex-McGill hospital officials in order to obtain a $1.3-billion contract.[12] Research indicates that most unethical activities within organizations are supported by an organizational culture that encourages employees to bend the rules.[13]

Many people—including entrepreneurs, employees, consumers, and social advocates—believe that businesses should not only make a profit but also consider the social implications of their activities. For example, the employees at the Montreal law firm Stikeman Elliott LLP formed a green committee to ensure that the company was minimizing its impact on the environment.[14] These employees are apparently not on their own, according to Nicholas Lamm, co-founder of Green Workplace, a Vancouver-based consulting firm. Lamm says, "As the go-green message increasingly gains footing, Canadians are looking for ways to make an environmental impact on their job."[15] Business owners may want to take note about the growing importance of acting in a socially responsible manner. In a recent poll, 78 percent of Canadians said that they would quit their jobs to work at a company that was more environmentally friendly.[16]

We define **social responsibility** as a business's obligation to maximize its positive impact and minimize its negative impact on society. Although many people use the terms *social responsibility* and *ethics* interchangeably, they do not mean the same thing. Business ethics relate to an *individual's* or a *work group's* decisions that society evaluates as right or wrong, whereas social responsibility is a broader concept that concerns the impact of the *entire business's* activities on society. From an ethical perspective, for example, we may be concerned about a drug company overcharging the government for its medications. From a social responsibility perspective, we might be concerned about the impact

social responsibility a business's obligation to maximize its positive impact and minimize its negative impact on society

> "Many people including entrepreneurs, employees, consumers, and social advocates believe that businesses should not only make a profit but also consider the social implications of their activities."

that this overcharging will have on the ability of the health care system to provide adequate services for all citizens.

The most basic ethical and social responsibility concerns have been codified as laws and regulations that encourage businesses to conform to society's standards, values, and attitudes. For example, in the early 2000s, corporate scandals involving Nortel, Atlas Cold Storage, Enron, WorldCom, Global Crossing, and Tyco, as well as several major auditing firms, including Arthur Andersen, resulted in hundreds of billions of dollars in corporate and investor losses and shook public confidence in the integrity of the public markets. To help restore confidence in corporations and markets, the U.S. Congress passed the Sarbanes-Oxley Act[17] and the Ontario government proclaimed Bill C-198, which criminalized securities fraud and stiffened penalties for corporate fraud. At a minimum, managers are expected to obey all laws and regulations. Yet even obeying laws is open to interpretation. In Canada, Rogers Communications was running advertisements noting that it offered consumers the fastest and most reliable cellphone service. Telus, one of Rogers' competitors, disagreed with the claim and brought the matter before the courts. Telus ultimately succeeded in getting Rogers to stop running the ads, but Rogers did not admit to any wrongdoing.[18] Essentially, both businesses felt that they were obeying the laws at the time. Most legal issues arise as choices that society deems unethical, irresponsible, or otherwise unacceptable. However, all actions deemed unethical by society are not necessarily illegal, and both legal and ethical concerns change over time (see Table 2.1). Business law refers to the laws and regulations that govern the conduct of business. Many problems and conflicts in business can be avoided if owners, managers, and employees know more about business law and the legal system. Together, business ethics, social responsibility, and legislation act as a compliance system requiring that businesses and employees act responsibly in society. In this chapter, we explore ethics and social responsibility; Appendix B addresses business law, including securities regulations.

The Role of Ethics in Business

You only have to pick up the *National Post* or *The Globe and Mail's Report on Business* to see examples of the growing concern about legal and ethical issues in business. Volkswagen, for example, installed software in some of its diesel cars to trick emission testers into thinking the cars were more environmentally friendly than they actually are. The result of its unethical and perhaps illegal behaviour led to cars being on the road emitting up to 40 times the allowable nitrogen oxide limits.[19] Other examples include XL Foods, which sold tainted meat

Table 2.1 A Timeline of Ethical and Socially Responsible Concerns

1960s	1970s	1980s	1990s	2000s
• Environmental issues	• Employee militancy	• Bribes and illegal contracting practices	• Sweatshops and unsafe working conditions in third-world countries	• Employee benefits
• Civil rights issues	• Human rights issues	• Influence peddling		• Privacy issues
• Increased employee-employer tension	• Covering up rather than correcting issues	• Deceptive advertising	• Rising corporate liability for personal damages (e.g., cigarette companies)	• Financial mismanagement
• Honesty	• Discrimination	• Financial fraud (e.g., savings and loan scandal)		• Abusive behaviour
• Changing work ethic	• Harassment			• Cyber crime
• Rising drug use		• Transparency issues	• Financial mismanagement and fraud	• Intellectual property theft

Source: Adapted from "Business Ethics Timeline," Copyright © 2003, *Ethics Resource Center* (n.d.), www.ethics.org, updated 2006.

products to Canadians, and Ontario-based Premier Fitness, whose advertising and collection methods were questioned. Premier Fitness customers noted they were often lured in for free fitness trials and then charged for mandatory physical assessments or continued to be billed after they cancelled their memberships. Interestingly, both XL Foods and Premier Fitness no longer operate under the same banners, with XL being sold and Premier Fitness closing its doors. Additionally, the rent-to-own store Aaron's installed spy software on people's laptops, which enabled Aaron's to record pictures and video of users at home or work without their knowledge. Regardless of what an individual believes about a particular action, if society judges it to be unethical or wrong, whether correctly or not, that judgment directly affects the organization's ability to achieve its business goals.[20]

Well-publicized incidents of unethical and illegal activity—from accounting fraud to using the Internet to steal another person's credit-card number, from deceptive advertising of food and diet products to unfair competitive

Consider the Following: The Occupy Movement

The Occupy Movement can be described as a global protest against social and economic inequality. The protestors believe that global corporations, especially financial institutions and wealthy individuals, have an unfair influence in politics leading to economic and social problems that undermine democracy. The movement, which originated in New York, spread quickly throughout North America as protestors built camps in highly visible areas such as in public parks or in front of government buildings. Critics of the movement have said that many of the protestors didn't understand the issues they were protesting, could not even name the companies they were upset with, and were taking over public space to run unsanitary camps. Early in the movement, politicians and law enforcement agencies let the camps exist, but as time passed, tolerance for the protestors started to wane. Citing concerns about the health and safety of the protestors and a desire to return public space back to the public, law enforcement agencies eventually tore down many camps throughout North America. Often the protestors refused to move and were arrested as a result. Today, people in the movement claim they are still working on ending economic disparity and note several major political themes, including higher minimum wage and the focus of politicians working for the "other 99 percent of Canadians and not the top 1 percent" was a direct result of the movement.

1. Some people in the Occupy Movement argued the practice of business itself is unethical. Do you agree or disagree?

2. Do you think law enforcement agencies were right to tear down camps? Why or why not?

3. Some protestors fought back when police officers came to evict them from their camps, including physically confronting officers and throwing objects. Do you think protestors were acting ethically? Why or why not?

4. Do you think minimum wage should be raised in your province? Why or why not? What are some of the potential pros and cons of setting a higher minimum wage?

Valeant Pharmaceuticals based in Laval, Quebec, has been in the news for much of 2015 for various reasons. First, the company, which manufactures and distributes roughly 500 drugs globally, became for a brief period of time the largest company in Canada by market cap.[21] The value of the business almost doubled in 2015 as investors were attracted to strong growth and what shareholders believe is a sound business model. Rather then develop new drugs, Valeant often prefers to purchase companies that have brought drugs from development to the approval process. Once Valeant purchases the companies, it uses its aggressive sales force to improve the sales of the drugs. The strategy is clearly working as Valeant's annual revenue is expected to be in the $8 to $9 billion dollar for 2015.

The business model on its own appears to be both ethical and practical. Developing drugs can take a significant amount of time and resources, and Valeant doesn't appear to have the capabilities to successfully bring its own drugs to market. Firms that successfully develop drugs normally do so at great cost, and once they are approved, they can lack both the resources and marketing abilities to successfully sell the drugs. Valeant purchases the firms and/or their drugs; the company's investors, entrepreneurs, and scientists normally get paid a premium for their time and investment; and Valeant makes money by using its marketing abilities to sell the drugs.

What brought Valeant into the news beyond its financial success is its pricing practices for newly acquired drugs. Valeant has been charged with unethically raising the price of acquired drugs. It is not uncommon for Valeant to raise the price by 100 percent or greater, and in rare cases as much as 500 percent. Valeant has been justifying the price hikes by noting the drugs were originally priced too low for market conditions.[22] On average, Valeant raised its drug prices in 2015 by 66 percent, which is five times more than similar-sized companies, and raised the price of

two new heart drugs it bought the rights to sell: Nitropress by 212 percent and Isuprel by 525 percent.[23] CEO Michael Pearson defends the company's drug-price policies, stating price increases do not drive the company's success as growth in the number of prescriptions being written for Valeant drugs is the major factor fuelling revenue growth, which is a direct result of its marketing and sales abilities.[24]

1. Is Valeant Pharmaceuticals an ethical company? Why or why not? Would you invest in the company based on its business model?

2. Do you think governments should regulate the prices that companies can charge for drugs? Why or why not?

3. What are some of the arguments for charging high drug prices?

4. The discussions about Valeant and ethics are likely to continue for years to come. Use Internet resources to review the current state of the company and whether any governments have started to regulate their pricing practices. Update the class on what you have found.

© Ingram Publishing/SuperStock

Canadian pharmaceutical giant, Valeant Pharmaceuticals has had its fair share of people question the ethics of the company over its practice of buying other drug businesses and then substantially raising the price of the drugs.

practices in the computer software industry—strengthen the public's perception that ethical standards and the level of trust in business need to be raised. Author David Callahan has commented, "[People] who wouldn't so much as shoplift a pack of chewing gum are committing felonies at tax time, betraying the trust of their patients, misleading investors, ripping off their insurance companies, lying to their clients, and much more."[25] Often, such charges start as ethical conflicts but evolve into legal disputes when cooperative conflict resolution cannot be accomplished. For example, Shirley Slesinger Lasswell, whose late husband acquired the rights to Winnie the Pooh and his friends from creator A. A. Milne in 1930, filed a lawsuit against the Walt Disney Company over merchandising rights to the

characters. Although Lasswell granted rights to use the characters to Walt Disney, she contended that the company cheated her and her family out of millions of dollars in royalties on video sales for two decades. Disney asserted that video sales were not specified in its agreement with Lasswell and declined to pay her a percentage of those sales. A California Superior Court judge dismissed the case after 13 years of negotiations and proceedings, effectively siding with Disney.[26] Indeed, many activities deemed unethical by society have been outlawed through legislation.

However, it is important to understand that business ethics go beyond legal issues. Ethical conduct builds trust among individuals and in business relationships, which validates and promotes confidence in business

> **"Ethical conduct builds trust among individuals and in business relationships, which validates and promotes confidence in business relationships."**

Senator Mike Duffy is one of the senators facing criminal charges as a result of the Senate expense scandal in Canada.

relationships. Establishing trust and confidence is much more difficult in organizations that have established reputations for acting unethically. If you were to discover, for example, that a manager had misled you about company benefits when you were hired, your trust and confidence in that company would probably diminish. And if you learned that a colleague had lied to you about something, you probably would not trust or rely on that person in the future.

Ethical issues are not limited to for-profit organizations, as evident by recent political scandals. In Canada, the Senate expense scandal was in the news in 2015 and 2016. The scandal started in 2012 when Senators Mike Duffy, Patrick Brazeau, Mac Harb, and Pamela Wallin claimed travel and living expenses that were deemed ineligible. While the senators repaid some of the money, Duffy, Brazeau, and Harb were criminally charged. Duffy's case captured the public interest when it was found that former Prime Minister Stephen Harper's chief of staff, Nigel Wright, wrote a personal cheque for $90,000 to help Duffy pay back his expenses. When news of the arrangement was made public, Wright was forced to resign as chief of staff, and many in the public were left wondering what if anything the prime minister knew about the payment. When Wright eventually testified at the Duffy trial in 2015, he stated the prime minister did not know about the arrangement and he was helping Duffy as he clearly could not pay the money back himself. Duffy, who is faced 31 charges of fraud, breach of trust, and bribery, continued to maintain his innocence during his trial, arguing that Senate rules were so poorly laid out and enforced that he should be found innocent of all charges. Ethical concerns are not just limited to actions in the Senate. During the 2011 national election in Canada, Elections Canada and the RCMP investigated a scandal and eventually laid charges against campaign workers for trying to manipulate election results. The scandal, commonly referred to as Robocall, involved people being called and told the place where they would cast their ballot had been changed—when this was not the case. Additionally, some of the callers pretended to be from the Liberal Party of Canada, and called late at night or used rude and/or racist statements. The calls were an attempt to dissuade people from voting for Liberal candidates in the election. Originally, the scandal was thought to be limited to a few areas, but the media has reported that up to 100 ridings were impacted.

Other government scandals include the federal sponsorship scandal. In 2004, Auditor General Sheila Fraser released a report saying taxpayer dollars were mismanaged during the federal sponsorship program.[27] Forensic accountants later said the government had spent $355 million on sponsorships to promote Canadian unity at sporting and cultural events in Quebec. A government-appointed commission was set up and Judge John Gomery, its chair, looked at how the scheme was abused for political ends, and in particular at how $147 million paid in fees and commissions to a dozen advertising and public relations firms found its way into the coffers of the Quebec Liberal Party. Five Crown corporations and agencies—the RCMP, VIA Rail, the Old Port of Montreal, the Business Development Bank of Canada, and Canada Post—were cited as involved in transferring money through dubious means since 1995. Stephen Harper's government later introduced the Accountability Act to crack down on unethical actions and make government transparent.

A number of Nova Scotia politicians landed in hot water when the provincial auditor general reviewed their expense reports. He discovered a number of questionable claims and referred the actions of four members to the RCMP for further investigation. In government, several politicians and some high-ranking officials have been forced to apologize and/or resign in disgrace over ethical indiscretions. For example, Nova Scotia politician Richard Hulbert resigned in 2010 after the above-mentioned review by the Nova Scotia auditor general revealed that he bought a $9,000 generator using provincial money. Hulbert had actually installed the generator in his home.[28] Irv Lewis "Scooter" Libby, a White House advisor, was indicted on five counts of criminal charges: one count of obstruction of justice, two counts of perjury, and two counts of making false statements. In 2007, he was convicted on four of those counts. Each count carried a $250,000 fine and maximum prison term of 30 years.[29] Several scientists have been accused of falsifying research data, which could invalidate later research based on their data and jeopardize trust in all scientific research. Hwang Woo-Suk was found to have faked some of his famous stem cell research, in which

Consider the Following: Are Social Media Sites Fair Game for Employers?

1. In a recent survey, 40 percent of employers admitted to visiting social media sites to pre-screen applicants who are applying for a job. Of the employers who pre-screen candidates, over 70 percent of them will not allow prospective applicants to explain questionable behaviour they see online. These companies simply remove the person from the pool of candidates they are considering for a job. While most people know that having pictures of yourself engaging in illegal activity is likely not a good idea for your Facebook page, employers are going even further than quickly reviewing photos. Many businesses are reading people's online posts to pre-determine if they have a good attitude and are friendly. Do you think it's ethical for companies to screen potential employees by viewing their social media sites such as Facebook, Twitter, and Instagram? Why or why not?

2. Tom comes to work and looks exhausted during a presentation he is giving to clients. Tom's boss later visits Tom's Facebook page where she discovers he was out partying the night before the presentation. How should she handle the situation? Should she have visited Tom's profile to determine what he was doing the day before the presentation? Why or why not?

3. A salesperson comes back from a tropical vacation. On her Facebook page she creates a folder with the title, "Close friends only! My vacation pics." In order to see the vacation pics you have to click on the folder. Her employer logs onto Facebook and visits the salesperson's profile. She notices the folder and clicks on it to view the pictures. She is outraged by the apparent lack of judgment by one of her employees engaging in questionable behaviour and then posting the pictures of this behaviour online. Was it right for her to view the pictures? Would it be right for her to discipline the employee?

4. An employee notes on his Facebook page that his boss is an idiot. The boss finds out about this through the office grapevine. How should the boss handle the situation?

he claimed to have created 30 cloned human embryos and made stem cell lines from skin cells of 11 people, as well as to have produced the world's first cloned dog. He also apologized for using eggs from his own female researchers, which was in breach of guidelines, but he still denied fabricating his research.[30] Even sports can be subject to ethical lapses. At many universities, for example, coaches and athletic administrators have been put on administrative leave after allegations of improper recruiting practices by team members came to light.[31] In some cases, even an entire team of athletes has engaged in ethical misconduct. Dalhousie University, the largest university in Atlantic Canada, recently suspended the majority of the players on its women's hockey team for engaging in unethical behaviour. The result was the team had to default the remainder of the season. In other examples, Montreal native Dick Pound recently completed an investigation on behalf of the World Anti-Doping Agency into the use of illegal drugs by Russian athletes in the latest Summer Olympic Games. Pound concluded, that the Russians were engaged in a massive doping cover-up as the majority of its track team was using performance-enhancing drugs. Pound noted that this was not the case of one or two athletes and stated that the governing body of the sport in Russia had to either have knowledge of the doping or aided in covering it up, saying, "It would be naïve in the extreme to think the massive cheating couldn't happen without government backing it." Asked whether it was state-supported doping, Mr. Pound said: "I don't see how you could call it anything else," adding that it was "not possible" for Russia's top sports bosses, to be unaware. While Russia has denied any doping allegations, the Olympic Committee is now being asked to ban Russian athletes from the next summer games unless they adopt major anti-doping reforms.[32]

© THE CANADIAN PRESS/Dave Chidley

Dick Pound, Montreal native and member of the World Anti-Doping Association, has found that Russian athletes engaged in the use of performance-enhancing drugs in the last Summer Olympic Games.

"Many business issues may seem straightforward and easy to resolve, but in reality, a person often needs several years of experience in business to understand what is acceptable or ethical."

Although we will not tell you in this chapter what you ought to do, others—your superiors, co-workers, and family—will make judgments about the ethics of your actions and decisions. Learning how to recognize and resolve ethical issues is an important step in evaluating ethical decisions in business.

Recognizing Ethical Issues in Business

LO2   Detect some of the ethical issues that may arise in business.

Learning to recognize ethical issues is the most important step in understanding business ethics. An **ethical issue** is an identifiable problem, situation, or opportunity that requires a person to choose from among several actions that may be evaluated as right or wrong, ethical or unethical. In business, such a choice often involves weighing monetary profit against what a person considers appropriate conduct. The best way to judge the ethics of a decision is to look at a situation from a customer's or

> **ethical issue** an identifiable problem, situation, or opportunity that requires a person to choose from among several actions that may be evaluated as right or wrong, ethical or unethical

competitor's viewpoint: Should liquid-diet manufacturers make unsubstantiated claims about their products? Should an engineer agree to divulge her former employer's trade secrets to ensure that she gets a better job with a competitor? Should a salesperson omit facts about a product's poor safety record in his presentation to a customer? Such questions require the decision maker to evaluate the ethics of his or her choice.

Many business issues may seem straightforward and easy to resolve, but in reality, a person often needs several years of experience in business to understand what is acceptable or ethical. For example, if you are a salesperson, when does offering a gift—such as season basketball tickets—to a customer become a bribe rather than just a sales practice? Clearly, there are no easy answers to such a question. But the size of the transaction, the history of personal relationships within the particular company, as well as many other factors may determine whether an action will be judged as right or wrong by others.

Ethics is also related to the culture in which a business operates. In Canada, for example, it would be inappropriate for a businessperson to bring an elaborately wrapped gift to a prospective client on their first meeting—the gift could be viewed as a bribe. In Japan, however, it is considered impolite *not* to bring a gift. Experience with the culture in which a business operates is critical to understanding what is ethical or unethical.

To help you understand ethical issues that perplex businesspeople today, we will take a brief look at some of them in this section. The vast number of news-format investigative programs has increased consumer and employee awareness of organizational misconduct. In addition, the multitude of cable channels and Internet resources has improved the awareness of ethical problems among the general public. The National Business Ethics Survey of more than 3,000 U.S. employees found that workers witness many instances

Consider the Following: When Is Organic Really Organic?

The organic food industry boasts that sales have surpassed $2.6 billion, with supermarkets and specialty stores often charging a premium price for products labelled as organic. In Canada, food with the organic label must be certified by the Canadian Food Inspection Agency (CFIA). Once certified, a company's products do not undergo any laboratory testing to confirm they are free of pesticides. The industry operates on what amounts to an honour system. The CFIA states that testing may be done as part of its annual monitoring program, but specific lab tests to confirm products are organic are not used. In one recent spot test, CFIA documents showed that 24 percent of organic apples contained pesticide residue. The CFIA theorized that many of the tainted apples likely resulted

from inadvertent contamination. The CFIA states that while it is not opposed to testing of products, it is not a proponent of excessive tests, arguing that too much testing will increase the price of organic food—something it says consumers do not want to see happen.[33]

1. Do you think the Canadian Food Inspection Agency is doing enough to ensure foods labelled as organic are actually organic?

2. Would you trust producers not to use pesticides in their operations? Why or why not?

3. Do you think consumers would be willing to pay more for organic food if a testing program ensured the food truly was organic? Why or why not?

Uber Technologies Inc., the ride-sharing company that allows regular people to turn their cars, better known as UberX vehicles, into unlicensed taxis has taken the personal transportation industry by storm. Uber, which was founded only five years ago, was recently valued at over $50 billion dollars and can boast it has reached the valuation two years faster than Facebook.[34] Uber ride sharing is available in 311 cities and 58 countries.[35]

The concept behind Uber is rather simple: Consumers download the Uber app and can use it to hail car owners who will take them to their desired location. All transactions are paid for electronically, eliminating the need for cash. Consumers like the concept as the consensus is drivers are more professional and their cars are cleaner than traditional taxis, you do not have to stand outside to hail a car, and in many instances, the Uber driver will text you when he arrives. Additionally, consumers can specify car types and can see driver reviews prior to agreeing to pick up. Uber drivers like the service as it enables them to basically operate as an unlicensed taxi, and they can earn extra money when they want to work and create their own schedule.

So while riders and drivers clearly like Uber's business model, government officials and traditional taxi drivers view the service very differently. In most, if not all, Canadian cities, taxi and limousine drivers are heavily regulated and drivers have to have a special licence or permit to operate. In many cities, such as Montreal, there is a limit on the number of legal taxis allowed on the road.[36] This limit in theory is to ensure that drivers earn a livable wage from their work. The result is that in most cities drivers treat their licences or permits as assets and can sell or rent them to other potential users. For example, in Montreal it is not uncommon to see a driver trying to sell his permit (licence) for upwards of $175,000.[37] Suni Johal, policy director at the Mowat Centre, a public-policy think

© ValeStock / Shutterstock.com

Uber drivers are everywhere in big cities in Canada. While many users prefer some of the Uber advantages, such as knowing who your driver is before he or she picks you up, taxi drivers often argue Uber is an illegal business that should be outlawed in Canada.

tank at the University of Toronto, and Vincent Geloso from the Montreal Economic Institute are in agreement that the traditional taxi industry should be deregulated as government should think about what's best for citizens and not maximizing taxi revenue.[38]

---

of ethical misconduct in their organizations (see Table 2.2). The most common types of observed misconduct were abusive/intimidating behaviour, lying, and placing employee interests over organizational interests.[43]

One of the principal causes of unethical behaviour in organizations is overly aggressive financial or business objectives. Many of these issues relate to decisions and concerns that managers have to deal with daily. It is not possible to discuss every issue, of course. However, a discussion of a few issues can help you begin to recognize the ethical problems with which businesspersons must deal. Many ethical issues in business can be

Table 2.2 Types and Incidences of Observed Misconduct

Type of Conduct Observed	Employees Observing It
Abusive or intimidating behaviour toward employees	21%
Lying to employees, customers, vendors, or the public	19
Situations placing employee interests over organizational interests	18
Violations of safety regulations	16
Misreporting of actual time worked	16
Discrimination on the basis of race, colour, gender, age, or similar categories	12
Stealing or theft	11
Sexual harassment	9

Source: "National Business Ethics Survey 2005," "Survey Documents State of Ethics in the Workplace," and "Misconduct," Ethics Resource Center (n.d.), www.ethics.org (accessed April 11, 2006).

Taxi owners and city officials do not agree with Johal and Geloso. Both sides point to the fact that traditional Canadian car insurance does not allow people to offer paid-for ride-sharing services, and there is a chance Uber drivers would have their insurance invalidated if they were involved in an accident leaving the driver personally liable for the car and its occupants.[39] The result is Uber riders may have to personally sue the driver to cover any health and/or legal claims. Taxi owners also claim that anyone can drive for Uber while the licensing process has checks in place to ensure that drivers are not a threat to passengers.

The Toronto City Council has recently decided Uber is offering an illegal service as drivers are operating without a taxi licence. Current Mayor John Tory admits that while he doesn't think drivers should continue to operate, shutting down Uber's 16,000 drivers and 400,000 riders is likely an impossible task and he is in favour of creating new regulations for ride-sharing companies. "I'm not okay with it, but I guess you have to sort of accept in this job, there's a lot of things that go on in the city every day where people are not in compliance, and we don't have the necessary resources to have every single one of those people overseen and charged. The practicality of having a huge portion of the police service devoted to cracking down on UberX drivers, the practicality of having a huge additional number or even existing bylaw officers cracking down to a point where we could stop the behaviour, I'm not sure is realistic."[40]

Traditional taxi and limousine drivers don't want the service regulated though. They want the service shut down. Dominik Konjevic, a Toronto taxi company owner, has filed a class-action lawsuit on behalf of Ontario taxi and limousine drivers, seeking $140 million in damages against Uber and a court injunction to shut down the service in Ontario. Mr. Konjevic states Uber conspired to break Ontario's Highway Traffic Act, which requires a licence to pick up people for money, and caused significant harm to taxi and limo drivers. "The defendants (Uber) and the UberX drivers knew, or ought to have known, that the natural result of their conspiracy would be injury to the ongoing legitimate business interests of the class members."[41]

Even as Toronto and other Canadian cities move to ban Uber, the company reports continued growth in Canada. More consumers continue to claim they prefer Uber drivers, that there is not enough taxis on the road—especially late at night and in the suburbs—and that they like knowing who their drivers are prior to pick-up. All of which is driving the demand for Uber services.

DISCUSSION QUESTIONS

1. In your opinion, are ride-sharing services like Uber ethical or unethical? Why?

2. Do you think all businesses should follow the same rules? Why or why not?

3. What are the implications of Uber being considered illegal in Canada? Should Uber riders be charged with a fine for using the service?

4. Do you prefer to have some choice in using a taxi or a ride sharing service? Why?

5. Uber is currently in discussions with Intact, one of Canada's largest insurance companies, to create ride-sharing insurance.[42] If the insurance is created, should governments allow Uber to operate as is? Why or why not?

Abusive or Intimidating Behaviour. Abusive or intimidating behaviour is the most common ethical problem for employees. The concepts can mean anything from physical threats, false accusations, being annoying, profanity, insults, yelling, harshness, or ignoring someone, to unreasonableness, and the meaning of these words can differ by person—you probably have some ideas of your own.

categorized in the context of their relation with abusive and intimidating behaviour, conflicts of interest, fairness and honesty, communications, and business associations.

"Bullying is associated with a hostile workplace when someone considered a target (or a group) is threatened, harassed, belittled, or verbally abused or overly criticized."

Abusive behaviour can be placed on a continuum from a minor distraction to a workplace disruption. For example, what one person may define as yelling might be another's definition of normal speech. Civility in our society has been a concern, and the workplace is no exception. The productivity level of many organizations has been damaged by the time spent unravelling abusive relationships.

Abusive behaviour is difficult to assess and manage because of diversity in culture and lifestyle. What does it mean to speak profanely? Is profanity only related to specific words or other such terms that are

© Image 100/Punchstock

Bullying, which was once something that occurred on the playground, has become a problem at work as abusive or intimidating behaviour continues to plague employees.

Table 2.3 Actions Associated with Bullies

1. Spreading rumours to damage others
2. Blocking others' communication in the workplace
3. Flaunting status or authority to take advantage of others
4. Discrediting others' ideas and opinions
5. Use of e-mails to demean others
6. Failing to communicate or return communication
7. Insults, yelling, and shouting
8. Using terminology to discriminate by gender, race, or age
9. Using eye or body language to hurt others or their reputation
10. Taking credit for others' work or ideas

Source: © O. C. Ferrell, 2011.

common in today's business world? If you are using words that are normal in your language but others consider profanity, have you just insulted, abused, or disrespected them?

Within the concept of abusive behaviour, intent should be a consideration. If the employee was trying to convey a compliment but the comment was considered abusive, then it was probably a mistake. The way a word is said (voice inflection) can be important. Add to this the fact that we now live in a multicultural environment—doing business and working with many different cultural groups—and the businessperson soon realizes the depth of the ethical and legal issues that may arise. There are problems of word meanings by age and within cultures. For example, an expression such as "Did you guys hook up last night?" can have various meanings, including some that could be considered offensive in a work environment.

Bullying is associated with a hostile workplace when someone considered a target (or a group) is threatened, harassed, belittled, or verbally abused or overly criticized. While bullying may create what some may call a hostile environment, this term is generally associated with sexual harassment. Although sexual harassment has legal recourse, bullying has little legal recourse at this time. Bullying can cause psychological damage that can result in health endangering consequences to the target. As Table 2.3 indicates, bullying can use a mix of verbal, nonverbal, and manipulative threatening expressions to damage workplace productivity. One may wonder why workers tolerate such activities; the problem is that 81 percent of workplace bullies are supervisors. A recent study by Jacqueline Power, an assistant professor of management at the University of Windsor's Odette School of Business, found that 40 percent of Canadians have experienced one or more acts of workplace bullying at least once a week for the last six months. Power has determined that bullying leads to the underperformance

of organizations as the injured parties can quit and go elsewhere or are prone to be less productive.[44]

Conflict of Interest. A conflict of interest exists when a person must choose whether to advance his or her own personal interests or those of others. For example, a manager in a corporation is supposed to ensure that the company is profitable so that its shareholder-owners receive a return on their investment. In other words, the manager has a responsibility to investors. If she instead makes decisions that give her more power or money but do not help the company, then she has a conflict of interest—she is acting to benefit herself at the expense of her company and is not fulfilling her responsibilities. To avoid conflicts of interest, employees must be able to separate their personal financial interests from their business dealings. For example, For example, Global Television suspended Toronto-based news anchor Leslie Roberts after it was revealed that he was a secret partner in public relations firm BuzzPR. BuzzPR was being paid by clients for publicity Roberts was providing them on the news and through his social media accounts. Roberts ultimately resigned over the matter.

As mentioned earlier, it is considered improper to give or accept **bribes**—payments, gifts, or special favours intended to influence the outcome of a decision. A bribe is a conflict of interest because it benefits an individual at the expense of an organization or society.

> **bribes** payments, gifts, or special favours intended to influence the outcome of a decision

Companies that do business overseas should be aware that bribes are a significant ethical issue and are in fact illegal in many countries. For example, Acres International of Oakville, Ontario, was convicted by the Lesotho High Court in Africa of bribing a local official to secure contracts.[45] Bribery is more prevalent in some countries than in others. For example, bribes are standard practice in Bangladesh, where Niko Resources, a Calgary-based company recently experienced trouble

© THE CANADIAN PRESS IMAGES/Frank Arcuri

Leslie Roberts, former Global News anchor, resigned when it was discovered he was being secretly paid to generate publicity for businesses and other clients.

when it was caught purchasing a $190,000 car for a government official.[46] Transparency International has developed a Corruption Perceptions Index (Table 2.4). Note there are eight countries perceived as less corrupt than Canada.

Table 2.4 Least Corrupt Countries

Rank	Country	2015 CPI Score*
1	Denmark	91
2	Finland	90
3	Sweden	89
4	New Zealand	88
5	Netherlands	87
5	Norway	87
7	Switzerland	86
8	Singapore	85
9	Canada	83
10	Germany	81
10	Luxembourg	81
10	United Kingdom	81
13	Australia	79
13	Iceland	79
15	Belgium	77
16	Austria	76
16	United States	76
18	Hong Kong	75
18	Ireland	75
18	Japan	75
21	Uruguay	74
22	Qatar	71

* CPI score relates to perceptions of the degree of corruption as seen by businesspeople and country analysts and ranges between 100 (highly clean) and 0 (highly corrupt).

Source: This information is extracted from the CPI; the CPI is measuring perceived public sector corruption. © Transparency International 2015. All Rights Reserved. For more information, visit http://www.transparency.org.

RESPONDING TO BUSINESS CHALLENGES | What Is Ethical When Bribes Are the Norm?

For years, bribes and corruption in foreign countries were customary and considered acceptable, meaning a Canadian company operating in a part of the world where bribery was the norm would be forgiven for following local customs and could pay bribes. This attitude started to change in 1999, when both the U.S. and Canadian governments started to pass tougher rules governing how North American companies conducted business globally. Like most of what happens in business though, things are not always straightforward. While large bribes are no longer considered acceptable, it still isn't clear about small bribes, often referred to as "facilitation payments," that get people to perform their jobs. For example, in some European countries it is not unusual for the mailman to knock on your door at Christmas looking for a cash gift. The norm is that you pay the gift or you don't get your mail anymore.

DISCUSSION QUESTIONS

1. Do you think it is ethical to pay a bribe in a country where it is a cultural norm? Why or why not?

2. Do you think "facilitation payments" should be considered bribes? If you ran a company in a country where these payments were the norm, would you pay them?

3. Do you think Canada's legal system should be investigating crimes such as bribes which occur in other countries? Why or why not?

Figure 2.1 Most Popular Office Supplies Employees Pilfer

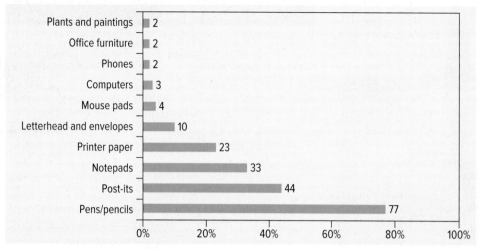

Category	Percentage
Plants and paintings	2
Office furniture	2
Phones	2
Computers	3
Mouse pads	4
Letterhead and envelopes	10
Printer paper	23
Notepads	33
Post-its	44
Pens/pencils	77

Source: Based on "More Employees Taking Supplies," *The (Wilmington, Del.) News Journal,* using data from Lawyers.com, April 1, 2007, http://www.usatoday.com/money/industries/retail/2007-03-30-supply_N.htm (accessed June 1, 2007).

Fairness and Honesty. Fairness and honesty are at the heart of business ethics and relate to the general values of decision makers. At a minimum, businesspersons are expected to follow all applicable laws and regulations. But beyond obeying the law, they are expected not to harm customers, employees, clients, or competitors knowingly through deception, misrepresentation, coercion, or discrimination. As discussed throughout the chapter, issues of ethics are not always clear, as in the case of probiotics, one of the trendiest health products over the past decade. Probiotics are being put into yogurt, sports drinks, and other food products with claims that they improve the digestive system. Advocates of the bacteria cite incidents of people's health improving as a result of ingesting the bacteria. Yet scientific research does not support these claims. The European Food Safety Authority (EFSA) has studied hundreds of health claims associated with probiotics and rejected them all. The EFSA is moving forward with plans to ban the use of the word *probiotics* on food labels. Yet some companies that produce these products point to research which they state proves their claim that probiotics are good for you. Other examples are a bit clearer cut such as the case of Volkswagen as mentioned above, which intentionally installed software on some of its diesel cars to cheat emission tests and then sold the cars as being more environmentally friendly. Other clear cases of dishonesty include Suzy Shier Inc. and The Forzani Group, owners and operators of SportChek and Sports Smart stores, who ended up on the receiving end of a number of consumer complaints as consumer groups noted that the stores frequently overstated the regular selling price on items to make the sales price look more attractive. The result was consumers felt that they were getting a larger bargain and spent more or bought items that they normally would not have bought. The Canadian Competition Bureau, an independent law enforcement agency that protects and promotes consumers, brought the matter before the courts; the result was

fines of $1 million for Suzy Shier Inc. and total fines and court costs of $1.7 million for The Forzani Group.[47] Vault. com found that 67 percent of employees have taken office supplies from work to use for matters unrelated to their job. Most employees do not view taking office supplies as stealing or dishonest, with 97 percent saying they have never gotten caught and it would not matter if they were found out. In addition, only 3.7 percent say they have taken items like keyboards, software, and memory sticks. Still, an employee should be aware of policies on taking items and recognize how these decisions relate to ethical behaviour.[48] Figure 2.1 provides an overview of the most pilfered office supplies.

One aspect of fairness relates to competition. Although numerous laws have been passed to foster competition and make monopolistic practices illegal, companies sometimes gain control over markets by using questionable practices that harm competition. Bullying can also occur between companies that are in intense competition. Even respected companies such as Intel have been accused of monopolistic bullying. A competitor, Advanced Micro Devices (AMD), claimed in a lawsuit that 38 companies,

© Keith Homan / Shutterstock.com

Consumers are flocking to buy products with added probiotics, hoping to improve their health. Unfortunately, research by the European Food Safety Authority and the U.S. Food and Drug Administration does not support any of these claims. Are companies pushing consumers to purchase probiotic products ethical?

including Dell and Sony, were strong-arming customers (such as Apple) into buying Intel chips rather than those marketed by AMD. The AMD lawsuit seeks billions of dollars and will take years to litigate. In many cases, the alleged misconduct not only can have monetary and legal implications but can threaten reputation, investor confidence, and customer loyalty. A front-cover *Forbes* headline stated "Intel to AMD: Drop Dead." An example of the intense competition and Intel's ability to use its large size won it the high-profile Apple account, displacing IBM and Free-scale. AMD said it had no opportunity to bid because Intel offered to deploy 600 Indian engineers to help Apple software run more smoothly on Intel chips.[49]

Another aspect of fairness and honesty relates to disclosure of potential harm caused by product use. For example, Maple Leaf Foods announced a series of recalls in 2008 after it discovered that some of its products were tainted with *Listeria monocytogenes*, a bacterium that can cause serious illness and even death if ingested. While a number of people did become ill and some in fact died, Maple Leaf CEO Michael McCain's handling of the situation was recognized as positive by the business press and many Canadians. McCain claimed full responsibility for the recall and was in constant communication with the public and the press. Right from the start of the outbreak, Maple Leaf reached out to the public using press conferences, web postings, and commercials to keep consumers informed. Testifying before a parliamentary committee on food safety McCain noted, "This tragedy was a defining moment for Maple Leaf Foods and for those that worked there. We are determined to make a terrible wrong, right."[50] Maple Leaf's efforts not only helped consumers realize they may have purchased tainted products but also helped the company's image and bottom line as the decline in the firm's value has not been as significant as industry experts thought it would be as a result of the recall. Toyota had to deal with an even larger issue in 2009 and 2010 when the company had to recall millions of cars and trucks due to problems with unintended acceleration, and again in 2013 when it had to recall 1.7 million vehicles, 75,000 of them in Canada, due to problems with airbags.[51] Toyota, much like Maple Leaf Foods, addressed the problem in the media and worked to find a solution.

Compare the responses of those companies to that of XL Foods, a Canadian beef processing plant where testing for *E. coli* was not stringent enough. The lack of testing resulted in infected food reaching the marketplace, causing consumers to become ill and requiring the company to institute a large recall of products. Rather than address the problem directly, the company basically went into a media blackout, ignoring requests for additional information. The result was no one trusted the few statements they heard from XL and rumours ran rampant in the press. A similar event occurred with Mitsubishi Motors, Japan's number-four automaker, which faced criminal charges and negative publicity after executives admitted that the company had systematically covered up customer complaints about tens of thousands of defective automobiles over a 20-year period to avoid

expensive and embarrassing product recalls.[52] Consumers seem willing to accept that mistakes, even deadly mistakes, will happen in the manufacturing of consumer goods. What upsets consumers, however, is when companies attempt to avoid the truth to limit financial damage. Both Toyota and Maple Leaf benefited from being honest with their customers.

While corrupt business practices in Canada are an issue, the country has recently improved its standing, according to the Corruption Perceptions Index from Transparency International, which annually ranks countries based on perceptions of corruption in business and government circles.[53] As of 2015, Canada is ranked ninth in the world, an improvement from our 14th place ranking a few years before. Lying was the most observed form of misconduct in the National Business Ethics Survey. Other examples of dishonesty include piracy. The Canadian Recording Industry Association has reported that net music sales in Canada have declined significantly in the past decade. The CRIA said the decline reflects an almost 15-year spiral paralleling the rise of music file sharing on the Internet, and continues unabated due to the failure of the Canadian government to enact much overdue copyright reform.[54] The music industry has been calling on the Canadian government to modernize copyright laws in this country in order to stem illegal downloading, and in June 2010, the government responded with Bill C-11 which passed in 2012. Research group Pollara says an estimated 1.6 billion illegal music files are shared online annually in Canada. Interestingly, a study released in March 2004 by Harvard Business School claims that Internet music piracy not only does not hurt legitimate CD sales, but may even boost sales of some types of music. The study provides evidence that file sharing alone cannot explain the decline in music sales in the last couple of years. In addition, music sales appear to have increased as file sharing has become even more popular. Even the Recording Industry Association of America (RIAA) now states that file sharing is only "one factor, along with economic conditions and competing forms of entertainment that is displacing legitimate sales."[55] The

© McGraw-Hill Companies, Inc. Mark Dierker, photographer

Toyota had to recall 9 million cars globally, including the popular hybrid Prius, after problems were uncovered with the accelerator.

Gary Fung, founder of Vancouver-based isoHunt, has recently agreed to pay a $110 million fine and shut down his website. The courts have found that Fung's company is much like a modern-day Napster for videos and music, allowing people to illegally share files on the Internet. Fung's opinion on the matter is very different. He argues his site operates just like Google in that it is a search engine that organizes information. It's not up to him to control what users do with the information his search engine produces. Supporters of Fung state that Google is not held responsible for the illegal content it organizes for people, so why should file-sharing sites be any different?[56]

1. Do you think it is ethical to download music, videos, and software? Why or why not?

2. Do you think Fung should be penalized for operating a website that helps facilitate the downloading of music, videos, and software?

3. In your opinion, is Fung's argument that the site is similar to Google, Bing, or other search engines a fair one to make? Why or why not?

© The Globe and Mail/CP Images

After a number of years of trying, the music and movie industry managed to shut down isoHunt, an online file-sharing site founded by Canadian Gary Fung.

contradictory evidence on the impact of file sharing reinforces the discussion at the start of the chapter that it can be difficult to judge ethical behaviour.

Dishonesty is not only found in business. According to the first major study of academic misconduct in Canada, cheating, deceit, and plagiarism were found to be serious problems. Julia Christensen Hughes of the University of Guelph and Donald McCabe of Rutgers University surveyed 14,913 undergraduate students, 1,318 graduate students, 683 teaching assistants, and 1,902 faculty from 11 Canadian post-secondary institutions across five provinces.

Students admitted to having engaged in some form of misconduct while completing their academic work. Seventy-three percent admitted to "serious" cheating while in high school and 53 percent of undergrads admitted they are still cheating in university.[57] If today's students are tomorrow's leaders, there is likely to be a correlation between acceptable behaviour today and tomorrow, adding to the argument that the leaders of today must be prepared for the ethical risks associated with this downward trend. According to a poll by Deloitte Touche of teenagers aged 13 to 18, when asked if people who practise good business ethics are more successful than those who don't, 69 percent of teenagers agreed.[58] The same poll found only 12 percent of teens think business leaders today are ethical. On the other hand, another survey indicated that many students do not define copying answers from another student's paper or downloading music or content for classroom work as cheating.[59]

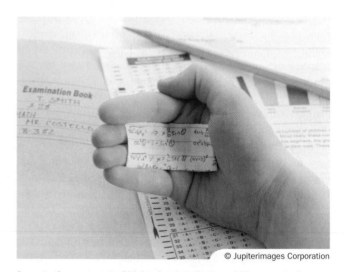

© Jupiterimages Corporation

Seventy-three percent of high school students and 53 percent of university students admitted to serious cheating.

Communications. Communications is another area in which ethical concerns may arise. False and misleading advertising, as well as deceptive personal-selling tactics, anger consumers and can lead to the failure of a business. Truthfulness about product safety and quality is also important to consumers. As discussed above, manufacturers of products with probiotics are starting to come under increased government scrutiny in Europe and the U.S. The bacteria was largely ignored in North America until Danone, producers of Activia yogurt, started spending upwards of $130 million annually to promote the health benefits of the product. The issue is that the benefits are not supported by any scientific research.[60] Claims about dietary supplements and weight-loss products can be particularly problematic. For example, Canada, Mexico, and the United States recently announced actions taken to fight weight-loss fraud: They had taken 734 compliance actions to combat companies promoting bogus and misleading weight-loss schemes. Canadian investigative news shows *Marketplace* and *W5* have spent considerable effort studying some of the claims of the weight loss industry with surprising results. CBC's *Marketplace* investigated Herbal Magic, one of the biggest weight loss companies in Canada—with more than 300 stores nationwide. The journalists discovered that Herbal Magic clients were being told to purchase two expensive dietary supplements to encourage weight loss. CBC brought the supplements to laboratories for independent testing and discovered that there was not enough scientific evidence to justify the claims. Since the airing of the show, Herbal Magic has announced it will replace the supplements with different formulations.[61] *W5* also uncovered questionable behaviour in its investigation of PhytoPharma, which became known for many weight-loss products including the popular Plant Macerate and Apple Cider Vinegar capsules by Naturalab. *W5* determined that there was no scientific evidence to support the claim that the products assisted in weight loss.[62]

Unscrupulous activity is not limited to just the diet industry. Governments in Canada, Mexico, and the United States launched 177 compliance and enforcement actions against companies promoting bogus diabetes products and services. Actions include prosecutions, recalls, seizures, import refusals, warnings, and other enforcement programs against false and misleading advertising and labelling, as well as the promotion of industry compliance.[63]

Some companies fail to provide enough information for consumers about differences or similarities between products. For example, driven by high prices for medicines, many consumers are turning to the Internet, Mexico, and overseas sources for drugs to treat a variety of illnesses and conditions. However, research suggests that a significant percentage of these imported pharmaceuticals may not actually contain the labelled drug, and the counterfeit drugs could even be harmful to those who take them. The issue of drug importation is particularly problematic in the United States where millions of people do not have health insurance. Unfortunately, as stated above, people do not always know what they are getting. In a recent FDA seizure, it was discovered that 85 percent of the drugs that were purported to be sold from Canada in fact came from other countries.[64]

Another important aspect of communications that may raise ethical concerns relates to product labelling. In Canada, anti-tobacco legislation requires cigarette manufacturers to include graphic pictures, health warnings, health information messages, and toxic emissions/constituents statements on their packages. The U.S. Surgeon General currently requires cigarette manufacturers to indicate clearly on cigarette packaging that smoking cigarettes is harmful to the smoker's health. In Europe, at least 30 percent of the front side of product packaging and 40 percent of the back needs to be taken up by the warning. The use of descriptors such as "light" or "mild" has been banned.[65] However, labelling of other products raises ethical questions when it threatens basic rights, such as freedom of speech and expression. This is the heart of the controversy surrounding the movement to require warning labels on movies and video games, rating their content, language, and appropriate audience age. Although people in the entertainment industry believe that such labelling violates their rights, other consumers—particularly parents—believe that such labelling is needed to protect children from harmful influences. Internet regulation, particularly that designed to protect children and the elderly, is at the forefront in consumer protection legislation. Because of the debate surrounding the acceptability of these business activities, they remain major ethical issues. The Canadian Radio-television and Telecommunications Commission, the body responsible for regulating broadcasting and telecommunications in Canada, does not regulate the Internet. However, certain obligations must be met under consumer protection laws when doing business with consumers on the Internet. Another highly polarized debate concerns the labelling of genetically modified (GM) foods in Canada. Currently, disclosure of GM foods among Canadian food manufacturers and retailers is not required, even though GM foods are said to be present in 60 to 70 percent of all processed foods on the market, according to the Food and Consumer Products Manufacturers of Canada.[66]

Opponents of GM foods argue that they might pose health risks for certain people (for example, foods could become metabolically dangerous or even toxic from the introduction of a fish gene in a plant). Proponents assert that GM foods will promise many health benefits (for example, farmers typically produce GM crops using fewer pesticides, herbicides, and fertilizers). Other arguments against GM crops are that the technology will hurt small farmers and harm the environment, that modification goes against

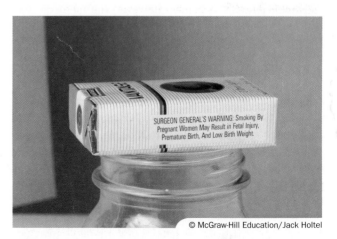

© McGraw-Hill Education/Jack Holtel

Cigarette labels now have to warn about health risks.

nature, that the industry suffers from poor oversight and regulation, and that biotech companies are profit-driven with little concern for potential risks to people or nature. Proponents maintain that farmers will reap great benefits from biotechnology; that the technology helps the environment, is completely natural, and uses the most thoroughly tested and highly regulated food plants; and that GM crops hold the greatest hope for adequately feeding a rapidly expanding population. Because of the debate surrounding the acceptability of these business activities, they remain major ethical issues.

"In Canada, corporate espionage is estimated to cost the economy upwards of $100 billion a year as secrets and confidential information is stolen."[70]

Business Relationships. The behaviour of businesspersons toward customers, suppliers, and others in their workplace may also generate ethical concerns. Ethical behaviour within a business involves keeping company secrets, meeting obligations and responsibilities, and avoiding undue pressure that may force others to act unethically.

Managers, in particular, because of the authority of their position, have the opportunity to influence employees' actions. For example, a manager can influence employees to use pirated computer software to save costs. The use of illegal software puts the employee and the company at legal risk, but employees may feel pressured to do so by their superior's authority. The Canadian Alliance Against Software Theft (CAAST) and the Business Software Alliance (BSA), watchdog groups that represent the world's leading software manufacturers, announced that some 11 Canadian companies from diverse industries have recently agreed to pay a total of $252,093 to settle claims that they were using unlicensed software. According to a study, 33 percent of software installed on computers in Canada was pirated, representing a loss of $943 million. It is estimated that, globally, software piracy resulted in a loss of $41 billion.[67]

It is the responsibility of managers to create a work environment that helps the organization achieve its objectives and fulfill its responsibilities. However, the methods that managers use to enforce these responsibilities should not compromise employee rights. Organizational pressures may encourage a person to engage in activities that he or she might otherwise view as unethical, such as invading others' privacy or stealing a competitor's secrets. For example, in 2004, when Air Canada found that WestJet had gained access to its internal website to acquire commercially sensitive data, it launched a $220 million lawsuit against the company. In return, WestJet filed a $5 million countersuit claiming that Air Canada had hired private investigators to pilfer the garbage of WestJet's co-founder, Mark Hill. After two years of arguments, WestJet apologized and admitted that its online snooping was unethical. It agreed to pay Air Canada $5.5 million to settle the allegations of corporate espionage, and to donate $10 million to children's charities in the name of both airlines. In return, Air Canada accepted WestJet's apologies and withdrew the legal claims.[68] Another example includes Betty Vinson, an accounting executive at WorldCom, who protested when her superiors asked her to make improper accounting entries to cover up the company's deteriorating financial condition. She acquiesced only after being told that it was the only way to save the troubled company. She, along with several other WorldCom accountants, pleaded guilty to conspiracy and fraud charges related to WorldCom's bankruptcy after the accounting improprieties came to light.[69] Alternatively, the firm may provide only vague or lax supervision on ethical issues, providing the opportunity for misconduct. Managers who offer no ethical direction to employees create many opportunities for manipulation, dishonesty, and conflicts of interest.

Plagiarism—taking someone else's work and presenting it as your own without mentioning the source—is another ethical issue. As a student, you may be familiar with plagiarism in school; for example, copying someone else's term paper or quoting from a published work or Internet source without acknowledging it. In business, an ethical issue arises when an employee copies reports or presents the work or ideas of others as his or her own. At *USA Today*, for example, an internal investigation into the work of veteran reporter Jack Kelley identified dozens of stories in which Kelley appeared to have plagiarized material from competing newspapers. The investigation also uncovered evidence Kelley fabricated significant portions of at least eight major stories and conspired to cover up his lapses in judgment. The newspaper later apologized to its readers, and Kelley resigned.[71] A manager attempting to take credit for a subordinate's ideas is engaging in another type of plagiarism.

plagiarism the act of taking someone else's work and presenting it as your own without mentioning the source

© Design Pics/Don Hammond

Air Canada and WestJet have both engaged in questionable practices as they fight for market share in Canada.

"It is the responsibility of managers to create a work environment that helps the organization achieve its objectives **and fulfill its responsibilities."**

Making Decisions About Ethical Issues

Although we've presented a variety of ethical issues that may arise in business, it can be difficult to recognize specific ethical issues in practice. Whether a decision maker recognizes an issue as an ethical one often depends on the issue itself. Managers, for example, tend to be more concerned about issues that affect those close to them, as well as issues that have immediate rather than long-term consequences. Thus, the perceived importance of an ethical issue substantially affects choices, and only a few issues receive scrutiny, while most receive no attention at all.[72]

Table 2.5 lists some questions you may want to ask yourself and others when trying to determine whether an action is ethical. Open discussion of ethical issues does not eliminate ethical problems, but it does promote both trust and learning in an organization.[73] When people feel that they cannot discuss what they are doing with their co-workers or superiors, there is a good chance that an ethical issue exists. Once a person has recognized an ethical issue and can openly discuss it with others, he or she has begun the process of resolving the ethical issue.

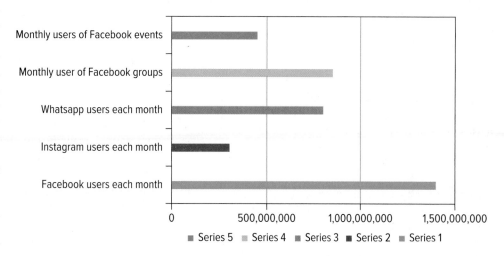

Based on data from "Facebook Beats in Q2 with $4.04B Revenue, Growth Slows to 3.47% QOQ to Hit 1.49B" by Josh Constine, *TechCrunch*, July 29, 2015.

Facebook reported revenues of over $4 billion in one quarter in 2015. While investors are happy, critics of the company maintain that most of the money is made from advertisers who are accessing users' personal information often without users' knowledge, let alone permission. Do you think this is ethical?

Consider the Following: Is Facebook Acting Ethically by Making Billions off Your Personal Information?

In quarter two, one three-month period, Facebook reported earnings of $4.04 billion and saw its total number of users reach almost 1.5 billion people.[74] Facebook, which also owns WhatsApp and Instagram, has seen steady growth in revenue and profits since its inception by Mark Zuckerberg 14 years ago. While investors in the company are quite happy with the results, there are a growing number of critics who contend that much of Facebook's advertising revenue is a direct result of Facebook using its users' personal information to sell to advertisers who create targeted ads based on users' browser history, likes, recommendations, and other information. These critics contend that Facebook is combining information from WhatsApp, Instagram, and location proximity apps to create even more detailed user profiles.[75] The end result is Facebook is making billions off people's personal information, and often people do not know that this is the case or the extent of personal information Facebook is selling.[76]

1. Do you think people are aware of the amount of personal information being collected by Facebook? Will awareness hurt the company's business model? Why or why not?

2. Do you think it's ethical for Facebook to collect and sell personal information of its roughly 1.5 billion users? Why or why not?

3. Facebook originally stated it would not combine the personal information from Facebook and Instagram to create even more detailed user profiles. After a brief period, Facebook have gone back on their word and started to combine user profiles. Is this ethical? Why or why not?

Table 2.5 Questions to Consider in Determining Whether an Action Is Ethical

Are there any potential legal restrictions or violations that could result from the action?

Does your company have a specific code of ethics or policy on the action?

Is this activity customary in your industry? Are there any industry trade groups that provide guidelines or codes of conduct that address this issue?

Would this activity be accepted by your co-workers? Will your decision or action withstand open discussion with co-workers and managers and survive untarnished?

How does this activity fit with your own beliefs and values?

Improving Ethical Behaviour in Business

LO3 Specify how businesses can promote ethical behaviour.

Understanding how people make ethical choices and what prompts a person to act unethically may reverse the current trend toward unethical behaviour in business. Ethical decisions in an organization are influenced by three key factors: individual moral standards, the influence of managers and co-workers, and the opportunity to engage in misconduct (Figure 2.2). While you have great control over your personal ethics outside the workplace, your co-workers and superiors exert significant control over your choices at work through authority and example. In fact, the activities and examples set by co-workers, along with rules and policies established by the firm, are critical in gaining consistent ethical compliance in an organization. If the company fails to provide good examples and direction for appropriate conduct, confusion and conflict will develop and result in the opportunity for misconduct. If your boss or co-workers leave work early, you may be tempted to do so as well. If you see co-workers making personal long-distance phone calls at work and charging them to the company, then you may be more likely to do so also. In addition, having sound personal values contributes to an ethical workplace.

Because ethical issues often emerge from conflict, it is useful to examine the causes of ethical conflict. Business managers and employees often experience some tension between their own ethical beliefs and their obligations to the organizations in which they work. Many employees utilize different ethical standards at work than they do at home. This conflict increases when employees feel that their company is encouraging unethical conduct or exerting pressure on them to engage in it.

It is difficult for employees to determine what conduct is acceptable within a company if the firm does not have ethics policies and standards. And without such policies and standards, employees may base decisions on how their peers and superiors behave. Professional **codes of ethics** are formalized rules and standards that describe what the company expects of its employees. Codes of ethics do not have to be so detailed that they take into account every situation, but they should provide guidelines and principles that can help employees achieve organizational objectives and address risks in an acceptable and ethical way. The development of a code of ethics should include not only a firm's executives and board of directors, but also legal staff and employees from all areas of a firm.[77] Table 2.6 lists some key things to consider when developing a code of ethics.

> **codes of ethics** formalized rules and standards that describe what a company expects of its employees

Codes of ethics, policies on ethics, and ethics training programs advance ethical behaviour because they prescribe which activities are acceptable and which are not, and they limit the opportunity for misconduct by providing punishments for violations of the rules and standards. According to the National Business Ethics Survey (NBES), employees in organizations that have written standards of conduct, ethics training, ethics offices or hotlines, and systems for anonymous reporting of misconduct are more likely to report misconduct when they observe it. The survey also found that such programs are associated with higher employee perceptions that they will be held accountable for ethical infractions.[78] The enforcement of such codes and policies through rewards and punishments increases the acceptance of ethical standards by employees.

One of the most important components of an ethics program is a means through which employees can report observed misconduct anonymously. The NBES found that although employees are increasingly reporting illegal and unethical activities they observe in the workplace, 59 percent of surveyed employees

> **"Many employees utilize different ethical standards at work than they do at home."**

Figure 2.2 Three Factors That Influence Business Ethics

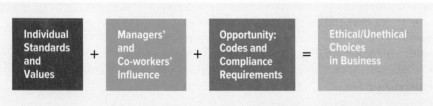

Individual Standards and Values + Managers' and Co-workers' Influence + Opportunity: Codes and Compliance Requirements = Ethical/Unethical Choices in Business

Table 2.6 Key Things to Consider in Developing a Code of Ethics

- Create a team to assist with the process of developing the code (include management and non-management employees from across departments and functions).

- Solicit input from employees from different departments, functions, and regions to compile a list of common questions and answers to include in the code document.

- Make certain that the headings of the code sections can be easily understood by all employees.

- Avoid referencing specific Canadian laws and regulations or those of specific countries, particularly for codes that will be distributed to employees in multiple regions.

- Hold employee group meetings on a complete draft version (including graphics and pictures) of the text using language that everyone can understand.

- Inform employees that they will receive a copy of the code during an introduction session.

- Let all employees know that they will receive future ethics training which will, in part, cover the important information contained in the code document.

Source: Based on William Miller, "Implementing an Organizational Code of Ethics," *International Business Ethics Review* 7 (Winter 2004), pp. 1, 6–10.

indicated they are unwilling to report misconduct because they fear that no corrective action will be taken or that their report will not remain confidential.[79] The lack of anonymous reporting mechanisms may encourage **whistleblowing**, which occurs when an employee exposes an employer's wrongdoing to outsiders, such as the media or government regulatory agencies. However, more companies are establishing programs to encourage employees to report illegal or unethical practices internally so that they can take steps to remedy problems before they result in legal action or generate negative publicity. The Federal Accountability Act, among other measures, provides public-sector workers legal protection against reprisals for reporting government wrongdoing. The legislation is "part of the government's broader commitment to ensure transparency, accountability, financial responsibility and ethical conduct."[80] Currently, whistleblowers in Canada also have special protection in respect of environmental and health and safety matters and there is a requirement for public companies to have confidential whistleblower hotlines and established procedures for anonymous reporting. Unfortunately, whistleblowers are often treated negatively in organizations.

The current trend is to move away from legally based ethical initiatives in organizations to cultural- or integrity-based initiatives that make ethics a part of core organizational values. Organizations recognize that effective business ethics programs are good for business

> **whistleblowing** the act of an employee exposing an employer's wrongdoing to outsiders, such as the media or government regulatory agencies

performance. Firms that develop higher levels of trust function more efficiently and effectively and avoid damaged company reputations and product images. Organizational ethics initiatives have been supportive of many positive and diverse organizational objectives, such as profitability, hiring, employee satisfaction, and customer loyalty.[81] Conversely, lack of organizational ethics initiatives and the absence of workplace values such as honesty, trust, and integrity can have a negative impact on organizational objectives. According to one report on employee loyalty and work practices, 79 percent of employees who questioned their bosses' integrity indicated that they felt uncommitted or were likely to quit soon.[82]

> "The Canadian government is hoping to encourage whistleblowers to inform them about tax cheats. Revenue Canada is offering whistleblowers a 15 percent commission on money collected as a result of tips."

The Nature of Social Responsibility

LO4 Explain the four dimensions of social responsibility.

There are four dimensions of social responsibility: economic, legal, ethical, and voluntary (including philanthropic) (Figure 2.3).[83] Earning profits is the economic foundation of the pyramid in Figure 2.3, and complying with the law is the next step. However, a business whose *sole* objective is to maximize profits is not likely to consider its social responsibility, although its activities will probably be legal. (We looked at ethical responsibilities in the first half of this chapter.) Finally, voluntary responsibilities are additional activities that may not be required but which promote human welfare or goodwill. Legal and economic concerns have long been acknowledged in business, but voluntary and ethical issues are more recent concerns.

Corporate citizenship is the extent to which businesses meet the legal, ethical, economic, and voluntary responsibilities placed on them by their various stakeholders. It involves the activities and organizational processes adopted by businesses to meet their social responsibilities. A commitment to corporate citizenship by a firm indicates a strategic focus on fulfilling the social responsibilities expected of it by its stakeholders.

> **corporate citizenship** the extent to which businesses meet the legal, ethical, economic, and voluntary responsibilities placed on them by their stakeholders

Figure 2.3 The Pyramid of Social Responsibility

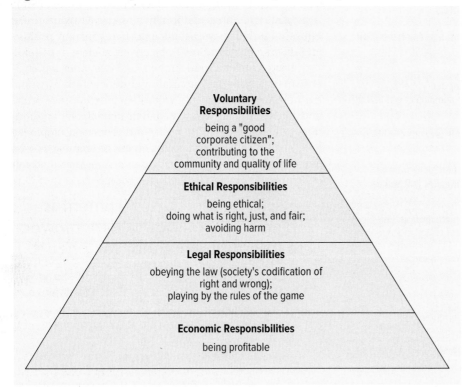

Source: Reprinted with permission from A. B. Carroll, "The Pyramid of Corporate Social Responsibility: Toward the Moral Management of Organizational Stakeholders," *Business Horizons,* July/August 1991. Copyright © 1991 by the Board of Trustees at Indiana University, Kelley School of Business.

The company recently donated $7.2 million. Nexen Inc. is rated one of the "Top 50 Companies to Work For in Canada"[84] and spearheaded the development of the "International Code of Ethics for Canadian Business" in 1997 as a template for Canadian businesses to follow when conducting business at home and abroad. Nexen received an award from the federal government for this initiative.[85] Nexen was recently taken over by Hong Kong–based CNOOC Limited.

Most companies today consider being socially responsible a cost of doing business. Corporate Knights, a Canadian-based media company with a focus on corporate responsibility, publishes an annual list of Canada's Best 50 Corporate Citizens based on 13 key indicators, such as reducing factory emissions, paying CEOs a fair wage relative to earnings, providing leadership opportunities to women and visible minorities, paying their fair share of taxes, avoiding work stoppages, and making sure workers' pension funds are properly funded.[86]

Corporate citizenship involves action and measurement of the extent to which a firm embraces the corporate citizenship philosophy and then follows through by implementing citizenship and social responsibility initiatives. Nexen, a Canadian-based, global energy company, follows the Imagine Canada guidelines, committing 1 percent of pre-tax earnings to community investment.

Although the concept of social responsibility is receiving more and more attention, it is still not universally accepted. Table 2.7 lists some of the arguments for and against social responsibility.

Table 2.7 The Arguments for and against Social Responsibility

For:

1. Business helped to create many of the social problems that exist today, so it should play a significant role in solving them, especially in the areas of pollution reduction and cleanup.

2. Businesses should be more responsible because they have the financial and technical resources to help solve social problems.

3. As members of society, businesses should do their fair share to help others.

4. Socially responsible decision making by businesses can prevent increased government regulation.

5. Social responsibility is necessary to ensure economic survival: If businesses want educated and healthy employees, customers with money to spend, and suppliers with quality goods and services in years to come, they must take steps to help solve the social and environmental problems that exist today.

Against:

1. It sidetracks managers from the primary goal of business—earning profits. Every dollar donated to social causes or otherwise spent on society's problems is a dollar less for owners and investors.

2. Participation in social programs gives businesses greater power, perhaps at the expense of particular segments of society.

3. Some people question whether business has the expertise needed to assess and make decisions about social problems.

4. Many people believe that social problems are the responsibility of government agencies and officials, who can be held accountable by voters.

"Organizations recognize that effective business ethics programs are good for business performance."

Social Responsibility Issues

As with ethics, managers consider social responsibility on a daily basis as they deal with real issues. Among the many social issues that managers must consider are their firms' relations with owners and shareholders, employees, consumers, the environment, and the community.

Social responsibility is a dynamic area with issues changing constantly in response to society's desires. There is much evidence that social responsibility is associated with improved business performance. Consumers are refusing to buy from businesses that receive publicity about misconduct. A number of studies have found a direct relationship between social responsibility and profitability, as well as that social responsibility is linked to employee commitment and customer loyalty—major concerns of any firm trying to increase profits.[87] This section highlights a few of the many social responsibility issues that managers face; as managers become aware of and work toward the solution of current social problems, new ones will certainly emerge.

LO5 Debate an organization's social responsibilities to owners, employees, consumers, the environment, and the community.

Relations with Owners and Shareholders. Businesses must first be responsible to their owners, who are primarily concerned with earning a profit or a return on their investment in a company. In a small business, this responsibility is fairly easy to fulfill because the owner(s) personally manages the business or knows the managers well. In larger businesses, particularly corporations owned by thousands of shareholders, ensuring responsibility to the owners becomes a more difficult task.

A business's responsibilities to its owners and investors, as well as to the financial community at large, include maintaining proper accounting procedures, providing all relevant information to investors about the current and projected performance of the firm, and protecting the owners' rights and investments. In short, the business must maximize the owners' investment in the firm.

Employee Relations. Another issue of importance to a business is its responsibilities to employees, for without employees a business cannot carry out its goals. Employees expect businesses to provide a safe workplace, pay them adequately for their work, and tell them what is happening in their company. They want

employers to listen to their grievances and treat them fairly. As noted at the start of the chapter, sometimes it is difficult to determine if businesses are acting ethically and responsibly to their employees as their motives often differ. Businesses usually want to maximize value for their shareholders while employees often want to maximize their own earnings. Thus there is often an ongoing debate about what is considered adequate pay. In Canada's auto sector, assembly workers earned approximately $80 an hour including benefits and received numerous other perks. When General Motors and Ford attempted to cut labour costs, the Canada Auto Workers Union (CAW) fought strongly against the move.[88] In order to engage employees, many business such as WestJet and Royal Bank offer employees an opportunity to own shares in their company.[89] The result is employees who feel more engaged and interested in the performance of the company. Employee ownership programs are not just limited to large businesses. *Profit* magazine, a Canadian publication that covers small- and mid-size businesses in Canada, has discovered that many small firms are encouraging employees to become shareholders in their company.

The Canadian government has passed several laws regulating safety in the workplace. Labour unions have also made significant contributions to achieving safety in the workplace and improving wages and benefits. Most organizations now recognize that the safety and satisfaction of their employees are critical ingredients in their success, and many strive to go beyond what is expected of them by the law. Healthy, satisfied employees supply more than just labour to their employers, however. Employers are beginning to realize the importance of obtaining input from even the lowest-level employees to help the company reach its objectives.

A major social responsibility for business is providing equal opportunities for all employees regardless of their sex, age, race, religion, or nationality. Women and minorities have been slighted in the past in terms of education, employment, and advancement opportunities; additionally, many of their needs have not been addressed by business. For example, as many as 1.6 million current and former female Walmart employees filed a class-action discrimination lawsuit accusing the giant retailer of paying them lower wages and salaries than men in comparable positions. Pretrial proceedings uncovered not only discrepancies between the pay of men and women, but also the fact that men dominate higher-paying store manager positions while women occupy more than 90 percent of cashier jobs, most of which pay about $14,000 a year. Walmart faces fines and penalties in the millions of dollars if found guilty of sexual discrimination.[90] Women, who continue to bear most child-rearing responsibilities, often experience conflict between those responsibilities and their duties as employees. Consequently, day care has become a major employment issue for women, and more companies are providing daycare facilities as part

If you search the Internet for information regarding Nestlé, you are likely to come across a large amount of documentation referring to a 30-year-old scandal involving infant formula and poor handling of the resolution of debt owed by Ethiopia. Critics argue that Nestlé's socially responsible activities serve only as cover-ups for these scandals. Whatever the truth may be, Nestlé appears to be a company learning from its past mistakes—sometimes, the errors of the past can be great motivators to do good in the future. In the past few years, Nestlé has been working to promote itself as a company focused more on wellness, and for many years—although perhaps overshadowed by negative publicity—the company has been heavily focused on helping to improve the lives of people in Africa.

Nestlé opened the first of 27 African factories in South Africa in 1927. Since that time, African consumers have come to view Nestlé products as familiar parts of their lives. The company employs around 11,500 people in Africa; only 120 of those people are from other countries. Companies working with Nestlé provide about 50,000 additional jobs. In 2004, the dean of the University of Ibadan's Faculty of Social Sciences found that in Nigeria, Nestlé employees earn above-average manufacturing wages. It was noted that more than 75 percent of those employees would decline to change jobs if given the option. Nestlé is reputed to be a large supporter of bettering the standard of living in African communities.

Nestlé does not own farmland in Africa, but it does work to help local farmers improve the quality of their crops and often their incomes. For example, Nestlé is the largest direct buyer of coffee in the world. The company also invests highly in research on how to help farmers improve the quality of their coffee crops. By improving the quality, the farmers can become more competitive in the global market.

In Africa, Nestlé is committed to improving the labour standards of farming, promoting local African products, preserving water, creating less waste, and offering nutritional education. Nestlé is also contributing to the United Nations' Millennium Development Goals in Africa to wipe out extreme poverty and hunger; ensure universal primary education; promote gender equality and empower women; reduce child mortality; improve maternal health; fight HIV/AIDS, malaria, and other diseases; and work toward environmental sustainability. Nestlé is committed, in a wide variety of ways, to helping people in Africa lead high-quality, healthy lives.[91]

DISCUSSION QUESTIONS

1. Do you think that Nestlé's socially responsible activities today have made up for possible mistakes involving infant formula in the past?

2. What has Nestlé done to improve its image in Africa?

3. What can Nestlé do to improve its commitment to Africa?

---

of their effort to recruit and advance women in the workforce. In addition, companies are considering alternative scheduling such as flex-time and job sharing to accommodate employee concerns. Telecommuting has grown significantly over the past five to ten years, as well. Many Canadians today believe business has a social obligation to provide special opportunities for women and minorities to improve their standing in society.

Consumer Relations. A critical issue in business today is business's responsibility to customers, who look to business to provide them with satisfying, safe products and to respect their rights as consumers. The activities that independent individuals, groups, and organizations undertake to protect their rights as consumers are known as **consumerism**. To achieve their objectives, consumers and their advocates write letters to companies, lobby government agencies, make public service announcements, and boycott companies whose activities they deem irresponsible.

Many of those involved in the consumer movement argue that consumers should have four specific rights. The *right to safety* means that a business must not knowingly sell anything that could result in personal injury or harm to consumers. Defective or dangerous products erode public confidence in the ability of business to serve society. They also result in expensive litigation that ultimately

> **consumerism** the activities that independent individuals, groups, and organizations undertake to protect their rights as consumers

increases the cost of products for all consumers. The right to safety also means businesses must provide a safe place for consumers to shop. In recent years, many large retailers have been under increasing pressure to improve safety in their large warehouse-type stores. At Home Depot, for example, three consumer deaths and numerous serious injuries have been caused by falling merchandise. One lawsuit brought against the company over injuries received in one of its stores resulted in a $1.5 million judgment. To help prevent further deaths, injuries, and litigation, Home Depot now has a corporate safety officer and has hired 130 safety managers to monitor store compliance with new safety measures.[92]

The *right to be informed* gives consumers the freedom to review complete information about a product before they buy it. This means that detailed information about ingredients, risks, and instructions for use are to be printed on labels and packages.

The *right to choose* ensures that consumers have access to a variety of products and services at competitive prices. The assurance of both satisfactory quality and service at a fair price is also a part of the consumer's right to choose. Some consumers are not being given the right to choose. Many are being billed for products and services they never ordered.

The *right to be heard* assures consumers that their interests will receive full and sympathetic consideration when the government formulates policy. It also ensures the fair treatment of consumers who voice complaints about a purchased product.

The role of provincial and federal governments is to protect consumers against unfair, deceptive, or fraudulent practices. Canada's Office of Consumer Affairs, a part of Industry Canada, works with both the public and private sectors, using information, research, and policy to complement and support consumer protection regulation.[93]

Environmental Issues. Environmental responsibility has become a leading issue as both business and the public acknowledge the damage done to the environment in the past. Today's consumers are increasingly demanding that businesses take a greater responsibility for their actions and how they impact the environment.

Animal Rights. One area of environmental concern in society today is animal rights. Probably the most controversial business practice in this area is the testing of cosmetics and drugs on animals that may be injured or killed as a result. Animal-rights activists, such as People for the Ethical Treatment of Animals, say such research is morally wrong because it harms living creatures. Consumers who share this sentiment may boycott companies that test products on animals and take their business instead to companies such as The Body Shop and John Paul Mitchell Systems, which do not use animal testing. However, researchers in the cosmetics and pharmaceutical industries argue that animal testing is necessary to prevent harm to human beings who will eventually use the products. Business practices that harm wildlife and their habitats are another environmental issue. The seal hunt is one such controversial issue in Canada and around the world. Many Canadians argue that hunting seals is the same as farming beef cows or pigs, while animal rights groups argue that it is unethical and cruel. The hunt of 25-day-old seals takes place every March in the waters off the coast of Newfoundland. The federal government says the landed value of seals was $26.5 million in 2006 when 350,000 seals were killed, and provides a "significant" source of income for thousands of sealers.[94] The International Fund for Animal Welfare (IFAW) describes the contribution of sealing to Newfoundland's GDP as "trivial" and says after costs and indirect subsidies are taken into account, Canadians would "likely find that the hunt actually costs the Canadian taxpayer money." It is a pointless activity, in

the view of the IFAW, which says, "the only economically valuable part of the seal is its fur, a non-essential luxury product that no one really needs."[95] Most of the pelts are exported to Russia and China where demand is strong and growing. IFAW and other interest groups, including many consumers, recently struck a blow to the sealing industry when the European Union banned imported seal products. This ban, along with milder weather that prevents sealers from going on the ice, has seriously limited the seal hunt in recent years.

"Related to the problem of land pollution is the larger issue of how to dispose of waste in an environmentally responsible manner."

Pollution. Another major issue in the area of environmental responsibility is pollution. Water pollution results from dumping toxic chemicals and raw sewage into rivers and oceans, oil spills, and the burial of industrial waste in the ground where it may filter into underground water supplies. Water pollution and oil spills dominated the news in 2010, with the BP oil spill overshadowing other disasters. The blowout of the Deep Horizon oil rig resulted in the release of almost 5 million barrels of oil into the Gulf of Mexico, and its effects have been felt around the world. Environmentalists and governments are worried about the long-term impact of the spill on marine life and small industries such as fishing that rely on the Gulf waters.[96] The spill has also impacted oil drilling in Canada. At the time of the spill, the Nova Scotia government was deciding whether it should allow deep-water oil drilling on George's Bank, an area known for its vast undersea wildlife. The government opted not to allow drilling for exploration wells until at least 2022 in order to give science more time to study the impact of underwater exploration. While the Nova Scotia government did not cite the BP oil spill in its news release announcing the moratorium, political pundits all agreed that it influenced the decision.[97] Fertilizers and insecticides used in farming and grounds maintenance also run off into water supplies with each rainfall. Water pollution problems are especially notable in heavily industrialized areas. Medical waste—such as used syringes, vials of blood, and AIDS-contaminated materials—has turned up on beaches in Toronto, Halifax, and Vancouver, as well as other places. In May of 2000, the water supply of Walkerton, Ontario, was contaminated with *E. coli* bacteria. The result was that seven people died and 2,300 were made ill. The suspected cause of the contamination was untreated manure from a dairy farm being carried into a municipal well by spring runoff. A judicial inquiry held that no regulations were broken by the farmer. As a result of such occurrences, society is demanding that regulations be enacted and enforced to safeguard clean, healthful water supplies. The inquiry resulted in

93 recommendations of which 50 were included in the Ontario Safe Drinking Water Act of 2002.[98]

Air pollution is usually the result of smoke and other pollutants emitted by manufacturing facilities, as well as carbon monoxide and hydrocarbons emitted by motor vehicles. In addition to the health risks posed by air pollution, when some chemical compounds emitted by manufacturing facilities react with air and rain, acid rain results. Acid rain has contributed to the deaths of many valuable forests and lakes in North America as well as in Europe. Air pollution may also contribute to global warming in which carbon dioxide collects in the earth's atmosphere, trapping the sun's heat and preventing the earth's surface from cooling. Chlorofluorocarbons also harm the earth's ozone layer, which filters out the sun's harmful ultraviolet light; this too may be a cause of the greenhouse effect.

In 1997, 39 of the world's richest countries agreed to curb greenhouse-gas emissions at the Kyoto Climate Change Conference. However, the resulting Kyoto Protocol, enacted in February 2005, had little impact because it did not require developing countries to cut their emissions, and because the U.S. was not a party to it. Although Canada, under the Liberals, was one of the countries to sign the Kyoto Protocol in 1998, the Conservative government reneged on that agreement to meet greenhouse-gas targets with the introduction of the Clean Air Act to regulate industrial pollutants. The legislation took effect in January 2010. At present, rich countries emit more CO_2 than developing countries. Nevertheless, developing countries as a whole will shortly overtake rich countries, and China, the most populous of the emerging economies, will become the world's biggest greenhouse-gas emitter by 2015. Every year, China builds 60 gigawatts of power-generation capacity, and four-fifths of Chinese power is generated by coal, the dirtiest source of electricity. China currently uses 40 percent of the world's coal—more than the U.S., Europe, and Japan put together.[99]

Land pollution is tied directly to water pollution because many of the chemicals and toxic wastes that are dumped on the land eventually work their way into the water supply. Land pollution results from the dumping of residential and industrial waste, strip mining, forest fires, and poor forest conservation. In Brazil and other South American countries, rain forests are being destroyed—at a rate of one hectare every two minutes—to make way for farms and ranches, at a cost of the extinction of the many animals and plants (some endangered species) that call the rain forest home. Large-scale deforestation also depletes the oxygen supply available to humans and other animals.

Related to the problem of land pollution is the larger issue of how to dispose of waste in an environmentally responsible manner. One specific solid waste problem is being created by rapid innovations in computer hardware that make many computers obsolete after just 18 months. By 2005, 350 million computers had reached obsolescence, and at least 55 million were expected to end up in landfills.[101] Computers contain toxic substances such as lead, mercury, and polyvinyl chloride, which can leach into the soil and contaminate the groundwater when disposed of improperly. In Europe, the Waste of Electrical and Electronic Equipment (WEEE) legislation aims to reduce the waste arising from this equipment. The key elements are that users recycle equipment free of charge, while producers (manufacturers, sellers, and distributors) are responsible for financing the collection, treatment, recovery, and disposal of WEEE from the recycling facilities.[102]

Response to Environmental Issues Partly in response to laws and partly due to consumer concerns, businesses are responding to environmental issues. Many small and large companies, including the Irving Group, Suncor, BlackBerry, Walt Disney Company, Chevron, and Scott Paper, have created new positions to help them achieve their business goals in an environmentally responsible manner. A survey indicated that 83.5 percent of *Fortune* 500 companies have a written environmental policy, 74.7 percent engage in recycling efforts, and 69.7 percent have made investments in waste-reduction efforts.[103] Many companies, including Alcoa, Dow Chemical, Phillips Petroleum, and Raytheon, now link executive pay to environmental performance.[104] Some companies are finding that environmental consciousness can save them money. DuPont saved more than $3 billion through energy conservation by replacing natural gas with methane in its industrial boilers in many of its plants.[105]

Many firms are trying to eliminate wasteful practices, the emission of pollutants, and/or the use of harmful chemicals. For example, Toronto-based Delta Hotels introduced Delta Greens, a national sustainability program aimed at improving environmental practices. Marriott Hotels of Canada also engaged in similar environmentally friendly practices by using low-energy light bulbs and low-flow showerheads in their guest rooms.[106] Other companies are seeking ways to improve their products to minimize the environmental impact. Lush Fresh Handmade Cosmetics, a Vancouver-based cosmetic retailer, has averted 6 million plastic bottles from landfills by selling shampoo in bars.[107]

Utility providers, for example, are increasingly supplementing their services with alternative energy

DID YOU KNOW?

It takes one barrel of oil to produce six barrels of oil from the Athabasca Tar Sands in Alberta.[100]

GOING GREEN | Fracking for Natural Gas: Clean Energy Solution or Environmental Catastrophe?

Hydraulic fracturing, known as fracking, has the potential to reduce Canada's dependence on foreign oil and create significant economic spinoffs. Fracking forces water, sand, and chemicals into underground tunnels of shale rock, bringing natural gas to the surface. Natural gas releases half the carbon dioxide of oil and is praised as a much more environmentally friendly fuel. Some provinces, such as Alberta and British Columbia, have benefited economically from fracking for years as the drilling creates jobs and increases tax revenue.

However, fracking does have a dark side. There have been instances where fracking chemicals have contaminated drinking water and increased levels of methane in water wells. People in the oil and gas industry argue that these cases occurred in the past and had more to do with companies not operating properly than the actual technology. Phil Knoll, former CEO of Corridor Resources, a Nova Scotia–based oil company, notes that fracking has been successfully and safely done for 20-plus years throughout Canada and the U.S.

Yet some provinces, most notably Quebec and recently Nova Scotia, have banned fracking over environmental concerns. While environmental groups have applauded such bans and are lobbying other provincial governments to stop fracking, many people in government and in the oil industry question the economic sense of the ban. Given that both Nova Scotia and Quebec would benefit from the increased tax revenue and investment fracking would bring, Knoll criticized the decision to ban fracking by the Nova Scotia government, stating the government ignored the science that fracking has been done safely for 20 years and turned away investment into the province, which is struggling economically. Cape Breton University President David Wheeler was commissioned by the Nova Scotia government to complete a report on fracking, and he estimated that fracking would likely result in an additional billion dollars a year in revenue through the creation of jobs, investment, and royalties to the government.[108] Interestingly, both Quebec and Nova Scotia receive money, better known as transfer payments, from other provinces that have stronger economies. In 2014, four provinces (Alberta, Saskatchewan, British Columbia, and Newfoundland) paid into the transfer payment program, which benefited Nova Scotia and Quebec.

All of these provinces have a successful oil and gas industry operating within their provincial boundaries and allow for fracking.

DISCUSSION QUESTIONS

1. What is the ethical issue involved with fracking, and why is it so hard to resolve?

2. Examine this issue from the perspective of the gas company as well as from the perspective of concerned stakeholders.

3. Why might a government ban fracking when science appears to indicate it can be safely done?

4. Do you think it is fair for some provinces to ban fracking yet turn around and take money from other provinces who allow for fracking?

5. Use Internet resources and find additional arguments for and against fracking. Present the findings to the class.

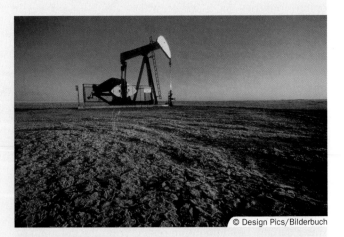

© Design Pics/Bilderbuch

The recent decision by the government of Nova Scotia to ban fracking has resulted in criticism from oil and gas companies who claim significant studies have proven that fracking is safe and would result in billions of economic opportunities for the struggling region.

British Petroleum (BP) has become synonymous with the worst oil leak disaster in U.S. waters to date. Simply put, BP failed to adequately prepare for a worst-case scenario. When the Deepwater Horizon oil rig exploded, killing 11 workers and pouring millions of litres of oil into the Gulf of Mexico, BP had no effective contingency plan. The crisis immediately spun out of control.

Not only did BP underestimate the risks, but some suggest it willfully cut corners to save money. A rig technician accused BP of knowing that the rig's blow-out preventer was leaking weeks prior to the explosion. Similar accusations of risky or negligent behaviour soon followed. Two months into the disaster, it was revealed that one-third of BP's deep water oil rig designs were deemed risky by government inspectors—a higher percentage than those of other oil companies.

Effective business ethics requires firms to identify risks and educate employees to deal with issues related to the risks. BP did not adequately acknowledge the risks despite warnings from industry experts. It also had no effective crisis management plan in place. BP did have a spill-response plan; however, its plan proved ineffective to handle the situation.

The disaster has undermined BP's reputation, and its ethics and social responsibility have been questioned by stakeholders. Many consumers responded by boycotting BP gas stations and products. The disaster has overshadowed BP's positive multimillion-dollar investments in renewable energy. BP has implemented a $20 billion Deepwater Horizon Oil Spill Trust to pay out claims and a $500 million Gulf of Mexico Research Initiative to fund the study of the impacts of the disaster, among other initiatives. BP has a long history of environmental

disasters and safety violations. What will it take to improve the reputation of BP?[109]

DISCUSSION QUESTIONS

1. Are BP's attempts at compensation enough to change the company's reputation in the eyes of consumers?

2. What are the ethical considerations that BP failed to recognize in its management of risks?

3. How important is BP's reputation for business success?

Photo by U.S. Coast Guard photo by Petty Officer 3rd Class Patrick Kelley

British Petroleum (BP) has become synonymous with the worst oil leak disaster in U.S. waters to date.

---

sources, including solar, wind, and geothermal power. Many businesses have turned to *recycling*, the reprocessing of materials—aluminum, paper, glass, and some plastic—for reuse. The above-mentioned Lush Fresh Handmade Cosmetics uses recycled material in its packaging 90 percent of the time. Such efforts to make products, packaging, and processes more environmentally friendly have been labelled "green" business or marketing by the public and media. Lumber products at Home Depot may carry a seal from the Forest Stewardship Council to indicate that they were harvested

from sustainable forests using environmentally friendly methods.[110] Likewise, most Chiquita bananas are certified through the Better Banana Project as having been grown with more environmentally and labour-friendly practices.[111]

It is important to recognize that, with current technology, environmental responsibility requires trade-offs. Society must weigh the huge costs of limiting or eliminating pollution against the health threat posed by the pollution. Environmental responsibility imposes costs on both business and the public. Although people

Turn the clock back: Imagine it's 2008 and the Canadian government is being asked to supply the Big Three automakers—Ford, General Motors (GM), and Chrysler—with approximately $3 billion in bailout money. The car companies are arguing that if they cease operations, it will cost the country more than 100,000 jobs.

The three automakers have had their business hurt in the recent recession and have made numerous management missteps that have added to their economic pain. All three auto companies failed to foresee rising consumer demand for fuel-efficient vehicles and continued to produce much larger cars than consumers wanted. The three companies also produce too many similar cars. For example, up until 2008, GM manufactured Saturn, GM, Saab, Cadillac, Hummer, and Pontiac brands and operated too many dealerships in the same geographic region. The three companies are hampered by high wages, with employee costs coming in at approximately $80 an hour, and they also suffer from a significant pension shortfall (meaning that they do not have enough money to pay their past employees their contracted pension). While their market share has continued to drop throughout the 1990s and 2000s, their competitors, including Honda, Toyota, and Hyundai, have increased their market share by producing cars that people want.

As the automakers were pressing their case for government money, arguing that thousands of jobs would be lost without the injection of funds, another Canadian giant was going through a financial crisis of its own. Nortel Networks Corp., a technology company that was once the darling of Canada's Internet boom, was seriously hurt by the downturn in the economy and years of financial mismanagement. Nortel managers, like senior executives from the car companies, were meeting with government officials and looking for bailout money to the tune of $3 billion. Nortel managers were no doubt pointing out to government officials in Ottawa that the tech giant still employs thousands of people in Canada, that it is the biggest corporate spender on research and development in the country, and that Nortel's spending may in fact be paying off as its next-generation Long Term Evolution, or LTE, wireless technology is expected to deliver top broadband speeds of 100 megabits per second for voice and data transmission to mobile phones—over 14 times quicker than the top networks currently operating across Canada.

Turn the clock to 2009 and you would discover that the Canadian government did supply General Motors and Chrysler with roughly $3 billion between them and gave Ford an operating line of credit. In addition, management has attempted to lower costs by renegotiating contracts with labour unions, reducing the number of cars that they manufacture, and focusing on building the fuel-efficient cars that consumers want. Industry analysts all agree that the companies are likely going to be succesful going forward because of the help from the government, improvements in operations and healtheir state of the economy. Nortel, on the other hand, did not receive a government bailout and the company was forced into bankruptcy in 2009. The company's assets were then auctioned off, including the licensing rights to LTE technology, which were sold to Ericsson (a Swedish company) for approximately $1.1 billion.[112]

Now fast-forward to 2015, Justin Trudeau has just been sworn in as prime minister and another large Canadian company is facing significant challenges. Bombardier, a Quebec-based manufacturer of trains and airplanes, is struggling in the face of growing competition and poor management. For years, Bombardier prospered by making smaller regional jets, airplanes that could seat between 30 and 90 people.

certainly do not want oil fouling beautiful waterways and killing wildlife, they insist on low-cost, readily available gasoline and heating oil. People do not want to contribute to the growing garbage-disposal problem, but they often refuse to pay more for "green" products packaged in an environmentally friendly manner, to recycle as much of their own waste as possible, or to permit the building of additional waste-disposal facilities (the "not in my backyard," or NIMBY, syndrome).

Managers must coordinate environmental goals with other social and economic ones.

Community Relations. A final, yet very significant, issue for businesses concerns their responsibilities to the general welfare of the communities and societies in which they operate. Many businesses want to make their communities better places for everyone to live and work. The most common way that businesses exercise

The two largest plane manufacturers, Boeing and Airbus, virtually ignored the market as they focused on making larger planes. Bombardier's success did not go unnoticed, and eventually Boeing and Airbus started to make smaller regional planes to compete with Bombardier. In response, Bombardier started to develop what would be its largest jet, better known as the C series, which could seat between 100 and 130 passengers depending on the model and burn 20 percent less fuel making it cheaper than similar jets to operate. But the development of the C series has been plagued by problems, including cost overruns, delays, and a lack of sales. This combined with a decline in sales for Bombardier's other planes has left the company in a cash crisis, and some experts predict it could run out of money in 2016.[113] In its most recent operating quarter, the company lost $4.9 billion, and investors seriously question if it will be profitable again.

In order to assist Bombardier, the Quebec provincial government invested $1 billion in return for 49.5 percent ownership of the C series planes.[114] The government notes that it is supporting a strategic industry that is important to Quebec's economy, much like the federal government's support for the auto industry. Critics of the investment state that Bombardier needs more than a billion dollars in investment and the company is in the midst of a 10- to 15-year decline brought on by poor management and not a short-term economic shock, which impacted the auto industry. Trudeau's newly sworn-in government is now being asked by the Quebec provincial government to match the investment. While Trudeau has stated he would consider helping the company, he has noted it must be based on a strong business case and not just a corporate handout. Critics of such investments state that the government rarely receives its money back when investing in corporate bailouts, and Bombardier's decline has more to do with emerging competition and poor management—things that cannot be fixed with a cash infusion.

© Art Babych / Shutterstock.com

Justin Trudeau's government is being asked to invest $1 billion in Bombardier, a Quebec-based manufacturer of trains and airplanes. Do you think governments should invest in corporate bailouts?

DISCUSSION QUESTIONS

1. What are some of the potential pitfalls with bailouts? Do you think the government is acting ethically when it spends taxpayers' dollars on bailouts? Why or why not?

2. Do you think Bombardier will survive in the coming years?

3. Did the government have an ethical obligation to invest in Nortel for the betterment of Canada's scientific community?

their community responsibility is through donations to local and national charitable organizations. Nationally, Statistics Canada reports that millions of individual and corporate donors contributed a record-high $10 billion in 2007. The number did drop sharply to just over $8 billion in 2008 as the economic crisis appeared to be hindering donations. However, corporate donations are once again on the rise. Examples of donations include Delta Hotels' support of Habitat for Humanity Canada, CIBC's sponsorship of MADD Canada, and significant contributions by Pfizer Canada and Boardwalk Realty to the Canadian Mental Health Association.[115]

"Many businesses want to make their communities better places for everyone to live and work."

TEAM EXERCISE

Sam Walton, founder of Walmart, had an early strategy for growing his business related to pricing. The "Opening Price Point" strategy used by Walton involved offering the introductory product in a product line at the lowest point in the market. For example, a minimally equipped microwave oven would sell for less than anyone else in town could sell the same unit. The strategy was that if consumers saw a product, such as the microwave, and saw it as a good value, they would assume that all of the microwaves were good values. Walton also noted that most people don't buy the entry-level product; they want more features and capabilities and often trade up.

Form teams and assign the role of defending this strategy or casting this strategy as an unethical act. Present your thoughts on either side of the issue.

LEARNING OBJECTIVES SUMMARY

LO1   Define business ethics and social responsibility and examine their importance.

Business ethics refers to principles and standards that define acceptable business conduct. Acceptable business behaviour is defined by customers, competitors, government regulators, interest groups, the public, and each individual's personal moral principles and values. Social responsibility is the obligation an organization assumes to maximize its positive impact and minimize its negative impact on society. Socially responsible businesses win the trust and respect of their employees, customers, and society, and in the long run, this practice increases profits. Ethics is important in business because it builds trust and confidence in business relationships. Unethical actions may result in negative publicity, declining sales, and even legal action.

LO2   Detect some of the ethical issues that may arise in business.

An ethical issue is an identifiable problem, situation, or opportunity requiring a person or organization to choose from among several actions that must be evaluated as right or wrong. Ethical issues can be categorized in the context of their relation with conflicts of interest, fairness and honesty, communications, and business associations.

LO3   Specify how businesses can promote ethical behaviour by employees.

Businesses can promote ethical behaviour by employees by limiting their opportunity to engage in misconduct. Formal codes of ethics, ethical policies, and ethics training programs reduce the incidence of unethical behaviour by informing employees of what is expected of them and providing punishments for those who fail to comply.

LO4   Explain the four dimensions of social responsibility.

The four dimensions of social responsibility are economic (being profitable), legal (obeying the law), ethical (doing what is right, just, and fair), and voluntary (being a good corporate citizen).

LO5   Debate an organization's social responsibilities to owners, employees, consumers, the environment, and the community.

Businesses must maintain proper accounting procedures, provide all relevant information about the performance of the firm to investors, and protect the owners' rights and investments. In relations with employees, businesses are expected to provide a safe workplace, pay employees adequately for their work, and treat them fairly. Consumerism refers to the activities undertaken by independent individuals, groups, and organizations to protect their rights as consumers. Increasingly, society expects businesses to take greater responsibility for the environment, especially with regard to animal rights, as well as water, air, land, and noise pollution. Many businesses engage in activities to make the communities in which they operate better places for everyone to live and work.

KEY TERMS

bribes
business ethics
codes of ethics
consumerism
corporate citizenship

ethical issue
plagiarism
social responsibility
whistleblowing

DESTINATION CEO DISCUSSION QUESTIONS

1. The Keystone and Energy East projects have been in the news for the past few years. Prior to reading the opening case, what was your opinion and knowledge of the issues at hand? After reading the case, do you think TransCanada Corp. has acted ethically throughout the process?

2. TransCanada Corp. has been relying on facts to argue the merits of Keystone XL and Energy East while many opponents have been making emotional arguments. What are some of the advantages and disadvantages of TransCanada's approach?

3. Given what you have read in the opening case, do you think either Keystone XL or Energy East will be approved for development?

SO YOU WANT A JOB *in Business Ethics and Social Responsibility*

In the words of Kermit the Frog, "It's not easy being green." It may not be easy, but green business opportunities abound. A popular catch phrase, "Green is the new black," indicates how fashionable green business is becoming. Consumers are more in tune with and concerned about green products, policies, and behaviours by companies than ever before. Companies are looking for new hires to help them see their business creatively and bring insights to all aspects of business operations. The American Solar Energy Society estimates that the number of green jobs could rise to 40 million in North America by 2030. Green business strategies not only give a firm a commercial advantage in the marketplace, but help lead the way toward a greener world. The fight to reduce our carbon footprint in an attempt to reverse climate change has opened up opportunities for renewable energy, recycling, conservation, and increasing overall efficiency in the way resources are used. New businesses that focus on hydro, wind, and solar power are on the rise and will need talented businesspeople to lead them. Carbon emissions trading is gaining popularity as large corporations and individuals alike seek to decrease their footprints. A job in this growing field

could be similar to that of a stock trader, or you could lead the search for carbon-efficient companies in which to invest.

In the ethics arena, current trends in business governance strongly support the development of ethics and compliance departments to help guide organizational integrity. This alone is a billion-dollar business, and there are jobs in developing organizational ethics programs, developing company policies, and training employees and management. An entry-level position might be as a communication specialist or trainer for programs in a business ethics department. Eventually there's an opportunity to become an ethics officer with typical responsibilities of meeting with employees, the board of directors, and top management to discuss and advise on ethics issues in the industry; developing and distributing a code of ethics; creating and maintaining an anonymous, confidential service to answer questions about ethical issues; taking actions on possible ethics code violations; and reviewing and modifying the code of ethics of the organization.

There are also opportunities to support initiatives that help companies relate social responsibility to stakeholder interests and needs. These jobs could involve coordinating and implementing philanthropic programs that give back to others important to the organization or developing a community volunteering program for employees. In addition to the human relations function, most companies develop programs to assist employees and their families to improve their quality of life. Companies have found that the healthier and happier employees are, the more productive they will be in the workforce.

Social responsibility, ethics, and sustainable business practices are not a trend; they are good for business and the bottom line. New industries are being created and old ones are adapting to the new market demands, opening up many varied job opportunities that will lead not only to a paycheque, but to the satisfaction of making the world a better place.[116]

BUILD YOUR BUSINESS PLAN

Business Ethics and Social Responsibility

Think about which industry you are considering competing in with your product/service. Are there any kind of questionable practices in the way the product has been traditionally sold? Produced? Advertised? Have there been any recent accusations regarding safety within the industry? What about any environmental concerns?

For example, if you are thinking of opening a lawn care business, you need to consider what possible effects the chemicals you are using will have on the client and the environment. You have a responsibility not to threaten your customers' health or safety. You also have the social responsibility to let the community know of any damaging effect you may be directly or indirectly responsible for.

CASE | Social Media and Privacy

As more and more people establish profile pages on social networking sites to kindle friendships (Facebook), create professional networks (LinkedIn), and inform people about the happenings in their day-to-day lives (Twitter), the line between public and private information has become blurred. While ten years ago much of this information may have been shared only with a small number of close friends, people now maintain online relationships that number in the thousands. This large network of contacts often includes professional relationships and employers.

Today, it is not uncommon to see people post risqué photos on Facebook, state their opinion about their job or employer, and update their online friends about their sexual orientation and drinking habits. Unfortunately for some people, employers or potential employers, family members, and friends have accessed online information

to help in evaluating a person's performance or potential performance; learn their opinions about work; determine who their friends are; and/or discover where they were the night before. The people who access and then use this information will often argue that the material is posted online in the public domain. For example, an employer may feel that it has just cause to discipline or fire an employee who criticizes the boss on Facebook or displays risqué photos from a recent vacation. Some social media users object to this behaviour and note that the information is not intended for public consumption. This begs the question: How can some people consider Facebook sites public and others consider them private? A recent exploratory study by Dr. Amy Thurlow, a professor at Halifax-based Mount Saint Vincent University, on the acceptable use of online information may shed some light on the opposing viewpoints. During the course of the study, Dr. Thurlow discovered that older people thought all information in the public domain, including information on social media sites, was public content, and it was fair to use such information any way that they see fit. Others, in particular younger students, indicated that it was not posters' responsibility to control what they put on their social media site; rather, the visitor of the site should be expected to know what is private and what is intended for public viewing. For example, if someone posts risqué photos or private information on his or her Facebook profile, the view of the students was that people likely know who this information is intended for, and visitors to Facebook should not view or use information that was not meant for their use.[117]

DISCUSSION QUESTIONS

1. Do you think employers should look at people's social media pages as part of the hiring process? Do you think employers should monitor employees' social media sites?

2. Who is responsible for privacy on social media sites—the person who posts the information or the person who visits the site?

3. Facebook, Twitter, and LinkedIn are valuable business tools. List some of the advantages and disadvantages that social media offers to: (1) students looking for a job; (2) businesses that are trying to market their products; (3) charities that are raising money.

LEARNING OBJECTIVES

After reading this chapter, you will be able to:

LO1 Explore some of the factors within the international trade environment that influence business.

LO2 Investigate some of the economic, legal-political, social, cultural, and technological barriers to international business.

LO3 Specify some of the agreements, alliances, and organizations that may encourage trade across international boundaries.

LO4 Summarize the different levels of organizational involvement in international trade.

LO5 Contrast two basic strategies used in international business.

DESTINATION CEO

Marc Kielburger is a Canadian social entrepreneur, author, and speaker. Marc and his brother Craig co-founded WE, an international charity and educational partner that empowers youth to achieve their fullest potential. Craig Kielburger is also a social entrepreneur. He is the co-founder of a family of organizations dedicated to shifting the world from 'me' to 'we.'

Craig Kielburger's story began at breakfast one morning when he noticed the picture of a boy on the front page of the *Toronto Star*. The headline read, "Battled Child Labour, Boy, 12, Murdered!" Craig, who was also 12, felt an immediate connection and grabbed the paper to read more. He had never heard of child labour before, and decided to do more research. There were more than 215 million child labourers in the world, many working in slave-like conditions.

Craig took the story to school and formed an activist group with fellow students. In 1999, Craig appeared on *Oprah* in an episode highlighting young people making a difference. The encounter eventually led to Oprah Winfrey partnering with WE to build schools around the world.

At 18, while working as a page in the House of Commons, Marc was invited on a trip to Thailand to volunteer in the slums of Bangkok. Marc stayed close to a year, teaching English and working with AIDS patients. He returned to Harvard to study international business, and was later awarded a Rhodes Scholarship and completed a law degree at Oxford University, with an emphasis on human rights law. He moved back to Canada to help found WE. "I owe an enormous debt of gratitude to Marc: He came at a critical moment and took a leadership role," says Craig.

As an international charity and educational partner, the organization—which has formed successful partnerships with top school boards and leading corporations, including Oprah's Angel Network, KPMG, and BlackBerry—has grown into a global network of more than 2 million young people committed to leading social change. Through its holistic and sustainable development model, WE has built more than 650 schools and school rooms in developing regions, providing education to more than 55,000 children every day. Its health and clean water initiatives have empowered more than 1 million beneficiaries.[1]

Introduction

Consumers around the world can drink Coca-Cola and Pepsi; eat at McDonald's and Pizza Hut; see movies from Mexico, England, France, Australia, and China; and watch CBC and Much Music on Samsung and Sony televisions. The products you consume today are just as likely to have been made in China, Korea, or Germany as in North America. Likewise, consumers in other countries buy Western electrical equipment, clothing, rock music, cosmetics, and toiletries, as well as computers, robots, and earth-moving equipment.

Many Canadian firms are finding that international markets provide tremendous opportunities for growth. Accessing these markets can promote innovation, while intensifying global competition spurs companies to market better and less expensive products. Today, the more than 7 billion people who inhabit the earth create one tremendous marketplace.

In this chapter, we explore business in this exciting global marketplace. First, we'll look at the nature of international business, including barriers and promoters of trade across international boundaries. Next, we consider the levels of organizational involvement in international business. Finally, we briefly discuss strategies for trading across national borders.

The Role of International Business

LO1 Explore some of the factors within the international trade environment that influence business.

International business refers to the buying, selling, and trading of goods and services across national boundaries. Falling political barriers and new technology are making it possible for more and more companies to sell their products overseas as well as at home. And as differences among nations continue to blur, the trend toward the globalization of business is becoming increasingly important. Starbucks, for example, serves millions of global customers a week at more than 5,500 coffee shops in 50 countries.[3] The Internet provides many companies easier entry to access global markets than opening bricks-and-mortar stores.[4] Amazon, an online retailer, has global fulfillment/distribution centres from Mississauga to Beijing that fill millions of orders a day and ship them to customers in every corner of the world. Proctor and Gamble's Febreze brand passed the $1 billion mark partially due to its strong growth overseas. While North American sales of air fresheners have fallen in recent years, global sales have seen an increase.[5] Indeed, most of the world's population and two-thirds of its total purchasing power are outside of North America.

international business
the buying, selling, and trading of goods and services across national boundaries

> ## DID YOU KNOW?
> McDonald's is the largest global franchise with over 36,000 units.[2]

"Falling political barriers and new technology are making it possible for more and more companies to sell their products overseas as well as at home."

When McDonald's sells a Big Mac in Moscow, Sony sells a stereo in Vancouver, or a small Swiss medical supply company sells a shipment of orthopedic devices to a hospital in Monterrey, Mexico, the sale affects the economies of the countries involved. The Canadian market, with 35 million consumers, makes up only a small part of the more than 7 billion people in the world to whom global

companies must consider marketing. Global marketing requires balancing your global brand with the needs of local consumers.[6] To begin our study of international business, we must first consider some economic issues: why nations trade, exporting and importing, and the balance of trade.

Why Nations Trade

Nations and businesses engage in international trade to obtain raw materials and goods that are otherwise unavailable to them or are available elsewhere at a lower price than that at which they themselves can produce. A nation, or individuals and organizations from a nation, sell surplus materials and goods to acquire funds to buy the goods, services, and ideas its people need. Poland and Hungary, for example, want to trade with Western nations so that they can acquire new technology and techniques to revitalize their formerly communist economies. Which goods and services a nation sells depends on what resources it has available.

Some nations have a monopoly on the production of a particular resource or product. Such a monopoly, or **absolute advantage**, exists when a country is the only source of an item, the only producer of an item,

absolute advantage
a monopoly that exists when a country is the only source of an item, the only producer of an item, or the most efficient producer of an item

© guli studio/iStock

Companies such as KFC have become widely popular in China. Some are making more sales in China than they are in North America.

or the most efficient producer of an item. Because South Africa has the largest deposits of diamonds in the world, one company, De Beers Consolidated Mines, Ltd., controls a major portion of the world's diamond trade and uses its control to maintain high prices for gem-quality diamonds. India, until recently, held an absolute advantage in operating call centres. But an absolute advantage not based on the availability of natural resources rarely lasts, and the Philippines is now challenging India in its call centre industry. Call-centre jobs are appealing to many Filipinos because the pay is almost as much as the average family income within the country. English is also one of the country's official languages, which makes it easier to communicate with English-speaking customers.[7]

comparative advantage the basis of most international trade, when a country specializes in products that it can supply more efficiently or at a lower cost than it can produce other items

outsourcing the transferring of manufacturing or other tasks—such as data processing—to countries where labour and supplies are less expensive

exporting the sale of goods and services to foreign markets

Most international trade is based on **comparative advantage**, which occurs when a country specializes in products that it can supply more efficiently or at a lower cost than it can produce other items. Canada has a comparative advantage in wood products, minerals, and hydroelectric generation. Until recently, the United States had a comparative advantage in manufacturing automobiles, heavy machinery, airplanes, and weapons; other countries now hold the comparative advantage for many of these products. Other countries, particularly India and Ireland, are also gaining a comparative advantage in the provision of some services, such as call-centre operations, engineering, and software programming. As a result, companies are increasingly **outsourcing**, or transferring manufacturing and other tasks to countries where labour and supplies are less expensive. Outsourcing has become a controversial practice because many jobs have moved overseas where those tasks can be accomplished for lower costs.

"Outsourcing has become a controversial practice in [many Western nations]"

Trade between Countries

To obtain needed goods and services and the funds to pay for them, nations trade by exporting and importing. **Exporting** is the sale of goods and services to foreign markets. Canada exported more than $528 billion in goods and services in 2014.[8] Canadian businesses export many goods and services, particularly energy products, industrial goods and materials (e.g., metals, chemicals, fertilizers),

and machinery and equipment products. **Importing** is the purchase of goods and services from foreign sources. Many of the goods you buy in Canada are likely to be imports or to have some imported components. Sometimes, you may not even realize they are imports. As shown in Table 3.1, Canada imported more than $524 billion in goods and services in 2014.[9]

Balance of Trade

You have probably read or heard about the fact that in some years Canada has a trade deficit. But what is a trade deficit? A nation's **balance of trade** is the difference in value between its exports and imports. Because some nations import more products than they export, they have a negative balance of trade, or **trade deficit**. Table 3.2 shows Canada's principal trading partners and whether Canada has a trade deficit or a trade surplus with them. In 2014, Canada had a trade surplus of about $4.8 billion, recovering from a trade deficit of $6.6 billion The trade deficit fluctuates according to such factors as the economic health of Canada and other countries, productivity, perceived quality, and exchange rates. In 2014, Canada had a $4.9 billion trade surplus with the United States and a $14.9 billion trade deficit with China.[10] Trade deficits are harmful because they can mean the failure of businesses, the loss of jobs, and a lowered standard of living.

importing the purchase of goods and services from foreign sources

balance of trade the difference in value between a nation's exports and its imports

trade deficit a nation's negative balance of trade, which exists when that country imports more products than it exports

balance of payments the difference between the flow of money into and out of a country

Of course, when a nation exports more goods than it imports, it has a favourable balance of trade, or trade surplus. Until 2008, Canada had a trade surplus due to trade in automotive products, machinery and equipment, and an abundance of natural resources, including crude oil and related energy products.[11]

The difference between the flow of money into and out of a country is called its **balance of payments**. A country's balance of trade, foreign investments, foreign aid, loans, military expenditures, and money spent by tourists

Table 3.1 Canada's Trade Balance, 2009–2014 (in millions of dollars)

	2009	2010	2011	2012	2013	2014
Exports	367,211	403,967	456.612	461,511	480,280	528,849
Imports	373,984	413,670	456,045	474,800	486,842	524,058
Balance	−6,773	−9,703	567	−13,289	−6,562	4,791

Source: Adapted from Statistics Canada, "Imports, exports and trade balance of goods on a balance-of-payments basis, by country or country grouping," http://www.statcan.gc.ca/tables-tableaux/sum-som/l0l/cst0l/gblec02a-eng.htm (accessed January 7, 2016).

Table 3.2 Canada's Top 10 Principal Trading Partners (2014)

Export Destinations	Import Sources	Trade Balance
1. United States	United States	$49.3
2. China	China	–15.0
3. Mexico	Mexico	–10.4
4. United Kingdom	United Kingdom	7.8
5. Japan	Japan	1.9
6. Germany	Germany	–9.6
7. South Korea	South Korea	–1.2
8. Hong Kong	Hong Kong	0.5
9. Netherlands	Netherlands	–0.3
10. France	France	–0.9

Source: Adapted from Statistics Canada, Table 1, "Annual merchandise trade: Canada's top 10 principal trading partners – Seasonally adjusted, current dollars," http://www.statcan.gc.ca/daily-quotidien/150402/t150402b001-eng.htm (accessed January 7, 2016).

comprise its balance of payments. As you might expect, a country with a trade surplus generally has a favourable balance of payments because it is receiving more money from trade with foreign countries than it is paying out. When a country has a trade deficit, more money flows out of the country than into it. If more money flows out of the country than into it from tourism and other sources, the country may experience declining production and higher unemployment, because there is less money available for spending.

International Trade Barriers

LO2 Investigate some of the economic, legal-political, social, cultural, and technological barriers to international business.

Completely free trade seldom exists. When a company decides to do business outside its own country, it will encounter a number of barriers to international trade. Any firm considering international business must research the other country's economic, legal, political, social, cultural, and technological background. Such research will help the company choose an appropriate level of involvement and operating strategies, as we will see later in this chapter.

Economic Barriers

When looking at doing business in another country, managers must consider a number of basic economic factors, such as economic development, infrastructure, and exchange rates.

Economic Development. When considering doing business abroad, businesspeople need to recognize that they cannot take for granted that other countries offer the same things as are found in *industrialized nations*—economically

advanced countries such as Canada, Japan, Great Britain, and the United States. Many countries in Africa, Asia, and South America, for example, are in general poorer and less economically advanced than those in North America and Europe; they are often called *less-developed countries (LDCs)*. LDCs are characterized by low per-capita income (income generated by the nation's production of goods and services divided by the population), which means that consumers are less likely to purchase non-essential products. Nonetheless, LDCs represent a potentially huge and profitable market for many businesses because they may be buying technology to improve their infrastructures, and much of the population may desire consumer products. For example, automobile manufacturers are looking toward LDCs as a way to expand their customer base. The rising middle class has caused many consumers in India and China to desire their own vehicles. Companies such as General Motors are partnering with domestic manufacturers to create electric vehicles for the Chinese market.[12]

A country's level of development is determined in part by its **infrastructure**, the physical facilities that support its economic activities, such as railroads, highways, ports, airfields, utilities and power plants, schools, hospitals, communication systems, and commercial distribution systems. When doing business in LDCs, for example, a business may need to compensate for rudimentary distribution and communication systems, or even a lack of technology.

"Devaluation decreases the value of currency in relation to other currencies."

Exchange Rates. The ratio at which one nation's currency can be exchanged for another nation's currency is the **exchange rate**. Exchange rates vary daily and can be found in newspapers and through many sites on the Internet. Familiarity with exchange rates is important because they affect the cost of imports and exports. When the value of the Canadian dollar declines relative to other currencies, such as the euro, the price of imports becomes relatively expensive for Canadian consumers. On the other hand, Canadian exports become relatively cheap for international markets—in this example, the European Union.

Occasionally, a government may alter the value of its national currency. Devaluation decreases the value of currency in relation to other currencies. If the Canadian government were to devalue

infrastructure the physical facilities that support a country's economic activities, such as railroads, highways, ports, airfields, utilities and power plants, schools, hospitals, communication systems, and commercial distribution systems

exchange rate the ratio at which one nation's currency can be exchanged for another nation's currency

China has made great strides in sustainability. The country has become the largest producer of wind turbines worldwide and has captured more than half of the market for solar technology. However, with 1.3 billion consumers and a growing middle class, pollution in China has also grown—with sometimes catastrophic results. The Ministry of Environmental Protection in Beijing has estimated that one-sixth of China's river water is dangerously polluted. Acid rain is also common in China, and less than one-fifth of its hazardous waste is properly treated each year. Perhaps most tragically, many cities located near factories have reported high incidences of cancer and other diseases.

The situation has prompted the Chinese government to take action. The government is closing many of the country's worst-polluting factories, is adopting stringent environmental laws, and has announced its intention of implementing a cap-and-trade system. Although most people would applaud China's attempt to reduce pollution, serious economic disadvantages come with better environmental enforcement. The loss of jobs that occurs when factories close is a major drawback. For example, one older steel mill employed 6,000 workers, many of whom were laid off when the factory closed. Additionally,

because the majority of China is still powered by coal (a dirtier source of energy), the nation is opening up new power plants even as it is closing less-efficient older ones. Finally, although China releases the most greenhouse gas emissions, each person in China is responsible for only one-third of the carbon emissions attributable to the average North American. Therefore, China's pollution problem not only involves the clash between economics and the environment but also brings up the issue of fairness.[13]

DISCUSSION QUESTIONS

1. Describe the environmental issues that China is facing.

2. Describe the clash between China's economic situation and the environment. Why is this such a major concern?

3. Do you feel that it is fair for China to receive attention for greenhouse gas emissions when North American people's activities cause more greenhouse gas emissions per capita?

---

the dollar, it would lower the cost of Canadian goods abroad and make trips to Canada less expensive for foreign tourists. Thus, devaluation encourages the sale of domestic goods and tourism. Mexico has repeatedly devalued the peso for this reason. Revaluation, which increases the value of a currency in relation to other currencies, occurs rarely.

Ethical, Legal, and Political Barriers

A company that decides to enter the international marketplace must contend with potentially complex relationships among the different laws of its own nation, international laws, and the laws of the nation with which it will be trading; various trade restrictions imposed on international trade; changing political climates; and different ethical values. Legal and ethical requirements for successful business are increasing globally. For instance, India has strict limitations on foreign retailers that want to operate within the country. Until recently, foreign retailers were required to partner with a domestic firm if they wanted to do business within India. Walmart partnered with Bharti Enterprises in order to gain entry into the country. India has now reduced the restrictions slightly. Single-brand retailers like Nike can now own their own stores in India without a partner, but multibrand retailers like Walmart

are still limited by the former restrictions. Although India represents a lucrative market for retailers, many multi-brand retailers such as IKEA are avoiding doing business within India because of the legal barriers.[14]

© McGraw-Hill Education/Christopher Kerrigan

The watch on the right, a knock-off developed by Digital Time Co., Ltd. in Thailand, received a special award for falsification. The dubious honour is given to the "best" product knock-offs by the organization Action Plagiarius in an effort to shame their makers. (The real watch was created by FORTIS Uhren AG in Grenchen, Switzerland.)

Laws and Regulations. Canada has a number of laws and regulations that govern the activities of Canadian firms engaged in international trade. For example, the Customs Act and the Reporting of Exported Goods Regulations require Canadian firms to report their exports. The three main objectives of the export reporting program are the following: to control the export of strategic and dangerous goods, as well as other controlled and regulated goods; to collect accurate information on Canadian exports; and to control the outbound movement of goods in transit through Canada.[15] Canada is a member of the World Trade Organization, which administers the rules governing trade among its 153 members. Canada also has a variety of international trade agreements with other nations, ranging from free trade agreements, to foreign investment promotion and protection agreements (FIPAs), to other types of agreements. These agreements allow business to be transacted among citizens of the specified countries. Some agreements also eliminate tariffs in a range of sectors, including for industrial, agricultural, forestry, fish, and seafood products.

Once outside Canadian borders, businesspeople are likely to find that the laws of other nations differ from those of Canada. Many of the legal rights that Canadians take for granted do not exist in other countries, and a firm doing business abroad must understand and obey the laws of the host country. Some countries have strict laws limiting the amount of local currency that can be taken out of the country and the amount of foreign currency that can be brought in; others forbid foreigners from owning real property outright. In Mexico, for example, foreigners cannot directly own property in what is known as the "Restricted Zone." The Restricted Zone includes land within 100 kilometres of Mexico's international borders along with land within 50 kilometres of Mexico's oceans and beaches. Foreigners who wish to use property in these areas must obtain a title through a bank title transfer or through a corporation.[16]

Some countries have copyright and patent laws that are less strict than those of Canada, and some countries fail to honour Canada's laws. Because copying is a tradition in China and Vietnam, and laws protecting copyrights and intellectual property are weak and minimally enforced, those countries are flooded with counterfeit videos, movies, CDs, computer software, furniture, and clothing. Companies are angry because the counterfeits harm not only their sales but also their reputations if the knock-offs are of poor quality. Such counterfeiting is not limited to China or Vietnam. It is estimated that nearly half of all software installed on personal computers worldwide is illegally pirated or copied, amounting to more than $50 billion in global revenue losses annually.[17] In countries where these activities occur, laws against them may not be sufficiently enforced, if counterfeiting is deemed illegal. Thus, businesses engaging in foreign trade may have to take extra steps to protect their products because local laws may be insufficient to do so.

Tariffs and Trade Restrictions. Tariffs and other trade restrictions are part of a country's legal structure but may be established or removed for political reasons. An **import tariff** is a tax levied by a nation on goods imported into the country. A *fixed tariff* is a specific amount of money levied on each unit of a product brought into the country, while an *ad valorem tariff* is based on the value of the item. Most countries allow citizens travelling abroad to bring home a certain amount of merchandise without paying an import tariff. A Canadian citizen may bring up to $200 worth of merchandise into Canada duty free after each absence of 24 hours, up to $800 worth of goods after each absence of 48 hours. After that, Canadian citizens must pay duty rates according to the goods imported, the country where the goods were

import tariff a tax levied by a nation on goods imported into the country

---

Consider the Following: The Loonie Has an Identity Crisis

The Canadian dollar dipped below 71 cents US in 2016, and for the first time since 2003. "Canada is in the midst of an identity crisis," Emanuella Enenajor, senior Canada economist for Bank of America Merrill Lynch, told Bloomberg. "In the 2000s, Canada was the commodity producer to the U.S. In the '90s, Canada was the manufacturer to the U.S. Today, Canada's identity is unclear."

There are other reasons for the decline in the Canadian dollar, among them the falling price of oil, a dimming outlook on China's growth prospects, and sabre rattling in the Middle East. A low dollar means consumers will

pay more for imports such as fruits, vegetables, and consumer electronics, but will help boost Canada's exports and foreign investment.

However, ripple effects in the economy will be seen. Canadian GDP dipped into recession territory in the first half of 2015 on the oil shock, and slumps in oil-rich provinces like Alberta, Saskatchewan, and Newfoundland are leaving a gaping wound. The energy sector has long driven Canada's trade surplus, papering over weakness elsewhere while soaking up large numbers of unemployed and underemployed people from regions like the Maritimes and hard-hit southwestern Ontario.[18]

made, and the country from which they are imported. Thus, identical items purchased in different countries might have different tariffs.

Countries sometimes levy tariffs for political reasons, as when they impose sanctions against other countries to protest their actions. However, import tariffs are more commonly imposed to protect domestic products by raising the price of imported ones. Such protective tariffs have become controversial, as governments become increasingly concerned over their trade deficits. Protective tariffs allow more expensive domestic goods to compete with foreign ones. For example, Canada has protectionist tariff walls sheltering poultry and dairy farmers from foreign competition.[19] The United States has had tariffs on imported sugar for almost two centuries. The European Union levies tariffs on many products, including some seafood imports.

Critics of protective tariffs argue that their use inhibits free trade and competition. Supporters of protective tariffs say they insulate domestic industries, particularly new ones, against well-established foreign competitors. Once an industry matures, however, its advocates may be reluctant to let go of the tariff that protected it. Tariffs also help when, because of low labour costs and other advantages, foreign competitors can afford to sell their products at prices lower than those charged by domestic companies. Some protectionists argue that tariffs should be used to keep domestic wages high and unemployment low.

Exchange controls Restrict the amount of currency that can be bought or sold. Some countries control their foreign trade by forcing business people to buy and sell foreign products through a central bank. If John

exchange controls regulations that restrict the amount of currency that can be bought or sold

Deere, for example, receives payments for its tractors in a foreign currency, it may be required to sell the currency to that nation's central bank. When foreign currency is in short supply, as it is in many less-developed and Eastern European countries, the government uses foreign currency to purchase necessities and capital goods and produces other products locally, thus limiting its need for foreign imports.

A **quota** limits the number of units of a particular product that can be imported into a country. A quota may be established by voluntary agreement or by government decree. In Canada, the Export and Import Controls Bureau is responsible for issuing permits and certificates for various products included on the Import Controls List. Products subject to quotas include agricultural products, firearms, textiles and clothing, and steel.[20]

An **embargo** prohibits trade in a particular product. Embargoes are generally directed at specific goods or countries and may be established for political, economic, health, or religious reasons. While the United States maintains a trade embargo with Cuba, European and Canadian hotel chains are engaged in a building boom on the Caribbean island, where tourism is the number-one industry. Until recently, U.S. tourists were forbidden by the U.S. government to vacation in Cuba, although the push to lift the government embargo is growing stronger all the time.[21] Health embargoes prevent the importing of various pharmaceuticals, animals, plants, and agricultural products. Other nations forbid the importation of alcoholic beverages on religious grounds.

quota a restriction on the number of units of a particular product that can be imported into a country

embargo a prohibition on trade in a particular product

(left): © Ryan McVay/Getty Images RF; (right): © Stockbyte RF

Dumping can spark trade wars. After the Obama administration imposed stiff tariffs on Chinese-made tires it alleged were being dumped on the U.S. market, China retaliated by slapping tariffs on U.S. chicken products exported to China.

One common reason for setting quotas or tariffs is to prohibit **dumping**, which occurs when a country or business sells products at less than what it costs to produce them. The European Union, for example, recently announced that it had opened the largest anti-dumping investigation ever, into imports of Chinese solar panels worth $26.5 billion last year. China retaliated by filing a case with the World Trade Organization accusing some European Union member countries of violating free trade rules.[22] A company may dump its products for several reasons. Dumping permits quick entry into a market. Sometimes dumping occurs when the domestic market for a firm's product is too small to support an efficient level of production. In other cases, technologically obsolete products that are no longer saleable in the country of origin are dumped overseas. Dumping is relatively difficult to prove, but even the suspicion of dumping can lead to the imposition of quotas or tariffs.

Political Barriers. Unlike legal issues, political considerations are seldom written down and often change rapidly. Nations that have been subject to economic sanctions for political reasons in recent years include Cuba, Iran, Syria, and North Korea. While these were dramatic events, political considerations affect international business daily as governments enact tariffs, embargoes, or other types of trade restrictions in response to political events.

Businesses engaged in international trade must consider the relative instability of countries such as Iraq, Haiti, and Venezuela. Political unrest in countries such as Pakistan, Somalia, and the Democratic Republic of the Congo may create a hostile or even dangerous environment for foreign businesses. Natural disasters, like the Haitian or Chilean earthquakes in 2010, can cripple a country's government, making the region even more unstable. Even Japan, a developed country, had its social, economic, and political institutions stressed by the 2011 earthquake and tsunamis. Finally, a sudden change in power can result in a regime that is hostile to foreign investment. Some businesses have been forced out of a country altogether, as when a socialist revolution in Venezuela forced out or took over foreign oil companies. Whether they like it or not, companies are often involved directly or indirectly in international politics.

Political concerns may lead a group of nations to form a **cartel**, a group of firms or nations that agree to act as a monopoly and not compete with each other, to generate a competitive advantage in world markets. Probably the most famous cartel is OPEC, the Organization of Petroleum Exporting Countries, founded in the 1960s to increase the price of petroleum throughout the world and to maintain high prices. By working to ensure stable oil prices, OPEC hoped to enhance the economies of its member nations. More recently, the decline in the price of oil led to deep divisions in the cartel, and it has been unable to reach an agreement on a notional ceiling for its production.

Social and Cultural Barriers

Most businesspeople engaged in international trade underestimate the importance of social and cultural differences, but these differences can derail an important transaction. For example, when Big Boy opened a restaurant in Bangkok, it quickly became popular with Western tourists, but the local Thais refused to eat there. Instead, they placed gifts of rice and incense at the feet of the Big Boy statue (a chubby boy holding a hamburger) because it reminded them of Buddha. In Japan, customers were forced to tiptoe around a logo painted on the floor at the entrance to an Athlete's Foot store because in Japan, it is considered taboo to step on a crest.[23] And in Russia, consumers found the Western-style energetic happiness of McDonald's employees insincere and offensive when the company opened its first stores there.[24] Unfortunately, cultural norms are rarely written down, and what is written down may well be inaccurate.

Cultural differences include differences in spoken and written language. Although it is certainly possible to translate words from one language to another, the true meaning is sometimes misinterpreted or lost. Consider some translations that went awry in foreign markets:

- Scandinavian vacuum manufacturer Electrolux used the following in an American campaign: "Nothing sucks like an Electrolux."

- The Coca-Cola name in China was first read as "Ke-kou-ke-la," meaning "bite the wax tadpole."

- In Italy, a campaign for Schweppes Tonic Water translated the name into Schweppes Toilet Water.[25]

Translators cannot just translate slogans, advertising campaigns, and website language; they must know the cultural differences that could affect a company's success.

Differences in body language and personal space also affect international trade. Body language is nonverbal, usually unconscious communication through gestures, posture, and facial expression. Personal space is the distance at which one person feels comfortable talking to another. Canadians tend to stand a moderate distance away from the person with whom they are speaking. Arab businessmen tend to stand face-to-face with the object of their conversation. Additionally, gestures vary from culture to culture, and gestures considered acceptable in Canadian society—pointing, for example—may be considered rude in others. Table 3.3 shows some of the behaviours considered rude or unacceptable in other countries. Such cultural differences may generate uncomfortable

Table 3.3 Cultural Behavioural Differences

Region	Gestures Viewed as Rude or Unacceptable
Japan, Hong Kong, Middle East	Summoning with the index finger
Middle and Far East	Pointing with index finger
Thailand, Japan, France	Sitting with soles of shoes showing
Brazil, Germany	Forming a circle with fingers (e.g., the "O.K." sign in North America)
Japan	Winking means "I love you"
Buddhist countries	Patting someone on the head

Source: Adapted from Judie Haynes, "Communicating with Gestures," *Everything ESL* (n.d.), www.everythingesl.net/inservice/body_language.php (accessed March 2, 2004).

feelings or misunderstandings when businesspeople of different countries negotiate with each other.

Family roles also influence marketing activities. Many countries do not allow children to be used in advertising, for example. Advertising that features people in non-traditional social roles may or may not be successful either. One airline featured advertisements with beautiful flight attendants serving champagne on a flight. The ad does not seem unusual in Western markets, but there was a major backlash in the Middle East. Saudi Arabia even considered restricting the airline from flights in that country. Not only is alcohol usage forbidden among Muslims, but unveiled women are not allowed to interact with men—especially without their husbands around. Some in Saudi Arabia saw the airline as being insensitive to their religious beliefs and customs.[26]

The people of other nations quite often have a different perception of time as well. Canadians value promptness; a business meeting scheduled for a specific time seldom starts more than a few minutes late. In Mexico and Spain, however, it is not unusual for a meeting to be delayed half an hour or more. Such a late start might produce resentment in a Canadian negotiating in Spain for the first time.

Companies engaged in foreign trade must observe the national and religious holidays and local customs of the host country. In many Islamic countries, for example, workers expect to take a break at certain times of the day to observe religious rites. Companies also must monitor their advertising to guard against offending customers. In Thailand and many other countries, public displays of affection between the sexes are unacceptable in advertising messages; in many Middle Eastern nations, it is unacceptable to show the soles of one's feet.[27] In Russia, smiling is considered appropriate only in private settings, not in business.

With the exception of the United States, most nations use the metric system. This lack of uniformity creates problems for both buyers and sellers in the international marketplace. American sellers, for instance, must produce goods destined for foreign markets in litres or metres, and

Japanese sellers must convert to the imperial system if they plan to sell a product in the United States. Tools also must be calibrated in the correct system if they are to function correctly. Hyundai and Honda service technicians need metric tools to make repairs on those cars.

The literature dealing with international business is filled with accounts of sometimes humorous but often costly mistakes that occurred because of a lack of understanding of the social and cultural differences between buyers and sellers. Such problems cannot always be avoided, but they can be minimized through research on the cultural and social differences of the host country.

Technological Barriers

Many countries lack the technological infrastructure found in North America, and some marketers are viewing such barriers as opportunities. For instance, marketers are targeting many countries such as India and China and some African nations where there are few private phone lines. Citizens of these countries are turning instead to wireless communication through cellphones. Technological advances are creating additional global marketing opportunities. Along with opportunities, changing technologies also create new challenges and competition. For example, out of the top five global PC companies—Hewlett-Packard, Dell, Acer, Lenovo, and Toshiba—three are from Asian countries. On the other hand, Apple Inc.'s iPad and other tablet computer makers have already begun eroding the market share of traditional personal computers, leading many to believe that personal computers have hit the maturity stage of the product life cycle.[28]

Trade Agreements, Alliances, and Organizations

LO3 Specify some of the agreements, alliances, and organizations that may encourage trade across international boundaries.

Although these economic, political, legal, and sociocultural issues may seem like daunting barriers to international trade, there are also organizations and agreements—such as the General Agreement on Tariffs and Trade, the World Bank, and the International Monetary Fund—that foster international trade and can help companies get involved in and succeed in global markets. Various regional trade agreements, such as the North American Free Trade

David Auerbach, Ani Vallabhaneni, and Lindsay Stradley

Business: Sanergy

Founded: 2011, in Kenya

Success: The idea for Sanergy won the three student entrepreneurs the $100,000 grand prize in MIT's annual Business Plan Competition, enabling them to start their Kenyan business.

Making money off human waste seems like an unusual (and disgusting) idea. But for recent MBA graduate David Auerbach, it is an opportunity to make money and meet critical needs in developing countries. According to the World Health Organization, 2.6 billion people lack proper sanitation facilities, a situation Auerbach witnessed when visiting China. Auerbach partnered with fellow students Ani Vallabhaneni and Lindsay Stradley to submit a business plan for a sanitation business in Kenya. They won MIT's annual Business Plan Competition and received $100,000 to start Sanergy.

Sanergy involves a four-step process. First, it builds the sanitation facilities, which include showers and toilets. The centres are then franchised to other entrepreneurs, who charge five cents for each use. The waste is collected daily and finally converted into electricity and fertilizer and sold. In this way, Sanergy can make a profit, create clean sanitation facilities for Kenyans, and generate jobs simultaneously.[29]

Agreement and the European Union, also promote trade among member nations by eliminating tariffs and trade restrictions. In this section, we'll look briefly at some of these agreements and organizations.

General Agreement on Tariffs and Trade (GATT)

During the Great Depression of the 1930s, nations established so many protective tariffs covering so many products that international trade became virtually impossible. By the end of World War II, there was considerable international momentum to liberalize trade and minimize the effects of tariffs. The **General Agreement on Tariffs and Trade (GATT)**, originally signed by 23 nations in 1947, provided a forum for tariff negotiations and a place where international trade problems could be discussed and resolved. More than 100 nations abided by its rules. GATT sponsored rounds of negotiations aimed at reducing trade restrictions. The Uruguay Round (1988–1994) further reduced trade barriers for most products and provided new rules to prevent dumping. The most recent round, the Doha Development Round, collapsed in 2008 after failing to agree on major issues. The main stumbling block was farm import rules, which allow countries to protect poor farmers by imposing a tariff on certain goods in the event of a drop in prices or a surge in imports.[30]

The **World Trade Organization (WTO),** an international organization dealing with the rules of trade between nations, was created in 1995 by the Uruguay Round. Key to the World Trade Organization are the WTO agreements, which are the legal ground rules for international commerce. The agreements were negotiated and signed by most of the world's trading nations and ratified by their legislative assemblies. The goal is to help producers of goods and services and exporters and importers conduct their business. In addition to administering the WTO trade agreements, the WTO presents a forum for trade negotiations, monitors national trade policies, provides technical assistance and training for developing countries, and cooperates with other international organizations. Based in Geneva, Switzerland, the WTO has also adopted a leadership role in negotiating

General Agreement on Tariffs and Trade (GATT) a trade agreement, originally signed by 23 nations in 1947, that provided a forum for tariff negotiations and a place where international trade problems could be discussed and resolved

World Trade Organization (WTO) international organization dealing with the rules of trade between nations

© The McGraw-Hill Companies, Inc./Barry Barker, photographer/DAL

The WTO facilitates trade among nations through the development of trade policies.

trade disputes among nations.[31] For example, the WTO investigated allegations that China was unfairly placing restrictions on the export of nine raw materials. The WTO eventually ruled that China was violating international trade rules.[32]

The North American Free Trade Agreement (NAFTA)

The **North American Free Trade Agreement (NAFTA)**, which went into effect on January 1, 1994, effectively merged Canada, the United States, and Mexico into one market of more than 440 million consumers. NAFTA was

> **North American Free Trade Agreement (NAFTA)** agreement that eliminates most tariffs and trade restrictions on agricultural and manufactured products to encourage trade among Canada, the United States, and Mexico

designed to eliminate virtually all tariffs on goods produced and traded among Canada, Mexico, and the United States to create a free trade area. The estimated annual output for this trade alliance is $14 trillion. NAFTA makes it easier for Canadian businesses to invest in the U.S. and Mexico; provides protection for intellectual property (of special interest to high-technology and entertainment industries); expands trade by requiring equal treatment of Canadian firms in both countries; and simplifies country-of-origin rules, hindering Japan's use of Mexico as a staging ground for penetration into Canadian and U.S. markets.

"NAFTA makes it easier for Canadian businesses to invest in the U.S. and Mexico."

The United States' 300 million consumers are extremely affluent, with a per capita GDP of $48,000.[33] Trade between the United States and Canada totals approximately $550 billion. About 80 percent of Canada's exports go to the United States, including gold, oil, and uranium.[34] In fact, Canada is the single largest trading partner of the United States.[35]

With a per capita GDP of $13,900, Mexico's 113 million consumers are less affluent than American consumers.[36] However, they bought $5 billion worth of Canadian products in 2014, making Mexico Canada's fifth-largest trading market. Mexico is on a course of a market economy, rule of law, respect for human rights, and responsible public policies. There is also a commitment to the environment and sustainable human development. Many Canadian and U.S. companies have taken advantage of Mexico's low labour costs and proximity to set up production facilities, sometimes called *maquiladoras*. Mexico is also attracting major technological industries, including electronics, software, and aerospace. Companies as diverse as Bombardier, Celestica, and Ford have set up facilities in Mexican states. With the maquiladoras and the influx

of foreign technological industries, Mexico became the world's 12th-largest economy.[37]

However, there is great disparity within Mexico. The country's southern states cannot seem to catch up with the more affluent northern states on almost any socio-economic indicator. For example, 47 percent of rural Mexicans in the south are considered extremely poor, compared with just 12 percent in the north. The disparities are growing, as can be seen comparing the south to the northern industrial capital of Monterrey, which is beginning to seem like south Texas.[38] However, drug gang wars threaten the economic stability and tourist industry of Mexico, especially in the northern states.

Despite its benefits, NAFTA has been controversial and disputes continue to arise over the implementation of the trade agreement. While many Canadians feared the agreement would erase jobs in Canada, Mexicans have been disappointed that the agreement failed to create more jobs. Moreover, Mexico's rising standard of living has increased the cost of doing business there; some 850 *maquiladoras* have closed their doors and transferred work to China and other nations where labour costs are cheaper. Indeed, China has become Canada's second-largest importer. On the other hand, high transportation costs, intellectual property theft, quality failures, and the difficulty management often incurs in controlling a business so far away and under a communist regime are now causing some manufacturers to reconsider opting for Mexican factories over China, even going so far as to relocate from China back to Mexico.[39]

Although NAFTA has been controversial, it has become a positive factor for North American firms wishing to engage in international marketing. Because licensing requirements have been relaxed under the pact, smaller businesses that previously could not afford to invest in Mexico and Canada will be able to do business in those markets without having to locate there. NAFTA's long phase-in period provides ample time for adjustment by those firms affected by reduced tariffs on imports. Furthermore, increased competition should lead to a more efficient market, and the long-term prospects of including most countries in the Western Hemisphere in the alliance promise additional opportunities for North American marketers.

The European Union (EU)

The **European Union (EU)**, also called the *European Community* or *Common Market*, was established in 1958 to promote trade among its members, which initially included Belgium, France, Italy, West Germany, Luxembourg, and the Netherlands. East and West Germany united in 1991, and by 1995 the United Kingdom, Spain, Denmark, Greece, Portugal, Ireland, Austria, Finland, and Sweden had joined as well. Cyprus, the Czech Republic, Estonia, Hungary, Latvia, Lithuania, Malta, Poland, Slovakia, and Slovenia

> **European Union (EU)** community established in 1958 to promote trade within Europe; as of 2013, has 27 member countries

joined in 2004. In 2007 Bulgaria and Romania also became members, which brought total membership to 27. Croatia, the former Yugoslav Republic of Macedonia, and Turkey are candidate countries that hope to join the European Union soon.[40] Until 1993, each nation functioned as a separate market, but at that time members officially unified into one of the largest single world markets, which today has nearly half a billion consumers with a GDP of more than $14 trillion.[41]

To facilitate free trade among members, the EU is working toward standardization of business regulations and requirements, import duties, and value-added taxes; the elimination of customs checks; and the creation of a standardized currency for use by all members. Many European nations (Austria, Belgium, Finland, France, Germany, Ireland, Italy, Luxembourg, the Netherlands, Portugal, and Spain) link their exchange rates together to a common currency, the *euro;* however, several EU members have rejected use of the euro in their countries. Although the common currency requires many marketers to modify their pricing strategies and will subject them to increased competition, the use of a single currency frees companies that sell goods among European countries from the nuisance of dealing with complex exchange rates.[42] The long-term goals are to eliminate all trade barriers within the EU, improve the economic efficiency of the EU nations, and stimulate economic growth, thus making the union's economy more competitive in global markets, particularly against Japan and other Pacific Rim nations, and North America. However, several disputes and debates still divide the member nations, and many barriers to complete free trade remain. The refugee crises and the subsequent return of border controls is threatening to disrupt the union. Consequently, it may take many years before the EU is truly one deregulated market.

The EU has also enacted some of the world's strictest laws concerning antitrust issues, which have had unexpected consequences for some non-European firms. For example, European antitrust regulators resisted the New York Stock Exchange's proposed merger with German marketplace organizer Deutsche Börse. They believed the merger would give the combined companies too much market power, thus decreasing competition.[43]

The prosperity of the EU has suffered in recent years. EU members experienced a severe economic crisis in 2010 that required steep bailouts from the International Monetary Fund (IMF). The first country to come to the forefront was Greece, which had so much debt that it risked default. With an increase in Greek bond yields and credit risks—along with a severe deficit and other negative economic factors—the country's economy plummeted. Since Greece uses the euro as its currency, the massive downturn served to decrease the euro's value. This had a profound effect on other countries in the Euro zone (the Euro zone refers collectively to European member countries that have adopted the euro as their form of currency). Ireland, Spain, and Portugal were particularly vulnerable

as they had some of the region's largest deficits.[44] Ireland began experiencing problems similar to Greece's, including a debt crisis, failing economic health, and rising bond yields.[45] Both Ireland and Portugal required bailout packages. In 2012, Spain and Cyprus also requested bailouts.

Greece continued to struggle even after the initial bailout because it did not have enough funds to repay its bondholders. Greece was forced to default. A default by one nation in the EU negatively affects the rest of the members by making them appear riskier as well.[46] In early 2012, the credit rating agency Standard & Poor's downgraded the sovereign debt of France, Austria, Spain, Portugal, Italy, Malta, Slovakia, Slovenia, and Cyprus. This means that these countries are perceived as riskier in terms of paying off their debt. Such downgrades could dissuade investors from investing in these countries.[47] Germany, on the other hand, has largely avoided the economic woes plaguing other countries. Germany has many exporting companies and has a smaller budget deficit and smaller household debt, which has enabled it to weather the crisis better than other EU members.[48] It was not downgraded but maintained its high ratings.[49]

Asia-Pacific Economic Cooperation (APEC)

The **Asia-Pacific Economic Cooperation (APEC)**, established in 1989, promotes open trade and economic and technical cooperation among member nations, which initially included Australia, Brunei Darussalam, Canada, Indonesia, Japan, Korea, Malaysia, New Zealand, the Philippines, Singapore, Thailand, and the United States. Since then the alliance has grown to include China, Hong Kong, Chinese Taipei, Mexico, Papua New Guinea, Chile, Peru, Russia, and Vietnam. The 21-member alliance represents approximately 41 percent of the world's population, 44 percent of world trade, and 54 percent of world GDP. APEC differs from other international trade alliances in its commitment to facilitating business and its practice of allowing the business/private sector to participate in a wide range of APEC activities.[50]

Asia-Pacific Economic Cooperation (APEC) community established in 1989 to promote international trade and facilitate business; as of 2013, has 21 member countries

Companies of the APEC countries have become increasingly competitive and sophisticated in global business in the last three decades. The Japanese and South Koreans in particular have made tremendous inroads on world markets for automobiles, motorcycles, watches, cameras, and audio and video equipment. Products from Samsung, Sony, Sanyo, Toyota, Daewoo, Mitsubishi, Suzuki, and Toshiba are sold all over the world and have set standards of quality by which other products are often judged. The People's Republic of China, a country of 1.3 billion people, has launched a program of economic reform to stimulate its economy by privatizing many industries, restructuring its banking system, and increasing public spending on infrastructure (including railways and telecommunications).[51]

As a result, China has become a manufacturing power-house, with an estimated economic growth rate of 8 to 10 percent a year.[52] China's export market has consistently outpaced its import growth in recent years and its GDP is the world's second-largest behind the United States.

Increased industrialization has also caused China to become the world's largest emitter of greenhouse gases as of 2008. China mainly uses coal-fired power plants; in fact, it builds a new one every ten days, so it has become the world's largest emitter of carbon dioxide. As companies transfer their manufacturing to China, they increase their CO_2 emissions because China emits 22 percent more than the global average of carbon per kilowatt-hour.[53] On the other hand, China has also begun a quest to become a world leader in green initiatives and renewable energy. This is an increasingly important quest as the country becomes more polluted.

Another risk area for China is the fact that the government owns or has stakes in so many enterprises. On the one hand, China's system of state-directed capitalism has benefited the country because reforms and decisions can be made more quickly. On the other hand, state-backed companies lack many of the competitors that private industries have. Remember that competition often spurs innovation and lowers costs. If China's firms lack sufficient competition, their costs may very likely increase.[54]

Less-visible Pacific Rim regions, such as Thailand, Singapore, Taiwan, Vietnam, and Hong Kong, have also become major manufacturing and financial centres. Vietnam, with one of the world's most open economies, has bypassed its communist government with private firms moving ahead despite bureaucracy, corruption, and poor infrastructure. In a country of 85 million barely able to feed themselves, Vietnamese firms now compete internationally with an agricultural miracle, making the country one of the world's main providers of farm produce. Coach, Inc. wants to increase its presence in Vietnam, while Guess, Inc. is considering an expansion of its production facilities in Vietnam along with Cambodia and Indonesia.[55]

Association of Southeast Asian Nations

The **Association of Southeast Asian Nations (ASEAN)**, established in 1967, promotes trade and economic integration among member nations in Southeast Asia, including Malaysia, the Philippines, Singapore, Thailand, Brunei Darussalam, Vietnam, Laos, Myanmar, and Cambodia.[56] The nine-member alliance represents 600 million people with a GDP of $2 trillion.[57] ASEAN's goals include the promotion of free trade, peace, and collaboration between its members.[58] In 1993, ASEAN began to reduce or phase out tariffs among countries and eliminate non-tariff trade barriers.[59] This elimination of tariffs will encourage additional trade among countries and could be beneficial to businesses that want to export to other countries in the trading bloc.

Association of Southeast Asian Nations (ASEAN) trade alliance that promotes trade and economic integration among member nations in Southeast Asia

However, ASEAN is facing challenges in becoming a unified trade bloc. Unlike members of the European Union, the economic systems of ASEAN members are quite different, with political systems including dictatorships (Myanmar), democracies (Philippines and Malaysia), constitutional monarchies (Thailand and Cambodia), and communism (Vietnam).[60] Major conflicts have also occurred between member-nations. For instance, in 2011 Thailand and Cambodia clashed militarily over disputed territory between the two nations.[61]

Despite these challenges, ASEAN increased economic integration and in 2015 established the AEC (ASEAN Economic Community), but unlike the European Union, it will not have a common currency or fully free labour flows between member-nations. In this way, ASEAN plans to avoid some of the pitfalls that occurred among nations in the EU during the latest worldwide recession.[62]

World Bank

The **World Bank**, more formally known as the International Bank for Reconstruction and Development, was established in 1946 to loan money to underdeveloped and developing countries.

It loans its own funds or borrows funds from member countries to finance projects ranging from road and factory construction to the building of medical and educational facilities. The World Bank and other multilateral development banks (banks with international support that provide loans to developing countries) are the largest source of advice and assistance for developing nations. The International Development Association and the International Finance Corporation are associated with the World Bank and provide loans to private businesses and member countries.

World Bank an organization established by the industrialized nations in 1946 to loan money to underdeveloped and developing countries; formally known as the International Bank for Reconstruction and Development

International Monetary Fund (IMF) organization established in 1947 to promote trade among member nations by eliminating trade barriers and fostering financial cooperation

International Monetary Fund

The **International Monetary Fund (IMF)** was established in 1947 to promote trade among member nations by eliminating trade barriers and fostering financial cooperation. It also makes short-term loans to member countries that have balance-of-payment deficits and provides foreign currencies to member nations. The International Monetary Fund also tries to avoid financial crises and panics by alerting the international community about countries that will not be able to repay their debts.

In 2008, Howard Schultz returned as CEO to re-anchor Starbucks after years of expansion. After closing almost 1,000 stores and cutting expenses, Starbucks is back on track. The company has become more discerning about where and how to expand by focusing on its international markets.

Starbucks operates in more than 50 countries, but its primary focus is on expansion in China. Starbucks first entered China in 1999. It now runs about 2,000 stores in 100 Chinese cities and plans to open 500 stores in China, every year for the next five years. Finding the right approach in China was challenging. Some have complained that Starbucks' early entrance was invasive and accused the company of pushing American culture along with its products. At one point, Starbucks closed its Forbidden City location after complaints circulated throughout the media. This time around, Schultz adapted stores to incorporate Chinese cultural expectations. Stores offered Chinese-inspired food items and more coffee-free beverages, because the Chinese are less drawn to coffee. In recent meetings with Chinese managers, Schultz has been honest about the company's challenges, thereby creating an impression of trust. The company has also opened a coffee farm and processing facilities in China. Schultz believes China might become the company's largest market. Therefore, he is changing the company's structure to include a China and Asia Pacific division. Will this focus on global expansion be Starbucks' recipe for further success?[63]

DISCUSSION QUESTIONS

1. What are some of the cultural barriers Starbucks encountered in its China expansion?

2. How has CEO Howard Schultz been able to resolve some of the differences between Chinese and American culture?

3. What are some ways that Starbucks is creating trust with its Chinese stakeholders?

The IMF's Internet site provides additional information about the organization, including news releases, frequently asked questions, and members.

The IMF is the closest thing the world has to an international central bank. If countries get into financial trouble, they can borrow from the World Bank. However, the global economic crisis created many challenges for the IMF as it was forced to significantly increase its loans to both emerging economies and more developed nations. The usefulness of the IMF for developed countries is limited because these countries use private markets as a major source of capital.[64] Yet the European debt crisis changed this somewhat. Greece, Ireland, and Portugal required billions of dollars in bailouts from the IMF to keep their economies afloat.

Getting Involved in International Business

LO4 Summarize the different levels of organizational involvement in international trade.

Businesses may get involved in international trade at many levels—from a small Kenyan firm that occasionally exports African crafts to a huge multinational corporation such as Shell Oil that sells products around the globe. The degree of commitment of resources and effort required increases according to the level at which a business involves itself in international trade. This section examines exporting and importing, trading companies, licensing and franchising, contract manufacturing, joint ventures, direct investment, and multinational corporations.

Exporting and Importing

Many companies first get involved in international trade when they import goods from other countries for resale in their own businesses. For example, a grocery store chain may import bananas from Honduras and coffee from Colombia. A business may get involved in exporting when it is called upon to supply a foreign company with a particular product. Such exporting enables enterprises of all sizes to participate in international business. Exporting to other countries becomes a necessity for established countries that seek to grow continually. Products often have higher sales growth potential in foreign countries than they have in the parent country. For example, Heinz exports its ketchup to other countries, including Mexico, Africa, and the Middle East, because there exists much greater potential for growth. Mexico in particular has become a crucial part of Heinz's growth strategy because Mexicans consume more ketchup than all but eight other nations.[67] Walmart experienced sales growth in international markets even as

Table 3.4 Canadian Exporters and Value by Company Size, 2013

	No. of Exporters	%	Value (C$ billions)	%
Large enterprises (> 500 employees)	1,216	3.13	314.3	74.7
Small and medium-sized enterprises	37,639	96.87	106.4	25.3
Total	38,855		420.7	

Source: Adapted from Statistics Canada, "Trade by Enterprise Characteristics Program, standard tables," http://www.statcan.gc.ca/daily-quotidien/150626/t001b-eng.htm (accessed January 7, 2016).

domestic sales were falling. Table 3.4 shows the number of Canadian exporters and the export value by company size, while Figure 3.1 shows some of the world's largest exporting countries.

Exporting sometimes takes place through **countertrade agreements**, which involve bartering products for other products instead of for currency. Such arrangements are fairly common in international trade, especially between Western companies and Eastern European nations. An estimated 40 percent or more of all international trade agreements contain countertrade provisions.

countertrade agreements foreign trade agreements that involve bartering products for other products instead of for currency

Although a company may export its wares overseas directly or import goods directly from their manufacturer, many choose to deal with an intermediary, commonly called an *export agent*. Export agents seldom produce goods themselves; instead, they usually handle international transactions for other firms. Export agents either purchase products outright or take them on consignment. If they purchase them outright, they generally mark up the price they have paid and attempt to sell the product in the international marketplace. They are also responsible for storage and transportation.

An advantage of trading through an agent instead of directly is that the company does not have to deal with foreign currencies or the red tape (paying tariffs and handling paperwork) of international business. A major disadvantage is that, because the export agent must make a profit, either the price of the product must be increased or the domestic company must provide a larger discount than it would in a domestic transaction.

trading company a firm that buys goods in one country and sells them to buyers in another country

Trading Companies

A **trading company** buys goods in one country and sells them to buyers in another country. Trading companies handle all activities required to move products from one country to another, including consulting, marketing research, advertising, insurance, product research and design, warehousing, and foreign exchange services to companies interested in selling their products in foreign markets. Trading companies are similar to export agents, but their role in international trade is larger. By linking sellers and buyers of goods in different countries, trading companies promote international trade. Canada has a few trading companies but one of the oldest is the Canadian Commercial Corporation (CCC), a federal Crown corporation in existence since 1946. Its primary goal is to promote and facilitate international trade on behalf of Canadian industry, particularly with government markets.[68] Export Development Canada (EDC) is another Crown corporation and Canada's export credit agency. It helps Canadian exporters and investors expand their international business among other services.[69]

Figure 3.1 Top Exporting Countries*

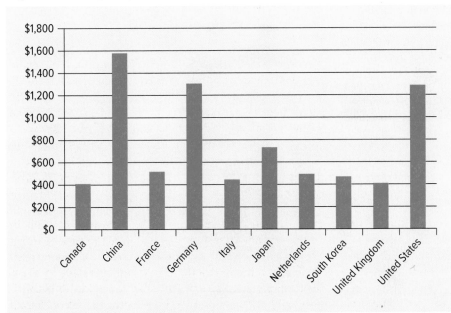

*2011 estimates in billions, calculated on an exchange rate basis

Source: "Country Comparison: Exports," *CIA World Factbook*, www.cia.gov/library/publications/the-world-factbook/rankorder/2078rank.html (accessed January 25, 2012).

© Glow Images

The ship *Cosco Ran* transports cargo from one side of the globe to the other.

Licensing and Franchising

Licensing is a trade arrangement in which one company—the *licensor*—allows another company—the *licensee*—to use its company name, products, patents, brands, trademarks, raw materials, and/or production processes in exchange for a fee or royalty. The Coca-Cola Company and PepsiCo frequently use licensing as a means to market their soft drinks, apparel, and other merchandise in other countries. Licensing is an attractive alternative to direct investment when the political stability of a foreign country is in doubt or when resources are unavailable for direct investment. Licensing is especially advantageous for small manufacturers wanting to launch a well-known brand internationally. Yoplait is a French yogurt that is licensed for production in Canada.

Franchising is a form of licensing in which a company—the *franchiser*—agrees to provide a *franchisee* a name, logo, methods of operation, advertising, products, and other elements associated with the franchiser's business, in return for a financial commitment and the agreement to conduct business in accordance with the franchiser's standard of operations. Subway, McDonald's, Pizza Hut, and Holiday Inn are well-known franchisers with international visibility. Table 3.5 lists some of the top global franchises.

Licensing and franchising enable a company to enter the international marketplace without spending large sums of money abroad or hiring or transferring personnel to handle overseas affairs. They also minimize problems associated with shipping costs, tariffs, and trade restrictions. And they allow the firm to establish goodwill for its products in a foreign market, which will help the company if it decides to produce or market its products directly in the foreign country at some future date. However, if the licensee (or franchisee) does not maintain high standards of quality, the product's image may be hurt; therefore, it is important for the licensor to monitor its products overseas and to enforce its quality standards.

Contract Manufacturing

Contract manufacturing occurs when a company hires a foreign company to produce a specified volume

licensing a trade agreement in which one company—the licensor—allows another company—the licensee—to use its company name, products, patents, brands, trademarks, raw materials, and/or production processes in exchange for a fee or royalty

franchising a form of licensing in which a company—the franchiser—agrees to provide a franchisee a name, logo, methods of operation, advertising, products, and other elements associated with a franchiser's business, in return for a financial commitment and the agreement to conduct business in accordance with the franchiser's standard of operations

contract manufacturing the hiring of a foreign company to produce a specified volume of the initiating company's product to specification; the final product carries the domestic firm's name

Table 3.5 Top Global Franchises

Franchise	Country	Ranking
McDonald's	United States	1
Subway	United States	2
KFC	United States	3
InterContinental Hotels & Resorts	United Kingdom	8
Groupe Casino	France	12
Kumon	Japan	40
Tim Hortons	Canada	42
Cartridge World	Australia	78
Engel & Völkers	Germany	89
Husse	Sweden	96

Source: "Top 100 Global Franchises—Ranking," *Franchise Direct,* www.franchisedirect.com/top100globalfranchises/rankings/ (accessed July 29, 2016).

© WENN Ltd / Alamy Stock Photo

The Canadian frozen yogurt franchise Yogen Fruz has operations on four continents.

of the firm's product to specification; the final product carries the domestic firm's name. Spalding, for example, relies on contract manufacturing for its sports equipment; Reebok uses Korean contract manufacturers to manufacture many of its athletic shoes.

Outsourcing

Earlier, we defined outsourcing as transferring manufacturing or other tasks (such as information technology operations) to companies in countries where labour and supplies are less expensive. Many international firms have outsourced tasks to India, Ireland, Mexico, and the Philippines, where there are many well-educated workers and significantly lower labour costs. Experts estimate that 80 percent of *Fortune* 500 companies have some relationship with an offshore company.[70]

Although outsourcing has become politically controversial in recent years amid concerns over jobs lost to overseas workers, foreign companies transfer tasks and jobs to North American companies—sometimes called *insourcing*. However, some firms are bringing their outsourced jobs back after concerns that foreign workers were not adding enough value. For example, some of the bigger banks are now choosing to set up offshore operations themselves rather than outsource. This has to do with increased regulations in foreign countries and concerns over data security. One instance of fraud at the Indian outsourcer Satyam amounted to more than $1 billion.[71]

Offshoring

Offshoring is the relocation of a business process by a company, or a subsidiary, to another country. Offshoring is different from outsourcing: the company retains control of the process because it is not subcontracting to a different company. Companies may choose to offshore for a number of reasons, ranging from lower wages, skilled labour, or taking advantage of time zone differences in order to offer services around the clock. Some banks have chosen not to outsource because of concerns about data security in other countries. These institutions may instead engage in offshoring, which allows a company more control over international operations because the offshore office is an extension of the company. Barclays Bank, for instance, has an international offshore banking unit called Barclays Wealth International. This branch helps the company better serve wealthy clients with international banking needs.[72]

offshoring the relocation of business processes by a company or subsidiary to another country; it differs from outsourcing because the company retains control of the offshored processes

Joint Ventures and Alliances

Many countries, particularly LDCs, do not permit direct investment by foreign companies or individuals. A company may also lack sufficient resources or expertise to operate elsewhere. In such cases, a company that wants to do business in another region or country may set up a **joint venture** by finding a local partner (occasionally, the host nation itself) to share the costs and operation of the business. For example, Brazilian conglomerate Odebrecht created a joint venture with state-owned oil company Petroleos de Venezuela. Odebrecht paid $50 million, or a 40 percent stake, to search for oil in the Venezuelan state of Zulia. Because the oil industry is nationalized in Venezuela, foreign oil companies must enter into joint ventures if they want to explore for and drill oil in the country.[73]

In some industries, such as automobiles and computers, strategic alliances are becoming the predominant means of competing. A **strategic alliance** is a partnership formed to create competitive advantage on a worldwide basis. In such industries, international competition is so fierce and the costs of competing on a global basis are so high that few firms have the resources to go it alone, so they collaborate with other companies. An example of a strategic alliance is the partnership between Australian airlines Virgin Blue and Skywest. By forming an alliance, the two airlines hope to tap into the increased demand from the mining industry for flights to distant mining sites. As part of the agreement, Skywest can use as many as 18 Virgin Blue turbo-prop aircraft for 10 years. In addition to penetrating a lucrative market, Virgin Blue hopes the alliance will help it extend its influence into regional markets and steal market share from its competitor QantasLink.[74]

Direct Investment

Companies that want more control and are willing to invest considerable resources in international business may consider **direct investment**, the ownership of overseas facilities. Direct investment may involve the development and operation of new facilities—such as when Starbucks opens a new coffee shop in Japan—or the purchase of all or part of an existing operation in a foreign country. India's Tata Motors purchased Jaguar and Land Rover from Ford Motor Company. Tata, a maker of cars and trucks, is attempting to broaden its global presence, including manufacturing these vehicles in the United Kingdom.[75]

The highest level of international business involvement is the **multinational corporation (MNC)**, a corporation, such as IBM or ExxonMobil, that operates on a worldwide

joint venture a partnership established for a specific project or for a limited time involving the sharing of the costs and operation of a business, often between a foreign company and a local partner

strategic alliance a partnership formed to create competitive advantage on a worldwide basis

direct investment the ownership of overseas facilities

multinational corporation (MNC) a corporation that operates on a worldwide scale, without significant ties to any one nation or region

© pcruciatti / Shutterstock.com

Walmart has chosen to directly invest in China. However, it must still make adjustments to fit with the local culture. For instance, Walmart, which is normally against trade unions, was pressured to allow its Chinese employees to unionize.

scale, without significant ties to any one nation or region. Table 3.6 lists the ten largest multinational corporations. MNCs are more than simple corporations. They often have greater assets than some of the countries in which they do business. General Motors, ExxonMobil, Ford Motors, and General Electric, for example, have sales higher than the GDP of many of the countries in which they operate. Nestlé, with headquarters in Switzerland, operates more than 400 factories around the world and receives revenues from Europe; North, Central, and South America; Africa; and Asia. The Royal Dutch/Shell Group, one of the world's major oil producers, is another MNC. Its main offices are located in The Hague and London. Other MNCs include BASF, British Petroleum, Cadbury Schweppes, Matsushita, Mitsubishi, Siemens, Texaco, Toyota, and Unilever. Many MNCs have been targeted by anti-globalization activists at global business forums, and some protests have turned violent. The activists contend that MNCs increase the gap between rich and poor nations, misuse and misallocate scarce resources, exploit the labour markets in LDCs, and harm their natural environments.[76]

International Business Strategies

LO5 Contrast two basic strategies used in international business.

Planning in a global economy requires businesspeople to understand the economic, legal, political, and socio-cultural realities of the countries in which they will operate. These factors will affect the strategy a business chooses to use outside its own borders.

Developing Strategies

Companies doing business internationally have traditionally used a **multinational strategy**, customizing their products, promotion, and distribution according to cultural, technological, regional, and national differences. To succeed in India, for example, McDonald's had to adapt its products to respect religious customs. McDonald's India does not serve beef or pork products and also has vegetarian dishes for its largely vegetarian consumer base. Many soap and detergent manufacturers have adapted their products to local water conditions, washing equipment, and washing habits. For customers in some less-developed countries, Colgate-Palmolive Co. has developed an inexpensive, plastic, hand-powered washing machine for use in households that have no electricity. Even when products are standardized, advertising often has to be modified to adapt to language and cultural differences. Also, celebrities used in advertising in the North America may be unfamiliar to foreign consumers and thus would not be effective in advertising products in other countries.

More and more companies are moving from this customization strategy to a **global strategy (globalization)**, which involves standardizing products (and, as much as possible, their promotion and distribution) for the whole world, as if it were a single entity. As it has become a global brand, Starbucks has standardized its products and stores. Starbucks was ranked as the world's most engaged brand in terms of online activities, even surpassing Coca-Cola, which is another global brand. Starbucks communicates with fans around the world via Facebook, Twitter, YouTube, and its company website.

Before moving outside their own borders, companies must conduct environmental analyses to evaluate

multinational strategy a plan, used by international companies, that involves customizing products, promotion, and distribution according to cultural, technological, regional, and national differences

global strategy (globalization) a strategy that involves standardizing products (and, as much as possible, their promotion and distribution) for the whole world, as if it were a single entity

Table 3.6 Top 10 Largest Corporations

Company	Revenue (in millions)	Country
1. Royal Dutch Shell	$484,489	Netherlands
2. ExxonMobil	452,926	United States
3. Walmart	446,950	United States
4. BP	386,463	Britain
5. Sinopec Group	375,214	China
6. China National Petroleum	352,338	China
7. State Grid	259,141	China
8. Chevron	245,621	United States
9. ConocoPhillips	237,272	United States
10. Toyota Motor	235,364	Japan

Source: Data from "Global 500: The World's Largest Corporations," July 23, 2012, *Fortune*, F-1.

the potential of and problems associated with various markets and to determine what strategy is best for doing business in those markets. Failure to do so may result in losses and even negative publicity. Some companies rely on local managers to gain greater insights and faster response to changes within a country. Astute business-people today "think globally, act locally." That is, while constantly being aware of the total picture, they adjust their firms' strategies to conform to local needs and tastes.

Managing the Challenges of Global Business

As we've pointed out in this chapter, many past political barriers to trade have fallen or been minimized, expanding and opening new market opportunities. Managers who can meet the challenges of creating and implementing effective and sensitive business strategies for the global marketplace can help lead their companies to success. For example, the Canadian Trade Commissioner Service is the global business solutions unit of Foreign Affairs and International Trade Canada that offers Canadian firms wide and deep practical knowledge of international markets and industries, a network of international business professionals, market intelligence, financial support, and expert advice.[77] As mentioned previously, Canadian Commercial Corporation (CCC) promotes and facilitates international trade on behalf of Canadian industry, and Export Development Canada provides Canadian exporters with financing, insurance, and bonding services as well as foreign market expertise. A major element of the assistance that these governmental organizations can provide firms (especially for small- and medium-sized firms) is knowledge of the internationalization process. Small businesses, too, can succeed in foreign markets when their managers have carefully studied those markets and prepared and implemented appropriate strategies. Being globally aware is therefore an important quality for today's managers and will become a critical attribute for managers of the twenty-first century.

TEAM EXERCISE

Visit Transparency International's Country Corruption Index website: www.transparency.org/. Form groups and select two countries. Research some of the economic, ethical, legal, regulatory, and political barriers that would have an impact on international trade. Be sure to pair a fairly ethical country with a fairly unethical country (e.g., Sweden with Myanmar, Ireland with Haiti). Report your findings.

LEARNING OBJECTIVES SUMMARY

LO1 Explore some of the factors within the international trade environment that influence business.

International business is the buying, selling, and trading of goods and services across national boundaries. Importing is the purchase of goods and services from another nation; exporting is the sale of goods and services to foreign markets. A nation's balance of trade is the difference in value between its exports and imports; a positive balance of trade is a trade surplus and a negative balance of trade is a trade deficit. The difference between the flow of money into and out of a country is called the balance of payments. An absolute or comparative advantage in trade may determine what products a company from a particular nation will export.

LO2 Investigate some of the economic, legal-political, social, cultural, and technological barriers to international business.

Companies engaged in international trade must consider the effects of economic, legal, political, social, and cultural differences between nations. Economic barriers are a country's level of development (infrastructure) and exchange rates. Wide-ranging legal and political barriers include differing laws (and enforcement), tariffs, exchange controls, quotas, embargoes, political instability, and war. Ambiguous cultural and social barriers involve differences in spoken and body language, time, holidays and other observances, and customs.

LO3 Specify some of the agreements, alliances, and organizations that may encourage trade across international boundaries.

Among the most important promoters of international business are the General Agreement on Tariffs and Trade, the World Trade Organization, the North American Free Trade Agreement, the European Union, the Asia-Pacific Economic Cooperation, the Association of Southeast Asian Nations, the World Bank, and the International Monetary Fund.

LO4 Summarize the different levels of organizational involvement in international trade.

A company may be involved in international trade at several levels, each requiring a greater commitment of resources and effort, ranging from importing/exporting to multinational corporations. Countertrade agreements occur at the import/export level and involve bartering products for other products instead of currency. At the next level, a trading company links buyers and sellers in different countries to foster trade. In licensing and franchising, one company agrees to allow a foreign company the use of its company name, products, patents, brands, trademarks, raw materials, and production processes, in exchange for a flat fee or royalty. Contract manufacturing occurs when a company hires a foreign company to produce a specified volume of the firm's product to specification; the final product carries the domestic firm's name. A joint venture is a partnership in which companies from different countries agree to share the costs and operation of the business. The purchase of overseas production and marketing facilities is direct investment. Outsourcing, a form of direct investment, involves transferring manufacturing to countries where labour and supplies are cheap. A multinational corporation is one that operates on a worldwide scale, without significant ties to any one nation or region.

LO5 Contrast two basic strategies used in international business.

Companies typically use one of two basic strategies in international business. A multinational strategy customizes products, promotion, and distribution according to cultural, technological, regional, and national differences. A global strategy (globalization) standardizes products (and, as much as possible, their promotion and distribution) for the whole world, as if it were a single entity.

KEY TERMS

absolute advantage
Asia-Pacific Economic Cooperation (APEC)
Association of Southeast Asian Nations (ASEAN)
balance of payments
balance of trade
cartel
comparative advantage
contract manufacturing
countertrade agreements
direct investment
dumping
embargo

European Union (EU)
exchange controls
exchange rate
exporting
franchising
General Agreement on Tariffs and Trade (GATT)
global strategy (globalization)
importing
import tariff
infrastructure
international business
International Monetary Fund (IMF)
joint venture

licensing
multinational corporation (MNC)
multinational strategy
North American Free Trade Agreement (NAFTA)
offshoring
outsourcing
quota
strategic alliance
trade deficit
trading company
World Bank
World Trade Organization (WTO)

DESTINATION CEO DISCUSSION QUESTIONS

1. What factors led to WE's growth?

2. What attributes led to the brothers' success as social entrepreneurs?

3. Do partnerships play a role in the expansion of the charity?

SO YOU WANT A JOB *in Global Business*

Have you always dreamt of travelling the world? Whether backpacking your way through Central America or sipping espressos at five-star European restaurants is your style, the increasing globalization of business might just give you your chance to see what the world has to offer. Most new jobs will have at least some global component, even if located within Canada, so being globally aware and keeping an open mind to different cultures is vital in today's business world. Think about the 1.3 billion consumers in China who have already purchased 500 million mobile phones. In the future, some of the largest markets will be in Asia.

Many jobs discussed in chapters throughout this book tend to have strong international components. For example, product management and distribution management are discussed as marketing careers in Chapter 12. As more and more companies sell products around the globe, their function, design, packaging, and promotions need to be culturally relevant to many different people in many different places. Products very often cross multiple borders before reaching the final consumer, both in their distribution and through the supply chain to produce the products.

Jobs exist in export and import management, product and pricing management, distribution and transportation, and advertising. Many "born global" companies such as Google operate virtually and consider all countries their market. Many companies sell their products through eBay and other Internet sites and never leave Canada. Today, communication and transportation facilitates selling and buying products worldwide with delivery in a few days. You may have sold or purchased a product on eBay outside Canada

without thinking about how easy and accessible international markets are to business. If you have, welcome to the world of global business.

To be successful you must have an idea not only of differing regulations from country to country, but of different languages, ethics, and communication styles and varying needs and wants of international markets. From a regulatory side, you may need to be aware of laws related to intellectual property, copyrights, antitrust, advertising, and pricing in every country. Translating is never only about translating the language. Perhaps even more important is ensuring that your message gets through. Whether on a product label or in advertising or promotional materials, the use of images and words varies widely across the globe.

BUILD YOUR BUSINESS PLAN

Business in a Borderless World

Think about the product/service you are contemplating for your business plan. If it is an already established product or service, try to find out if the product is currently being sold internationally. If not, can you identify opportunities to do so in the future? What countries do you think would respond most favourably to your product? What problems would you encounter if you attempted to export your product to those countries?

If you are thinking of creating a new product or service for your business plan, think about the possibility of

eventually marketing that product in another country. What countries or areas of the world do you think would be most responsive to your product?

Does Canada have trade agreements or alliances with countries that would make your entry into the market easier? What would be the economic, social, cultural, and technological barriers you would have to recognize before entering the prospective country(ies)? Think about the specific cultural differences that would have to be considered before entering the prospective market.

CASE | P&G Steps Up Its International Expansion

Four billion global customers may seem like a lot, but for Procter & Gamble CEO David Taylor, it's just the beginning. In the past, management has been criticized for being too slow in reacting to changing trends in key markets. The company now sees growth in key markets, such as China, and in emerging economies, like India and the Philippines. The company is seeking to make the most of China's removal of its one-child policy and a growing preference to premium-priced products. Economies in which income is as low as $1 per day require P&G to adapt its marketing strategy. To work within this constraint, P&G offers no frills packages to low-income global consumers.

Of the countries targeted by P&G, India stands out for its 1.2 billion consumers. To expand, it is focusing on needs-based innovation and products new to the country. For example, P&G sells single-serving packets of many products to accommodate lower incomes. It is also working to change the lifestyles of Indian consumers. After recognizing that most Indians go to the barber for shaves, P&G introduced the "Women Against Lazy Stubble" campaign. The campaign indicated that women prefer clean shaves and introduced Gillette's Mac3 razor as an alternative to the barber. P&G gained nearly half of the Indian razor market in two years.

The second challenge for P&G is finding a way to get its innovative products onto shelves. With few large retailers in India, small stores with limited space can easily stock P&G items like razors and toothbrushes. Disposable diapers, however, take up more room. Competition is another problem. In India, P&G must fight against major competitors like Unilever and Colgate-Palmolive. P&G's Indian sales have been growing steadily, but it lags behind Unilever with sales of $800 million versus $3.8 billion. The trick for P&G will be to balance its products with the needs of its Indian customers—both retailers and end-users.[78]

DISCUSSION QUESTIONS

1. Why is Procter & Gamble expanding into places such as India and the Philippines?

2. How is Procter & Gamble tailoring its products to meet the needs of Indian consumers?

3. What are some of the social and economic barriers P&G is facing in its expansion into India?

CHAPTER 4

Options for Organizing Business

LEARNING OBJECTIVES

After reading this chapter, you will be able to:

LO1 Define and examine the advantages and disadvantages of the sole proprietorship form of organization.

LO2 Identify three types of partnership, and evaluate the advantages and disadvantages of the partnership form of organization.

LO3 Describe the corporate form of organization, and cite the advantages and disadvantages of corporations.

LO4 Define and debate the advantages and disadvantages of mergers, acquisitions, and leveraged buyouts.

DESTINATION CEO

Heather Reisman If you walk into any Chapters or Indigo book-store in Canada, you are likely to see some books flagged as "Heather's Picks." Heather, in case you don't know, is Heather Reisman, founder of Indigo Books and Music and the current CEO of Canada's largest retail chain of bookstores, Indigo, which includes Chapters, Indigo, and Coles branded stores. Reisman maintains she has always had a deep love of books and she had originally intended to be a major investor in bringing Borders, an American bookstore, to Canada. Borders' attempts to enter the Canadian market failed to gain approval from the Canadian government, and Reisman opted to start her own book retailer.

During Indigo's early years, the company battled for market share with what at the time was its main rival, Chapters. This competitive rivalry changed dramatically in 2001 when Indigo, under Reisman's leadership, launched a hostile takeover of Chapters. While Chapters' management tried to prevent the sale of the company to Indigo, Reisman was ultimately successful. The acquisition, or merger, gave Indigo a virtual monopoly of retail bookstores in Canada. With 221 stores under the Indigo, Chapters, and Coles brands, Reisman's company sells most of the retail books in Canada. Yet since the takeover, Indigo has been under increased pressure from the emergence of both online retailers, including Amazon, and e-books, which have hurt sales of traditional store-bought printed books. For a period of time, many investors were of the opinion that this would become another failed merger,[1] and *Metro News* actually published an article titled, "Are Canadian bookstores headed towards extinction?"[2]

Reisman responded to the challenge by improving Indigo and Chapter's online presence and shifting its merchandise mix to include electronics such as Apple products, household items, giftware, stationery, baby gifts, and toys, all with the hopes of increasing its revenue. The change in merchandising is apparently working as Indigo's book sales now account for only 50 percent of its revenue, and store sales have been on the rise over the last three quarters.[3] In fact, Reisman is now eyeing further expansion, with many thinking Indigo will soon expand into U.S. and other international markets.[4]

Introduction

The legal form of ownership taken by a business is seldom of great concern to you as a customer. When you eat at a restaurant, you probably don't care whether the restaurant is owned by one person (a sole proprietorship), has two or more owners who share the business (a partnership), or is an entity owned by many shareholders (a corporation); all you want is good food. If you buy a foreign car, you probably don't care whether the company that made it has laws governing its form of organization that are different from those for businesses in Canada. You are buying the car because it is well made, fits your price range, or appeals to your sense of style. Nonetheless, a business's legal form of ownership affects how it operates, how much tax it pays, and how much control its owners have.

This chapter examines three primary forms of business ownership—sole proprietorship, partnership, and corporation—and weighs the advantages and disadvantages of each. These forms are the most often used whether the business is a traditional "bricks and mortar" company, an online-only one, or a combination of both. We also take a look at cooperatives and discuss some trends in business ownership. You may wish to refer to Table 4.1 to compare the various forms of business ownership mentioned in the chapter.

Table 4.1 Various Forms of Business Ownership

Structure	Ownership	Taxation	Liability	Use
Sole proprietorship	1 owner	Individual income taxed	Unlimited	Individual starting a business and easiest way to conduct business
Partnership	2 or more owners	Individual owners' income taxed	Unlimited (unless it is a limited partnership)	Easy way for two individuals to conduct business
Private corporation	Any number of shareholders	Corporate and shareholder income taxed	Varies between limited and unlimited	A legal entity with shareholders or stakeholders
Public corporation	Any number of shareholders	Corporate and shareholder income taxed	Limited	A legal entity with shareholders or stakeholders

Sole Proprietorships

LO1 Define and examine the advantages and disadvantages of the sole proprietorship form of organization.

Sole proprietorships, businesses owned and operated by one individual, are the most common form of business organization in Canada. Common examples include service firms, restaurants, hair salons, flower shops, doggie day cares, and independent retail stores. For example, stay-at-home mom Sandra Wilson of Vancouver started making form-fitted leather shoes

sole proprietorships
businesses owned and operated by one individual; the most common form of business organization in Canada

for toddlers when she was unable to find traditional shoes that would stay on her son's feet. Wilson made 20 pairs of shoes in her basement and started selling them at local trade shows. The company, which shares its name with the shoes—Robeez—was eventually sold for $27.5 million.[5] While most sole proprietors stay small, stories like Wilson's are not uncommon. Where Wilson's tale is unique is that most sole proprietors focus on services—small retail stores, financial counselling, appliance repair, child care, and the like—rather than on the manufacture of goods, which often requires large amounts of money not available to small businesses.

Sole proprietorships are typically small businesses employing fewer than 50 people. (We'll look at small businesses in greater detail in Chapter 5.) There are approximately 2.3 million businesses in Canada, of which the majority are sole proprietorships.

> "Common examples include many restaurants, hair salons, flower shops, doggie day cares, and independent retail stores."

Advantages of Sole Proprietorships

Sole proprietorships are generally managed by their owners. Because of this simple management structure, the owner/manager can make decisions quickly. This is just one of many advantages of the sole proprietorship form of business.

Ease and Cost of Formation. Forming a sole proprietorship is relatively easy and inexpensive. In some instances, all the entrepreneur has to do is to start selling a product or service. For example, when Chris Neville of Sydney, Nova Scotia, started his online business, www.lifeofsports.com, he simply started running his business online. Neville now owns and operates several online companies, including University Poker Championship. Neville is no doubt trying to follow in the footsteps of other entrepreneurs who made it big starting with a small company. For example, Frank Stronach of Magna International Inc. and Brian Scudamore of 1-800-GOT-JUNK? both started small companies in Canada, and grew them into large successful enterprises. Other proprietorships, such as barbershops and restaurants, may require provincial and local licences and permits because of the nature of the business. The cost of these permits may run from $25 to $1,000. No lawyer is needed to create such enterprises, and the owner can usually take care of the required paperwork.

Of course, an entrepreneur starting a new sole proprietorship must find a suitable site from which to operate the business. Some sole proprietors look no farther than their garage or a spare bedroom that they can convert into a workshop or office. Among the more famous businesses that sprang to life in their founders' homes are Robeez (which we discussed above), Spin Master (Canada's largest private toy company, which can trace its origins to a poster business in a dorm room), Google, Dell, eBay, and Mattel.[6] Computers, personal copiers, fax machines, and other high-tech gadgets have been a boon for home-based businesses, permitting them to interact quickly with customers, suppliers, and others. Many independent salespersons and contractors can perform their work using a tablet computer or smartphone as they travel. E-mail and cellphones have made it possible for many proprietorships to develop in the services area.

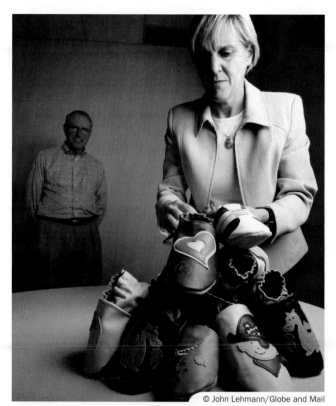
© John Lehmann/Globe and Mail

While most sole proprietorships stay small, some experience tremendous success. Sandra Wilson sold her business, Robeez, for $27 million.

approval. This control allows the owner to respond quickly to competitive business conditions or to changes in the economy. Jim Pattison, one of Canada's most successful entrepreneurs and owner of the Pattison Group (www. jimpattison.com), a private corporation that is managed very much like a sole proprietorship, has frequently stated that his company has remained private as it allows him to make quick decisions that focus on the long term without having to answer to a board of directors or shareholders like publicly owned corporate operators.

Government Regulation. Sole proprietorships have the most freedom from government regulation. Many government regulations—federal, provincial, and local—apply only to businesses that have a certain number of employees, and securities laws apply only to corporations that issue shares. Nonetheless, sole proprietors must ensure that they follow all laws that do apply to their business.

Taxation. Profits from the business are considered personal income to the sole proprietor and are taxed at individual tax rates. The owner pays one income tax. In addition, owners of sole proprietorships can deduct losses from their business against other forms of income. For example, Bill, a high school teacher, starts a part-time business sealing driveways and loses $10,000 in his first year of operations. He can now deduct $10,000 from the $80,000 he makes as an educator and only pay tax on $70,000. A sole proprietor who works from his or her home can also deduct expenses such as their home office from their business income. Another tax benefit is that a sole proprietor is allowed to establish a tax-exempt retirement account. Such accounts are exempt from current income tax, but payments taken after retirement are taxed when they are received.

Closing the Business. A sole proprietorship can be dissolved easily. No approval of co-owners or partners is necessary. When Mary Drain of Sudbury, Ontario, closed her home-based craft business, she only told her friends and family she was closing. No other formal notice was required.

Disadvantages of Sole Proprietorships

What is seen as an advantage by one person may turn out to be a disadvantage to another. The goals and talents of the individual owner are the deciding factors in determining the success of a sole proprietorship. For profitable businesses managed by capable owners, many of the following factors do not cause problems. On the other hand, proprietors starting out with little management experience and little money are likely to encounter many of the disadvantages.

Unlimited Liability. The sole proprietor has unlimited liability in meeting the debts of the business. In other words, if the business cannot pay its creditors, the owner may be forced to use personal, non-business holdings such as a car or

Internet connections also allow small businesses to establish websites to promote their products and even to make low-cost long-distance phone calls with voice over Internet protocol (VOIP) technology such as Skype.

> "Sole proprietorships have the most freedom from government regulation."

Secrecy. Sole proprietorships allow for the greatest degree of secrecy. The proprietor, unlike the owners of a partnership or corporation, does not have to share his or her operating plans, minimizing the possibility that competitors can obtain trade secrets. Financial reports need not be disclosed, as do the financial reports of publicly owned corporations. For example, when David Reynolds of Halifax, Nova Scotia, founded his sole proprietorship QuickSnap, selling a unique shoe-fastening device that was later featured on CBC's hit TV series *Dragons' Den,* he did not have to share information on how the product was constructed or his financial results with anyone.

Distribution and Use of Profits. All profits from a sole proprietorship belong exclusively to the owner. He or she does not have to share them with any partners or shareholders. The owner alone decides how the profits are used, which could include to expand the business, to increase salaries, or to find new customers.

Flexibility and Control of the Business. The sole proprietor has complete control over the business and can make decisions on the spot without anyone else's

a home to pay off the debts. Furthermore, the sole proprietor may also be legally responsible for any claims made against the business. For example, if a person walks into a retail store and slips, he or she will be able to personally sue the sole proprietor for the accident. The more wealth an individual has, the greater is the disadvantage of unlimited liability.

Limited Sources of Funds. Among the relatively few sources of money available to the sole proprietorship are banks, friends, family, some government programs, and/ or his or her own funds. The owner's personal financial condition determines his or her credit standing. Additionally, sole proprietorships may have to pay higher interest rates on funds borrowed from banks than do large corporations because they are considered greater risks. Often, the only way a sole proprietor can borrow for business purposes is to pledge a house, other real estate, or other personal assets to guarantee the loan. If the business fails, the owner may lose the personal assets as well as the business. Publicly owned corporations, in contrast, not only can obtain funds from banks but can sell shares and bonds to the public to raise money. If a public company goes out of business, the owners do not lose personal assets.

"The sole proprietor has unlimited liability in meeting the debts of the business."

Limited Skills. The sole proprietor must be able to perform many functions and possess skills in diverse fields such as management, marketing, finance, accounting, bookkeeping, and personnel. Business owners can rely on specialized professions for advice and services, such as accountants and attorneys. Musicians, for example, can turn to agents for assistance in navigating through the complex maze of the recording business. One start-up firm specializing in this type of assistance for online musicians and bands is the Digital Artists Agency, which researches, markets, and cultivates online music talent in exchange for a commission on their online sales of music, tickets, and merchandise.[7] In the end, however, it is up to the owner to make the final decision in all areas of the business, and not everyone has the skills to be successful on their own.

Lack of Continuity. The life expectancy of a sole proprietorship is directly related to that of the owner and his or her ability to work. The serious illness of the owner could result in failure if competent help cannot be found.

It is difficult to arrange for the sale of a proprietorship and at the same time assure customers that the business will continue to meet their needs. For instance, how does one sell

Consider the Following: Microlending Helps Small Entrepreneurs Start Businesses

Sending food and money to disadvantaged communities meets immediate needs, but ending long-term poverty is more difficult. Kiva.org is one business that seeks to tackle this problem head on. Founded by Stanford University graduates with an interest in business and technology, Kiva was first designed to lend money to impoverished Ugandan entrepreneurs. It soon expanded its reach to include other developing countries. Kiva is a microfinance business, which means it provides small loans—as little as $25 for equipment, for example—to individuals to start their own businesses.

Kiva partners with microfinance institutions worldwide. These field partners approve entrepreneurs and send their profiles to Kiva. The entrepreneurs' profiles are then posted on Kiva's website, and people who want to lend to an entrepreneur send their donations through the site. Kiva's field partners distribute the loans, work with the entrepreneurs, and collect repayments. Kiva.org does not earn returns on investments for lenders, but it does charge interest rates of between 23 and 48 percent. These interest rates cover loan costs, transaction costs, defaults, and inflation rates—and are much lower than rates charged by informal lenders or predatory lenders who typically supply loans to those who do not qualify for bank loans.

Kiva and over 560,000 lenders have succeeded in providing loans to over half a million entrepreneurs since 2005. The company has lent entrepreneurs a total of $813,647,450 since its inception, with an average loan of $412.84 and a repayment rate of 98.39 percent. Kiva wants to go even further and has established a five-year plan, aiming to reach $1 billion in global loans, help 2 million entrepreneurs, and achieve organizational sustainability.[8] The buzz about Kiva is positive, and Kiva.org's future looks bright as microlending continues to receive favourable press.[9]

DISCUSSION QUESTIONS

1. Kiva.org has been very successful at extending microlending to entrepreneurs in need. What about Kiva.org has helped make it so successful?

2. What is unique about the way Kiva.org is organized that sets it apart from more traditional businesses?

3. Do you think the Kiva.org model of giving loans would work for larger loans, or even for other kinds of businesses?

a veterinary practice? A veterinarian's major asset is patients. If the vet dies suddenly, the equipment can be sold, but the patients will not necessarily remain loyal to the office. On the other hand, a veterinarian who wants to retire could take in a younger partner and sell the practice to the partner over time.

Taxation. Although we listed taxation as an advantage for sole proprietorships, it can also be a disadvantage, depending on the proprietor's income. Under current tax rates, sole proprietors pay a higher marginal tax rate than do small corporations. This means sole proprietors may pay more in tax than small corporations.

Partnerships

LO2 Identify three types of partnership, and evaluate the advantages and disadvantages of the partnership form of organization.

One way to minimize the disadvantages of a sole proprietorship and maximize its advantages is to have more than one owner. For example, Mississauga-based Dekalam Hire Learning—a provider of online training to help people with pre-employment exams for policing, the public service, and so forth—was founded by three partners who brought complementary skills to the business: Adam Cooper had testing experience, Kalpesh Rathod brought IT experience, and Deland Jessop worked in law enforcement. Cooper says, "We went into business together because our skill set was so complementary."[10] Other times, partnerships are formed because people share a passion for the same type of business or hobby. For example, Mark Lampert and Chris Ye founded Uken games after they met at a Facebook development camp. The pair shared an interest in IT and gaming and soon created a gifting app where people could engage in online trick or treating at virtual locations.[11] The app went viral and reached over a million users and companies paid for in-game advertisements. Today the company has ten games including hits Bingo Pop, Crime Inc., Age of Legends, and Forces of War, and boasts over 35 million game installs, 1 million monthly active users, and millions in revenue.[12]

In Canada, partnerships are formed when two or more people fill out simple forms registering their business with the provincial governments to form partners. The partnership would then be governed by the Partnership Act (see Table 4.2), which outlines the rights and duties of partners toward one another. The rules of the Partnership Act apply unless the partners have signed a *partnership agreement*. A **partnership** can be defined as an association of two or more persons who carry on as co-owners of a business for profit. Partnerships are the least used form of business organization in Canada. They are typically larger than sole proprietorships but smaller than corporations.

partnership a form of business organization defined as an association of two or more persons who carry on as co-owners of a business for profit

Table 4.2 The Partnership Act

The following rules can be found in the Ontario statute of the Partnership Act, which is similar to those of other provinces:

- All partners are entitled to share equally in the capital and profits of the business and must contribute equally toward the losses, whether of capital or otherwise, sustained by the firm
- All money or property brought into or acquired by the partnership becomes partnership property
- No partner should be entitled to remuneration for acting in the partnership of the business
- No person may be introduced as a partner without the consent of existing partners

Types of Partnership

There are three basic types of partnership: general partnership, limited partnership, and a limited liability partnership. A **general partnership**

general partnership a partnership that involves a complete sharing in both the management and the liability of the business

© Nathan King/Alamy Stock Photo

Cirque du Soleil started with a small partnership between Quebec street performers and has grown into a global company with millions in sales.

David Reynolds

Business: Quicksnap

Founded: 2003

Success: Since his appearance on Season III of *Dragons'
Den*, sales have risen more than twofold, with online
orders originating from as far away as Australia and
New Zealand.

When David Reynolds of Halifax, Nova Scotia, started
university he was like most students, unsure about what
he wanted to do with his life. Reynolds notes, "I had no
idea why I was even enrolled in university other than it was
what everyone does." Shortly after attending a lecture
on entrepreneurship, Reynolds became enthralled with
the idea of starting his own company, saying, "I loved
the idea of being my own boss, thoughts of getting rich
with something I created." Reynolds searched for an
idea and a short time later found one as he was getting
tired of waiting for his friend to tie his shoes. Reynolds
states, "People hate tying their shoes. What if they didn't
have to do this? What if there was a way to clip the laces
together?" A short time later, Quicksnap (www.Quick-
snap.ca), a shoe-fastening device, was born. When the
company first started, it was structured as a sole proprietorship; as Reynolds quips, "It was just me and my idea."
A short time later, Reynolds realized he needed some
help managing his business as well as some extra funding, and recruited two friends to join his company. Thus,
the sole proprietor became a partner. Reynolds says that
forming a partnership was cheaper and easier than forming a corporation. "We drafted a partnership agreement,
we all signed it, and we became partners." Like most
start-ups, the business eventually needed more funding,
and Reynolds found himself looking for outside inves-

tors. Reynolds notes, "At this time I knew that we needed
a formal structure and the business went through the
process of incorporating. We needed the advantages of a
private corporation, we needed to be able to issue shares
to investors, ensure that everyone involved in the ownership group had limited liability and so forth." The business
has been featured on the hit CBC series *Dragons' Den*
and the product is being sold nationally in various stores.
Reynolds is no longer CEO, but still owns shares in the
business that he founded as a 19-year-old with an idea he
had while watching his friend struggle to tie his shoes.[13]

Young entrepreneur David Reynolds established QuickSnap while
growing tired watching his friend try to tie his shoes.

involves a complete sharing in the management of a business. In a general partnership, each partner has unlimited
liability for the debts of the business. For example, Cirque du
Soleil grew from a group of Quebec street performers, who
acted as partners, into a half-billion-dollar global company.[14]

Professionals such as lawyers,
accountants, and architects
often join together in general
partnerships.

A **limited partnership** has
at least one general partner, who assumes unlimited
liability, and at least one
limited partner, whose liability is limited to his or her

investment in the business. Limited partnerships exist for
risky investment projects where the chance of loss is great.
The general partners accept the risk of loss; the limited partners' losses are limited to their initial investment. Limited
partners do not participate in the management of the business, but share in the profits in accordance with the terms
of a partnership agreement. Usually the general partner
receives a larger share of
the profits after the limited
partners have received their
initial investment back.
Popular examples are oil-
drilling partnerships and real
estate partnerships. A **limited
liability partnership (LLP)** is a

limited partnership a
business organization that has
at least one general partner,
who assumes unlimited liability,
and at least one limited
partner, whose liability is
limited to his or her investment
in the business

**limited liability
partnership (LLP)** a
partnership agreement where
partners are not responsible for
losses created by other partners

unique partnership agreement where non-negligent partners are not personally responsible for losses created by other partners. This type of partnership is available only in some provinces and is popular among legal and accounting firms.

Partnership Agreement

A **partnership agreement** is a legal document that sets forth the basic agreement between partners. Unless partners sign a partnership agreement, their partnership will be bound by the rules outlined in their provincial Partnership Act. While not legally required, it makes good sense for partners to sign and follow such an agreement. Partnership agreements usually list the money or assets that each partner has contributed (called *partnership capital*), state each partner's individual management role or duty, specify how the profits and losses of the partnership will be divided among the partners, and describe how a partner may leave the partnership, as well as any other restrictions that might apply to the agreement. Table 4.3 lists some of the issues and provisions that should be included in articles of partnership.

partnership agreement
document that sets forth the basic agreement between partners

Table 4.3 Issues and Provisions in Articles of Partnership

1. Name, purpose, location
2. Duration of the agreement
3. Authority and responsibility of each partner
4. Character of partners (i.e., general or limited, active or silent)
5. Amount of contribution from each partner
6. Division of profits or losses
7. Salaries of each partner
8. How much each partner is allowed to withdraw
9. Death of partner
10. Sale of partnership interest
11. Arbitration of disputes
12. Required and prohibited actions
13. Absence and disability
14. Restrictive covenants
15. Buying and selling agreements

Source: Adapted from "Partnership Agreement Sample," State of New Jersey, http://www.state.nj.us/njbusiness/start/biztype/partner/agreement_sample.shtml (accessed June 13, 2007).

Advantages of Partnerships

Law firms, accounting firms, and investment firms with several hundred partners have partnership agreements that are quite complicated in comparison with the partnership agreement among two or three people owning a computer repair shop. The advantages must be compared with those offered by other forms of business organization, and not all apply to every partnership.

Ease of Organization. Starting a partnership requires little more than filling out some basic forms with the provincial government including the registration of the business's name. While a partnership agreement is highly recommended, it is not required as the provincial Partnership Act provides rules for the business to follow. As evident in the Entrepreneurship in Action box above, forming a partnership is relatively simple.

Combined Knowledge and Skills. Successful partners acknowledge each other's talents and avoid confusion and conflict by specializing in a particular area of expertise such as marketing, production, accounting, or service. The diversity of skills in a partnership makes it possible for the business to be run by a management team of specialists instead of by a generalist sole proprietor. For example, Mike Lazaridis (founder of Research In Motion—better known as RIM, and now called Black-Berry, and manufacturer of the BlackBerry line of smartphones) brought Jim Balsillie in as partner. Lazaridis notes, "I asked Jim to join RIM in 1992 because I needed a partner with finance expertise. The decision to go with a co-CEO structure is based on a trust of each other's strengths and an appreciation for the complexity of running a fast-growing global company."[15] Lazaridis and

© Brett Gundlock

Tracey Bochner, co-owner of Paradigm Public Relations, pictured here with her partner Michael Abbass, states that a good partner will help you solve problems and keep you from making stupid mistakes.

Balsillie successfully ran the company under this structure for over nine years before leaving in 2012. Tracey Bochner, co-owner of Paradigm Public Relations, a Toronto-based PR firm, states that a good partnership enables you to achieve more than you could on your own. Boucher says, "In my experience, if you share, the net result can be so much better than what you can achieve alone." She states partners can help you become better problem solvers and prevent you from making stupid mistakes.[16] Service-oriented partnerships in fields such as law, financial planning, and accounting may attract customers because clients may think that the service offered by a diverse team is of higher quality than that provided by one person. Larger law firms, for example, often have individual partners who specialize in certain areas of the law—such as family, bankruptcy, corporate, entertainment, and criminal law.

"When a business has several partners, it has the benefit of a combination of talents."

Availability of Capital and Credit. When a business has several partners, it has the benefit of a combination of talents and skills and pooled financial resources. The pooling of financial resources is particularly attractive to new firms as they are heavily dependent on the personal investment of the owner for start-up financing. As discussed in Chapter 5, personal investment of the owner is responsible for 66 percent of the money raised by new ventures. Partnerships tend to be larger than sole proprietorships and therefore have greater earning power and better credit ratings.

Decision Making. Small partnerships can react more quickly to changes in the business environment than can large partnerships and corporations. Such fast reactions are possible because the partners are involved in day-to-day operations and can make decisions quickly after consultation. Examples of this quick decision making can often be seen by partners on CBC's hit series *Dragons' Den* or ABC's *Shark Tank* where entrepreneurs are looking to raise money for a fledging business or idea. Often partners are given very little time to make decisions about selling a percentage of their business for much-needed capital. This was the situation in which the owners of Atomic Tea, a Calgary-based specialty tea store, found themselves while pitching on the show. The sister and brother partnership—Jessica and Russell Bohrson— were offered a $120,000 investment for 50.1 percent of their business. The pair had to make the decision in minutes and opted to accept the money and give up a large percentage of their business.[17] While the Bohrsons' decision-making process was obviously more dramatic because it occurred on television, viewers did get to see how quickly small partners can react to changes in their environment.

© Design Pics Inc/Alamy Stock Photo

Mike Lazaridis, on the right, and Jim Balsillie, on the left, were likely the most famous Canadian business partners in recent years. The former co-CEOs of Research In Motion combined their expertise to build one of the top technology companies in the world.

Regulatory Controls. Like a sole proprietorship, a partnership has fewer regulatory controls affecting its activities than does a corporation. A partnership does, however, have to abide by all laws relevant to the industry or profession in which it operates, as well as provincial and federal laws relating to hiring and firing, food handling, and so on, just as the sole proprietorship does.

Disadvantages of Partnerships

Partnerships have many advantages compared to sole proprietorships and corporations, but they also have some disadvantages. Limited partners have no voice in the management of the partnership, and they may bear most of the risk of the business while the general partner reaps a larger share of the benefits. There may be a change in the goals and objectives of one partner but not the other, particularly when the partners are multinational organizations. This can cause friction, giving rise to an enterprise that fails to satisfy both parties or even forcing an end to the partnership. Many partnership disputes wind up in court or require outside mediation. For example, a quarrel among the partners who owned the Montreal Expos baseball team moved to U.S. District Court after new general partner Jeffrey Loria moved the team to Florida and renamed it the Florida Marlins. Twelve of the team's limited partners sued Loria, accusing him of buying the Expos with the intent of moving the team, diluting their share in the team, and effectively destroying "the economic viability of baseball in Montreal."[18] In such cases, the ultimate solution may be dissolving the partnership. Major disadvantages of partnerships include the following.

Disagreements among Partners. A partnership is similar to any relationship including a close friendship or a marriage. Partners often work together on a daily basis and disagreements are inevitable. Smaller firms are more likely to suffer from such disagreements as their size often prevents a clear distinction of duties that can be found in larger partnerships. Often disagreements are minor and they can be successfully managed or resolved. For example, Babak Barkhodaei and his brother Arash started SkyPrep, an online training company. The pair split the duties, with Babak focusing on sales and Arash on product development. While it seemed like the perfect match, Babak admits the partnership was far from perfect as he was so focused on sales he often failed to consider if Arash could actually develop the finished product. Babak says, "We had so many conflicts. I was thinking about growing the business, so any time a person wanted a feature, I would say to Arash, 'do it, do it.' I was focused on getting business and didn't consider the complexity of the solution. At one point, Arash just got really fed up." Rather than end the partnership, the pair brought in another partner, their brother Sepand, who understood their points of view and implemented a conflict resolution system.[19] Sometimes disputes can go much further and actually spell the end of a partnership, a friendship, and a business. This is what happened to the highly successful partnership of Michel Boucher and Chuck Buchanan. The pair operated Flightexec, a company based in London, Ontario that went from bankruptcy to $20 million in annual sales in 10 years. But when the two partners differed over the long-term strategy for the company, it ended the partnership, and Buchanan was forced to leave the business. Partnership disputes can occur in large companies as well. One of the most talked about disputes in Canadian business history was the succession battle at the multibillion-dollar McCain Foods frozen food empire. Harrison and Wallace McCain co-managed the business for years with Harrison looking after sales and growth and his brother Wallace dealing with managing the manufacturing facilities. When the pair started to look for a successor, Wallace was insistent that his son Michael receive the job while Harrison objected to the idea. The succession battle ended with Harrison removing Wallace as his co-CEO, the brothers' relationship being in tatters, and Wallace buying a large interest in Maple Leaf Foods where his son Michael was eventually named CEO. Table 4.4 lists some suggestions for building a successful partnership.

Table 4.4 Keys to Success in Business Partnerships

1. Keep profit sharing and ownership at 50/50, or you have an employer/employee relationship.
2. Partners should have different skill sets to complement one another.
3. Honesty is critical.
4. Maintain face-to-face communication in addition to phone and e-mail.
5. Maintain transparency, sharing more information over time.
6. Be aware of funding constraints and do not put yourself in a situation where neither you nor your partner can secure additional financial support.
7. To be successful, you need experience.
8. Whereas family should be a priority, be careful to minimize the number of associated problems.
9. Do not become too infatuated with "the idea" as opposed to its implementation.
10. Couple optimism with realism in sales and growth expectations and planning.

Source: Abstracted from J. Watananbe, "14 Reasons Why 80 Percent of New Business Partnerships Would Fail Within Their First 5 Years of Existence," http://ezinearticles.com/?14-Reasons-Why-80-Percent-Of-New-Business-Partnerships-Would-Fail-Within-Their-First-5-Years-Of-Exis&id=472498 (accessed June 20, 2013).

Unlimited Liability. In general partnerships, the general partners have unlimited liability for the debts incurred by the business, just as the sole proprietor has unlimited liability for his or her business. Such unlimited liability can be a distinct disadvantage to one partner if his or her personal financial resources are greater than those of the others. A potential partner should make sure that all partners have comparable resources to help the business in times of trouble. This disadvantage is eliminated for limited partners, who can lose only their initial investment.

Brothers Babak, Arash, and Sepand Barkhodaei, partners in the online-training company SkyPrep, admit their initial partnership suffered from a lot of disagreements before they implemented a conflict management system.

© Stavros Rougas

Business Responsibility. All partners are responsible for the business actions of all others. Partners may have the ability to commit the partnership to a contract without approval of the other partners. A bad decision by one partner may put the other partners' personal resources in jeopardy. Personal problems such as a divorce can eliminate a significant portion of one partner's financial resources and weaken the financial structure of the whole partnership.

Life of the Partnership. A partnership is terminated when a partner dies or withdraws. In a two-person partnership, if one partner withdraws, the firm's liabilities would be paid off and the assets divided between the partners. Obviously, the partner who wishes to continue in the business would be at a serious disadvantage. The business could be disrupted, financing would be reduced, and the management skills of the departing partner would be lost. The remaining partner would have to find another partner or reorganize the business as a sole proprietorship. In very large partnerships such as those found in law firms and investment banks, the continuation of the partnership may be provided for in the articles of partnership. The provision may simply state the terms for a new partnership agreement among the remaining partners. In such cases, the disadvantage to the other partners is minimal.

"All partners are responsible for the business actions of all others."

Selling a partnership interest has the same effect as the death or withdrawal of a partner. It is difficult to place a value on a partner's share of the partnership. No public value is placed on the partnership, as there is on publicly owned corporations. What is a law firm worth? What is the local hardware store worth? Coming up with a fair value to which all partners can agree is not easy. For example, in the McCain partnership dispute discussed above, Wallace maintained 35 percent ownership in the business even after being fired as co-CEO because he could not sell his stake in the company. No buyer wanted to purchase his minority stake in the company, and he and his brother Harrison could never agree on a price for the shares.[20] Selling a partnership interest is easier if the articles of partnership specify a method of valuation. Even if there is not a procedure for selling one partner's interest, the old partnership must still be dissolved and a new one created. In contrast, in the corporate form of business, the departure of owners has little effect on the financial resources of the business, and the loss of managers does not cause long-term changes in the structure of the organization.

Distribution of Profits. Profits earned by the partnership are distributed to the partners in the proportions specified in the articles of partnership. This may be a disadvantage if the division of the profits does not reflect the work each partner puts into the business. You may have encountered this disadvantage while working on a student group project: You may have felt that you did most of the work and that the other students in the group received grades based on your efforts. Even the perception of an unfair profit-sharing agreement may cause tension between the partners, and unhappy partners can have a negative effect on the profitability of the business.

Limited Sources of Funds. As with a sole proprietorship, the sources of funds available to a partnership are limited. Because no public value is placed on the business (such as the current trading price of a corporation's shares), potential partners do not know what one partnership share is worth. Moreover, because partnership shares cannot be bought and sold easily in public markets, potential owners may not want to tie up their money in assets that cannot be readily sold on short notice, as is evident in the McCain dispute. Accumulating enough funds to operate a national business, especially a business requiring intensive investments in facilities and equipment, can be difficult. Partnerships also may have to pay higher interest rates on funds borrowed from banks than do large corporations because partnerships may be considered greater risks.

Taxation of Partnerships

Partnerships do not pay taxes when submitting the partnership tax return to the Canada Revenue Agency. Partners must report their share of profits on their individual tax returns and pay taxes at the income tax rate for individuals. Much like sole proprietors, partners can deduct losses from their partnership against other sources of income, but often pay more in taxes compared to corporations due to their tax rate.

Corporations

LO3 Describe the corporate form of organization, and cite the advantages and disadvantages of corporations.

When you think of a business, you probably think of a huge corporation such as Bell Canada, Tim Hortons, Shoppers Drug Mart, or the Royal Bank because most of your consumer dollars go to such corporations. A **corporation** is a legal entity, created under law either provincially or federally, whose assets and liabilities are separate from its owners'. As a legal entity, a corporation has many of the rights, duties, and powers of a person, such as the right to receive, own, and transfer property. Corporations can enter into contracts with individuals or

corporation a legal entity, whose assets and liabilities are separate from its owners'

"Should partners have a shotgun?" Perhaps the question makes you think of the Old West or organized crime movies, but the term *shotgun* has a very different meaning in partnership agreements.

Essentially the term is used to describe a clause where one business partner can make a cash offer for the other partner's share of the business. The person being offered the money for their share of the business is usually left with only two choices: (1) Accept the offer and take the money; or (2) match the partner's offer and assume the partner's share of the business.

People's opinions of shotgun clauses in partnerships differ. Some argue that they are useful tools, which allow for a quick end to a partnership that is no longer working. Furthermore, the cash offer is usually at a premium as the person making the offer risks getting removed from the business if they make a low offer. Others argue that shotgun clauses are often used too quickly when other dispute resolutions could be used to save partnerships, and that shotguns favour the partner with the most resources.

Joyce Groote, owner of Vancouver-based Holey Soles, did not start the business that she currently runs with her husband. Groote, who was very successful in the pharmaceutical industry, was asked to join the company to offer the founders managerial assistance. Groote eventually invested some cash in the business and ultimately exercised a shotgun clause to oust the founding partners. Groote noted that while her partners were good at starting a company, they were often too slow at making decisions, which negatively impacted growth.

The use of shotgun clauses is not limited to small business, as evident in the case of Tim Hortons and its partner, the Swiss specialist bakery conglomerate Aryzta AG. Tim Hortons and Aryzta AG had formed a partnership whereby the companies jointly owned a baking facility in Brantford, Ontario, that supplied all of the Tim Hortons stores with baked goods. Unexpectedly, the Swiss firm exercised a shotgun clause forcing Tim Hortons to either pay a substantial amount of money for a key production facility that is essential to its operation or allow Aryzta AG to assume control over an essential part of Tim Hortons' business. Tim Hortons eventually accepted the $475 million offer after Aryzta agreed to continue to supply product to the company until 2016.[21]

DISCUSSION QUESTIONS

1. If you were ever to join a partnership, would you want to have a shotgun clause?

2. What are some of the advantages and disadvantages of a shotgun clause?

3. What alternatives would you suggest to using a shotgun clause?

4. Would exercising the shotgun clause negatively impact Aryzta AG's ability to form partnerships in the future? Why or why not?

---

with other legal entities, and they can sue and be sued in court.

Corporations account for the majority of Canadian sales and employment. Thus, most of the dollars you spend as a consumer probably go to incorporated businesses (see Table 4.5 for the largest corporations in Canada). Not all corporations are mega-companies like Encana Corp. or Manulife; even small businesses can incorporate and share in many of the advantages of being an incorporated company. In fact, as businesses grow, it is normal for its legal ownership structure to change. As discussed above, many business start as a sole proprietorship or a partnership but as sales climb and the firm and its owner takes on more liability risk it is considered routine for entrepreneurs and/or managers to incorporate their business. *Globe and Mail* business columnist Chris Griffiths sums up this sentiment when he writes, "For most businesses, the question is not if, but when, to incorporate."[22]

Table 4.5 Market Cap: Top 10 Snapshot

The largest corporations in Canada by market cap from largest to smallest are as follows.[23] Since the information in the table can change quickly, students may want to use Internet resources to see what companies have moved up or down the list.

Royal Bank of Canada

Toronto Dominion Bank

Valeant Pharaceuticals

Bank of Nova Scotia

Canadian National Railway Company

General Motors Company

Suncor

Enbridge Inc.

Bank of Montreal

BCE

shares shares of a corporation that may be bought or sold

dividends profits of a corporation that are distributed in the form of cash payments to shareholders

Corporations are typically owned by individuals and organizations who own **shares** of the business sometimes referred to as stocks (thus, corporate owners are often called *shareholders* or *stockholders*). Shareholders can buy, sell, give or receive as gifts, or inherit their shares of stock. As owners, the shareholders are entitled to all profits that are left after all the corporation's other obligations have been paid. These profits may be distributed in the form of cash payments called **dividends**. For example, if a corporation earns $100 million after expenses and taxes and decides to pay the owners $40 million in dividends, the shareholders receive 40 percent of the profits in cash dividends. However, not all after-tax profits are paid to shareholders in dividends. In this example, the corporation retained $60 million of profits to finance expansion.

Creating a Corporation

A corporation is created, or incorporated, under the laws of the provincial or federal government. A business that is incorporated provincially does so under its provincial corporations legislation and can conduct business only in the province in which it is incorporated. Businesses that are incorporated federally do so under the Canada Business Corporations Act and can conduct business in all provinces and territories provided that they register their corporation in all the provinces where they carry on business. The main advantages of incorporating federally are the ability to operate anywhere in Canada and to use the same company name. Federal corporations do cost more to start than provincial corporations and have extra paperwork, including filings required by the federal Directors of Corporations Branch and all the filings required by the provinces.

The individuals creating the corporation are known as *incorporators*. Each provincial government and the federal government have specific procedures, sometimes called *chartering the corporation*, for incorporating a business. The first step is often choosing the name of the company, which must have the following:

- Distinctive portion to identify the business

- Descriptive portion that assists in identifying the activities of the company

- Legal element that identifies the business as a corporation, including Limited, Incorporated, or Corporation

After a name is chosen, a search is conducted to determine if the name is original and suitable.

The incorporators must then file legal documents including the *Memorandum*, which lays out the rules for

the company's conduct; the *Articles of Incorporation*, which are the rules and regulations that the company's members and directors must follow; and the *Notice of Officers*, which states the location of the required offices for the company—the registered office and the records office. Corporations that are incorporating under federal law must also prepare a *Notice of Directors* with the appropriate provincial or federal government. The following information is necessary when filing for a corporation:

- Name and address of the corporation

- Address for the Registered and Records Office

- Description of the classes of shares and the maximum number of shares that will be issued, as well as a clear description of the rights, privileges, and restrictions for each class of share

- Restrictions on share transfers, which must specify whether shares can be sold or transferred

- Number of directors

- Restrictions on the company's business activities

- Other provisions (While there is no requirement to include this, some incorporators do so to satisfy requirements from other provinces or regulatory agencies.)

Based on the information in the articles of incorporation, the provincial or federal government approves the corporation by issuing a **certificate of incorporation**. After securing approval, the owners hold an organizational meeting at which they establish the corporation's bylaws and elect a board of directors. The bylaws might set up committees of the board of directors and describe the rules and procedures for their operation.

Types of Corporations

A corporation may be privately or publicly owned. A **private corporation** is owned by just one or a few people who are closely involved in managing the business. These people, sometimes a family, own the majority if not all of the corporation's shares, and shares are not sold on any of the public stock exchanges. Shares in private corporations can be sold but the details of the transactions usually remain private. Many corporations are quite large, yet remain private, including the Irving Group of New Brunswick. Irving is one of the largest and most diversified companies in Canada with interests in shipbuilding,

certificate of incorporation a legal document that the provincial or federal government issues to a company based on information the company provides in the articles of incorporation

private corporation a corporation owned by just one or a few people who are closely involved in managing the business

Shares/stocks can be sold but the details of the transactions usually remain private.

owned corporations must disclose financial information to the public under specific laws that regulate the trade of stocks and other securities.

> ### "Privately owned corporations are not required to disclose financial information publicly, **but they must, of course, pay taxes.**"

A private corporation sometimes goes public to obtain more financing through the sale of shares, to allow the founders of the company to realize the value of the business, to raise money to pay off debt, to invest the proceeds in the firm, or to enhance the company's ability to raise capital in the future. A company goes public through an **initial public offering (IPO),** that is, becoming a public corporation by selling its shares so that it can be traded in public markets. For example, Google, the popular Internet search engine, went public with an initial public offering in 2004 and raised US$1.66 billion.[24] Facebook's IPO surpassed Google's, and raised US$16 billion, valuing the company at US$104.2 billion. As a result of the IPO, Facebook founder Mark Zuckerberg became the 19th-richest person on Earth, with a net worth of roughly US$19 billion. Unfortunately for Zuckerberg, and many of the company's initial investors, Facebook's share price did not increase dramatically in value after its IPO and actually declined.[25] The stock has since recovered as Facebook has managed to make more money from mobile advertising than was originally expected. Pizza Pizza Ltd., one of Canada's largest fast-food restaurants, went public and raised in excess of C$150 million. The owners of Pizza Pizza took the company public so they could realize some of the value in the company. They initially sold 75 percent of the shares in the business. Toronto-based Spin Master Toys completed an IPO in 2015 and raised over $200 million. The management of the company intends to re-invest the money into acquisitions to fuel future growth.[26] Hudson's Bay Company (HBC) has recently become a public corporation again after being taken private a short time ago by an American firm. HBC raised roughly $350 million in its IPO, of which 20 percent will be used to pay down debt; the rest of the money will be re-invested in improving stores in the face of increased competition.

Sometimes, privately owned firms are forced to go public with share offerings when a majority owner dies and the company's family members cannot decide on how best to manage the company or settle a large tax bill due as a result of the owner's death. The Irving Group discussed above has a long history of being a "very private" corporation—meaning very little information about the company was ever shared with the outside world. The family-owned business is currently controlled

> **initial public offering (IPO)** selling a corporation's shares on public markets for the first time

© Kobby Dagan/Shutterstock.com

Facebook CEO Mark Zuckerberg saw the company's share price fall shortly after taking the company public. The share price has recovered and risen sharply as Facebook has managed to increase its revenue through advertising.

newspapers, tissue paper, transportation, and oil and gas, yet it remains a large private corporation. Privately owned corporations are not required to disclose financial information publicly, but they must, of course, pay taxes.

> ### "A corporation may be privately or publicly owned."

A **public corporation** is one whose shares anyone may buy, sell, or trade on a public stock exchange such as the Toronto Stock Exchange (www.tmx.com). In large public corporations, such as the Royal Bank, the shareholders are often far removed from the management of the company. In other public corporations, the managers are often the founders and the majority shareholders. For example, the late Ted Rogers, founder of Rogers Communications, ran Rogers Communications right up until the time of his death. Other Canadian companies that have been or still are controlled by their founders include Magna International (Frank Stronach), Power Corporation of Canada (Paul Desmarais), and Onex Corporation (Gerald Schwartz). Publicly

> **public corporation** a corporation whose shares anyone may buy, sell, or trade

Public Cor. — Anyone may buy/sell or trade stocks/shares on a public stock exchange.

© Hand-out/TMX Group Limited/Newscom

Canadian toy giant Spin Master Toys recently completed an IPO raising over $200 million, which management plans to re-invest into future growth opportunities.

by the three sons of founder KC Irving, but they are apparently considering taking the company public in order to assist in long-term planning for the business and to ensure that all family members are properly compensated. Another example occurred at Adolph Coors Inc. When brewer Adolph Coors died, his business went public and his family sold shares of stock to the public to pay the estate taxes. Interestingly enough, KC Irving actually changed his place of residence from Canada to Bermuda to avoid paying large estate taxes.

Often when students see the letters IPO they may recall media stories describing the large amounts of money investors were willing to pay for the initial public offerings of companies such as Facebook, Spin Master Toys, Hudson's Bay Company, Google, or Boston Pizza. But these figures are not always the norm. In fact, sometimes the money raised is not as significant as you might imagine, and often the companies are not well known. Listed below are some of the companies that completed IPOs in Canada between 2013 and 2016.[27] How many of these have you heard of? Consider using the Internet to find out how much money their IPOs raised and what they did with the proceeds.

- Spin Master Toys
- Shopify
- BitGold Inc
- Seven Generations Energy Ltd.
- Cara Operations Ltd.
- Innova Gaming Group Inc.
- Xenon Pharmaceuticals Inc.

On the other hand, public corporations can be "taken private" when one or a few individuals (perhaps the management of the firm) purchase all the firm's shares so that it can no longer be sold publicly. For example, the founder and CEO of Hollywood Video, Mark Wattles, took the video rental chain private in 2004 by buying up all the shares for $14 each.[28] Taking a corporation private may be desirable when new owners want to exert more control over the firm, or when they want to avoid the necessity of public disclosure

of future activities for competitive reasons. For example, Frank Stronach opted to privatize two Canadian auto component manufacturing companies he owns, Intier and Decoma, to avoid the increased scrutiny public companies are now facing in North America. Michael Dell, the founder of computer company Dell Inc., is currently attempting to take the computer company that bears his name private. Dell, who resumed duties as CEO when the company's fortunes continued to fade in recent years, believes that increased pressure from investors for short-term results is negatively impacting the company's ability to innovate and plan for long-term success. Taking a corporation private is also one technique for avoiding a takeover by another corporation.

Two other types of corporations are Crown corporations and non-profit corporations. **Crown corporations** are owned by the provincial or federal government, such as Canada Post, and focus on providing a service to citizens, such as mail delivery, rather than earning a profit. Examples of federal Crown corporations include the Royal Canadian Mint and Via Rail Canada Inc. Provincial examples often include providers of electricity such as BC Hydro, lottery corporations, and liquor boards, such as the LCBO in Ontario.

Like Crown corporations, **non-profit corporations** focus on providing a service rather than earning a profit, but

Crown corporations
corporations owned and operated by government (federal or provincial)

non-profit corporations
corporations that focus on providing a service rather than earning a profit but are not owned by a government entity

Courtesy GMAC Financial Services

Habitat for Humanity is a non-profit, non-denominational Christian housing organization that builds simple, decent, and affordable houses in partnership with those who lack adequate shelter. Chosen families work alongside volunteers to build their own home.

they are not owned by a government entity. Organizations such as the Children's Wish Foundation, the United Way, the Canadian Cancer Society, museums, and private schools provide services without a profit motive. To fund their operations and services, non-profit organizations sometimes charge for their services (private schools), solicit donations from individuals and companies, and apply for grants from the government and other charitable foundations.

Elements of a Corporation

The Board of Directors. A **board of directors**, elected by the shareholders to oversee the general operation of the corporation, sets the long-range objectives of the corporation. It is the board's responsibility to ensure that the objectives are achieved on schedule. Board members are legally liable for the mismanagement of the firm or for any misuse of funds. An important duty of the board of directors is to hire corporate officers, such as the president and the chief executive officer (CEO), who are responsible to the directors for the management and daily operations of the firm. The role and expectations of the board of directors took on greater significance after the accounting scandals of the early 2000s and the passage of much tougher regulation in Canada by the provincial regulatory boards and the Sarbanes-Oxley Act in the United States.[29] As a result, the duties and the workload of board members has increased substantially along with their accountability. Allen Shaw, chairman of the Shaw Group and a director at the Bank of Nova Scotia, says, "Fifteen years ago, it wouldn't have been unusual for very little paper to be sent out before a meeting. Directors could prepare for lots of meetings in an hour. Today it is not unusual to spend a day or more reading documents and studying financial statements while preparing for board meetings."[30] An example of this increased accountability and scrutiny occurred when former Newfoundland premier Brian Tobin recruited Kevin O'Leary, a well-known TV personality and investor, along with former Ontario premier Mike Harris, Nova Scotia seafood king John Risley, and Toronto governance expert Timothy Rowley, to serve on the board at Environmental Management Solutions Inc. (EMS), today known as EnGlobe Corp. Tobin had agreed to assist then-CEO Frank D'Addario in building a board and quickly built what many would consider an all-star team of directors. The public reacted strongly to the move and the company's shares soared. Unfortunately, the new directors quickly learned about what they characterized as financial misdeeds by D'Addario and were forced to fire him from his post. Some of the new board members considered leaving the company due to the financial mess they inherited, but after hearing from their lawyers that they could be held responsible for the

board of directors a group of individuals, elected by the shareholders to oversee the general operation of the corporation, who set the corporation's long-range objectives

© Thomas Barwick/Getty Images

After the accounting scandals of the early 2000s and the passage of much tougher regulations, directors on public corporations' boards are expected to be more involved in the running of the company and highly scrutinize management decisions.

mismanagement of the company, the board stayed on and dealt with the company's problems.

Directors can be employees of the company (*inside directors*) or people unaffiliated with the company (*outside directors*). Inside directors are usually the officers responsible for running the company. For example, when Frank Stronach of Magna sat on its board of directors and acted as CEO, he would have been considered an inside director. Outside directors are often top executives from other companies, lawyers, bankers, or even professors. Directors today are increasingly chosen for their expertise, competence, and ability to bring diverse perspectives to strategic discussions. Outside directors are also thought to bring more independence to the monitoring function because they are not bound by past allegiances, friendships, a current role in the company, or some other issue that may create a conflict of interest. Many of the corporate scandals uncovered in recent years might have been prevented if each of the companies' boards of directors had been better qualified, more knowledgeable, and more independent. A survey by *USA Today* found that corporate boards have considerable overlap. More than 1,000 corporate board members sit on four or more company boards, and of the nearly 2,000 boards of directors, more than 22,000 board members are linked to boards of more than one company.[31] According to Phil Purcell, CEO of Morgan Stanley, "Some director overlap is inevitable when shareholders demand the highest-calibre directors for their board."[32] This overlap creates the opportunity for conflicts of interest in decision making and limits the independence of individual boards of directors. For example, the telecommunications firm Verizon, which shares four board members with prescription-drug producer Wyeth, withdrew from non-profit organization Business for Affordable Medicine, which had been criticized by Wyeth because of its stance on bringing generic drugs to market sooner.[33]

preferred shares a special type of share whose owners, though not generally having a say in running the company, have a claim to profits before other shareholders do

common shares shares whose owners have voting rights in the corporation, yet do not receive preferential treatment regarding dividends

Share Ownership. Corporations issue two types of shares: preferred and common. Owners of **preferred shares** are a special class of owners because, although they generally do not have any say in running the company, they have a claim to any profits before any other shareholders do. Other shareholders do not receive any dividends unless the preferred shareholders have already been paid. Dividend payments on preferred shares are usually a fixed percentage of the initial issuing price (set by the board of directors). For example, if a preferred share originally cost $100 and the dividend rate was stated at 7.5 percent, the dividend payment will be $7.50 per share per year. Dividends are usually paid quarterly. Most preferred shares carry a cumulative claim to dividends. This means that if the company does not pay preferred-share dividends in one year because of losses, the dividends accumulate to the next year. Such dividends unpaid from previous years must also be paid to preferred shareholders before other shareholders can receive any dividends.

Although owners of **common shares** do not get such preferential treatment with regard to dividends, they do get some say in the operation of the corporation. Their ownership gives them the right to vote for members of the board of directors and on other important issues. Common share dividends may vary according to the profitability of the business, and some corporations do not issue dividends at all, but instead plough their profits back into the company to fund expansion.

Common shareholders are the voting owners of a corporation. They are usually entitled to one vote per share. During an annual shareholders' meeting, common shareholders elect a board of directors. Because they can choose the board of directors, common shareholders have some say in how the company will operate. Common shareholders may vote by *proxy*, which is a written authorization by which shareholders assign their voting privilege to someone else, who then votes for his or her choice at the shareholders' meeting. It is a normal practice for management to request proxy statements from shareholders who are not planning to attend the annual meeting. Most owners do not attend annual meetings of the very large companies, such as Encana or Suncor, unless they live in the city where the meeting is held.

Common shareholders have another advantage over preferred shareholders. Sometimes when the corporation decides to sell new common shares in the marketplace, common shareholders have the first right, called a

> ## "Corporations issue two types of shares: preferred and common."

> ## "Common shareholders are the voting owners of a corporation."

preemptive right, to purchase new shares from the corporation. A preemptive right is often included in the articles of incorporation. This right is important because it allows shareholders to purchase new shares to maintain their original positions. For example, if a shareholder owns 10 percent of a corporation that decides to issue new shares, that shareholder has the right to buy enough of the new shares to retain the 10 percent ownership.

Advantages of Corporations

Because a corporation is a separate legal entity, it has some very specific advantages over other forms of ownership. The biggest advantage may be the limited liability of the owners.

Limited Liability. Because the corporation's assets (money and resources) and liabilities (debts and other obligations including legal) are separate from its owners', in most cases the shareholders are not held responsible for the firm's debts if it fails. Their liability or potential loss is limited to the amount of their original investment. Although a creditor can sue a corporation for not paying its debts, even forcing the corporation into bankruptcy, it cannot make the shareholders pay the corporation's debts out of their personal assets. This advantage is rarely extended to small private corporations when borrowing money. Most banks and credit unions will insist that the owners of a private corporation pledge personal assets to secure a loan for the corporation unless the business has a long successful history; this would be most unusual for a public corporation. The main advantage of limited liability to small business is against loss to trade creditors/suppliers who granted the business credit and against legal liability.

Ease of Transfer of Ownership. Shareholders in public corporations can sell or trade shares to other people

© Chris Batson/Alamy Stock Photo

RBC is currently Canada's third-largest public corporation.

without causing the termination of the corporation, and they can do this without the prior approval of other shareholders. The transfer of ownership (unless it is a majority position) does not affect the daily or long-term operations of the corporation. Private corporations also allow shareholders to sell or transfer shares, but the transfer is not always easy, as is evident from the discussion about McCain Foods Ltd. Private corporations often face the same hurdles as partnerships when people are trying to sell shares or a stake in the business.

Perpetual Life. A corporation usually is chartered to last forever unless its articles of incorporation stipulate otherwise. The existence of the corporation is unaffected by the death or withdrawal of any of its shareholders. It survives until the owners sell it or liquidate its assets. However, in some cases, bankruptcy ends a corporation's life. Bankruptcies occur when companies are unable to compete and earn profits. Eventually, uncompetitive businesses must close or seek protection from creditors in bankruptcy court while the business tries to reorganize.

External Sources of Funds. Of all the forms of business organization, the public corporation finds it easiest to raise money. When a corporation needs to raise more money, it can sell more shares or issue bonds (corporate "IOUs," which pledge to repay debt), attracting funds from anywhere in North America and even overseas. The larger a corporation becomes, the more sources of financing are available to it. We take a closer look at some of these in Chapter 16. Research has indicated that a private corporation's ability to raise funds has more to do with the history of the company than its business structure. A private corporation such as the Irving Group or Chapman's Ice Cream (Canada's largest ice cream seller) would have little trouble raising money. A small corporation with an unproven business record would likely face the same hurdles in raising funds that a sole proprietor or partnership would have.

Expansion Potential. Because large public corporations can find long-term financing readily, they can easily expand into national and international markets. And as a legal entity, a corporation can enter into contracts without as much difficulty as a partnership.

Tax Advantages. Corporations have a number of tax advantages. Public corporations pay a lower tax rate than sole proprietorships and partnerships. Smaller private corporations also pay a lower tax rate, and their owners can often defer tax by leaving money in the corporation, splitting income through payment of dividends to spouses or children, and, if the business is sold, realizing tax-free capital gains of up to $750,000.

Disadvantages of Corporations

Corporations have some distinct disadvantages resulting from tax laws and government regulation.

Double Taxation. As a legal entity, the corporation must pay taxes on its income just like you do. When after-tax corporate profits are paid out as dividends to the shareholders, the dividends are taxed a second time as part of the individual owner's income. This process creates double taxation for the shareholders of dividend-paying corporations. Often, the disadvantage of double taxation is offset by the Dividend Tax Credit program, a tax credit that allows the Canada Revenue Agency to tax dividend income at a lower rate than personal income. For example, if a private corporation earns $200,000, the money is taxed at 16 percent, which creates a $32,000 tax bill. If the owner then pays himself the remaining $168,000 as dividends, which are taxed at 15 percent, his take-home pay will be $142,800. If the owner of the business was a sole proprietor, all of the $200,000 would be taxed at personal rates, which can be as high as 49 percent. Double taxation does not occur with the other forms of business organization.

Forming a Corporation. The formation of a corporation can be costly. There are filing fees associated with forming a corporation, and often a lawyer is needed. The total costs of forming a corporation are usually in excess of $1,000.

Disclosure of Information and Regulations. Corporations must make information available to their owners, usually through an annual report to shareholders. The annual report contains financial information about the firm's profits, sales, facilities and equipment, and debts, as well as descriptions of the company's operations, products, and plans for the future. Public corporations must also file reports with the public stock exchanges and the various provincial exchange commissions. As discussed above, tougher corporate governance laws and increased scrutiny in Canada and the United States means corporations are faced with increased paperwork and regulations. In fact, some of Canada's most prominent business leaders, including Paul Desmarais, owner of Power Corp., and Dominic D'Allessandro, former CEO of Manulife, have stated that the increased regulations have hindered corporate growth by draining time and money away from the company. Frank Stronach, former CEO of the publicly traded Canadian automobile component manufacturing company Magna, notes, "The time we spend complying with regulations is now enormous."[34]

Impact on Management Decisions. Shareholders of publicly traded companies are becoming much more aggressive in demanding share appreciation and short-term

> "Of all the forms of business organization, the public corporation finds it easiest to raise money."

results from management teams. As a result, management sometimes feels pressure to make decisions that are beneficial in the short term, but are not good long-term decisions. When Rogers Communications invested hundreds of millions of dollars in 3G technology, shareholders and stock market analysts questioned the decision and some attempted to pressure management to halt the costly project. As a result of the investment, Rogers became the technological leader among cellphone companies in Canada. This leadership position is what allowed the company to be the first cellphone provider to sell the popular iPhone in Canada, giving Rogers a substantial advantage over its competitors, but this shareholder pressure is why some owners prefer to remain private. Jim Pattison of Jim Pattison Group sums up the advantages of remaining private: "We can make better decisions as the owner of a private enterprise where we don't have to worry about daily share prices and analysts' expectations."[35]

Employee–Owner Separation. Many employees are not shareholders of the company for which they work. This separation of owners and employees may cause employees to feel that their work benefits only the owners. Employees without an ownership stake do not always see how they fit into the corporate picture and may not understand the importance of profits to the health of the organization. If managers are part owners but other employees are not, management–labour relations take on a different, sometimes difficult, aspect from those in partnerships and sole proprietorships. However, this situation is changing as more corporations establish employee share ownership plans (ESOPs), which give employees shares in the company. Such plans build a partnership between employee and employer and can boost productivity because they motivate employees to work harder so that they can earn dividends from their hard work as well as from their regular wages. In fact, of the 100 fastest-growing businesses in Canada identified by *Profit* magazine, 47 percent run ESOPs.[36]

Other Types of Ownership

In this section we will take a brief look at joint ventures and cooperatives—businesses formed for special purposes.

Joint Ventures

A **joint venture** is a partnership established for a specific project, often for a limited time. The partners in a joint venture may be individuals or organizations, as in the case of the international joint ventures discussed in Chapter 3. Control of a joint venture may be shared equally, or one partner may control decision making. Joint ventures are especially popular in situations that call for large investments, such as extraction of natural resources, and are quite common in the Alberta

joint venture a partnership established for a specific project or for a limited time involving the sharing of the costs and operation of a business, often between a foreign company and a local partner

oil patch. For example, Husky Energy and BP plc formed a 50/50 joint venture in the Athabasca Oil Sands in Alberta. BP plc agreed to bring its excess refinery capacity to the agreement and Husky Energy brought its reserves from the oil patch. Joint ventures are also common in the development of new products. Ballard Power, a B.C.-based alternative energy company, has been in various joint ventures and strategic partnerships with such companies as Ford and Mercedes-Benz as they strive to replace traditional car engines. One of the better-known retail joint ventures in recent years was the partnership between Tim Hortons and Cold Stone Creamery. Tim Hortons and Cold Stone had agreed to include Cold Stone ice cream in over 150 stores in Canada and Tim Hortons' coffee in some of the more prominent Cold Stone stores in the United States. The venture allowed Cold Stone to quickly gain access to the Canadian market through a proven retailer, and Tim Hortons was able to offer a product with strong summer sales to its customers and franchise owners. Tim Hortons also gained access to some of Cold Stone's U.S. locations as a result of the arrangement.[37] This joint venture didn't last as Tim Hortons ended the partnership rather abruptly in 2014. While ice cream did diversify its in-store sales, the premium price attached to Cold Stone products did not seem to fit in Tim Hortons restaurants, which are known for value food.[38]

Successful retail partnerships are not limited to the food industry, as illustrated by the partnership between Loblaws and Joe Fresh, the Canadian clothing company. The partnership allows Joe Fresh to sell its products in 300 supermarket locations, and Loblaws gets access to a popular consumer brand. Joe Fresh hoped to create the same type of relationship in the U.S. when it announced a partnership with JC Penney to carry its line in stores throughout America.[39] Other examples include MovieLink, a joint venture of the film studios MGM, Paramount, Sony, Universal,

© Manor Photography/Alamy Stock Photo

When first announced, Tim Hortons' joint venture with Cold Stone Creamery seemed like a perfect match of complementary products. But value-seeking Tim Hortons customers did not like the premium pricing of Cold Stone products, and the venture ultimately failed.

and Warner Bros. that was developed as a competitor to Netflix, the popular online movie-rental source.[40] While the theory supporting joint ventures such as the pooling of resources and/or the sharing of expertise is sound in principle, many studies indicate that over 50 percent of joint ventures fail and most will not last five years.

Cooperatives

Another form of organization in business is the **cooperative or co-op,** an organization composed of individuals or small businesses that have banded together to reap the benefits of belonging to a larger organization. In cooperatives, the owners usually are limited to one share per person—although the share structure can be altered to reflect the level of a member's contribution to the co-op. There are currently over 9,000 co-ops in Canada that provide services to 18 million members and employ over 150,000 people.[41] Well-known Canadian co-ops include Farmers Dairy, which is a co-operative of milk producers in Atlantic Canada; the Toronto Renewable Energy Co-operative (TREC), which was Canada's first green power community co-operative; SSQ Groupe Financier in Quebec, which stands out in the financial services industry as its clients are also the company's owners; and Community Health Co-operative

GOING GREEN | CSAs for Everyone

As people become more and more concerned about the state of the environment, *sustainable*, *local*, and *green* are just some of the words being tossed around with increasing frequency. Individuals are looking for ways to reduce their carbon footprint, protect the land, and take better care of their own health. To this end, community-supported agriculture (CSA) is becoming a popular alternative to large-chain grocery stores. The CSA is not a new idea. It originated in Japan around 30 years ago and was adopted in Canada in the 1980s.

A CSA is a way for local farmers to bypass the bureaucracy of traditional corporate grocery stores and to conduct business directly with consumers. Under this model, a farmer first creates a budget for the growing season that includes all costs (such as land payments, seeds, salaries, equipment, and so on). The farmer then divides this budget into the number of shares of crops available for purchase. Usually a CSA share is designed to feed a family of four for a week. People become members of a farm's CSA by purchasing shares. They will then receive a portion of local, often organic, produce each week during the growing season. The CSA creates a sustainable relationship in which members receive quality produce and farmers have a reliable method for distributing their crops.

How does the CSA benefit the environment and contribute to health? The farms offering CSAs are usually small and dedicated to ecologically sound farming practices, such as permaculture and avoiding chemical pesticides. Because the cost of distribution is lower for these farmers, members often receive produce at prices competitive with conventional produce sold in grocery stores. Farmers, knowing that their basic costs are covered, can focus their full attention on growing high-quality produce rather than searching for distributors. In addition, because deliveries are made locally, produce is fresher. The local aspect of delivery also cuts

© Ocean/Corbis

Farmers and consumers are embracing community-supported agriculture, in which consumers invest in farms and get paid in produce.

down on pollution because the products do not need to travel great distances.

In a world where people are looking to take better care of themselves and the environment, as well as to understand where their food came from, the CSA is becoming a popular alternative to traditional stores.[42] While Agriculture Canada has yet to determine the number of CSAs in existence, an Internet search reveals that they exist in every province and news articles indicate that they are growing in popularity with consumers.

DISCUSSION QUESTIONS

1. What are some of the benefits farmers gain by switching to the CSA model?

2. Why are people opting to use CSAs over traditional grocery stores?

3. Can you think of any drawbacks to the CSA model?

Federation in Saskatchewan, which aims to reform health policy and provide community-oriented alternatives to traditional care. A co-op is set up not to make money as an entity but so that its members can become more profitable or save money. Co-ops are generally expected to operate without profit or to create only enough profit to maintain the co-op organization. For example, Mountain Equipment Co-op is the largest retailer co-operative in Canada, and its goal is to provide accessible and fairly priced outdoor gear to its members. At the end of the year, any surplus money is returned to shareholders.

Many cooperatives exist in small farming communities. The co-op stores can market grain; order large quantities of fertilizer, seed, and other supplies at discounted prices; and reduce costs and increase efficiency with good management. A co-op can purchase supplies in large quantities and pass the savings on to its members. It also can help distribute the products of its members more efficiently than each could on an individual basis. A cooperative can advertise its members' products and thus generate demand. Ace Hardware, a cooperative of independent hardware store owners, allows its members to share in the savings that result from buying supplies in large quantities; it also provides advertising, which individual members might not be able to afford on their own.

RESPONDING TO BUSINESS CHALLENGES | Heartland Farm Foods Co-op Helps Preserve Beef—and a Way of Life

Jim Farmer, a lifelong livestock producer, wants his son and two daughters to be able to carry on the family farm. To help achieve this goal, he formed the Heartland Farm Foods Co-op with about three dozen beef producers to turn 1,000 cattle a year into canned beef. The co-op form of organization is not unusual for small businesses that band together to obtain the benefits of a larger organization. The co-op is not set up to make money as an organization, but rather so that all the ranchers involved can become more profitable or, in this case, continue to maintain a lifestyle that they enjoy. In the face of intense competition from large commercial feedlots, Farmer's idea was to offer a different kind of product and to market and support it through the co-op, which has the support of the local Beef Industry Council, and the Department of Agriculture.

The co-op's canned, precooked ground and chunked beef products contain just one ingredient—beef, with no preservatives, not even salt. Any harmful bacteria are removed through a pressure-cooking process. Each animal yields 400 to 500 cans of federally inspected beef from cattle raised without steroids, hormone additives, or routine antibiotics. The precooked beef is targeted at outdoor enthusiasts—from hikers and hunters to anglers and campers. Thanks to a shelf life of two to five years, the cans can be stowed in tackle boxes or backpacks, or even stored in storm shelters in case of a disaster.

The co-op has constructed a 415-square-metre plant on 4 hectares to process the beef. Construction of this facility and first-year operating capital needs were estimated at approximately $750,000. Some of these expenses were partially offset by grants that the co-op received; co-ops that foster economic development in a region often receive grants or other financial support from provincial or federal development initiatives.

Currently, Heartland's canned beef is primarily available in local supermarkets and convenience stores and online at www.heartlandfoods.com. Prices range from $2.69 to $3.99 on the website, although retailers sell the product for $4.99 per can. At this price, consumers surely demand a quality product, but Heartland believes the product's convenience and ingredients support sales. The co-op recently released five new products—Nacho Express, Zesty Beef'n Bean, Beef'n Bean Chili, Chili Con Queso, and Hearty Taco Beef—and is selling steaks to local restaurants and markets. Heartland's initiative offers an example of creativity in bringing back a product—canned meat—that was once a pantry staple before the era of refrigeration. The co-operative form of organization has made it possible for small ranchers to join together to make this product a reality.[43]

DISCUSSION QUESTIONS

1. Why did Heartland Foods employ a cooperative form of organization?

2. What are the advantages for ranchers who belong to the cooperative?

3. Can you think of any other industries where the cooperative form of business ownership would be beneficial?

Toronto Do...

TD canada Trust.

Trends in Business Ownership: Mergers and Acquisitions

LO4 — Define and debate the advantages and disadvantages of mergers, acquisitions, and leveraged buyouts.

Companies large and small achieve growth and improve profitability by expanding their operations, often by developing and selling new products or selling current products to new groups of customers in different geographic areas. Such growth, when carefully planned and controlled, is usually beneficial to the firm and ultimately helps it reach its goal of enhanced profitability. But companies also grow by merging with or purchasing other companies.

A **merger** occurs when two companies (usually corporations) combine to form a new company. An **acquisition** occurs when one company purchases another, generally by buying its shares. The acquired company may become a subsidiary of the buyer, or its operations and assets may be merged with those of the buyer. For example, in 2014 Burger King bought Tim Hortons for $14.6 billion, much to the dismay of many Canadians who expressed mild surprise to outrage that their beloved Canadian icon would be owned by the U.S. restaurant operator.[44]

merger the combination of two companies (usually corporations) to form a new company

acquisition the purchase of one company by another, usually by buying its shares

Other examples include the Molson family and a group of investors buying the Montreal Canadiens, Bell Centre, and Gillett Entertainment for $500 million. One of the better-known recent acquisitions involved Disney purchasing Lucasfilm Ltd., including the rights to the *Star Wars* movies for $4.01 billion.[45] Disney has already released the newest *Star Wars* movie, *The Force Awakens*, and announced plans to expand the successful movie franchise, ensuring children will be playing with light sabres for years to come.[46]

Acquisitions and mergers are generally driven by (1) *economies of scale*, where a larger company can reduce its costs and offer the same products or level or service at a lower cost; (2) *increased market share*, when the company is acquiring a competitor; (3) *cross-selling*, where the acquired firm can sell different products to the same customer; (4) *integration*, where the acquired firm can act as a supplier or a distributor for the firms' products; and (5) *diversification*, where a firm acquires another firm that operates in a different industry to hedge against an industry downturn. As previously discussed, even when one or more of these advantages are evident in an acquisition/merger, studies indicate that they are only successful 50 percent of the time. Common reasons cited for the lack of success include unanticipated expenses, overestimation of cost savings, and conflicting corporate cultures.

Recent examples of mergers and acquisitions in Canada or featuring Canadian companies include the following:

- Burger King acquires Tim Hortons for $14.6 billion.
- Talisman Energy was acquired by Spanish energy firm Repsol for $15.7 billion.
- Encana purchased Athlon Energy for $7.8 billion.
- Valeant Pharmaceuticals' $2.6 billion acquisition of Medicis Pharmaceuticals.
- Royal Bank of Canada acquired U.S.-based City National Corporation for $3.2 billion.

When firms that make and sell similar products to the same customers merge, it is known as a *horizontal merger*, as when Toronto-Dominion Bank merged with another financial service company, Canada Trust, to form TD Canada Trust. Horizontal mergers, however, reduce the number of corporations competing within an industry and, for this reason, usually are reviewed

© Cal Sport Media/Alamy Stock Photo

One of the most discussed acquisitions in recent memory was that of the Montreal Canadiens, Bell Centre, and Gillett Entertainment by the Molson family.

carefully by federal regulators before the merger is allowed to proceed. After the TD Canada Trust merger, a number of Canadian banks attempted to merge, including Royal Bank with the Bank of Montreal and CIBC with TD, but the federal government blocked these mergers noting that they would be unfair to consumers. Given that the federal government does not appear to be willing to allow any mergers or acquisitions between the largest banks in Canada, many of them have gone shopping for other companies. It is estimated that Canadian banks were involved in over 50 acquisitions between 2011 and 2013, and some examples include Royal Bank paying $4.1 billion for Ally,[47] a Canadian auto lending company, and TD Bank spending $6 billion for Target's credit card business.[48] Sometimes firms purchase other companies and allow them to continue operating under their brand and to maintain some form of independence. This often happens when the competitor's brand is strong, and it resonates with consumers. For example, the Bank of Nova Scotia/Scotiabank recently purchased ING Direct's Canadian operations for $3.1 billion. Scotia plans to continue to operate the company under the ING brand as it has 1.8 million loyal followers in Canada and 1,100 employees.[49]

Since most mergers and acquisitions result in larger companies and reduce the level of competition, the government through various regulatory agencies often has to approve mergers. As discussed above, and in the case at the end of the chapter, various regulatory boards review acquisitions to ensure that a level, competitive playing field exists, that consumers are not negatively impacted as a result of the merger, and (in the case of foreign takeovers of Canadian companies) that the result is of net benefit to Canada. Recently, the Canadian Radio-television and Telecommunications Commission (CRTC) rejected Bell Canada's proposed $3.4 billion takeover of Astral Media, saying it would place too much power in the hands of one company and threaten the competitive media landscape in Canada. Bell then submitted a revised proposal that included the sale of several television and radio stations; the proposal was ultimately approved.[50]

Perhaps one of the stranger acquisition-rejection stories may end up not being a rejection at all. Lowes, an American hardware retailer, launched a $1.8 billion takeover bid for Rona Inc., which was Canada's largest hardware store in 2012 continuing into 2013. The government of Quebec, where Rona maintains its head office, stated that Rona was of significant value to the province, and the government would do everything in its power to block the bid. Lowes eventually walked away from the takeover, but many business analysts questioned the province's statements. Derek DeCloet, of the *Globe and Mail* stated, "Rona became a target for a reason. The company was plagued by poor management and its share price was underappreciated as a result."[51] Many journalists in the press agreed with DeCloet,

arguing that the Quebec government was misguided and Lowes could have bought Rona and improved the company—with the end result being more Canadian jobs and lower prices for consumers. But Lowes was undeterred and in 2016 launched another bid for Rona, this time valuing the company at $2.3 billion. Unlike the last bid, Rona's management and board of directors are fully supportive of the sale. Yet some politicians in Quebec are once again denouncing the sale, including Pierre-Karl Péladeau, the leader of the Parti Québécois. Given that the Liberal Party is in power provincially and has a very pro-business approach, analysts believe the deal sale will be finalized sometime in 2016.[52]

When companies operating at different but related levels of an industry merge, it is known as a *vertical merger*. In many instances, a vertical merger results when one corporation merges with one of its customers or suppliers. For example, if Tim Hortons were to purchase a large coffee bean farm—to ensure a ready supply of beans for its coffee—a vertical merger would result. Vertical mergers allow for quick growth and were a key strategy used by KC Irving to grow the Irving Group. Irving noted that he started selling cars, and since cars needed gas, he opened a gas station. Since gas needed refined oil, he started an oil company, and since oil had to be transported, he entered into the transportation and shipping industry.

A *conglomerate merger* results when two firms in unrelated industries merge. For example, the purchase of the Toronto Blue Jays in the 1990s by brewer Labatt and the CIBC represents a conglomerate merger because the two companies are in different industries.

When a company (or an individual), sometimes called a *corporate raider*, wants to acquire or take over another company, it first offers to buy some or all of the other company's shares at a premium over its current price in a *tender offer*. Most such offers are "friendly," with both groups agreeing to the proposed deal, but some are "hostile," when the second company does not want to be taken over. For example, Potash Corp. of Saskatchewan, which is discussed in the case at the end of the chapter, opposed the US$38.6 billion hostile takeover bid by BHP Billiton Ltd. The bid was ultimately unsuccessful as the Canadian government refused to allow the takeover, arguing the bid was not in the best interest of Canadians. As discussed in the CEO profile at the start of the chapter, Indigo, a Canadian book retailer, made a hostile bid for Chapters, its largest Canadian competitor. Initially, management at Chapters tried to avert the bid using a number of techniques including looking for a white knight (see below), which they thought they found in Future Shop, but Indigo was persistent in its pursuit of the company and raised the initial offer price. Ultimately, Indigo successfully acquired Chapters.

To head off a hostile takeover attempt, a threatened company's managers may use one or more of several techniques. They may ask shareholders not to sell to the

Do you Skype? If you do, you likely use its free video-calling feature. Thanks to this feature, Skype has approximately 150 million monthly users. Sensing its potential, eBay purchased Skype in 2005 for $2.5 billion. Four years later, venture capitalists purchased 70 percent of the company. Despite changes in ownership, Skype has flourished, prompting Microsoft to purchase it for $8.5 billion. However, this acquisition has created concern over Skype's future.

Analysts are skeptical that Skype can survive being consumed by such a large corporation. Many question why Microsoft would want a video-conferencing site when it already provides video/voice software on two platforms. Skype's 8 million customers who use its pay-based services do not seem to justify Microsoft's willingness to pay more than $8 billion for the company. Additionally, major acquisitions often fail because stock prices tend to decrease due to investor uncertainty over whether the venture will succeed. Microsoft's decision to pay so much for Skype without a seemingly logical explanation concerns analysts and investors. Although new opportunities for Skype are emerging, such as its integration into school curriculums, are these market opportunities enough to quell investor fears and create a successful acquisition?[53]

© Ken Wolter/Shutterstock.com

Microsoft recent $8.5 billion acquisition of Skype has many business analysts wondering how the company will recoup its investment.

DISCUSSION QUESTIONS

1. Why do you think Microsoft decided to purchase Skype?

2. Why do analysts appear unsure about the success of the acquisition?

3. What are some of the risks involved with acquiring a new company?

raider; file a lawsuit in an effort to abort the takeover; institute a *poison pill* (in which the firm allows shareholders to buy more shares at prices lower than the current market value) or *shark repellant* (in which management requires a large majority of shareholders to approve the takeover); or seek a *white knight* (a more acceptable firm that is willing to acquire the threatened company). In some cases, management may take the company private or even take on more debt so that the heavy debt obligation will "scare off" the raider. The result of companies taking actions such as these has been a reduction in the success rate of hostile bids—only 46 percent of hostile takeovers are successful.[54] As a result, the popularity of hostile takeovers has declined sharply since their heyday in the 1990s. From 2006 to 2015 only 5 percent of takeovers would be classified as hostile. In the case of the initial hostile bid by Sanofi for Aventis, for example, Aventis initially instituted several measures to thwart the takeover attempt, including asking a rival Swiss firm, Novartis, to bid for Aventis. Only when Sanofi significantly raised its offer did Aventis's board of directors recommend that its shareholders accept the revised offer from Sanofi.[55]

In a **leveraged buyout (LBO)**, a group of investors borrows money from banks and other institutions to acquire a company (or a division of one), using the assets of the purchased company to guarantee repayment of the loan. In some LBOs, as much as 95 percent of the buyout price is paid with borrowed money, which eventually must be repaid. The new management then engages in a number of strategies including selling assets, cutting costs including termination of employees, and/or breaking up businesses to restore value to the acquired business. The company uses its improved balance sheet to pay off the debt and the business is often sold at a much higher price than the original purchase price. In Canada, Gerry Schwartz, CEO of Onex Corporation, has made billions by buying distressed businesses, making changes, and then selling the improved companies. Examples of Schwartz's work include Sky Chefs and

leveraged buyout (LBO) a purchase in which a group of investors borrows money from banks and other institutions to acquire a company (or a division of one), using the assets of the purchased company to guarantee repayment of the loan

Loews Cineplex, two companies that he bought at deep discounts using debt and eventually sold for millions in profit.

With the explosion of mergers, acquisitions, and leveraged buyouts in the 1980s and 1990s, some financial journalists coined the term *merger mania*. Many companies joined the merger mania simply to enhance their own operations by consolidating them with the operations of other firms. Mergers and acquisitions enabled these companies to gain a larger market share in their industries, acquire valuable assets, such as new products or plants and equipment, and lower their costs. Mergers also represent a means of making profits quickly, as was the case during the 1980s when many companies' shares were undervalued. Quite simply, such companies represent a bargain to other companies that can afford to buy them. Additionally, deregulation of some industries has permitted consolidation of firms within those industries for the first time, as is the case in the banking and airline industries.

Some people view mergers and acquisitions favourably, pointing out that they boost corporations' share prices and market value, to the benefit of their shareholders. In many instances, mergers enhance a company's ability to meet foreign competition in an increasingly global marketplace. And, companies that are victims of hostile takeovers generally streamline their operations, reduce unnecessary staff, cut costs, and otherwise become more efficient with their operations, which benefits their shareholders whether or not the takeover succeeds.

Critics, however, argue that mergers hurt companies because they force managers to focus their efforts on avoiding takeovers rather than managing effectively and profitably. Some companies have taken on a heavy debt burden to stave off a takeover, later to be forced into bankruptcy when economic downturns left them unable to handle the debt. Mergers and acquisitions also can damage employee morale and productivity, as well as the quality of the companies' products.

Many mergers have been beneficial for all involved; others have had damaging effects for the companies, their employees, and customers. No one can say if mergers will continue to slow, but many experts say the utilities, telecommunications, financial services, natural resources, computer hardware and software, gaming, managed health care, and technology industries are likely targets.

TEAM EXERCISE

Form groups and find examples of mergers and acquisitions. Mergers can be broken down into traditional mergers, horizontal mergers, and conglomerate mergers. When companies are found, note how long the merger or acquisition took, if there were any requirements by the government before approval of the merger or acquisition, and if any failed mergers or acquisitions were found that did not receive government approval. Report your findings to the class, and explain what the companies hoped to gain from the merger or acquisition.

LEARNING OBJECTIVES SUMMARY

LO1 Define and examine the advantages and disadvantages of the sole proprietorship form of organization.

LO2 Identify three types of partnership, and evaluate the advantages and disadvantages of the partnership form of organization.

Sole proprietorships—businesses owned and managed by one person—are the most common form of organization. Their major advantages are the following: (1) They are easy and inexpensive to form, (2) they allow a high level of secrecy, (3) all profits belong to the owner, (4) the owner has complete control over the business, (5) government regulation is minimal, (6) taxes are paid only once, and (7) the business can be closed easily. The disadvantages include: (1) The owner may have to use personal assets to borrow money, (2) limited source of external funds, (3) often owners have a limited skill set, (4) lack of continuity, and (5) successful sole proprietors pay a higher tax than they would under the corporate form of business.

Partnership is a form of business organization defined as an association of two or more persons who carry on as co-owners of a business for profit. There are three basic types of partnership: general partnership, limited partnership, and limited liability partnership.

Partnerships offer the following advantages: (1) They are easy to organize, (2) partners can complement their skills, (3) they may have more access to capital, (4) partnerships can make decisions faster than larger businesses, and (5) government regulations are few. Partnerships also have several disadvantages: (1) All partnerships have to deal with disagreements, (2) general partners have unlimited liability for the debts of the partnership, (3) partners are responsible for each other's decisions, (4) the death or termination of one partner requires a new partnership agreement to be drawn up, (5) it is difficult to sell a partnership interest at a fair price, (6) the distribution of profits may not correctly reflect the amount of work done by each partner, and (7) partnerships may be taxed at a higher rate than corporations.

LO3 Describe the corporate form of organization, and cite the advantages and disadvantages of corporations.

A corporation is a legal entity created by the province or federal government, whose assets and liabilities are separate from those of its owners. Corporations have a board of directors made up of corporate officers or people from outside the company. Corporations, whether private or public, are owned by shareholders. Common shareholders have the right to elect the board of directors. Preferred shareholders do not have a vote but get preferential dividend treatment over common shareholders.

Advantages of the corporate form of business include: (1) The owners have limited liability, (2) ownership (stock) can be easily transferred, (3) corporations usually last forever, (4) raising money is easier than for other forms of business, and (5) expansion into new businesses is simpler because of the ability of the company to enter into contracts. Corporations also have disadvantages: (1) The company is taxed on its income, and owners pay a second tax on any profits received as dividends although the combined amount of tax paid may still be less than what would be paid by other forms of business, (2) forming a corporation can be expensive, (3) corporations have to disclose a great deal of information to the public (such as future plans) and comply with various government regulations, (4) corporations sometimes make decisions to appease shareholders' goals, and (5) owners and managers are not always the same and can have different goals.

LO4 Define and debate the advantages and disadvantages of mergers, acquisitions, and leveraged buyouts.

A merger occurs when two companies (usually corporations) combine to form a new company. An acquisition occurs when one company buys most of another company's stock. In a leveraged buyout, a group of investors borrows money to acquire a company, using the assets of the purchased company to guarantee the loan. They can help merging firms to gain a larger market share in their industries, acquire valuable assets such as new products or plants and equipment, and lower their costs. Consequently, they can benefit shareholders by improving the companies' market value and stock prices. However, they also can hurt companies if they force managers to focus on avoiding takeovers at the expense of productivity and profits. They may lead a company to take on too much debt and can harm employee morale and productivity.

KEY TERMS

acquisition
board of directors
certificate of incorporation
common shares
cooperative or co-op
corporation
Crown corporations
dividends
general partnership
initial public offering (IPO)
joint venture
leveraged buyout (LBO)

limited liability partnership (LLP)
limited partnership
merger
non-profit corporations
partnership
partnership agreement
preferred shares
private corporation
public corporation
shares
sole proprietorships

DESTINATION CEO DISCUSSION QUESTIONS

1. What do you think would be some of the advantages and disadvantages of Indigo taking over Chapters from a business perspective?

2. From a consumer perspective, what is the danger of Indigo having a virtual monopoly of retail bookstores in Canada? Should the Canadian government have stepped in and prevented the takeover?

3. How do you think Indigo will do as they face ever-increasing competition from both online stores such as Amazon and traditional retailers like Walmart and Target who are allocating significant shelf space to books?

4. Do you think Reisman's strategy of shifting the merchandising mix to include household items, giftware, stationery, baby gifts, and toys will be successful? Why or why not?

SO YOU WANT TO *Start a Business*

If you have a good idea and want to turn it into a business, you are not alone. Small businesses are popping up all over Canada and the concept of entrepreneurship is hot. Entrepreneurs seek opportunities and creative ways to make profits. Business emerges in a number of different organizational forms, each with its own advantages and disadvantages. Sole proprietorships are the most common form of business organization in Canada. They tend to be small businesses and can take pretty much any form—anything from a hair salon to a scuba shop, from an organic produce provider to a financial advisor. Proprietorships are everywhere serving consumers' wants and needs. Proprietorships have a big advantage in that they tend to be simple to manage—decisions get made quickly when the owner and the manager are the same person and they are fairly simple and inexpensive to set up. Rules vary by province, but at most all you will need is a licence from the province.

Many people have been part of a partnership at some point in their life. Group work in school is an example of a partnership. If you ever worked as a DJ on the weekend with your friend and split the profits, then you have experienced a partnership. Partnerships can be either general or limited. General partnerships have unlimited liability and share completely in the management, debts, and profits of the business. Limited partners, on the other hand, consist of at least one general partner and one or more limited partners who do not participate in the management of the company, but share in the profits. This form of partnership is used more often in risky investments where the limited partner stands only to lose his or her initial investment. Real estate limited partnerships are an example of how investors can minimize their financial exposure. Although it has its advantages, partnership is the least utilized form of business. Part of the reason is that all partners are responsible for the actions and decisions of all other partners, whether or not all of the partners were involved. Usually, partners will have to write up articles of partnership that outline respective responsibilities in the business. Unlike a corporation, proprietorships and partnerships both expire upon the death of one or more of those involved.

Corporations tend to be larger businesses, but do not need to be. A corporation can consist of nothing more than a small group of family members. In order to become a corporation, you have to file in the province in which you wish to incorporate. Each province has its own procedure for incorporation, meaning there are no general guidelines to follow. You can make your corporation private or public, meaning the company issues stocks and shareholders are the owners. While incorporating is a popular form of organization because it gives the company an unlimited lifespan and limited liability (meaning that if your business fails you cannot lose personal funds to make up for losses), there is a downside. You will be taxed as a corporation and as an individual, resulting in double taxation. No matter what form of organization suits your business idea best, there is a world of options out there for you if you want to be or experiment with being an entrepreneur.

BUILD YOUR BUSINESS PLAN

Options for Organizing a Business

As discussed above, there are a variety of legal structures for organizing your own business. In addition to reviewing the material in this chapter, students may want to talk to some small-business owners and see what structure they selected and why. Students should ask these entrepreneurs if they are happy with their form of business organization and what they see as its advantages and disadvantages. Students could also describe their business to the entrepreneur and ask them what form of business they would recommend.

Foreign companies looking to complete an acquisition in Canada are starting to learn that regulatory approval is not as easy to obtain as it once was.

Former Prime Minister Stephen Harper's Conservative government and the Liberal government it replaced both were advocates of free trade and foreign investment in Canada and regularly approved foreign takeovers of Canadian companies. However, from 2005 to 2009, after a series of deals saw Canadian mining firms, such as Inco, Falconbridge, and Alcan, taken over by large global players, public sentiment about foreign firms buying Canadian companies started to turn negative.

A significant turning point in public perception was Australia-based BHP Billiton Ltd.'s US$38.6 billion hostile bid for Potash Corp. of Saskatchewan. Potash, which is used in fertilizers, is a rare resource, and Potash Corp. owns vast reserves in Saskatchewan. Saskatchewan's premier, Brad Wall, rallied support against the deal when he stated, "The people of Saskatchewan are justifiably proud of Potash Corp. and the success it has achieved here and around the world. Do we want to add Potash Corp. to that list of once-proud Canadian companies that are now under foreign control?"[56] While BHP stated it would keep the company's head office in Saskatchewan, it would allow global prices (not the provincial marketing board) to set the price for potash, likely resulting in lower prices and less tax revenue for the province. Other provinces quickly supported Saskatchewan's position, as did the opposition parties in Ottawa. The federal government, citing the Investment Act, opted to block the deal in 2010. One of the rules governing foreign takeovers in the Act is that the result must offer Canadians a positive net benefit, and the federal government determined this was not the case in the BHP bid. This marked only the second time a foreign takeover failed to meet the standards in the Act.

The arguments against foreign investment include keeping Canadian companies in the hands of Canadians who will protect Canadian interests (which include jobs and access to resources) and ensure that Canada's rules and regulations govern operations. Proponents of foreign investment in Canada counter that Canada really is a country built on foreign investment; Canadian companies often need the capital injection that foreign investment brings; and shareholders ultimately should decide whether they sell the company, not government. Furthermore, research indicates that countries which are open to foreign investment usually have economies that outperform countries who limit such investments.

Foreign takeovers became a hot button topic again in 2012–13 when Chinese giant CNOOC Ltd. successfully bought Canadian oil and gas company Nexen, and the Malaysian state-owned company Petronas purchased Alberta's Progress Energy for $6 billion. Public sentiment across the country was decidedly negative to the deals as many Canadians argued that Canada's greatest natural resource—the oil sands—would soon be controlled by foreign governments. The proponents of the takeover stated that both Canadian companies were poorly run and needed the injection of capital that could come from the foreign firms, and that the true owners of the company—the shareholders—were in favour of the deals. While the federal government eventually approved these takeovers, then–Prime Minister Stephen Harper noted that this was not the beginning of a trend but the end of one. Harper stated, "While Canada is open for business, we do not mean that Canada is for sale to foreign governments....To be blunt, Canadians have not spent years reducing ownership of sectors of the economy by our own governments only to see them bought and controlled by foreign governments instead,"[57] As part of this pledge, Harper made changes to the Investment Act, where foreign investors have to do more than prove a net benefit to Canada as a result of a takeover in the oil sands. Foreign companies, especially those controlled by governments, will only be granted approval to take over oil sand companies in exceptional circumstances. These new rules seem to make everyone unhappy. People opposed to foreign investment in the country stated that they did not go far enough and that tougher rules should apply to all takeovers, not just those in the oil sands. Those opposed to government interference in foreign takeovers felt that these new rules amounted to unneeded government interference into private industry.[58]

DISCUSSION QUESTIONS

1. What do you think are some of the advantages and disadvantages of foreign takeovers?

2. Why do you think Stephen Harper and the Conservative government changed their opinion on foreign takeovers and drafted stricter regulations?

3. Given that shareholders own the company, if they approve a takeover, should the government have the ability to step in and block the approved takeover? Is this ethical or unethical?

4. Some people have argued that the new takeover rules do not go far enough and that foreign takeovers of resource companies should be banned. What would be some of the advantages and disadvantages of barring such takeovers?

5. Use Internet resources to determine if Prime Minister Justin Trudeau's stance and record on approving takeovers is any different than Stephen Harper's. Do you think Trudeau will ultimately make any changes to the Investment Act? Why or why not?

LEARNING OBJECTIVES

After reading this chapter, you will be able to:

LO1 Define entrepreneurship and small business.

LO2 Investigate the importance of small business in the Canadian economy and why certain fields attract small business.

LO3 Specify the advantages of small-business ownership.

LO4 Summarize the disadvantages of small-business ownership, and analyze why many small businesses fail.

LO5 Describe how you go about starting a small business and what resources are needed.

LO6 Evaluate the demographic, technological, and economic trends that are affecting the future of small business.

LO7 Explain why many large businesses are trying to "think small."

Kevin O'Leary "You may lose your wife, you may lose your dog, [and] your mother may hate you. None of those things matter. What matters is that you achieve success and become free. Then you can do whatever you like."[1]

Kevin O'Leary,
Business News Network

Chances are if you watch the Business News Network (BNN), *Shark Tank* on ABC, or re-runs of CBC's *Dragons' Den* you likely have seen and formed an opinion about Kevin O'Leary. O'Leary, while not being Canada's richest entrepreneur, is likely one of the best known and perhaps the brashest. In Canada, O'Leary is almost famous for being famous, he currently hosts his own show on BNN, aptly titled *Ask O'Leary* and previously he starred on the hit show *Dragons' Den* on CBC, where he also hosted a daily show, *The Lang and O'Leary Exchange*. O'Leary is also a regular on U.S. television as he stars on ABC's *Shark Tank*. In *Dragons' Den* and *Shark Tank*, O'Leary plays the role of a smart investor who will provide business owners with money and his much-sought-after advice in exchange for a part of their company. During both shows, entrepreneurs stand in front of a panel and describe their business, hoping one of the Dragons or Sharks will invest in their company. While O'Leary is not the most active investor in either show, he made himself famous with his somewhat brutal assessment of what he perceives as poor business ideas and the entrepreneurs behind them. O'Leary has occasionally asked guests if they are nuts, has called them cockroaches, has informed entrepreneurs that their product is ugly and a bad idea, and even has told crying guests that there is no value in their tears and that they mean nothing. O'Leary is clear: His sole mandate on the show is to make money and he won't waste his time or hard-earned dollars on bad ideas. On the news show on BNN, viewers get more of the same: O'Leary comments on the stock market and stories that appear in the news, always with a right wing, capitalistic edge. This is something Chris Hedges, a *New York Times* correspondent, found out when he was on the show defending the Occupy Movement, which was a global protest against big business and government. O'Leary's response was to call the protestors "nothing burgers who couldn't name the companies they were upset with" and to tell Hedges he sounded like "a left-wing nutbar" for defending the protestors.

O'Leary's first successful entrepreneurial venture was SoftKey Software Products Inc., a company he co-founded in his basement with a $10,000 investment from his mother. O'Leary and his partner eventually moved the company to Boston where he kick-started sales by selling the company's software in big box stores at a deep discount compared to what other companies were selling their products for in computer stores. While the practice did not make O'Leary any friends in the computer industry, he did manage to grow revenue and eventually expanded his company into educational products. SoftKey eventually purchased The Learning Centre (TLC), another software company, and started operating under its name. TLC grew to become the biggest educational software company in the world, with sales of $800 million. In 1999, toy giant

Mattel purchased TLC for $4 billion and asked O'Leary to stay on and manage the educational software business. While the two parted ways a short time later, O'Leary had his first major success under his belt.

O'Leary went on to other entrepreneurial ventures with a mixed degree of success, and in 2003 he called BNN and offered his own self-assessment that he would be good on TV. BNN felt O'Leary was a natural and eventually gave him his own nightly news show. While popular with viewers of BNN, O'Leary really hit the big time when he was cast in *Dragons' Den* in 2006. O'Leary quickly became "villain judge," the person all either love or love to hate. After all, how often do you hear comments like, "Business is war. I go out there, [and] I want to kill the competitors. I want to make their lives miserable. I want to steal their market share. I want them to fear me and I want everyone on my team thinking we're going to win."[2] O'Leary's on-air presence eventually captured the eye of Mark Burnett, who created the hit reality TV show *Survivor*, and he cast O'Leary in *Shark Tank*—America's version of *Dragons' Den*.

O'Leary soon realized that while he was making money and creating a brand on TV, he had a real opportunity to capitalize on his fame, and he started to build businesses that he could personally brand. His first foray into creating a business to build on his brand was O'Leary Funds, a mutual fund for which he acted as the main spokesman whenever a camera was placed in front of him. While O'Leary did not personally manage the funds, he did a great job of promoting his new investment products, and money poured into his company. O'Leary did not stop with O'Leary Funds and has since introduced O'Leary Mortgages and O'Leary Fine Wines, offers public-speaking services, has authored three books, and is apparently developing other products and concepts. O'Leary has recently mentioned he has been inspired by Donald Trump's run for president of the United Sates and may one day run for prime minister of Canada. Whether you love him or love to hate him, O'Leary has come a long way from a $10,000 investment and a video game company he started in his basement.

Introduction

Although many business students go to work for large corporations upon graduation, others may choose to start their own business or find employment opportunities in small businesses with 500 or fewer employees. There are more than 2.3 million small businesses operating in Canada today.[3] Each small business represents the vision of its entrepreneurial owners to succeed by providing new or better products. Small businesses are the heart of the Canadian economic and social system because they offer opportunities and express the freedom of people to make their own destinies. *Profit* magazine's editor-in-chief, Ian Portsmouth, states, "Canada is in the middle of an entrepreneurial boom . . . and Canada and the world [will be] full of opportunities . . . in coming years."[4] Today, the entrepreneurial spirit is growing around the world, from India and China to Germany, Brazil, and Mexico.

This chapter surveys the world of entrepreneurship and small business. First we define entrepreneurship and small business and examine the role of small business in the Canadian economy. Then we explore the advantages and disadvantages of small-business ownership and analyze why small businesses succeed or fail. Next, we discuss how an entrepreneur goes about starting a small business and the challenges facing small business today. Finally, we look at entrepreneurship in larger businesses.

As you study this chapter, you may be asking yourself why you should study entrepreneurship. Research indicates students who study entrepreneurship are likely to experience the following benefits:

- Be three to four times more likely to start a business

- Earn 20 to 30 percent more than students studying in other fields

- Gain valuable entrepreneurial skills such as business planning, networking, and sales, which are valued by employers

- Improve their ability to think critically and become better problem solvers

- Improve their chance of landing their dream job because entrepreneurial students have many of the characteristics that employers are looking for

- Gain knowledge to supplement their income

Other reasons for studying entrepreneurship include:

- Entrepreneurs have unlimited earning potential.

- Many of society's problems today require entrepreneurial solutions. In fact, charity workers, nurses, and social workers often need to think entrepreneurially in order to solve problems. These people are sometimes referred to as social entrepreneurs.

- Ninety-nine percent of businesses in Canada are in fact small or medium-sized enterprises (SMEs), so even if you don't start an SME, you will probably end up working for one. By studying entrepreneurship, you will understand how to succeed at such a firm.

The Nature of Entrepreneurship and Small Business

LO1 Define entrepreneurship and small business.

In Chapter 1, we defined an entrepreneur as a person who risks his or her wealth, time, and effort to develop for profit an innovative product or way of doing something. **Entrepreneurship** is the process of creating and managing a business to achieve desired objectives.

entrepreneurship
the process of creating and managing a business to achieve desired objectives

Many large businesses you may recognize—Rogers Communications, Tim Hortons, 1-800-GOT-JUNK?, Magna International Inc., and Pizza Pizza—all began as small businesses based on the entrepreneurial visions of their founders. Some entrepreneurs who start small businesses have the ability to see emerging trends; in response, they create a company to provide a product that serves customer needs. For example, rather than inventing a major new technology, an innovative company may take advantage of an existing technology to create markets that did not exist before, such as Amazon.com.[5] Or they may offer something familiar but improved or repackaged, such as what Vancouver-based 1-800-GOT-JUNK? did with junk removal. Prior to Brian Scudamore founding and subsequently franchising 1-800-GOT-JUNK?, most junk and garbage removal was done by small independent operators whose customer service practices were often questionable. Scudamore's approach was to first professionalize the service and then franchise the concept, which he has done successfully over 250 times in three different countries. The company that Scudamore started as a university student now generates millions of dollars in annual revenue.[6] Or they may innovate by focusing on a particular market segment and delivering a combination of features that consumers in that segment could not find anywhere else (e.g., REI Outdoor

© Ryan Holmes, CEO of Hootsuite. Photograph courtesy of Hootsuite.

Ryan Holmes is the founder and CEO of Hootsuite. He started the company in 2008 and has helped grow it into the world's most widely used social relationship platform, with 10-million-plus users, including 800 of the Fortune 1000 companies.

Gear & Clothing for camping, hiking, backpacking, and more).

Of course, smaller businesses do not have to evolve into such highly visible companies to be successful, but those entrepreneurial efforts that result in rapidly growing businesses become more visible with their success. Entrepreneurs who have achieved success—like Gerry Schwartz (Onex Corp.), Jim Pattison (Pattison Group), Mike Lazaridis (Blackberry), Ryan Holmes (Hootsuite.com), Tobias Lütke (Shopify.com), Ken Rowe (IMP Group), Michael Dell (Dell Inc.), and Bill Gates (Microsoft)—are the most visible.

The entrepreneurship movement is accelerating with many new, smaller businesses emerging. Technology once available only to the largest firms can now be acquired by a small business. The Internet and cloud computing have reshaped the business landscape and levelled the playing field between large and small businesses by allowing small businesses to offer products globally, present professional marketing campaigns, and conduct customer service at a fraction of what it used to cost. A recent article in the *National Post* sums this up when the author notes, "The Web has lowered the bar for people with skills and ideas. People don't need a development team or a big budget; they just need a good idea and a laptop."[7] For example, Mike McDerment of Toronto

---

Consider the Following: What Is the Difference between an Entrepreneur and a Small Business Person?

This common question can result in much discussion. The authors of the book think an entrepreneur is someone who is always looking to seize opportunities. Whether through expansion of a business or finding better ways to do things, an entrepreneur is consistently looking to create something new. A small business person is someone who works in a small business. They may have even started the company and engaged in one act of entrepreneurship, but if they do not continue to look for additional opportunities to create something new then they stop being an entrepreneur and become a manager. The question for you is: How would you define an entrepreneur and a small business person? Do you think they are different, as we believe?

Consider the Following: Should You Start Your Own Business?

Each day, thousands of individuals ask the difficult question, "Should I start my own business?" When queried, 85 percent of the populace said they would like to be in business for themselves. The driving force behind this desire to start a new venture is the desire to be one's own boss, to be independent. Since there is no definitive measurement developed that allows an individual to determine if he or she can be a successful entrepreneur, each individual needs to carefully appraise his or her situation through several different methods and self-assessment models. One way to determine whether you have what it takes to be an entrepreneur is to fill out the questionnaire below. If you find that you are answering "yes" to most of the questions, you might have all the qualities to be a great entrepreneur. If you answer "no" to many of the questions, it likely means you could still be an entrepreneur and do very well, but you may have to work on some of your weaknesses. There are many exceptions, and there is no such person as a "typical" entrepreneur.

1. Can you start a project and see it through to completion in spite of a myriad of obstacles? _____ Yes _____ No

2. Can you make a decision on a matter and then stick to the decision even when challenged? _____ Yes _____ No

3. Do you like to be in charge and be responsible? _____ Yes _____ No

4. Do other people you deal with respect and trust you? _____ Yes _____ No

5. Are you in good physical health? _____ Yes _____ No

6. Are you willing to work long hours with little immediate compensation? _____ Yes _____ No

7. Do you like meeting and dealing with people? _____ Yes _____ No

8. Can you communicate effectively and persuade people to go along with your dream? _____ Yes _____ No

9. Do others easily understand your concepts and ideas? _____ Yes _____ No

10. Have you had extensive experience in the type of business you wish to start? _____ Yes _____ No

11. Do you know the mechanics and forms of running a business (tax records, payroll records, income statements, balance sheets)? _____ Yes _____ No

12. Is there a need in your geographic area for the product or service you are intending to market? _____ Yes _____ No

13. Do you have skills in marketing and/or finance? _____ Yes _____ No

14. Are other firms in your industrial classification doing well in your geographic area? _____ Yes _____ No

15. Do you have a location in mind for your business? _____ Yes _____ No

16. Do you have enough financial backing for the first year of operation? _____ Yes _____ No

17. Do you have enough money to fund the start-up of your business or have access to it through family or friends? _____ Yes _____ No

18. Do you know the suppliers necessary for your business to succeed? _____ Yes _____ No

19. Do you know individuals who have the talents and expertise you lack? _____ Yes _____ No

20. Do you really want to start this business more than anything else? _____ Yes _____ No

Source: Hisrich et al., *Entrepreneurship*, 2/C/e. McGraw-Hill Ryerson.

founded FreshBooks, an online accounting company aimed at servicing small businesses throughout North America. While the company is based in Ontario, it now boasts 5 million subscribers—most of them paying $19.95 a month for accounting services—and bills itself as the world's No. 1 cloud-based accounting specialist. Fresh-Books has grown from four employees to over 100 who service clients from all over the world using the Internet. Vincent Cheung founded Shape Collage Inc. as a student at the University of Toronto. Cheung's website allows people to take hundreds of photos and, in seconds, automatically arrange them into a collage in any shape. His software has been downloaded over a million times so far. Not only has he managed to pay himself a full salary, but he also captured the 2010 Ontario Entrepreneur of the Year student award.[8] Much like Cheung, Cameron Laker started Vancouver-based Mindfield Group when he was in his 20s. Within three years, the company had grown to be one of the leading retail human resource staffing firms in Canada. Laker notes that the Internet, in particular social media sites, is important to the company's success: "Social media has allowed us to get our name out there very quickly. . . . Every one of our deals, except for . . . one, has been attracted to us originally because of our use of social media."[9] The Internet also allows smaller companies to find great employees no matter where their head office is located. For example, Empire Avenue, an Edmonton-headquartered social media company, uses the Internet to link its employees together. The company's employees live all over the world, working collaboratively using the Internet to create value for clients. Empire Avenue CEO Duleepa Wijayawardhana says, "All of us are scattered all over the country. We run the company remotely." Other technological advances such as tablet computers, smartphones, high-speed printers, fax machines, copiers, voicemail, computer bulletin boards and networks, cellular phones, and even overnight delivery services enable small businesses to be more competitive with today's giant corporations. Small businesses can also form alliances with other companies to produce and sell products in domestic and global markets.

Entrepreneur Characteristics

While entrepreneurs can come from various backgrounds, many of them share certain characteristics including the following:

- Strong desire to act independently
- High need for achievement
- Willingness to take some risks
- Energetic

Do you think you have some of these characteristics? Do you think entrepreneurs need all of them to be successful? Why or why not?

What Is a Small Business?

This question is difficult to answer because smallness is relative. While recent research has found that the most consistent determinant of business size is the number of employees, there is no consistency in identifying the actual number of employees that make up a small business. Furthermore, researchers and government agencies often consider other variables, such as upper limits on revenue, limits on rank in the industry, and so forth, when determining whether a business is small. In this book, we will define a **small business** as any independently owned and operated business that is not dominant in its competitive area and does not employ more than 500 people. A local Mexican restaurant may be the most patronized Mexican restaurant in your community, but because it does not dominate the restaurant industry as a whole, the restaurant can be considered a small business. This definition is similar to the one used by Statistics Canada, which uses 500 employees as the cut-off separating small and large businesses.[10] Interestingly, the Canadian Federation of Independent Businesses (CFIB) also defines small business by the number of employees but uses less than 250 employees as its cut-off. The CFIB website (www.cfib.ca) offers advice on starting a small business and offers a wealth of information to current and potential small-business owners.[11]

> **small business** any independently owned and operated business that is not dominant in its competitive area and does not employ more than 500 people

The Role of Small Business in the Canadian Economy

LO2 Investigate the importance of small business in the Canadian economy and why certain fields attract small business.

No matter how you define small business, one fact is clear: Small businesses are vital to the soundness of the Canadian economy. As you can see in Table 5.1, more than 99 percent of all Canadian firms are classified as small businesses, and they employ 48 percent of private workers.[12] Small firms are also important as exporters, representing roughly 97 percent of Canadian exporters of goods.[13] In addition, small businesses are largely responsible for fuelling job creation and innovation. Small businesses also provide opportunities for women to succeed in business. There are 910,000 women entrepreneurs in Canada with an ownership interest in approximately 1 million small businesses.[14] For example, Christine Magee, co-founder and president

© Deborah Baic/CPimages

Christine Magee is one of the better-known female entrepreneurs in Canada. She co-founded Sleep Country Canada in 1994 and has grown the company from one store to 240 today.

of Sleep Country Canada, started the specialty store in 1994. The firm, which specializes in mattress sales, was purchased in 2008 for $356 million.[15] Today, Magee remains as president of the company, which has become famous for its slogan, "Why buy a mattress anywhere else?"

Table 5.1 Facts about Small Businesses

- Represent 99.7 percent of all employer firms.

- Employ 5 million people, or 48 percent of all private-sector employees.

- In 2008, small businesses created roughly 70,000 jobs, accounting for over 50 percent of the jobs created in Canada.

- Between 2002 and 2006, approximately 130,000 new small businesses were created each year.

- Approximately 15 percent of the population is self-employed.

- Seventy-five percent of small businesses are in the service sector.

- Small firms spend approximately $4 billion on R&D annually.

Sources: http://www.ic.gc.ca/eic/site/sbrp-rppe.nsf/eng/rd01238.html and http://www.cfib-fcei.ca/cfib-documents/rr3093.pdf.

Job Creation. The energy, creativity, and innovative abilities of small-business owners have resulted in jobs for other people. In fact, in the last decade, between 60 and 80 percent of net new jobs annually were created by small businesses.[16] Table 5.2 indicates that 99.7 percent of all businesses employ fewer than 500 people.

Many small businesses today are being started because of encouragement from larger ones. Many jobs are being created by big-company/small-company alliances. Whether through formal joint ventures, supplier relationships, or product or marketing cooperative projects, the rewards of collaborative relationships are creating many jobs for small-business owners and their employees. Some publishing companies, for example, contract out almost all their editing and production to small businesses. Row House Publishing Services is a small business in Toronto, Ontario, that provides editorial services for educational publishers, and government and corporate clients.[17]

Innovation. Perhaps one of the most significant strengths of small businesses is their ability to innovate and bring significant changes and benefits to customers. Small firms produce approximately 55 percent of innovations and invest significant resources in the development of new products and services.[18] For example, Alberta-based Western Manufacturing, which builds fuel storage containers, has seen its business grow by 25,719 percent in five years, attributing much of its success to being innovative. CEO Lonny Thiessen states, "Even today, with the current state of the oil and gas industry, we're still making significant investments into new technology and different ways of doing things. . . . In the slow and challenging times, differentiation becomes even more important."[19] Among important twentieth-century innovations by Canadian small firms are smartphones,

Table 5.2 Number of Businesses by Firm Size (Number of Employees), December 2008

Number of Employees	Cumulative Percent of Employer Businesses	TOTAL
Indeterminate		1,233,595
Employer Business Total	100.0	1,080,968
1–4	54.9	593,014
5–9	75.2	219,852
10–19	87.4	131,666
20–49	95.2	84,643
50–99	97.9	28,644
100–199	99.1	13,375
200–499	99.7	6,748
500+	100.0	3,026
TOTAL:		2,314,563

Sources: http://www.ic.gc.ca/eic/site/sbrp-rppe.nsf/eng/rd02300.html and http://www.cfib-fcei.ca/cfib-documents/rr3093.pdf.

© Western Manufacturing Ltd.

CEO Lonny Thiessen states that his firm, Western Manufacturing, continues to invest in innovation even as the price of oil declines.

insulin, the snowmobile, the pacemaker, the washing machine, the IMAX movie system, and television. Ballard Power, a British Columbia alternative energy company, may be working on one of the most important twenty-first century innovations: a car that runs without gas or oil. Although currently still in the testing phase, the company hopes one day to replace the oil combustion engine with one that is powered by batteries.[20]

The innovation of successful firms takes many forms. For example, a group of entrepreneurs and filmmakers noticed how popular multi-screen films were at EXPO '67 in Montreal and decided to build a system using a large screen and a powerful projector. The result of the invention was the IMAX screen and projection system.[21] As mentioned in Chapter 1, Ryan Holmes, CEO of Vancouver-based HootSuite, felt that companies should be able to manage their social media messages from one central location. Holmes created a social-media dashboard that is now being used by almost 80 out of the largest 100 companies in America.[22] Small-businessman Ray Kroc found a new way to sell hamburgers and turned his ideas into one of the most successful fast-food franchises in the world—McDonald's. Much like Kroc, Ron Joyce, longtime owner of Tim Hortons, found a way to sell doughnuts and coffee along with other quick-serve items from one store. Joyce's aggressive growth strategy resulted in Canada having more doughnut stores per capita than anywhere else in the world and the company name becoming a cultural icon.[23] James Dyson spent time from 1979 to 1984 developing a prototype of a dual-cyclone, bagless vacuum cleaner. As a matter of fact, he built more than 5,000 versions before manufacturing his G Force, which made the front cover of *Design* magazine in 1983. Today, the company outsells its leading rival, Hoover, by capturing 21 percent of the U.S. dollars spent on upright vacuum cleaners versus 16 percent for Hoover. Dyson's vacuums sell for $400 to $600 each, whereas Hoover's sell for $69 to $389. Hoover,

however, still sells more overall units than Dyson. Dyson's designs are featured in the Metropolitan Museum of Art, New York; the Science Museum, London; and the Victoria and Albert Museum, London, to name a few.[24] Small businesses have become an integral part of our lives. They provide fresh ideas and usually have greater flexibility to change than do large companies.

Industries That Attract Small Business

Small businesses are found in nearly every industry, but retailing and wholesaling, services, manufacturing, and high technology are especially attractive to entrepreneurs because they are relatively easy to enter and require low initial financing. Small-business owners also find it easier to focus on a specific group of consumers in these fields than in others, and new firms in these industries suffer less from heavy competition, at least in the early stages, than do established firms.

Retailing and Wholesaling.
Retailers acquire goods from producers or wholesalers and sell them to consumers. Main streets, shopping strips, and shopping malls are lined with independent music stores, sporting-goods shops, dry cleaners, boutiques, drugstores, restaurants, caterers, service stations, and hardware stores that sell directly to consumers. Retailing attracts entrepreneurs because gaining experience and exposure in retailing is relatively easy. Additionally, an entrepreneur opening a new retailing store does not have to spend the large sums of money for the equipment and distribution systems that a manufacturing business requires. All that a new retailer needs is a lease on store space, merchandise, enough money to sustain the business, knowledge about prospective customers' needs and desires, the ability to use promotion to generate awareness, and basic management skills. Some small retailers are

© CP PHOTO/Aaron Harris

Ron Joyce, longtime owner of Tim Hortons, grew the company from a local coffee shop to a national chain. Joyce eventually sold the company to Wendy's in 1995.

© Christine Deslauriers

eBay has enabled Canadians, such as eBay Entrepreneur of the Year Christine Deslauriers, to start successful retail businesses without establishing a physical location.

taking their businesses online. For example, Christine Deslauriers, of Sudbury, Ontario, recently won the 2015 Canadian eBay Entrepreneur of the Year Award. Deslauriers, founder of Boutique Step Up, an online eBay store that started out selling figure-skating equipment, has seen sales grow by 470 percent in two years. As a result of her success, Deslauriers has expanded her product line to gymnastic and dance equipment and opened a bricks-and-mortar store.[25]

Wholesalers supply products to industrial, retail, and institutional users for resale or for use in making other products. Wholesaling activities range from planning and negotiating for supplies, promoting, and distributing (warehousing and transporting) to providing management and merchandising assistance to clients. Wholesalers are extremely important for many products, especially consumer goods, because of the marketing activities they perform. Although it is true that wholesalers themselves can be eliminated, their functions must be passed on to some other organization, such as the producer or another intermediary, often a small business. For example, FouFou Dog was founded by Cheryl Ng from Richmond Hill, Ontario, to produce trendy, affordable, and high-quality pet clothes. After Ng started manufacturing and designing her own pet clothes, she expanded the business to act as a distributor for other manufacturers of similar products, including Rolf C. Hagen Inc., the world's largest pet products company.[26] Frequently, small businesses are closer to the final customers and know what it

takes to keep them satisfied. Some smaller businesses start out manufacturing but find their real niche as a supplier or distributor of larger firms' products. One of the better-known Canadian success stories is Spin Master Toys, the firm founded by Ronnen Harary, Anton Rabie, and Ben Varadi after they graduated from university. They started manufacturing Earth Buddies, small pantyhose heads filled with grass seed, and built the business into the largest private toy company in Canada through in-house product development and by acting as a distributor/licensee for the Canadian market for large and small international toy firms. Today the company sells or distributes a variety of well-known toys including Air Hogs, Aqua Doodle, Bella Dancerella, Nano Speed, and the highly acclaimed Bakugan Battle Brawlers. Gerrick Johnson, an expert in the toy industry, notes, "They don't have to develop the toys themselves. If someone brings them the right idea, they'll develop it."[27] In fact, their latest hot toy, Bakugan Battle Brawlers, was acquired from an inventor who had no ties to the company. Anton Rabie states, "We have no ego about where the idea comes from. Lots of ideas come from in-house, but even more come from outside."[28]

Services. Services include businesses that work for others but do not actually produce tangible goods. They represent one of the fastest-growing sectors of the Canadian economy, accounting for 66 percent of the economy and employing roughly 75 percent of the workforce.[29] Real estate, insurance, and personnel agencies; barbershops; banks; television and computer repair shops; copy centres; dry cleaners; and accounting firms are all service businesses. Services also attract individuals—such as beauticians, morticians, jewellers, doctors, and veterinarians—whose skills are not usually required by large firms. Service businesses are attractive to start as the upfront costs are often quite low and potential profits can be quite high. If entrepreneurs are willing to complete the services themselves, then they don't even need employees. Of the 50 fastest-growing companies in Canada as identified in *Profit* magazine, nine of the top ten are service-based businesses. *Profit* recently expanded its study of Canada's fastest-growing companies to 200 firms and discovered that 111 of the companies would be classified as service-based firms.[30] In 2006, four of the top five businesses had revenues less than $75,000.[31] Today, the top four service companies all have revenue in excess of $1 million. For example, Total Debt Freedom Inc., a Markham, Ontario, firm, assists consumers in getting rid of their debt by negotiating for settlements with various credit card holders. This service business,

"Services include businesses that work for others **but** do not actually produce tangible goods.**"**

which promises to reduce unsecured debt by at least 40 percent, has grown from $300,000 to over $1 million in revenue in a few short years.[32]

Manufacturing. Manufacturing goods can provide unique opportunities for small businesses. While start-up costs can be higher for manufacturing businesses, entrepreneurs may be able to focus on a specific niche and keep costs down. Such products include custom artwork, jewellery, clothing, and furniture. For example, Canada Goose has carved a niche for itself by manu-facturing warm stylish coats in Northern Canada. The company has managed to build a premium brand and sell its products at a premium through marketing and free celebrity endorsements. Other examples include Classic Cabinets Ltd., based in Medicine Hat, Alberta, and Fluidconcepts & Design Inc., from Mississauga, Ontario. Both companies focus on niche markets, with Classic Cabinets Ltd. manufacturing high-end cabinets specifi-cally designed for customers. The company grew its revenue from slightly over $110,000 to $3.4 million in two years by focusing on the custom marketplace.[33] Fluid-concepts & Design Inc. designs and builds contemporary office furniture. The company, which had revenues of less than $400,000 in 2003, recently reported revenues in excess of $4 million.[34]

Technology. *Technology* was once a broad term used to describe businesses that depend heavily on advanced scientific and engineering knowledge. Today, the term also refers to businesses that make use of the Inter-net and cloud computing to create opportunities for entrepreneurs. As mentioned at the start of the chap-ter, the Internet has substantially levelled the playing field between large and small business. Whereas people previously needed substantial money to engineer new technology products, this is not the case anymore. People who can innovate or identify new markets in the fields of computers (smartphones and tablets), biotechnology, genetic engineering, robotics, and other markets have the opportunity to become today's high-tech giants. For example, Toronto-based XMG Studios, creator of mobile games such as Cows vs. Aliens and Powder Monkeys, believes it is taking advantage of a growing niche in the gaming industry. XMG, which has grown from five employ-ees to 35 in a few short years, has deter-mined that there will be 1.5 billion smartphone users by 2015, most of whom will be people who would have some interest in casual games.[35] And unlike conven-tional video games, which can cost on average $20 million to create, casual games can be created for a fraction of this cost and offered for sale on an iPhone after paying Apple's $99 developer fee. Mike Lazaridis, founder of Research In Motion (RIM) now known as BlackBerry, managed to create a billion-dollar busi-ness when he took notice of the popularity of e-mail and designed a device to allow people to read and respond to e-mail on their telephones or smartphones. Other well-known examples include Michael Dell, who started building personal computers in his University of Texas dorm room at age 19. His Dell Inc. is now one of the leading PC companies in the world and the world's number-one direct-sale computer vendor with annual sales of more than $55 billion.[36] Apple Computer began in a garage. The Apple prototype was financed by the proceeds Steven Wozniak received from selling his Hewlett-Packard calculator and Steven Jobs got from selling his van.[37] In general, high-tech businesses require greater capital and have higher initial start-up costs than do other small businesses. The advent of the Internet is starting to change this, however, as the technology is reducing start-up costs and allowing entrepreneurs to reach consumers all over the globe. Jason DeZwirek of Toronto used the Internet to start an online media company, Kaboose.com, which appealed to parents—specifically mothers. Within a few short years, the company had a global audience and interna-tional advertisers. In 2009, Disney purchased the busi-ness for C$23.3 million.[38]

Advantages of Small-Business Ownership

LO3 Specify the advantages of small-business ownership.

There are many advantages to establishing and running a small business. These can be categorized as personal advantages and business advantages.

Independence

According to Statistics Canada, inde-pendence is the leading reason that entre-preneurs choose to go into business for themselves. Being a small-business owner means being your own boss. Many people start their own businesses because they believe they will do better for themselves than they could do by remaining with their current employer or by changing jobs. Kenzie MacDonald left his job as vice president at Colliers International, a global commer-cial real estate firm, to branch off and start his own company in Halifax. MacDonald stated the main reason for leaving his job was a strong desire to be his own

> **DID YOU KNOW?**
>
> Thirty-nine percent of high-tech jobs are in small businesses.[39]

Entrepreneurs do not just operate in business. The entrepreneurial spirit can also be found in the social sector. A social entrepreneur is someone who is driven to create social change by identifying and implementing solutions to social problems. Emphasis is being placed on the social entrepreneur as a necessary component for future economic growth. One of the most famous social entrepreneurs is Muhammad Yunus, founder of microfinance bank Grameen. Another example is Canadian Jeff Skoll, founder of the Skoll Foundation, which invests in social entrepreneurs who are helping solve some of the world's most pressing problems. The foundation is the world's largest organization of its type in the world and makes annual grants of $40 million to social entrepreneurs and organizations throughout the world.[40]

Although social entrepreneurship has long been privately funded, governments are recognizing its importance. For example, the Canadian government and many of its provincial counterparts are in the process of implementing Social Impact Bonds (SIB). The bonds would have private investors lend money to organizations that are trying to make improvements in society, such as increasing literacy rates for prisoners. If the organization succeeds, the government would then pay for the service and the organization could pay back its investors plus interest. In 2014, Saskatchewan, became the first province to approve SIBs as they were approached by Don Meikle, the executive

director of EGADZ, a non-profit that provides programs for families. Meikle wanted to build a home for displaced young single mothers, and the province couldn't provide the financing. What they did do was approve an SIB bond, and a short time later, Sweet Dreams shelter was open thanks to a $1 million raised through SIBs.[41] SIBs are expanding to other provinces including Ontario, which recently started a large-scale pilot project to determine the feasibility of SIBs.[42]

DISCUSSION QUESTIONS

1. What are the potential benefits of social entrepreneurship in our society?

2. What are some of the advantages and disadvantages of SIBs?

3. Should the government do more to encourage social enterprise? Why or why not?

4. If you were an investor, would you invest money in SIBs? Why or why not?

5. Use the Internet to see what progress SIBs have made in Canada. What other provinces have adopted SIBs? See if you can find what projects are being funded and share them with your class.

boss: "I wanted to be in charge, to do things the way I wanted to do them . . . when you work as an employee for years you always answer to someone . . . it's nice to be able to make all the decisions, to be in control."[43] Sometimes people who venture forth to start their own small business are those who simply cannot work for someone else. Such people may say that they just do not fit the "corporate mould."

More often, small-business owners just want the freedom to choose whom they work with, the flexibility to pick where and when to work, and the option of working in a family setting. The availability of the computer, copy machine, business telephone, and fax machine has permitted many people to work at home. Only a few years ago, most of them would have needed the support that an office provides. The desire for flexible work has given rise to a new type of entrepreneur or small-business owner—the *mompreneur*. Mompreneurs are mothers who are running a business either full-time or part-time and taking care of their children. Mompreneurs often start businesses rather than choose traditional employment as they can establish their own hours and schedule. Kathryn Bechthold, a mompreneur

Mompreneur Victoria Turner of Toronto, creator of Pippalily baby slings, was attracted to entrepreneurship as a career choice as it enabled her to work at home with her child.

© Victoria Turner

herself, founded *The Mompreneur*, a Canadian magazine dedicated to this niche group, noting that she wanted to assist other mompreneurs in balancing their family life and business.[44]

Enjoyment

One of the most commonly cited advantages of owning a business, whether big or small, is how much entrepreneurs enjoy their chosen careers. In fact, over 90 percent of Canadian entrepreneurs would start their business again if given the chance. Colin MacDonald, co-founder of Clearwater—a Halifax-based fish wholesale business that he founded out of the back of a pickup truck—notes that one of his biggest motivations in growing his business was how much he enjoyed working. "I really enjoyed the job, the responsibility, the growth," says MacDonald. Today, Clearwater is a publicly traded company and MacDonald says, "I still enjoy running the company . . . there is good and bad but I truly enjoy it."[45] Young entrepreneur James Cuthbert, founder of the Port Moody, B.C.–based Rocky Point Kayak Ltd., echoes MacDonald's comments. "I love being an entrepreneur because it gives me the ability to earn a living in an area I love. It gives me an opportunity to be flexible with my time and pursue other personal and business interests."[46]

Financial Rewards

Often people are drawn to entrepreneurship with the hopes of earning a higher salary. Small-business owners know that their earnings are limited only by their skills as an entrepreneur. There is an old saying, "You can't get rich working for someone else." While there are no guarantees you will become wealthy by running your own business— you just may.

Low Start-Up Costs

As already mentioned, small businesses often require less money to start and maintain than do large ones. Obviously, a service firm with just five people will spend less money on wages and salaries, rent, utilities, and other expenses than does a firm employing tens of thousands of people in several large facilities. And, rather than maintain the expense and staff of keeping separate departments for accounting, advertising, and legal counselling, small businesses can hire other firms (often small businesses themselves) to supply these services as they are needed. Additionally, small-business owners trying to produce a difficult project can sometimes rely on the volunteer efforts of friends and family members in order to save money.

Management

Small businesses usually have only one layer of management—the owners. With small size comes the flexibility to adapt to changing market demands, the ability to build employee relations, and the capacity to create

© Joaquin Palting/Getty Images

Entrepreneurs like James Cuthbert, founder of Rocky Point Kayak Ltd., enjoy the freedom of being an entrepreneur.

a strong corporate culture. Since decisions can be made and carried out quickly, small firms can change direction faster than larger businesses. For example, Targray Technology International Inc., a Quebec manufacturer of CD and DVD components, noticed the trend toward green energy and started making inputs for solar panel makers. Solar power parts now account for more than half of the company's $225 million in revenue.[47] A similar situation occurred on a smaller scale for David Ciccarelli, who was acting as an agent and trying to market voice-over work for his wife. Ciccarelli noticed that no firms were offering what he thought was the appropriate level of service to voice-over artists. He quickly changed the focus of his work from drumming up business for his wife to building www.voices.com, a website that markets roughly 35,000 voice-over artists to *Fortune* 500 companies, advertising agencies, and various types of media.[48] If David had been working for a large marketing agency, this decision might have taken months if not years to come to fruition. In larger firms, decisions about even routine matters can take weeks because they must pass through two or more levels of management before action is authorized. When McDonald's introduces a new product, for example, it must first research what consumers want, then develop the product and test it carefully before introducing it nationwide, a process that sometimes takes years. An independent snack shop, however, can develop and introduce a new product (perhaps to meet a customer's request) in a much shorter time. Another advantage of being small is that business owners can build strong relationships with their employees, which can distinguish their business from larger competitors. Since managers/ owners in smaller firms get to know their employees better than larger counterparts, they can use this knowledge to differentiate themselves from larger competitors. Grant McKeracher of Keen Technology Consulting, a Toronto-based IT staffing agency, states that by being small, they get to know their employees, can monitor them more closely, and provide customers with better service: "It's easy to compete when your company is small. You can easily monitor the quality of work of people you are hiring and the work that's going on, because it's all happening right in front of you."[49] Small-business owners also get to create their company's corporate culture. In larger, more-established businesses, the culture of the business can be hard to influence and/or change. In smaller firms, especially new companies, the owner can create the culture desired and often use it to his or her advantage. For example, VersaPay Corp., a credit card and debt payment processing company based in Vancouver, uses its employee ownership program to motivate existing employees and to attract new talent. Michael Gokturk, the CEO, says he wanted to create employees that are owners of his company right from the start: "I went into this with a very Warren Buffett mindset. If you read his annual report . . . employee ownership is one of the main reasons his subsidiary companies do so well. . . . At our company we use our stock as currency to incentivize our current employees."[50]

Focus

Small firms can focus their efforts on a few key customers or on a precisely defined market niche—that is, a specific group of customers. Many large corporations must compete in the mass market or for large market segments. Smaller firms can develop products for particular groups of customers or to satisfy a need that other companies have not addressed. For example, Fatheadz focuses on producing sunglasses for people with big heads. To be an official "fathead," you need a ball cap size of at least 7⅝ and a head circumference above the ear of at least 23.5 inches. The idea arose when Rico Elmore was walking down the Las Vegas strip with his brother and realized that he had lost his sunglasses. He went to a nearby sunglass shop, and out of 300 pairs of glasses, he could not find one that fit. Customers include the entire starting line of the Indianapolis Colts, Rupert Boneham (of *Survivor* fame), and Tim Sylvia, former heavyweight title holder of Ultimate Fighting Championship.[51] By targeting small niches or product needs, small businesses can sometimes avoid fierce competition from larger firms, helping them to grow into stronger companies.

Reputation

Small firms, because of their capacity to focus on narrow niches, can develop enviable reputations for quality and service. For example, the above-mentioned VersaPay Corp. knew it was entering a market dominated by the large Canadian banks. The co-founders, Michael Gokturk and Kevin Short, felt that they could capture market share by offering superior customer service at lower fees—especially to smaller firms that frequently complain about how large banks treat them. The company's strategy appears to be paying off as it has grown from less than $50,000 in sales to $5.1 million in two years.[52] Another example of a small business with a formidable

© Scott T. Baxter/Getty Images

Small-business owners, such as dentists, know that maintaining a high-quality reputation is essential to their success.

reputation is W. Atlee Burpee and Co., which has the U.S.'s premier bulb and seed catalogue. Burpee has an unqualified returns policy (complete satisfaction or your money back) that demonstrates a strong commitment to customer satisfaction.[53]

Disadvantages of Small-Business Ownership

LO4 Summarize the disadvantages of small-business ownership, and analyze why many small businesses fail.

The rewards associated with running a small business are so enticing that it's no wonder many people dream of it. However, as with any undertaking, small-business ownership has its disadvantages.

High Stress Level

A small business is likely to provide a living for its owner, but this often comes with an increase in stress. There are always worries about competition, employee problems, new equipment, expanding inventory, rent increases, or changing market demand. In addition to other stresses, small-business owners tend to be victims of physical and psychological stress. The small-business person is often the owner, manager, sales force, shipping and receiving clerk, bookkeeper, and custodian. Figure 5.1 shows the five biggest challenges and goals of small and medium-sized businesses. Many creative persons fail, not because of their business concepts, but rather because of difficulties in managing their business.

Limited Financial Rewards

While many people start a business with dreams of becoming wealthy, research indicates that this does not always

Figure 5.1 Top Five Biggest Challenges, Concerns, and Goals of Small and Medium-Sized Businesses

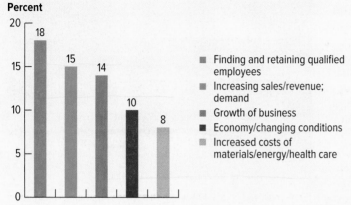

Source: Based on "Entrepreneurial Challenges Survey Results," *Entrepreneur*, http://www.entrepreneur.com/encyclopedia/businessstatistics/article81812.html (accessed June 14, 2007).

happen. Royal Bank of Canada recently released a study that shows only 34 percent of entrepreneurs were making more money than they made as a paid employee.[54] In a larger study, Statistics Canada determined that the median income of self-employed individuals was only 91.4 percent of the median income of paid employees.[55] Young entrepreneur Brandon Turner came to a similar conclusion that being a paid employee resulted in more money than being an entrepreneur. Turner, who started his own real estate investing website, RealEstateInYour Twenties.com, left the company to take a job with www. BiggerPockets.com, an online real estate social network. Turner says he could get paid more as an employee and as a result he can invest that money into creating more wealth in the future and enjoy life. "While most of the world would simply buy a larger house, a nicer car, and better wardrobe, I've been sinking this cash into several other more productive avenues, including more real estate investments, paying off debt, and going on some relaxing vacations. Simply put: I'm leveraging this job to create even greater wealth in my future."[56]

Time Demands

Entrepreneurship usually involves a significant investment in time from the entrepreneur, Statistics Canada, *Profit*, and the U.S. Census all have produced research indicating that entrepreneurs work longer hours than paid employees. For example, Ambareen Musa, founder of Souqalmal. com, a financial website, states, "There's no such thing as a 9-to-5 schedule for the company founder and no holiday when he or she can take a complete break from work . . . and when it comes to maternity leave, forget it. When my second child was born this past summer, I took one week off."[57] Given the time demands of entrepreneurship and the low pay, entrepreneurs must really love what they do. Serial entrepreneur, Chris Neville of Sydney, Nova Scotia, sums up his feelings on entrepreneurship: "I work longer

hours and likely get paid less than I would make as an employee. But I love going to work and wouldn't have it any other way."[58]

High Failure Rate

Despite the importance of small businesses to our economy, there is no guarantee of small-business success. Roughly 90 percent of all new businesses fail within the first five years.[59] Neighbourhood restaurants are a case in point. Look around your own neighbourhood and you can probably spot the locations of several restaurants that are no longer in business.

Small businesses fail for many reasons (see Table 5.3). A poor business concept—such as insecticides for garbage cans (research found that consumers are not concerned with insects in their garbage)—will produce disaster nearly every time. Expanding a hobby into a business may work if a genuine market niche exists, but all too often people start such a business without identifying a real need for the goods or services. Other notable causes of small-business failure include the burdens imposed by government regulation, insufficient funds to withstand

Table 5.3 Most Common Mistakes Made by Start-Up Businesses

- Failing to spend enough time researching the business idea to see if it's viable.
- Miscalculating market size, timing, ease of entry, and potential market share.
- Underestimating financial requirements and timing.
- Over-projecting sales volume and timing.
- Making cost projections that are too low.
- Hiring too many people and spending too much on offices and facilities.
- Lacking a contingency plan for a shortfall in expectations.
- Bringing in unnecessary partners.
- Hiring for convenience rather than skill requirements.
- Neglecting to manage the entire company as a whole.
- Accepting that it's "not possible" too easily rather than finding a way.
- Focusing too much on sales volume and company size rather than profit.
- Seeking confirmation of your actions rather than seeking the truth.
- Lacking simplicity in your vision.
- Lacking clarity of your long-term aim and business purpose.
- Lacking focus and identity.
- Lacking an exit strategy.

Source: Based on John Osher, in Mark Henricks, "What Not to Do," *Entrepreneur*, February 2004, www.entrepreneur.com/article/0,4621,312661,00.html.

slow sales, and vulnerability to competition from larger companies. However, four major causes of small-business failure deserve a close look: external shocks, undercapitalization, managerial inexperience or incompetence, and inability to cope with growth; roughly 90 percent of small-business failures can be attributed to these faults.[60]

External Shocks. Approximately 68 percent of businesses fail in Canada due to what is described as **external shocks**. These are events that occur in a company's external environment that the company could not control. Consider restaurants that operate in Windsor, Ontario, a region of the country that has seen a significant increase in the unemployment rate with the loss of numerous jobs in the auto sector. Dan Young, a food and beverage manager for a Windsor-based restaurant, notes, "We have managed to stay open, but many competitors have closed, revenue is down at almost every restaurant in town, and there is very little restaurant owners can do about it."[61] Examples of external shocks include downturns in the economy, new competitors, customers going out of business, loss of suppliers, energy prices, and so forth.

external shocks unanticipated events that occur in a firm's external environment that hurt the company's business

undercapitalization the lack of funds to operate a business normally

Undercapitalization. The shortest path to failure in business is **undercapitalization**, the lack of funds to operate a business normally. Too many entrepreneurs think that all they need is enough money to get started, that the business can survive on cash generated from sales soon thereafter. But almost all businesses suffer from seasonal variations in sales, making cash tight, and few businesses make money from the start. Without sufficient funds, the best small-business idea in the world will fail.

Managerial Inexperience or Incompetence. Poor management is the cause of many business failures. Just because an entrepreneur has a brilliant vision for a small business does not mean he or she has the knowledge or experience to manage a growing business effectively. A person who is good at creating great product ideas and marketing them may lack the skills and experience to make good management decisions in hiring, negotiating, finance, and control. Moreover, entrepreneurs may neglect those areas of management they know little about or find tedious, at the expense of the business's success.

Inability to Cope With Growth. Sometimes, the very factors that are advantages turn into serious disadvantages when the time comes for a small business to grow. Growth often requires the owner to give up a certain amount of direct authority, and it is frequently hard for someone who has called all the shots to give up control.[62] For example, Rebecca MacDonald, founder of Toronto–based Energy

© Brent Jones

The failure rate for small businesses is very high.

Saving Income Fund, says that when she first started the business she did everything, but as the company grew she had to let other people do more and more. MacDonald notes that the transition was tough: "It was almost like letting a child leave home. It was hard for me. But I wanted to allow my talented people to do what they were hired to do."[63] Similarly, growth requires specialized management skills in areas such as credit analysis and promotion—skills that the founder may lack or not have time to apply. David Cynamon, CEO of KIK Corp., a private-label cleaning product producer, openly questions if he has the ability to manage the company as it grows: "It becomes a different game. . . . At 700 people (current number of employees), it becomes difficult; 3,000 people might be beyond my capability." Cynamon has accepted that fact that his company may outgrow his ability to manage it. "It's not about the job (CEO), it's about the longevity and success of KIK forever. The status of the job means nothing to me."[64]

Poorly managed growth probably affects a company's reputation more than anything else, at least initially. And products that do not arrive on time or goods that are poorly made can quickly reverse a company's success.

Starting a Small Business

LO5 Describe how you go about starting a small business and what resources are needed.

We've told you how important small businesses are, and why they succeed and fail, but *how do you go about* starting your own business? To start any business, large or small, you must first have an idea. Sam Walton, founder of Walmart, had an idea for a discount retailing enterprise and spawned the world's largest retailing empire, also changing the way traditional companies look at their business. Next, you need to assess whether the idea is in fact an opportunity that is worth pursuing as a business—the two are not one and the same. You may have an idea to build an amusement park in space, but due to financial and resource limitations, it is unlikely to be considered an opportunity for an entrepreneur. An opportunity is an idea that can be turned into a profitable company. Writing a business plan to guide planning and development in the business comes next. Finally, you must make decisions about form of ownership, the financial resources needed, and whether to buy an existing business, start a new one, or buy a franchise.

Idea Generation

Ideas can come from anywhere—past jobs and hobbies are two of the most common sources of business ideas, as 80 percent of new businesses in Canada can trace their beginnings to the entrepreneur's previous business experience. For example, Michelle Strum, owner of the Halifax Backpackers Hostel, came up with the idea of a locally owned hostel after travelling extensively overseas and staying and working in different countries.[65] Similarly, Costa Elles, co-owner of Ela, a Greek restaurant that is expanding rapidly in Atlantic Canada, relied heavily on his 10-plus years of work experience in the food and beverage industry to shape the design and management of his restaurants.[66]

Ideas can also come from watching television shows like CBC's *Dragons' Den*, observing consumers as they shop, or paying close attention to emerging trends by following reports by trend watchers such as www.wired.com, www.springwise.com, and www.trendwatching.com. For example, Jay Cho of Coma Food Truck, a gourmet Korean-Mexican-American food-truck operating in Vancouver, states he was inspired to open his business after seeing the popularity of the trucks in Los Angeles. Cho says he always wanted to open his own restaurant but could never come up with the start-up money. The food-truck business allows him to enter the restaurant business at much lower costs than opening a bricks-and-mortar establishment.[67] Coma Food Truck opened to rave reviews from customers, but Cho eventually closed the business after a dispute with the city. The growing number of tutoring companies, especially online tutoring, is a direct result of entrepreneurs watching trends and using the Internet to first reach customers and offer an improved experience. At one time, tutoring was used by struggling students to pass, but more and more parents are including tutoring as part of their children's extracurricular activities with the hope that the extra attention will lead to long-term success. For example, Christopher Ide, co-founder of Pax Learning, is currently offering both in-home and online tutoring in Toronto; his selling point is personalized engagement. "I don't think we need a white paper to tell us that kids' lives are totally immersed in technology these days," he says. "Having a background in the educational-technology sector, I knew that tablets, computers, and smartphones could make learning much more enjoyable for kids."[68] Other business ideas can come from a deliberate search, where entrepreneurs are engaging in formal methods to generate new ideas. For example, Dr. A.K. Kirumira of BioMedical, a Windsor, Nova Scotia–based diagnostic equipment company, says that when he needs new ideas

© Vanhawks

Ali Zahid, Sohaib Zahid, and Niv Yahel co-founded Vanhawks, a smart bicycle manufacturer in Toronto. Personal experience along with observing fellow bike riders led them to conclude people would buy a smartbike with such safety features as blind spot detection.

he starts with a formal review of medical journals, old files, and research to look for opportunities that others may have missed.[69]

Opportunity Identification and Assessment

All entrepreneurs start with an idea that they hope can be an opportunity. An "opportunity" to an entrepreneur is an idea that can be turned into a profitable business. Prior to spending significant time on the development of an idea, an entrepreneur should first conduct an opportunity assessment. An opportunity assessment is a screening tool that can be used to determine if an entrepreneur should write a full business plan or go back to the drawing board and consider another idea. An opportunity assessment consists of the following:

1. Describing the business and the marketing mix (price, product, place, and promotion).

2. Assessing his or her own skills. Does the potential entrepreneur know enough about the industry and have the skills necessary to run this type of business? Additionally, the entrepreneur should want to work in this type of industry.

3. Determining if there is a need for the business. While entrepreneurs do not have to engage in market research at this point, they may want to talk to

Josh Brandley and Hamid Abbas

Business: Parsel

Founded: 2014

Success: The business has recently raised $1.2 million to fuel expansion.[70]

Josh Brandley and Hamid Abbas recognized that many of the people with significant YouTube and Instagram followings were not making money off their content. In fact, it was Internet giants Google and Facebook that were making the money off people's content, such as their pictures, YouTube channels, and so forth. "We realized it's the distribution platforms that are really making the money out of this—Google owns YouTube and Facebook owns Instagram," Brandley says.[71] So Brandley and his partner founded Parsel to help the social media stars make money from their success. Parsel matches up companies who are looking for online personalities with significant followers to endorse their products or services. These companies pay a fee per endorsement or product placement. Additionally, Parsel will help online stars create web pages to sell the products they are endorsing. Parsel boasts that it pre-screens people

before allowing them to use its services, and that its average creator has 100,000 YouTube subscribers, with some at over a million.[72] For example, Sylvia Ta, whose YouTube channel has more than 186,000 subscribers, says she has made enough money to pay for a condo in downtown Toronto as a result of working with Parsel.[73]

© JuliusKielaitis/Shutterstock.com

Josh Brandley founded Parsel after he realized online YouTube stars were making very little off their popular videos. Parsel helps online stars monetize their content through the use of endorsements and online stores.

friends, family, knowledgeable lawyers, accountants, and industry experts.

4. Identifying the competition and assessing their strengths and weaknesses. Start to determine how they would react to a new competitor.

5. Calculating start-up costs, annual expenses, and potential revenue to determine if the idea makes financial sense.

6. Determining if the entrepreneur has the ability to bring together the financial and human resources to start the company.

After completing a thorough opportunity assessment, an entrepreneur should have enough facts to decide if the idea is still worth pursuing. If the idea looks promising, the entrepreneur may proceed and write a business plan.

The Business Plan

A key element of business success is a **business plan**—a precise statement of the rationale for the business and a step-by-step explanation of how it will achieve its goals. The business plan should include an explanation of the business, an analysis of the competition, estimates of income and expenses, and other information. It should

establish a strategy for acquiring sufficient funds to keep the business going. Indeed, many financial institutions decide whether to loan money to a small business based on its business plan. However, the business plan should act as a guide and reference document—not a shackle to limit the business's flexibility and decision making. Finally, the business plan should be revised periodically to ensure that the firm's goals and strategies can adapt to changes in the environment. Julian Brass, founder and CEO of Notable.com, an online company that informs people about notable events and people in and around Canada, sums up this sentiment: "Every entrepreneur needs to start with a business plan, and like when you're seeking advice and mentorship, it's an ongoing process. You can say, 'This is a golden plan and we're going to be rich in a year,' but often times when you hit the market things are very different than what you perceived before starting out. It's then that you have to return to the drawing board and tweak some things and go from there."[74]

Numerous websites provide information on how to write a business plan, including www.bdc.ca and

> **business plan** a precise statement of the rationale for a business and a step-by-step explanation of how it will achieve its goals

Consider the Following: Check Your Creativity

The entrepreneurial success stories in this chapter are about people who used their creative abilities to develop innovative products or ways of doing something that became the basis of a new business. Of course, being creative is not just for entrepreneurs or inventors; creativity is an important tool to help you find the optimal solutions to the problems you face on a daily basis. Employees rely heavily on their creativity skills to help them solve daily workplace problems.

According to brain experts, the right-brain hemisphere is the source of creative thinking, and the creative part of the brain can "atrophy" from lack of use. Let's see how much "exercise" you're giving your right-brain hemisphere.

TASK:

1. Take the following self-test to check your Creativity Quotient.[75]

2. Write the appropriate number in the box next to each statement according to whether the statement describes your behaviour always (3), sometimes (2), once in a while (1), or never (0).

3. Check your score using the following scale:

   30–36   High creativity. You are giving your right-brain hemisphere a regular workout.

   20–29   Average creativity. You could use your creativity capacity more regularly to guard against "creativity atrophy."

   10–19   Low creativity. You could benefit from reviewing the questions you answered "never" in the assessment and selecting one or two of the behaviours that you could start practising.

   0–9   Undiscovered creativity. You have yet to uncover your creative potential.

	Always 3	Sometimes 2	Once in a While 1	Never 0
1. I am a curious person who is interested in other people's opinions.				
2. I look for opportunities to solve problems.				
3. I respond to changes in my life creatively by using them to redefine my goals and revising plans to reach them.				
4. I am willing to develop and experiment with ideas of my own.				
5. I rely on my hunches and insights.				
6. I can reduce complex decisions to a few simple questions by seeing the "big picture."				
7. I am good at promoting and gathering support for my ideas.				
8. I think further ahead than most people I associate with by thinking long term and sharing my vision with others.				
9. I dig out research and information to support my ideas.				
10. I am supportive of the creative ideas from my peers and subordinates and welcome "better ideas" from others.				
11. I read books and magazine articles to stay on the "cutting edge" in my areas of interest. I am fascinated by the future.				
12. I believe I am creative and have faith in my good ideas.				
Subtotal for each column				
	Grand Total			

From dumpster-diving to $1.5 million in revenue—this is the story behind EcoScraps. EcoScraps was founded by college students Craig Martineau, Dan Blake, and Brandon Sargent. After realizing how much was wasted at restaurants and groceries, the three began experimenting with ways to turn food waste into compost. This often required them to dumpster dive to collect the necessary scraps. The trio conducted composting research in their dorm parking lot and soon discovered a process that converts fruit and vegetable waste to compost in three weeks.

With their proprietary process in hand, the founders approached businesses and offered to pick up their food waste at a discounted rate. They also partnered with garbage haulers to drop off waste at their facilities for free. This saves the haulers money because landfills charge dumping fees. EcoScraps collects 30 tonnes of old fruit and vegetables every day from across Utah and Arizona. After composting the waste, EcoScraps resells it as organic potting soil to nurseries and stores like Whole Foods and Costco. According to Blake, EcoScraps' emphasis on sustainability means finding "a balance between financial viability, environmental responsibility, and being meaningful for everyone involved."[76]

DISCUSSION QUESTIONS

1. Why did the three entrepreneurs decide to found EcoScraps?

2. How has EcoScraps' proprietary process contributed to its success?

3. Why is EcoScraps' partnership with garbage haulers so beneficial?

© Notable.ca, @MrBrass

Julian Brass, founder of Notable, a website for young, professional and connected people, says entrepreneurs should start their business with a plan.

www.scotiabank.com. The major points covered in a business plan include the following:

- Executive summary
- Industry analysis
- Description of the venture
- Production plan
- Operational plan
- Marketing plan
- Organizational plan
- Assessment of risk
- Financial plan

Forms of Business Ownership

After developing a business plan, the entrepreneur has to decide on an appropriate legal form of business ownership—whether it is best to operate as a sole proprietorship, partnership, or corporation—and examine the many factors that affect that decision, which we explored in Chapter 4.

Financial Resources

The old adage "It takes money to make money" holds true in developing a business enterprise. To make money from a small business, the owner must first provide or obtain money (capital) to start the business and keep it running smoothly. Often, the small-business owner has to put up a significant percentage of the necessary capital. Few new business owners have the entire amount, however, and must look to other sources for additional financing. Students should recognize that while finding money to start a business is hard, it is never impossible—the world is full of entrepreneurs who came up with creative fundraising techniques. For example, Susan Squires-Hutchings, owner of a St. John's, Newfoundland, pottery business, was turned down for financing on more than 50 occasions prior to convincing her landlord to lend her the money to get her company off the ground.[77] Jim Treliving and George Melville of Boston Pizza fame did not originally create the restaurant; rather they purchased the rights to be the franchisor from the original owner. The pair raised the funds needed by convincing two friends to lend them half the money and then persuading the founder to lend them the other half.[78]

Equity Financing. The most important source of funds for any new business is the owner. Many owners include among their personal resources ownership of a home or the accumulated value in a life-insurance policy or a savings account. A new business owner may sell or borrow against the value of such assets to obtain funds to operate a business. Gerry Schwartz, one of the richest men in Canada and founder of Onex Corp., says that people should invest in themselves—they shouldn't fear risking their assets if it means attempting to realize their dreams.[79] Additionally, the owner may bring useful personal assets such as a computer, desks and other furniture, or a car or truck as part of his or her ownership interest in the firm. Such financing is referred to as *equity financing* because the owner uses real personal assets rather than borrowing funds from outside sources to get started in a new business. The owner can also provide working capital by reinvesting profits into the business or simply by not drawing a full salary. These thoughts are evident in the words of Michael Cerny, CEO of Creative Building Maintenance Inc. in Mississauga, Ontario, and Huck Owen, CEO of Toronto-based Owen Media Partners Inc. Cerny states, "The reality is that any grade-A financial institution is going to expect you to put up some kind of your own money up front to show your commitment and belief in your venture."[80] "Be prepared not to get paid,"[81] says Owen, who admits he is the last person in the company to get paid.

"The most important source of funds for any new business is the owner."

Small businesses can also obtain equity financing by finding investors for their operations. They may sell stock in the business to family members, friends, employees, or other investors. For example, when Eryn Green and Tamar Wagman—founders of Sweetpea Baby Food, an Ontario company that sells frozen organic baby food—needed money, they asked their family and friends to help out. The pair managed to raise $150,000 by selling a 10 percent stake in the company.[82]

Other sources of equity financing include the informal risk-capital market or business **angel investors** and venture capitalists. Angels are private, wealthy investors who

angel investors private investors who supply equity financing for businesses

typically invest anywhere from $10,000 to $500,000 in a business for an equity stake in the company. Angels in Canada are typically older males with entrepreneurship experience and most will want to invest in companies where they can provide some management assistance or mentoring. While little research has been done in Canada on the total value of dollars invested by angels, research in the U.S. has found that the amount far exceeds the total venture capital pool in the country. Examples of angel investors can be seen on CBC's *Dragons' Den* where entrepreneurs pitch their ideas to wealthy investors with hopes of receiving cash and business mentoring.[83] While the CBC version of angel investing has been spiced up for TV, it does provide some insight into what angel investors are looking for in a company—a motivated owner, strong business plan and presentation skills, an idea where they can add some expertise, and growth potential. A new trend in angel investing is the formation of angel groups or clubs. These are small organizations of investors who meet on a regular basis to hear pitches from aspiring entrepreneurs. Some of the better-known clubs in Canada include National Angel Capital Organization, Angel One Investor Network, BC Angel Forum, and the First Angel Network. **Venture capitalists** are businesses or organizations that agree to provide some funds for a new business in exchange for an ownership interest or stock. Venture capitalists hope to purchase the stock of a small business at a low price and then sell the stock for a profit after the business has grown successful. A teenage dance club that only exists online has been a real hit with venture capitalists. Doppelganger raised $11 million in one year from venture capitalists. What's so attractive about the site? Users to the club enter a three-dimensional, virtual world with custom characters meant to replicate their real-world counterparts. Entry is free, but inside they encounter plenty of advertising from marketers. The only public advertiser that Doppelganger has acknowledged is Vivendi Universal's Interscope Records.[84]

venture capitalists persons or organizations that agree to provide some funds for a new business in exchange for an ownership interest or stock

A new form of investment has emerged in Canada in recent years—crowdfunding. Rather than one or two large investors, groups of small investors, or a crowd pool their money and invest in a business. While crowdfunding was originally started as way for entertainers or social entrepreneurs to raise money in the form of donations, it quickly evolved. For example, the Brooklyn Warehouse, a popular Halifax-based eatery, engaged in a crowdfunding campaign where they asked people for a donation to expand their business. In return, people received free meals and their picture on the wall of the restaurant.[85] Soon entrepreneurs were using popular crowdfunding sites such as Kickstarter (www.kickstarter.com) and Indiegogo (www.indiegogo.com) to pre-sell product ideas. For example, Canadian Eric Migicovsky made use of Kickstarter to pre-sell his Pebble

"Stop the madness! You are a crazy chicken and this is a really bad idea," barks Kevin O'Leary at one entrepreneur. Jim Treliving tells another, "This idea is awful." Do these quotes sound like words from angels? Well, it depends on how you see the world. Both O'Leary and Treliving have starred on CBC's show, *Dragons' Den*, where entrepreneurs pitch their ideas to five angel investors in the hopes of receiving much-needed cash and business mentoring. Successful pitches may receive funding and often more than one new partner in their business, while unsuccessful pitches (poor products) are sometimes lambasted by the Dragons. Many viewers of the popular show are left to wonder if pitching ideas to angel investors even remotely resembles this process and if all investors are indeed as greedy as these so called angels appear to be.

The questions are not easy to answer. Yes, entrepreneurs may pitch their ideas to a group of angel investors in a relatively short time period as seen on the show. Yes, the investors will be mostly interested in the numbers, want a large return, and expect entrepreneurs to know their business inside and out. But the really poor ideas or the unprepared entrepreneurs often seen in the show would almost never get an opportunity to pitch to a group of angel investors. Almost all angel investors thoroughly pre-screen ideas (by reading a business plan) and would not consider listening to any of the poor, albeit entertaining, concepts that make their way onto the CBC. Furthermore, most angel investors do not want

control of a company, whereas these investors almost always do. The question concerning greed is much more difficult to answer. Let's look at two examples, PeerFX and Atomic Tea. Both companies came looking for money and mentorship.

PeerFX, an online peer-to-peer currency exchange, allows customers to exchange money via the Internet at a substantially lower fee than traditional banks charge. At the time of their pitch to the Dragons, 22-year-old business students Robert Dunlop and Florence Leung were presenting an idea to make money, not operate a business. The pair had hoped to receive an investment of $200,000 for 25 percent of their business. What they ended up with was $200,000 but for 50.1 percent of their company and partners with the knowledge and contacts to bring the project to life. The Dragons, especially Kevin O'Leary, negotiated very strongly with the two students and perhaps bullied them a bit. But both students admitted later that they are soft-spoken and may need a partner like O'Leary to get the business operating successfully. So, were the investors helpful angels or greedy dragons in this case? You decide.

Atomic Tea, an innovative tea company owned by Jessica and Russell Bohrson, presented the Dragons with an operating company and a vision of becoming the next Starbucks, albeit with teas. The brother and sister team hoped to raise $120,000 for 25 percent of their company and use the funds to franchise their business. During the

---

smartwatch and successfully raised over $10 million. Growth in crowdfunding has been significant as contributions on Kickstarter topped $2.18 billion in 2016, up a significant amount from $320 million in 2012.[86,87] Up until 2015, only Ontario allowed entrepreneurs to actually sell equity in their business using crowdfunding. This all changed when British Columbia, Saskatchewan, Manitoba, Quebec, New Brunswick, and Nova Scotia all agreed to permit the practice. Entrepreneurs are now allowed to raise upwards of $500,000 a year for their company using crowdfunding in these provinces.[88]

Although these forms of equity financing have helped many small businesses, they require that the small-business owner share the profits of the business—and sometimes control, as well—with the investors. The trade-off in profits and control may well be worth the risk as research in Canada and the United States has found that businesses that make use of equity investors (angels/venture capitalists) are more financially successful, hire more employees, and bring more products to market than firms that do not use equity financing.

Debt Financing. Businesses often borrow the funds necessary to start and run their business. Banks are the main suppliers of external financing to small businesses. Business owners can also borrow money from some government sources such as the Business Development Centre or have some of their bank loans guaranteed by government programs such as the Canadian Small Business Financing Program. Other sources of debt financing can include family and friends, money borrowed from equity investors, and peer-to-peer lending (see the Responding to Business Challenges box below), which is relatively new in Canada. If the business owner manages to borrow money from family or friends, he or she may be able to structure a favourable repayment schedule and sometimes negotiate an interest rate below current bank rates. If the business goes bad, however, the emotional losses for all concerned may greatly exceed the money involved. Anyone lending a friend or family member money for a venture should state the agreement clearly in writing.

The amount a bank or other institution is willing to loan depends on its assessment of the venture's likelihood

course of their pitch, the Dragons all stated that they loved Atomic Tea's products and all of them appeared interested in investing in the fledging company. Jim Treliving spoke first, offering them $120,000 for 51 percent of the company. Laurence Lewin spoke next and offered to pair with Treliving and invest $75,000 each for a total of $150,000 for 50.1 percent of the business. Before the Bohrsons could respond, Dragon Robert Herjavec jumped in and stated that he believed Atomic Tea would need more money to franchise successfully and offered to join Treliving and Lewin in an investing syndicate that would invest $225,000 in the business for 50.1 percent equity in the company. While the three investors were contemplating their offer, fellow Dragon Arlene Dickinson offered the Bohrsons $120,000 for only 40 percent of the business. Meanwhile, the only Dragon not heard from, Kevin O'Leary, told the two Atomic Tea owners to go back behind the curtain and consider their options. The pair left thinking they were going to come back and choose between two offers—one for $225,000 for 50.1 percent of the company, and one for $120,000 for 40 percent of their company.

Back in the Den, the investors were listening to a pitch of a different kind from O'Leary that would see the investors withdraw both offers and counter with a new take-it-or-leave-it, single offer from all the Dragons. When the Atomic Tea owners reappeared in front of the Dragons, they were surprised to hear that both original offers were now gone and they could accept a one-time offer of $120,000 for 50.1 percent of their business. The Bohrsons tried to get the investors to revisit one of the previous offers and were told by O'Leary that they could "take or leave the new offer" as it was the only one that they would get. After some thought, the Bohrsons accepted the terms and shook on the deal. After the show, Internet chat rooms and blogs were filled with people questioning the ethics of the Dragons and stating the Bohrsons should have walked away from the offer. But the Bohrsons have since stated time and time again that they are happy with the terms and the Dragons' vast experience was worth giving up 50.1 percent of their company.

So, were the investors helpful angels or greedy dragons in this case? You decide.[89]

DISCUSSION QUESTIONS

1. If you represented PeerFX or Atomic Tea, would you have agreed to the deals proposed by the Dragons?

2. Did the investors act ethically?

3. Using Internet resources such as YouTube, review some *Dragons' Den* episodes. What were the pitches about? Were they successful? What were the terms of the offer? Communicate your findings to the class.

of success and of the entrepreneur's ability to repay the loan. The bank will often require the entrepreneur to put up *collateral*, a financial interest in the property or fixtures of the business, to guarantee payment of the debt. Additionally, the small-business owner may have to offer some personal property as collateral, such as his or her home, in which case the loan is called a *mortgage.* If the small business fails to repay the loan, the lending institution may eventually claim and sell the collateral (or the owner's home, in the case of a mortgage) to recover its loss.

Banks and other financial institutions can also grant a small business a *line of credit*—an agreement by which a financial institution promises to lend a business a predetermined sum on demand. A line of credit permits an entrepreneur to take quick advantage of opportunities that require a bank loan. Small businesses may obtain funding from their suppliers in the form of a *trade credit*—that is, suppliers allow the business to take possession of the needed goods and services and pay for them at a later date or in installments. Occasionally, small businesses engage in *bartering*—trading their own products for the goods and services offered by other businesses. For example, an accountant may offer accounting services to an office supply firm in exchange for printer paper and CDs.

Entrepreneurs know that being persistent is a requirement for raising money. If the idea is sound and an entrepreneur has a strong business plan, then raising debt and/or equity is always possible. For example, when Christopher Frey, Kisha Ferguson, and Matt Robinson began searching for the $300,000 they needed to fund their Toronto-based, Canadian adventure travel magazine *Outpost*, they had to be determined. During a three-month period, the partners telephoned over 200 potential investors. While the trio were initially unsuccessful in raising all the money, they did manage to come up with $50,000—enough to get started. Two years later, the company managed to raise $1 million from BHVR Communications, a Montreal media and entertainment company.[90] See Table 5.4 for a list of funds requested by Canadian small and medium-sized enterprises (SMEs) in 2015.

Table 5.4 Small Business Funding Requested by SMEs

Trade Credit	29%
Bank Debt (Banks, Credit Unions, Government)	28%
Lease Financing	8%
Government Financing (non-debt)	4%
Equity Financing	1%

Source: Based on data from "Survey on Financing and Growth of Small and Medium Enterprises, 2014," Innovation, Science and Economic Development Canada.

Approaches to Starting a Small Business

Starting from Scratch versus Buying an Existing Business. Although entrepreneurs often start new small businesses from scratch, much as we have discussed in this section, they may elect instead to buy an already existing business. This has the advantage of providing a network of existing customers, suppliers, and distributors and reducing some of the guesswork inherent in starting a new business. However, an entrepreneur buying an existing business must also deal with whatever problems the business already has, such as human resource issues, declining business, and increasing competition. In addition, it is often difficult to determine a price for a business that satisfies both the buyer and seller.

Family Business. Another common method of starting a business is to engage in a family-run business. Entrepreneurs may join an existing family business, start their own family-orientated company, or inherit a firm. In Canada, family businesses account for 80 to 90 percent of all firms, create 50 percent of all new jobs, and represent 40 percent of the largest 100 companies.[91] The advantages of starting or joining a family business include the following:

- Family businesses outperform non-family businesses in terms of profit and longevity.

- Family members' strengths can be combined.

- Family members tend to be more loyal to a firm than non-family members.

- Owners of family businesses are often more driven to succeed than traditional business owners.

- Family members tend to trust each other more.

Even with these advantages, the long-term survival rate of family businesses is not as high as some people think—in fact, only one-third of family businesses survive to be passed on to the founder's children and fewer than 10 percent of those make it to the third generation. As the founder exits the business, the new owner(s) may not be as competent, the external environment can change,

or issues may arise over succession planning that could result in the demise of the business. The Irving Group represents an example of what can happen to a family business over time. K.C. Irving, the original founder of the company, noted that his succession plan was rather simple. He had three male children and they would inherit the business equally with his oldest son in charge. While the eldest Irving's approach was rather traditional, it did work and the Irving Empire continued to grow into a multibillion-dollar firm. Eventually, Irving's sons started to hand the company down to their children, but instead of three successors there were many more heirs. Still, the company remained relatively intact. Now, with the company going through another succession plan, there is loud talk that the firm will break up into separate companies as the family can no longer agree to a succession plan and there are too many shareholders at the table vying for their interests.[92]

Besides the problems with succession planning, there are other disadvantages associated with family businesses, including disputes among family members, family ties preventing people from being honest with one another, the inability of participants to separate work from home, problems in establishing fair remuneration policies, and difficulty in attracting qualified non-family workers. Still, even with these problems, people gravitate to starting or joining family businesses. For example, when Tyler Gompf of Winnipeg came up with the idea of a customer management company called Tell Us About Us Inc., he enlisted his brother Kirby to help start and eventually manage the business. The brothers have grown TUAU into a full-service customer-feedback research firm. The pair agree that there are advantages and disadvantages of working with family as they communicate easily and trust one another. But they admit that they do argue, which can strain family relations. Their solution was for Tyler to assume the role of CEO and for Kirby to become chief operating officer (COO).[93]

Franchising. Many small-business owners find entry into the business world through franchising. A licence to sell another's products or to use another's name in business, or both, is a **franchise**. The company that sells a franchise is the **franchiser**. Tim Hortons, Nurse Next Door, and Boston Pizza are well-known franchisers with national visibility. The purchaser of a franchise is called a **franchisee**.

franchise a licence to sell another's products or to use another's name in business, or both

franchiser the company that sells a franchise

franchisee the purchaser of a franchise

"**Many** small-business owners find entry into the business world **through franchising.**"

As discussed above, entrepreneurs are starting to take advantage of new sources of obtaining capital. Rather than finding one or two large investors or lenders, business owners are taking to the Internet to pitch their business to groups of people. These groups of people or crowds are asked to pool their small investments together and either purchase equity in a business, which is called crowdfunding, or lend the business money, which is known as peer-to-peer lending.

Up until recently, both practices were considered illegal in most provinces in Canada. Businesses owners could only sell equity or borrow money from financial institutions, their family or friends, or accredited investors. Accredited investors are individuals with an annual income in excess of $250,000 a year and some financial literacy. Essentially, provincial governments, which set the rules for lending and investing, were more or less of the opinion that the average citizen lacked the business knowledge to decide if an opportunity was a good or bad idea. Therefore, in order to protect people from themselves, they had adopted strict rules essentially forbidding most people from investing or lending to entrepreneurs.

But this all changed in 2015 when British Columbia, Saskatchewan, Manitoba, Quebec, New Brunswick, and Nova Scotia joined Ontario in permitting equity crowdfunding. Part of the approval process was to limit the amount a firm can raise in one year to $500,000 and to establish some rules to protect investors. Investors have a limit on how much they can invest in one business, they can cancel their investment within a time period, and the proposal from the entrepreneur must be clear and transparent.[94] In Canada, Seed-Ups has emerged as the most popular equity funding website, but it is relatively small compared to some of its global counterparts, such as EquityNet, Wefunder, and EarlyShares.

The rules on peer-to-peer lending have not officially changed, but this hasn't stopped Cato Pastoll from opening up the LendingLoop.ca, the first online website for businesses in Canada. Now entrepreneurs can fill out a simple one-page online application, have their creditworthiness approved by Lending Loop, and post the amount of money they wish to borrow along with any terms. Similarly, lenders with as little as $50 to lend can fill out an online application and once approved they can view profiles of firms looking to borrow money, the interest rate the companies will pay, and all other repayment terms. Pastoll says, "We are confident that our platform will prove to be a compelling alternative to high-cost private lenders and overly conservative Canadian banks for small businesses that are looking for flexible financing at fair rates."[95]

DISCUSSION QUESTIONS

1. Prior to reading this feature, did you know about crowdfunding and peer-to-peer lending?
2. If crowdfunding and peer-to-peer lending grows, what are some of the advantages and potential pitfalls to this source of funds?
3. Do you think the provincial governments mentioned above should have changed their laws to allow for equity-based crowdfunding? Why or why not?
4. Currently there are no peer-to-peer lending laws in Canada. Should the government create laws to protect investors and entrepreneurs? Why or why not?
5. Is it ethical for lenders to earn as much as 15 percent from a loan to an entrepreneur when bank rates are much lower?
6. Lending Loop is only allowing business who have been operating for two years to borrow money using their site. Why do you think they are not allowing start-ups to register and borrow funds?
7. Use the Internet to find some crowdfunding and/or peer-to-peer lending opportunities. Report back to the class the type of opportunities you found, including the amount of money entrepreneurs are trying to raise, when investors will receive their money back, and any other details. Indicate what opportunities you would personally invest in and why?

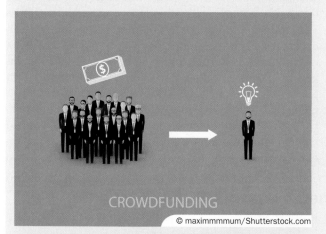
CROWDFUNDING
© maximmmmum/Shutterstock.com

Crowdfunding and peer-to-peer lending allow groups of people to pool small funds together to invest in a business.

franchising grew especially rapidly during the 1960s, when it expanded to more diverse industries. Table 3.5 lists a selection of the top 100 global franchises from 2016.

There are both advantages and disadvantages to franchising for the entrepreneur. Franchising allows a franchisee the opportunity to set up a small business relatively quickly, and because of its association with an established brand, a franchise outlet often reaches the break-even point faster than an independent business would. Franchisees often report the following advantages:[96]

- Management training and support
- Brand-name appeal
- Standardized quality of goods and services
- National advertising programs
- Financial assistance
- Proven products and business formats
- Centralized buying power
- Site selection and territorial protection
- Greater chance for success

However, the franchisee must sacrifice some freedom to the franchiser. Furthermore, research has found that franchisees fail at the same rate as traditional small and medium-sized firms. Some shortcomings experienced by some franchisees include:[97]

- Franchise fees and profit sharing with the franchiser
- Strict adherence to standardized operations
- Restrictions on purchasing
- Limited product line
- Possible market saturation
- Less freedom in business decisions

Strict uniformity is the rule rather than the exception. Entrepreneurs who want to be their own bosses are often frustrated with a franchise. In addition, entrepreneurs should recognize that not all franchises offer the same advantages to their franchisees. While there is value in the brand recognition and training of large franchises such as Tim Hortons, Quiznos, and Subway, an entrepreneur has to question if it is worthwhile to pay the extra costs and ongoing royalties associated with buying into a small, lesser-known company. Often the entrepreneur could start a business from scratch and create a name and brand for less money than is required to purchase a franchise. For example, a Halifax woman purchased a Western Canada–based tanning franchise. She assumed that buying into a franchise would provide her with training and that she would receive some ongoing assistance for the royalties (fees) she paid to the franchiser. Soon after buying the franchise she received her training, which amounted to a small manual. She then learned that since all of the other franchisees were located in Western provinces, the

© yellowdog/Getty Images

Curves is designed for women. It's not a fast-food franchise—it's a fast-exercise franchise.

The franchisee acquires the rights to a name, logo, methods of operation, national advertising, products, and other elements associated with the franchiser's business in return for a financial commitment and the agreement to conduct business in accordance with the franchiser's standard of operations. Depending on the franchise, the initial fee to join a system varies. In addition, franchisees buy equipment, pay for training, and obtain a mortgage or lease. The franchisee also pays the franchiser a monthly or annual fee based on a percentage of sales or profits. In return, the franchisee often receives building specifications and designs, site recommendations, management and accounting support, and perhaps most importantly, immediate name recognition. Visit the website of the International Franchise Association or the Canadian Franchise Association to learn more about this topic.

The practice of franchising first began in the United States when Singer used it to sell sewing machines in the nineteeenth century. It soon became commonplace in the distribution of goods in the automobile, gasoline, soft drink, and hotel industries. The concept of

"Entrepreneurs can learn critical marketing, management, and finance skills in seminars and university/college courses."

franchise would not assist her in advertising her company until more franchises were sold in her region.[98]

Help for Small-Business Managers

Because of the crucial role that small business and entrepreneurs play in the Canadian economy, a number of organizations offer programs to improve the small-business owner's ability to compete. These include entrepreneurial training programs and programs sponsored by Industry Canada and the Business Development Centre. Such programs provide small-business owners with invaluable assistance in managing their businesses, often at little or no cost to the owner.

Entrepreneurs can learn critical marketing, management, and finance skills in seminars and university/college courses. In addition, knowledge, experience, and judgment are necessary for success in a new business. While knowledge can be communicated and some experiences can be simulated in the classroom, good judgment must be developed by the entrepreneur. Local chambers of commerce and provincial and federal economic development offices offer information and assistance helpful in operating a small business. National publications such as *Profit, Inc.*, and *Entrepreneur* share statistics, advice, tips, and success/failure stories. Additionally, many urban areas—including Halifax, Montreal, Ottawa, Toronto, Calgary, and Vancouver—have weekly or monthly business journals or newspapers that provide stories on local businesses as well as on business techniques that a manager or small business can use.

Additionally, the small-business owner can obtain advice from other small-business owners, suppliers, and even customers. A customer may approach a small business it frequents with a request for a new product, for example, or a supplier may offer suggestions for improving a manufacturing process. Networking—building relationships and sharing information with colleagues—is vital for any businessperson, whether you work for a huge corporation or run your own small business. Communicating with other business owners is a great way to find ideas for dealing with employees and government regulation, improving processes, or solving problems. New technology is making it easier to network. For example, some regions are setting up computer bulletin boards for the use of their businesses to network and share ideas.

The Future for Small Business[99]

LO6 Evaluate the demographic, technological, and economic trends that are affecting the future of small business.

Although small businesses are crucial to the economy, they can be more vulnerable to turbulence and change in the marketplace than large businesses. Next, we take a brief look at the demographic, technological, and economic trends that will have the most impact on small business in the future.

Demographic Trends

Canada's baby boom started in 1946 and ended in 1964. The earliest baby boomers are already past 65, and in the next few years, millions more will pass that mark. The baby boomer generation numbers about 10 million, or 30 percent of Canadian citizens.[100] This segment of the population is probably the wealthiest, and the one that is often pursued by small businesses. For example, Atlantic Tours, a Halifax-based travel company, offers numerous tours aimed at this market. Industries such as travel, financial planning, and health care will continue to grow as baby boomers age. Many experts think that this demographic is the market of the future. For example, Calgary-based Masterpiece Inc., a developer and operator of retirement homes, has enjoyed revenue growth of 7,710 percent over a five-year period.[101] Nurse Next Door, a Canadian home care franchiser, is hoping the trend of seniors' spending money on their care will grow significantly as the company embraces a major expansion campaign. The baby boom will also influence the labour market in Canada as many boomers are considering retirement options. The results of this are a shortage of highly trained and skilled labour in various regions, which is a contributing factor to the growth in staffing agencies such as PEOPLEsource Staffing Solutions Inc. and MGA Computer Consulting Ltd., both in Toronto. In fact, when companies were surveyed for a recent *Profit* magazine poll, they noted the lack of skilled workers as the biggest barrier to future growth.[102]

Another market with huge potential for small business is the echo generation, that is, the children of the baby boomers. They are sometimes referred to as Millennials or Generation Y. Born between 1977 and 1994, there are about 6 million people in Canada in this age group. Typically, they shop frequently and spend lavishly on clothing, entertainment, and food.[103] Companies that have the most success with this group are ones that cater to the teens' and young adults' lifestyles. Some successful small businesses aimed at this market include Sylvan Learning Centre, a franchise that offers after-school tutoring; Alien Workshop, which designs and distributes skateboards and apparel; Burton Snowboards, a manufacturer of snowboards and accessories; and Femme Arsenal, which develops and distributes cosmetics.

Yet another trend is the growing number of immigrants living in Canada, as 260,000 people immigrate to this country each year.[104] This vast number of people provides still another greatly untapped market for small businesses. Retailers who specialize in ethnic products, and service providers who offer bi- or multilingual employees, can find vast potential in this market. Table 5.5 ranks the top cities for doing business in Canada.

Table 5.5 Top Cities for Doing Business in Canada

1. Quebec	6. Saint John
2. Charlottetown	7. Edmonton
3. Saguenay	8. Markham
4. Laval	9. Halifax
5. St. John's	10. Sherbrooke

Source: Based on data from http://www.findmapping.com/canadian_business_cities/bestcitiesforbusiness.php.

Technological and Economic Trends

Advances in technology have opened up many new markets to small businesses. As previously discussed, the Internet has revolutionized business and allows small firms to compete with larger counterparts. One of the hot areas will be the Internet infrastructure area that enables companies to improve communications with employees, suppliers, and customers.

Technological advances and an increase in service exports have created new opportunities for small companies to expand their operations abroad. Changes in communications and technology can allow small companies to customize their services quickly for international customers. Also, free trade agreements and trade alliances are helping to create an environment in which small businesses have fewer regulatory and legal barriers.

In recent years, economic turbulence has provided both opportunities and threats for small businesses. As large information technology companies such as Cisco and Oracle had to recover from an economic slowdown and an oversupply of Internet infrastructure products, some smaller firms found new niche markets. Smaller companies can react quickly to change and can stay close to their customers. While many well-funded dot-coms were failing, many small businesses were learning how to use the Internet to promote their businesses and sell products online. For example, many arts and crafts dealers and

makers of specialty products found they could sell their wares on existing websites, such as eBay. Service providers related to tourism, real estate, and construction also found they could reach customers through their own or existing websites.

Interest in alternative fuels and fuel conservation has spawned many small businesses. Earth First Technologies Inc. produces clean-burning fuel from contaminated water or sewage. Southwest Windpower Inc. manufactures and markets small wind turbines for producing electric power for homes, sailboats, and telecommunications. Solar Attic Inc. has developed a process to recover heat from home attics to use in heating hot water or swimming pools. As entrepreneurs begin to realize that worldwide energy markets are valued in the hundreds of billions of dollars, the number of innovative companies entering this market will increase. In addition, many small businesses have the desire and employee commitment to purchase such environmentally friendly products.

The future for small business remains promising. The opportunities to apply creativity and entrepreneurship to serve customers are unlimited. While large organizations such as Walmart, which has more than 1.8 million employees,[105] typically must adapt to change slowly, a small business can adapt to customer and community needs and changing trends immediately. This flexibility provides small businesses with a definite advantage over large companies.

Making Big Businesses Act "Small"

LO7 Explain why many large businesses are trying to "think small."

The continuing success and competitiveness of small businesses through rapidly changing conditions in the business world have led many large corporations to take a closer look at what makes their smaller rivals tick. More and more firms are emulating small businesses in an effort to improve their own bottom line. Beginning in the 1980s and continuing through the present, the buzzword in business has been to *downsize,* or more recently, to *right-size;* to reduce management layers, corporate staff, and work tasks in order to make the firm more flexible, resourceful, and innovative like a smaller business. Many well-known Canadian companies—including Nortel, Bell Canada, and Air Canada—have downsized to improve their competitiveness, as have American, German, British, and Japanese firms. Other firms have sought to make their businesses "smaller" by making their operating units function more like independent small businesses,

© epa european pressphoto agency b.v./Alamy Stock Photo

Sirius created value for a product and a market that didn't previously exist.

with each being responsible for its profits, losses, and resources. For example, when John Bell, CEO and president of an auto parts manufacturing business, assumed the role of board chair at Cambridge Hospital in Ontario, he managed to turn a $2 million deficit into a $3.5 million profit in one year. Bell first streamlined services and eliminated 29 management jobs and then hired an entrepreneur—Julia Dumanian—to assume the day-to-day operations of the hospital. Under their joint leadership, the pair eliminated services that were provided elsewhere in the region for annual savings of $1.6 million.[106] Of course, some large corporations, such as WestJet Airlines, have acted like small businesses from their inception, with great success.

Trying to capitalize on small-business success in introducing innovative new products, more and more companies are attempting to instill a spirit of entrepreneurship into even the largest firms. In major corporations, **intrapreneurs**, like entrepreneurs, take responsibility for, or "champion," the development of innovations of any kind *within* the larger organization.[107] Often, they use company resources and time to develop a new product for the company.

> **intrapreneurs** individuals in large firms who take responsibility for the development of innovations within the organizations

TEAM EXERCISE

Explore successful franchises. Go to the companies' websites and find the requirements for applying for three franchises. This chapter provides examples of successful franchises. What do these companies provide, and what is expected to be provided by the franchiser? Compare and contrast each group's findings for the franchises researched. For example, at Subway, the franchisee is responsible for the initial franchise fee, finding locations, leasehold improvements and equipment, hiring employees and operating restaurants, and paying an 8 percent royalty to the company and a fee into the advertising fund. The company provides access to formulas and operational systems, store design and equipment ordering guidance, a training program, an operations manual, a representative on-site during opening, periodic evaluations and ongoing support, and informative publications.

LEARNING OBJECTIVES SUMMARY

LO1 Define entrepreneurship and small business.

Entrepreneurship is the process of creating and managing a business to achieve desired objectives. Small business is any independently owned and operated business that is not dominant in its competitive area and does not employ more than 500 people.

LO2 Investigate the importance of small business in the Canadian economy and why certain fields attract small business.

No matter how you define small business, one fact is clear: Small businesses are vital to the soundness of the Canadian economy as more than 99 percent of all Canadian firms are classified as small businesses, and they employ 48 percent of private workers. Small firms are also important as exporters, representing roughly 97 percent of Canadian exported goods. In addition, small businesses are largely responsible for fuelling job creation and innovation.

LO3 Specify the advantages of small-business ownership.

Small-business ownership has many advantages, including (1) independence—the leading reason that entrepreneurs choose to go into business for themselves; (2) enjoyment of chosen career—one of the most commonly cited advantages of owning a business whether big or small; (3) realization that earnings are limited only by their skills as an entrepreneur—they can become wealthy; (4) the requirement for less money to start and maintain a small business compared to a large one; (5) small businesses usually have only one layer of management—the owners—which gives them flexibility to adapt to changing market demands, the ability to build strong employee relations, and the capacity to create a strong corporate culture; (6) the ability to focus efforts on a few key customers or on a precisely defined market niche—that is, a specific group of customers; and (7) the ability, with that narrow focus, to develop enviable reputations for quality and service.

LO4 Summarize the disadvantages of small-business ownership, and analyze why many small businesses fail.

Small businesses have many disadvantages for their owners, such as expense, physical and psychological stress, and a high failure rate. Small businesses fail for many reasons: undercapitalization, external shocks, management inexperience or incompetence, neglect, disproportionate burdens imposed by government regulation, and vulnerability to competition from larger companies.

LO5 Describe how you go about starting a small business and what resources are needed.

First you must have an idea for developing a small business. You must decide whether to start a new business from scratch, enter into a family business, buy an existing company, or buy a franchise operation. Next, you need to devise a business plan to guide planning and development of the business. Then you must decide what form of business ownership to use: sole proprietorship, partnership, or corporation. Small-business owners are expected to provide some of the funds required to start their businesses, but funds also can be obtained from friends and family, financial institutions, other businesses in the form of trade credit, investors (angels and or venture capitalists), and government organizations.

LO6 Evaluate the demographic, technological, and economic trends that are affecting the future of small business.

Changing demographic trends that represent areas of opportunity for small businesses include more elderly people as baby boomers age; a large group known as echo boomers, Millennials, or Generation Y; and an increasing number of immigrants to Canada. Technological advances and an increase in service exports have created new opportunities for small companies to expand their operations abroad, while trade agreements and alliances have created an environment in which small business has fewer regulatory and legal barriers. Economic turbulence presents both opportunities and threats to the survival of small business.

LO7 Explain why many large businesses are trying to "think small."

More large companies are copying small businesses in an effort to make their firms more flexible, resourceful, and innovative, and generally to improve their bottom line. This effort often involves downsizing (reducing management layers, laying off employees, and reducing work tasks) and intrapreneurship, where an employee takes responsibility for (champions) developing innovations of any kind within the larger organization.

KEY TERMS

angel investors
business plan
entrepreneurship
external shocks
franchise
franchisee

franchiser
intrapreneurs
small business
undercapitalization
venture capitalists

DESTINATION CEO DISCUSSION QUESTIONS

1. Re-read the opening quote in the profile at the beginning of this chapter. Would you live your life as described in the quote if you were guaranteed to be worth millions of dollars in the future?

2. How does O'Leary's sometimes "villainous" role help him sell himself and products to consumers? Would you

buy products just because they were endorsed by a celebrity?

3. How did O'Leary try to capitalize on the brand he was building on TV? Some of the products and companies he is branding are quite different; for example, wine is very different from mortgages.

What are some of the advantages and disadvantages of this?

4. After reading the opening profile, would you describe Kevin O'Leary's business practices as ethical?

5. Use the Internet to research O'Leary and his companies. Has he added his name to any new products? What is the status of his businesses?

SO YOU WANT TO BE *an Entrepreneur or Small-Business Owner*

In times when jobs are scarce, many people turn to entrepreneurship as a way to find employment. As long as there are unfulfilled needs from consumers, there will be a demand for entrepreneurs and small businesses. Entrepreneurs and small-business owners have been, and will continue to be, a vital part of the Canadian economy, whether in retailing, wholesaling, manufacturing, technology, or services. Creating a business around your idea has a lot of advantages. For many people, independence is the biggest advantage of forming their own small business, especially for those who do not work well in a corporate setting and like to call their own shots. Smaller businesses are also cheaper to start up than large ones in terms of salaries, infrastructure, and equipment. Smallness also provides a lot of flexibility to change with the times. If consumers suddenly start demanding new and different products or services, a small business is more likely to deliver quickly.

Starting your own business is not easy, especially in slow economic times. Even in a good economy, taking a good idea and turning it into a business has a very high failure rate. The possibility of failure can increase even more when money is tight. Reduced revenues and expensive material can hurt a small business more than a large one because small businesses have fewer resources. When people are feeling the pinch from rising food and fuel prices, they tend to cut back on other expenditures—which could potentially harm your small business. However, several techniques can help your company survive.

Set clear payment schedules for all clients. Small businesses tend to be worse about collecting payments than large ones, especially if the clients are acquaintances. However, you need to keep cash flowing into the company in order to keep business going.

Take the time to learn about tax breaks. A lot of people do not realize all of the deductions they can claim on items such as equipment.

Focus on your current customers, and don't spend a lot of time looking for new ones. It is far less expensive for a company to keep its existing customers happy.

Although entrepreneurs and small-business owners are more likely to be friends with their customers, do not let this be a temptation to give things away for free. Make it clear to your customers what the basic price is for what you are selling and charge for extra features, extra services, etc.

Make sure the office has the conveniences employees need—like a good coffee maker and other drinks and snacks. This will not only make your employees happy, but it will also help maintain productivity by keeping employees closer to their desks.

Use your actions to set an example. If money is tight, show your commitment to cost cutting and making the business work by doing simple things like taking the bus to work and bringing your lunch every day.

Don't forget to increase productivity in addition to cutting costs. Try not to focus so much attention on cost cutting that you don't try to increase sales.

In unsure economic times, these measures should help new entrepreneurs and small-business owners sustain their businesses. Learning how to run a business on a shoestring is a great opportunity to cut the fat and establish lean, efficient operations.[108]

BUILD YOUR BUSINESS PLAN

Small Business, Entrepreneurship, and Franchising

Now you can get started writing your business plan! Refer to the "Business Plan Development" section following Chapter 1, which provides you with an outline for your business plan. As you are developing your business plan, keep in mind that potential investors might be reviewing it. Or you might have plans to participate in some of the government opportunities aimed at supporting youth in entrepreneurship, such as the Futerpreneurs loans program.

At this point in the process, you should think about collecting information from a variety of (free) resources. For example, if you are developing a business plan for a local business, product, or service, you might want to check out any of the following sources for demographic information: the local Chamber of Commerce,

Economic Development Office, or the Statistics Canada website.

Go on the Internet and see if any recent studies or articles have focused on your specific type of business, especially in your area. Remember, you always want to explore any secondary data before trying to conduct your own research.

CASE | Finding a Niche in the Golf Apparel Business

Like lots of golf enthusiasts, Linda Hipp loves to golf and played as much as she could. The more she played, though, the less she liked traditional women's golf apparel. Hipp notes that the clothes were mostly baggy shirts and shorts and the colours were bland. Hipp was certain that she could mesh the colours and styles from fashion runways into her own line of golf clothing. She started to do some research on the idea and discovered that a market was emerging for stylish golf clothing. "After doing research, I found that there was a huge upswing in younger women taking up the game and I thought there would be a demand for more fashionable apparel," says Hipp. Based on this market research, Hipp started manufacturing clothing under the brand name Hyp Golf.

Shortly after starting her firm, Hipp started to realize that she was right; there was in fact a significant market for fashionable women's golf clothing. Retailers were signing up to sell her clothes, and that year, Pearl Sinn became the first of many women on the LPGA tour to embrace the brand. "Our customers are women who are fit. They care about what they look like and they care about their health and well-being. They want to look good no matter what they're doing, whether taking kids to school, or out on a golf course or out to dinner."

Hipp, now armed with positive consumer reaction in Canada, started to look south of the border to the U.S. for expansion opportunities. She says, "We started off in Canada. We made sure that, one, we could sell the product, and second, that we could manufacture and provide the goods completely and on time to customers." Hipp admits that she was hesitant to expand into the U.S. as many people advised her against the idea. "I had a lot of people tell me that we shouldn't [enter the U.S. market], that a Canadian company can never make it into the U.S." But Hipp could see the huge potential for her products, especially in the southern states where golf is played 12 months a year.

Rather than rush into the market, Hipp opted to spend considerable time conducting research and planning on the right market-entry strategy. "To mitigate the risk, we spent a lot of time researching and finding the right people, and finding the right two or three markets that had the most potential." Hipp also designed a unique marketing program to help her break into new territories using a three-step approach. The first step is to identify market

© Linda Hipp

influencers in the geographical area, such as golf pros, and provide them with free clothes to create awareness for the brand. The second stage involves securing media coverage by targeting newspapers, radio, television, and Internet companies, providing them with free product and encouraging them to write about the company. The final step involves a manager from head office contacting three to five key accounts and establishing a relationship with them and securing an initial order. Only once a relationship is established with key retailers, along with appropriate demand for the product, does the company find a sales representative to serve the area.

Hyp Golf's entry into the U.S. market has been a huge success, and today the market accounts for more than 75 percent of the company's sales. Hipp has since rebranded her business and product line under the brand LIJA and expanded into yoga, tennis, running, and studio apparel.[109] LIJA has continued to expand globally and has launched its brand into Dubai, the United Arab Emirates, South Africa, and the United Kingdom.

DISCUSSION QUESTIONS

1. What are some of Linda Hipp's strengths as an entrepreneur? Does she have any apparent weaknesses?

2. Why do you think Hipp was advised to avoid the American market? What did she do to ensure that she would be successful?

3. What are some of the advantages and disadvantages of dropping the Hyp Golf name and rebranding her products under the LIJA name?

4. Given the company's success in the U.S., what are some of the advantages of continuing to expand into other countries? What would some of the challenges be?

5. Hyp's original product, fashionable clothes for young female golfers, could be characterized as a niche product. She has now expanded her product line to include products that compete against much larger competitors such as Nike and Lululemon. Why do you think she diversified her product line? Do you think adding new products is a wise strategy?

LEARNING OBJECTIVES

After reading this chapter, you will be able to:

LO1 Define management and explain its role in the achievement of organizational objectives.

LO2 Describe the major functions of management.

LO3 Distinguish among three levels of management and the concerns of managers at each level.

LO4 Specify the skills managers need in order to be successful.

LO5 Summarize the systematic approach to decision making used by many business managers.

DESTINATION CEO

As chief operating officer of social networking phenomenon Facebook, **Sheryl Sandberg** is a powerful woman—so much so that she was listed in *Fortune* as being among the 50 most powerful women in business. She is in charge of controlling Facebook's massive user growth and increasing the site's earning capacity. Thus, the management of Facebook is no easy task. As second in command to CEO Mark Zuckerberg, Sandberg must deal with lawsuits, privacy issues, potential legislation to regulate the collection of user information, the decision over whether to enter China, and more. Sandberg handles all these decisions while maintaining positive relationships with important stakeholders. This makes her the perfect foil for Zuckerberg, who is reputed to lack people skills.

Sandburg's pedigree is impressive—a Harvard graduate with time spent at the World Bank, in Washington, and at Google. At Harvard, she honed her leadership skills by co-founding and leading the group Women in Economics and Government as a way to encourage more women to tackle these male-dominated fields. Sandberg caught the attention of Google, becoming the company's vice president of global online sales and operations. She was hired away by Facebook in 2008. Sandberg is still passionate about supporting women in business, giving speeches and regularly holding Women in Silicon Valley events at her home.

Sandberg announced her next big task: attract more small businesses to Facebook. Under Sandberg's leadership, Facebook unveiled a strategy in which it will offer small companies $50 in advertising credits before starting to charge for ads. She hopes that small businesses will become hooked when they find that marketing through Facebook will help grow their customer base. Known for her down-to-earth, intelligent, and compassionate nature, it may well be Sandberg's passion and openness that have led to her success.[1]

Introduction

For any organization—small or large, for profit or non-profit—to achieve its objectives, it must have equipment and raw materials to turn into products to market, employees to make and sell the products, and financial resources to purchase additional goods and services, pay employees, and generally operate the business. To accomplish this, it must also have one or more managers to plan, organize, staff, direct, and control the work that goes on.

This chapter introduces the field of management. It examines and surveys the various functions, levels, and areas of management in business. The skills that managers need for success and the steps that lead to effective decision making are also discussed.

The Importance of Management

LO1 Define management and explain its role in the achievement of organizational objectives.

Management is a process designed to achieve an organization's objectives by using its resources effectively and efficiently in a changing environment. *Effectively* means having the intended result; *efficiently* means accomplishing the objectives with a minimum of resources. **Managers** make decisions about the use of the organization's resources and are concerned with planning, organizing, staffing, directing, and controlling the organization's activities so as to reach its objectives (see Figure 6.1). When Dani Reiss became CEO of Snow Goose, he made two key decisions that impacted the company's long-term growth. The first was to change the company's name to Canada Goose. The other was to continue to manufacture in Canada at a time when most Canadian garment companies were leaving to produce goods in Asia. Reiss believed the "made in Canada" label could be a major selling point as customers would associate the label to their ideal view of Canada's wilderness. "My whole life was like a focus group," he says. "I realized people had an emotional response to 'made in Canada.' The experience of owning one of these jackets was like trying on a piece of Canada."[2] The result of these two key decisions has been sales upwards of $200 million annually. Management is universal. It takes place not only in businesses of all sizes, but also in government, the military, labour unions, hospitals, schools, and religious groups—any organization requiring the coordination of resources.

Every organization, in the pursuit of its objectives, must acquire resources (people, raw materials and equipment, money, and information) and coordinate their use to turn out a final good or service. Employees are one of the most important resources in helping a business attain its objectives. Successful companies recruit, train, compensate, and provide benefits (such as shares of stock and health insurance) to foster employee loyalty. Acquiring suppliers is another important part of managing resources and in ensuring that products are made available to customers. As firms reach global markets, companies such as Walmart, IKEA, and Dell enlist hundreds of diverse suppliers that provide goods and services to support operations. A good supplier maximizes efficiencies and provides creative solutions to help the company reduce expenses and reach its objectives. Finally, the manager needs adequate financial resources to pay for essential activities. Primary funding comes from owners and shareholders, as well as banks and other financial institutions. Organizations must have adequate resources of all types, and managers must carefully coordinate the use of these resources if they are to achieve the organization's objectives.

> **management** a process designed to achieve an organization's objectives by using its resources effectively and efficiently in a changing environment

> **managers** those individuals in organizations who make decisions about the use of resources and who are concerned with planning, organizing, staffing, directing, and controlling the organization's activities to reach its objectives

> **planning** the process of determining the organization's objectives and deciding how to accomplish them; the first function of management

Management Functions

LO2 Describe the major functions of management.

To harmonize the use of resources so that the business can develop, make, and sell products, managers engage in a series of activities: planning, organizing, staffing, directing, and controlling (Figure 6.1). Although we describe each separately, these five functions are interrelated, and managers may perform two or more of them at the same time.

Planning

Planning, the process of determining the organization's objectives and deciding how to accomplish them, is the first function of management. Planning is a crucial activity, for it designs the map that lays the groundwork for the other functions. It involves

Figure 6.1 The Functions of Management

Managers

Planning	Organizing	Staffing	Directing	Controlling
activities to achieve the organization's objectives	resources and activities to achieve the organization's objectives	the organization with qualified people	employees' activities toward achievement of objectives	the organization's activities to keep it on course

forecasting events and determining the best course of action from a set of options or choices. The plan itself specifies what should be done, by whom, where, when, and how. For example, Canada Goose CEO Dani Reiss was engaged in planning in the above-mentioned example when he opted to keep manufacturing his jackets in Canada. Reiss had a set of choices: He could move manufacturing to Asia and reduce costs, or he could continue to manufacture in Canada at higher costs but use this choice as part of the company's marketing. By making the decision to continue manufacturing in Canada and communicate this to customers, Reiss's plans provided direction to his entire organization. After making one successful decision to keep manufacturing in Canada, Reiss was faced with another decision—whether he should expand his growing company beyond winter jackets. Reiss once again considered his options and decided to start manufacturing spring and fall jackets along with accessories.

Mission.   A **mission**, or mission statement, is a declaration of an organization's fundamental purpose and basic philosophy. It seeks to answer the question: "What business are we in?" Good mission statements are clear and concise statements that explain the organization's reason for existence. A well-developed mission statement, no matter what the industry or size of business, will answer five basic questions:

mission the statement of an organization's fundamental purpose and basic philosophy

1. Who are we?
2. Who are our customers?
3. What is our operating philosophy (basic beliefs, values, ethics, etc.)?
4. What are our core competencies and competitive advantages?
5. What are our responsibilities with respect to being a good steward of environmental, financial, and human resources?

A mission statement that delivers a clear answer to these questions provides the foundation for the development of a strong organizational culture, a good marketing plan, and a coherent business strategy. Sustainable cleaning products company Seventh Generation states that its mission is to "inspire a revolution that nurtures the health of the next seven generations."[3]

Goals.   A goal is the result that a firm wishes to achieve. A company almost always has multiple goals, which illustrates the complex nature of business. A goal has three key components: an attribute sought, such as profits, customer satisfaction, or product quality; a target to be achieved, such as the volume of sales or extent of management training to be achieved; and a time frame, which is the time period in which the goal is to be achieved.

Walmart, for example, set goals of improving its reputation as an environmentally friendly company. Some of its goals involve reducing greenhouse gas emissions, increasing the fuel efficiency of its fleet, and requiring its suppliers to use less packaging. To be successful, company goals should be specific. Walmart planned to improve the fuel efficiency of its truck fleet by 25 percent within a specified time frame. It also implemented systems to measure its progress toward these goals. To be successful at achieving goals, it is necessary to know what is to be achieved, how much, when, and how succeeding at a goal is to be determined.

Objectives.   Objectives are the ends or results desired by an organization; they derive from the organization's mission. A business's objectives may be elaborate or simple. Common objectives relate to profit, competitive advantage, efficiency, and growth. The principal difference between goals and objectives is that objectives are generally stated in such a way that they are measurable. Organizations with profit as an objective want to have money and assets left over after paying off business expenses. Objectives regarding competitive advantage are generally stated in terms of percentage of sales increase and market share, with the goal of increasing those figures. Efficiency objectives involve making the best use of the organization's resources. Dalhousie University has developed energy calculators for small and medium-sized businesses to help them become more aware of their energy usage and to reduce their energy expenditure. Growth objectives relate to an organization's ability to adapt and to get new products to the marketplace in a timely fashion. Objectives provide direction for all managerial decisions; additionally, they establish criteria by which performance can be evaluated.

"Objectives are the ends or results desired by the organization."

Plans.   There are three general types of plans for meeting objectives—strategic, tactical, and operational. A firm's highest managers develop its **strategic plans**, which establish the long-range objectives and overall strategy or course of action by which the firm fulfills its mission and vision statement while attempting to stay true to its values. Strategic plans generally cover periods ranging from two to ten years or even longer. They include plans to add products, purchase companies, sell unprofitable segments of the business, issue stock, and move into international markets. For example, Ford sold its Volvo division to China's Geely automotive group to acquire new resources and increase profits. Strategic plans must take into account the organization's capabilities and resources,

strategic plans those plans that establish the long-range objectives and overall strategy or course of action by which a firm fulfills its mission

the changing business environment, and organizational objectives. Plans should be market-driven, matching customers' desire for value with operational capabilities, processes, and human resources.[4]

Planning is a continuous process that defines the organization's objectives, assesses the internal and external environment, implements the strategy, evaluates the progress, and makes the necessary adjustments to stay on track. Basically, planning answers two fundamental questions:

- Where does the organization want to go?

- How does it get there?

Guided by the business vision, managers then set the financial and strategic objectives. Assessing the environment includes an analysis of the firm, the industry, and the external macroenvironment. A framework that helps to identify the organization's strengths, weaknesses, opportunities, and threats is the SWOT analysis (Figure 6.2).

- *Strengths* are things the company does well or characteristics that give it an important capability—for example, access to unique resources.

- *Weaknesses* are things the company does not have or does poorly, or are conditions where it is at a disadvantage—for example, a deteriorating financial position.

- *Opportunities* are found in the external environment and could potentially be an avenue for growth or a source of competitive advantage—for example, online sales.

- *Threats* are also potentially present in the external environment—for example, future demographic changes that would curtail demand for the product the company sells.

For example, strengths for Tim Hortons could include its profits, brand, and reputation as a respected employer. Weaknesses could include the company's reliance on the Canadian market and its main product, coffee. Under opportunities, there is the potential for global expansion, as well as new products and services or menus. Threats could be changing consumer tastes; price increases of commodities like coffee, sugar, and milk; and the entry of new competition.

Figure 6.2 SWOT Framework

An industry analysis can be performed using a framework known as Porter's five forces, shown in Figure 6.3. This framework evaluates entry barriers, suppliers, customers, substitute products, and industry rivalry. For example, industry rivals for Tim Hortons include other coffee retailers, ranging from local operators to national chains such as McDonald's and Starbucks; while the threat of substitutes is pushing Tim Hortons to develop rival strategies in order to keep up with other expanding fast-food restaurants.[5]

- *Threat of new entrants.* How easy is it for new competitors to enter the market? For example, the Internet has made it easy to enter the publishing industry.

Figure 6.3 Porter's Five Forces Framework

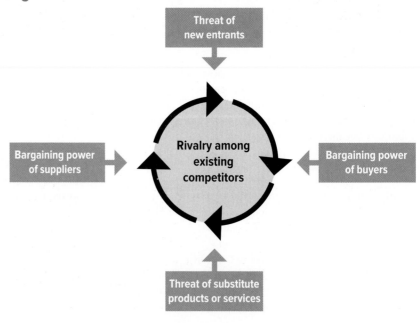

- *Threat of substitutes.* How easy is it for customers to find an alternative to this product or service? For example, there are many substitutes in the soft drinks market.

- *Buyer power.* How strong is the position of buyers? Do they control the market? For example, airlines are very large buyers of jet fuel.

- *Supplier power.* How strong is the position of suppliers? Can they drive up input prices? For example, OPEC can control the supply of oil and oil prices.

- *Rivalry.* Is there strong competition or are there dominant players? For example, the top five suppliers of sugar control 99 percent of market share.[6]

The external macroenvironment can be analyzed using a PEST analysis. A PEST (political, economic, social, technology) analysis is a macro framework for expanding a SWOT analysis to include political and regulatory issues, economic factors, social norms and attitudes as well as demographics, and technological developments. Some organizations expand the PEST analysis to include legal and environmental concerns (PESTEL).[7]

Strategic plans are then developed from the information gathered in the environmental assessment to help the organization keep a competitive advantage over its rivals. A competitive advantage exists when a firm can deliver the same benefits as competitors at a lower cost (cost advantage), or deliver benefits that exceed those of competing products (differentiation advantage). This results in profits that exceed the industry average.[8]

Strategic plans must take into account the organization's capabilities and resources, the changing business environment, and organizational objectives. Plans should be market-driven, matching customers' desire for value with operational capabilities, processes, and human resources.[9]

Tactical plans are short-range plans designed to implement the activities and objectives specified in the strategic plan. These plans, which usually cover a period of one year or less, help keep the organization on the course established in the strategic plan. Because tactical plans permit the organization to react to changes in the environment while continuing to focus on the company's overall strategy, management must periodically review and update them. Declining performance or failure to meet objectives set out in tactical plans may be one reason for revising them. As part of changes to its tactical planning, Cisco made the decision to "slim down" different areas of the company. This included reducing its number of councils (internal committees) to three main ones whose focus will be setting direction for projects rather than engaging in tactical planning. Tactical planning will be more decentralized.[10]

The differences between the two types of planning result in different activities in the short-term versus the long-term. For instance, a strategic plan might include the use of social media to reach consumers. A tactical plan could involve finding ways to increase traffic to the site or promoting premium content to those who visit the site. A fast-paced and ever-changing market requires companies to develop short-run or tactical plans to deal with the changing environment.

A retailing organization with a five-year strategic plan to invest $5 billion in 500 new retail stores may develop

tactical plans short-range plans designed to implement the activities and objectives specified in the strategic plan

---

ENTREPRENEURSHIP IN ACTION | Australis Aquaculture Discovers Sustainable Fish

Josh Goldman

Business: Australis Aquaculture

Founded: 2004, in Turner Falls, Massachusetts

Success: Australis Aquaculture's barramundi fish are sold in 3,000 supermarkets and have been promoted by celebrities such as television show host Dr. Oz and actress Nicole Kidman.

Josh Goldman's goal was to find the perfect fish for aquaculture. Because 32 percent of the world's fish stock is overexploited, aquaculture—or fish farming—may be the key to feeding our growing population. However, aquaculture presents many issues, including water contamination and using wild fish stock to feed farmed fish (many farmed fish are carnivores). Therefore, Goldman developed strict criteria that would ensure sustainable fish of high quality.

He soon found that implementing his criteria would not be easy. For 20 years, Goldman explored fish options with little success. Then in 2000, an entrepreneur introduced him to the Australian fish barramundi. Not only does barramundi thrive in aquaculture, its omnivorous nature allows Goldman to use less than 20 percent of fish meal and oil as feed. Goldman opened Australis Aquaculture in 2004 by creating a vertically integrated fish facility that uses a closed system to reduce waste. As a manager, Goldman has the responsibility of convincing Americans to eat an unfamiliar fish. Yet, so far, demand for barramundi has risen, enabling Australis to expand into Indonesia and Vietnam.[11]

© Dmitriy Shironosov/Shutterstock

Businesses have to rely on contingency plans when disaster strikes.

five tactical plans (each covering one year) specifying how much to spend to set up each new store, where to locate, and when to open each new store. Tactical plans are designed to execute the overall strategic plan. Because of their short-term nature, they are easier to adjust or abandon if changes in the environment or the company's performance so warrant.

Operational plans are very short term and specify what actions specific individuals, work groups, or departments need to accomplish to achieve the tactical plan and ultimately the strategic plan. They may apply to just one month, week, or even day. For example, a work group may be assigned a weekly production quota to ensure there are sufficient products available to elevate market share (tactical goal) and ultimately help the firm be number one in its product category (strategic goal). Returning to our retail store example, operational plans may specify the schedule for opening one new store, hiring new employees, obtaining merchandise, training new employees, and opening for actual business.

Another element of planning is **crisis management or contingency planning**, which deals with potential disasters such as product tampering, oil spills, fire, earthquake, computer viruses, or even a reputation crisis due to unethical or illegal conduct by one or more employees. Unfortunately, many businesses do not have updated contingency plans to handle the types of crises that their companies might encounter. Businesses that have correct and well-thought-out contingency plans tend to respond more effectively when problems occur than do businesses who lack such planning.

operational plans very short-term plans that specify what actions individuals, work groups, or departments need to accomplish in order to achieve the tactical plan and ultimately the strategic plan

crisis management or contingency planning an element in planning that deals with potential disasters such as product tampering, oil spills, fires, earthquakes, computer viruses, or airplane crashes

Many companies, including H. J. Heinz, and Johnson & Johnson, have crisis management teams to deal specifically with problems, permitting other managers to continue to focus on their regular duties. Some companies even hold periodic disaster drills to ensure that their employees know how to respond when a crisis does occur. After the horrific earthquake in Japan, companies in earthquake zones reevaluated their crisis management plans. Crisis management plans generally cover maintaining business operations throughout a crisis and communicating with the public, employees, and officials about the nature of and the company's response to the problem. Communication is especially important to minimize panic and damaging rumors; it also demonstrates that the company is aware of the problem and plans to respond.

Organizing

Rarely are individuals in an organization able to achieve common goals without some form of structure. **Organizing** is the structuring of resources and activities to accomplish objectives in an efficient and effective manner. Managers organize by reviewing plans and determining what activities are necessary to implement them; then, they divide the work into small units and assign it to specific individuals, groups, or departments. As companies reorganize for greater efficiency, more often than not, they are organizing work into teams to handle core processes such as new product development instead of organizing around traditional departments such as marketing and production. Organizing occurs continuously because change is inevitable.

organizing the structuring of resources and activities to accomplish objectives in an efficient and effective manner

Organizing is important for several reasons. It helps create synergy, whereby the effect of a whole system equals more than that of its parts. It also establishes lines of authority, improves communication, helps avoid duplication of resources, and can improve competitiveness by speeding up decision making. When Japanese consumer electronics firm Panasonic decided to reorganize its business, it reduced its workforce, formed overseas alliances to expand into new product areas such as industrial-use solar systems, and stopped investing in less profitable areas. Although eliminating jobs was a difficult move, Panasonic believed that it must reduce redundancies and streamline operations to create a more efficient business.[12] Because organizing is so important, we'll take a closer look at it in Chapter 7.

Staffing

Once managers have determined what work is to be done and how it is to be organized, they must ensure that the organization has enough employees with appropriate skills to do the work. Hiring people to carry out the

staffing the hiring of people to carry out the work of the organization

downsizing the elimination of a significant number of employees from an organization

work of the organization is known as **staffing**. Beyond recruiting people for positions within the firm, managers must determine what skills are needed for specific jobs, how to motivate and train employees to do their assigned jobs, how much to pay employees, what benefits to provide, and how to prepare employees for higher-level jobs in the firm at a later date. These elements of staffing will be explored in detail in Chapters 9 and 10.

Another aspect of staffing is **downsizing**, the elimination of significant numbers of employees from an organization, which has been a pervasive and much-talked-about trend. Staffing can be outsourced to companies that focus on hiring and managing employees. For instance, Adecco Employment Services Limited provides search and staffing services, workforce solutions, and consulting services. Adecco has a network of over 50 branch locations stretching from coast to coast.[13] Many firms downsize by outsourcing production, sales, and technical positions to companies in other countries with lower labour costs. Downsizing has helped numerous firms reduce costs quickly and become more profitable (or become profitable after lengthy losses) in a short period of time. Whether it is called downsizing, right-sizing, trimming the fat, or the new reality in business, the implications of downsizing have been dramatic. During the recessions, many companies lay off workers to cut costs.

Downsizing and outsourcing, however, have painful consequences. Obviously, the biggest casualty is those who lose their jobs, along with their incomes, insurance, and pensions. Some find new jobs quickly; others do not. Another victim is the morale of the employees at downsized firms who get to keep their jobs. Those left behind often feel insecure, angry, and sad, and their productivity

© The McGraw-Hill Companies, Inc./Mark Dierker, photographer

Some companies choose to recruit people to hire through online job websites such as Monster.com. Monster.com is one of the world's largest employment websites. Using websites like Monster.com would fall under the staffing function of management.

may decline as a result, the opposite of the effect sought. Studies have found that firms that lay off more than 10 percent of their surviving workforce can expect to see turnover increase to 15.5 percent versus 10.4 percent at firms that do not have layoffs.[14]

After a downsizing situation, an effective manager will promote optimism and positive thinking and minimize criticism and fault-finding. Management should also build teamwork and encourage positive group discussions. Honest communication is important during a time of change and will lead to trust. Truthfulness about what has happened and also about future expectations is essential.

Directing

Once the organization has been staffed, management must direct the employees. **Directing** is motivating and leading employees to achieve organizational objectives. Good directing involves telling employees what to do and when to do it through the implementation of deadlines, and then encouraging them to do their work. For

directing motivating and leading employees to achieve organizational objectives

example, as a sales manager, you would need to learn how to motivate salespersons, provide leadership, teach sales teams to be responsive to customer needs, and manage organizational issues as well as evaluate sales results. Finally, directing also involves determining and administering appropriate rewards and recognition. All managers are involved in directing, but it is especially important for lower-level managers who interact daily with the employees operating the organization. For example, a front-line manager or foreperson with Suncor, one of Canada's largest oil sands companies, must ensure that the workers know how to use their equipment properly and have the resources needed to carry out their jobs, and must motivate the workers to achieve their expected output.

Managers may motivate employees by providing incentives—such as the promise of a raise or promotion—for them to do a good job. But most workers want more than money from their jobs: They need to know that their employer values their ideas and input. Managers should give younger employees some decision-making authority as soon as possible. Smart managers, therefore, ask workers to contribute ideas for reducing costs, making equipment more efficient, improving customer service, or even developing new products. For example, Travelocity has made employee engagement a top priority to bring customer service to the highest level. This participation makes workers feel important, and the company benefits. Recognition and appreciation are often the best motivators. Employees who understand more about their effect on the financial success of the company may be induced to work harder for that success, and managers who understand the needs and desires of workers can encourage their employees to work harder and more productively. The motivation of employees is discussed in detail in Chapter 9.

"Participation makes workers feel important, and the company benefits."

Controlling

Planning, organizing, staffing, and directing are all important to the success of an organization, whether its objective is earning a profit or something else. But what happens when a firm fails to reach its goals despite a strong planning effort? **Controlling** is the process of evaluating and correcting activities to keep the organization on course. Controlling involves five activities: (1) measuring performance, (2) comparing present performance with standards or objectives, (3) identifying deviations from the standards, (4) investigating the causes of deviations, and (5) taking corrective action when necessary.

controlling the process of evaluating and correcting activities to keep the organization on course

Controlling and planning are closely linked. Planning establishes goals and standards. By monitoring performance and comparing it with standards, managers can determine whether performance is on target. When performance is substandard, management must determine why and take appropriate actions to get the firm back on course. In short, the control function helps managers assess the success of their plans. You might relate this to your performance in this class. If you did not perform as well on early projects or exams, you must take corrective action such as increasing studying or using website resources to achieve your overall objective of getting an A or B in the course. When the outcomes of plans do not meet expectations, the control process facilitates revision of the plans. Control can take many forms such as visual inspections, testing, and statistical modeling processes. The basic idea is to ensure that operations meet requirements and are satisfactory to reach objectives.

The control process also helps managers deal with problems arising outside the firm. For example, if a firm is the subject of negative publicity, management should use the control process to determine why and to guide the firm's response.

Types of Management

LO3 Distinguish among three levels of management and the concerns of managers at each level.

All managers—whether the sole proprietor of a jewellery store or the hundreds of managers of a large company such as the CBC—perform the five functions just discussed. In the case of the jewellery store, the owner

© YURIKO NAKAO/AFP/Getty Images

Interestingly, Mark Zuckerberg is an example of a CEO who does not receive high annual compensation. In 2012, it was announced that Zuckerberg would go from a base salary of $600,000 to an annual pay of just $1 per year.

handles all the functions, but in a large company with more than one manager, responsibilities must be divided and delegated. This division of responsibility is generally achieved by establishing levels of management and areas of specialization—finance, marketing, and so on.

Levels of Management

As we have hinted, many organizations have multiple levels of management—top management, middle management, and first-line, or supervisory management. These levels form a pyramid, as shown in Figure 6.4. As the pyramid shape implies, there are generally more middle managers than top managers, and still more first-line managers. Very small organizations may have only one manager (typically, the owner), who assumes the responsibilities of all three levels. Large businesses have many managers at each level to coordinate the use of the organization's resources. Managers at all three levels perform all five management functions, but the amount of time they spend on each function varies, as we shall see (Figure 6.5).

Top Management. In businesses, **top managers** include the president and other top executives, such as the chief executive officer (CEO), chief financial officer (CFO), and chief operations officer (COO), who have overall responsibility for the organization. For example, Mark Zuckerberg, CEO and founder of Facebook, manages the overall strategic direction of the company and plays a key role in representing the company to stakeholders. Sheryl Sandberg, Facebook's

top managers the president and other top executives of a business, such as the chief executive officer (CEO), chief financial officer (CFO), chief operations officer (COO), and, more recently, chief privacy officer (CPO), who have overall responsibility for the organization

Patagonia founder and owner Yvon Chouinard proves that ethical business practices and product quality can lead to profitability. Founded more than 35 years ago, Patagonia earns more than $300 million in revenue. The company's values are minimalistic and reflect those of a business founded by climbers and surfers.

Patagonia sells durable and eco-friendly outdoor gear and clothing. Its adoption of organic cotton and its recycling efforts are a few of the reasons consumers are loyal. Since the inception of its "cradle to cradle" Common Threads recycling program, most of its products, when they do finally reach the ends of their lifespans, may be returned to Patagonia and made into new products. Chouinard is currently working to create a sustainability index for clothing.

Chouinard sees saving the planet as an ongoing and evolving quest. The decisions that he makes to promote sustainability reinforce the values upon which the company was founded. He recently established the Patagonia Music Collective, a group of more than 100 artists (many of them A-listers) who donate their iTunes fees to various environmental groups. Patagonia takes no cut. Chouinard is also working to implement a new Patagonia food division called Patagonia Provisions. Its first project is partnering with British Columbia fishermen to harvest local wild salmon to be turned into smoked and jerky products under sustainable conditions. Under Yvon Chouinard's strong leadership, Patagonia demonstrates what can happen when high ethical and social standards are maintained.[15]

DISCUSSION QUESTIONS

1. What initiatives has Patagonia taken to promote its value of sustainability?

2. Describe why consumers tend to be more loyal to "green," environmentally friendly companies.

3. Under Yvon Chouinard's leadership, Patagonia launched the Patagonia Music Collective. How does this new venture relate back to the company's green values?

Figure 6.4 Levels of Management

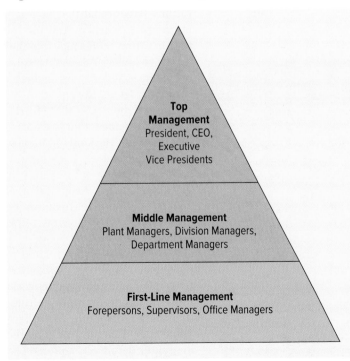

Top Management
President, CEO, Executive Vice Presidents

Middle Management
Plant Managers, Division Managers, Department Managers

First-Line Management
Forepersons, Supervisors, Office Managers

chief operating officer, is responsible for the daily operation of the company. The COO reports to the CEO and is often considered to be number two in command. In public corporations, even chief executive officers such as Bradley Shaw have a boss—the firm's board of directors. With technological advances continuing and privacy concerns increasing, some companies are adding a new top management position—chief privacy officer (CPO). The number of CPOs is expected to rise over the next few years in response to growing concerns about privacy as well as a requirement in the Personal Information Protection and Electronic Documents Act (PIPEDA) that organizations appoint individuals to be accountable for their privacy practices. Among the companies that have appointed CPOs are Bell Canada, CIBC, Nexen, and Rogers Communications.[16] In government, top management refers to the prime minister, a premier, or a mayor or city manager; in education, a chancellor of a university or a school board's superintendent of education.

Top-level managers spend most of their time planning. They make the organization's strategic decisions, decisions that focus on an overall scheme

Figure 6.5 Importance of Management Functions to Managers in Each Level

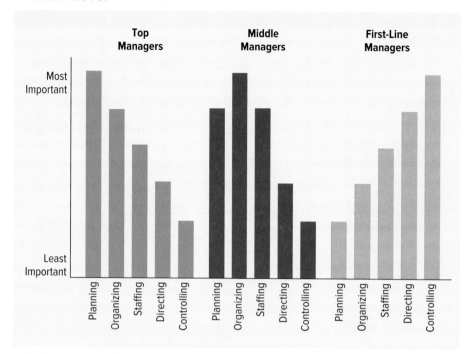

or key idea for using resources to take advantage of opportunities. They decide whether to add products, acquire companies, sell unprofitable business segments, and move into foreign markets. Top managers also represent their company to the public and to government regulators.

Given the importance and range of top management's decisions, top managers generally have many years of varied experience and command top salaries. In addition to salaries, top managers' compensation packages typically include bonuses, long-term incentive awards, stock, and stock options. Table 6.1 lists the ten highest-paid CEOs, including bonuses, stock options, and other compensation. Top management may also get perks and special treatment that is criticized by stakeholders.

Compensation committees are increasingly working with boards of directors and CEOs to attempt to keep pay in line with performance in order to benefit stockholders and key stakeholders. The majority of major companies cite their concern about attracting capable leadership for the CEO and other top executive positions in their organizations. However, many firms are trying to curb criticism of excessive executive compensation by trying to align CEO compensation with performance. In other words, if the company performs poorly, the CEO will not be paid as well. According to a report by the Canadian Centre for Policy Alternatives, the average executive now earns 184 times as much as the average blue-collar worker.[17] Some CEOs, however, limit the level of compensation that they and other top managers can receive to minimize the disparity between the levels of employees and to show social responsibility with respect to their compensation.

Workforce diversity is an important issue in today's corporations. Effective managers at enlightened corporations have found that diversity is good for workers and for the bottom line. Putting together different kinds of people to solve problems often results in better solutions Irene Rosenfeld, CEO of Kraft Foods, said that "fostering a workplace that welcomes diversity of all kinds—perspectives, experiences, backgrounds and cultures—is a proven way to attract and keep talented people and inspire them to do great things."[18] A diverse workforce is better at making decisions regarding issues related to consumer diversity. Managers from companies devoted to workforce diversity devised five rules that make diversity work (see Table 6.2). Diversity is explored in greater detail in Chapter 10.

Table 6.1 The Ten Highest-Paid CEOs

Rank	Name	Organization Name	Total Reported Compensation (millions)
1	John Chen	BlackBerry Ltd	$89.7
2	Donald Walker	Magna International Inc	$23.4
3	Gerald Schwartz	Onex Corporation	$21.1
4	Hunter Harrison	Canadian Pacific Railway Ltd	$17.6
5	Mark Thierer	Catamaran Corp	$16.3
6	Donald Guloien	Manulife Financial Corp	$14.5
7	John Thornton	Barrick Gold Corp	$14.2
8	Paul Wright	Eldorado Gold Corp	$13.8
9	Bradley Shaw	Shaw Communications Inc	$13.3
10	Steven Williams	Suncor Energy Inc	$12.4

Source: Based on Graham F. Scott, "Canada's Top 100 highest-paid CEOs," *Canadian Business*, January 4, 2016, http://www.canadianbusiness.com/lists-and-rankings/richest-people/canadas-top-100-highest-paid-ceos-2016 (accessed January 10, 2016).

Table 6.2 Five Rules of Successful Diversity Recruiting

Rule	Action
1. Get everyone involved.	Educate all employees on the tangible benefits of diversity recruiting to garner support and enthusiasm for those initiatives.
2. Showcase your diversity.	Prospective employees are not likely to become excited about joining your company just because you say that your company is diversity-friendly; they need to see it.
3. Work with diversity groups within your community.	By supporting community-based diversity organizations, your company will generate the priceless word-of-mouth publicity that will lead qualified diversity candidates to your company.
4. Spend money.	If you are serious about diversity recruiting, you will need to spend some money getting your message out to the right places.
5. Sell, sell, sell—and measure your return on investment.	Employers need to sell their company to prospective diversity employees and present them with a convincing case as to why their company is a good fit for the diversity candidate.

Source: Based on Annie Finnigan, "Different Strokes," *Working Woman*, April 2001, pp. 42-48.

Middle Management. Rather than making strategic decisions about the whole organization, **middle managers** are responsible for tactical planning that will implement the general guidelines established by top management. Thus, their responsibility is more narrowly focused than that of top managers. Middle managers are involved in the specific operations of the organization and spend more time organizing than other managers. In business, plant managers, division managers, and department managers make up middle management. The product manager for laundry detergent at a consumer products manufacturer, the department chairperson in a university, and the head of a regional public health department are all middle managers. The ranks of middle managers have been shrinking as more and more companies downsize to be more productive.

First-Line Management. Most people get their first managerial experience as **first-line managers**, those who supervise workers and the daily operations of the organization. They are responsible for implementing the plans established by middle management and directing workers' daily performance on the job. They spend most of their time directing and

> DID YOU KNOW?
>
> Women represent 8.5 percent of executive positions in Canadian companies and just 3 percent are CEOs.[19]

controlling. Common titles for first-line managers are foreperson, supervisor, and office manager.

Areas of Management

At each level, there are managers who specialize in the basic functional areas of business: finance, production and operations, human resources (personnel), marketing, and administration.

Financial Management. **Financial managers** focus on obtaining the money needed for the successful operation of the organization and using that money in accordance with organizational goals. Among the responsibilities of financial managers are projecting income and expenses over a specified period, determining short- and long-term financing needs and finding sources of financing to fill those needs, identifying and selecting appropriate ways to invest extra funds, monitoring the flow of financial resources, and protecting the financial resources of the organization. A financial manager at Ford, for example, may be asked to analyze the costs and revenues of a car model to determine its contribution to Ford's profitability. All organizations must have adequate financial resources to acquire the physical and human resources that are necessary to create goods and services. Consequently, financial resource management is of the utmost importance.

Production and Operations Management. **Production and operations managers** develop and administer the activities involved in transforming resources into goods, services, and ideas ready for the marketplace. Production and operations managers are typically involved in planning and designing production facilities, purchasing raw materials and supplies, managing inventory, scheduling processes to meet demand, and ensuring that products meet quality standards. Because no business can exist without the production of goods and services, production and operations

middle managers those members of an organization responsible for the tactical planning that implements the general guidelines established by top management

first-line managers those who supervise both workers and the daily operations of an organization

financial managers those who focus on obtaining needed funds for the successful operation of an organization and using those funds to further organizational goals

production and operations managers those who develop and administer the activities involved in transforming resources into goods, services, and ideas ready for the marketplace

"Most people get their first managerial experience as first-line managers."

© NAN104/iStockphoto

This financial manager of a city hedge fund analyzes data from financial charts. Financial managers are responsible for obtaining the necessary funding for organizations to succeed, both in the short term and in the long term.

Marketing Management. **Marketing managers** are responsible for planning, pricing, and promoting products and making them available to customers through distribution. The marketing manager who oversees Samsung televisions, for example, must make decisions regarding a new television's size, features, name, price, and packaging, as well as plan what type of stores to distribute the television through and the advertising campaign that will introduce the new television to consumers. The chief marketing officer for Gap Inc. is repositioning the company's clothing lines by focusing on denim as the core product. Its line of 1969 jeans has been positioned as a product that represents Gap's strong heritage in the fashion industry.[20] Within the realm of marketing, there are several areas of specialization: product development and management, pricing, promotion, and distribution. Specific jobs are found in areas such as marketing research, advertising, personal selling, retailing, telemarketing, and Internet marketing.

Information Technology (IT) Management. **Information technology (IT) managers** are responsible for implementing, maintaining, and controlling technology applications in business, such as computer networks. Google, the world's largest online search engine, employs more than 30,000 employees, many of whom are IT managers. Google searches for IT managers and employees who are enthusiastic about their field and Google's products. To keep their engineers motivated, Google allows them to spend up to 20 percent of their time working on personal projects.[21] One major task in IT management is securing computer systems from unauthorized users while making the system easy to use for employees, suppliers, and others

managers are vital to an organization's success. Production can be a complicated process because companies, no matter what the size, must balance different considerations such as cost, performance, extra features, and styling. For example, the Ford Mustang is faster than the Chevrolet Camaro, but it does not handle as well. Both Ford and General Motors face the challenges inherent in producing products that balance high performance and maintaining quality standards in order to gain competitive advantage from their designs, production, and operations excellence. An additional challenge to small companies is to do all these things while remaining profitable.

> "IT managers are also responsible for teaching and helping employees use technology resources efficiently **through training and support.**"

Human Resources Management. **Human resources managers** handle the staffing function and deal with employees in a formalized manner. Once known as personnel managers, they determine an organization's human resource needs; recruit and hire new employees; develop and administer employee benefits, training, and performance appraisal programs; and deal with government regulations concerning employment practices. For example, some companies recognize that their employees' health affects their health care costs. Therefore, more progressive companies provide health care facilities and outside health club memberships, encourage proper nutrition, and discourage smoking in an effort to improve employee health and lower the costs of providing health care benefits.

who have legitimate reason to access the system. Another crucial task is protecting the data, even during a disaster such as a fire. IT managers are also responsible for teaching and helping employees use technology resources efficiently through training and support. At many companies, some aspects of IT management are outsourced to third-party firms that can perform this function expertly and efficiently.

Administrative Management. **Administrative managers** are not specialists; rather they manage an entire business or a major segment of a business. Such managers coordinate the activities of

human resources managers those who handle the staffing function and deal with employees in a formalized manner

marketing managers those who are responsible for planning, pricing, and promoting products and making them available to customers

information technology (IT) managers those who are responsible for implementing, maintaining, and controlling technology applications in business, such as computer networks

administrative managers those who manage an entire business or a major segment of a business; they are not specialists but coordinate the activities of specialized managers

specialized managers, which would include marketing managers, production managers, and financial managers. Because of the broad nature of their responsibilities, administrative managers are often called general managers. However, this does not mean that administrative managers lack expertise in any particular area. Many top executives have risen through the ranks of financial management, production and operations management, or marketing management; but most top managers are actually administrative managers, employing skills in all areas of management.

Skills Needed by Managers

LO4 Specify the skills managers need in order to be successful.

Managers are typically evaluated as to how effective and efficient they are. Managing effectively and efficiently requires certain skills—leadership, technical expertise, conceptual skills, analytical skills, and human relations skills. Table 6.3 describes some of the roles managers may fulfill.

Leadership

Leadership is the ability to influence employees to work toward organizational goals. Strong leaders manage and pay attention to the culture of their organizations and the needs of their customers. Table 6.4 offers some tips for successful leadership while Table 6.5 lists the world's ten most admired companies and their CEOs. The list is compiled annually for *Fortune* magazine by executives and analysts who grade companies according to nine attributes, including quality of management.

Managers often can be classified into three types based on their leadership style. *Autocratic leaders* make all the decisions and then tell employees what must be done and how to do it. They generally use their authority and economic rewards to get employees to comply with their directions. Martha Stewart is an example of an autocratic leader. She built up her media empire by paying close attention to every detail.[22] *Democratic leaders* involve their employees in decisions. The manager presents a situation and encourages his or her subordinates to express

leadership the ability to influence employees to work toward organizational goals

Table 6.3 Managerial Roles

Type of Role	Specific Role	Examples of Role Activities
Decisional	Entrepreneur	Commit organizational resources to develop innovative goods and services; decide to expand internationally to obtain new customers for the organization's products
	Disturbance handler	Move quickly to take corrective action to deal with unexpected problems facing the organization from the external environment, such as a crisis like an oil spill, or from the internal environment, such as producing faulty goods or services
	Resource allocator	Allocate organizational resources among different functions and departments of the organization; set budgets and salaries of middle and first-level managers
	Negotiator	Work with suppliers, distributors, and labour unions to reach agreements about the quality and price of input, technical, and human resources; work with other organizations to establish agreements to pool resources to work on joint projects
Informational	Monitor	Evaluate the performance of managers in different functions and take corrective action to improve their performance; watch for changes occurring in the external and internal environment that may affect the organization in the future
	Disseminator	Inform employees about changes taking place in the external and internal environment that will affect them and the organization; communicate to employees the organization's vision and purpose
	Spokesperson	Launch a national advertising campaign to promote new goods and services; give a speech to inform the local community about the organization's future intentions
Interpersonal	Figurehead	Outline future organizational goals to employees at company meetings; open a new corporate headquarters building; state the organization's ethical guidelines and the principles of behaviour employees are to follow in their dealings with customers and suppliers
	Leader	Provide an example for employees to follow; give direct commands and orders to subordinates; make decisions concerning the use of human and technical resources; mobilize employee support for specific organizational goals
	Liaison	Coordinate the work of managers in different departments; establish alliances between different organizations to share resources to produce new goods and services

Source: Based on Gareth R. Jones and Jennifer M. George, *Essentials of Contemporary Management* (Burr Ridge, IL: McGraw-Hill/Irwin, 2004), p. 14.

Table 6.4 Seven Tips for Successful Leadership

- Build effective and responsive interpersonal relationships.
- Communicate effectively—in person, print, e-mail, etc.
- Build the team and enable employees to collaborate effectively.
- Understand the financial aspects of the business.
- Know how to create an environment in which people experience positive morale and recognition.
- Lead by example.
- Help people grow and develop.

Source: Based on Susan M. Heathfield, "Seven Tips About Successful Management," About.com, http://humanresources.about.com/cs/managementissues/qt/mgmtsuccess.htm (accessed February 25, 2010).

Table 6.5 Canada's Most Admired Corporate Cultures (Enterprise - 2015)

Cineplex
GoodLife Fitness
Longos
Loyalty One
Manulife
National Leasing
OpenText
PCL Construction
Telus
WestJet

Source: Based on "Canada's 10 Most Admired Corporate Cultures Winners List, Enterprise - 2015," Canada's Most Admired website, n.d., http://www.canadasmostadmired.com/full-winners.html (accessed January 10, 2016).

© Jen Grantham/iStock

A product mishap with pants led to the resignation of Lululemon CEO Christine Day.

> ## "Employees who have been involved in decision making generally require less supervision than those not similarly involved."

opinions and contribute ideas. The manager then considers the employees' points of view and makes the decision. Clive Beddoe, co-founder of WestJet Airlines, had a democratic leadership style. Under his leadership, employees were encouraged to discuss concerns and provide input. *Free-rein leaders* let their employees work without much interference. The manager sets performance standards and allows employees to find their own ways to meet them. For this style to be effective, employees must know what the standards are, and they must be motivated to attain them. The free-rein style of leadership can be a powerful motivator because it demonstrates a great deal of trust and confidence in the employee. Larry Page, CEO and co-founder of Google, exhibits free-rein leadership among employees, who are encouraged to pursue any and all ideas.

The effectiveness of the autocratic, democratic, and free-rein styles depends on several factors. One consideration is the type of employees. An autocratic style of leadership is generally needed to stimulate unskilled, unmotivated employees; highly skilled, trained, and motivated employees may respond better to democratic or free-rein leaders. Employees who have been involved in decision making generally require less supervision than those not similarly involved. Other considerations are the manager's abilities and the situation itself. When a situation requires quick decisions, an autocratic style of leadership may be best because the manager does not have to consider input from a lot of people. If a special task force must be set up to solve a quality-control problem, a normally democratic manager may give free rein to the task force. Many managers, however, are unable to use more than one style of leadership. Some are unable to allow their subordinates to participate in decision making, let alone make any decisions. Thus, what leadership style is "best" depends on specific circumstances, and effective managers strive to adapt their leadership style as circumstances warrant. Many organizations offer programs to develop leadership skills. When plans fail, very often leaders are held responsible for what goes wrong. For example, Lululemon chief product officer Sheree Waterson and chief executive officer Christine Day left the company following a product mishap with Lululemon pants.[23]

Technical Expertise

Managers need **technical expertise**, the specialized knowledge and training needed to perform jobs that are related to their area of

technical expertise the specialized knowledge and training needed to perform jobs that are related to particular areas of management

management. Accounting managers need to be able to perform accounting jobs, and production managers need to be able to perform production jobs. Although a production manager may not actually perform a job, he or she needs technical expertise to train employees, answer questions, provide guidance, and solve problems. Technical skills are most needed by first-line managers and least critical to top-level managers.

Today, most organizations rely on computers to perform routine data processing, simplify complex calculations, organize and maintain vast amounts of information to communicate, and help managers make sound decisions. For this reason, most managers have found computer expertise to be an essential skill.

Conceptual Skills

Conceptual skills, the ability to think in abstract terms, and to see how parts fit together to form the whole, are needed by all managers, but particularly top-level managers. Top management must be able to evaluate continually where the company will be in the future. Conceptual skills also involve the ability to think creatively. Recent scientific research has revealed that creative thinking, which is behind the development of many innovative products and ideas, including fibre optics and compact disks, can be learned. As a result, top firms hire creative consultants to teach their managers how to think creatively.

conceptual skills the ability to think in abstract terms and to see how parts fit together to form the whole

Consider the Following: CEO Leads Rona's Recovery

Rona, the 500-store national chain of hardware, garden, and home-renovation centres, had not seen an improvement in same store sales in several years. A poorly managed expansion plan had resulted in five consecutive years of declining revenues, even as the larger market grew. In 2013, in an attempt to revitalize the company, a new CEO joined the team.

Robert Sawyer turned things around. By 2015, this driven CEO had raised sales 5.4 percent in same store sales and net income by 19 percent—the largest increase in more than three years. The company is also getting back into growth mode, opening seven stores in 2015 and planning for 10 more in 2016.

Although Sawyer never attended university, he seemed destined for a career in retail. At 14, he delivered beer and groceries on his bike for a corner store in Montreal, where he grew up. He started working for Steinberg's catalogue distribution business at age 16, and by 19, he was foreman of one of its warehouses. He moved on to Metro in 1979, as director of a fruit and vegetable warehouse, and rose through the ranks of the Montreal-based grocer. Those who have worked with him view him as very direct and demanding. "With him, you always know where you are headed. There are no grey zones: It's either white or it's black," says Christian Bourbonnière, Metro's first vice-president, Quebec division. "He is demanding to the extreme."

In approaching the issues facing Rona, Sawyer took the simple path. Under his leadership, the company cut 375 administrative positions, closed 11 unprofitable stores, sold most of its commercial and professional market division, shaved $110 million from expenses, and developed separate business plans for the four divisions. Sawyer took over just as the job and housing markets were slowing. "If you don't know where to cut, I'm giving you two weeks," he told his new team.

But it wasn't all about cutting costs. Sawyer also searched for where he could invest to help Rona achieve some wins. He focused on underperforming assets in Quebec, as well as a poorly executed integration of Totem Building Supplies in Calgary. The real focus has been on Réno-Dépôt, one of the company's banners in Quebec, which expanded its seasonal merchandise and put a greater emphasis on big-ticket, high-end products. Even parking spaces were widened to better accommodate trucks driven by contractors—Réno-Dépôt's primary customers.

In 2015, two years after taking the helm at Rona, Sawyer was named Top Turnaround CEO of the Year by *Canadian Business* magazine. In 2016, Lowe's Canada took control of Rona in a friendly takeover bid. Robert Sawyer, who departed after the $3.2 billion transaction, gained more than $22 million from his equity holdings in Rona.[24]

DISCUSSION QUESTIONS

1. How was Sawyer a strong leader in helping Rona's recovery?

2. What areas of management do you think Sawyer emphasized in his attempt to re-establish Rona as a leader in home improvement products ?

3. What are the challenges for a new CEO when trying to ensure a company such as Rona continues to stay successful?

Analytical Skills

Analytical skills refer to the ability to identify relevant issues and recognize their importance, understand the relationships between them, and perceive the underlying causes of a situation. When managers have identified critical factors and causes, they can take appropriate action. All managers need to think logically, but this skill is probably most important to the success of top-level managers. To be analytical, it is necessary to think about a broad range of issues and to weigh different options before taking action. Because analytical skills are so important, questions that require analytical skills are often a part of job interviews. Questions such as "Tell me how you would resolve a problem at work if you had access to a large amount of data?" may be part of the interview process. The answer would require the interviewee to try to explain how to sort data to find relevant facts that could resolve the issue. Analytical thinking is required in complex or difficult situations where the solution is often not clear. Resolving ethical issues often requires analytical skills.

analytical skills the ability to identify relevant issues, recognize their importance, understand the relationships between them, and perceive the underlying causes of a situation

human relations skills the ability to deal with people, both inside and outside the organization

Human Relations Skills

People skills, or **human relations skills**, are the ability to deal with people, both inside and outside the organization. Those who can relate to others, communicate well with others, understand the needs of others, and show a true appreciation for others are generally more successful than managers who lack human relations skills. People skills are especially important in hospitals, airline companies, banks, and other organizations that provide services. For example, Westjet's motto is "We succeed because I care." The company believes that highly engaged employees, or in its case, owners, will go above and beyond to provide a truly memorable experience. Its strategy has earned WestJet a spot alongside only five other companies in Canada's Most Admired Corporate Cultures Hall of Fame, J.D. Power has recognized it as a customer service champion, and it is one of the most profitable airlines in North America.[25]

Where Do Managers Come From?

Good managers are not born; they are made. An organization acquires managers in three ways: promoting employees from within, hiring managers from other organizations, and hiring managers who have recently graduated.

Promoting people within the organization into management positions tends to increase motivation by showing

© Compassionate Eye Foundation/Getty Images

WestJet Airlines has been able to successfully differentiate itself from its competitors by way of no-frills and low-price fares. But WestJet also is known for its human relations skills. Jovial flight crews often crack jokes over the intercom system to their captive audiences.

employees that those who work hard and are competent can advance in the company. Internal promotion also provides managers who are already familiar with the company's goals and problems. Procter & Gamble prefers to promote managers from within, which creates managers who are familiar with the company's products and policies and builds company loyalty. Promoting from within, however, can lead to problems: It may limit innovation. The new manager may continue the practices and policies of previous managers. Thus it is vital for companies—even companies committed to promotion from within—to hire outside people from time to time to bring fresh ideas to the table.

"Good managers are not born; they are made."

Finding managers with the skills, knowledge, and experience required to run an organization or department is sometimes difficult. Specialized executive employment agencies—sometimes called headhunters, recruiting managers, or executive search firms—can help locate candidates from other companies. The downside is that even though outside people can bring fresh ideas to a company, hiring them may cause resentment among existing employees as well as involve greater expense in relocating an individual to another city or province.

Colleges and universities provide a large pool of potential managers, and entry-level applicants can be screened for their developmental potential. People with specialized management skills, such as those with an MBA (master of business administration) degree, may be good candidates. Business students in the twenty-first century must remain flexible during their job searches. Before applying for a job, graduates should understand the company, the people, and the company's core values to ascertain whether they would be a good fit. Students may not have the exact skills for which the company is searching, but if they fit well with the culture, they can be trained.

On-the-job training and socialization can help new recruits achieve success in their position and can help them reach their objectives. Finding employees who are trainable and a good fit with corporate culture means that organizations have a workforce staffed with potential future managers. Businesses that are recovering from the most recent economic recession should be willing to embrace new ideas and new employees willing to undergo change.

Figure 6.6 Steps in the Decision-Making Process

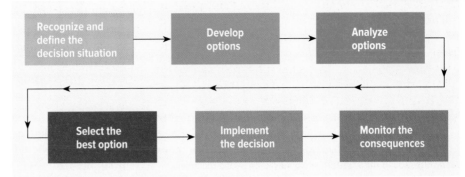

Decision Making

LO5   Summarize the systematic approach to decision making used by many business managers.

Managers make many different kinds of decisions, such as what office hours to set, which employees to hire, what products to introduce, and what price to charge for a product. Decision making is important in all management functions at all levels, whether the decisions are on a strategic, tactical, or operational level. A systematic approach using these six steps usually leads to more effective decision making: (1) recognizing and defining the decision situation, (2) developing options to resolve the situation, (3) analyzing the options, (4) selecting the best option, (5) implementing the decision, and (6) monitoring the consequences of the decision (Figure 6.6).

RESPONDING TO BUSINESS CHALLENGES | Managers and Employees See Different Corporate Cultures

Many top managers believe that their organizations have values-based cultures in which employees can grow and make ethical decisions. However, employees disagree. In a recent study of the American workplace, 43 percent of employee respondents described the workplace as "command-and-control" or "top-down management." This indicates a management style in which the top managers make the rules and employees follow them. However, employers were eight times more likely to respond that their organizations allow employees to make decisions based upon organizational values, thus contributing to a values-based organizational culture.

In a traditional top-down chain of command, managers perform most of the planning, organizing, and directing functions of the firm. However, as views toward management change and employees are expected to take on greater roles, stakeholders are advocating for a self-governance approach. Such an approach calls for employee engagement, a greater emphasis on employee well-being, and the adoption of a culture that inspires through values rather than strictly rules. Additionally, managers must look beyond the bottom line when providing rewards.

The good news is that managers are recognizing the benefits of this system. The bad news is that according to employees, managers are not successfully implementing this new management style. Better communication is needed to understand employee concerns, disseminate corporate values throughout the company, and create an incentives system that rewards the successful practice of these values in the workplace.[26]

DISCUSSION QUESTIONS

1. How does a values-based culture differ from a top-down chain of command?

2. Why do you think more managers want to adopt a values-based corporate culture?

3. How can managers make sure that they are successfully implementing a values-based managerial approach?

© Aaron M. Sprecher/Bloomberg via Getty Images

General Electric's excellent managerial training programs are renowned around the world. The company knows good managers aren't born. They are made.

Recognizing and Defining the Decision Situation

The first step in decision making is recognizing and defining the situation. The situation may be negative—for example, huge losses on a particular product—or positive—for example, an opportunity to increase sales.

Situations calling for small-scale decisions often occur without warning. Situations requiring large-scale decisions, however, generally occur after some warning signals. Effective managers pay attention to such signals. Declining profits, small-scale losses in previous years, inventory buildup, and retailers' unwillingness to stock a product are signals that may warn of huge losses to come. If managers pay attention to such signals, problems can be contained.

Once a situation has been recognized, management must define it. Huge losses reveal a problem—for example, a failing product. One manager may define the situation as a product quality problem; another may define it as a change in consumer preference. These two definitions may lead to vastly different solutions to the problem. The first manager, for example, may seek new sources of raw materials of better quality. The second manager may believe that the product has reached the end of its lifespan and decide to discontinue it. This example emphasizes the importance of carefully defining the problem rather than jumping to conclusions.

Developing Options

Once the decision situation has been recognized and defined, the next step is to develop a list of possible courses of action. The best lists include both standard courses of action and creative ones. As a general rule, more time and expertise are devoted to the development stage of decision making when the decision is of major importance. When the decision is of lesser importance, less time and expertise will be spent on this stage. Options may be developed individually, by teams, or through analysis of similar situations in comparable

organizations. Creativity is a very important part of selecting the best option. Creativity depends on new and useful ideas, regardless of where the idea originates or the method used to create the ideas. The best option can range from a required solution to an identified problem to a volunteered solution to an observed problem by an outside work group member.[27]

Analyzing Options

After developing a list of possible courses of action, management should analyze the practicality and appropriateness of each option. An option may be deemed impractical because of a lack of financial resources to implement it, legal restrictions, ethical and social responsibility considerations, authority constraints, technological constraints, economic limitations, or simply a lack of information and expertise to implement the option. For example, a small computer manufacturer may recognize an opportunity to introduce a new type of computer but lack the financial resources to do so. Other options may be more practical for the computer company: It may consider selling its technology to another computer company that has adequate resources or it may allow itself to be purchased by a larger company that can introduce the new technology.

> "After developing a list of possible courses of action, management should analyze the practicality and appropriateness of each option."

When assessing appropriateness, the decision maker should consider whether the proposed option adequately addresses the situation. When analyzing the consequences

© The McGraw-Hill Companies, Inc./Mark Dierker, photographer

Technology such as the BlackBerry smartphone can help managers maintain an agenda, analyze options, and aid in decision making.

of an option, managers should consider the impact the option will have on the situation and on the organization as a whole. For example, when considering a price cut to boost sales, management must consider the consequences of the action on the organization's cash flow and consumers' reaction to the price change.

Selecting the Best Option

When all courses of action have been analyzed, management must select the best one. Selection is often a subjective procedure because many situations do not lend themselves to mathematical analysis. Of course, it is not always necessary to select only one option and reject all others; it may be possible to select and use a combination of several options.

Implementing the Decision

To deal with the situation at hand, the selected option or options must be put into action. Implementation can be fairly simple or very complex, depending on the nature of the decision. Effective implementation of a decision to abandon a product, close a plant, purchase a new business, or something similar requires planning. For example, when a product is dropped, managers must decide how to handle distributors and customers and what to do with the idle production facility. Additionally, they should anticipate resistance from people within the organization (people tend to resist change because they fear the unknown). Finally, management should be ready to deal with the unexpected consequences. No matter how well planned implementation is, unforeseen problems will arise. Management must be ready to address these situations when they occur.

Monitoring the Consequences

After managers have implemented the decision, they must determine whether the decision has accomplished the desired result. Without proper monitoring, the consequences of decisions may not be known quickly enough to make efficient changes. If the desired result is achieved, management can reasonably conclude that it made a good decision. If the desired result is not achieved, further analysis is warranted. Was the decision simply wrong, or did the situation change? Should some other option have been implemented?

If the desired result is not achieved, management may discover that the situation was incorrectly defined from the beginning. That may require starting the decision-making process all over again. Finally, management may determine that the decision was good even though the desired results have not yet shown up or it may determine a flaw in the decision's implementation. In the latter case, management would not change the decision but would change the way in which it was implemented.

The Reality of Management

Management is not a cut-and-dried process. There is no mathematical formula for managing an organization, although many managers passionately wish for one! Management is a widely varying process for achieving organizational goals. Managers plan, organize, staff, direct, and control, but management expert John P. Kotter says even these functions can be boiled down to two basic activities:

1. Figuring out what to do despite uncertainty, great diversity, and an enormous amount of potentially relevant information, and

2. Getting things done through a large and diverse set of people despite having little direct control over most of them.[28]

Managers spend as much as 75 percent of their time working with others—not only with subordinates but with bosses, people outside their hierarchy at work, and people outside the organization itself. In these interactions they discuss anything and everything remotely connected with their business.

> ### "Managers spend a lot of time establishing and updating an agenda of goals and plans for carrying out their responsibilities."

Managers spend a lot of time establishing and updating an agenda of goals and plans for carrying out their responsibilities. An **agenda** contains both specific and vague items, covering short-term goals and long-term objectives. Like a calendar, an agenda helps the manager figure out what must be done and how to get it done to meet the objectives set by the organization. Technology tools such as personal digital assistants (PDAs) can help managers manage their agendas, contacts, and time.

Managers also spend a lot of time **networking**— building relationships and sharing information with colleagues who can help them achieve the items on their agendas. Managers spend much of their time communicating with a variety of people and participating in activities that on the surface do not seem to have much to do with the goals of their organization. Nevertheless, these activities are crucial to getting the job done. Networks are

agenda a calendar, containing both specific and vague items, that covers short-term goals and long-term objectives

networking the building of relationships and sharing of information with colleagues who can help managers achieve the items on their agendas

not limited to immediate subordinates and bosses; they include other people in the company as well as customers, suppliers, and friends. These contacts provide managers with information and advice on diverse topics. Managers ask, persuade, and even intimidate members of their network in order to get information and to get things done. Networking helps managers carry out their responsibilities. Social media sites have increased the ability of both managers and subordinates to network. Internal social networks allow employees to connect with one another, while social networks such as Facebook or Twitter enable managers to connect with customers. Sales managers are even using social networks to communicate with their distributors. LinkedIn has been used for job networking and is gaining in popularity among the younger generation as an alternative to traditional job hunting. Some speculate that social networks might eventually replace traditional résumés and job boards.[29]

Finally, managers spend a great deal of time confronting the complex and difficult challenges of the business world today. Some of these challenges relate to rapidly changing technology (especially in production and information processing), increased scrutiny of individual and corporate ethics and social responsibility, the changing nature of the workforce, new laws and regulations, increased global competition and more challenging

© JuliusKielaitis/Shutterstock.com

Websites like LinkedIn are helping managers and employees network with one another to achieve their professional goals.

foreign markets, declining educational standards (which may limit the skills and knowledge of the future labour and customer pool), and time itself—that is, making the best use of it. But such diverse issues cannot simply be plugged into a computer program that supplies correct, easy-to-apply solutions. It is only through creativity and imagination that managers can make effective decisions that benefit their organizations.

TEAM EXERCISE

Form groups and research examples of crisis management implementation for companies dealing with natural disasters (explosions, fires, earthquakes, etc.), technology disasters (viruses, plane crashes, compromised customer data, etc.) or ethical or legal disasters. How did these companies communicate with key stakeholders? What measures did the company take to provide support to those involved in the crisis? Report your findings to the class.

LEARNING OBJECTIVES SUMMARY

LO1 Define management and explain its role in the achievement of organizational objectives.

Management is a process designed to achieve an organization's objectives by using its resources effectively and efficiently in a changing environment. Managers make decisions about the use of the organization's resources and are concerned with planning, organizing, staffing, directing, and controlling the organization's activities so as to reach its objectives.

LO2 Describe the major functions of management.

Planning is the process of determining the organization's objectives and deciding how to accomplish them.

Organizing is the structuring of resources and activities to accomplish those objectives efficiently and effectively. Staffing obtains people with the necessary skills to carry out the work of the company. Directing is motivating and leading employees to achieve organizational objectives. Controlling is the process of evaluating and correcting activities to keep the organization on course.

LO3 Distinguish among three levels of management and the concerns of managers at each level.

Top management is responsible for the whole organization and focuses primarily on strategic planning. Middle management develops plans for specific operating areas and carries out the general guidelines set by top management. First-line, or supervisory, management supervises the workers and day-to-day operations. Managers can also be categorized as to their area of responsibility: finance, production and operations, human resources, marketing, or administration.

LO4 Specify the skills managers need in order to be successful.

To be successful, managers need leadership skills (the ability to influence employees to work toward organizational goals), technical expertise (the specialized knowledge and training needed to perform a job), conceptual skills (the ability to think in abstract terms and see how parts fit together to form the whole), analytical skills (the ability to identify relevant issues and recognize their importance, understand the relationships between issues, and perceive the underlying causes of a situation), and human relations (people) skills.

LO5 Summarize the systematic approach to decision making used by many business managers.

A systematic approach to decision making follows these steps: recognizing and defining the situation, developing options, analyzing options, selecting the best option, implementing the decision, and monitoring the consequences.

KEY TERMS

administrative managers
agenda
analytical skills
conceptual skills
controlling
crisis management or contingency planning
directing
downsizing
financial managers
first-line managers
human relations skills
human resources managers
information technology (IT) managers
leadership
management

managers
marketing managers
middle managers
mission
networking
operational plans
organizing
planning
production and operations managers
staffing
strategic plans
tactical plans
technical expertise
top managers

DESTINATION CEO DISCUSSION QUESTIONS

1. Why is Sheryl Sandberg's job as chief operating officer so important?

2. How do you think that Sandberg's job as a Google executive prepared her to help run Facebook?

3. Why do you think Facebook is trying to attract small businesses?

SO YOU WANT TO BE *a Manager: What Kind?*

Managers are needed in a wide variety of organizations. Experts suggest that employment will increase by millions of jobs by 2016. But the requirements for the jobs become more demanding with every passing year—with the speed of technology and communication increasing by the day, and the stress of global commerce increasing pressures to perform. However, if you like a challenge and if you have the right kind of personality, management remains a viable field. Even as companies are forced to restructure, management remains a vital role in business.

Salaries for managerial positions remain strong overall. While pay can vary significantly depending on your level of experience, the firm where you work, and the province where you live.

In short, if you want to be a manager, there are opportunities in almost every field. There may be fewer middle management positions available in firms, but managers remain a vital part of most industries and will continue to be long into the future—especially as navigating global business becomes ever more complex.

BUILD YOUR BUSINESS PLAN

The Nature of Management

The first thing you need to be thinking about is "What is the mission of your business? What is the shared vision your team members have for this business? How do you know if there is demand for this particular business?" Remember, you need to think about the customer's *ability and willingness* to try this particular product.

Think about the various processes or stages of your business in the creation and selling of your product or service. What functions need to be performed for these processes to be completed? These functions might include buying, receiving, selling, customer service, and/or merchandising.

Operationally, if you are opening up a retail establishment, how do you plan to provide your customers with superior customer service? What hours will your customers expect you to be open? At this point in time, how many employees are you thinking you will need to run your business? Do you (or one of your partners) need to be there all the time to supervise?

CASE | Lululemon Practises Crisis Management and Perhaps Marketing All at the Same Time

Lululemon, the Burnaby, British Columbia–based, North American retailer of yoga clothes, engaged in a massive recall of its "Luon" yoga pants in 2013, after determining the pants were too sheer. According to the company, "The ingredients, weight and longevity qualities of the women's black Luon bottoms remain the same but the coverage does not, resulting in a level of sheerness in some of our women's black Luon bottoms that falls short of our very high standards." The recalled pants accounted for 17 percent of all women's pants in the stores, and resulted in a $67 milllion loss and shaved 6 percent off the stock price.

Lululemon, rather than just pulling the pants from store shelves, issued a number of press releases about the recall and produced a lengthy FAQ on its website. CEO Christine Day said that while regretting the inconvenience, the recall was necessary to protect "the quality of our fabrics." In a press release she also stated, "We will accept nothing less than the very highest quality we are known for." Lululemon appears to be following sound public relations advice as it has communicated openly with the public and has offered customers who bought the pants a full refund.[30]

Some marketing and public relations experts have even considered that Lululemon may be pushing the story as a way to garner free publicity from what others would classify as a problem. The story was covered by all major media outlets throughout North America and received in-depth TV coverage for what would be considered a relatively simple recall by a company. In 2015, Lululemon went on to recall more than 318,000 women's tops due to dangerous hoodie drawstrings. Many experts agree that the recalls don't hurt the brand with its target market. For example, Simon Fraser University marketing professor Lindsay Meredith said a recall that ties the company to revealing clothing would do nothing to hurt the Lululemon brand with its target market—women aged 18 to 35.[31]

The recall story went "viral" on the Internet, receiving coverage from almost every online source of news, and people have been discussing the "Luon" pants on Twitter, Facebook, YouTube, and various other social media sites. Front and centre in most news stories is a quote or two from the company, bringing attention to the high quality of its products and its desire to offer consumers nothing but the best. These news stories often end with some company information stating how successful the retailer has been, the number of stores it has in North America, and that business analysts see this recall as just a blip.

DISCUSSION QUESTIONS

1. Do you think the recall damaged the image of the store with consumers?

2. After reading the chapter, especially the sections on contingency planning and crisis management, do you think Lululemon should have recalled the pants quietly? Why or why not?

3. Do you think it is possible that Lululemon turned the recall into an opportunity for free publicity which will benefit the company in the long run? What are the pros and cons associated with doing this?

DESTINATION CEO

When **Galen G. Weston** took over his family's Loblaw Cos. Ltd. grocery chain in 2006, at the age of 33, he also took on an obligation to restore value to a good company that had lost its way. Galen utilized centralized authority and crafted a restructuring strategy that scaled back the company's lineup of non-food products. His main objectives have been a greater assortment of foods to attract customers, an improved customer experience, and lower costs. To achieve those goals, the company cut 700 jobs, or approximately 10 percent of its head office and administrative staff, and spent more than $2 billion making its technology and supply chains more efficient.

Under Galen's leadership, his team adopted a business model designed to strengthen its brand and to position itself for growth. To do so, a number of strategic decisions were undertaken, including moving into the higher-margin clothing business, introducing the Joe Fresh clothing line; strengthening the President's Choice (PC) brand; developing organic foods under the PC umbrella; and engineering a takeover of Shoppers Drug Mart. The company also introduced a number of environmentally and socially responsible initiatives, including charging for plastic grocery bags, selling reusable cloth grocery bags, and being the first grocery chain to have unsold produce converted into energy. What sets the company apart is its ability to pounce on consumer trends early and its willingness to spend big to see its concepts through.

The 96-year-old grocery store was named one of Canada's Most Innovative Companies in 2015, which shows that companies don't have to be young to hatch new ideas.[1]

Introduction

An organization's structure determines how well it makes decisions and responds to problems, and influences employees' attitudes toward their work. Even companies that operate within the same industry may utilize different organizational structures. For example, in the medical device industry, 3M is organized by line of business (health care products, office products, security tools), whereas Medtronic has similar business groups, but it also has top-level, functional units that focus on legal issues, strategy, and human resources operating above each of the lines of business.[2]

Because a business's structure can so profoundly affect its success, this chapter will examine organizational structure in detail. First, we discuss how an organization's culture affects its operations. Then we consider the development of structure, including how tasks and responsibilities are organized through specialization and departmentalization. Next, we explore some of the forms organizational structure may take. Finally, we consider communication within business.

Organizational Culture

One of the most important aspects of organizing a business is determining its **organizational culture**, a firm's shared values, beliefs, traditions, philosophies, rules, and role models for behaviour. Also called corporate culture, an organizational culture exists in every organization, regardless of size, organizational type, product, or profit objective. A firm's culture may be expressed formally through its mission statement, codes of ethics, memos, manuals, and ceremonies, but it is more commonly expressed informally. Examples of informal expressions of culture include dress codes (or the lack thereof), work habits, extracurricular activities, and stories. Employees often learn the accepted standards through discussions with co-workers.

organizational culture
a firm's shared values, beliefs, traditions, philosophies, rules, and role models for behaviour

TOMS Shoes' organizational culture is determined by the founder's desire to provide as many shoes as possible to children in developing countries (where shoeless children walk for miles to get water, food, and medical care). Blake Mycoskie gives hundreds of thousands of shoes to children around the world each year, creating a strong organizational culture of giving back and corporate social responsibility. His company operates with a program that for every shoe purchased, a shoe will be donated to children in need.[3] Disneyland/Disney World and McDonald's have organizational cultures focused on cleanliness, value, and service. The company Zappos.com created a culture of "fun and a little weirdness." Zappos has a flexible work environment with very few rules, and employees are encouraged to socialize and engage in unique activities (such as ringing cowbells when visitors arrive). Zappos' goal is to make both employees and customers feel good. Customer service is such a must at Zappos that new hires must work for one month at a call centre, even if the new employees are not going to be interacting with customers normally.[4] When such values and philosophies are shared by all members of an organization, they will be expressed in its relationships with stakeholders. However, organizational cultures that lack such positive values may result in employees who are unproductive and indifferent and have poor attitudes, which will be reflected externally to customers. The corporate culture may have contributed to the misconduct at a number of well-known companies. A survey found that executives in financial and technology companies are mostly cutthroat in collecting intelligence about competition, creating a corporate culture in which unethical acts might be tolerated if it means beating the competition.[5]

© Joshua Rainey Photography/Shutterstock.com

The organizational structure at TOMS Shoes consists of two parts. The for-profit component of the company manages overall operations. Its non-profit component, Friends of TOMS, is responsible for volunteer activities and shoe donations.

Organizational culture helps ensure that all members of a company share values and suggests rules for how to behave and deal with problems within the organization. Table 7.1 confirms that executives in this study believe that corporate culture has a significant impact on organizational performance and the ability to retain good employees. The key to success in any organization is satisfying stakeholders, especially customers. Establishing a positive organizational culture sets the tone

Table 7.1 Impact of Corporate Culture on Business Performance

Culture has a strong or very strong impact on an organization's performance.	82%
My corporate culture has a strong impact on the ability to retain top talent.	68%
My organization's culture drives sales and increases revenue.	61%
My organization's culture creates a sense of belonging.	57%
My organization's culture lowers turnover.	53%

Based on "Ten Most Admired Corporate Cultures," February 10, 2010, http://cthrc.ca/en/member_area/member_news/ten_most_admired_corporate_cultures.aspx (accessed March 1, 2010).

After surveys indicated that customers wanted Best Buy to provide sustainable solutions to the electronic waste (e-waste) problem, the company set out to do just that. However, successfully implementing such a program requires collaboration among the company, its employees, and its partners.

Best Buy has a culture based on teamwork and open communication. The company also encourages employees to improve the company's products and operations. This cohesive work environment enables employees to work together to support Best Buy's green initiatives and come up with sustainable solutions. Communication of the company's sustainability goals is also essential. For this reason, Best Buy created a Sustainability and Corporate Responsibility Scorecard that provides employees with metrics enabling them to measure their progress toward the company's sustainability initiatives.

Best Buy's attempts to incorporate sustainability throughout its operations require employee participation as the company incorporates eco-friendly product lines and business practices. When Energy Star products were first introduced to Best Buy, employees underwent training so that they could educate consumers concerning Energy Star benefits. As part of Best Buy's energy conservation program, the company has set a goal to reduce operations emissions, which requires employees to change their behaviours by not leaving the engines of delivery trucks idling outside Best Buy locations.

Best Buy also teams up with recycling companies to tackle the problem of e-waste. Best Buy collects consumers' used electronics, and its partners work to give these products a "second life" by repairing them or using their parts for other products. Best Buy also monitors its recyclers to make sure they are following safe recycling practices. The collaboration among Best Buy, its employees, and its partners (including consumers) is reducing the e-waste in landfills one item at a time.[6]

DISCUSSION QUESTIONS

1. Why did Best Buy feel the need to embrace sustainability?

2. Why is communication so important in achieving Best Buy's sustainability goals?

3. Describe how Best Buy has used teamwork to increase sustainability within its operations.

for all other decisions, including building an efficient organizational structure.

Developing Organizational Structure

LO1 Define organizational structure, and relate how organizational structures develop.

structure the arrangement or relationship of positions within an organization

Structure is the arrangement or relationship of positions within an organization. Rarely is an organization, or any group of individuals working together, able to achieve common objectives without some form of structure, whether that structure is explicitly defined or only implied. A professional baseball team such as the Toronto Blue Jays is a business organization with an explicit formal structure that guides the team's activities so that it can increase game attendance, win games, and sell souvenirs such as T-shirts. But even an informal group playing softball for fun has an organization that specifies who will pitch, catch, bat, coach, and so on.

Governments and non-profit organizations also have formal organizational structures to facilitate the achievement of their objectives. Getting people to work together efficiently and coordinating the skills of diverse individuals requires careful planning. Developing appropriate organizational structures is therefore a major challenge for managers in both large and small organizations.

An organization's structure develops when managers assign work tasks and activities to specific individuals or work groups and coordinate the diverse activities required to reach the firm's objectives. When Sears, for example, has a sale, the store manager must work with the advertising department to make the public aware of the sale, with department managers to ensure that extra salespeople are scheduled to handle the increased customer traffic, and with merchandise buyers to ensure that enough sale merchandise is available to meet expected consumer demand. All the people occupying these positions must work together to achieve the store's objectives.

The best way to begin to understand how organizational structure develops is to consider the evolution of a new business such as a clothing store. At first, the business is a sole proprietorship in which the owner does everything—buys, prices, and displays the merchandise; does the accounting and tax records; and assists customers. As the business grows, the owner hires a salesperson and perhaps a merchandise buyer to help run the store. As the business continues to grow, the owner hires more salespeople. The growth and success of the business now require the owner to be away from the store frequently, meeting with suppliers, engaging in public relations, and attending trade shows. Thus, the owner must designate someone to manage the salespeople and maintain the accounting, payroll, and tax functions. If the owner decides to expand by opening more stores, still more managers will be needed. Figure 7.1 shows these stages of growth with three **organizational charts** (visual displays of organizational structure, chain of command, and other relationships).

organizational charts visual displays of the organizational structure, lines of authority (chain of command), staff relationships, permanent committee arrangements, and lines of communication

Growth requires organizing—the structuring of human, physical, and financial resources to achieve objectives in an effective and efficient manner. Growth necessitates hiring people who have specialized skills. With more people and greater specialization, the organization needs to develop a formal structure to function efficiently. Consider Cirque du Soleil, which started in 1984 with 20 ambitious street artists. Today, with 3,000 employees and 40 nationalities, creativity and business must be balanced through some structure. Cirque returns 10 percent of its profits to employees, and the core team meets 10 times a year to recruit and keep the right people in a team-focused corporate culture.[7] As we shall see, structuring an organization requires that management assign work tasks to specific individuals and departments and assign responsibility for the achievement of specific organizational objectives.

"Growth requires organizing—the structuring of human, physical, and financial resources to achieve objectives in an effective and efficient manner."

Assigning Tasks

LO2 Describe how specialization and departmentalization help an organization achieve its goals.

For a business to earn profits from the sale of its products, its managers must first determine what activities are required to achieve its objectives. At Celestial Seasonings, for example, employees must purchase herbs from suppliers, dry the herbs and place them in tea bags, package and label the tea, and then ship the packages to grocery stores around the country. Other necessary activities include negotiating with supermarkets and other retailers for display space, developing new products, planning advertising, managing finances, and managing employees. All these activities must be coordinated, assigned to work groups, and controlled. Two important aspects of assigning these work activities are specialization and departmentalization.

Figure 7.1 The Evolution of a Clothing Store, Phases I, 2, and 3

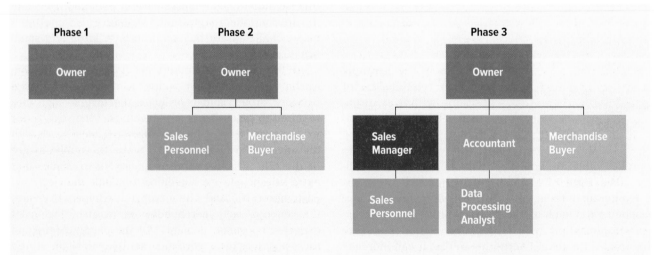

Henry Ford, the founder of Ford Motor Company, revolutionized manufacturing by creating assembly lines like this one to specialize the tasks his workers performed.

© Library of Congress

Specialization means workers don't waste time shifting from one job to another, and training is easier. However, efficiency is not the only motivation for specialization. Specialization also occurs when the activities that must be performed within an organization are too numerous for one person to handle. Recall the example of the clothing store. When the business was young and small, the owner could do everything; but when the business grew, the owner needed help waiting on customers, keeping the books, and managing other business activities.

Overspecialization can have negative consequences. Employees may become bored and dissatisfied with their jobs, and the result of their unhappiness is likely to be poor-quality work, more injuries, and high employee turnover. In extreme cases, employees in crowded specialized electronic plants are unable to form working relationships with one another. At Foxconn, a multinational electronics manufacturing firm and one of the suppliers of Apple iPhones and iPods, the lack of working relationships, long work hours, low pay, and other conditions have resulted in employee dissatisfaction and, tragically, depression and even suicide.[10] This is why some manufacturing firms allow job rotation so that employees do not become dissatisfied and leave. Although some degree of specialization is necessary for efficiency, because of differences in skills, abilities, and interests, all people are not equally suited for all jobs. We examine some strategies to overcome these issues in Chapter 9.

Specialization

After identifying all activities that must be accomplished, managers then break these activities down into specific tasks that can be handled by individual employees. This division of labour into small, specific tasks and the assignment of employees to do a single task is called **specialization**.

specialization the division of labour into small, specific tasks and the assignment of employees to do a single task

The rationale for specialization is efficiency. People can perform more efficiently if they master just one task rather than all tasks. In *The Wealth of Nations*, eighteenth-century economist Adam Smith discussed specialization, using the manufacture of straight pins as an example. Individually, workers could produce 20 pins a day when each employee produced complete pins. Thus, 10 employees working independently of each other could produce 200 pins a day. However, when one worker drew the wire, another straightened it, a third cut it, and a fourth ground the point, 10 workers could produce 48,000 pins per day.[8] To save money and achieve the benefits of specialization, some companies outsource and hire temporary workers to provide key skills. Many highly skilled workers with diverse experience are available through temp agencies.[9]

Departmentalization

After assigning specialized tasks to individuals, managers next organize workers doing similar jobs into groups to make them easier to manage. **Departmentalization** is the grouping of jobs into working units usually called departments, units, groups, or divisions. As we shall see, departments are commonly organized by function, product, geographic region, or customer (Figure 7.2). Most companies use more than one departmentalization plan to enhance productivity. For

departmentalization the grouping of jobs into working units usually called departments, units, groups, or divisions

instance, many consumer goods manufacturers have departments for specific product lines (beverages, frozen dinners, canned goods, and so on) as well as departments dealing with legal, purchasing, finance, human resources, and other business functions. For smaller companies, accounting can be set up online, almost as an automated department. Accounting software can handle electronic transfers so that you never have to worry about a late bill.[11] Many city governments also have departments for specific services (e.g., police, fire, waste disposal) as well as departments for legal, human resources, and other business functions. Figure 7.3 depicts the organizational chart for the city of Yellowknife, Northwest Territories, showing these departments.

Figure 7.2 Departmentalization

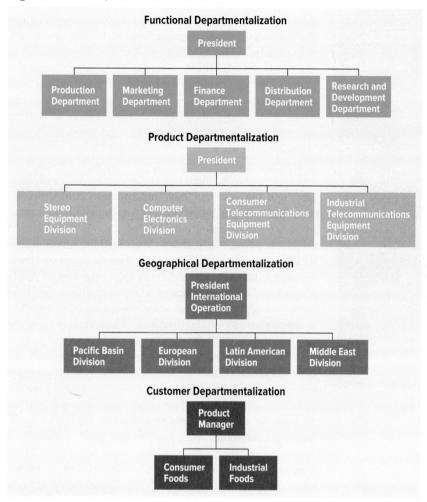

Functional Departmentalization

President

- Production Department
- Marketing Department
- Finance Department
- Distribution Department
- Research and Development Department

Product Departmentalization

President

- Stereo Equipment Division
- Computer Electronics Division
- Consumer Telecommunications Equipment Division
- Industrial Telecommunications Equipment Division

Geographical Departmentalization

President International Operation

- Pacific Basin Division
- European Division
- Latin American Division
- Middle East Division

Customer Departmentalization

Product Manager

- Consumer Foods
- Industrial Foods

"Specialization means workers do not waste time shifting from one job to another, and training is easier."

Functional Departmentalization. Functional departmentalization groups jobs that perform similar functional activities, such as finance, manufacturing, marketing, and human resources. Each of these functions is managed by an expert in the work done by the department—an engineer supervises the production department; a financial executive supervises the finance department. This approach is common in small organizations. A weakness of functional departmentalization is that, because it tends to emphasize departmental units rather than the organization as a whole, decision making that involves more than one department may be slow, and it requires greater coordination. Thus,

as businesses grow, they tend to adopt other approaches to organizing jobs.

Product Departmentalization. Product departmentalization, as you might guess, organizes jobs around the products of the firm. Procter & Gamble has global units, such as laundry and cleaning products, paper products, and health care products. Each division develops and implements its own product plans, monitors the results, and takes corrective action as necessary. Functional activities—production, finance, marketing, and others—are located within each product division. Consequently, organizing by products duplicates functions and resources and emphasizes the product rather than the achievement of the organization's overall objectives. However, it simplifies decision making and helps coordinate all activities related to a product or product group.

In 2015, Campbell's reorganized its "enterprise structure" into three segments. First, the Americas Simple Meals and Beverages business includes Campbell's U.S. retail and food service businesses, Plum, and the company's simple meals and shelf-stable beverage businesses in Canada, Mexico, and Latin America. The second segment is the Global Biscuits and Snacks business, which includes the company's Pepperidge Farm, Arnott's, and Kelsen businesses. This division also includes the company's businesses in Asia Pacific and Asia, including its soup and broth business in Hong Kong and China. Finally, the Packaged Fresh division includes Bolthouse Farms' portfolio of fresh carrots, super-premium beverages and salad dressings, and Campbell's retail refrigerated soup business. Campbell's has actually adopted a combination of two types of departmentalization. While it clearly separates baking and snacking products from soups and beverages, the company also chooses to divide its segments into geographic regions—a type of geographic departmentalization.[12]

Geographical Departmentalization. Geographical departmentalization groups jobs according to geographic location, such as state or province, region, country, or continent. FritoLay, for example, is

functional departmentalization the grouping of jobs that perform similar functional activities, such as finance, manufacturing, marketing, and human resources

product departmentalization the organization of jobs in relation to the products of the firm

geographical departmentalization the grouping of jobs according to geographic location, such as state or province, region, country, or continent

Figure 7.3 An Organizational Chart for the City of Yellowknife

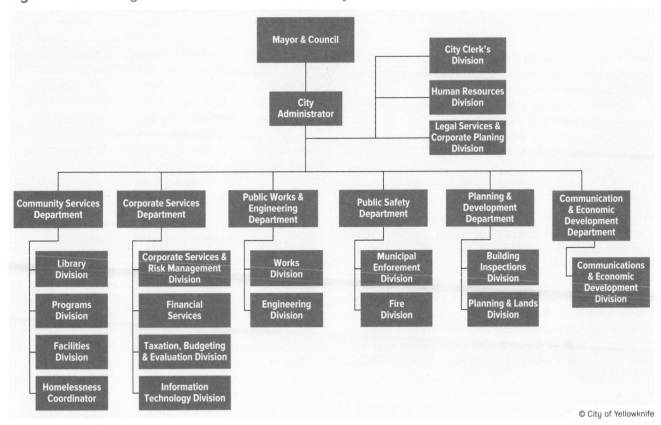

© City of Yellowknife

© Bloomberg via Getty Images

The Campbell Soup Company uses product departmentalization to organize its company. However, the firm also engages in a type of geographical departmentalization for various regions.

organized into four regional divisions, allowing the company to get closer to its customers and respond more quickly and efficiently to regional competitors. Multinational corporations often use a geographical approach because of vast differences between different regions. Coca-Cola, General Motors, and Caterpillar are organized by region. However, organizing by region requires a large administrative staff and control system to coordinate operations, and tasks are duplicated among the different regions.

Customer Departmentalization. **Customer departmentalization** arranges jobs around the needs of various types of customers. Banks, for example, typically have separate departments for commercial banking activities and for consumer or retail banking. This permits the bank to address the unique requirements of each group. Airlines, such as WestJet and Air Canada, provide prices and services customized for either business/frequent travellers or infrequent/vacationing customers. Customer departmentalization, like geographical departmentalization, does not focus on the organization as a whole and therefore requires a large administrative staff to coordinate the operations of the various groups.

customer departmentalization the arrangement of jobs around the needs of various types of customers

Assigning Responsibility

LO3 Determine how organizations assign responsibility for tasks and delegate authority.

After all workers and work groups have been assigned their tasks, they must be given the responsibility to carry them out. Management must determine to what extent it will delegate responsibility throughout the organization and how many employees will report to each manager.

Delegation of Authority

Delegation of authority means not only giving tasks to employees but also empowering them to make commitments, use resources, and take whatever actions are necessary to carry out those tasks. Let's say a marketing manager at Nestlé has assigned an employee to design a new package that is less wasteful (more environmentally responsible) than the current package for one of the company's frozen dinner lines. To carry out the assignment, the employee needs access to information and the authority to make certain decisions on packaging materials, costs, and so on. Without the authority to carry out the assigned task, the employee would have to get the approval of others for every decision and every request for materials.

As a business grows, so do the number and complexity of decisions that must be made; no one manager can handle them all. Hotels such as Westin Hotels and Resorts and the Ritz-Carlton give authority to service providers, including front desk personnel, to make service decisions such as moving a guest to another room or providing a discount to guests who experience a problem at the hotel. Delegation of authority frees a manager to concentrate on larger issues, such as planning or dealing with problems and opportunities.

Delegation also gives a **responsibility**, or obligation, to employees to carry out assigned tasks satisfactorily and holds them accountable for the proper execution of their assigned work. The principle of **accountability** means that employees who accept an assignment and the authority to carry it out are answerable to a superior for the outcome. Returning to the Nestlé example, if the packaging design prepared by the employee is unacceptable or late, the employee must accept the blame. If the new design is innovative, attractive, and cost-efficient, as well as environmentally responsible, or is completed ahead of schedule, the employee will accept the credit.

The process of delegating authority establishes a pattern of relationships and accountability between a superior and his or her subordinates. The president of a firm delegates responsibility for all marketing activities to the vice president of marketing. The vice president accepts this responsibility and has the authority to obtain all relevant information, make certain decisions, and delegate any or all activities to his or her subordinates. The vice president, in turn, delegates all advertising activities to the advertising manager, all sales activities to the sales manager, and so on. These managers then delegate specific tasks to their subordinates. However, the act of delegating authority to a subordinate does not relieve the superior of accountability for the delegated job. Even though the vice president of marketing delegates work to subordinates, he or she is still ultimately accountable to the president for all marketing activities.

Degree of Centralization

The extent to which authority is delegated throughout an organization determines its degree of centralization.

Centralized Organizations. In a **centralized organization**, authority is concentrated at the top, and very little decision-making authority is delegated to lower levels. Although decision-making authority in centralized organizations rests with top levels of management, a vast amount of responsibility for carrying out daily and routine procedures is delegated to even the lowest levels of the organization. Many government organizations and Crown corporations, including the Canadian Armed Forces, Canada Post, and the Canada Revenue Agency, are centralized.

Businesses tend to be more centralized when the decisions to be made are risky and when low-level managers are not highly skilled in decision making. In the banking industry, for example, authority to make routine car loans is given to all loan managers, while the authority to make high-risk loans, such as for a large residential development, may be restricted to upper-level loan officers.

Overcentralization can cause serious problems for a company, in part because it may take longer for the organization as a whole to implement decisions and to respond to changes and problems on a regional scale. McDonald's, for example, was one of the last chains to introduce a chicken sandwich because of the amount of research, development, test marketing, and layers of approval the product had to go through.

Decentralized Organizations. A **decentralized organization** is one in which decision-making authority is delegated as far down the chain of command as possible. Decentralization is characteristic of organizations that operate in complex, unpredictable environments. Businesses that face intense

delegation of authority giving employees not only tasks, but also the power to make commitments, use resources, and take whatever actions are necessary to carry out those tasks

responsibility the obligation, placed on employees through delegation, to perform assigned tasks satisfactorily and be held accountable for the proper execution of work

accountability the principle that employees who accept an assignment and the authority to carry it out are answerable to a superior for the outcome

centralized organization a structure in which authority is concentrated at the top, and very little decision-making authority is delegated to lower levels

decentralized organization an organization in which decision-making authority is delegated as far down the chain of command as possible

John Baker

Business: D2L

Founded: 1999, in Kitchener, Ontario

Success: D2L is already leading a major shift in educational software: It's harnessing data and analytics to become the Netflix of education.

D2L was founded in 1999 by John Baker. His engineering class was being challenged to look at the world in new ways by coming up with questions that no one had asked before. John Baker started to imagine designing software that could automatically grade student assignments to provide instant feedback, as well as perform other tasks. In his third year of university, Baker founded D2L to put some of his ideas into practice. Later, Baker signed his first big client, the University of Guelph, which incorporated tools he designed into its new MBA program. These features, which included a way to take notes online, an instant-messaging client, and a discussion board, formed the core of the company's software. Today, D2L has 15 million students using its platform worldwide and employs 900 staff in offices across Canada, the United States, Europe, Australia, Brazil, and Singapore.[13]

competition often decentralize to improve responsiveness and enhance creativity. Lower-level managers who interact with the external environment often develop a good understanding of it and thus are able to react quickly to changes.

Delegating authority to lower levels of managers may increase the organization's productivity. Decentralization requires that lower-level managers have strong decision-making skills. In recent years the trend has been toward more decentralized organizations, and some of the largest and most successful companies, including Google and Nike, have decentralized decision-making authority. McDonald's, realizing most of its growth is outside North America, is becoming increasingly decentralized and "glo-cal," varying products in specific markets to better meet consumer demands. This change in organizational structure for McDonald's is fostering greater innovation and local market success. McDonald's, which was long known for the homogeneity of its products, has embraced local cuisine on a limited scale. For instance, because cows are sacred in India, McDonald's has introduced the McVeggie and the Veg McMuffin. It also sells the Spicy Paneer wrap, made with chicken, paneer cheese, and spicy batter, to appeal to Indians' preferences for spicy food.[14] Diversity and decentralization seem to be McDonald's keys to being better, not just bigger. Non-profit organizations benefit from decentralization as well.

Span of Management

How many subordinates should a manager manage? There is no simple answer. Experts generally agree, however, that top managers should not directly supervise more than four to eight people, while lower-level managers who supervise routine tasks are capable of managing a much larger number of subordinates. For example, the manager of the finance department may supervise 25 employees, whereas the vice president of finance may supervise only five managers. **Span of management** refers to the number of subordinates who report to a particular manager. A *wide span of management* exists when a manager directly supervises a very large number of employees.

A *narrow span of management* exists when a manager directly supervises only a few subordinates (Figure 7.4). At Whole Foods, the best employees are recruited and placed in small teams in one of eight departments. Employees are empowered to discount, give away, and sample products, as well as to assist in creating a respectful workplace where goals are achieved, individual employees succeed, and customers are core in

span of management the number of subordinates who report to a particular manager

Figure 7.4 Span of Management: Wide Span and Narrow Span

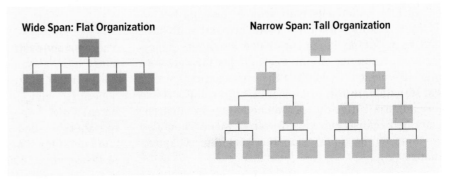

Wide Span: Flat Organization

Narrow Span: Tall Organization

business decisions. This approach allows Whole Foods to offer unique and "local market" experiences in each of its stores. This level of customization is in contrast to more centralized national supermarket chains.[15]

Should the span of management be wide or narrow? To answer this question, several factors need to be considered. A narrow span of management is appropriate when superiors and subordinates are not in close proximity, the manager has many responsibilities in addition to the supervision, the interaction between superiors and subordinates is frequent, and problems are common. However, when superiors and subordinates are located close to one another, the manager has few responsibilities other than supervision, the level of interaction between superiors and subordinates is low, few problems arise, subordinates are highly competent, and a set of specific operating procedures governs the activities of managers and their subordinates, a wide span of management will be more appropriate. Narrow spans of management are typical in centralized organizations, while wide spans of management are more common in decentralized firms.

"A company with many layers of managers is considered tall."

Organizational Layers

Complementing the concept of span of management are **organizational layers**, the levels of management in an organization.

A company with many layers of managers is considered tall; in a tall organization, the span of management is narrow (see Figure 7.4). Because each manager supervises only a few subordinates, many layers of management are necessary to carry out the operations of the business. McDonald's, for example, has a tall organization with many layers, including store managers, district managers, regional managers, and functional managers (finance, marketing, and so on), as well as a chief executive officer and many vice presidents. Because there are more managers in tall organizations than in flat organizations, administrative costs are usually higher. Communication is slower because information must pass through many layers.

Organizations with few layers are flat and have wide spans of management. When managers supervise a large number of employees, fewer management layers are needed to conduct the organization's activities. Managers in flat organizations typically perform more administrative duties than managers in tall organizations because there are fewer of them. They also spend more time supervising and working with subordinates.

organizational layers the levels of management in an organization.

Many of the companies that decentralized also flattened their structures and widened their spans of management, often by eliminating layers of middle management. Other corporations, including Avon and Ford Motor Company, embraced a more decentralized structure to reduce costs, speed up decision making, and boost overall productivity.

Forms of Organizational Structure

LO4 Compare and contrast some common forms of organizational structure.

Along with assigning tasks and the responsibility for carrying them out, managers must consider how to structure their authority relationships—that is, what structure the organization itself will have and how it will appear on the organizational chart. Common forms of organization include line structure, line-and-staff structure, multidivisional structure, and matrix structure.

Line Structure

The simplest organizational structure, **line structure**, has direct lines of authority that extend from the top manager to employees at the lowest level of the organization. For example, a convenience store employee at 7-Eleven may report to an assistant manager, who reports to the store manager, who reports to a regional manager, or, in an independent store, directly to the owner (Figure 7.5). This structure has a clear chain of command, which enables managers to make decisions quickly. A mid-level manager facing a decision must consult only one person, his or her immediate supervisor. However, this structure requires that managers possess a wide range of knowledge and skills. They are responsible for a variety of activities and must be knowledgeable about them all. Line structures are most common in small businesses.

Line-and-Staff Structure

The **line-and-staff structure** has a traditional line relationship between superiors and subordinates, and specialized managers—called staff managers—are available to assist line managers

line structure the simplest organizational structure in which direct lines of authority extend from the top manager to the lowest level of the organization

line-and-staff structure a structure having a traditional line relationship between superiors and subordinates and also specialized managers—called staff managers—who are available to assist line managers

Figure 7.5 Line Structure

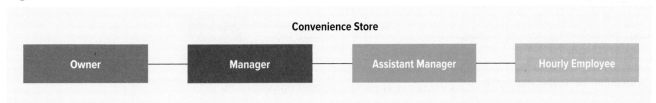

Convenience Store

Owner — Manager — Assistant Manager — Hourly Employee

(Figure 7.6). Line managers can focus on their area of expertise in the operation of the business, while staff managers provide advice and support to line departments on specialized matters such as finance, engineering, human resources, and the law. In the city of Yellowknife (Figure 7.3), for example, the city administrator is a line manager who oversees groups of related departments. However, the heads of the Human Resources Division, Legal Services and Corporate Planning Division, Community Services Department, etc., are effectively staff managers who report directly to the city administrator (the city equivalent of a business chief executive officer). Staff managers do not have direct authority over line managers or over the line manager's subordinates, but they do have direct authority over subordinates in their own departments. However, line-and-staff organizations may experience problems with overstaffing and ambiguous lines of communication. Additionally, employees may become frustrated because they lack the authority to carry out certain decisions.

Multidivisional Structure

As companies grow and diversify, traditional line structures become difficult to coordinate, making communication difficult and decision making slow. When the weaknesses of the structure—the "turf wars," miscommunication, and working at cross-purposes—exceed the benefits, growing firms tend to restructure, often into the divisionalized form. A **multidivisional structure** organizes departments into larger groups called divisions. Just as departments might be formed on the basis of geography, customer, product, or a combination of these, so too divisions can be formed based on any of these methods of organizing. Within each of these divisions, departments may be organized by product, geographic region, function, or some combination of all three. Indra Nooyi, CEO of PepsiCo, rearranged the company's organizational structure. Prior to her tenure, PepsiCo was organized geographically. She created new units—PepsiCo Americas Foods (PAF), PepsiCo Americas Beverages (PAB), PepsiCo Europe, and PepsiCo Asia, Middle East & Africa—that span international boundaries and make it easier for employees in different geographic regions to share business practices.[16]

Multidivisional structures permit delegation of decision-making authority, allowing divisional and department

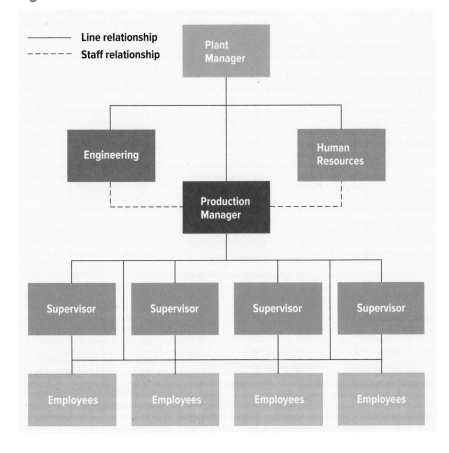

multidivisional structure
a structure that organizes departments into larger groups called divisions

Need help understanding this concept? Check out an informational video! Log into Connect, go to Resources, and click on the Videos page.

Figure 7.6 Line-and-Staff Structure

——— **Line relationship**
------ **Staff relationship**

Plant Manager

Engineering

Human Resources

Production Manager

Supervisor · Supervisor · Supervisor · Supervisor

Employees · Employees · Employees · Employees

managers to specialize. They allow those closest to the action to make the decisions that will affect them. Delegation of authority and divisionalized work also mean that better decisions are made faster, and they tend to be more innovative. Most importantly, by focusing each division on a common region, product, or customer, each is more likely to provide products that meet the needs of its particular customers. However, the divisional structure inevitably creates work duplication, which makes it more difficult to realize the economies of scale that result from grouping functions together.

Matrix Structure

Another structure that attempts to address issues that arise with growth, diversification, productivity, and competitiveness is the matrix. A **matrix structure**, also called a project-management structure, sets up teams from different departments, thereby creating two or more intersecting lines of authority (see Figure 7.7). One of the first organizations to design and implement a matrix structure was NASA for the U.S. space program because it needed to coordinate different projects at the same time. The matrix structure superimposes project-based departments on the more traditional, function-based departments. Project teams bring together specialists from a variety of areas to work together on a single project, such as developing a new fighter jet. In this arrangement, employees are responsible to two managers—functional managers and project managers. Matrix structures are usually temporary: Team members typically go back to their functional or line department after a project is finished. However, more firms are becoming permanent matrix structures, creating and dissolving project teams as needed to meet customer needs. The aerospace industry was one of the first to apply the matrix structure, but today it is used by universities and schools, accounting firms, banks, and organizations in other industries.

Matrix structures provide flexibility, enhanced cooperation, and creativity, and they enable the company to respond quickly to changes in the environment by giving special attention to specific projects or problems. However, they are generally expensive and quite complex, and employees may be confused as to whose authority

matrix structure a structure that sets up teams from different departments, thereby creating two or more intersecting lines of authority; also called a project-management structure

Figure 7.7 • Matrix Structure

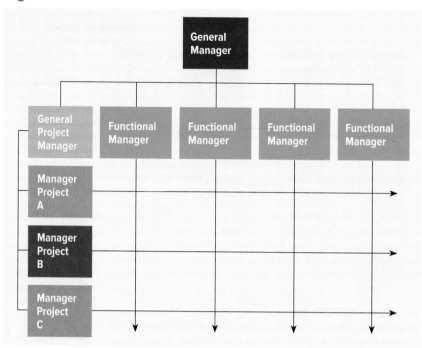

has priority—the project manager's or the immediate supervisor's.

The Role of Groups and Teams in Organizations

LO5 Distinguish between groups and teams, and identify the types of groups that exist in organizations.

Regardless of how they are organized, most of the essential work of business occurs in individual work groups and teams, so we'll take a closer look at them now. Although some experts do not make a distinction between groups and teams, in recent years there has been a gradual shift toward an emphasis on teams and managing them to enhance individual and organizational success. Some experts now believe that highest productivity results only when groups become teams.[17]

Traditionally, a **group** has been defined as two or more individuals who communicate with one another, share a common identity, and have a common goal. A **team** is a small group whose members have complementary skills; have a common purpose, goal,

group two or more individuals who communicate with one another, share a common identity, and have a common goal

team a small group whose members have complementary skills; have a common purpose, goal, and approach; and hold themselves mutually accountable

Table 7.2 Differences Between Groups and Teams

Working Group	Team
Has strong, clearly focused leader	Has shared leadership roles
Has individual accountability	Has individual and group accountability
Has the same purpose as the broader organizational mission	Has a specific purpose that the team itself delivers
Creates individual work products	Creates collective work products
Runs efficient meetings	Encourages open-ended discussion and active problem-solving meetings
Measures its effectiveness indirectly by its effects on others (e.g., financial performance of the business)	Measures performance directly by assessing collective work products
Discusses, decides, and delegates	Discusses, decides, and does real work together

Source: Robert Gatewood, Robert Taylor, and O. C. Ferrell, *Management: Comprehension Analysis and Application*, 1995, p. 427. Copyright © 1995 Richard D. Irwin, a Times Mirror Higher Education Group, Inc., company. Reproduced with permission of the McGraw-Hill Companies.

and approach; and hold themselves mutually accountable.[18] All teams are groups, but not all groups are teams. Table 7.2 points out some important differences between them. Work groups emphasize individual work products, individual accountability, and even individual leadership. Salespeople working independently for the same company could be a work group. In contrast, work teams share leadership roles, have both individual and mutual accountability, and create collective work products. In other words, a work group's performance depends on what its members do as individuals, while a team's performance is based on creating a knowledge centre and a competency to work together to accomplish a goal. On the other hand, it is also important for team members to retain their individuality and avoid becoming just "another face in the crowd." According to former corporate lawyer and negotiations consultant Susan Cain, the purpose of teams should be toward collaboration versus collectivism. Although the team is working toward a common goal, it is important that all team members actively contribute their ideas and work together to achieve this common goal.[19]

The type of groups an organization establishes depends on the tasks it needs to accomplish and the situation it faces. Some specific kinds of groups and teams include committees, task forces, project teams, product-development teams, quality-assurance teams, and self-directed work teams. All of these can be *virtual teams*—employees in different locations who rely on e-mail, audio conferencing, fax, Internet, video-conferencing, or other technological tools to accomplish

their goals. One survey found that almost 48 percent of workers have participated in virtual teams.[20] Virtual teams have also opened up opportunities for different companies. Not only does Cisco Systems Inc. work in virtual teams, but the company makes networking technology to support video conferencing. At Cisco Europe, 10,000 employees across 21 countries developed a set of team operating principles to aid team collaboration.[21]

DID YOU KNOW?

A survey of managers and executives found that they feel 28 percent of meetings are a waste of time and that information could be communicated more effectively using other methods.[22]

Committees

A **committee** is usually a permanent, formal group that does some specific task. For example, many firms have a compensation or finance committee to examine the effectiveness of these areas of operation as well as the need for possible changes. Ethics committees are formed to develop and revise codes of ethics, suggest methods for implementing ethical standards, and review specific issues and concerns.

Task Forces

A **task force** is a temporary group of employees responsible for bringing about a particular change. They typically come from across all departments and levels of an organization. Task force membership is usually based on expertise rather than organizational position. Occasionally, a task force may be formed from individuals outside a company. When Toyota experienced a major product recall, the president, Akio Toyoda, formed and led a Global Quality Task Force to conduct quality improvements throughout the worldwide operations of the company. With massive recalls looming, the company focused on (1) improving the quality inspection process, (2) enhancing customer research, (3) establishing an automotive centre of quality excellence, (4) utilizing external industry experts, (5) increasing the frequency of communication

committee a permanent, formal group that performs a specific task

task force a temporary group of employees responsible for bringing about a particular change

with regional authorities, and (6) improving regional autonomy.[23]

Teams

Teams are becoming far more common in the Canadian workplace as businesses strive to enhance productivity and global competitiveness. In general, teams have the benefit of being able to pool members' knowledge and skills and make greater use of them than can individuals working alone. Team building is becoming increasingly popular in organizations, with around half of executives indicating their companies had team-building training. Teams require harmony, cooperation, synchronized effort, and flexibility to maximize their contribution.[24] Teams can also create more solutions to problems than can individuals. Furthermore, team participation enhances employee acceptance of, understanding of, and commitment to team goals. Teams motivate workers by providing internal rewards in the form of an enhanced sense of accomplishment for employees as they achieve more, and external rewards in the form of praise and certain perks. Consequently, they can help get workers more involved. They can help companies be more innovative, and they can boost productivity and cut costs.

According to psychologist Ivan Steiner, team productivity peaks at about five team members. People become less motivated and group coordination becomes more difficult after this size. Jeff Bezos, Amazon.com CEO, says that he has a "two-pizza rule": If a team cannot be fed by two pizzas, it is too large. Keep teams small enough that everyone gets a piece of the action.[25]

Project Teams. **Project teams** are similar to task forces, but normally they run their operation and have total control of a specific work project. Like task forces, their membership is likely to cut across the firm's hierarchy and be composed of people from different functional areas. They are almost always temporary, although a large project, such as designing and building a new airplane at Boeing Corporation, may last for years.

Product-development teams are a special type of project team formed to devise, design, and implement a new product. Sometimes product-development teams exist within a functional area—research and development—but now they more frequently include people from numerous functional areas and may even include

> **project teams** groups similar to task forces that normally run their operation and have total control of a specific work project

> **product-development teams** a specific type of project team formed to devise, design, and implement a new product

> "Teams are becoming far more common in the workplace as businesses strive to enhance productivity and global competitiveness."

customers to help ensure that the end product meets the customers' needs.

Quality-Assurance Teams. **Quality-assurance teams (or quality circles)** are fairly small groups of workers brought together from throughout the organization to solve specific quality, productivity, or service problems. Although the *quality circle* term is not as popular as it once was, the concern about quality is stronger than ever. Companies such as IBM and Xerox as well as companies in the automobile industry have used quality circles to shift the organization to a more participative culture. The use of teams to address quality issues will no doubt continue to increase throughout the business world.

> **quality-assurance teams (or quality circles)** small groups of workers brought together from throughout the organization to solve specific quality, productivity, or service problems

> **self-directed work team (SDWT)** a group of employees responsible for an entire work process or segment that delivers a product to an internal or external customer

Self-Directed Work Teams. A **self-directed work team (SDWT)** is a group of employees responsible for an entire work process or segment that delivers a product to an internal or external customer.[26] SDWTs permit the flexibility to change rapidly to meet the competition or respond to customer needs. The defining characteristic of an SDWT is the extent to which it is empowered or given authority to make and implement work decisions. Thus, SDWTs are designed to give employees a feeling of "ownership" of a whole job. With shared team responsibility for work outcomes, team members often have broader job assignments and cross-train to master other jobs, thus permitting greater team flexibility.

Communicating in Organizations

LO6 Describe how communication occurs in organizations.

Communication within an organization can flow in a variety of directions and from a number of sources, each using both oral and written forms of communication. The success of communication systems within the organization has a tremendous effect on the overall success of the firm. Communication mistakes can lower productivity and morale.

Alternatives to face-to-face communications—such as meetings—are growing thanks to technology such

It seems unlikely that businesses would encourage employees to engage in social networking, but clients of Yammer do just that. Yammer supplies internal social networking for organizations. These internal networks provide many benefits. For example, Yammer enables global employees to communicate easily in real time, cutting down significantly on e-mail. Yammer CEO David Sacks says employees using his service more easily develop relationships and a commitment to their companies—a claim bolstered by research. Although the networks are designed for conducting business, employees often share jokes, light banter, and personal information. Many companies also use Yammer and the equivalent to track ideas from conception through production and beyond in a streamlined fashion.

Despite advantages, internal social networking has pitfalls. Disadvantages primarily affect employees, who may be too free with their comments. Anything posted on an internal social network is potentially admissible during performance reviews, promotion decisions, and legal proceedings.

More than 100,000 companies currently use Yammer, and most love it. They do agree, however, that it's important to implement user guidelines to avoid trouble. For instance, the technology company Xerox states that employees should use discretion, professionalism, and common sense in the tone an aunt might use with a favourite nephew. With gentle guidance, Yammer and others can enhance company culture and the workplace experience. As social networking continues to grow, it's likely the internal version will thrive as well.[29]

DISCUSSION QUESTIONS

1. How does Yammer contribute to a firm's corporate culture?

2. How can Yammer be used as a way to improve productivity?

3. What are some potential pitfalls of Yammer, and how can these pitfalls be avoided?

---

as voice-mail, e-mail, and online newsletters. Many companies use internal networks called intranets to share information with employees. Intranets increase communication across different departments and levels of management and help with the flow of everyday business activities. Another innovative approach is cloud computing. Rather than using physical products, companies using cloud computing technology can access computing resources and information over a network. Cloud computing allows companies to have more control over computing resources and can be less expensive than hardware or software. Salesforce.com uses cloud computing in its customer relationship management solutions.[27] Companies can even integrate aspects of social media into their intranets, allowing employees to post comments and pictures, participate in polls, and create group calendars. However, increased access to the Internet at work has also created many problems, including employee abuse of company mail and Internet access.[28]

Formal Communication

Formal channels of communication are intentionally defined and designed by the organization. They represent the flow of communication within the formal organizational structure, as shown on organizational charts. Traditionally, formal communication patterns were classified as vertical and horizontal, but with the increased use of teams and matrix structures, formal communication may occur in a number of patterns (Figure 7.8).

Upward communication flows from lower to higher levels of the organization and includes information such as progress reports, suggestions for improvement, inquiries, and grievances. *Downward communication* refers to the traditional flow of information from upper organizational levels to lower levels. This type of communication typically involves directions, the assignment of tasks and responsibilities, performance feedback, and certain details about the organization's strategies and goals. Speeches, policy and procedures manuals, employee handbooks, company leaflets, telecommunications, and job descriptions are examples of downward communication.

Horizontal communication involves the exchange of information among colleagues and peers on the same organizational level, such as across or within departments. Horizontal information informs, supports, and coordinates activities both within the department and with other departments. At times, the business will formally require horizontal communication among particular organizational members, as is the case with task forces or project teams.

Figure 7.8 The Flow of Communication in an Organizational Hierarchy

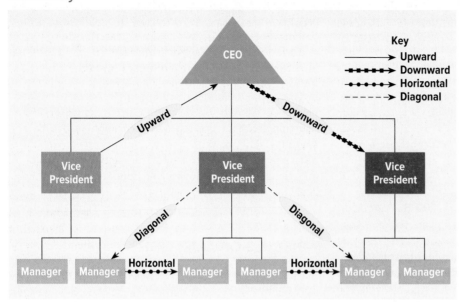

Informal Communication Channels

Along with the formal channels of communication shown on an organizational chart, all firms communicate informally as well. Communication between friends, for instance, cuts across department, division, and even management–subordinate boundaries. Such friendships and other non-work social relationships comprise the *informal organization* of a firm, and their impact can be great.

The most significant informal communication occurs through the **grapevine**, an informal channel of communication, separate from management's formal, official communication channels. Grapevines exist in all organizations. Information passed along the grapevine may relate to the job or organization, or it may be gossip and rumours unrelated to either. The accuracy of grapevine information has been of great concern to managers.

grapevine an informal channel of communication, separate from management's formal, official communication channels

Additionally, managers can turn the grapevine to their advantage. Using it as a "sounding device" for possible new policies is one example. Managers can obtain valuable information from the grapevine that could improve decision making. Some organizations use the grapevine to their advantage by floating ideas, soliciting feedback, and reacting accordingly. People love to gossip, and managers need to be aware that grapevines exist in every organization. Managers who understand how the grapevine works also can use it to their advantage by feeding it facts to squelch rumours and incorrect information.

With more and more companies downsizing and increasing the use of self-managed work teams, many workers are being required to communicate with others in different departments and on different levels to solve problems and coordinate work. When these individuals from different units and organizational levels communicate, it is *diagonal communication*. One benefit of companies doing more with fewer employees is that productivity (output per work hour) increased by 9.5 percent in one year. Increased productivity allows companies to increase wages and leads to increased standards of living.[30]

"Grapevines exist in all organizations. Information passed along the grapevine may relate to the job or organization, or it may be gossip and rumours unrelated to either."

Monitoring Communications

Technological advances and the increased use of electronic communication in the workplace have made monitoring its use necessary for most companies Many companies require that employees sign and follow a

© chrisdorney / Shutterstock.com

Online sites such as wikis are allowing employee teams to share information and work collaboratively on documents. The most well-known wiki is the online encyclopedia Wikipedia.

policy on appropriate Internet use. These agreements often require that employees will use corporate computers only for work-related activities. Additionally, several companies use software programs to monitor employee computer usage.[31] Instituting practices that show respect for employee privacy but do not abdicate employer responsibility are increasingly necessary in today's workplace. Several websites provide model policies and detailed guidelines for conducting electronic monitoring, including the Guide for Businesses and Organizations, "Your Privacy Responsibilities," on the Privacy Commissioner of Canada site.

Improving Communication Effectiveness

Without effective communication, the activities and overall productivity of projects, groups, teams, and individuals will be diminished. Communication is an important area for a firm to address at all levels of management. Apple supplier Foxconn is one example of how essential communication is to a firm. Despite criticisms of unfair labour conditions, the Fair Labor Association determined that Foxconn had formal procedures in place at its factories to prevent many major accidents. However, it concluded that the firm had a communication problem. These procedures were not being communicated to the factory workers, contributing to unsafe practices and two tragic explosions.[32]

One of the major issues of effective communication is in obtaining feedback. If feedback is not provided, then communication will be ineffective and can drag down overall performance. Managers should always encourage feedback, including concerns and challenges about issues. Listening is a skill that involves hearing, and most employees listen much more than they actively communicate to others. Therefore, managers should encourage employees to provide feedback—even if it is negative. This will allow the organization to identify strengths and weaknesses and make adjustments when needed. At the same time, strong feedback mechanisms help to empower employees as they feel that their voices are being heard.

Interruptions can be a serious threat to effective communication. Various activities can interrupt the message. For example, interjecting a remark can create discontinuance in the communication process or disrupt the uniformity of the message. Even small interruptions can be a problem if the messenger cannot adequately understand or interpret the communicator's message. One suggestion is to give the communicator space or time to make another statement rather than quickly responding or making your own comment.

Strong and effective communication channels are a requirement for companies to distribute information to different levels of the company. Businesses have several channels for communication, including face-to-face, e-mail, phone, and written communication (for example, memos). Each channel has advantages and disadvantages, and some are more appropriate to use than others. For instance, a small task requiring little instruction might be communicated through a short memo or e-mail. An in-depth task would most likely require a phone conversation or face-to-face contact. E-mail has become especially helpful for businesses, and both employees and managers are increasingly using e-mail rather than memos or phone conversations. However, it is important that employees use e-mail correctly. It is quite easy to send the wrong e-mail to the wrong person, and messages sent over e-mail can be misinterpreted. Inappropriate e-mails can be forwarded without a second thought, and employees have gotten in trouble for sending personal e-mails in the workplace. It is therefore important for companies to communicate their e-mail policies throughout the organization. Communicators using e-mail, whether managers or employees, must exert caution before pushing that "Send" button.

Communication is necessary in helping every organizational member understand what is expected of him or her. Many business problems can be avoided if clear communication exists within the company. Even the best business strategies are of little use if those who will oversee them cannot understand what is intended. Communication might not seem to be as big of a concern to management as finances, human resources, and marketing, but in reality it can make the difference between successful implementation of business activities or failure.

TEAM EXERCISE

Assign the responsibility of providing the organizational structure for a company one of your team members has worked for. Was your organization centralized or decentralized in terms of decision making? Would you consider the span of control to be wide or narrow? Were any types of teams, committees, or task forces utilized in the organization? Report your work to the class.

LEARNING OBJECTIVES SUMMARY

LO1 Define organizational structure, and relate how organizational structures develop.

Structure is the arrangement or relationship of positions within an organization; it develops when managers assign work activities to work groups and specific individuals and coordinate the diverse activities required to attain organizational objectives. Organizational structure evolves to accommodate growth, which requires people with specialized skills.

LO2 Describe how specialization and departmentalization help an organization achieve its goals.

Structuring an organization requires that management assign work tasks to specific individuals and groups. Under specialization managers break labour into small, specialized tasks and assign employees to do a single task, fostering efficiency. Departmentalization is the grouping of jobs into working units (departments, units, groups, or divisions). Businesses may departmentalize by function, product, geographic region, or customer, or they may combine two or more of these.

LO3 Determine how organizations assign responsibility for tasks and delegate authority.

Delegation of authority means assigning tasks to employees and giving them the power to make commitments, use resources, and take whatever actions are necessary to accomplish the tasks. It lays responsibility on employees to carry out assigned tasks satisfactorily and holds them accountable to a superior for the proper execution of their assigned work. The extent to which authority is delegated throughout an organization determines its degree of centralization. Span of management refers to the number of subordinates who report to particular manager. A wide span of management occurs in flat organizations; a narrow one exists in tall organizations.

LO4 Compare and contrast some common forms of organizational structure.

Line structures have direct lines of authority that extend from the top manager to employees at the lowest level of the organization. The line-and-staff structure has a traditional line relationship between superiors and subordinates, and specialized staff managers are to assist line managers. A multidivisional structure gathers departments into larger groups called divisions. A matrix, or project-management, structure sets up teams from different departments, thereby creating two or more intersecting lines of authority.

LO5 Distinguish between groups and teams, and identify the types of groups that exist in organizations.

A group is two or more persons who communicate, share a common identity, and have a common goal. A team is a small group whose members have complementary skills, a common purpose, goals, and approach; and who hold themselves mutually accountable. The major distinction is that individual performance is most important in groups, while collective work group performance counts most in teams. Special kinds of groups include task forces, committees, project teams, product-development teams, quality-assurance teams, and self-directed work teams.

LO6 Describe how communication occurs in organizations.

Communication occurs both formally and informally in organizations. Formal communication may be downward, upward, horizontal, and even diagonal. Informal communication takes place through friendships and the grapevine.

KEY TERMS

accountability

centralized organization

committee

customer departmentalization

decentralized organization

delegation of authority

departmentalization

functional departmentalization

geographical departmentalization

grapevine

group

line-and-staff structure

line structure

matrix structure

multidivisional structure

organizational charts

organizational culture

organizational layers

product departmentalization

product-development teams

project teams

quality-assurance teams (or quality circles)

responsibility

self-directed work team (SDWT)

span of management

specialization

structure

task force

team

DESTINATION CEO DISCUSSION QUESTIONS

1. What are the most important factors contributing to Galen Weston's success?

2. What prepared Galen Weston for his role as CEO of Loblaw?

3. How does innovation contribute to the growth of the company?

SO YOU WANT A JOB IN GLOBAL BUSINESS *Managing Organizational Culture, Teamwork, and Communication*

Jobs dealing with organizational culture and structure are usually at the top of the organization. If you want to be a CEO or high-level manager, you will help shape these areas of business. On the other hand, if you are an entrepreneur or small-business person, you will need to make decisions about assigning tasks, departmentalization, and assigning responsibility. Even managers in small organizations have to make decisions about decentralization, span of management, and forms of organizational structure. While these decisions may be part of your job, there are usually no job titles dealing with these specific areas. Specific jobs that attempt to improve organizational culture could include ethics and compliance positions as well as those who are in charge of communicating memos, manuals, and policies that help establish the culture. These positions will be in communications, human resources, and positions that assist top organizational managers.

Teams are becoming more common in the workplace, and it is possible to become a member of a product-development group or quality-assurance team. There are also human resources positions that encourage teamwork through training activities. The area of corporate communications provides lots of opportunities for specific jobs that facilitate communication systems. Thanks to technology, there are job positions to help disseminate information through online newsletters, intranets, or internal computer networks to increase collaboration. In addition to the many advances using electronic communications, there are technology concerns that create new job opportunities. Monitoring workplace communications such as the use of e-mail and the Internet have created new industries. There have to be internal controls in the organization to make sure that the organization does not engage in any copyright infringement. If this is an area of interest, there are specific jobs that provide an opportunity to use your technological skills to assist in maintaining appropriate standards in communicating and using technology.

If you go to work for a large company with many divisions, you can expect a number of positions dealing with the tasks discussed here. If you go to work for a small company, you will probably engage in most of these tasks as a part of your position. Organizational flexibility requires individual flexibility, and those employees willing to take on new domains and challenges will be the employees who survive and prosper in the future.

BUILD YOUR BUSINESS PLAN

Organization, Teamwork, and Communication

Developing a business plan as a team is a deliberate move of your instructor to encourage you to familiarize yourself with the concept of teamwork. You need to realize that you are going to spend a large part of your professional life working with others. At this point, you are working on the business plan for a grade, but after graduation you will be "teaming" with co-workers, and the success of your endeavour may determine whether you get a raise or a bonus. It is important that you be comfortable as soon as possible with working with others and holding them accountable for their contributions.

Some people are natural "leaders" and leaders often feel that if team members are not doing their work, they take it upon themselves to "do it all." This is not leadership, but rather micro-managing.

Leadership means holding members accountable for their responsibilities. Your instructor may provide ideas on how this could be implemented, possibly by utilizing peer reviews. Remember you are not doing team members any favours by doing their work for them.

If you are a "follower" (someone who takes directions well) rather than a leader, try to get into a team where others are hard workers and you will rise to their level. There is nothing wrong with being a follower; not everyone can be a leader!

CASE | Keurig Green Mountain Empowers Employees

Keurig Green Mountain (GMCR) Inc., based in Delaware, is a leader in the specialty coffee industry. The company sells coffee and beverage selections through a coordinated, multichannel distribution network of wholesale and consumer direct operations. It also sells Keurig single-pack coffee packets and Keurig brewers, which are single-cup brewing systems that have exploded in popularity. The demand for GMCR products has led the company to expand rapidly.

GMCR employs more than 2,100 people, but it has a decentralized and flat organizational structure with few layers of management. This structure gives all employees responsibility for implementation. Although it has functional departments that vary across the company, there is an openness of communication that allows employees regular access to all levels of the organization. The company uses voicemail or e-mail to inform groups of decisions and encourages employees to voice their opinions and ideas in response. In this way, the company has achieved a culture in which people are involved in creating ideas and coming up with better solutions together.

This employee empowerment means that the company may sometimes seem chaotic. However, the communication across channels ensures that the collaborative nature of getting things done is spread equally throughout the company. Although there are many meetings at which employees are encouraged to share their views, following an agenda ensures that there is efficient decision making occurring seamlessly across the GMCR.

With its growth, GMCR must carefully manage its communication channels to ensure that employees will continue to be heard. Accusations that GMCR has become less transparent along with investigations regarding some accounting practices indicate that GMCR is facing challenges as it expands. GMCR also faces competition from Starbucks, which is selling its own single-serve coffee brewer. However, by embedding communication and employee participation into its culture, GMCR continues to be listed as a top workplace for employees.[33]

DISCUSSION QUESTIONS

1. Describe how Green Mountain Coffee Roasters (GMCR) uses a decentralized and flat organizational structure.

2. How does empowerment work at GMCR?

3. What are some of the challenges GMCR must overcome as it continues to expand?

DESTINATION CEO

Gerald Schwartz is founder, chairman, and CEO of Onex, Canada's largest private equity firm. The only son of a Winnipeg auto parts dealer and a lawyer, Schwartz spent his childhood in an apartment upstairs from his grandparents and worked at his father's auto parts store on Friday nights and Saturdays. His high school ambition, he says, was to be "an executive and to have a big job that would pay at least $10,000 a year." He studied law at the University of Manitoba, and later moved to Boston to earn a Harvard MBA. From there, he went to New York City, where he became part of a team of investment bankers that pioneered leveraged-buyout techniques on Wall Street.

In the late 1970s, Schwartz and a partner, Izzy Asper, founded a media company, later known as CanWest Global Communications. He left CanWest in 1983 and went on to establish Onex. His preference for friendly acquisitions has helped Onex amass a group of companies with 110,000 employees and $17 billion in revenue. Notable components of the $20 billion portfolio are the Cineplex movie chain and Celestica, the huge electronics manufacturer. His most important tips for starting a new business include starting a business in a field that you want to be working in and not being afraid to start small. He also believes that the key business principle is integrity: "It's real simple, do the right thing, always."

An honorary director at the Bank of Nova Scotia, Schwartz also serves as a director of Indigo Books & Music, where his wife, Indigo Books & Music Inc. founder Heather Reisman, is CEO. They own homes in Toronto, Malibu, Nantucket, and Palm Beach—where he keeps his 19-foot dinghy, *Know Heather*, named after his wife. Schwartz and Reisman donated $15 million to the Mount Sinai Hospital in Toronto in 2013, taking their total giving to the institution to $28 million.[1]

Introduction

All organizations create products—goods, services, or ideas—for customers. Thus, organizations as diverse as Toyota, Campbell Soup, UPS, and a hospital share a number of similarities relating to how they transform resources into the products we consume. Most hospitals use similar admission procedures, while online social media companies, like Facebook and Twitter, use their technology and operating systems to create social networking opportunities and sell advertising. Such similarities are to be expected. But even organizations in unrelated industries take similar steps in creating goods or services. The check-in procedures of hotels and commercial airlines are comparable, for example. The way Subway assembles a sandwich and the way GMC assembles a truck are similar (both use automation and an assembly line). These similarities are the result of operations management, the focus of this chapter.

Here, we discuss the role of production or operations management in acquiring and managing the resources necessary to create goods and services. Production and operations management involves planning and designing the processes that will transform those resources into finished products, managing the movement of those resources through the transformation process, and ensuring that the products are of the quality expected by customers.

The Nature of Operations Management

LO1 Define operations management, and differentiate between operations and manufacturing.

Operations management (OM), the development and administration of the activities involved in transforming resources into goods and services, is of critical importance. Operations managers oversee the transformation process and the planning and designing of operations systems, managing logistics, quality, and productivity. Quality and productivity have become fundamental aspects of operations management because a company that cannot make products of the quality desired by consumers, using resources efficiently and effectively, will not be able to remain in business. OM is the "core" of most organizations because it is responsible for the creation of the organization's goods or services.

Historically, operations management has been called "production" or "manufacturing" primarily because of the view that it was limited to the manufacture of physical goods. Its focus was on methods and techniques required to operate a factory efficiently. The change from "production" to "operations" recognizes the increasing importance of organizations that provide services and ideas. Additionally, the term *operations* represents an interest in viewing the operations function as a whole rather than simply as an analysis of inputs and outputs.

Today, OM includes a wide range of organizational activities and situations outside of manufacturing, such as health care, food service, banking, entertainment, education, transportation, and charity. Thus, we use the terms **manufacturing** and **production** interchangeably to represent the activities and processes used in making *tangible* products, whereas we use the broader term **operations** to describe those processes used in the making of *both tangible and intangible products*. Manufacturing provides tangible products such as Hewlett-Packard's latest printer, and operations provides intangibles such as a stay at Wyndham Hotels and Resorts.

The Transformation Process

At the heart of operations management is the transformation process through which **inputs** (resources such as labour, money, materials, and energy) are converted into **outputs** (goods, services, and ideas). The transformation process combines inputs in predetermined ways using different equipment, administrative procedures, and technology to create a product (Figure 8.1). To ensure that this process generates quality products efficiently, operations managers control the process by taking measurements (feedback) at various points in the transformation process and comparing them to previously established standards. If there is any deviation between the actual and desired outputs, the manager may take some sort of corrective action. All adjustments made to create a satisfying product are a part of the transformation process.

Transformation may take place through one or more processes. In a business that manufactures oak furniture, for example, inputs pass through several processes before being turned into the final outputs—furniture that has been designed to meet the desires of customers (Figure 8.2). The furniture maker must first strip the oak trees of their bark and saw them

> **operations management (OM)** the development and administration of the activities involved in transforming resources into goods and services

> **manufacturing** the activities and processes used in making tangible products; also called production

> **production** the activities and processes used in making tangible products; also called manufacturing

> **operations** the activities and processes used in making both tangible and intangible products

> **inputs** the resources—such as labour, money, materials, and energy—that are converted into outputs

> **outputs** the goods, services, and ideas that result from the conversion of inputs

> **connect**
> Need help understanding this concept? Check out an informational video! Log into Connect, go to Resources, and click on the Videos page.

Figure 8.1 The Transformation Process of Operations Management

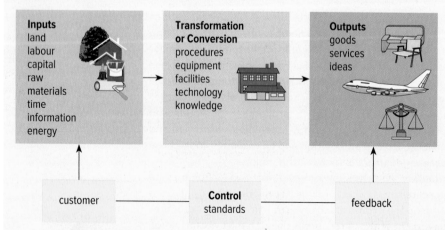

Figure 8.2 Inputs, Outputs, and Transformation Processes in the Manufacture of Oak Furniture

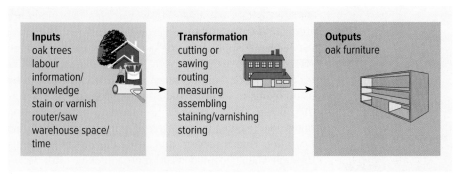

Inputs
oak trees
labour
information/
knowledge
stain or varnish
router/saw
warehouse space/
time

Transformation
cutting or
sawing
routing
measuring
assembling
staining/varnishing
storing

Outputs
oak furniture

into appropriate sizes—one step in the transformation process. Next, the firm dries the strips of oak lumber, a second form of transformation. Third, the dried wood is routed into its appropriate shape and made smooth. Fourth, workers assemble and treat the wood pieces, then stain or varnish the piece of assembled furniture. Finally, the completed piece of furniture is stored until it can be shipped to customers at the appropriate time. Of course, many businesses choose to eliminate some of these stages by purchasing already processed materials—lumber, for example—or outsourcing some tasks to third-party firms with greater expertise.

Operations Management in Service Businesses

LO2 Explain how operations management differs in manufacturing and service firms.

Different types of transformation processes take place in organizations that provide services, such as airlines, universities or colleges, and most non-profit organizations. An airline transforms inputs such as employees, time, money, and equipment through processes such as booking flights, flying airplanes, maintaining equipment, and training crews. The output of these processes is flying passengers and/or packages to their destinations. In a non-profit organization like Habitat for Humanity, inputs such as money, materials, information, and volunteer time and labour are used to transform raw materials into homes for needy families. In this setting, transformation processes include fundraising and promoting the cause in order to gain new volunteers and donations of supplies, as well as pouring concrete, raising walls, and setting roofs. Transformation processes occur in all organizations, regardless of their products or their objectives. For most organizations, the ultimate objective is for the produced outputs to be worth more than the combined costs of the inputs.

Unlike tangible goods, services are effectively actions or performances that must be directed toward the consumers who use them. Thus, there is a significant customer-contact component to most services. Examples of high-contact services include health care, real estate, tax preparation, and food service. Low-contact services, such as Amazon, often have a strong high-tech component.

Regardless of the level of customer contact, service businesses strive to provide a standardized process, and technology offers an interface that creates an automatic and structured response. The ideal service provider will be high-tech and high-touch. WestJet, for example, strives to maintain an excellent website; friendly, helpful customer contact; and live satellite TV service at every seat on board most of the Boeing Next-Generation 737 aircraft. Thus, service organizations must build their operations around good execution, which comes from hiring and training excellent employees, developing flexible systems, customizing services, and maintaining adjustable capacity to deal with fluctuating demand.[2]

Another challenge related to service operations is that the output is generally intangible and even perishable. Few services can be saved, stored, resold, or returned.[3] A seat on an airline or a table in a restaurant, for example, cannot be sold or used at a later date. Because of the perishability of services, it can be extremely difficult for service providers to accurately estimate the demand to match the right supply of a service. If an airline overestimates demand, for example, it will still have to fly each plane even with empty seats. The flight costs the same regardless of whether it is 50 percent full or 100 percent full, but the former will result in much higher costs per passenger. If the airline underestimates demand, the result can be long lines of annoyed customers or even the necessity of bumping some customers off of an overbooked flight.

Businesses that manufacture tangible goods and those that provide services or ideas are similar yet different. For example, both types of organizations must make design and operating decisions. Most goods are manufactured prior to purchase, but most services are performed after purchase. Flight attendants at Air Canada, hotel service personnel, and even the Montreal Canadiens hockey team engage in performances that are a part of the total product. Though manufacturers and service providers often perform similar activities, they also differ in several respects. We can classify these differences in five basic ways:

1. Nature and consumption of output
2. Uniformity of inputs
3. Uniformity of output
4. Labour required
5. Measurement of productivity

Although service organizations tend to vary depending on the service provider, businesses strive to standardize operations to ensure a high level of quality. The waitstaff at this hotel wear uniforms and are trained to behave a certain way when interacting with customers.

© Digital Vision/Alamy

sayings such as "Do it right the first time," and "Make the first time you do it the only time anyone has to do it." The quality of the service experience is often controlled by a service contact employee. However, some hospitals are studying the manufacturing processes and quality control mechanisms applied in the automotive industry in an effort to improve their service quality. By analyzing work processes to find unnecessary steps to eliminate, and by using teams to identify and address problems as soon as they occur, these hospitals are slashing patient waiting times, decreasing inventories of wheelchairs, readying operating rooms sooner, and generally moving patients through their hospital visit more quickly, with fewer errors, and at a lower cost.

Uniformity of Inputs. A second way to classify differences between manufacturers and service providers has to do with the uniformity of inputs. Manufacturers typically have more control over the amount of variability of the resources they use than do service providers. For example, each customer calling Service Canada is likely to require different services due to differing needs, whereas many of the tasks required to manufacture a Ford Focus are the same across each unit of output. Consequently, the products of service organizations tend to be more "customized" than those of their manufacturing counterparts. Consider, for example, a haircut versus a bottle of shampoo. The haircut is much more likely to incorporate your specific desires (customization) than is the bottle of shampoo.

Uniformity of Output. Manufacturers and service providers also differ in the uniformity of their output, the final product. Because of the human element inherent in providing services, each service tends to be performed differently. Not all grocery cashiers, for example, wait on customers in the same way. If a barber or stylist performs 15 haircuts in a day, it is unlikely that any two of them will be exactly the same. Consequently, human and technological elements associated with a service can result in a different day-to-day or even hour-to-hour performance of that service. The service experience can even vary at McDonald's or Burger King despite the fact that the two chains employ very similar procedures and processes. Moreover, no two customers are exactly alike in their perception of the service experience. Health care offers another excellent example of this challenge. Every diagnosis, treatment, and surgery varies because every individual is different. In manufacturing, the high degree of automation available allows manufacturers to generate uniform outputs and, thus, the operations are more effective and efficient. For example, we would expect every TAG Heuer or Rolex watch to maintain very high standards of quality and performance.

Nature and Consumption of Output. First, manufacturers and service providers differ in the nature and consumption of their output. For example, the term *manufacturer* implies a firm that makes tangible products. A service provider, on the other hand, produces more intangible outputs such as Canada Post's delivery of priority mail or a business stay in a Hyatt hotel. As mentioned earlier, the very nature of the service provider's product requires a higher degree of customer contact. Moreover, the actual performance of the service typically occurs at the point of consumption. At the Fairmont Chateau Laurier, the business traveller may evaluate in-room communications and the restaurant. Automakers, on the other hand, can separate the production of a car from its actual use. Manufacturing, then, can occur in an isolated environment, away from the customer. On the other hand, service providers, because of their need for customer contact, are often more limited than manufacturers in selecting work methods, assigning jobs, scheduling work, and exercising control over operations. At FedEx, the quality improvement process (QIP) includes

> **"The actual performance of the service typically occurs at the point of consumption."**

Labour Required. A fourth point of difference is the amount of labour required to produce an output. Service providers are generally more labour-intensive (require more labour) because of the high level of customer contact, perishability of the output (must be consumed immediately), and high degree of variation of inputs and outputs (customization). For example, Adecco provides temporary support personnel. Each temporary worker's performance determines Adecco's product quality. A manufacturer, on the other hand, is likely to be more capital-intensive because of the machinery and technology used in the mass production of highly similar goods. For instance, it would take a considerable investment for Ford to make an electric car that has batteries with a longer life.

Measurement of Productivity. The final distinction between service providers and manufacturers involves the measurement of productivity for each output produced. For manufacturers, measuring productivity is fairly straightforward because of the tangibility of the output and its high degree of uniformity. For the service provider, variations in demand (e.g., higher demand for air travel in some seasons than in others), variations in service requirements from job to job, and the intangibility of the product make productivity measurement more difficult. Consider, for example, how much easier it is to measure the productivity of employees involved in the production of Intel computer processors as opposed to serving the needs of CIBC's clients.

It is convenient and simple to think of organizations as being either manufacturers or service providers as in the preceding discussion. In reality, however, most organizations are a combination of the two, with both tangible and intangible qualities embodied in what they produce. For example, Porsche provides customer services such as toll-free hotlines and warranty protection, while banks may sell cheques and other tangible products that

© ValeStock/Shutterstock.com

Subway's inputs are sandwich components such as bread, tomatoes, and lettuce, while its outputs are customized sandwiches.

complement their primarily intangible product offering. Thus, we consider "products" to include tangible physical goods as well as intangible service offerings. It is the level of tangibility of its principal product that tends to classify a company as either a manufacturer or a service provider. From an OM standpoint, this level of tangibility greatly influences the nature of the company's operational processes and procedures.

Planning and Designing Operations Systems

LO3 Describe the elements involved in planning and designing an operations system.

Before a company can produce any product, it must first decide what it will produce and for what group of customers. It must then determine what processes it will use to make these products as well as the facilities it needs to produce them. These decisions comprise operations planning. Although planning was once the sole realm of the production and operations department, today's successful companies involve all departments within an organization, particularly marketing and research and development, in these decisions.

Planning the Product

Before making any product, a company first must determine what consumers want and then design a product to satisfy that want. Most companies use marketing research (discussed in Chapter 11) to determine the kinds of goods and services to provide and the features they must possess. Twitter and Facebook provide new opportunities for businesses to discover what consumers want, and then design the product accordingly. For instance, mineral-based makeup company Bare Escentuals Cosmetics uses Facebook to interact with its customers and generate feedback. From Facebook, Bare Escentuals learned that customers preferred makeup packaging that was more portable so it would be easier to take the makeup with them. This feedback led the company to redesign its packaging by adopting the more portable "Click, Lock, Go" container. By listening to its customers, Bare Escentuals was able to meet their needs more effectively, leading to greater customer satisfaction.[5] Marketing research can also help gauge the demand for a product and how much consumers are willing to pay for it.

Developing a product can be a lengthy, expensive process. For example, in the automobile industry, developing the new technology for night vision, bumper-mounted sonar systems that make parking easier, and a satellite service that locates and analyzes car problems has been a lengthy, expensive process. Most companies work to reduce development time and costs. For example, through Web collaboration, faucet manufacturer Moen has reduced the time required to take an idea to a finished product in stores to just 16 months, a drop of 33 percent.[6] Once management has developed an idea for a product that customers will buy, it must then plan how to produce the product.

Within a company, the engineering or research and development department is charged with turning a product idea into a workable design that can be produced economically. In smaller companies, a single individual (perhaps the owner) may be solely responsible for this crucial activity. Regardless of who is responsible for product design, planning does not stop with a blueprint for a product or a description of a service; it must also work out efficient production of the product to ensure that enough is available to satisfy consumer demand. How does a lawn mower company transform steel, aluminum, and other materials into a mower design that satisfies consumer and environmental requirements? Operations managers must plan for the types and quantities of materials needed to produce the product, the skills and quantity of people needed to make the product, and the actual processes through which the inputs must pass in their transformation to outputs.

Designing the Operations Processes

Before a firm can begin production, it must first determine the appropriate method of transforming resources into the desired product. Often, consumers' specific needs and desires dictate a process. Customer needs, for example, require that all ¾-inch bolts have the same basic thread size, function, and quality; if they did not, engineers and builders could not rely on ¾-inch bolts in their construction projects. A bolt manufacturer, then, will likely use a standardized process so that every ¾-inch bolt produced is like every other one. On the other hand, a bridge often must be customized so that it is appropriate for the site and expected load; furthermore, the bridge must be constructed on site rather than in a factory. Typically, products are designed to be manufactured by one of three processes: standardization, modular design, or customization.

Standardization. Most firms that manufacture products in large quantities for many customers have found that they can make them more quickly and at lower cost by standardizing designs. **Standardization** is making identical, interchangeable components or even complete products. With standardization, a customer may not get exactly what he or she wants, but the product generally costs less than a custom-designed product. Television sets, ballpoint pens, and tortilla chips are standardized products; most are manufactured on an assembly line. Standardization speeds up production and quality control and reduces production costs. And, as in the example of the ¾-inch bolts, standardization provides consistency so that customers who need certain products to function uniformly all the time will get a product that meets their expectations. Standardization becomes more complex

standardization the making of identical interchangeable components or products

Tony and Maureen Wheeler

Business: Lonely Planet

Founded: Early 1970s

Success: A sense of adventure led to Lonely Planet with offices in Melbourne, London, and Oakland; 500 staff members; and 300 authors.

Tony and Maureen met on a park bench in London, England, and married a year later. For their honeymoon, they decided to attempt what few people thought possible—crossing Europe and Asia overland, all the way to Australia. It took them several months and all the money they could earn, beg, or borrow, but they made it. It was too amazing an experience to keep to themselves. Urged on by their friends, they stayed up nights at their kitchen table writing, typing, and stapling together their very first travel guide, *Across Asia on the Cheap*. Within a week they had sold 1,500 copies and Lonely Planet was born. They wrote their second book, *South-East Asia on a Shoestring*, in a backstreet hotel in Singapore, which led to books on Nepal, Australia, Africa, and India. Maureen and Tony decided to settle in Australia where

Maureen went to La Trobe University in Melbourne and received a bachelor's degree in social work. Faced with a choice between her social work and travelling, she chose to make travel her career. Travelling with children became a way of life for the Wheelers after the births of their children. This prompted Maureen to write a guidebook about it, *Travel With Children*, which is the result of years of experience on the road with the kids. As Lonely Planet became a globally loved brand, Tony and Maureen received several offers for the company. But it was not until 2007 that they found a partner whom they trusted to remain true to Lonely Planet's principles. In October of that year, BBC Worldwide acquired a 75 percent share in Lonely Planet, pledging to uphold Lonely Planet's commitment to independent travel, trustworthy advice, and editorial independence. Tony and Maureen are still actively involved with Lonely Planet. They are travelling more often than ever, and they are devoting their spare time to charitable projects. And the company is still driven by the philosophy in *Across Asia on the Cheap*: "All you've got to do is decide to go and the hardest part is over. So go!"[8]

on a global scale because different countries have different standards for quality. To help solve this problem, the International Organization for Standardization (ISO) has developed a list of global standards that companies can adopt to assure stakeholders that they are complying with the highest quality, environmental, and managerial guidelines.

Modular Design. **Modular design** involves building an item in self-contained units, or modules, that can be combined or interchanged to create different products. Dell laptops, for example, are composed of a number of components—LCD screen, AC adapter, keyboard, motherboard, etc.—that can be installed in different configurations to meet customers' needs.[7] Because many modular components are produced as integrated units, the failure of any portion of a modular component usually means replacing the entire component. Modular design allows products to be repaired quickly, thus reducing the cost of labour, but the component itself is expensive, raising the cost of repair materials. Many automobile manufacturers use modular

> **modular design** the creation of an item in self-contained units, or modules, that can be combined or interchanged to create different products

design in the production process. Manufactured homes are built on a modular design and often cost about one-fourth the cost of a conventionally built house.

Customization. **Customization** is making products to meet a particular customer's needs or wants. Products produced in this way are generally unique. Such products include repair services, photocopy services, custom artwork, jewellery, and furniture, as well as large-scale products such as bridges, ships, and computer software. Custom designs are used in communications and service products. Ship design is another industry that uses customization. Builders generally design and build each ship to meet the needs of the customer who will use it. Orca Houseboats, for example, custom-builds each houseboat to the customer's exact specifications and preferences for things like fireplaces, hot tubs, spiral staircases, and water slides. The Vancouver-based company has delivered houseboats up to 23 metres long.[9] Mass customization relates to making products that meet the needs or wants of a large number of individual customers. The customer can select the model, size, colour, style, or design of the product.

> **customization** making products to meet a particular customer's needs or wants

> **DID YOU KNOW?**
> Hershey's has the production capacity to make 80 million Hershey's kisses per day.[10]

Dell can customize a computer with the exact configuration that fits a customer's needs. Services such as fitness programs and travel packages can also be custom designed for a large number of individual customers. For both goods and services, customers get to make choices and have options to determine the final product.

Planning Capacity

Planning the operational processes for the organization involves two important areas: capacity planning and facilities planning. The term **capacity** basically refers to the maximum load that an organizational unit can carry or operate. The unit of measurement may be a worker or machine, a department, a branch, or even an entire plant. Maximum capacity can be stated in terms of the inputs or outputs provided. For example, an electric plant might state plant capacity in terms of the maximum number of kilowatt-hours that can be produced without causing a power outage, while a restaurant might state capacity in terms of the maximum number of customers who can be effectively—comfortably and courteously—served at any one particular time.

> **capacity** the maximum load that an organizational unit can carry or operate

Efficiently planning the organization's capacity needs is an important process for the operations manager. Capacity levels that fall short can result in unmet demand, and consequently, lost customers. On the other hand, when there is more capacity available than needed, operating costs are driven up needlessly due to unused and often expensive resources. To avoid such situations, organizations must accurately forecast demand and then plan capacity based on these forecasts. Another reason for the importance of efficient capacity planning has to do with long-term commitment of resources. Often, once a capacity decision—such as factory size—has been implemented, it is very difficult to change the decision without incurring substantial costs. Large companies have come to realize that although change can be expensive, not adjusting to future demand and stakeholder desires will be more expensive in the long run. For this reason, Honda has begun to adopt ISO 14001 guidelines for environmental management systems in its factories. These systems help firms monitor their impact on the environment. Thirteen of Honda's 14 North American factories have received certification.[11]

Planning Facilities

Once a company knows what process it will use to create its products, it then can design and build an appropriate facility in which to make them. Many products are manufactured in factories, but others are produced in stores, at home, or where the product ultimately will be used. Companies must decide where to locate their operations facilities, what layout is best for producing their particular product, and even what technology to apply to the transformation process.

Many firms are developing both a traditional organization for customer contact and a virtual organization. RBC Financial Group maintains traditional branches and has developed complete telephone and Internet services for customers. Through its website, clients can obtain banking services and trade securities without leaving their home or office.

Facility Location. Where to locate a firm's facilities is a significant question because, once the decision has been made and implemented, the firm must live with it due to the high costs involved. When a company decides to relocate or open a facility at a new location, it must pay careful attention to factors such as proximity to market, availability of raw materials, availability of transportation, availability of power, climatic influences, availability of labour, community characteristics (quality of life), and taxes and inducements. Inducements and tax reductions have become an increasingly important criterion in recent years. When selecting a site for a contact centre to serve customers throughout Canada and the Americas, Dell chose Edmonton for its good quality of life, highly skilled workers, and world-class training programs. eBay chose to locate its new customer-support centre in Burnaby, British Columbia, out of 100 other communities that were vying for the centre, because of the combination of the educated workforce, quality of life, and easy access to eBay's headquarters in San Jose, California.[12] Apple has followed the lead of other major companies by locating its manufacturing facilities in China to take advantage of lower labour and production costs. The facility-location decision is complex because it involves the evaluation of many factors, some of which cannot be measured with precision. Because of the long-term impact of the decision, however, it is one that cannot be taken lightly.

© China Photos/Getty Images

Apple stores are designed to make the most efficient use of space. The layout of the stores allows customers to test Apple's products before purchasing.

Facility Layout. Arranging the physical layout of a facility is a complex, highly technical task. Some industrial architects specialize in the design and layout of certain types of businesses. There are three basic layouts: fixed-position, process, and product.

A company using a **fixed-position layout** brings all resources required to create the product to a central location. The product—perhaps an office building, house, hydroelectric plant, or bridge—does not move. A company using a fixed-position layout may be called a **project organization** because it is typically involved in large, complex projects such as construction or exploration. Project organizations generally make a unique product, rely on highly skilled labour, produce very few units, and have high production costs per unit.

Firms that use a **process layout** organize the transformation process into departments that group related processes. A metal fabrication plant, for example, may have a cutting department, a drilling department, and a polishing department. A hospital may have an X-ray unit, an obstetrics unit, and so on. These types of organizations are sometimes called **intermittent organizations**, which deal with products of a lesser magnitude than do project organizations, and their products are not necessarily unique but possess a significant number of differences. Doctors, makers of custom-made cabinets, commercial printers, and advertising agencies are intermittent organizations because they tend to create products to customers' specifications and produce relatively few units of each product. Because of the low level of output, the cost per unit of product is generally high.

The **product layout** requires that production be broken down into relatively simple tasks assigned to workers, who are usually positioned along an assembly line. Workers remain in one location, and the product moves from one worker to another. Each person in turn performs his or her required tasks or activities. Companies that use assembly lines are usually known as **continuous manufacturing organizations**, so named because once they are set up, they run continuously, creating products with many similar characteristics. Examples of products produced on assembly lines are automobiles, television sets, vacuum cleaners, toothpaste, and meals from a cafeteria. Continuous manufacturing organizations using a product layout are characterized by the standardized product they produce, the large number of units produced, and the relatively low unit cost of production.

Many companies actually use a combination of layout designs. For example, an automobile manufacturer may rely on an assembly line (product layout) but may also use a process layout to manufacture parts.

Technology. Every industry has a basic, underlying technology that dictates the nature of its transformation process. The steel industry continually tries to improve steelmaking techniques. The health care industry performs research into medical technologies and pharmaceuticals to improve the quality of health care service. Two developments that have strongly influenced the operations of many businesses are computers and robotics.

Computers have been used for decades and on a relatively large scale since IBM introduced its 650 series in the late 1950s. The operations function makes great use of computers in all phases of the transformation process. **Computer-assisted design (CAD)**, for example, helps engineers design components, products, and processes on the computer instead of on paper. **Computer-assisted manufacturing (CAM)** goes a step further, employing specialized computer systems to actually guide and control the transformation processes. Such systems can monitor the transformation process, gathering information about the equipment used to produce the products and about the product itself as it goes from one stage of the transformation process to the next. The computer provides information to an operator who may, if necessary, take corrective action. In some highly automated systems, the computer itself can take corrective action. At Dell's OptiPlex Plant, electronic instructions are sent to double-decker conveyor belts that speed computer components to assembly stations. Two-member teams are told by computers which PC or server to build, with initial assembly taking only three to four minutes. Then more electronic commands move the products (more than 20,000 machines on a typical day) to a finishing area to be customized, boxed, and sent to waiting delivery trucks. Although the plant covers over 18,500 square metres, enough to enclose 23 football fields, it is managed almost entirely by a network of computers.[13]

---

fixed-position layout a layout that brings all resources required to create the product to a central location

project organization a company using a fixed-position layout because it is typically involved in large, complex projects such as construction or exploration

process layout a layout that organizes the transformation process into departments that group related processes

intermittent organizations organizations that deal with products of a lesser magnitude than do project organizations; their products are not necessarily unique but possess a significant number of differences

product layout a layout requiring that production be broken down into relatively simple tasks assigned to workers, who are usually positioned along an assembly line

continuous manufacturing organizations companies that use continuously running assembly lines, creating products with many similar characteristics

computer-assisted design (CAD) the design of components, products, and processes on computers instead of on paper

computer-assisted manufacturing (CAM) manufacturing that employs specialized computer systems to actually guide and control the transformation processes

> ## "Every industry has a basic, underlying technology that dictates the nature of its transformation process."

Using **flexible manufacturing**, computers can direct machinery to adapt to different versions of similar operations. For example, with instructions from a computer, one machine can be programmed to carry out its function for several different versions of an engine without shutting down the production line for refitting.

Robots are also becoming increasingly useful in the transformation process. These "steel-collar" workers have become particularly important in industries such as nuclear power, hazardous-waste disposal, ocean research, and space construction and maintenance, in which human lives would otherwise be at risk. Robots are used in numerous applications by companies around the world. Many assembly operations—cars, television sets, telephones, stereo equipment, and numerous other products—depend on industrial robots. Researchers continue to create more sophisticated robots, and some speculate that in the future robots will not be limited to space programs and production and operations, but will also be able to engage in farming, laboratory research, and even household activities. Moreover, robotics is increasingly being used in the medical field. Voice-activated robotic arms operate video cameras for surgeons. Similar technology assists with biopsies, as well as heart, spine, and nervous system procedures. A heart surgeon at London Health Science Centre in Ontario uses a surgical robot to perform bypass operations on patients without opening their chests, except for five tiny incisions, while their hearts continue beating. More than 400 surgeons around the world currently use surgical robots with far fewer postoperative complications than encountered in conventional operations.[14] There are an estimated 1 million robots being used in manufacturing around the world, most of them in high-tech industries.

When all these technologies—CAD/CAM, flexible manufacturing, robotics, computer systems, and more—are integrated, the result is **computer-integrated manufacturing (CIM)**, a complete system that designs products, manages machines and materials, and controls the operations function. Companies adopt CIM to boost productivity and quality and reduce costs. Such technology, and computers in particular, will continue to make strong inroads into operations on two fronts—dealing with the technology involved in manufacturing, and dealing with the administrative functions and processes used by operations managers.

flexible manufacturing the direction of machinery by computers to adapt to different versions of similar operations

computer-integrated manufacturing (CIM) a complete system that designs products, manages machines and materials, and controls the operations function

The operations manager must be willing to work with computers and other forms of technology and to develop a high degree of computer literacy.

Sustainability and Manufacturing

Manufacturing and operations systems are moving quickly to establish environmental sustainability and minimize negative impact on the natural environment. Sustainability deals with reducing the consumption of resources and the long-term well-being of the planet, including natural entities and the interactions of individuals, organizations, and businesses. Sustainability issues are becoming increasingly important to stakeholders and consumers, as they pertain to the future health of the planet. Some sustainability issues include pollution of the land, air, and water; climate change; waste management; deforestation; urban sprawl; protection of biodiversity; and genetically modified foods.

For example, Johnson Controls has incorporated sustainability into many different facets of its operations. The company purchases green energy, works with suppliers to "green" its supply chain, and designs more eco-friendly products. Overseeing these activities is Johnson Control's Global Environmental Sustainability Council, which measures the company's progress toward its sustainability goals.

The outdoor clothing company Patagonia is always looking for a greener way to design, produce, and recycle its products. The company's mission statement: *Build the best product, cause no unnecessary harm, and use business to inspire and implement solutions to the environmental crisis.*

Johnson Controls also opened a battery recycling facility to encourage stakeholders to recycle their lead-acid batteries rather than disposing of them improperly.[15] Molson Coors Brewing Company was the first major brewer in Canada to convert its brewing by-products, such as spent yeast and waste beer, into fuel-grade ethanol. Molson aluminum cans are made with a minimum 67 percent recycled content (up from 42 percent in 2007), while kegs are refilled more than 200 times over their 25-year lifespan.[16]

Johnson Controls and Molson Coors demonstrate that reducing waste, recycling, conserving, and using renewable energy not only protect the environment but also can gain the support of stakeholders. Green operations and manufacturing can improve a firm's reputation along with customer and employee loyalty, leading to improved profits.

Much of the movement to green manufacturing and operations is the belief that global warming and climate change must decline. The McKinsey Global Institute (MGI) says that just by investing in existing technologies, the world's energy use could be reduced by 50 percent by 2020. Just creating green buildings and more fuel-efficient cars could yield $900 billion in savings per year by 2020.[17] Companies such as Canadian National Railway Co. are integrating hybrid and alternative fuel vehicles into its fleet, which are up to 20 percent more fuel efficient and produce 40 percent fewer nitrogen oxides. The company provides customers with web-based carbon emissions and carbon credit calculators to estimate the environmental impact of their rail shipments.[18] Green products produced through green operations and manufacturing are our future. Government initiatives provide space for businesses to innovate their green operations and manufacturing.

Managing the Supply Chain

LO4 Specify some techniques managers may use to manage the logistics of transforming inputs into finished products.

A major function of operations is **supply chain management**, which refers to connecting and integrating all parties or members of the distribution system to satisfy customers.[19] Also called logistics, supply chain management includes all the activities involved in obtaining and managing raw materials and component parts, managing finished products, packaging them, and getting them to customers. Sunny Delight had to quickly re-create its supply chain after spinning off from Procter & Gamble. This means it had to develop ordering, shipping, billing, and warehouse management systems as well as transportation, so it could focus on growing and managing the Sunny Delight brand.[20] The supply chain integrates firms such as raw material

supply chain management connecting and integrating all parties or members of the distribution system in order to satisfy customers

suppliers, manufacturers, retailers, and ultimate consumers into a seamless flow of information and products.[21] Some aspects of logistics (warehousing, packaging, distributing) are so closely linked with marketing that we will discuss them in Chapter 12. In this section, we look at purchasing, managing inventory, outsourcing, and scheduling, which are vital tasks in the transformation of raw materials into finished goods. To illustrate logistics, consider a hypothetical small business—we'll call it Rushing Water Canoes Inc.—that manufactures aluminum canoes, which it sells primarily to sporting goods stores and river-rafting expeditions. Our company also makes paddles and helmets, but the focus of the following discussion is the manufacture of the company's quality canoes as they proceed through the logistics process.

Purchasing

Purchasing, also known as procurement, is the buying of all the materials needed by the organization. The purchasing department aims to obtain items of the desired quality in the right quantities at the lowest possible cost. Rushing Water Canoes, for example, must procure not only aluminum and other raw materials, and various canoe parts and components, but also machines and equipment, manufacturing supplies (oil, electricity, and so on), and office supplies to make its canoes. People in the purchasing department locate and evaluate suppliers of these items. They must constantly be on the lookout for new materials or parts that will do a better job or cost less than those currently being used. The purchasing function can be quite complex and is one area made much easier and more efficient by technological advances.

purchasing the buying of all the materials needed by the organization; also called procurement

Not all companies purchase all the materials needed to create their products. Often, they can make some components more economically and efficiently than can an outside supplier. Coors, for example, manufactures its own cans at a subsidiary plant. On the other hand, firms sometimes find that it is uneconomical to make or purchase an item, and instead arrange to lease it from another organization. Some airlines, for example, lease airplanes rather than buy them. Whether to purchase, make, or lease a needed item generally depends on cost, as well as on product availability and supplier reliability.

"A major function of operations is supply chain management, which refers to connecting and integrating all parties or members of the distribution system in order to satisfy customers."

Managing Inventory

Once the items needed to create a product have been procured, some provision has to be made for storing them until they are needed. Every raw material, component, completed or partially completed product, and piece of equipment a firm uses—its **inventory**—must be accounted for, or controlled. There are three basic types of inventory. *Finished-goods inventory* includes those products that are ready for sale, such as a fully assembled automobile ready to ship to a dealer. *Work-in-process inventory* consists of those products that are partly completed or are in some stage of the transformation process. At McDonald's, a cooking hamburger represents work-in-process inventory because it must go through several more stages before it can be sold to a customer. *Raw materials inventory* includes all the materials that have been purchased to be used as inputs for making other products. Nuts and bolts are raw materials for an automobile manufacturer, while hamburger patties, vegetables, and buns are raw materials for the fast-food restaurant. Our fictional Rushing Water Canoes has an inventory of materials for making canoes, paddles, and helmets, as well as its inventory of finished products for sale to consumers. **Inventory control** is the process of determining how many supplies and goods are needed and keeping track of quantities on hand, where each item is, and who is responsible for it.

Operations management must be closely coordinated with inventory control. The production of televisions, for example, cannot be planned without some knowledge of the availability of all the necessary materials—the chassis, picture tubes, colour guns, and so forth. Also, each item held in inventory—any type of inventory—carries with it a cost. For example, storing fully assembled televisions in a warehouse to sell to a dealer at a future date requires not only the use of space, but also the purchase of insurance to cover any losses that might occur due to fire or other unforeseen events.

Inventory managers spend a great deal of time trying to determine the proper inventory level for each item. The answer to the question of how many units to hold in inventory depends on variables such as the usage rate of the item, the cost of maintaining the item in inventory, the cost of paperwork and other procedures associated with ordering or making the item, and the cost of the item itself. For example, the price of

© Katie N. Gardner for the Washington Post via Getty Images

At Walmart, managing inventory involves finding the right balance between excess inventory and not enough inventory. Walmart uses just-in-time inventory management to minimize inventory costs and become more efficient.

copper has fluctuated between $1.50 and $4 per pound over the last five years. Firms using copper wiring for construction or copper pipes for plumbing, and other industries requiring copper, have to analyze the trade-offs between inventory costs and expected changes in the price of copper. Several approaches may be used to determine how many units of a given item should be procured at one time and when that procurement should take place.

The Economic Order Quantity Model. To control the number of items maintained in inventory, managers need to determine how much of any given item they should order. One popular approach is the **economic order quantity (EOQ) model**, which identifies the optimum number of items to order to minimize the costs of managing (ordering, storing, and using) them.

Just-In-Time Inventory Management. An increasingly popular technique is **just-in-time (JIT) inventory management**, which eliminates waste by using smaller quantities of materials that arrive "just in time" for use in the transformation process and therefore require less storage space and other inventory management expense. JIT minimizes inventory by providing an almost continuous flow of items from suppliers to the

inventory all raw materials, components, completed or partially completed products, and pieces of equipment a firm uses

inventory control the process of determining how many supplies and goods are needed and keeping track of quantities on hand, where each item is, and who is responsible for it

economic order quantity (EOQ) model a model that identifies the optimum number of items to order to minimize the costs of managing (ordering, storing, and using) them

just-in-time (JIT) inventory management a technique using smaller quantities of materials that arrive "just in time" for use in the transformation process and therefore require less storage space and other inventory management expense

production facility. While first used by Toyota, many companies now have adopted JIT to reduce costs and boost efficiency.

Let's say that Rushing Water Canoes uses 20 units of aluminum from a supplier per day. Traditionally, its inventory manager might order enough for one month at a time: 440 units per order (20 units per day times 22 workdays per month). The expense of such a large inventory could be considerable because of the cost of insurance coverage, recordkeeping, rented storage space, and so on. The just-in-time approach would reduce these costs because aluminum would be purchased in smaller quantities, perhaps in lot sizes of 20, which the supplier would deliver once a day. Of course, for such an approach to be effective, the supplier must be extremely reliable and relatively close to the production facility.

needed to make the product. The basic components of MRP are a master production schedule, a bill of materials, and an inventory status file. At Rushing Water Canoes, for example, the inventory-control manager will look at the production schedule to determine how many canoes the company plans to make. He or she will then prepare a bill of materials—a list of all the materials needed to make that quantity of canoes. Next, the manager will determine the quantity of these items that RWC already holds in inventory (to avoid ordering excess materials) and then develop a schedule for ordering and accepting delivery of the right quantity of materials to satisfy the firm's needs. Because of the large number of parts and materials that go into a typical production process, MRP must be done on a computer. It can be, and often is, used in conjunction with just-in-time inventory management.

material-requirements planning (MRP) a planning system that schedules the precise quantity of materials needed to make the product

Material-Requirements Planning. Another inventory management technique is **material-requirements planning (MRP)**, a planning system that schedules the precise quantity of materials

Outsourcing

Increasingly, outsourcing has become a component of supply chain management in operations. As we mentioned in Chapter 3, outsourcing refers to the contracting of manufacturing or other tasks to independent companies, often overseas. Many companies elect to outsource some aspects of their operations to companies that can provide

---

GOING GREEN | UPS Adds Green Practices to Its Logistics

UPS is doing more with less. In 2010, the company increased its package volume by 1.8 percent. Normally, such an increase requires more resources, but not so at UPS; the company actually reduced its fuel consumption by 3.3 percent for each package. It also decreased its absolute water consumption in the United States by 11 percent. UPS hired Scott Wicker to be its corporate sustainability officer (CSO) to oversee its initiatives and embed sustainability into its operations. According to Wicker, "Sustainability means we operate not only for the present, but for the future as well."

How has UPS been able to increase its productivity and sustainability at the same time? UPS uses technology and data measurements to calculate the resources it consumes and determine ways to be more efficient. For instance, the company has been investing in more fuel-efficient vehicles for years. Additionally, UPS has made slight changes in operations, such as reducing the number of stops and only making right turns to decrease driving time and save fuel. Although these

methods may not seem like much, UPS was able to cut more than 11.5 million litres of fuel and 68,000 tonnes of emissions from its logistics operations. The company is also targeting eco-minded consumers with services such as a carbon neutral service for U.S. deliveries. UPS is creating a competitive advantage by becoming expert at incorporating green practices into all facets of its operations.[22]

DISCUSSION QUESTIONS

1. How is UPS using sustainability to cut costs?

2. Which stakeholders have the ability to benefit from UPS's green practices?

3. How can UPS's green practices act as a model for other companies to improve their operations?

these products more efficiently, at a lower cost, and with greater customer satisfaction. Globalization has put pressure on supply chain managers to improve speed and balance resources against competitive pressures. Companies outsourcing to China, in particular, face heavy regulation, high transportation costs, inadequate facilities, and unpredictable supply chain execution. Therefore, suppliers need to provide useful, timely, and accurate information about every aspect of the quality requirements, schedules, and solutions to dealing with problems. Companies that hire suppliers must also make certain that their suppliers are following company standards; failure to do so could lead to criticism of the parent company. For example, Hershey was criticized for sourcing from suppliers that used child labour on chocolate plantations. Although suppliers are responsible for hiring underage workers, it is ultimately the responsibility of Hershey to ensure the compliance of suppliers in its supply chain.[23]

Many high-tech firms have outsourced the production of memory chips, computers, and telecom equipment to Asian companies.[24] The hourly labour costs in countries such as China, India, and Vietnam are far less than in Canada, Europe, or even Mexico. These developing countries have improved their manufacturing capabilities, infrastructure, and technical and business skills, making them more attractive regions for global sourcing. On the other hand, the cost of outsourcing halfway around the world must be considered in decisions.[25] While information technology is often outsourced today, transportation, human resources, services, and even marketing functions can be outsourced. Our hypothetical Rushing Water Canoes might contract with a local janitorial service to clean its offices and with a local accountant to handle routine bookkeeping and tax-preparation functions.

Outsourcing, once used primarily as a cost-cutting tactic, has increasingly been linked with the development of competitive advantage through improved product quality, speeding up the time it takes products to get to the customer, and overall supply-chain efficiencies. Table 8.1 provides the world's top five outsourcing providers that assist mainly in information technology. Outsourcing allows companies to free up time and resources to focus on what they do best and to create better opportunities to focus on customer satisfaction. Many executives view outsourcing as an innovative way to boost productivity and remain competitive against low-wage offshore factories. However, outsourcing may create conflict with labour and negative public opinion when it results in North American workers being replaced by lower-cost workers in other countries.

Table 8.1 The World's Top Five Outsourcing Providers

Company	Services
Alsbridge	Global advisory services
KPMG	Audit, tax, and advisory services
TPI	Information services and market intelligence
Kirkland & Ellis	Law services
EquaTerra (since acquired by KPMG)	Information technology and business process transformation advisory services

Source: "IAOP Announces 2010 Rankings for the World's Best Outsourcing Providers and Advisors," International Association of Outsourcing Professionals, www.iaop.org/content/23/152/2042/ (accessed February 22, 2012).

> **"Many executives view** outsourcing as an innovative way to boost productivity and remain competitive against low-wage offshore factories."

Routing and Scheduling

After all materials have been procured and their use determined, managers must then consider the **routing**, or sequence of operations

routing the sequence of operations through which the product must pass

© AP Photo/Richard Vogel

Many athletic shoe manufacturers such as Nike outsource production to China and Vietnam to take advantage of lower labour costs.

Figure 8.3 A Hypothetical PERT Diagram for a McDonald's Big Mac

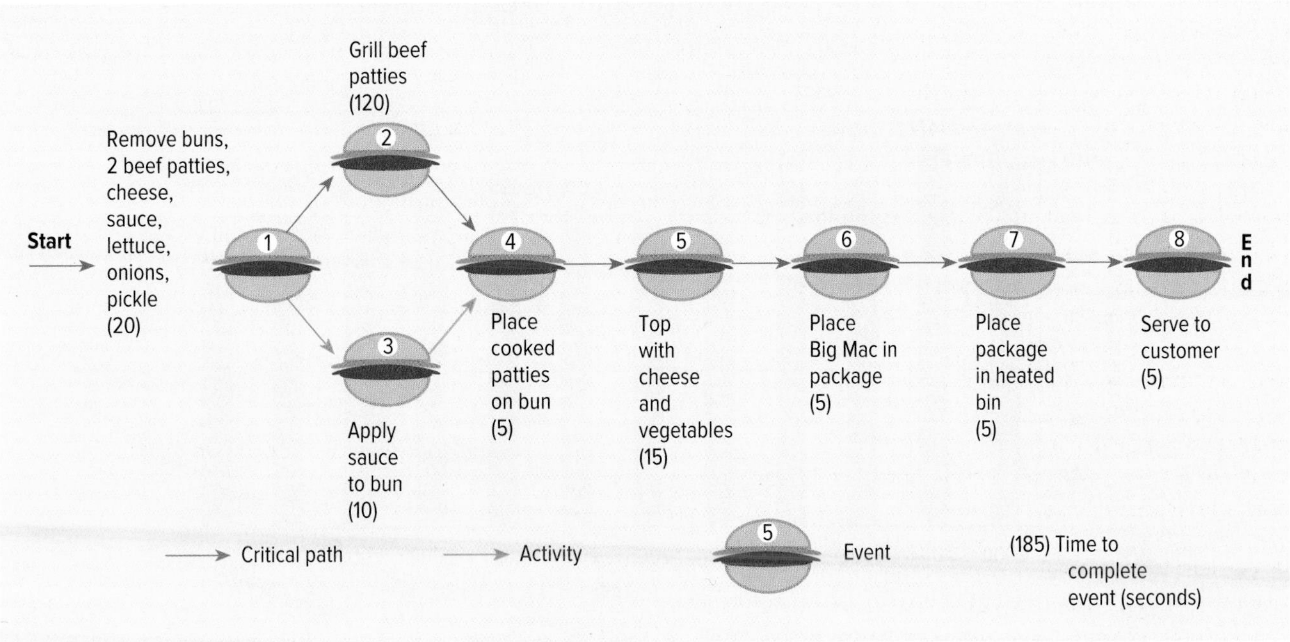

through which the product must pass. For example, before employees at Rushing Water Canoes can form aluminum sheets into a canoe, the aluminum must be cut to size. Likewise, the canoe's flotation material must be installed before workers can secure the wooden seats. The sequence depends on the product specifications developed by the engineering department of the company.

Once management knows the routing, the actual work can be scheduled. **Scheduling** assigns the tasks to be done to departments or even specific machines, workers, or teams. At Rushing Water, cutting aluminum for the company's canoes might be scheduled to be done by the "cutting and finishing" department on machines designed especially for that purpose.

scheduling the assignment of required tasks to departments or even specific machines, workers, or teams

Many approaches to scheduling have been developed, ranging from simple trial and error to highly sophisticated computer programs. One popular method is the *Program Evaluation and Review Technique (PERT)*, which identifies all the major activities or events required to complete a project, arranges them in a sequence or path, determines the critical path, and estimates the time required for each event. Producing a McDonald's Big Mac, for example, involves removing meat, cheese, sauce, and vegetables from the refrigerator; grilling the hamburger patties; assembling the ingredients; placing the completed Big Mac in its package; and serving it to the customer (Figure 8.3). The cheese, pickles, onions, and sauce cannot be put on before the hamburger patty is completely grilled and placed on the bun. The path that requires the longest time from start to finish is called the *critical path* because it determines the minimum amount of time in which the process can be completed. If any of the activities on the critical path for production of the Big Mac fall behind schedule, the sandwich will not be completed on time, causing customers to wait longer than they usually would.

Managing Quality

LO5 Assess the importance of quality in operations management.

Quality, like cost and efficiency, is a critical element of operations management, for defective products can quickly ruin a firm. Quality reflects the degree to which a good or service meets the demands and requirements of customers. Customers are increasingly dissatisfied with the quality of service provided by many airlines. There are thousands of air travel complaints every year. Determining quality can be difficult because it depends on customers' perceptions of how well the product meets or exceeds their expectations. For example, customer satisfaction on airlines can vary wildly depending on individual customers' perspectives. However, the

Figure 8.4 J. D. Power & Associates Initial Automobile Quality Study

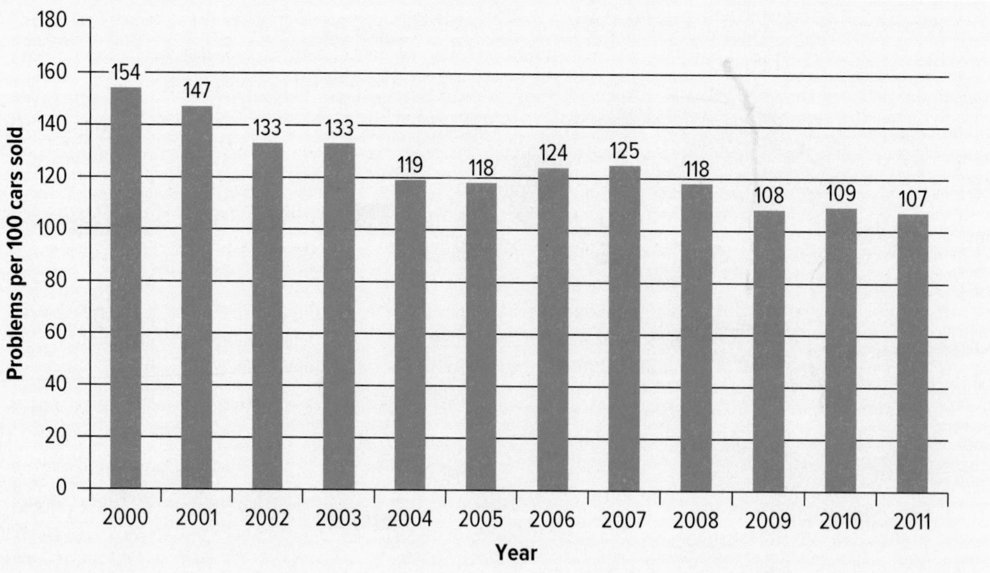

Source: J. D. Power & Associates 2011 Initial Quality Study, JDPower.com, June 23, 2011, www.jdpower.com/news/pressrelease.aspx?id52011089 (accessed February 22, 2012).

airline industry is notorious for its dissatisfied customers. Flight delays are a common subject of complaints from airline passengers; 20 percent of all flights arrive more than 15 minutes late. However, most passengers do not select an airline based on how often flights arrive on time.[26]

The fuel economy of an automobile or its reliability (defined in terms of frequency of repairs) can be measured with some degree of precision. Although automakers rely on their own measures of vehicle quality, they also look to independent sources such as the J. D. Power & Associates annual initial quality survey for confirmation of their quality assessment as well as consumer perceptions of quality, as indicated in Figure 8.4.

It is especially difficult to measure quality characteristics when the product is a service. A company has to decide exactly which quality characteristics it considers important and then define those characteristics in terms that can be measured. The inseparability of production and consumption and the level of customer contact influence the selection of characteristics of the service that are most important. Employees in high-contact services such as hairstyling, education, legal services, and even the barista at Starbucks are an important part of the product.

The Malcolm Baldrige National Quality Award is given each year to companies that meet rigorous standards of quality. The Baldrige criteria are (1) leadership, (2) information and analysis, (3) strategic planning, (4) human resource development and management, (5) process management, (6) business results, and (7) customer focus and satisfaction. The criteria have become a worldwide framework for driving business improvement.

Quality is so important that we need to examine it in the context of operations management. **Quality control** refers to the processes an organization uses to maintain its established quality standards. Kia recognized the importance of quality control when it sought to revamp its image. For years, Kia vehicles were seen as low quality. To change consumer perceptions of the Kia brand, the company had its quality-control managers provide final approval for its products instead of sales executives, implemented benchmarks for improving product quality, developed strong marketing campaigns promoting the brand, and cut dealers that they did not feel were supporting the Kia franchise. Kia's quality efforts were largely successful; its overall sales grew 27 percent in a one-year period.[27] Quality has become a major concern in many organizations, particularly in light of intense foreign competition and increasingly demanding customers. To regain a competitive edge, a number of firms have adopted a total quality management approach. **Total quality management (TQM)** is a philosophy that uniform commitment to quality in all areas of

quality control the processes an organization uses to maintain its established quality standards

total quality management (TQM) a philosophy that uniform commitment to quality in all areas of an organization will promote a culture that meets customers' perceptions of quality

the organization will promote a culture that meets customers' perceptions of quality. It involves coordinating efforts to improve customer satisfaction, increase employee participation and empowerment, form and strengthen supplier partnerships, and foster an organizational culture of continuous quality improvement. TQM requires continuous quality improvement and employee empowerment.

Continuous improvement of an organization's goods and services is built around the notion that quality is free; by contrast, *not* having high-quality goods and services can be very expensive, especially in terms of dissatisfied customers.[28] A primary tool of the continuous improvement process is *benchmarking*, the measuring and evaluating of the quality of the organization's goods, services, or processes as compared with the quality produced by the best-performing companies in the industry.[29] Benchmarking lets the organization know where it stands competitively in its industry, thus giving it a goal to aim for over time. Now that online digital media are becoming more important in businesses, companies such as Compuware Gomez offer benchmarking tools so that companies can monitor and compare the success of their websites. Such tools allow companies to track traffic to the site versus competitors' sites. Studies have shown a direct link between website performance and online sales, meaning this type of benchmarking is important.[30]

Companies employing total quality management (TQM) programs know that quality control should be incorporated throughout the transformation process, from the initial plans to develop a specific product through the product and production facility design processes to the actual manufacture of the product. In other words, they view quality control as an element of the product itself, rather than as simply a function of the operations process. When a company makes the product correctly from the outset, it eliminates the need to rework defective products, expedites the transformation process itself, and allows employees to make better use of their time and materials. One method through which many companies have tried to improve quality is **statistical process control**, a system in which management collects and analyzes information about the production process to pinpoint quality problems in the production system.

Establishing Standards—ISO 9000

Regardless of whether a company has a TQM program for quality control, it must first determine what standard of quality it desires and then assess whether its products meet that standard. Product specifications and quality standards must be set so the company can create a product that will compete in the marketplace. Rushing Water Canoes, for example, may specify that each of its canoes has aluminum walls of a specified uniform thickness, that the front and back of each canoe be reinforced with a specified level of steel, and that each canoe contain a specified amount of flotation material for safety. Production facilities must be designed that can build products with the desired specifications.

Quality standards can be incorporated into service businesses as well. A hamburger chain, for example, may establish standards relating to how long it takes to cook an order and serve it to customers, how many fries are in each order, how thick the burgers are, or how many customer complaints might be acceptable. Once the desired quality characteristics, specifications, and standards have been stated in measurable terms, the next step is inspection.

Consider the Following: Stella & Chewy's: The Food Dogs Love

After being told that her dog Chewy was deathly ill, Marie Moody's only chance of saving him was to change his diet. She began purchasing organic meat and vegetables to create her own dog food. Almost immediately, Chewy's health improved. Moody began feeding her other dog, Stella, the same mixture and noticed positive results in her as well. Stella & Chewy's dog food, consisting of fresh meats and organic produce, was born.

Moody began in her apartment kitchen and later expanded manufacturing. She developed partnerships with organic and antibiotic-free meat producers and hired animal scientists to help create technology to keep the food pathogen-free. Today, Stella & Chewy's uses hydrostatic high pressure to pasteurize without removing nutrients and taste. The company has a third party test each batch of food. Maintaining quality is critical to a raw food diet and for building a product that consumers trust. Stella & Chewy's has flourished, becoming the dog food of choice for many pet lovers.[31]

The International Organization for Standardization (ISO) has created a series of quality management standards—**ISO 9000**—designed to ensure the customer's quality standards are met. The standards provide a framework for documenting how a certified business keeps records, trains employees, tests products, and fixes defects. To obtain ISO 9000 certification, an independent auditor must verify that a business's factory, laboratory, or office meets the quality standards spelled out by the International Organization for Standardization. The certification process can require significant investment, but for many companies, the process is essential to being able to compete. Thousands of companies have been certified, and many more are working to meet the standards. Certification has become a virtual necessity for doing business in Europe in some high-technology businesses. ISO 9002 certification was established for service providers.

ISO 14000 is a comprehensive set of environmental standards that encourages a cleaner and safer world. ISO 14000 is a valuable standard because, currently, considerable variation exists between the regulations in different nations, and even regions within a nation. These variations make it difficult for organizations committed to sustainability to find acceptable global solutions to problems. The goal of the ISO 14000 standards is to promote a more uniform approach to environmental management and to help companies attain and measure improvements in their environmental performance.

ISO 9000 a series of quality assurance standards designed by the International Organization for Standardization (ISO) to ensure consistent product quality under many conditions

ISO 14000 a comprehensive set of environmental management standards determined by the ISO that help companies attain and measure improvements in their environmental performance

Inspection

Inspection reveals whether a product meets quality standards. Some product characteristics may be discerned by fairly simple inspection techniques—weighing the contents of cereal boxes or measuring the time it takes for a customer to receive a hamburger. As part of the ongoing quality assurance program at Hershey Foods, all wrapped Hershey Kisses are checked, and all imperfectly wrapped kisses are rejected.[32] Other inspection techniques are more elaborate. Automobile manufacturers use automated machines to open and close car doors to test the durability of latches and hinges. The food-processing and pharmaceutical industries use various chemical tests to determine the quality of their output. Rushing Water Canoes might use a special device that can precisely measure the thickness of each canoe wall to ensure that it meets the company's specifications.

Organizations normally inspect purchased items, work-in-process, and finished items. The inspection of purchased items and finished items takes place after the fact; the inspection of work-in-process is preventive. In other words, the purpose of inspection of purchased items and finished items is to determine what the quality level is. For items that are being worked on—an automobile moving down the assembly line or a canoe being assembled—the purpose of the inspection is to find defects before the product is completed so that necessary corrections can be made.

Sampling

An important question relating to inspection is how many items should be inspected. Should all canoes produced by Rushing Water be inspected or just some of them? Whether to inspect 100 percent of the output or only part of it is related to the cost of the inspection process, the destructiveness of the inspection process (some tests last until the product fails), and the potential cost of product flaws in terms of human lives and safety.

© Kent Knudson/PhotoLink/Getty Images

The ISO 9000 standards are international standards that relate to quality management. ISO 14000 standards relate to environmental management—managing businesses to minimize harmful effects to the environment.

Some inspection procedures are quite expensive, use elaborate testing equipment, destroy products, and/or require a significant number of hours to complete. In such cases, it is usually desirable to test only a sample of the output. If the sample passes inspection, the inspector may assume that all the items in the lot from which the sample was drawn would also pass inspection. By using principles of statistical inference, management can employ sampling techniques that assure a relatively high probability of reaching the right conclusion—that is, rejecting a lot that does not meet standards and accepting a lot that does. Nevertheless, there will always be a risk of making an incorrect conclusion—accepting a population that *does not* meet standards (because the sample was satisfactory) or rejecting a population that *does* meet standards (because the sample contained too many defective items).

Sampling is likely to be used when inspection tests are destructive. Determining the life expectancy of lightbulbs by turning them on and recording how long they last would be foolish: There is no market for burned-out lightbulbs. Instead, a generalization based on the quality of a sample would be applied to the entire population of lightbulbs from which the sample was drawn. However, human life and safety often depend on the proper functioning of specific items, such as the navigational systems installed in commercial airliners. For such items, even though the inspection process is costly, the potential cost of flawed systems—in human lives and safety—is too great not to inspect 100 percent of the output.

Integrating Operations and Supply Chain Management

Managing operations and supply chains can be complex and challenging due to the number of independent organizations that must perform their responsibilities in creating product quality. Managing supply chains requires constant vigilance and the ability to make quick tactical changes. For example, an Australian firm experienced severe supply chain problems when it sent 50 goldfish to media companies as part of a public relations campaign. The fish died in transit, requiring the company to issue an apology and donate money to animal protection organizations.[33] Even Apple Inc., the most admired company in the world, has had supply chain problems. Reports of forced overtime, underage workers, and dangerous conditions at its Chinese supplier factories have resulted in negative publicity for the company.[34] Therefore, managing the various partners involved in supply chains and operations is important because many stakeholders hold the firm responsible for appropriate conduct related to product quality. This requires that the company exercise oversight over all suppliers involved in producing a product. Encouraging suppliers to report problems, issues, or concerns requires excellent communication systems to obtain feedback. Ideally, suppliers will report potential problems before they reach the next level of the supply chain, which reduces damage.

Despite the challenges of monitoring global operations and supply chains, there are steps businesses can take to manage these risks. All companies who work with global suppliers should adopt a Global Supplier Code of Conduct and ensure that it is effectively communicated. Additionally, companies should encourage compliance and procurement employees to work together to find ethical suppliers at reasonable costs. Those in procurement are concerned with the costs of obtaining materials for the company. As a result, supply chain and procurement managers must work together to make operational decisions to ensure the selection of the best suppliers from an ethical and cost-effective standpoint. Businesses must also work to make certain that their supply chains are diverse. Having only a few suppliers in one area can disrupt operations should a disaster strike. Finally, companies must perform regular audits on its suppliers and take action against those found to be in violation of company standards.[35]

TEAM EXERCISE

Form groups and assign the responsibility of finding companies that outsource their production to other countries. What are the key advantages of this outsourcing decision? Do you see any drawbacks or weaknesses in this approach? Why would a company not outsource when such a tactic can be undertaken to cut manufacturing costs? Report your findings to the class.

LO1 Define operations management and differentiate between operations and manufacturing.

Operations management (OM) is the development and administration of the activities involved in transforming resources into goods and services. Operations managers oversee the transformation process and the planning and designing of operations systems, managing logistics, quality, and productivity. The terms *manufacturing* and *production* are used interchangeably to describe the activities and processes used in making tangible products, whereas *operations* is a broader term used to describe the process of making both tangible and intangible products.

LO2 Explain how operations management differs in manufacturing and service firms.

Manufacturers and service firms both transform inputs into outputs, but service providers differ from manufacturers in several ways: They have greater customer contact because the service typically occurs at the point of consumption; their inputs and outputs are more variable than manufacturers', largely because of the human element; service providers are generally more labour intensive; and their productivity measurement is more complex.

LO3 Describe the elements involved in planning and designing an operations system.

Operations planning relates to decisions about what product(s) to make, for whom, and what processes and facilities are needed to produce them. OM is often joined by marketing and research and development in these decisions. Common facility layouts include fixed-position layouts, process layouts, or product layouts. Where to locate operations facilities is a crucial decision that depends on proximity to the market, availability of raw materials, availability of transportation, availability of power, climatic influences, availability of labor, and community characteristics. Technology is also vital to operations, particularly computer-assisted design, computer-assisted manufacturing, flexible manufacturing, robotics, and computer-integrated manufacturing.

LO4 Specify some techniques managers may use to manage the logistics of transforming inputs into finished products.

Logistics, or supply chain management, includes all the activities involved in obtaining and managing raw materials and component parts, managing finished products, packaging them, and getting them to customers. The organization must first make or purchase (procure) all the materials it needs. Next, it must control its inventory by determining how many supplies and goods it needs and keeping track of every raw material, component, completed or partially completed product, and piece of equipment, how many of each are on hand, where they are, and who has responsibility for them. Common approaches to inventory control include the economic order quantity (EOQ) model, the just-in-time (JIT) inventory concept, and material-requirements planning (MRP). Logistics also includes routing and scheduling processes and activities to complete products.

Quality is a critical element of OM because low-quality products can hurt people and harm the business. Quality control refers to the processes an organization uses to maintain its established quality standards. To control quality, a company must establish what standard of quality it desires and then determine whether its products meet that standard through inspection.

KEY TERMS

capacity
computer-assisted design (CAD)
computer-assisted manufacturing (CAM)
computer-integrated manufacturing (CIM)
continuous manufacturing organizations
customization
economic order quantity (EOQ) model
fixed-position layout
flexible manufacturing
inputs
intermittent organizations
inventory
inventory control
ISO 9000
ISO 14000
just-in-time (JIT) inventory management
manufacturing

material-requirements planning (MRP)
modular design
operations
operations management (OM)
outputs
process layout
product layout
production
project organization
purchasing
quality control
routing
scheduling
standardization
statistical process control
supply chain management
total quality management (TQM)

DESTINATION CEO DISCUSSION QUESTIONS

1. What led to Gerald Schwartz's success?

2. What business principles does Schwatrz subscribe to?

3. Who was Schwartz's earliest role model?

While you might not have been familiar with terms such as *supply chain* or *logistics* or *total quality management* before taking this course, careers abound in the operations management field. You will find these careers in a wide variety of organizations—manufacturers, retailers, transportation companies, third-party logistics firms, government agencies, and service firms. Closely managing how a company's inputs and outputs flow from raw materials to the end consumer is vital to a firm's success. Successful companies also need to ensure that quality is measured and actively managed at each step.

Supply chain managers have a tremendous impact on the success of an organization. These managers are engaged in every facet of the business process, including planning, purchasing, production, transportation, storage and distribution, customer service, and more. Their performance helps organizations control expenses, boost sales, and maximize profits.

Warehouse managers are a vital part of manufacturing operations. A typical warehouse manager's duties include overseeing and recording deliveries and pickups, maintaining inventory records and the product tracking system, and adjusting inventory levels to reflect receipts and disbursements. Warehouse managers also have to consider customer service and employee issues. Warehouse managers can earn up to $60,000 in some cases.

Operations management is also required in service businesses. With more than 80 percent of the North American economy in services, jobs exist for services operations. Many service contact operations require standardized processes that often use technology to provide an interface that provides an automatic quality performance. Consider jobs in health care, the travel industry, fast food, and entertainment. Think of any job or task that is a part of the final product in these industries. Even an online retailer such as Amazon has a transformation process that includes information technology and human activities that facilitate a transaction. These services have a standardized process and can be evaluated based on their level of achieved service quality.

Total quality management is becoming a key attribute for companies to ensure that quality pervades all aspects of the organization. Quality-assurance managers may make salaries in the $55,000 to $65,000 range. These managers monitor and advise on how a company's quality management system is performing and publish data and reports regarding company performance in both manufacturing and service industries.

BUILD YOUR BUSINESS PLAN

Managing Service and Manufacturing Operations

For your business you need to determine if you are providing raw materials that will be used in further production, or you are a reseller of goods and services, known as a retailer. If you are the former, you need to determine what processes you go through in making your product.

The text provides ideas of breaking the process into inputs, transformation processes, and outputs. If you are a provider of a service or a link in the supply chain, you need to know exactly what your customer expectations are. Services are intangible so it is all the more important to better understand what exactly the customer is looking for in resolving a problem or filling a need.

When it comes to the drive-thru, Taco Bell is a master. Taco Bell employees average 164 seconds per customer order from the time the customer arrives to departure. With an assembly line of food items to construct, six different types of wrappers, and detailed procedures for every step of the process, Taco Bell is now among the top for speed, accuracy, and efficiency.

The company was founded in 1962. It focused on mass-produced food and now serves its south-of-the-border fare in 5,600 stores. In 2011, fast-food sales hit $168 billion. However, Taco Bell was not always so successful with its drive-thru operations. Workers lacked specific directions and the preparedness to efficiently handle the fast-paced drive-thru. Because 70 percent of customers use the drive-thru—designating it as the fast-food industry's make-it-or-break-it element—Taco Bell was at a disadvantage.

Taco Bell's solution to this problem was similar to what would be found in a major factory: standardize procedures, eliminate bottlenecks, and work to optimize staff efficiency. Employees at Taco Bell are divided into two categories: service champions (drive-thru) and food champions (food preparation). Service champions are trained to follow a specific script as they greet customers and take orders. They enter orders into the point-of-sale system, make drinks when needed, and handle payments. When processing orders for more complex menu items, service champions may assist food champions in food preparation.

The script goes a long way toward eliminating botched orders. Beyond that, it comes down to teamwork, to everyone working together to create a seamless process free from mistakes. In this instance, speed and accuracy of service are as much a part of quality as the finished food. Taco Bell has essentially maximized its service speed, unless, miraculously, it can figure out how to speed up its customers.

DISCUSSION QUESTIONS

1. Why was it so important for Taco Bell to create a seamless drive-thru process?

2. How does the Taco Bell drive-thru process manage for quality?

3. Why is speed and accuracy of service just as important as the quality of finished food for Taco Bell?

KERENSA CLARKE

CHAPTER

9 Motivating the Workforce

© Deborah Gillis

LEARNING OBJECTIVES

After reading this chapter, you will be able to:

LO1 Define human relations, and determine why its study is important.

LO2 Summarize early studies that laid the groundwork for understanding employee motivation.

LO3 Compare and contrast the human-relations theories of Abraham Maslow and Frederick Herzberg.

LO4 Investigate various theories of motivation, including theories X, Y, and Z; equity theory; and expectancy theory.

LO5 Describe some of the strategies that managers use to motivate employees.

DESTINATION CEO

Deborah Gillis, president and CEO of Catalyst, a leading research and advisory organization, wants to boost the number of female executives in C-suites and on corporate boards. She is the fourth president in Catalyst's 53-year history—and the first from outside the United States. In Canada, where she served as executive director from 2006 to 2011, she launched the Catalyst Accord, which asks companies to commit to increasing female representation on their boards to 25 percent by 2017.

In North America, the number of women on boards of publicly traded companies sits at about 20 percent and only 14 percent of publicly listed Canadian firms have a formal plan for promoting women to their boards. In anticipation of the current attention to board diversity challenges in Canada, Gillis led Catalyst's initiative to increase women in the boardroom, resulting in the successful launch of the Catalyst Accord and Catalyst's first acquisition, Women On Board®.

Growing up in Cape Breton, Nova Scotia, Gillis was an outspoken defender of women's rights early on in life. She still has the notes from a Grade 12 civics debate—"Be It Resolved that Women Earn the Same as Men"—and recalls feminists pushing for gender equality to be included in the Canadian Charter of Rights and Freedoms.

Today Ms. Gillis is a recognized advocate and expert on expanding opportunities for women and business. She is frequently quoted in the media globally, including the *Wall Street Journal*, BBC, CNBC, CNN, and the *Globe and Mail*, on issues related to talent and women's leadership. She regularly addresses senior leaders around the world in a variety of business, academic, and public policy venues. In 2016 she was named one of Canada's most powerful business people.[1]

Introduction

Because employees do the actual work of the business and influence whether the firm achieves its objectives, most top managers agree that employees are an organization's most valuable resource. To achieve organizational objectives, employees must have the motivation, ability (appropriate knowledge and skills), and tools (proper training and equipment) to perform their jobs. Chapter 10 covers topics related to managing human resources, such as those listed earlier. This chapter focuses on how to motivate employees.

We examine employees' needs and motivation, managers' views of workers, and several strategies for motivating employees. Managers who understand the needs of their employees can help them reach higher levels of productivity and thus contribute to the achievement of organizational goals.

Nature of Human Relations

LO1 Define human relations, and determine why its study is important.

What motivates employees to perform on the job is the focus of **human relations**, the study of the behaviour of individuals and groups in organizational settings. In business, human relations involves motivating employees to achieve organizational objectives efficiently and effectively. The field of human relations has become increasingly important over the years as businesses strive to understand how to boost workplace morale, maximize employees' productivity and creativity, and motivate their ever more diverse employees to be more effective.

human relations the study of the behaviour of individuals and groups in organizational settings

motivation an inner drive that directs a person's behaviour toward goals

Motivation is an inner drive that directs a person's behaviour toward goals. A goal is the satisfaction of some need, and a need is the difference between a desired state and an actual state. Both needs and goals can be motivating. Motivation explains why people behave as they do; similarly, a lack of motivation explains, at times, why people avoid doing what they should do. Motivating employees to do the wrong things or for the wrong reasons can be problematic, however. Encouraging employees to take excessive risks through high compensation, for example, led to the downfall of AIG. Also, encouraging employees to lie to customers or to create false documentation is unethical and could even have legal ramifications. A person who recognizes or feels a need is motivated to take action to satisfy the need and achieve a goal (Figure 9.1). Consider a person who takes a job in sales. If his or her performance is far below other salespeople's, he or she will likely recognize a need to increase sales. To satisfy that need and achieve success, the person may try to acquire new insights from successful salespeople or obtain additional training to improve sales skills. In addition, a sales manager might try different means to motivate the salesperson to work harder and improve his or her skills. Human relations is concerned with the needs of employees, their goals and how they try to achieve them, and the impact of those needs and goals on job performance.

Effectively motivating employees helps keep them engaged in their work. Engagement involves emotional involvement and commitment. Being engaged results in carrying out the expectations and obligations of employment. Many employees are actively engaged in their jobs, while others are not. Some employees do the minimum amount of work required to get by, and some employees are completely disengaged. Motivating employees to stay engaged is a key responsibility of management. For example, to test if his onsite production managers were fully engaged in their jobs, former Van Halen frontman David Lee Roth placed a line in the band's rider asking for a bowl of M&Ms with the brown ones removed. It was a means for the band to test local stage production crews' attention to detail. Because Van Halen's shows were highly technical, Roth would demand a complete recheck of everything if he found brown M&Ms in the bowl.[3]

One prominent aspect of human relations is **morale**—an employee's attitude toward his or her job, employer, and colleagues. High morale contributes to high levels of productivity, high returns to stakeholders, and employee loyalty. Conversely, low morale may cause high rates of absenteeism and turnover (when employees quit or are fired and must be replaced by new employees). Google recognizes the value of happy, committed employees and strives to engage in practices that will minimize turnover. Employees have the opportunity to have a massage every other week; onsite laundry service; free all-you-can-eat gourmet meals and snacks; and the "20 percent a week" rule, which allows engineers to work on whatever project they want for one day each week.[4]

Employees are motivated by their perceptions of

morale an employee's attitude toward his or her job, employer, and colleagues

intrinsic reward the personal satisfaction and enjoyment felt from attaining a goal

DID YOU KNOW?

Absenteeism costs the Canadian economy more than $16 billion a year.[2]

Figure 9.1 The Motivation Process

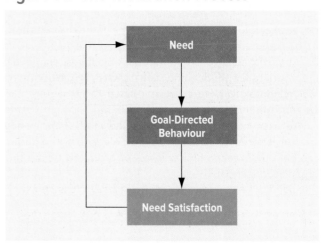

extrinsic reward a benefit and/or recognition received from someone else

extrinsic and intrinsic rewards. An **intrinsic reward** is the personal satisfaction and enjoyment that you feel from attaining a goal. For example, in this class you may feel personal enjoyment in learning how business works and aspire to have a career in business or to operate your own business one day. An **extrinsic reward** is a benefit and/or recognition that you receive from someone else. In this class, your grade is an extrinsic recognition of your efforts and success in the class. In business, praise and recognition, pay increases, and bonuses are extrinsic rewards. If you believe that your job provides an opportunity to contribute to society or the environment, then that aspect would represent an intrinsic reward. Both intrinsic and extrinsic rewards contribute to motivation that stimulates employees to do their best in contributing to business goals.

Respect, involvement, appreciation, adequate compensation, promotions, a pleasant work environment, and a positive organizational culture are all morale boosters. Table 9.1 lists some ways to retain good employees. Nike seeks to provide a comprehensive compensation and benefits package, which includes traditional elements such as medical, dental, vision, life and disability insurance, paid holidays and time off, sabbaticals, and team as well as individual compensation plans. More comprehensive benefits include employee discounts on Nike products, scholarships for children of employees, employee

© IT Stock Free/Alamy

Many companies offer onsite daycare as a benefit for employees who have children. Company benefits such as these tend to increase employee satisfaction and motivation.

assistance plans, tuition assistance, group legal plans, and matching gift programs. At its headquarters, Nike employees may take advantage of onsite daycare and fitness centres, onsite cafés and restaurants, an onsite hair and nail salon, discounted annual transit passes, and several other work–life resources.[5] Ericsson Canada Inc., has an onsite daycare facility for parents in Montreal; and the Bank of Canada encourages employees to keep fit with free memberships to an onsite fitness facility in Ottawa.[6]

Many companies offer a diverse array of benefits designed to improve the quality of employees' lives and increase their morale and satisfaction. Some of the best companies to work for offer onsite day care, concierge services (e.g., dry cleaning, shoe repair, prescription renewal), and fully paid sabbaticals. Table 9.2 offers suggestions as to how leaders can motivate employees on a daily basis.

Table 9.1 Top 10 Ways to Retain Great Employees

1. Satisfied employees know clearly what is expected from them every day at work.
2. The quality of the supervision an employee receives is critical to employee retention.
3. The ability of the employee to speak his or her mind freely within the organization is another key factor in employee retention.
4. Talent and skill utilization is another environmental factor your key employees seek in your workplace.
5. The perception of fairness and equitable treatment is important in employee retention.
6. Employees must have the tools, time, and training necessary to do their jobs well—or they will move to an employer who provides them.
7. The best employees, those employees you want to retain, seek frequent opportunities to learn and grow in their careers, knowledge, and skill.
8. Take time to meet with new employees to learn about their talents, abilities, and skills. Meet with each employee periodically.
9. No matter the circumstances, never, never, ever threaten an employee's job or income.
10. Staff members must feel rewarded, recognized, and appreciated.

Based on Susan M. Heathfield, "Top Ten Ways to Retain Your Great Employees," *About. com*, http://humanresources.about.com/od/retention/a/more_retention.htm (accessed February 18, 2010).

Table 9.2 You Can Make Their Day: Tips for the Leader about Employee Motivation

1. Use simple, powerful words.
2. Make sure people know what you expect.
3. Provide regular feedback.
4. People need positive and not so positive consequences.
5. It's about discipline, not magic.
6. Continue learning and trying out new ideas for employee motivation.
7. Make time for people.
8. Focus on the development of people.
9. Share the goals and the context: communicate.

Based on Susan M. Heathfield, "You Can Make Their Day: Ten Tips for the Leader About Employee Motivation," *About.com*, http://humanresources.about.com/od/motivationsucces3/a/lead_motivation.htm (accessed February 18, 2010).

Historical Perspectives on Employee Motivation

LO2 Summarize early studies that laid the groundwork for understanding employee motivation.

Throughout the twentieth century, researchers have conducted numerous studies to try to identify ways to motivate workers and increase productivity. From these studies have come theories that have been applied to workers with varying degrees of success. A brief discussion of two of these theories—the classical theory of motivation and the Hawthorne studies—provides a background for understanding the present state of human relations.

Classical Theory of Motivation

The birth of the study of human relations can be traced to time and motion studies conducted at the turn of the century by Frederick W. Taylor and Frank and Lillian Gilbreth. Their studies analyzed how workers perform specific work tasks in an effort to improve the employees' productivity. These efforts led to the application of scientific principles to management.

According to the **classical theory of motivation**, money is the sole motivator for workers. Taylor suggested that workers who were paid more would produce more, an idea that would benefit both companies and workers. To improve productivity, Taylor thought that managers should break down each job into its component tasks (specialization), determine the best way to perform each task, and specify the output to be achieved by a worker performing the task. Taylor also believed that incentives would motivate employees to be more productive. Thus, he suggested that managers link workers' pay directly to their output. He developed the piece-rate system, under which employees were paid a certain amount for each unit they produced; those who exceeded their quota were paid a higher rate per unit for all the units they produced.

We can still see Taylor's ideas in practice today in the use of mathematical models, statistics, and incentives. Moreover, companies are increasingly striving to relate pay to performance at both the hourly and managerial level. Incentive planners choose an individual incentive to motivate and reward their employees. In contrast, team incentives are used to generate partnership and collaboration to accomplish organizational goals. Boeing develops sales teams for most of its products, including commercial airplanes. The team dedicated to each product shares in the sales incentive program.

More and more corporations are tying pay to

© Jason Smith/iStock

Even small symbols of recognition, such as an "Employee of the Month" parking space, can serve as strong motivators for employees.

performance in order to motivate—even up to the CEO level. The topic of executive pay has become controversial in recent years, and many corporate boards of directors have taken steps to link executive compensation more closely to corporate performance. Despite these changes, many top executives still receive large compensation packages. Onex CEO Gerry Schwartz, is one of the highest-paid executives in Canada, with total compensation of \$87.9 million.[7]

Like most managers of the early twentieth century, Taylor believed that satisfactory pay and job security would motivate employees to work hard. However, later studies showed that other factors are also important in motivating workers.

The Hawthorne Studies

Elton Mayo and a team of researchers from Harvard University wanted to determine what physical conditions

> **"Taylor believed that** satisfactory pay and job security would motivate employees to work hard. **However, later** studies showed that other factors are also important **in motivating workers."**

classical theory of motivation theory suggesting that money is the sole motivator for workers

Whole Foods is well known for being a customer-centric organization that sells organic and natural produce. The company is 100 percent powered by renewable energy and ranked among *Forbes'* "America's Greenest Companies." Whole Foods also works hard to create an inviting, informative store environment for the customer.

However, truly creating a quality store experience requires dedication from the company's in-store employees. For this reason, Whole Foods employees are empowered to make decisions that will achieve the company's goals. Employees often work in small self-directed teams to discuss issues and develop solutions to improve the company's operations. Additionally, Whole Foods wants its employees to feel like they are an important component of the company's success. Employees therefore have access to all the company's books, including the compensation report. Whole Foods also implemented a voluntary program to encourage employees to stay healthy. Employees already receive

a 20 percent discount on Whole Foods products, and under the Whole Foods Healthy Living Challenge, employees are eligible to receive an additional 10 percent discount. Its support for employee empowerment, sustainability, and healthy living has earned Whole Foods a place on *Fortune's* "100 Best Companies to Work For" for 14 consecutive years.[9]

DISCUSSION QUESTIONS

1. How does Whole Foods use teams to improve its operations?

2. What are some ways that Whole Foods empowers its employees?

3. What are some of the benefits of the Whole Foods Healthy Living Challenge?

---

in the workplace—such as light and noise levels—would stimulate employees to be most productive. From 1924 to 1932, they studied a group of workers at the Hawthorne Works Plant of the Western Electric Company and measured their productivity under various physical conditions.

What the researchers discovered was quite unexpected and very puzzling: Productivity increased regardless of the physical conditions. This phenomenon has been labelled the Hawthorne effect. When questioned about their behaviour, the employees expressed satisfaction because their co-workers in the experiments were friendly and, more importantly, because their supervisors had asked for their help and cooperation in the study. In other words, they were responding to the attention they received, not the changing physical work conditions. The researchers concluded that social and psychological factors could significantly affect productivity and morale. Medtronic, often called the "Microsoft of the medical-device industry," has a built-in psychological factor that influences employee morale. The company makes life-saving medical devices, such as pacemakers, neurostimulators, and stents. New hires at Medtronic receive medallions inscribed with a portion of the firm's mission statement, "alleviate pain, restore health, and extend life." There is an annual party where people whose bodies function thanks to Medtronic devices give testimonials.[8] Obviously, Medtronic employees feel a sense of satisfaction in their jobs. Figure 9.2 indicates what executives consider to be most valuable in maintaining an effective work–life balance.

© Sarah M. Golonka/Brand X Pictures/PunchStock

Working conditions are important. However, the Hawthorne studies, which were carried out at the electric company shown here beginning in the 1920s, found that the workers became more productive because of the attention they received—regardless of their working conditions.

The Hawthorne experiments marked the beginning of a concern for human relations in the workplace. They revealed that human factors do influence workers' behaviour and that managers who understand the needs, beliefs, and expectations of people have the greatest success in motivating their workers.

Figure 9.2 Job Aspects Important to Employee Satisfaction

Besides salary, which one of the aspects of your job in the graph below is most tied to your satisfaction?

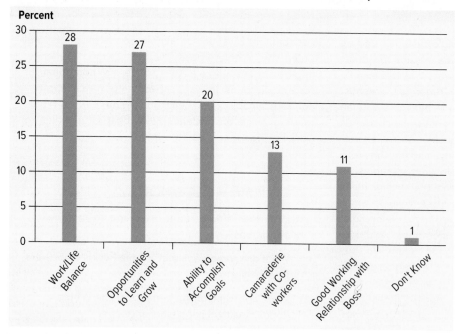

Source: "OfficeTeam Survey: Work/Life Balance, Learning Opportunities Have Greatest Impact on Job Satisfaction," PR Newswire, January 26, 2012, www.prnewswire.com/news-releases/officeteam-survey-worklife-balance-learning-opportunities-have-greatest-impact-on-job-satisfaction-138116108.html (accessed February 23, 2012).

Theories of Employee Motivation

LO3 Compare and contrast the human-relations theories of Abraham Maslow and Frederick Herzberg.

The research of Taylor, Mayo, and many others has led to the development of a number of theories that attempt to describe what motivates employees to perform. In this section, we will discuss some of the most important of these theories. The successful implementation of ideas based on these theories will vary, of course, depending on the company, its management, and its employees. It should be noted, too, that what worked in the past may no longer work today. Good managers must have the ability to adapt their ideas to an ever-changing, diverse group of employees.

Maslow's hierarchy a theory that arranges the five basic needs of people—physiological, security, social, esteem, and self-actualization—into the order in which people strive to satisfy them

Maslow's Hierarchy of Needs

Psychologist Abraham Maslow theorized that people have five basic needs: physiological, security, social, esteem, and self-actualization. **Maslow's** **hierarchy** arranges these needs into the order in which people strive to satisfy them (Figure 9.3).

Physiological needs, the most basic and first needs to be satisfied, are the essentials for living—water, food, shelter, and clothing. According to Maslow, humans devote all their efforts to satisfying physiological needs until they are met. Only when these needs are met can people focus their attention on satisfying the next level of needs—security.

Security needs relate to protecting yourself from physical and economic harm. Actions that may be taken to achieve security include reporting a dangerous workplace condition to management, maintaining safety equipment, and purchasing insurance with income protection in the event you become unable to work. Once security needs have been satisfied, people may strive for social goals.

Social needs are the need for love, companionship, and friendship—the desire for acceptance by others. To fulfill social needs, a person may try many things: making friends with a co-worker, joining a group, volunteering at a hospital, or throwing a party. Once their social needs have been satisfied, people attempt to satisfy their need for esteem.

Esteem needs relate to respect—both self-respect and respect from others. One aspect of esteem needs is competition—the need to feel that you can do something better than anyone else. Competition often motivates people to increase their productivity. Esteem needs are not as easily satisfied as the needs at lower levels in Maslow's hierarchy because they do not always provide tangible evidence of success. However, these needs can be realized through rewards and increased involvement in organizational activities. Until esteem needs are met, people focus their attention on achieving respect. When they feel they have achieved some measure of respect, self-actualization becomes the major goal of life.

physiological needs the most basic human needs to be satisfied—water, food, shelter, and clothing

security needs needs to protect oneself from physical and economic harm

social needs needs for love, companionship, and friendship—the desire for acceptance by others

esteem needs needs for respect—both self-respect and respect from others

Figure 9.3 Maslow's Hierarchy of Needs

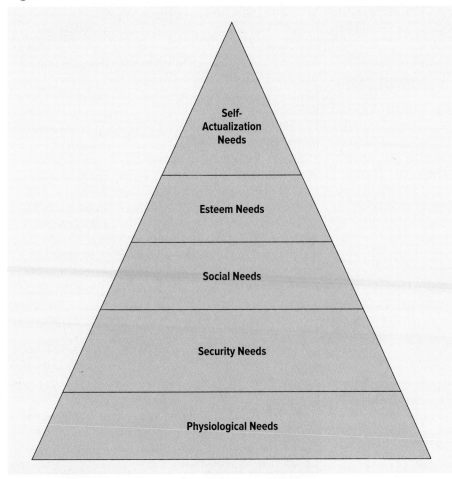

Source: Adapted from Abraham H. Maslow, "A Theory of Human Motivation," *Psychology Review* 50 (1943), pp. 370–396. American Psychology Association.

Self-actualization needs, at the top of Maslow's hierarchy, mean being the best you can be. Self-actualization involves maximizing your potential. A self-actualized person feels that she or he is living life to its fullest in every way. For author Stephen King, self-actualization might mean being praised as the best fiction writer in the world; for actress Halle Berry, it might mean winning an Oscar.

Maslow's theory maintains that the more basic needs at the bottom of the hierarchy must be satisfied before higher-level goals can be pursued. Thus, people who are hungry and homeless are not concerned with obtaining respect from

> "Maslow's theory maintains that the more basic needs at the bottom of the hierarchy must be satisfied before higher-level goals can be pursued."

self-actualization needs needs to be the best one can be; at the top of Maslow's hierarchy

their colleagues. Only when physiological, security, and social needs have been more or less satisfied do people seek esteem. Maslow's theory also suggests that if a low-level need is suddenly reactivated, the individual will try to satisfy that need rather than higher-level needs. Many laid-off workers probably shift their focus from high-level esteem needs to the need for security. When unemployment reached 8.3 percent during the last recession and the job market appeared increasingly insecure, many employees, particularly those in manufacturing, banking, and finance, felt they had to shift their focus back to security needs. Managers should learn from Maslow's hierarchy that employees will be motivated to contribute to organizational goals only if they are able to first satisfy their physiological, security, and social needs through their work.

Herzberg's Two-Factor Theory

In the 1950s, psychologist Frederick Herzberg proposed a theory of motivation that focuses on the job and on the environment where work is done. Herzberg studied various factors relating to the job and their relation to employee motivation and concluded that they can be divided into hygiene factors and motivational factors (Table 9.3).

Hygiene factors, which relate to the work setting and not to the content of the work, include adequate wages, comfortable and safe working conditions, fair company policies, and job security. These factors do not necessarily motivate employees to excel, but their absence may be a potential source of dissatisfaction and high turnover. Employee safety and comfort are clearly hygiene factors.

Many people feel that a good salary is one of the

hygiene factors aspects of Herzberg's theory of motivation that focus on the work setting and not the content of the work; these aspects include adequate wages, comfortable and safe working conditions, fair company policies, and job security

Several organizations offer paid time off to part-time workers rather than creating full-time positions, which come with their own share of costs.

Companies that reward employees with extra time off include Travelzoo (a global travel deal website), Ontario Public Service (a provincial government entity), and Patagonia (an outdoor gear and clothing company). Travelzoo offers its employees of more than one year an annual $1,500 to $3,000 with three extra vacation days and the chance to snatch up a deal listed on its site. In return, employees are merely required to submit pictures and brief write-ups to the company's subscriber newsletter. The Ontario Public Service manages a unique volunteer opportunity for high-potential employees to be seconded for a 15-week period to work for United Way (with regular pay).[10] After one year of employment, Patagonia covers up to 60 days' worth of an employee's salary to allow the employee to volunteer with a grassroots organization. Like those at Travelzoo, employees are asked to report back about their experiences.

Studies have suggested that these types of incentives boost bottom-line profits and enhance employee retention. Points of Light Foundation claims that over 80 percent of companies feel that volunteering raises profits. This may be due to the fact that consumers are increasingly doing business with socially responsible companies. Employees also become committed to companies that give back to communities and appreciate their efforts.[11]

Table 9.3 Herzberg's Hygiene and Motivational Factors

Hygiene Factors	Motivational Factors
Company policies	Achievement
Supervision	Recognition
Working conditions	Work itself
Relationships with peers, supervisors, and subordinates	Responsibility
Salary	Advancement
Security	Personal growth

© WorldFoto/Alamy

The *Dirty Jobs* television series recognizes individuals who take on society's undesirable, but essential, jobs.

most important job factors, even more important than job security and the chance to use one's mind and abilities. Salary and security, two of the hygiene factors identified by Herzberg, make it possible for employees to satisfy the physiological and security needs identified by Maslow. However, the presence of hygiene factors is unlikely to motivate employees to work harder.

Motivational factors, which relate to the content of the work itself, include achievement, recognition, involvement, responsibility, and advancement. The absence of motivational factors may not result in dissatisfaction, but their presence is likely to motivate employees to excel. Many companies are beginning to employ methods to give employees more responsibility and control and to involve them more in their work, which serves to motivate them to higher levels of productivity and quality. Chubb Insurance Company of Canada has a 430-member workforce that boasts a 98 percent employee retention rate for high-performance hires—one of the industry's highest. Chubb backs employees who want to volunteer, offering time to do everything from helping out at their child's school to spending weeks away with Habitat for Humanity. Most employees work long hours, but they feel it's a partnership with Chubb.[12]

Herzberg's motivational factors and Maslow's esteem and self-actualization needs are similar. Workers' low-level needs (physiological and security) have largely been satisfied by minimum-wage laws and occupational-safety standards set by various government agencies and are therefore not motivators. Consequently, to improve productivity, management should focus on satisfying workers' higher-level needs (motivational factors) by

motivational factors
aspects of Herzberg's theory of motivation that relate to the content of the work itself, include achievement, recognition, involvement, responsibility, and advancement

providing opportunities for achievement, involvement, and advancement and by recognizing good performance.

McGregor's Theory X and Theory Y

LO4 Investigate various theories of motivation, including Theories X, Y, and Z; equity theory; and expectancy theory.

In *The Human Side of Enterprise*, Douglas McGregor related Maslow's ideas about personal needs to management. McGregor contrasted two views of management—the traditional view, which he called Theory X, and a humanistic view, which he called Theory Y.

According to McGregor, managers adopting **Theory X** assume that workers generally dislike work and must be forced to do their jobs. They believe that the following statements are true of workers:

1. The average person naturally dislikes work and will avoid it when possible.
2. Most workers must be coerced, controlled, directed, or threatened with punishment to get them to work toward the achievement of organizational objectives.
3. The average worker prefers to be directed and to avoid responsibility, has relatively little ambition, and wants security.[13]

Managers who subscribe to the Theory X view maintain tight control over workers, provide almost constant supervision, try to motivate through fear, and make decisions in an autocratic fashion, eliciting little or no input from their subordinates. The Theory X style of management focuses on physiological and security needs and virtually ignores the higher needs discussed by Maslow. Foxconn, a manufacturing company that creates components for tech products such as the Apple iPad, is a company that adopted the Theory X perspective. In China, Foxconn workers live in crowded dorms and often work more than 60 hours per week.

The Theory X view of management does not take into account people's needs for companionship, esteem, and personal growth, whereas Theory Y, the contrasting view of management, does. Managers subscribing to the **Theory Y** view assume that workers like to work and that under proper conditions employees will seek out responsibility in an attempt to satisfy their social, esteem, and self-actualization needs.

Theory X McGregor's traditional view of management whereby it is assumed that workers generally dislike work and must be forced to do their jobs

Theory Y McGregor's humanistic view of management whereby it is assumed that workers like to work and that under proper conditions employees will seek out responsibility in an attempt to satisfy their social, esteem, and self-actualization needs

McGregor describes the assumptions behind Theory Y in the following way:

1. The expenditure of physical and mental effort in work is as natural as play or rest.
2. People will exercise self-direction and self-control to achieve objectives to which they are committed.
3. People will commit to objectives when they realize that the achievement of those goals will bring them personal reward.
4. The average person will accept and seek responsibility.
5. Imagination, ingenuity, and creativity can help solve organizational problems, but most organizations do not make adequate use of these characteristics in their employees.
6. Organizations today do not make full use of workers' intellectual potential.[14]

Obviously, managers subscribing to the Theory Y philosophy have a management style very different from managers subscribing to the Theory X philosophy. Theory Y managers maintain less control and supervision, do not use fear as the primary motivator, and are more democratic in decision making, allowing subordinates to participate in the process. Theory Y managers address the high-level needs in Maslow's hierarchy as well as physiological and security needs. For instance, Google is one well-known example of a company that has adopted the Theory Y philosophy. From its famous employee perks to the 20 percent time it gives its employees to pursue company projects they find interesting, Google believes that its employees are motivated and creative enough to significantly profit the company.[15] Today, Theory Y enjoys widespread support and may have displaced Theory X.

> "Theory Y managers maintain less control and supervision, do not use fear as the primary motivator, and are more democratic in decision making."

Theory Z

Theory Z is a management philosophy that stresses employee participation in all aspects of company decision making. It was first described by William Ouchi in his book *Theory Z—How American Business Can Meet the Japanese Challenge*.

Theory Z incorporates many elements associated with the Japanese approach to management, such as trust and intimacy, but Japanese ideas have been

Theory Z a management philosophy that stresses employee participation in all aspects of company decision making

Jason Tham, Jason Yuen, and Sean Kirby

Business: Nulogy

Founded: 2002, in Toronto, Ontario

Success: Since 2011, the company has seen top-line growth in excess of 350 percent, and was named one of Deloitte's Fast 50 in 2015.

Nulogy, a Toronto-based software supplier, puts new hires through an intensive orientation. They get face time with the CEO, who explains the company's vision. They are taken to customer sites to see first-hand how the company's software is being used. This process not only shows new employees how much they matter but also creates transparency around the company's operations and demonstrates how their work contributes to the whole.

The company also empowers workers to solve problems for themselves. For example, teams vote on disputed issues, like whether a meeting should last five minutes or an hour. By giving employees a clear, formal process to achieve decisions among their peers, they feel a greater sense of ownership and accomplishment in their projects. Plus, a collaborative workforce is a happier workforce.[16]

adapted for use in North America. In a Theory Z organization, managers and workers share responsibilities, the management style is participative, and employment is long term and often lifelong. Japan has faced a significant period of slowing economic progress and competition from China and other Asian nations. This has led to experts questioning Theory Z, particularly at firms such as Sony and Toyota. Theory Z results in employees feeling organizational ownership. Research has found that such feelings of ownership may produce positive attitudinal and behavioural effects for employees.[17] In a Theory Y organization, managers focus on assumptions about the nature of the worker. The two theories can be seen as complementary. Table 9.4 compares the traditional American management style, the Japanese management style, and Theory Z (the modified Japanese management style).

Variations on Theory Z

Theory Z has been adapted and modified for use in a number of Canadian companies. One adaptation involves workers in decisions through quality circles. Quality circles (also called quality-assurance teams) are small, usually having five to eight members who discuss ways to reduce waste, eliminate problems, and improve quality, communication, and work satisfaction. Such quality teams are a common technique for harnessing the knowledge and creativity of hourly employees to solve problems in companies. As Theory Z has questioned the use of quality circles, their prevalence has declined. Quality circles have been replaced with quality methods.

Even more involved than quality circles are programs that operate under names such as *participative management*,

Table 9.4 Comparison of North American, Japanese, and Theory Z Management Styles

	North American	Japanese	Theory Z
Duration of employment	Relatively short term; workers subject to layoffs when business slows	Lifelong; no layoffs	Long term; layoffs rare
Rate of promotion	Rapid	Slow	Slow
Amount of specialization	Considerable; worker develops expertise in one area only	Minimal; worker develops expertise in all aspects of the organization	Moderate; worker learns all aspects of the organization
Decision making	Individual	Consensual; input from all concerned parties is considered	Consensual; emphasis on quality
Responsibility	Assigned to the individual	Shared by the group	Assigned to the individual
Control	Explicit and formal	Less explicit and less formal	Informal but with explicit performance measures
Concern for workers	Focus is on work only	Focus extends to worker's whole life	Focus includes worker's life and family

Source: Adapted from William Ouchi, Theory *Z—How American Business Can Meet the Japanese Challenge*, p. 58. © 1981 by Addison-Wesley Publishing Company, Inc. Reprinted by permission of Perseus Books Publishers, a member of Perseus Books, L.L.C.

employee involvement, or self-directed work teams. Regardless of the term used to describe such programs, they strive to give employees more control over their jobs while making them more responsible for the outcome of their efforts. Such programs often organize employees into work teams of 5 to 15 members who are responsible for producing an entire product item. Team members are cross-trained and can therefore move from job to job within the team. Each team essentially manages itself and is responsible for its quality, scheduling, ordering and use of materials, and problem solving. Many firms have successfully employed work teams to boost morale, productivity, quality, and competitiveness.

Equity Theory

According to **equity theory**, how much people are willing to contribute to an organization depends on their assessment of the fairness, or equity, of the rewards they will receive in exchange. In a fair situation, a person receives rewards proportional to the contribution he or she makes to the organization. However, in practice, equity is a subjective notion. Each worker regularly develops a personal input–output ratio by taking stock of his or her contributions (inputs) to the organization in time, effort, skills, and experience and assessing the rewards (outputs) offered by the organization in pay, benefits, recognition, and promotions. The worker compares his or her ratio to the input–output ratio of some other person—a "comparison other," who may be a co-worker, a friend working in another organization, or an "average" of several people working in the organization. If the two ratios are close, the individual will feel that he or she is being treated equitably.

Let's say you have a high-school education and earn $25,000 a year. When you compare your input–output ratio with that of a co-worker who has a college degree and makes $35,000 a year, you will probably feel that you are being paid fairly. However, if you perceive that your personal input–output ratio is lower than that of your college-educated co-worker, you may feel that you are being treated unfairly and be motivated to seek change. But, if you learn that the co-worker who makes $35,000 has only a high-school diploma, you may feel cheated by your employer. To achieve equity, you could try to increase your outputs by asking for a raise or promotion. You could also try to have your co-worker's inputs increased or his or her outputs decreased. Failing to achieve equity, you may be motivated to look for a job at a different company or in a different city. Table 9.5 shows the top Canadian cities to work and live in from a strictly economic perspective.

Equity theory might explain why many consumers are upset about CEO compensation. Although the job of the

equity theory an assumption that how much people are willing to contribute to an organization depends on their assessment of the fairness, or equity, of the rewards they will receive in exchange

Table 9.5 Best Places to Live in Canada

Overall Rank	City
1	Ottawa, Ont.
2	Burlington, Ont.
3	Oakville, Ont.
4	St. Albert, Alta.
5	Boucherville, Que.
6	Blainville, Que.
7	West Vancouver, B.C.
8	North Vancouver, B.C.
9	Levis, Que.
10	Waterloo, Ont.

Based on *MoneySense*, "Canada's Best Places to Live 2016." Retrieved August 16, 2016, from http://www.moneysense.ca/canadas-best-places-to-live-2016-full-ranking/

CEO can be incredibly stressful, the fact that they take home millions in compensation, bonuses, and stock options has been questioned. The high unemployment rate coupled with the misconduct that occurred at some large corporations prior to the recession contributed largely to the Occupy Wall Street protests. To counter this perception of pay inequality, several corporations have now begun to tie CEO compensation with company performance. If the company performs poorly for the year, then firms will cut bonuses and other compensation.[18] While lower compensation rates might appease the general public, some companies are worried that lower pay might deter talented individuals from wanting to assume the position of CEO at their firms.

Because almost all the issues involved in equity theory are subjective, they can be problematic. Author David Callahan has argued that feelings of inequity may underlie some unethical or illegal behaviour in business. For example, due to employee theft and shoplifting, Walmart experiences billions in inventory losses every year. Some employees may take company resources to restore what they perceive to be equity. Theft of company resources is a major ethical issue, based on a survey by the Ethics Resource Center.[19] Callahan believes that employees who do not feel they are being treated equitably may be motivated to equalize the situation by lying, cheating, or otherwise "improving" their pay, perhaps by stealing.[20] Managers should try to avoid equity problems by ensuring that rewards are distributed on the basis of performance and that all employees clearly understand the basis for their pay and benefits.

Expectancy Theory

Psychologist Victor Vroom described **expectancy theory**, which states that motivation depends not only on how

expectancy theory the assumption that motivation depends not only on how much a person wants something but also on how likely he or she is to get it

© Jack Hollingsworth/Corbis RF

Your motivation depends not only on how much you want something, but how likely you believe you are to get it.

much a person wants something but also on the person's perception of how likely he or she is to get it. A person who wants something and has reason to be optimistic will be strongly motivated. For example, say you really want a promotion. And, let's say because you have taken some night classes to improve your skills, and moreover, have just made a large, significant sale, you feel confident that you are qualified and able to handle the new position. Therefore, you are motivated to try to get the promotion. In contrast, if you do not believe you are likely to get what you want, you may not be motivated to try to get it, even though you really want it.

Strategies for Motivating Employees

LO5 Describe some of the strategies that managers use to motivate employees.

Based on the various theories that attempt to explain what motivates employees, businesses have developed several strategies for motivating their employees and boosting morale and productivity. Some of these techniques include behaviour modification and job design, as well as the already described employee involvement programs and work teams.

Behaviour Modification

Behaviour modification involves changing behaviour and encouraging appropriate actions by relating the consequences of behaviour to the behaviour itself. The concept of behaviour

behaviour modification changing behaviour and encouraging appropriate actions by relating the consequences of behaviour to the behaviour itself

modification was developed by psychologist B. F. Skinner, who showed that there are two types of consequences that can modify behaviour—reward and punishment. Skinner found that behaviour that

is rewarded will tend to be repeated, while behaviour that is punished will tend to be eliminated. For example, employees who know that they will receive a bonus, such as an expensive restaurant meal, for making a sale over $2,000 may be more motivated to make sales. Workers who know they will be punished for being tardy are likely to make a greater effort to get to work on time.

However, the two strategies may not be equally effective. Punishing unacceptable behaviour may provide quick results but may lead to undesirable long-term side effects, such as employee dissatisfaction and increased turnover. In general, rewarding appropriate behaviour is a more effective way to modify behaviour.

Job Design

Herzberg identified the job itself as a motivational factor. Managers have several strategies that they can use to design jobs to help improve employee motivation. These include job rotation, job enlargement, job enrichment, and flexible scheduling strategies.

Job Rotation. **Job rotation** allows employees to move from one job to another in an effort to relieve the boredom that is often associated with job specialization. Businesses often turn to specialization in hopes of increasing productivity, but there is a negative side effect to this type of job design: Employees become bored and dissatisfied, and productivity declines. Job

job rotation movement of employees from one job to another in an effort to relieve the boredom often associated with job specialization

rotation reduces this boredom by allowing workers to undertake a greater variety of tasks and by giving them the opportunity to learn new skills. With job rotation, an employee spends a specified amount of time performing one job and then moves on to another, different job. The worker eventually returns to the initial job and begins the cycle again. World Vision Canada, manages an internal secondment policy allowing employees to try a new role within the organization for up to six months while holding their original position.[21]

PriceWaterhouseCoopers recommends six make-or-break rules for relocation overseas:

1. Find the right candidate, technically, and address the soft issues such as family as well.

2. Offer a set of benefits that supports the transition; be flexible and consider taxes.

3. Provide cultural orientation and language training for the family.

4. Provide support after the move including security and even shopping locations.

5. Address spousal work issues; most households are now dual income so help both persons.

6. Plan for repatriation; help them reintegrate when they return.[22]

Job rotation is a good idea, but it has one major drawback. Because employees may eventually become bored with all the jobs in the cycle, job rotation does not totally eliminate the problem of boredom. Job rotation is extremely useful, however, in situations where a person is being trained for a position that requires an understanding of various units in an organization.

McCain Foods uses job rotation to train both management trainees and potential senior managers in all aspects of the company. The management trainee program at McCain has employees switching jobs or divisions every four to six months for the first couple of years in the company prior to the employer and employee agreeing to a more permanent set of duties and placement in the company. Eli Lilly is also a strong believer in the benefits of job rotation. The company leaves employees in their current jobs and asks them to take on short-term assignments outside their field of expertise or interest. The results of the process have been positive, and Nokia is trying the same process with similar outcomes.[23] Many executive training programs require trainees to spend time learning a variety of specialized jobs. Job rotation is also used to cross-train today's self-directed work teams.

Job Enlargement. **Job enlargement** adds more tasks to a job instead of treating each task as separate. Like job rotation, job enlargement was developed to overcome the boredom associated with specialization. The rationale behind this strategy is that jobs are more satisfying as the number of tasks performed by an individual increases. Employees sometimes enlarge, or craft, their jobs by noticing what needs to be done and then changing tasks and relationship boundaries to adjust. Individual orientation and motivation shape opportunities to craft new jobs and job relationships.[24] Job enlargement strategies have been more successful in increasing job satisfaction than have job rotation strategies.

Job Enrichment. **Job enrichment** incorporates motivational factors, such as opportunity for achievement, recognition, responsibility, and advancement, into a job. It gives workers not only more tasks within the job but more control and authority over the job. Job enrichment programs enhance a worker's feeling of responsibility and provide opportunities for growth and advancement when the worker is able to take on the more challenging tasks. Statistics Canada allows employees who have been with the firm for four years a chance to request "career broadening" where they request an assignment in another department to build their skill set.[25] The potential benefits of job enrichment are great, but it requires careful planning and execution.

Flexible Scheduling Strategies. Many Canadians work a traditional 40-hour workweek consisting of five 8-hour days with fixed starting and ending times. Facing problems of poor morale and high absenteeism as well as a diverse workforce with changing needs, many managers have turned to flexible scheduling strategies such as flextime, compressed workweeks, job sharing, part-time work, and telecommuting. A survey by CareerBuilder.com showed that 40 percent of working fathers were offered flexible work schedules versus 53 percent of working mothers.[26]

Flextime is a program that allows employees to choose their starting and ending times, as long as they are at work during a specified core period (Figure 9.4). It does not reduce the total number of hours that employees work; instead, it gives employees more flexibility in choosing which hours they work. A firm may specify that employees must be present from 10:00 a.m. to 3:00 p.m. One employee may choose to come in at 7:00 a.m. and leave at the end of the core time, perhaps to attend classes at a nearby college after work. Another employee, a mother who lives in the suburbs, may come in at 9:00 a.m. to have time to drop off her children at a daycare centre and commute by public transportation to her job. Flextime provides many benefits, including improved ability to recruit and retain workers who wish to balance work and home life. Customers can be better served by allowing more coverage of customers over longer hours, workstations and facilities can be better utilized by staggering employee use, and rush hour traffic may be reduced. In addition, flexible schedules have been associated with an increase in healthy behaviours on the part of employees. More flexible schedules are associated

flextime a program that allows employees to choose their starting and ending times, provided that they are at work during a specified core period

job enlargement the addition of more tasks to a job instead of treating each task as separate

job enrichment the incorporation of motivational factors, such as opportunity for achievement, recognition, responsibility, and advancement, into a job

Figure 9.4 Flextime, Showing Core and Flexible Hours

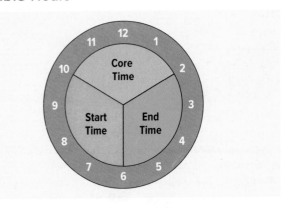

"Flextime provides many benefits, including improved ability to recruit and retain workers who wish to balance work and home life."

with healthier lifestyle choices such as increased physical activity and healthier sleep habits.[27]

Related to flextime are the scheduling strategies of the compressed workweek and job sharing. The **compressed workweek** is a four-day (or shorter) period in which an employee works 40 hours. Under such a plan, employees typically work 10 hours per day for four days and have a three-day weekend. The compressed workweek reduces the company's operating expenses because its actual hours of operation are reduced. It is also sometimes used by parents who want to have more days off to spend with their families. Cameco Corp., in Saskatoon, encourages employees' work–life balance with alternative work arrangements including flexible hours, telecommuting, and shortened and compressed workweek options.[28]

compressed workweek
a four-day (or shorter) period during which an employee works 40 hours

job sharing performance of one full-time job by two people on part-time hours

Job sharing occurs when two people do one job. One person may work from 8:00 a.m. to 12:30 p.m.; the second person comes in at 12:30 p.m. and works until 5:00 p.m. Job sharing gives both people the opportunity to work, as well as time to fulfill other obligations, such

© Vancouver Island Technology Park by Sandy Beaman, Patrician Ventures Ltd.

Vancouver Island Technology Park encourages employees to access more than 100 acres of walking and running trails, as well outdoor sports fields and a community garden.

as parenting or school. With job sharing, the company has the benefit of the skills of two people for one job, often at a lower total cost for salaries and benefits than one person working eight hours a day would be paid.

Two other flexible scheduling strategies attaining wider use include allowing full-time workers to work part time for a certain period and allowing workers to work at home

Consider the Following:
Enhancing Productivity: What's Mine Is Yours and What's Yours Is Mine

Five years ago, Sharonie was returning from maternity leave and was wondering how she was going to manage her academic role as undergraduate hospital program director at North York General Hospital in Toronto, Ontario; her practice; and her young family. Jordana, having covered the role for the year as a locum, wanted to keep her hand in academia. Both women want to work, but not full time. Both women work six separate but identical rotations. The arrangement began when they reconciled the workload dilemma with career aspirations, and proposed a job to share the position.

The two are typical of most job sharers—they are women in administrative positions who, for varying personal reasons, do not want full-time work. Job sharing is a small, but important part of the changes being made in the way people work. Flexibility is the key word and the number one priority for an increasing number of employees who are trying to mesh careers with personal lives. More and more employers are viewing flexibility as a necessity and realizing it can be used as a benefit to attract and retain satisfied employees. Keeping employees happy and loyal to a company can

go right to the bottom line. Studies show that employee loyalty correlates to customer loyalty, which correlates to greater profits and growth. A firm may actually get greater output from two part-time successful job sharers than from one full-time employee. Job sharers are diligent, often focusing intently on the job and maximizing the hours while there.

The arrangement works well for Sharonie and Jordana, and their employer is pleased with the results. Today, not only must employers attract top talent, but they must work to retain it. To do that, organizations must create environments that support employees' family and lifestyle issues.[29]

DISCUSSION QUESTIONS

1. What jobs would lend themselves to this kind of arrangement? Which would not?

2. What limitations are there to this type of arrangement? To the organization? To the employee?

either full or part time. Employees at some firms may be permitted to work part time for several months in order to care for a new baby or an elderly parent or just to slow down for a little while to "recharge their batteries." When the employees return to full-time work, they are usually given a position comparable to their original full-time position. Other firms are allowing employees to telecommute or telework (work at home a few days of the week), staying connected via computers, modems, and telephones. Today, 11.2 million Canadians are teleworkers, working most often from home.[30]

Although many employees ask for the option of working at home to ease the responsibilities of caring for family members, some have discovered that they are more productive at home without the distractions of the workplace. An assessment of 12 company telecommuting programs found that positive productivity changes occurred. Traveler's Insurance Company reports its telecommuters to be 20 percent more productive than its traditional employees.[31] Other employees, however, have discovered that they are not suited for working at home. Human resource management executives are split as to whether telecommuting helps or hurts employees' careers. Thirty percent feel telecommuting helps their careers, while 25 percent feel that it hurts, whereas 39 percent feel it does neither.[32] Still, work-at-home programs do help reduce overhead costs for businesses. For example, some companies used to maintain a surplus of office space but have reduced the surplus through employee telecommuting, "hoteling" (being assigned to a desk through a reservation system), and "hot-desking" (several people using the same desk but at different times).

Companies are turning to flexible work schedules to provide more options for employees who are trying to juggle their work duties with other responsibilities and needs. Preliminary results indicated that flexible scheduling plans increase job satisfaction, which, in turn, leads to increases in productivity. Some recent research, however, has indicated there are potential problems with telecommuting. Some managers are reluctant to adopt the practice because the pace of change in today's workplace is faster than ever, and telecommuters may be left behind or actually cause managers more work in helping them stay abreast of changes. Some employers also worry that telecommuting workers create a security risk by creating more opportunities for computer hackers or equipment thieves. Some employees have found that working outside the office may hurt career advancement opportunities, and some report that instead of helping them balance work and family responsibilities, telecommuting increases the strain by blurring the barriers between the office and home. Co-workers call at all hours, and telecommuters are apt to continue to work when they are not supposed to (after regular business hours or during vacation time).[33]

Importance of Motivational Strategies

Motivation is more than a tool that managers can use to foster employee loyalty and boost productivity. It is a

© Tony May/Stone/Getty Images

Single working-parent families face a tough challenge in balancing work and home life. For single parents, business travel and other routine demands of a corporate career—including overtime and interoffice transfers—can turn life upside down. Sometimes single parents decline promotions or high-profile assignments to preserve time with their children. In some organizations, experts say, it may be assumed single-mom staffers can't handle new duties because of the responsibilities they're shouldering at home.

process that affects all the relationships within an organization and influences many areas such as pay, promotion, job design, training opportunities, and reporting relationships. Employees are motivated by the nature of the relationships they have with their supervisors, by the nature of their jobs, and by characteristics of the organization.

© Noel Hendrickson/Digital Vision/Getty Images

Businesses have come up with different ways to motivate employees, including rewards such as trophies and plaques to show the company's appreciation.

There is no getting around it: Bad moods produce bad results. Employees who come to work unhappy tend to carry that unhappiness throughout the day. Until recently, just how much bad moods affect the work environment was not clear. However, a study by business professor Steffanie Wilk found that employees who start the day in a bad mood can see their productivity levels reduced by more than 10 percent. Additionally, bad moods tend to be contagious, affecting other employees and customers and reducing the bottom line.

This does not bode well for companies in the current work climate. The Gallup-Healthways Well-Being Index reveals that employees are becoming unhappier with their jobs. Much of this can be attributed to economic uncertainty. With businesses cutting back, employees are often expected to take on greater roles with fewer benefits. As a result, employees experience more dissatisfaction with their jobs and a less positive relationship with their employers. The upshot is that managers can take steps to improve employees' moods in simple ways.

Some companies offer very small incentives that make employees feel appreciated.

3M, for instance, gives its employees time to pursue their own projects, an act that not only increases employee morale but has also yielded some of 3M's greatest product ideas. Employers might also encourage short periods of socialization among employees, which can improve moods and build cohesiveness. It seems like carrots, not sticks, are the key to creating a more productive work environment.[34]

DISCUSSION QUESTIONS

1. Why might an uncertain economic climate contribute to decreased productivity?

2. Why do employee bad moods have such a negative effect on an organization?

3. What can employers do to improve the moods of their employees?

Table 9.6 shows the top 10 Canadian companies to work for, according to the *Financial Post*. Even the economic environment can change an employee's motivation. In a slow growth or recession economy, sales can flatten or decrease and morale can drop because of the need to cut jobs. In the most recent recession, many workers feared losing their jobs and increased the amount they were saving. The firm may have to work harder to keep good employees and to motivate all employees to work to overcome obstacles. In good economic times, employees may be more demanding and be on the lookout for better opportunities. New rewards or incentives may help motivate workers in such economies. Motivation tools, then, must be varied as well. Managers can further nurture motivation by being honest, supportive, empathetic, accessible, fair, and open. Motivating employees to increase satisfaction and productivity is an important concern for organizations seeking to remain competitive in the global marketplace.

Table 9.6 Best Companies to Work For

Bayer
Canadian National Railway Company / CN
CIBC
EllisDon Corporation
Enbridge Inc.
Ford Motor Company of Canada, Limited
Nature's Path Foods, Inc.
OpenText Corporation
Samsung Electronics Canada Inc.
Siemens Canada Limited

Based on *Financial Post's* 10 Best Companies to Work for 2016.

TEAM EXERCISE

Form groups and outline a compensation package that you would consider ideal in motivating an employee, recognizing performance, and assisting the company in attaining its cost-to-performance objectives. Think about the impact of intrinsic and extrinsic motivation and recognition. How can flexible scheduling strategies be used effectively to motivate employees? Report your compensation package to the class.

LO1 Define human relations, and determine why its study is important.

Human relations is the study of the behaviour of individuals and groups in organizational settings. Its focus is what motivates employees to perform on the job. Human relations is important because businesses need to understand how to motivate their increasingly diverse employees to be more effective, boost workplace morale, and maximize employees' productivity and creativity.

LO2 Summarize early studies that laid the groundwork for understanding employee motivation.

Time and motion studies by Frederick Taylor and others helped them analyze how employees perform specific work tasks in an effort to improve their productivity. Taylor and the early practitioners of the classical theory of motivation felt that money and job security were the primary motivators of employees. However, the Hawthorne studies revealed that human factors also influence workers' behaviour.

LO3 Compare and contrast the human-relations theories of Abraham Maslow and Frederick Herzberg.

Abraham Maslow defined five basic needs of all people and arranged them in the order in which they must be satisfied: physiological, security, social, esteem, and self-actualization. Frederick Herzberg divided characteristics of the job into hygiene factors and motivational factors. Hygiene factors relate to the work environment and must be present for employees to remain in a job. Motivational factors—recognition, responsibility, and advancement—relate to the work itself. They encourage employees to be productive. Herzberg's hygiene factors can be compared to Maslow's physiological and security needs; motivational factors may include Maslow's social, esteem, and self-actualization needs.

LO4 Investigate various theories of motivation, including Theories X, Y, and Z; equity theory; and expectancy theory.

Douglas McGregor contrasted two views of management: Theory X (traditional) suggests workers dislike work, while Theory Y (humanistic) suggests that workers not only like work but seek out responsibility to satisfy their higher-order needs. Theory Z stresses employee participation in all aspects of company decision making, often through participative management programs and self-directed work teams. According to equity theory, how much people are willing to contribute to an organization depends on their assessment of the fairness, or equity, of the rewards they will receive in exchange. Expectancy theory states that motivation depends not only on how much a person wants something but also on the person's perception of how likely he or she is to get it.

LO5 Describe some of the strategies that managers use to motivate employees.

Strategies for motivating workers include behaviour modification (changing behaviour and encouraging appropriate actions by relating the consequences of behaviour to the behaviour itself) and job design. Among the job design strategies businesses use are job rotation (allowing employees to move from one job to another to try to relieve the boredom associated with job specialization), job enlargement (adding tasks to a job instead of treating each task as a separate job), job enrichment (incorporating motivational factors into a job situation), and flexible scheduling strategies (flextime, compressed workweeks, job sharing, part-time work, and telecommuting).

Working from your computer

behaviour modification
classical theory of motivation
compressed workweek
equity theory
esteem needs
expectancy theory
extrinsic reward
flextime
human relations
hygiene factors
intrinsic reward
job enlargement
job enrichment

job rotation
job sharing
Maslow's hierarchy
morale
motivation
motivational factors
physiological needs
security needs
self-actualization needs
social needs
Theory X
Theory Y
Theory Z

DESTINATION CEO DISCUSSION QUESTIONS

1. What are the pros and cons of having a diversity strategy on corporate boards?

2. What motivated Deborah Gillis from an early age and led to her current position as CEO of Catalyst?

3. Do companies have a moral obligation to increase board diversity?

SO YOU THINK *You May be Good at Motivating a Workforce*

If you are good at mediation, can smooth over conflict, and have a good understanding of motivation and human relations theories, then you might be a good leader, human resource manager, or training expert. Most organizations, especially as they grow, will need to implement human relations programs. These are necessary to teach employees about sensitivity to other cultures, religions, and beliefs, as well as for teaching the workforce about the organization so that they understand how they fit in the larger picture. Employees need to appreciate the benefits of working together to make the firm run smoothly, and they also need to understand how their contributions help the firm. To stay motivated, most employees need to feel like what they do each day contributes something of value to the firm. Disclosing information and including employees in decision-making processes will also help employees feel valuable and wanted within the firm.

There are many different ways employers can reward and encourage employees. However, employers must be careful when considering what kinds of incentives to use. Different cultures value different kinds of incentives more highly than others. For example, a Japanese worker would probably not like it if she were singled out from the group and given a large cash bonus as a reward for her work. Japanese workers tend to be more group oriented, and therefore anything that singles out individuals would not be an effective way of rewarding and motivating. Canadian workers, on the other hand, are very individualistic, and a raise and public praise might be more effective. However, what might motivate a younger employee (bonuses, raises, and perks) may not be the same as what motivates a more seasoned, experienced, and financially successful employee (recognition, opportunity for greater influence, and increased training). Motivation is not an easy thing to understand, especially as firms become more global and more diverse.

Another important part of motivation is enjoying where you work and your career opportunities. Review Table 9.5 for the "Best Places to Live in Canada." Chances are, workers in these places have encountered fewer frustrations than those in places at the bottom of the list and, therefore, would probably be more content with where they work.

BUILD YOUR BUSINESS PLAN

Motivating the Workforce

As you determine the size of your workforce, you are going to face the reality that you cannot provide the level of financial compensation that you would like to your employees, especially when you are starting your business.

Many employees are motivated by other things than money. Knowing that they are appreciated and doing a good job can bring great satisfaction to employees. Known as "stroking," it can provide employees with internal gratification that can be valued even more than financial incentives. Listening to employees' suggestions, involving them in discussions about future growth, and valuing their input can go a long way toward building loyal employees and reducing employee turnover.

Think about what you could do in your business to motivate your employees without spending much money. Maybe you will have lunch brought in once a week or offer tickets to a local sporting event to the employee with the most sales. Whatever you elect to do, you must be consistent and fair with all your employees.

CASE | Is It Possible Your Dog Could Increase Business Productivity?

In an age in which companies are cutting back health care benefits due to a sluggish economy, many employers are turning to low-cost perks to keep workers happy. In addition to perks such as gym and spa facilities and weight-loss programs, an increasing number of companies are actually allowing employees to bring their pets to work. A recent survey conducted by Dogster (an online dog forum) and Simply Hired indicates that two-thirds of all dog owners surveyed would work longer hours if allowed to bring their dogs to work. One-third claimed they would accept a 5 percent pay deduction if allowed to bring their dogs to work. Maybe this is because another survey indicated that 69 percent of dog owners view their dog as part of the family.

Having dogs and cats in the workplace can provide many benefits, including a more relaxed and flexible atmosphere, increased staff morale, and even increased employee retention. One company's spokesperson indicated that its pet policy gives employees individual flexibility and shows that the company respects employees enough to let them make choices about their work environment. The American Psychological Association has even honoured companies such as Small Dog Electronics, a computer merchant with 27 employees, as psychologically healthy workplaces in part because of their pet-friendly policies. At this time, many pet-friendly companies have 50 or fewer employees, although a few *Fortune* 500 companies such as Amazon and Google have pet-friendly policies. At Planet Dog, a company allowing pets in the office daily, the company consists, so to speak, of 16 employees and 14 dogs.

A pet-friendly workplace can be a definite advantage in recruiting and retaining employees. Small Dog Electronics, for example, has boasted an employee turnover rate of 1 percent compared with its industry average of 11 percent. Even non-pet owners often appreciate the informal, flexible environments that characterize workplaces with pets. To some extent, being pet-friendly helps define a corporate culture—as it does at AutoDesk, a software provider. A Pet Products Manufacturers Association survey revealed that 73 percent of surveyed companies believed allowing pets at work increased productivity—compared with a 42 percent productivity increase due to business development or management training. Even when it is not possible for employees to bring pets to work every day, some companies allow them to bring their pets to work occasionally for short periods of time.

Many small businesses, particularly retailers, established pet-friendly policies out of personal necessity. Indeed many small retailers, such as antique dealers and bookstore owners, often have "store cats" or "store dogs" that are appreciated as much by customers as by employees. Although legislation prohibits allowing pets in restaurants in Canada and the United States, many European restaurants allow customers to have their dogs right at their tables where food is served.

While bringing your pet to work can definitely improve morale, there are a few challenges. People with allergies or who are afraid of animals may get distracted from their jobs. Of course, there may be the concern that a dog may bite a person or another dog. However, research by attorneys at Ralston Purina found that lawsuits related to pets in the work environment are quite rare. As long as good judgment is used, allowing animals in the workplace appears to be a great move.[35]

DISCUSSION QUESTIONS

1. Why can a non-financial benefit such as being able to bring your dog to work motivate employees?

2. What types of businesses are appropriate for a pet-friendly workplace policy?

3. How do you personally feel about having other people's pets in an office where you work or store where you shop?

DESTINATION CEO

For two decades, **Jack Welch** was at the helm of the most admired company in the world—GE. Now that he is retired, he and his wife, Suzy, have written the book *Winning*.

Welch's secret for success, he says, is recruiting and hiring people who are smarter than he is and who have a lot of energy, those with an edge and who can be energized to pursue the goals of the company. Welch describes three categories of employees—the top performers, the middle 70 percent, and the "others." Success, he says, is about maintaining the energy of the top performers. When asked how he motivates the middle 70 percent, he says that his approach is controversial. Welch maintains that it is important for that group to know what it takes for them to move up in the organization. Welch believes that it is important for all members of the organization to know where they stand. As for the "other" group, he says that more often than not, they will move on. Welch firmly believes that the job of the leader is to focus on the followers—not on your own success.

The most exciting thing about being a manager or a leader is helping people to grow and providing them the opportunity to change their lives. The hardest part, he says, is letting people go. Overall, however, it is important that no one in the organization is ever surprised about their performance review. Constant feedback, letting people know where they stand, is the most important role of the manager. In short, Welch says that once you are a manager, "It's about them, not about you."[1]

Introduction

If a business is to achieve success, it must have sufficient numbers of employees who are qualified and motivated to perform the required duties. Thus, managing the quantity (from hiring to firing) and quality (through training, compensating, and so on) of employees is an important business function. Meeting the challenge of managing increasingly diverse human resources effectively can give a company a competitive edge in a global marketplace.

This chapter focuses on the quantity and quality of human resources. First, we look at how human resources managers plan for, recruit, and select qualified employees. Next, we look at training, appraising, and compensating employees, aspects of human resources management designed to retain valued employees. Along the way, we'll also consider the challenges of managing unionized employees and workplace diversity.

The Nature of Human Resources Management

LO1 Define human resources management, and explain its significance.

Chapter 1 defined human resources as labour, the physical and mental abilities that people use to produce goods and services. **Human resources management (HRM)** refers to all the activities involved in determining an organization's human resources needs, as well as acquiring, training, and compensating people to fill those needs. Human resources managers are concerned with maximizing the satisfaction of employees and motivating them to meet organizational objectives productively. In some companies, this function is called personnel management.

human resources management (HRM) all the activities involved in determining an organization's human resources needs, as well as acquiring, training, and compensating people to fill those needs

HRM has increased in importance over the last few decades, in part because managers have developed a better understanding of human relations through the work of Maslow, Herzberg, and others. Moreover, the human resources themselves are changing. Employees today are concerned not only about how much a job pays; they are concerned also with job satisfaction, personal performance, leisure, the environment, and the future. Once dominated by white men, today's workforce includes significantly more women, African Canadians, Chinese Canadians, and other minorities, as well as disabled and older workers. Human resources managers must be aware of these changes and make the best use of them to increase the productivity of their employees. Every manager practises some of the functions of human resources management at all times.

Planning for Human Resources Needs

When planning and developing strategies for reaching the organization's overall objectives, a company must consider whether it will have the human resources necessary to carry out its plans. After determining how many employees and what skills are needed to satisfy the overall plans, the human resources department (which may range from the owner in a small business to hundreds of people in a large corporation) ascertains how many employees the company currently has and how many will be retiring or otherwise leaving the organization during the planning period. With this information, the human resources manager can then forecast how many more employees the company will need to hire and what qualifications they must have. HRM planning also requires forecasting the availability of people in the workforce who will have the necessary qualifications to meet the organization's future needs. The human resources manager then develops a strategy for satisfying the organization's human resources needs. As organizations strive to increase efficiency through outsourcing, automation, or learning to effectively use temporary workers, hiring needs can change dramatically.

job analysis the determination, through observation and study, of pertinent information about a job—including specific tasks and necessary abilities, knowledge, and skills

Next, managers analyze the jobs within the organization so that they can match the human resources to the available assignments. **Job analysis** determines, through observation and study, pertinent information about a job—the specific tasks that comprise it; the knowledge, skills, and abilities necessary to perform it; and the environment in which it will be performed. Managers use the information obtained through a job analysis to develop job descriptions and job specifications.

A **job description** is a formal, written explanation of a specific job that usually includes job title, tasks to be performed (for instance, waiting on customers), relationship with other jobs, physical and mental skills required (such as lifting heavy boxes or calculating data), duties,

job description a formal, written explanation of a specific job, usually including job title, tasks, relationship with other jobs, physical and mental skills required, duties, responsibilities, and working conditions

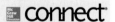

connect

Need help understanding this concept? Check out an informational video! Log into Connect, go to Resources, and click on the Videos page

© David Lees/Digital Vision/Getty Images

Today's organizations are more diverse, with a greater range of women, minorities, and older workers.

job specification a description of the qualifications necessary for a specific job, in terms of education, experience, and personal and physical characteristics

recruiting forming a pool of qualified applicants from which management can select employees

responsibilities, and working conditions. Job seekers might turn to online websites or databases to help find job descriptions for specific occupations. For instance, the Labour Market Information (LMI) service helps Canadians find information about occupations and labour market trends and outlooks, including skill or labour shortages and surpluses.[2] A **job specification** describes the qualifications necessary for a specific job, in terms of education (some jobs require a post-secondary degree), experience, personal characteristics (newspaper ads frequently request outgoing, hardworking persons), and physical characteristics. Both the job description and job specification are used to develop recruiting materials such as newspaper and online advertisements.

Recruiting and Selecting New Employees

LO2 Summarize the processes of recruiting and selecting human resources for a company.

After forecasting the firm's human resources needs and comparing them to existing human resources, the human resources manager should have a general idea of how many new employees the firm needs to hire. With the aid of job analyses, management can then recruit and select employees who are qualified to fill specific job openings.

Recruiting

Recruiting means forming a pool of qualified applicants from which management can select employees. There are two sources from which to develop this pool of applicants—the internal and external.

Internal sources of applicants include the organization's current employees. Many firms have a policy of giving first consideration to their own employees—or promoting from within. The cost of hiring current employees to fill job openings is inexpensive when compared with the cost of hiring from external sources, and it is good for employee morale. However, hiring from within creates another job vacancy to be filled.

External sources consist of advertisements in newspapers and professional journals, employment agencies, colleges, vocational schools, recommendations from current employees, competing firms, unsolicited applications, and online. Internships are also a good way to solicit for potential employees. Many companies hire university students or recent graduates for low-paying internships that give them the opportunity to get hands-on experience on the job. If the intern proves to be a good fit, an organization may then hire the intern as a full-time worker. There are also hundreds of websites where employers can post job openings and job seekers can post their résumés, including Workopolis.com, Monster.com, and CareerBuilder.com. Employers seeking employees for specialized jobs can use more focused sites such as computerwork.com. Increasingly, companies can turn to their own websites for potential candidates. Employers can also use social networking sites such as LinkedIn to post jobs and search for candidates. Many consumers believe social networking sites may eventually supplant traditional résumés. Using external sources of applicants is generally more expensive than hiring from within, but it may be necessary if there are no current employees who meet the job specifications or if there are better-qualified people outside of the organization. Recruiting for entry-level managerial and professional positions is often carried out on college and university campuses. For managerial or professional positions above the entry level, companies sometimes depend on employment agencies or executive search firms, sometimes called headhunters, which specialize in luring qualified people away from other companies. Employers are also increasingly using professional social networking sites such as LinkedIn and Viadeo as recruitment tools.

Selection

Selection is the process of collecting information about applicants and using that information to decide which ones to hire. It includes the application itself, as well as interviewing, testing, and reference checking. This process can be quite lengthy and expensive. At Procter & Gamble, for example, the steps include application submission, screening and comprehensive interviews, day visits/site visits, and for international applicants, a problem-solving test to ensure that P&G attracts and retains high-quality employees.[3] Such rigorous scrutiny is necessary to find those applicants who can do the work expected and fit into the firm's structure and culture. If an organization finds the "right" employees through its recruiting and selection process, it will not have to spend as much money later in recruiting, selecting, and training replacement employees.

selection the process of collecting information about applicants and using that information to make hiring decisions

The Application. In the first stage of the selection process, the individual fills out an application form and perhaps has a brief interview. The application form asks for the applicant's name, address, telephone number, education, and previous work experience. The goal of this stage of the selection process is to get acquainted with the applicants and to weed out those who are obviously not qualified for the job. Figure 10.1 indicates how much time human resources managers spend reviewing applications.

Figure 10.1 How Much Time Do Human Resource Managers Spend Reviewing Applications?

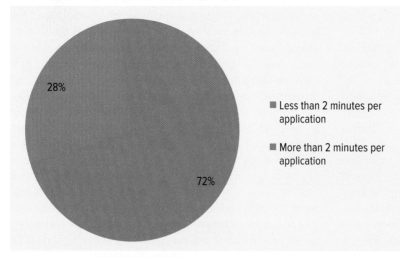

- 28% ■ Less than 2 minutes per application
- 72% ■ More than 2 minutes per application

Source: CareerBuilder survey of 2,662 hiring managers. Reprinted in *USA Today*, September 28, 2011.

For employees with work experience, most companies ask for the following information before contacting a potential candidate: current salary, reason for seeking a new job, years of experience, availability, and level of interest in the position. In addition to identifying obvious qualifications, the application can provide subtle clues about whether a person is appropriate for a particular job. For instance, an applicant who gives unusually creative answers may be perfect for a position at an advertising agency; a person who turns in a sloppy, hurriedly scrawled application probably would not be appropriate for a technical job requiring precise adjustments. Many companies now accept online applications. The online application at Target is designed not only to collect biographical data but to create a picture of the applicant and how the person might contribute within the company. The completion of the survey takes about 45 minutes, depending on the position. To get a better view of the fit between the applicant and the company, the online application contains a questionnaire that asks applicants for more specific information, from how they might react in a certain situation to personality attributes like self-esteem or ability to interact with people.[4]

The Interview. The next phase of the selection process involves interviewing applicants. Interviews allow management to obtain detailed information about the applicant's experience and skills, reasons for changing jobs, attitudes toward the job, and an idea of whether the person would fit in with the company. Table 10.1 provides some insights on finding the right work environment. Interviews allow management to obtain detailed information about the applicant's experience and skills, reasons for changing jobs, attitudes toward the job, and an idea of whether the person would fit in with the company. Table 10.2 lists some of the most common questions asked by interviewers while Table 10.3 reveals some common mistakes candidates make in interviewing. Furthermore,

the interviewer can answer the applicant's questions about the requirements for the job, compensation, working conditions, company policies, organizational culture, and so on. A potential employee's questions may be just as revealing as his or her answers. Today's students might be surprised to have an interviewer ask them, "What's on your Facebook account?" or have them show the interviewer their Facebook accounts. Currently, these are legal questions for an interviewer to ask.

Testing. Another step in the selection process is testing. Ability and performance tests are used to determine whether an applicant has the skills necessary for the job. Aptitude, IQ, or personality tests may be used to assess an applicant's potential for a certain kind of work and his or her ability to fit into the organization's culture. One of the most commonly used tests is the Myers-Briggs Type Indicator, which is used more than 2.5 million times each

Table 10.1 Interviewing Tips

1. Evaluate the work environment. Do employees seem to get along and work well in teams?
2. Evaluate the attitude of employees. Are employees happy, tense, or overworked?
3. Are employees enthusiastic and excited about their work?
4. What is the organizational culture, and would you feel comfortable working there?

Source: Adapted from "What to Look for During Office Visits," http://careercenter.tamu.edu/guides/interviews/lookforinoffice.cfm?sn=parents (accessed April 23, 2012).

Table 10.2 Top 10 Interview Questions

1. Tell me about yourself.
2. Why should I hire you?
3. Please tell me about your future objectives.
4. Has your education prepared you for your career?
5. Have you been a team player?
6. Did you encounter any conflict with your previous professors or employer? What are the steps that you have taken to resolve this issue?
7. What is your biggest weakness?
8. How would your professors describe you?
9. What are the qualities that a manager should possess?
10. If you could turn back time, what would you change?

Based on "Job Interview Skills Training: Top Ten Interview Questions for College Graduates," February 17, 2010, www.articlesbase.com/business-articles/job-interview-skills-training-top-ten-interview-questions-for-college-graduates-1871741.html (accessed April 13, 2011).

Table 10.3 Mistakes Made in Interviewing

1. Not taking the interview seriously

2. Not dressing appropriately (dressing down)

3. Not appropriately discussing experience, abilities, and education

4. Being too modest about your accomplishments

5. Talking too much

6. Too much concern about compensation

7. Speaking negatively of a former employer

8. Not asking enough or appropriate questions

9. Not showing the proper enthusiasm level

10. Not engaging in appropriate follow-up to the interview

Source: "Avoid the Top 10 Job Interview Mistakes," All Business, https://www.allbusiness.com/slideshow/avoid-the-top-10-job-interview-mistakes-16568835-1.html (April 23, 2012).

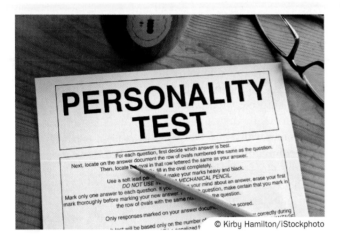
© Kirby Hamilton/iStockphoto

Personality tests such as Myers-Briggs are used to assess an applicant's potential for a certain kind of job. For instance, extroversion and a love of people would be good qualities for a sales or retail job. Interestingly, there does not seem to be any difference between introversion and extroversion in making a good manager.

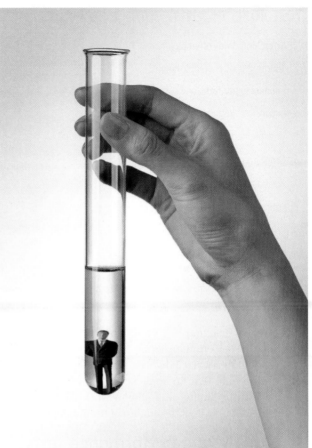
© Jeffrey Coolidge/Digital Vision/Getty Images

Some jobs require potential hires to undergo physical examinations such as alcohol tests.

year, according to a survey by *Workforce Management*. Applicants may also undergo physical examinations to determine their suitability for some jobs. One difference between Canadian and American human resource practices revolves around the use of drug testing—the practice is no longer legal in Canada (with some exceptions for government positions), but in the United States many companies require applicants to be screened for illegal drug use. In Canada, employers can screen for alcohol but not drugs.[5] Small businesses may have a higher percentage of these employees because they do not engage in systematic drug testing. If you employ a drug or alcohol abuser, you can expect a 33 percent loss in productivity from this employee.

Because computer knowledge is a requirement for many jobs today, certain companies also require an applicant to take a typing test or tests to determine their knowledge of Microsoft Word, Excel, PowerPoint, and/or other necessary programs. Like the application form and the interview, testing serves to eliminate those who do not meet the job specifications.

Reference Checking. Before making a job offer, the company should always check an applicant's references. Reference checking usually involves verifying educational background and previous work experience. Background checking is important because applicants may misrepresent themselves on their applications or résumés. The star of *Dinner: Impossible* on the Food Network fabricated portions of his résumé, including the claim that he cooked for Britain's royal family. The Food Network, upon learning of these errors, did not renew Robert Irvine's contract, indicating that viewers place trust in the network and the accuracy of information that it provides and that Irvine "challenged that trust."[6] Irvine had to work for months to apologize and set the record straight about his chef credentials. The Food Network ultimately did rehire him to host *Dinner: Impossible*. As Table 10.4 illustrates, some of the most common types of résumé lies include the faking of credentials, overstatements of skills or accomplishments, lies concerning education/degrees, omissions of past employment, and the falsification of references.[7]

Table 10.4 Top 10 Résumé Lies

1. Stretching dates of employment
2. Inflating past accomplishments and skills
3. Enhancing job titles and responsibilities
4. Education exaggeration and fabricating degrees
5. Unexplained gaps and periods of "self employment"
6. Omitting past employment
7. Faking credentials
8. Fabricating reasons for leaving previous job
9. Providing fraudulent references
10. Misrepresenting military record

Based on Christopher T. Marquet and Lisa J. B. Peterson, "Résumé Fraud: The Top 10 Lies," www.marquetinternational.com/pdf/Resume%20Fraud-Top%20Ten%20Lies.pdf (accessed April 13, 2011).

Reference checking is a vital, albeit often overlooked, stage in the selection process. Managers charged with hiring should be aware, however, that many organizations will confirm only that an applicant is a former employee, perhaps with beginning and ending work dates, and will not release details about the quality of the employee's work.

> ## "Ability and performance tests are used to determine whether an applicant has the skills necessary for the job."

Legal Issues in Recruiting and Selecting

Legal constraints and regulations are present in almost every phase of the recruitment and selection process, and a violation of these regulations can result in lawsuits and fines. Therefore, managers should be aware of these restrictions to avoid legal problems. The Charter of Rights and Freedoms guarantees that all people are treated the same way under the law, and the Canadian Human Rights Act ensures that all people have equal opportunities for employment.[8] The Human Rights Act is applicable for all federally regulated organizations including banks and airlines. Individual provinces and territories have their own laws to protect workers in non-regulated businesses.[9] Another important law which businesses have to be aware of is the Employment Equity Act, signed in 1986, which ensures that federally regulated

employers with more than 100 employees do not disadvantage women, visible minorities, disabled people, and Aboriginals. Furthermore, organizations have to make special accommodations to assist people in these categories in gaining meaningful employment. Additionally, if an employer or organization had a disproportionate number of male employees, then they had to develop a plan to balance out the gender of their employees. The same concept applies to skin colour and/or cultural background.[10] Recently, a new category of workers has gone before human rights boards to fight for their rights. Baby boomers, who have been forced to retire due to the mandatory retirement age in Canada being set at 65, have successfully challenged the law under the Charter of Rights and Freedoms, and mandatory retirement has effectively been abolished in most of Canada as a result.[11] Figure 10.2 shows the percentage of women who hold top leadership positions at *Fortune* 500 Companies.

Developing the Workforce

Once the most qualified applicants have been selected and offered positions, and they have accepted their offers, they must be formally introduced to the organization and trained so they can begin to be productive members of the workforce. **Orientation** familiarizes the newly hired employees with fellow workers, company procedures, and the physical properties of the company. It generally includes a tour of the

> **orientation** familiarizing newly hired employees with fellow workers, company procedures, and the physical properties of the company

Figure 10.2 Women Leaders at *Fortune* 500 Companies

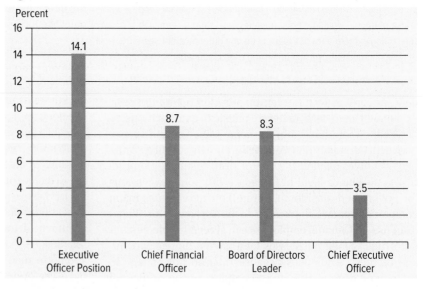

Source: Catalyst®, Women on Boards, 2012, www.catalyst.org/file/589/qt_women_on_boards.pdf (accessed April 4, 2012); Catalyst®, Women on Financial Services, 2012, www.catalyst.org/file/577/qt_women_in_financial_services.pdf (accessed April 4, 2012); Catalyst®, "Women CEOs of the Fortune 1000," March 2012, www.catalyst.org/publication/271/women-ceos-of-the-fortune-1000 (accessed April 4, 2012); Rachel Soares, Baye Cobb, Ellen Lebow, Allyson Regis, Hannah Winsten, and Veronica Wojnas, "2011 Catalyst Census: Fortune 500 Women Executive Officers and Top Earners," Catalyst®, December 2011, www.catalyst.org/publication/516/2011-catalyst-census-fortune-500-women-executive-officers-and-top-earners (accessed April 4, 2012).

building; introductions to supervisors, co-workers, and subordinates; and the distribution of organizational manuals describing the organization's policy on vacations, absenteeism, lunch breaks, company benefits, and so on. Orientation also involves socializing the new employee into the ethics and culture of the new company. Many larger companies show videos of procedures, facilities, and key personnel in the organization to help speed the adjustment process.

Training and Development

LO3 Discuss how workers are trained and their performance appraised.

Although recruiting and selection are designed to find employees who have the knowledge, skills, and abilities the company needs, new employees still must undergo **training** to learn how to do their specific job tasks. On-the-job training allows workers to learn by actually performing the tasks of the job, while *classroom training* teaches employees with lectures, conferences, videos, case studies, and web-based training. For instance, McDonald's trains those interested in company operations and leadership development at the Fred L. Turner Training Center, otherwise known as Hamburger University. Hamburger University employs full-time professors to train students in a variety of topics, including crew development, restaurant management, middle management, and executive development. Training includes classroom instruction, hands-on instruction, and computer e-learning.[12] **Development** is training that augments the skills and knowledge of managers and professionals. Training and development are also used to improve the skills of employees in their present positions and to prepare them for increased responsibility and job promotions. Training is therefore a vital function of human resources management. Use of role-plays, simulations, and online training methods are becoming increasingly popular in employee training.

training teaching employees to do specific job tasks through either classroom development or on-the-job experience

development training that augments the skills and knowledge of managers and professionals

Assessing Performance

Assessing an employee's performance—his or her strengths and weaknesses on the job—is one of the most difficult tasks for managers. However, performance appraisal

© Tannen Maury/Bloomberg via Getty Images

McDonald's has expanded its famous Hamburger University into China. This branch of Hamburger University will train a new generation of Chinese students in such areas as restaurant management, leadership development, and other skills.

is crucial because it gives employees feedback on how they are doing and what they need to do to improve their performance. It also provides a basis for determining how to compensate and reward employees, and it generates information about the quality of the firm's selection, training, and development activities. Table 10.5 identifies 16 characteristics that may be assessed in a performance review.

Table 10.5 General Performance Characteristics

- **Productivity**—rate at which work is regularly produced
- **Quality**—accuracy, professionalism, and deliverability of produced work
- **Job knowledge**—understanding of the objectives, practices, and standards of work
- **Problem solving**—ability to identify and correct problems effectively
- **Communication**—effectiveness in written and verbal exchanges
- **Initiative**—willingness to identify and address opportunities for improvement
- **Adaptability**—ability to become comfortable with change
- **Planning and organization skills**—reflected through the ability to schedule projects, set goals, and maintain organizational systems
- **Teamwork and cooperation**—effectiveness of collaborations with co-workers
- **Judgment**—ability to determine appropriate actions in a timely manner
- **Dependability**—responsiveness, reliability, and conscientiousness demonstrated on the job
- **Creativity**—extent to which resourceful ideas, solutions, and methods for task completion are proposed
- **Sales**—demonstrated through success in selling products, services, yourself, and your company
- **Customer service**—ability to communicate effectively with customers, address problems, and offer solutions that meet or exceed their expectations
- **Leadership**—tendency and ability to serve as a doer, guide, decision maker, and role model
- **Financial management**—appropriateness of cost controls and financial planning within the scope defined by the position

Source: "Performance Characteristics," Performance Review from www.salary.com/Careerresources/docs/related_performance_review_part2_popup.html (accessed June 12, 2001). Used with permission.

Performance appraisals may be objective or subjective. An objective assessment is quantifiable. For example, a Westinghouse employee might be judged by how many circuit boards he typically produces in one day or by how many of his boards have defects. A Century 21 real estate agent might be judged by the number of houses she has shown or the number of sales she has closed. A company can also use tests as an objective method of assessment. Whatever method they use, managers must take into account the work environment when they appraise performance objectively.

When jobs do not lend themselves to objective appraisal, the manager must relate the employee's performance to some other standard. One popular tool used in subjective assessment is the ranking system, which lists various performance factors on which the manager ranks employees against each other. Although used by many large companies, ranking systems are unpopular with many employees. Qualitative criteria, such as teamwork and communication skills, used to evaluate employees are generally hard to gauge. Such grading systems have triggered employee lawsuits that allege discrimination in grade/ranking assignments. For example, one manager may grade a company's employees one way, while another manager grades a group more harshly depending on the managers' grading style. If layoffs occur, then employees graded by the second manager may be more likely to lose their jobs. Other criticisms of grading systems include unclear wording or inappropriate words that a manager may unintentionally write in a performance evaluation, like *young* or *pretty* to describe an employee's appearance. These liabilities can all be fodder for lawsuits

should employees allege that they were treated unfairly. It is therefore crucial that managers use clear language in performance evaluations and be consistent with all employees. Several employee grading computer packages have been developed to make performance evaluations easier for managers and clearer for employees.[13]

Another performance appraisal method used by many companies is the 360-degree feedback system, which provides feedback from a panel that typically includes superiors, peers, and subordinates. Because of the tensions it may cause, peer appraisal appears to be difficult for many. However, companies that have success with 360-degree feedback tend to be open to learning and willing to experiment and are led by executives who are direct about the expected benefits as well as the challenges.[14] Managers and leaders with a high emotional intelligence (sensitivity to their own as well as others' emotions) assess and reflect upon their interactions with colleagues on a daily basis. In addition, they conduct follow-up analysis on their projects, asking the right questions and listening carefully to responses without getting defensive of their actions.[15]

Whether the assessment is objective or subjective, it is vital that the manager discuss the results with the employee, so that the employee knows how well he or she is doing the job. The results of a performance appraisal become useful only when they are communicated, tactfully, to the employee and presented as a tool to allow the employee to grow and improve in his or her position and beyond. Performance appraisals are also used to determine whether an employee should be promoted, transferred, or terminated from the organization.

Consider the Following: Morale among the Survivors

Medallion Corporation manufactures quality carpeting and linoleum. A recession and subsequent downturn in home sales has sharply cut the company's sales. Medallion found itself in the unenviable position of having to lay off hundreds of employees in the home office (the manufacturing facilities) as well as many salespeople. Employees were called in on Friday afternoon and told about their status in individual meetings with their supervisors. The laid-off employees were given one additional month of work and two weeks' severance pay per year of service, along with the opportunity to sign up for classes to help with the transition, including job search tactics and résumé writing.

Several months after the cutbacks, morale was at an all-time low for the company, although productivity had improved. Medallion brought in consultants, who suggested that the leaner, flatter organizational structure would be suitable for more team activities. Medallion therefore set up task forces and teams to

deal with employee concerns, but the diversity of the workforce led to conflict and misunderstandings among team members. Medallion is evaluating how to proceed with this new team approach.[16]

DISCUSSION QUESTIONS

1. What did Medallion's HRM department do right in dealing with the employees who were laid off?

2. What are some of the potential problems that must be dealt with after an organization experiences a major trauma such as massive layoffs?

3. What can Medallion do to make the team approach work more smoothly? What role do you think diversity training should play?

> "The results of a performance appraisal become useful only when they are communicated, tactfully, to the employee and presented as a tool to allow the employee to grow and improve in his or her position and beyond."

© Stephanie De Sakutin/AFP/Getty Images

Amazon holds a job fair in the virtual world Second Life. Companies have started using digital media for posting job applications, holding job fairs, and even training employees.

Turnover

LO4 Identify the types of turnover companies may experience, and explain why turnover is an important issue.

Turnover, which occurs when employees quit, or are fired, promoted, or transferred and must be replaced by new employees, results in lost productivity from the vacancy, fees to recruit replacement employees, management time devoted to interviewing, and training costs for new employees. Some companies are able to manage their employees more effectively to minimize turnover. However, some companies have created innovative solutions for reducing turnover. After learning that its employees felt micromanaged, Best Buy implemented a system for some of its employees called Results Only Work Environment (ROWE) to reduce turnover and increase employee morale. Under this program, employees who were able to do their work away from the workplace could choose to do so. The initiative offered flexibility and a better work–life balance for employees. A study that analyzed the impact that ROWE had upon employee turnover found that turnover had decreased by 45 percent.[17] Part of the reason for turnover may be overworked employees as a result of downsizing and a lack of training and advancement opportunities.[18]

Figure 10.3 provides some of the top reasons employees give for leaving the company. Of course, turnover is not always an unhappy occasion when it takes the form of a promotion or transfer.

Many companies in recent years are choosing to downsize by eliminating jobs. Reasons for downsizing might be due to financial constraints or the need to become more productive and competitive.

A **job promotion** is an advancement to a higher-level position with increased authority, responsibility, and pay. In some companies and most labour unions, seniority—the length of time a person has been with the company or at a particular job classification—is the key issue in determining who should be promoted. Most managers base promotions on seniority only when they have candidates with equal qualifications: Managers prefer to base promotions on merit.

turnover occurs when employees quit, or are fired, promoted, or transferred, and must be replaced by new employees

job promotion advancement to a higher-level position with increased authority, responsibility, and pay

Figure 10.3 Reasons Employees Do Not Work Out in a Position (aside from poor performance)

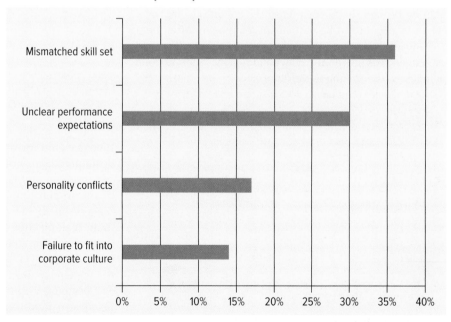

Based on Robert Half Finance & Accounting survey of 1,400 chief financial officers. Reprinted in *USA Today*, October 26, 2011.

A **transfer** is a move to another job within the company at essentially the same level and wage. Transfers allow workers to obtain new skills or to find a new position within an organization when their old position has been eliminated because of automation or downsizing.

Separations occur when employees resign, retire, are terminated, or are laid off. Employees may be terminated, or fired, for poor performance, violation of work rules,

transfer a move to another job within the company at essentially the same level and wage

separations employment changes involving resignation, retirement, termination, or layoff

absenteeism, and so on. Businesses have traditionally been able to fire employees *at will*, that is, for any reason other than for race, religion, sex, or age, or because an employee is a union organizer. However, recent legislation and court decisions now require that companies fire employees fairly, for just cause only. Managers must take care, then, to warn employees when their performance is unacceptable and may lead to dismissal. They should also document all problems and warnings in employees' work records. To avoid the possibility of lawsuits from individuals who may feel they have been fired unfairly, employers should provide clear, business-related reasons for any firing, supported by written documentation if possible. Employee disciplinary procedures should be carefully explained to all employees and should be set forth in employee handbooks. Table 10.6 illustrates what not to do when you are terminated.

Many companies have downsized in recent years, laying off tens of thousands of employees in their effort to become more productive and competitive. For example, Target had to lay off more than 17,000 workers after it decided to close 133 stores in the Canada. Declining sales convinced Target to adapt its marketing strategy and suspend its Canadian operations.[19] Layoffs are sometimes temporary; employees may be brought back when business conditions improve. When layoffs are to be permanent, employers often help employees find other jobs and may extend benefits while the employees search for new employment. Such actions help lessen the trauma of the layoffs.

Table 10.6 What to Avoid When Leaving Your Job

1. Do not tell off your boss and co-workers, even if you think they deserve it.
2. Do not damage company property or steal something.
3. Do not forget to ask for a reference.
4. Do not badmouth your employer or any of your co-workers to your replacement.
5. Do not badmouth your employer to a prospective employer when you go on a job interview.

Source: Dawn Rosenberg McKay, "Five Things Not to Do When You Leave Your Job," http://careerplanning.about.com/od/jobseparation/a/leave_mistakes.htm (accessed April 13, 2011).

© thodonal88/Shutterstock

Some companies are able to manage their employees more effectively to minimize turnover.

A well-organized human resources department strives to minimize losses due to separations and transfers because recruiting and training new employees is very expensive. For example, Loblaw Cos. Ltd. shifted more of its employees to full-time work with plans to convert 10,000 part-time positions to full-time work in the coming years. The company says that the move should reduce staff turnover and improve productivity.[20] Note that a high turnover rate in a company may signal problems either with the selection and training process, the compensation program, or even the type of company. To help reduce turnover, companies have tried a number of strategies, including giving employees more interesting job responsibilities (job enrichment), allowing for increased job flexibility, and providing more employee benefits.

Compensating the Workforce

LO5 Specify the various ways a worker may be compensated.

People generally don't work for free, and how much they are paid for their work is a complicated issue. Also, designing a fair compensation plan is an important task because pay and benefits represent a substantial portion of an organization's expenses. Wages that are too high may result in the company's products being priced too high, making them uncompetitive in the market. Wages that are too low may damage employee morale and result in costly turnover. Remember that compensation is one of the hygiene factors identified by Herzberg.

Designing a fair compensation plan is a difficult task because it involves evaluating the relative worth of all jobs within the business while allowing for individual efforts. Compensation for a specific job is typically

wage/salary survey a study that tells a company how much compensation comparable firms are paying for specific jobs that the firms have in common

wages financial rewards based on the number of hours the employee works or the level of output achieved

determined through a **wage/salary survey**, which tells the company how much compensation comparable firms are paying for specific jobs that the firms have in common. Compensation can also vary amongst employees within the same job category based on productivity.

Financial Compensation

Financial compensation falls into two general categories—wages and salaries. **Wages** are financial rewards based on the number of hours the employee works or the level of output achieved. Wages based on the number of hours worked are called time wages. In Canada, the general minimum wage varies by province or territory, with a high of $13 per hour in Nunavut and a low of $10.50 per hour in Saskatchewan and Newfoundland and Labrador (as of October 2016).[21] Table 10.7 compares the minimum wage across the country. As previously discussed in this chapter, the impending shortage of labour will result in increased levels of compensation especially for skilled workers in Canada.

Time wages are appropriate when employees are continually interrupted and when quality is more important than quantity. Assembly-line workers, clerks, and

maintenance personnel are commonly paid on a time-wage basis. The advantage of time wages is the ease of computation. The disadvantage is that time wages provide no incentive to increase productivity. In fact, time wages may encourage employees to be less productive.

To overcome these disadvantages, many companies pay on an incentive system, using piece wages or commissions. Piece wages are based on the level of output achieved. A major advantage of piece wages is that they motivate employees to supervise their own activities and to increase output. Skilled craftworkers are often paid on a piece-wage basis.

The other incentive system, **commission**, pays a fixed amount or a percentage of the employee's sales. At Good-Life Fitness trainers are paid minimum wage for the hours they are in clubs prospecting for new clients. For training sessions, they split the hourly rate with GoodLife, from about 40/60 to 50/50, and get paid a 10 percent commission on sales.[22] This method motivates employees to sell as much as they can. Some companies combine payment based on commission with time wages or salaries.

A **salary** is a financial reward calculated on a weekly, monthly, or annual basis. Salaries are associated with white-collar workers such as office personnel,

commission an incentive system that pays a fixed amount or a percentage of the employee's sales

salary a financial reward calculated on a weekly, monthly, or annual basis

Table 10.7 Provincial/Territorial Minimum Wage, October 2016

Jurisdiction	Wage (C$/h)	Effective Date	Comments
Alberta	12.20	1 October 2016	$10.70 for liquor servers.
British Columbia	11.25	15 September 2017	$9.60 for liquor servers.
Manitoba	11.00	1 October 2015	Workers involved in construction have a higher starting minimum wage.
New Brunswick	10.65	1 April 2016	
Newfoundland and Labrador	10.50	1 October 2015	
Northwest Territories	12.50	1 June 2015	
Nova Scotia	10.70	1 April 2016	Rate is adjusted by percent change in the Consumer Price Index.
Nunavut	13.00	1 April 2016	Highest in Canada.
Ontario	11.40	1 October 2016	Students (under age 18, working 28 hours or under per week while school is in session or work when there is a school break): $10.70. • Liquor servers: $9.90. • Home workers (includes students and supersedes the student wage): $12.55.
Prince Edward Island	11.00	1 October 2016	
Quebec	10.75	1 May 2016	Workers receiving gratuities receive $9.20.
Saskatchewan	10.50	1 October 2015	Rate is adjusted by percent change in the Consumer Price Index.
Yukon	11.07	1 April 2016	Rate is adjusted by percent change in the Consumer Price Index.

Source: Government of Canada. Retrieved October 20, 2016, from http://srv116.services.gc.ca/dimt-wid/sm-mw/rptl.aspx;and Wikipedia, "Minimum Wage in Canada." Retrieved October 20, 2016, from https://en.wikipedia.org/wiki/Minimum_wage_in_Canada.

executives, and professional employees. Although a salary provides a stable stream of income, salaried workers may be required to work beyond usual hours without additional financial compensation.

In addition to the basic wages or salaries paid to employees, a company may offer **bonuses** for exceptional performance as an incentive to increase productivity further. Many workers receive a bonus as a "thank you" for good work and an incentive to continue working hard. Many owners and managers are recognizing that simple bonuses and perks foster happier employees and reduce turnover. For example, Canadian Western Bank offers employees a number of incentives, including contributions to RSPs and an employee share-purchase plan. Atlantic Canada–based Maritime Travel offers employees free trips and other travel rewards if they meet their sales targets.[23]

Another form of compensation is **profit sharing**, which distributes a percentage of company profits to the employees whose work helped to generate those profits. Some profit-sharing plans involve distributing shares of company stock to employees. Usually referred to as ESOPs—employee stock ownership plans—they have been gaining popularity in recent years. One reason for the popularity of ESOPs is the sense of partnership that they create between the organization and employees. Profit sharing can also motivate employees to work hard, because increased productivity

bonuses monetary rewards offered by companies for exceptional performance as incentives to further increase productivity

profit sharing a form of compensation whereby a percentage of company profits is distributed to the employees whose work helped to generate them

© JGI/Tom Grill/Getty Images

An onsite fitness centre is just one of the benefits that large companies have begun to offer employees. Such onsite benefits as fitness and child care centres are particularly important for employees who work long hours or who struggle to maintain a healthy work-life balance.

and sales mean that the profits or the stock dividends will increase. WestJet management attributes much of its success to the fact that approximately 85 percent of its employees own shares in the company. Senior management has noted that employees who own shares in the business have a vested interest in the company succeeding, and they will often go the extra mile to ensure that customers are happy.[24] Many organizations offer employees a stake in the company through stock purchase plans, ESOPs, or stock investments through RRSP plans. Various studies show that 7 to 10 percent of Canadian workers participate in some form of employee ownership. For instance, Flynn Canada, a Toronto-based trade contractor that makes and installs the outer layers of buildings, known as the building envelope, has some 60 owners.[25] Employees below senior management

---

GOING GREEN | Google Rewards Employees for Being Sustainable

For employees at Google, it pays to be green. Google employees can save money, donate to charities, and receive discounts on eco-friendly technology by taking advantage of the company's green incentives. For instance, employees can save fuel costs by riding to work on Google's biodiesel shuttles. They can also use Google's GFleet car-sharing program, GBikes, or GRide taxi service for travelling across the company campus or attending meetings offsite. For employees who choose to bike, walk, or pogo to work, the company provides them with digital stamps, which can be redeemed for company donations to the employee's favourite charity.

Many of Google's green initiatives help both employees and society. In 2011, Google announced that it was creating a $280 million fund for SolarCity in a partnership to support the installation of solar panels on residential homes. While it may be difficult to convince the average consumer to adopt solar technology, Google offers

its employees discounts. The company also created the largest corporate electronic-vehicle charging station in the country, not only to support the electric vehicles in its GFleet but also to inspire employees to purchase their own. Google seeks to make a difference in the field of sustainability—starting with its employees.[26]

DISCUSSION QUESTIONS

1. Describe some of Google's green initiatives.

2. How is Google rewarding employees for adopting greener behaviours?

3. Why do you think it might be beneficial for Google to subsidize the cost of installing solar panels on employee houses, even if it costs the company money?

levels rarely received stock options, until recently. Companies are adopting broad-based stock option plans to build a stronger link between employees' interests and the organization's interests. ESOPs have met with enormous success over the years, and employee-owned stock has even outperformed the stock market during certain periods. Many businesses have found employee stock options a great way to boost productivity and increase morale.

Benefits

Benefits are non-financial forms of compensation provided to employees, such as pension plans for retirement; health, disability, and life insurance; holidays and paid days off for vacation or illness; credit union membership; health programs; child care; elder care; assistance with adoption; and more. According to Statistics Canada, the total cost of employee benefits has risen faster than wages with costs to employers increasing two to three times the rate of inflation. Legally required benefits—Canada Pension Plan, workers' compensation, and Employment Insurance—account for some of the increase in costs, but increases in non-mandatory benefits such as health and dental plans account for the majority of the increase.[27] Such benefits increase employee security and, to a certain extent, morale and motivation.

> **benefits** non-financial forms of compensation provided to employees, such as pension plans, health insurance, paid vacation and holidays, and the like

Table 10.8 lists some of the benefits that Google offers its employees. Surveys have revealed that with the decrease in benefits comes a decrease in employee loyalty. Only 42 percent of employees say they feel a strong sense of loyalty to their employers. However, more than half of respondents indicated that employee benefits were important in decisions to stay with the company. Benefits are particularly important to younger generations of employees.[28] Starbucks recognizes the importance of how benefits can significantly impact an employee's health and well-being. As a result, it is the only fast-food company to offer its part-time employees health insurance.

"The most common counselling services offered include drug and alcohol-abuse treatment programs, fitness programs, smoking cessation clinics, stress-management clinics, financial counselling, family counselling, and career counselling."

A benefit increasingly offered is the employee assistance program (EAP). Each company's EAP is different, but most offer counselling for and assistance with those employees' personal problems that might hurt their job performance if not addressed. The most common counselling services offered include drug and alcohol-abuse treatment programs, fitness programs, smoking cessation clinics, stress-management clinics, financial counselling, family counselling, and career counselling. EAPs help reduce costs associated with poor productivity, absenteeism, and other workplace issues by helping employees deal with personal problems that contribute to these issues. For example, exercise and fitness programs reduce health insurance costs by helping employees stay healthy. Family counselling may help workers trying to cope with a divorce or other personal problems better focus on their jobs.

Companies try to provide the benefits they believe their employees want, but diverse people may want different things. In recent years, some single workers have felt that co-workers with spouses and children seem to get "special breaks" and extra time off to deal with family issues. Some companies use flexible benefit programs to allow employees to choose the benefits they would like, up to a specified amount.

Fringe benefits include sick leave, vacation pay, pension plans, health plans, and any other extra compensation. Soft benefits include perks that help balance life

Table 10.8 Google's Employee Benefits

- Health insurance:
  - Dental insurance
  - Vision insurance
- Vacation (15 days per year for one to three years' employment; 20 days off for four to five years' employment; 25 days for more than six years' employment)
- Twelve paid holidays/year
- Savings plans
- Disability and life insurance
- Employee assistance program
- Free lunches and snacks
- Massages, gym membership, hair stylist, fitness class, and bike repair
- Weekly activities
- Maternity leave
- Adoption assistance
- Tuition reimbursement
- Employee referral plan
- Onsite doctor
- Backup child care
- Holiday parties, health fair, credit union, roller hockey, outdoor volleyball court, discounts for local attractions

Based on "Google Benefits," www.google.com/intl/en/jobs/lifeatgoogle/benefits (accessed April 13, 2012).

and work. They include onsite child care, spas, food service, and even laundry services and hair salons. These soft benefits motivate employees and give them more time to focus on their jobs.

Cafeteria benefit plans provide a financial amount to employees so that they can select the specific benefits that fit their needs. The key is making benefits flexible, rather than giving employees identical benefits. As firms go global, the need for cafeteria or flexible benefit plans becomes even more important. For some employees, benefits are a greater motivator and differentiator in jobs than wages.

Over the last two decades, the list of fringe benefits has grown dramatically, and new benefits are being added every year.

Managing Unionized Employees

LO6 Discuss some of the issues associated with unionized employees, including collective bargaining and dispute resolution.

Employees who are dissatisfied with their working conditions or compensation have to negotiate with management to bring about change. Dealing with management on an individual basis is not always effective, however, so employees may organize themselves into **labour unions** to deal with employers and to achieve better pay, hours, and working conditions. Organized employees are backed by the power of a large group that can hire specialists to represent the entire union in its dealings with management. The Canadian Auto Workers, for example, has considerable power in its negotiations with Ford Motor Company and General Motors. Canada has a 31.5 percent unionization rate.[29]

labour unions employee organizations formed to deal with employers for achieving better pay, hours, and working conditions

However, union growth has slowed in recent years, and prospects for improvement do not look good. One reason is that most blue-collar workers, the traditional members of unions, have already been organized. Factories have become more automated and need fewer blue-collar workers. Canada has shifted from a manufacturing to a service economy, further reducing the demand for blue-collar workers. Moreover, in response to foreign competition, Canadian companies are scrambling to find ways to become more productive and cost efficient. Job enrichment programs and participative management have blurred the line between management and workers. Because workers' say in the way plants are run is increasing, their need for union protection is decreasing.

Nonetheless, labour unions have been successful in organizing blue-collar manufacturing, government, and health care workers, as well as smaller percentages of employees in other industries. Consequently, significant aspects of HRM, particularly compensation, are dictated to a large degree by union contracts at many companies. Therefore, we'll take a brief look at collective bargaining and dispute resolution in this section.

Collective Bargaining

Collective bargaining is the negotiation process through which management and unions reach an agreement about compensation, working hours, and working conditions for the bargaining unit (Figure 10.4). The objective of negotiations is to reach agreement about a **labour contract**, the formal, written document that spells out the relationship between the union and management for a specified period of time, usually two or three years.

collective bargaining the negotiation process through which management and unions reach an agreement about compensation, working hours, and working conditions for the bargaining unit

labour contract the formal, written document that spells out the relationship between the union and management for a specified period of time—usually two or three years

In collective bargaining, each side tries to negotiate an agreement that meets its demands; compromise is frequently necessary. Management tries to negotiate a labour contract that permits the company to retain control over things like work schedules; the hiring and firing of workers; production standards; promotions, transfers, and separations; the span of management in each department; and discipline. Unions tend to focus on contract issues such as magnitude of wages; better pay rates for overtime, holidays, and undesirable shifts; scheduling of pay increases; and benefits. These issues will be spelled out in the labour contract, which union members will vote to either accept (and abide by) or reject.

Many labour contracts contain a *cost-of-living allowance (COLA)*, or cost-of-living escalator clause, which calls for automatic wage increases during periods of inflation to protect the "real" income of the employees. During tough economic times, unions may be forced to accept *givebacks*—wage and benefit concessions made to employers to allow them to remain competitive or, in some cases, to survive and continue to provide jobs for union workers.

Resolving Disputes

Sometimes, management and labour simply cannot agree on a contract. Most labour disputes are handled through collective bargaining or through grievance procedures. When these processes break down, however, either

Figure 10.4 The Collective Bargaining Process

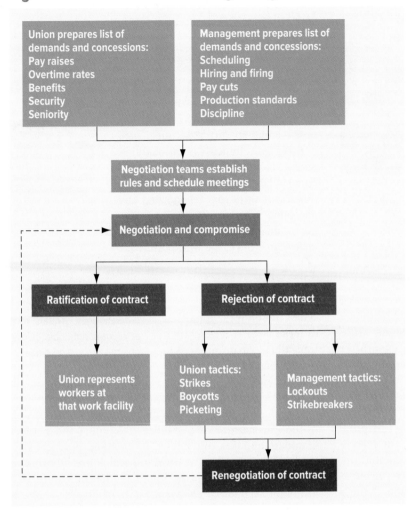

Union prepares list of demands and concessions:
- Pay raises
- Overtime rates
- Benefits
- Security
- Seniority

Management prepares list of demands and concessions:
- Scheduling
- Hiring and firing
- Pay cuts
- Production standards
- Discipline

Negotiation teams establish rules and schedule meetings

Negotiation and compromise

Ratification of contract

Rejection of contract

Union represents workers at that work facility

Union tactics:
- Strikes
- Boycotts
- Picketing

Management tactics:
- Lockouts
- Strikebreakers

Renegotiation of contract

United Kingdom experienced significant disruption with closed schools, refusals to collect refuse, and the suspension of non-emergency hospital services after 2 million public-sector workers staged a strike. The workers were protesting against government announcements to change public-sector worker pension plans. Such disruption in daily operations is one reason both unions and companies try to avoid strikes.[30] The threat of a strike is often enough to get management to back down. In fact, the number of worker-days actually lost to strikes is less than the amount lost to the common cold.

A **boycott** is an attempt to keep people from purchasing the products of a company. In a boycott, union members are asked not to do business with the boycotted organization. Some unions may even impose fines on members who ignore the boycott. To gain further support for their objectives, a union involved in a boycott may also ask the public—through picketing and advertising—not to purchase the products of the picketed firm.

Management Tactics. Management's version of a strike is the **lockout**; management actually closes a worksite so that employees cannot go to work. Lockouts are used, as a general rule, only when a union strike has partially shut down a plant and it seems less expensive for the plant to close completely. Caterpillar locked out workers from its 62-year-old plant in Ontario, after failure to reach an agreement with unionized employees over wages. In a controversial move, Caterpillar then announced it would close the plant entirely and relocate to Indiana. The wages of factory workers in Indiana would not be as high as those paid to the company's Canadian workers.[31]

Strikebreakers, called "scabs" by striking union members, are people hired by management to replace striking employees. Managers hire strikebreakers to continue operations and reduce the losses associated with strikes—and to show the unions that they will not bow to their demands. Strikebreaking is generally a last-resort measure for management because it

---

side may resort to more drastic measures to achieve its objectives.

Labour Tactics. **Picketing** is a public protest against management practices and involves union members marching (often waving anti-management signs and placards) at the employer's plant. Picketing workers hope that their signs will arouse sympathy for their demands from the public and from other unions. Picketing may occur as a protest or in conjunction with a strike.

Strikes (employee walkouts) are one of the most effective weapons labour has. By striking, a union makes carrying out the normal operations of a business difficult at best and impossible at worst. Strikes receive widespread publicity, but they remain a weapon of last resort. For example, the

picketing a public protest against management practices that involves union members marching and carrying anti-management signs at the employer's plant

strikes employee walkouts; one of the most effective weapons labour has

boycott an attempt to keep people from purchasing the products of a company

lockout management's version of a strike, wherein a worksite is closed so that employees cannot go to work

strikebreakers people hired by management to replace striking employees; called "scabs" by striking union members

© Justin Sullivan/Getty Images

Unions urged people to boycott the Hyatt hotel chain to protest allegedly abusive working conditions for Hyatt employees.

The Importance of Workforce Diversity

LO7 Describe the importance of diversity in the workforce.

Customers, employees, suppliers—all the participants in the world of business—come in different ages, genders, races, ethnicities, nationalities, and abilities, a truth that business has come to label **diversity**. Understanding this diversity means recognizing and accepting differences as well as valuing the unique perspectives such differences can bring to the workplace.

Mc Graw Hill Education **connect**

▶ Need help understanding this concept? Check out an informational video! Log into Connect, go to Resources, and click on the Videos page.

The Characteristics of Diversity

diversity the participation of different ages, genders, races, ethnicities, nationalities, and abilities in the workplace

When managers speak of diverse workforces, they typically mean differences in gender and race. While gender and race are important characteristics of diversity, others are also important. We can divide these differences into primary and secondary characteristics of diversity. In the lower segment of Figure 10.5, age, gender, race, ethnicity, abilities, and sexual orientation represent *primary characteristics* of diversity which are inborn and cannot be changed. In the upper section of Figure 10.5 are eight *secondary characteristics* of diversity—work background, income, marital status, military experience, religious beliefs, geographic location, parental status, and education—which *can* be changed. We acquire, change, and discard them as we progress through our lives.

Defining characteristics of diversity as either primary or secondary enhances our understanding, but we must remember that each person is defined by the interrelation of all characteristics. In dealing with diversity in the workforce, managers must consider the complete person—not one or a few of a person's differences.

Why Is Diversity Important?

The Canadian workforce is becoming increasingly diverse. More and more companies are trying to improve HRM programs to recruit, develop, and retain more diverse employees to better serve their diverse customers. Some firms are providing special programs such as sponsored affinity groups, mentoring programs, and special career development opportunities. Corporate Canada is also aware of the upcoming labour shortage and is becoming increasingly aware that eliminating barriers to potential employees could eliminate part of this problem. In fact, a recent study completed by RBC found that eliminating age, gender, and cultural barriers could bring an additional 1.6 million Canadians to the workforce.[32]

does great damage to the relationship between management and labour.

Outside Resolution. Management and union members normally reach mutually agreeable decisions without outside assistance. Sometimes though, even after lengthy negotiations, strikes, lockouts, and other tactics, management and labour still cannot resolve a contract dispute. In such cases, they have three choices: conciliation, mediation, and arbitration. **Conciliation** brings in a neutral third party to keep labour and management talking. The conciliator has no formal power over union representatives or over management. The conciliator's goal is to get both parties to focus on the issues and to prevent negotiations from breaking down. Like conciliation, **mediation** involves bringing in a neutral third party, but the mediator's role is to suggest or propose a solution to the problem. Mediators have no formal power over either labour or management. With **arbitration**, a neutral third party is brought in to settle the dispute, but the arbitrator's solution is legally binding and enforceable. Generally, arbitration takes place on a voluntary basis—management and labour must agree to it, and they usually split the cost (the arbitrator's fee and expenses) between them. Occasionally, management and labour submit to *compulsory arbitration*, in which an outside party (usually the federal government) requests arbitration as a means of eliminating a prolonged strike that threatens to disrupt the economy.

conciliation a method of outside resolution of labour and management differences in which a third party is brought in to keep the two sides talking

mediation a method of outside resolution of labour and management differences in which the third party's role is to suggest or propose a solution to the problem

arbitration settlement of a labour/management dispute by a third party whose solution is legally binding and enforceable

Astute

Effectively managing diversity in the workforce involves cultivating and valuing its benefits and minimizing its problems. Companies that are championing diversity are also becoming aware of the impact a diverse workforce can have on their financial performance. (For a list of top Canadian companies that practise diversity in hiring, go to the Canada's Best Diversity Employers website at www.canadastop100.com/diversity.)

The Benefits of Workforce Diversity

There are a number of benefits to fostering and valuing workforce diversity, including the following:

1. More productive use of a company's human resources. *make it possible to identify skills/knowledge that are useful*
2. Reduced conflict among employees of different ethnicities, races, religions, and sexual orientations as they learn to respect each other's differences. *and use them to achieve organization goal*
3. More productive working relationships among diverse employees as they learn more about and accept each other.
4. Increased commitment to and sharing of organizational goals among diverse employees at all organizational levels.
5. Increased innovation and creativity as diverse employees bring new, unique perspectives to decision-making and problem-solving tasks.
6. Increased ability to serve the needs of an increasingly diverse customer base.34

Companies that do not value their diverse employees are likely to experience greater conflict, as well as prejudice and discrimination. Among individual employees, for example, racial slurs and gestures, sexist comments, and other behaviours by co-workers harm the individuals at whom

© Michael Dwyer/Alamy

Some of the major benefits of diversity include a wider range of employee perspectives, greater innovation and creativity, and the ability to target a diverse customer base more effectively.

Figure 10.5 Characteristics of Diversity

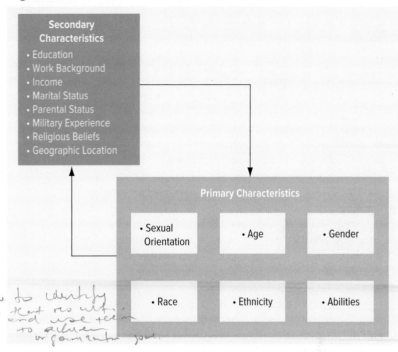

Source: Marilyn Loden and Judy B. Rosener, *Workforce America! Managing Employee Diversity as a Vital Resource,* 1991, p. 20. Used with permission. Copyright © 1991 The McGraw-Hill Companies.

such behaviour is directed. The victims of such behaviour may feel hurt, depressed, or even threatened and suffer from lowered self-esteem, all of which harm their productivity and morale. In such cases, women and minority employees may simply leave the firm, wasting the time, money, and other resources spent on hiring and training them. When discrimination comes from a supervisor, employees may also fear for their jobs. A discriminatory atmosphere not only can harm productivity and increase turnover, but may also subject a firm to costly lawsuits and negative publicity.

Astute business leaders recognize that they need to modify their human resources management programs to target the needs of *all* their diverse employees as well as the needs of the firm itself. They realize that the benefits of diversity are long term in nature and come only to those organizations willing to make the commitment. Most importantly, as workforce diversity becomes a valued organizational asset, companies spend less time managing conflict and more time accomplishing tasks and satisfying customers, which is, after all, the purpose of business.

> "Companies that do not value their diverse employees are likely to experience greater conflict, as well as prejudice and discrimination."

Employment Equity

Employee equity emerged in Canada in 1986. The Employment Equity Act is designed to ensure that women, Aboriginals, the disabled, and visible minorities

For years, companies have offered wellness plans aimed at improving employee health and reducing health care costs. Many of these plans include smoking cessation programs to help employees kick the habit. Statistics reveal that smokers cost smokers cost businesses 18 percent more than non-smokers. With health care costs rising, companies are concocting ways to tackle the smoking problem. Many employers are instituting additional insurance charges on employees who smoke. Employees participating in smoking cessation clinics can have their insurance costs deferred. Those who successfully kick the habit—roughly 25 percent—never pay. However, a growing number of employers such as Union Pacific, Scotts Miracle-Gro, and the Cleveland Clinic simply refuse to hire smokers.

These choices raise questions concerning employee rights. Critics are accusing these companies of discrimination. They point to the fact that tobacco use is not illegal, and the decision to use it is a private one. However, smoking is not a right protected by law, and legal reactions to this topic are mixed. While a number of courts have backed companies refusing to hire smokers, certain states have passed laws forbidding the practice. Those studying the issue feel the hiring ban is ineffective. They argue that to reduce the number of smokers, one must help them quit. A number of smokers agree, but others are thankful for the incentive to kick a highly addictive habit.[33]

DISCUSSION QUESTIONS

1. Why are employers worried about the health care costs of employees who smoke?

2. What are some initiatives employers are adopting to persuade smokers to kick the habit?

3. Do you think it is ethical for employers to create disincentives for smoking?

receive the same employment opportunities as all Canadians.

Trends in Management of the Workforce

Because of economic uncertainty, austerity has pervaded the workplace and inflated productivity. While companies are squeezing workers to cut costs, they are also drawing clear lines between workers and managers and are reducing privileges and benefits.

The nature of the workplace is changing as well. The increasing use of smart phones and tablet computers are blurring the lines between leisure and work time, with some employers calling employees after hours.[35] Employees themselves are mixing work and personal time by using social media in the office. In fact, theft of time is the number one ethical issue recorded by the Ethics Resource Center.[36] This is requiring companies to come up with new policies that limit how employees can use social media in the workplace. Clearly, technology is changing the dynamics of the workplace in both positive and negative ways.

It is important for human resources managers to be aware of legal issues regarding worker rights. Interestingly, although it might currently be legal for employers to request an applicant's Facebook password, employees who "rant" about their employers on Facebook can receive some form of legal protection. Threats, on the other hand, are not protected.[37] Hence, human resources managers should understand these issues to ensure that an employee is not wrongfully terminated.

Despite the grim outlook of the past few years, hiring trends appear to be on the rise. Companies are finding that as consumer demands rise, their current employees are hitting the limits of productivity, requiring firms to hire more workers.[38] This will require firms to not only know about relevant employee laws, but also to understand how benefits and employee morale can contribute to overall productivity. Many of the most successful firms have discovered ways to balance costs with the well-being of their employees.

TEAM EXERCISE

Form groups and go to monster.com and look up job descriptions for positions in business (account executive in advertising, marketing manager, human resources director, production supervisor, financial analyst, bank teller, etc). What are the key requirements for the position that you have been assigned (education, work experience, language/computer skills, etc.)? Does the position announcement provide a thorough understanding of the job? Was any key information omitted that you would have expected to see? Report your findings to the class.

LO1 Define human resources management, and explain its significance.

Human resources, or personnel, management refers to all the activities involved in determining an organization's human resources needs and acquiring, training, and compensating people to fill those needs. It is concerned with maximizing the satisfaction of employees and improving their efficiency to meet organizational objectives.

LO2 Summarize the processes of recruiting and selecting human resources for a company.

First, the human resources manager must determine the firm's future human resources needs and develop a strategy to meet them. Recruiting is the formation of a pool of qualified applicants from which management will select employees; it takes place both internally and externally. Selection is the process of collecting information about applicants and using that information to decide which ones to hire; it includes the application, interviewing, testing, and reference checking.

LO3 Discuss how workers are trained and their performance appraised.

Training teaches employees how to do their specific job tasks; development is training that augments the skills and knowledge of managers and professionals, as well as current employees. Appraising performance involves identifying an employee's strengths and weaknesses on the job. Performance appraisals may be subjective or objective.

LO4 Identify the types of turnover companies may experience, and explain why turnover is an important issue.

A promotion is an advancement to a higher-level job with increased authority, responsibility, and pay. A transfer is a move to another job within the company at essentially the same level and wage. Separations occur when employees resign, retire, are terminated, or are laid off. Turnovers due to separation are expensive because of the time, money, and effort required to select, train, and manage new employees.

LO5 Specify the various ways a worker may be compensated.

Wages are financial compensation based on the number of hours worked (time wages) or the number of units produced (piece wages). Commissions are a fixed amount or a percentage of a sale paid as compensation. Salaries are compensation calculated on a weekly, monthly, or annual basis, regardless of the number of hours worked or the number of items produced. Bonuses and profit sharing are types of financial incentives. Benefits are non-financial forms of compensation, such as vacation, insurance, and sick leave.

LO6 Discuss some of the issues associated with unionized employees, including collective bargaining and dispute resolution.

Collective bargaining is the negotiation process through which management and unions reach an agreement on a labour contract—the formal, written document that spells out the relationship between the union and management. If labour and management cannot agree on a contract, labour union members may picket, strike, or boycott the firm, while management may lock out striking employees, hire strikebreakers, or form employers' associations. In a deadlock, labour disputes may be resolved by a third party—a conciliator, mediator, or arbitrator.

LO7 Describe the importance of diversity in the workforce.

When companies value and effectively manage their diverse workforces, they experience more productive use of human resources, reduced conflict, better work relationships among workers, increased commitment to and sharing of organizational goals, increased innovation and creativity, and enhanced ability to serve diverse customers.

KEY TERMS

arbitration	collective bargaining
benefits	commission
bonuses	conciliation
boycott	development

diversity
human resources management (HRM)
job analysis
job description
job promotion
job specification
labour contract
labour unions
lockout
mediation
orientation
picketing

profit sharing
recruiting
salary
selection
separations
strikebreakers
strikes
training
transfer
turnover
wage/salary survey
wages

DESTINATION CEO DISCUSSION QUESTIONS

1. According to Jack Welch, what is the most important aspect of being a leader?

2. How does Welch deal with the bottom group of employees in an organization?

3. What is the most exciting thing about being a boss, according to Welch?

SO YOU WANT TO WORK *in Human Resources*

Managing human resources is a challenging and creative facet of a business. It is the department that handles the recruiting, hiring, training, and firing of employees. Because of the diligence and detail required in hiring and the sensitivity required in firing, human resources managers have a broad skill set. Human resources, therefore, is vital to the overall functioning of the business because without the right staff a firm will not be able to effectively carry out its plans. Like in basketball, a team is only as strong as its individual players, and those players must be able to work together and to enhance strengths and downplay weaknesses. In addition, a good human resources manager can anticipate upcoming needs and changes in the business, hiring in line with the dynamics of the market and organization.

Once a good workforce is in place, human resources managers must ensure that employees are properly trained and oriented and that they clearly understand some elements of what the organization expects. Hiring new people is expensive, time-consuming, and turbulent; thus, it is imperative that all employees are carefully selected, trained, and motivated so that they will remain committed and loyal to the company. This is not an easy task, but it is one of the responsibilities of the human resources manager. Even with references, a résumé, background checks, and an interview, it can be hard to tell how a person will fit into the organization; the HR manager needs to be able to anticipate how every individual will "fit in." Human resources jobs include compensation, labour relations, benefits, training, ethics, and compliance managers. All of

the tasks associated with the interface with hiring, developing, and maintaining employee motivation come into play in human resources management. Jobs are diverse and salaries will depend on responsibilities, education, and experience.

One of the major considerations for an HR manager is workforce diversity. A multicultural, multiethnic workforce consisting of men and women will help bring a variety of viewpoints and improve the quality and creativity of organizational decision making. Diversity is an asset and can help a company from having blindspots or too much harmony in thought, background, and perspective, which stifles good team decisions. However, a diverse workforce can present some management challenges. Human resources management is often responsible for managing diversity training and compliance to make sure employees do not violate the ethical culture of the organization or break the law. Different people have different goals, motivations, and ways of thinking about issues that are informed by their culture, religion, and the people closest to them. No one way of thinking is more right or more wrong than others, and they are all valuable. A human resources manager's job can become very complicated, however, because of diversity. To be good at human resources, you should be aware of the value of differences, strive to be culturally sensitive, and ideally should have a strong understanding of and appreciation for different cultures and religions. Human resources managers' ability to manage diversity and those differences will affect their overall career success.

Managing Human Resources

Now is the time to start thinking about the employees you will need to hire to implement your business plan. What kinds of background/skills are you going to look for in potential employees? Are you going to require a certain amount of work experience?

When you are starting a business you are often only able to hire part-time employees because you cannot afford to pay the benefits for a full-time employee. Remember at the end of the last chapter we discussed how important it is to think of ways to motivate your employees when you cannot afford to pay them what you would like.

You need to consider how you are going to recruit your employees. When you are first starting your business,

it is often a good idea to ask people you respect (and not necessarily members of your family) for any recommendations of potential employees they might have. You probably won't be able to afford to advertise in the classifieds, so announcements in sources such as church bulletins or community bulletin boards or on social networking sites should be considered as an excellent way to attract potential candidates with little, if any, investment.

Finally, you need to think about hiring employees from diverse backgrounds—especially if you are considering targeting diverse consumer segments. The more diverse your employees, the greater the chance you will be able to draw in diverse customers.

CASE | Recruiters Embrace Non-traditional Recruitment Methods

Traditionally, recruiters have used résumés to gauge applicants' fit for a job. However, some organizations are realizing that initially judging applicants' suitability for jobs based on résumés—and immediately discarding those that do not fit the criteria—is a flawed system that can overlook talented candidates. George Anders, author of *The Rare Find: Spotting Exceptional Talent Before Everyone Else*, tells many stories of applicants with stellar résumés who have failed at jobs requiring different skill sets or character traits. And hiring the wrong person, no matter how talented he or she might appear, can cost a company greatly.

Part of the problem with using résumés and traditional recruiting methods is their inflexibility. Many recruiters insist that applicants have specific educational achievements or experience to be eligible. Unfortunately, this might eliminate inexperienced candidates who, with training, could become valuable employees. According to Anders, because employees can often learn skills on the job, character is a better predictor of employee success than experience. Some of the best candidates are not the ones with great GPAs or job backgrounds, but those who possess analytical and conceptual skills to think outside of the box.

For this reason, some businesses are changing their recruitment approaches, including using more employee

referrals or accessing social networking sites like LinkedIn to search for potential candidates. Others are taking more unique approaches. Natural-gas company Range Resources Corp. arranges cookouts and other events to identify candidates who have a passion for the field. Facebook sends out coding puzzles for potential programmers to solve; this enables candidates interested in programming to test their abilities despite their previous work background. Several of Facebook's programmers have gotten hired after coming up with innovative solutions to puzzles. As the recruiting industry evolves, alternative means of recruitment might supplant the traditional résumé.[39]

DISCUSSION QUESTIONS

1. Why might a person with a stellar résumé still fail at a job?

2. What are some potential problems of using traditional résumés in the hiring process?

3. Describe some ways that companies are using non-traditional ways of evaluating applicants.

After reading this chapter, you will be able to:

LO1 Define marketing and describe the exchange process.

LO2 Specify the functions of marketing.

LO3 Explain the marketing concept and its implications for developing marketing strategies.

LO4 Examine the development of a marketing strategy, including market segmentation and marketing mix.

LO5 Investigate how marketers conduct marketing research and study buying behaviour.

LO6 Summarize the environmental forces that influence marketing decisions.

DESTINATION CEO

Ronnen Harary and Anton Rabie are living what for many would be a childhood dream. The close friends are co-CEOs of their own toy company—Spin Master Toys. The pair, along with their third partner Ben Varadi, who is the chief creative officer, started the business with a mere $10,000 as university students[1] and have built an international children's entertainment company that is valued at $1.86 billion.[2]

Spin Master has taken the toy world by storm over the last 18 years with such hot brands as Zoomer, including Zoomer Dino and Zoomer Kitty; Paw Patrol toys and games; Star Wars toys, including a talking and interactive Yoda; and Air Hogs, planes that fly on air power. In addition, the company has signed partnership agreements with some of the biggest companies in North America, including Disney and McDonald's, to develop such toys as the SpongeBob SquarePants–inspired Bounce 'Rounds (inflatable, portable play gyms) and a McDonald's McFlurry Maker. The company is on pace to exceed $1 billion in sales in 2016.

One of the first and most common questions people ask after hearing the accomplishments of the two entrepreneurs is, "How did they break into a North American toy market that is characterized by large operators with equally large product development and marketing budgets?" The answer is somewhat surprising. They relied on ingenuity and a combination of public relations (PR) and grassroots marketing.

The company's first product was Earth Buddy, a small head constructed of pantyhose and filled with grass seed that would sprout grass when watered. With no money for a major marketing campaign, the entrepreneurs set out to spread their story using non-traditional marketing and PR, selling the product and their story to anyone who would listen. The product was a huge success and they were on their way. They followed the product with Devil Sticks, a game for children, and they managed to sell 250,000 units in six months without using any traditional promotional campaigns. Instead they hired college and university students to demonstrate the game at playgrounds, local events, and malls, which created a huge demand for the product.

With Devil Sticks becoming a commercial success, the company received its biggest break when it was approached by two inventors with the idea of an air-powered airplane. The concept was simple enough: Children pump the plane full of air and then launch it, watching it soar upward of 15 metres. The result was a flying plane called Air Hogs. Rather than launch a massive retail and marketing campaign, Spin Master decided to focus on selling the product to specialty educational toy stores and through the Sears catalogue, using what the company did well: PR and unconventional marketing methods. It built a suitcase to serve as a press kit and filled it with not only the plane but also a plastic airline cup, a bag of peanuts, and a barf bag, sending it out to numerous writers and editors. The campaign worked wonders; both *Time* and *Popular Science* magazines wrote stories on the airplane, with *Popular Science* calling it one of the best products of the year. Spin Master again hired students to travel from air show to air show demonstrating the product and creating a buzz among airplane enthusiasts. Sales were starting to boom. But the best was yet to come as the PR team at Spin Master managed to get the product on NBC's *Today* and Rosie O'Donnell's talk show, creating major demand. The following year the company was ready to launch Air Hogs in traditional retailers, and the toy became a runaway hit.

A key to Spin Master's ongoing success has been its ability to pay attention to feedback better known as market research and emerging trends to develop winning ideas. The toy market is an extremely fickle one, where toys can be popular one year, and busts the next. As such, Spin Master must be extremely shrewd in developing toys and licensing products. For example, one Spin Master toy, aimed at 2015 holiday shoppers, was created to capture the interest of children and fans who had seen the recently released *Star Wars* movie. The company created an almost life-size interactive Yoda that could speak and teach users to be a Jedi Knight. During product development, Spin Master not only tested the toy with children but also brought in key retailers to provide feedback on important elements of the marketing mix such as price and promotion. By paying attention to customer and retail feedback, Spin Master is more likely to create products that will sell. In fact, the average development time for a Spin Master toy is 18 to 24 months, if not longer, and normally involves the creation of multiple prototypes and the use of play labs and focus groups.[3]

Paying attention to trends has also resulted in the evolution of the company from one being focused on toys to children's entertainment. The founders noticed a significant change in how children were playing in the past decade with a shift from children playing with tradition toys

to spending more time online, playing video and mobile games and watching television. The co-CEOs concluded that children still want toys, but toys that are connected to their favourite television shows and websites have the most appeal. Spin Master responded with television shows, websites, a popular YouTube channel, a mobile games division, and of course, toys built with all of this in mind. For example, Spin Master produces the hit television show *Paw Patrol*, sells Paw Patrol toys and mobile games, and has an interactive website aimed at children.[4] By paying attention to consumer trends and market research Spin Master appears to be well poised to be successful for years to come.

Introduction

Marketing involves planning and executing the development, pricing, promotion, and distribution of ideas, goods, and services to create exchanges that satisfy individual and organizational goals. These activities ensure that the products consumers want to buy are available at a price they are willing to pay and that consumers are provided with information about product features and availability. Organizations of all sizes and objectives engage in these activities.

In this chapter, we focus on the basic principles of marketing. First we define and examine the nature of marketing. Then we look at how marketers develop marketing strategies to satisfy the needs and wants of their customers. Next we discuss buying behaviour and how marketers use research to determine what consumers want to buy and why. Finally we explore the impact of the environment on marketing activities.

Nature of Marketing

LO1 Define marketing and describe the exchange process.

A vital part of any business undertaking, **marketing** is a group of activities designed to expedite transactions by creating, distributing, pricing, and promoting goods, services, and ideas. These activities create value by allowing individuals and organizations to obtain what they need and want. A business cannot achieve its objectives unless it provides something that customers value. McDonald's, for example, introduced an adult "Happy Meal" with a premium salad, water, exercise booklet, and a "stepometer" to satisfy adult consumers' desires

marketing a group of activities designed to expedite transactions by creating, distributing, pricing, and promoting goods, services, and ideas

© Radharc Images/Alamy Stock Photo

Tim Hortons introduced a breakfast sandwich so customers can get a hot breakfast with their morning coffee.

to improve their eating habits and health.[5] EastLink, an Atlantic Canada communications company, recently introduced cell and smartphone service to its Internet, cable, and telephone business to accommodate customers who wanted to purchase all of their communication services with one carrier.[6] Tim Hortons introduced breakfast sandwiches to accommodate people who wanted a hot breakfast with their morning coffee.[7] But just creating an innovative product that meets many users' needs isn't sufficient in today's volatile global marketplace. Products must be conveniently available, competitively priced, and uniquely promoted.

Of all the business concepts covered in this text, marketing may be the hardest for organizations to master. Businesses try to respond to consumer wants and needs and to anticipate changes in the marketplace. Unfortunately, it is difficult to understand and predict what consumers want. Businesses have found that by using market research (studies of consumers' needs and wants), they can improve their ability to predict consumers' ever-changing desires.

It is important to note what marketing is not: It is not manipulating consumers to get them to buy products they don't want. It is not just selling and advertising. It is a systematic approach to satisfying consumers. Marketing focuses on the many activities—planning, pricing, promoting, and distributing products—that foster exchanges.

The Exchange Relationship

At the heart of all business is the **exchange**, the act of giving up one thing (money, credit, labour, goods) in return for something else (goods, services, or ideas). Businesses exchange their goods, services, or ideas for money or credit supplied by customers in a voluntary *exchange relationship*, illustrated in Figure 11.1. The buyer must feel good about the purchase, or the exchange will not continue. If your local dry cleaner cleans your nice suit properly, on time, and without damage, you will probably feel good about using its services. But if your suit is damaged or isn't ready on time, you will probably use another dry cleaner next time.

> **exchange** the act of giving up one thing (money, credit, labour, goods) in return for something else (goods, services, or ideas)

For an exchange to occur, certain conditions are required. As indicated by the arrows in Figure 11.1, buyers and sellers must be able to communicate about the "something of value" available to each. An exchange does not necessarily take place just because buyers and sellers have something of value to exchange. Each participant must be willing to give up his or her respective "something of value" to receive the "something" held by the other. You are willing to exchange your "something of value"—your money or credit—for the latest technological gadgets, soft drinks, hockey tickets, or new shoes because you consider those products more valuable or more important than holding on to your cash or credit potential.

Figure 11.1 The Exchange Process: Giving Up One Thing in Return for Another

When you think of marketing products, you may think of tangible things—cars, stereo systems, or tablets, for example. What most consumers want, however, is a way to get a job done, solve a problem, or gain some enjoyment. You may purchase a Booster Juice drink—not because you want a fruit smoothie, but because you are thirsty and want some nourishment. Second Cup provides coffee drinks at a premium price, providing convenience, quality, and an inviting environment. Therefore, the tangible product itself may not be as important as the image or the benefits associated with the product. This intangible "something of value" may be capability gained from using a product or the image evoked by it, such as 7 for All Mankind jeans, which can sell for nearly $300.

> "A business cannot achieve its objectives unless it provides something that customers value."

Functions of Marketing

LO2 Specify the functions of marketing.

Marketing focuses on a complex set of activities that must be performed to accomplish objectives and generate exchanges. These activities include buying, selling, transporting, storing, grading, financing, marketing research, and risk taking.

Buying. Everyone who shops for products (consumers, stores, businesses, governments) decides whether and what to buy. A marketer must understand buyers' needs and desires to determine what products to make available.

Selling. The exchange process is expedited through selling. Marketers usually view selling as a persuasive activity that is accomplished through promotion (advertising, personal selling, sales promotion, publicity, and packaging). For example, when Jim Balsillie—former co-CEO of Research In Motion (now renamed BlackBerry after its proprietary smartphone)—first introduced the product to the marketplace, he travelled across corporate circles personally selling businesspeople on the virtues of the product.

Transporting. Transporting is the process of moving products from the seller to the buyer. Marketers focus on transportation costs and services.

Storing. Like transporting, storing is part of the physical distribution of products and includes warehousing goods. Warehouses hold some products for lengthy periods in order to create time utility. Consumers want frozen orange juice year-round, for example, although the production season for oranges is only a few months out of the year. This means that sellers must arrange cold storage for frozen orange juice concentrate all year.

Grading. Grading refers to standardizing products and displaying and labelling them so that consumers clearly understand their nature and quality. Many products, such as meat, steel, and fruit, are graded according to a set of standards that often are established by the federal or provincial government.

Financing. For many products, especially large items such as automobiles, refrigerators, and new homes, the marketer arranges credit to expedite the purchase.

Marketing Research. Through research, marketers ascertain the need for new goods and services. By gathering information regularly, marketers can detect new trends and changes in consumer tastes.

Risk Taking. Risk is the chance of loss associated with marketing decisions. Developing a new product creates a chance of loss if consumers do not like it enough to buy it. Spending money to hire a sales force or to conduct marketing research also involves risk. The implication of risk is that most marketing decisions result in either success or failure.

The Marketing Concept

LO3 Explain the marketing concept and its implications for developing marketing strategies.

A basic philosophy that guides all marketing activities is the **marketing concept**, the idea that an organization should try to satisfy customers' needs through coordinated activities that also allow it to achieve its own goals. According to the marketing concept, a business must find out what consumers

marketing concept the idea that an organization should try to satisfy customers' needs through coordinated activities that also allow it to achieve its own goals

need and want and then develop the good, service, or idea that fulfills those needs or wants. The business must then get the product to the customer. In addition, the business must continually alter, adapt, and develop products to keep pace with changing consumer needs and wants. This is sometimes referred to as relationship marketing or customer relationship management—where the company aims to build a mutually beneficial relationship with a customer that lasts a lifetime. Rather than focus on one sale, a company aims to determine a customer's ever-changing needs and meet those needs over the consumer's lifetime. Art Wilson, a sales consultant, states that firms of all sizes can compete effectively as long as they focus on building relations with customers. Walter Hachborn, president emeritus and co-founder of Home Hardware, which operates over 1,000 stores across Canada, states that "… retailing is all about customer relationships … recognize customers, give customers what they want, and stand behind your products."[8] Simons, the Quebec-based retailer that has recently expanded to Alberta and is eyeing locations in Toronto, is hoping its commitment to customer relations and dedication to knowing its customers' needs and wants will allow the company to successfully expand across Canada.[9] McDonald's, as already mentioned, faces increasing pressure to provide more healthful fast-food choices; in addition to introducing its Go Active! Happy Meal, the company has eliminated supersized fries and soft drinks from its menu to address these concerns.[10] McDonald's was also the first fast-food chain to put nutritional information on its food packaging.[11] Over the years, the fast-food giant has experimented with healthier fare, but consumers often rejected these items. To remain competitive, the company must be prepared to add to or adapt its menu to satisfy customers' desires for new fads or changes in eating habits. Each business must determine how best to implement the marketing concept, given its own goals and resources.

> "According to the marketing concept, a business must find out what consumers need and want and then develop the good, service, or idea that fulfills those needs or wants."

Although customer satisfaction is the goal of the marketing concept, a business must also achieve its own objectives, such as boosting productivity, reducing costs, or achieving a percentage of a specific market. If it does not, it will not survive. For example, Bell Canada could sell smartphones for five dollars and give customers a lifetime guarantee, which would be great for customers but not so great for Bell. Obviously, the company must strike a balance between achieving organizational objectives and satisfying customer needs and wants. Doug Kerr, founder and CEO of Vancouver-based Kerr Construction, embraced the marketing concept when he faced a slowing

Dave Luba & Kalen Emsley

Business: tentree

Founded: 2012

Success: Dave Luba and Kalen Emsley have created a branded apparel company that plants 10 trees for every item sold. To date, they have planted over 8 million trees in places such as Madagascar, Nepal, and Ethiopia.[12]

When Dave Luba went on a student exchange to Hawaii, he never imagined it would lead to the start of an environmentally friendly company. Like most Hawaiian students, he was studying hard and, in his free time, enjoying the majestic island and, of course, sharing pictures with his friends on Facebook. Luba's friend Kalen was following his friend's photos and was so taken with the beauty of the island that he decided he had to experience Hawaii first-hand. As the pair experienced all the islands had to offer, including hiking, surfing, and swimming, they started to think about companies that give back to society to not only make a profit but also to make the world a better place. One company that stood out was TOMS, a shoe company that donates one pair of shoes for every pair it sells. Luba and Emsley, inspired by TOMS, came up with the idea of tentree based on a similar model. The pair would develop lifestyle apparel, and for each item of clothing sold, they would plan 10 trees, hence the name tentree. The idea took off, and soon after returning to Canada, they managed to convince 30 retailers to carry its tentree branded clothing. The big break for the company occurred when the entrepreneurs appeared

on CBC's television show, *Dragons' Den*. At that time, dragons Arlene Dickinson and Bruce Croxon teamed up to invest $100,000 for a 20 percent stake in the business. Dickinson says, "They are social entrepreneurs to the 10th degree. They are the real deal. They are doing that has serious impact and I think that will resonate with people."[13] From the appearance, Tentree used the publicity to quickly roll out to other retailers and develop online sales. Now the company, whose motto is "Protect the World You Play In," is hoping to further expand globally while protecting the environment at the same time.[14]

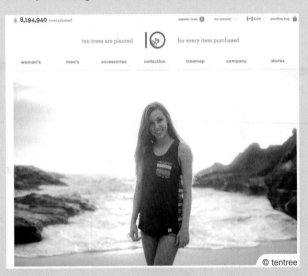

Dave Luba and Kalen Emsley, two Canadian social entrepreneurs, started Tentree, a company dedicated to protecting the environment.

construction market in that city. Rather than give up, Kerr surveyed his customers to better understand their wants and needs and increased his marketing efforts. During this slow period, 75 percent of his business came from previous clients. Kerr increased his focus on customer service to earn even more repeat business, which allowed Kerr Construction to post annual growth rates of 20 to 25 percent while many competitors went out of business.[15]

To implement the marketing concept, a firm must have good information about what consumers want, adopt a consumer orientation, and coordinate its efforts throughout the entire organization; otherwise, it may be awash with goods, services, and ideas that consumers do not want or need. Robb Chase, CEO of London, Ontario–based Herbal Magic, says, "It's always critical to know what customers' needs are. . . . You need to have a monitoring, information-gathering, and communication system to understand what those needs are and if they change you need to be able to adapt your value proposition."[16] It may be getting easier to learn what customers' needs are according to *Profit*

© Prathan Chorruangsak/Shutterstock.com

By determining what customers want and coordinating their efforts, Apple was able to create iPhones that have changed the way people use their phones. To date, Apple has sold over 600 million iPhones.

magazine, which is aimed at Canadian entrepreneurs and managers. The publication recently noted that customers now expect to be heard, and companies must let them know that they are listening. Minh Ngo, CEO of Memory Express Computer Products Inc., a Calgary-based retailer, allows customers to post comments on products directly on his website, much like Canadian Tire and Sears. Ngo, like other marketing managers, knows that companies can gain valuable information from customer comments, including their thoughts on product quality, price, and after-sale service. Companies are also actively monitoring third-party customer review sites, such as Yelp, TripAdvisor, Angie's List, ConsumerSearch, and Epinions, as well as social media sites, such as Facebook, Twitter, and Pinterest, to determine if customers are satisfied and to identify future consumer wants and needs. In fact, businesses are starting to consider it essential to monitor social media sites to understand their customers and identify opportunities, with 42 percent of companies considering social media monitoring one of their top three priorities.[17] As a result, a number of new businesses have emerged. Meltwater Group has created products such as Meltwater Buzz, a digital private investigator that scans thousands of sites to determine what people are saying about specific issues or companies. Businesses can use the information from Buzz to see if consumers are satisfied or not, spot developing trends, and address changes in public opinions. Canadian-based HootSuite, much like Buzz, offers companies a vast array of reports and information it gleans from monitoring social media sites.

Successfully implementing the marketing concept requires that a business view customer value as the ultimate measure of work performance and improving value, and the rate at which this is done as the measure of success.[18] Everyone in the organization who interacts with customers—*all* customer-contact employees—must know what customers want. They are selling ideas, benefits, philosophies, and experiences—not just goods and services. For example, Calgary-based Print Audit, which develops software to track and reduce printing costs, separates itself from the competition by focusing on customer relationships. CEO and founder John MacInnes requires that employees do everything possible to satisfy customers and if the customer remains unsatisfied they get a refund, no questions asked. MacInnes's firm also surveys clients 15 days after they purchased his products and 15 days later to determine if they are happy. In addition, each employee has access to flower and gift accounts to send thank-you gifts to customers or to mark key events in their lives.[19]

Someone once said that if you build a better mousetrap, the world will beat a path to your door. Suppose you do build a better mousetrap. What will happen? Actually, consumers are not likely to beat a path to your door because the market is too competitive. A coordinated effort by everyone involved with the mousetrap is needed to sell the product. Your company must reach out to customers and tell them about your mousetrap, especially how your mousetrap works better than those offered by competitors. If you do not make the benefits of your product widely known, in most cases, it will not be successful. Consider Apple's retail stores, which market computers and electronics in a way unlike any other computer manufacturer or retail store. The upscale stores, located in high-rent shopping districts, show off Apple's products in sparse, stylish settings to encourage consumers to try new things—like making a movie on a computer. The stores also offer special events like concerts and classes to give customers ideas on how to maximize their use of Apple's products.[20] You must also find—or create—stores willing to sell your mousetrap to consumers. You must implement the marketing concept by making a product with satisfying benefits and making it available and visible.

Orville Wright said that an airplane is "a group of separate parts flying in close formation." This is what most companies are trying to accomplish: They are striving for a team effort to deliver the right good or service to customers. A breakdown at any point in the organization—whether it be in production, purchasing, sales, distribution, or advertising—can result in lost sales, lost revenue, dissatisfied customers. Dissatisfied customers lead directly to lost sales as reported by Toronto-based research firm Ipsos-Reid, which has found that 84 percent of Canadians will stop making purchases from a company after just one negative experience.[21]

Evolution of the Marketing Concept

The marketing concept may seem like the obvious approach to running a business and building relationships with customers. However, businesspeople are not always focused on customers when they create and operate businesses. Many companies fail to grasp the importance of customer relationships and fail to implement customer strategies. One survey indicated that only 46 percent of executives believe that their firm is committed to customers, but 67 percent of executives frequently meet with customers.[22] Our society and economic system have changed over time, and marketing has become more important as markets have become more competitive.

The Production Orientation.   During the second half of the nineteenth century, the Industrial Revolution was well under way in Canada. New technologies, such as electricity, railroads, internal combustion engines, and mass-production techniques, made it possible to manufacture goods with ever increasing efficiency. Together with new management ideas and ways of using labour, products poured into the marketplace, where demand for manufactured goods was strong.

The Sales Orientation.   By the early part of the twentieth century, supply caught up with and then exceeded demand, and businesspeople began to realize they would have to "sell" products to buyers. During the first half of the twentieth century, businesspeople viewed sales as the major means of increasing profits, and this period came to have a sales orientation. They believed that the most important marketing activities were personal selling and advertising. Today some people still inaccurately equate marketing with a sales orientation.

The Marketing Orientation. By the 1950s, some businesspeople began to recognize that even efficient production and extensive promotion did not guarantee sales. These businesses, and many others since, found that they must first determine what customers want and then produce it rather than making the products first and then trying to persuade customers that they need them. Managers at General Electric first suggested that the marketing concept was a companywide philosophy of doing business. As more organizations realized the importance of satisfying customers' needs, Canadian and U.S. businesses entered the marketing era, one of marketing orientation.

marketing orientation an approach requiring organizations to gather information about customer needs, share that information throughout the firm, and use that information to help build long-term relationships with customers

A **marketing orientation** requires organizations to gather information about customer needs, share that information throughout the entire firm, and use that information to help build long-term relationships with customers. Top executives, marketing managers, non-marketing managers (those in production, finance, human resources, and so on), and customers all become mutually dependent and cooperate in developing and carrying out a marketing orientation. Non-marketing managers must communicate with marketing managers to share information important to understanding the customer. Consider Tim Hortons; the coffee chain started out by selling coffee and doughnuts. Based on market research and feedback from customers, managers expanded the menu to include cookies, bagels, and sandwiches. Recently the company started to offer breakfast sandwiches as the one-time coffee shop has transformed itself into a restaurant that specializes in coffee, breakfast, and lunch.

Trying to assess what customers want is difficult to begin with, and is further complicated by the rate at which trends, fashions, and tastes can change. Businesses today want to satisfy customers and build meaningful long-term relationships with them. It is more efficient to retain existing customers and even increase the amount of business each customer provides the organization than to find new customers. As discussed above, Vancouver-based Kerr Construction at one time was securing over 75 percent of its sales from repeat customers. Most companies' success depends on increasing the amount of repeat business, and many

companies are turning to technologies associated with customer-relationship management to help build relationships and boost business with existing customers.

> **"Businesses today want to** satisfy customers and build meaningful long-term relationships **with them."**

Communication remains a major element of any strategy to develop and manage long-term customer relationships. By providing multiple points of interaction with customers—that is, websites, telephone, fax, e-mail, and personal contact—companies can personalize customer relationships.[23] Like many online retailers, Chapters.ca collects, stores, and analyzes purchase data to understand each customer's interests. This information helps the retailer improve its ability to satisfy individual customers and thereby increase sales of books, music, movies, and other products to each customer. The ability to identify individual customers allows marketers to shift their focus from targeting groups of similar customers to increasing their share of an individual customer's purchases. Regardless of the medium through which communication occurs, customers should ultimately be the drivers of marketing strategy because they understand what they want. Customer relationship management systems should ensure that marketers listen to customers to respond to their needs and concerns and build long-term relationships.

Social Media Era

While the marketing orientation era is not over, some would argue that it is slowly being replaced or complemented by the social media era. Social media is redefining marketing, as it allows for the building of online communities, which encourage participation and communication among members. Consumers can communicate in real time with companies, share information with their associates and friends, and search for unbiased product opinions online. The results have been significant as Facebook, Twitter, LinkedIn, YouTube, Pinterest, blogs, wikis, and podcasts have become both communication and business tools. Some entrepreneurs, like Ryan Holmes, founder of HootSuite, think that social media is creating a new type of economy, and businesses will have to adapt as social media is vastly changing how business is conducted.[24] Others are less convinced that social media represents a new era in marketing and view social media as a tool, one that complements marketing orientation concepts. After all, social media allows companies to communicate with customers and learn about their wants and needs, and offers another means to establish a long-term relationship with clients—these are some of the major characteristics associated with a marketing orientation.

Developing a Marketing Strategy

LO4 Examine the development of a marketing strategy, including market segmentation and marketing mix.

marketing strategy a plan of action for developing, pricing, distributing, and promoting products that meet the needs of specific customers

market a group of people who have a need, purchasing power, and the desire and authority to spend money on goods, services, and ideas

✳ **target market** a specific group of consumers on whose needs and wants a company focuses its marketing efforts

To implement the marketing concept and customer relationship management, a business needs to develop and maintain a **marketing strategy**, a plan of action for developing, pricing, distributing, and promoting products that meet the needs of specific customers. This definition has two major components: selecting a target market and developing an appropriate marketing mix to satisfy that target market.

notes that the key to running a successful retail store is "a maniacal focus on your target customers." Under Sherman's leadership, Bonnie Brooks was hired as president and CEO of The Bay, and spent several months reviewing data from over 7,000 shopper interviews before determining that the retailer would focus on fashion customers who want high-end labels, pragmatists who want good-quality apparel, and value-shoppers who want the best price. The Bay's target market selection then influenced store design, allocation of advertising dollars, and product selection.[27] The approach at The Bay is no different than the one taken by another Canadian retailer, Shoppers Drug Mart, which had experienced similar business woes over a decade ago. Shoppers spent considerable resources on segmenting and redefining its target markets. The move has paid off and Shoppers is a Canadian retail success story.

Some firms use a **total-market approach**, in which they try to appeal to everyone and assume that all buyers have similar needs and wants. Sellers of salt, sugar, and

total-market approach an approach whereby a firm tries to appeal to everyone and assumes that all buyers have similar needs

Selecting a Target Market

A **market** is a group of people who have a need, purchasing power, and the desire and authority to spend money on goods, services, and ideas. A **target market** is a more specific group of consumers on whose needs and wants a company focuses its marketing efforts. Nike, for example, introduced a line of golf clubs targeted at recreational golfers.[25] Marketing managers may define a target market as a relatively small number of people, or they may define it as the total market (Figure 11.2). Rolls-Royce, for example, targets its products at a small, very exclusive, high-income market—people who want the ultimate in prestige in an automobile. General Motors, on the other hand, manufactures vehicles ranging from the Impala to Cadillac to GMC trucks in an attempt to appeal to varied tastes, needs, and desires. Likewise, Reitmans Canada Ltd., which has grown to include over 950 stores nationwide, operates under seven divisions: Reitmans, Smart Set, Penningtons, Thyme Maternity, Addition Elle, Hyba, and RW & Co., and uses different store concepts to appeal to different target markets.[26] Effective managers realize that selecting a target market can ultimately determine the success of a company. The Hudson's Bay Company is in the midst of a business turnaround that began in 2009 and has been attributed to the work of recently retired retail expert, Jeff Sherman. Sherman

Figure II.2 Target Market Strategies

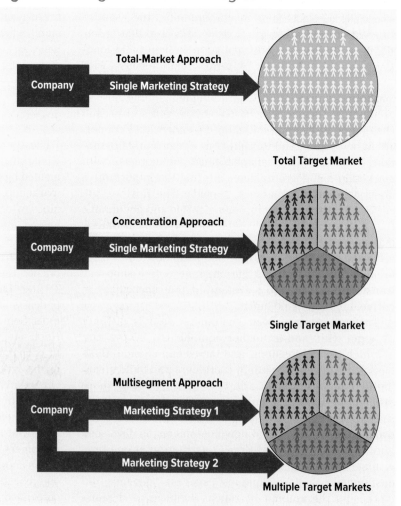

Total-Market Approach

Company — Single Marketing Strategy → Total Target Market

Concentration Approach

Company — Single Marketing Strategy → Single Target Market

Multisegment Approach

Company — Marketing Strategy 1
Marketing Strategy 2 → Multiple Target Markets

market segmentation a strategy whereby a firm divides the total market into groups of people who have relatively similar product needs

market segment a collection of individuals, groups, or organizations who share one or more characteristics and thus have relatively similar product needs and desires

concentration approach a market segmentation approach whereby a company develops one marketing strategy for a single market segment

many agricultural products use a total-market approach because everyone is a potential consumer of these products. Most firms, though, use **market segmentation** and divide the total market into groups of people who have relatively similar product needs. A **market segment** is a collection of individuals, groups, or organizations who share one or more characteristics and thus have relatively similar product needs and desires. Prior to selecting its three target markets, The Bay had broken Canada into 12 distinct consumer groups. The Bay then looked internally at its own resources. Women are the largest market segment, with 51 percent of the Canadian population. At the household level, segmentation can unlock each woman's social and cultural characteristics and stage in life to determine preferences and needs.[28] One market segment that many marketers are focusing on is the growing immigrant population. As immigration rates rise, more and more companies are altering their products or promotion to appeal to this important group. For example, Oakville, Ontario–based FlightNetwork.com hires recent immigrants to speak to customers in their native language, such as Swahili, Russian, and German. The company notes that many of its top call centre agents have the poorest English skills.[29] Another example is Staples, which has gained a footing in the immigrant market with a program aimed at helping immigrant entrepreneurs succeed. The seminar program teaches immigrants about accounting, taxes, and running a small business.[30] Companies use market segmentation to focus their efforts and resources on specific target markets so that they can develop a productive marketing strategy. Two common approaches to segmenting markets are the concentration approach and the multi-segment approach.

> **"One** market segment **that many marketers are** focusing on **is the** growing immigrant population.**"**

Market Segmentation Approaches. In the **concentration approach**, a company develops one marketing strategy for a single market segment. The concentration approach allows a firm to specialize, focusing all its efforts on the one market segment. Porsche, for example, focuses all its marketing efforts toward high-income individuals who want to own high-performance vehicles. A firm can generate a large sales volume by penetrating a single market segment deeply. The concentration approach may be especially effective

© HTT Pléthore

A Quebec car company manufactures the Pléthore, which sells for upwards of $798,000 and is an example of a niche product.

when a firm can identify and develop products for a particular segment ignored by other companies in the industry.

In the **multi-segment approach**, the marketer aims its marketing efforts at two or more segments, developing a marketing strategy for each. Many firms use a multi-segment approach that includes different advertising messages for different segments. RBC targets many different segments including teens, university students and recent grads, families, baby boomers, and retirees. The bank has products such as mortgages, which appeal to families; RRSPs, which appeal to people saving for their retirement; and student accounts. RBC also targets its promotional efforts to appeal to various customers by communicating through social media, offering services such as Internet banking, and promoting specific products through various commercials. BlackBerry used to focus primarily on the corporate segment when advertising and selling its smartphones. Now, with competition in the marketplace, particularly from Apple with its iPhone, BlackBerry has increased

multi-segment approach a market segmentation approach whereby the marketer aims its efforts at two or more segments, developing a marketing strategy for each

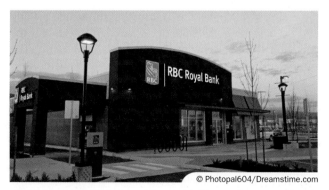

© Photopal604/Dreamstime.com

RBC targets many different segments with different products and methods of product promotion, as well as different means of communicating with customers.

A few years ago, Leonard Asper was the CEO of CanWest Global Communications, a media giant that controlled such assets as television stations Global Television, Showcase, Slice, and HGTV Canada, as well as other valuable media assets, such as the *National Post*. CanWest was relying on an aggressive acquisition strategy, and when the financial crisis hit, advertising revenue dried up, and CanWest's balance sheet, already strapped with a heavy debt load, became unsustainable and the company filed for creditor protection. As a result, Asper stepped down as CEO.

The financial crisis though was only part of the story; traditional television viewers have spent the better part of the past decade changing the way they watch programming. No longer are viewers wedded to one show or network; viewers are looking for highly specialized content, and if they cannot find it on television, they can find it online. This point was not lost on Asper, who says during the final days of CanWest that the only stations making money were HGTV and the Food Network. Asper says, "You need targeted destinations for communities that are passionate about the subject."[32]

After leaving CanWest, Asper was unsure what direction he would go professionally, but eventually decided to return to what he knew best—media—and bought a controlling interest in Anthem Media Group Inc., which at the time owned the Fight Network.[33] Asper was now intent on creating a new media empire, one with a lot more focus on a partic-

© Monkey Business Images/Shutterstock

ular audience. At the time, advertisers were telling Asper, and whoever would listen, that reaching men between the ages of 18 and 65—both on television and online—was increasingly difficult as there were very few stations or shows that targeted this important group. Asper's approach for Anthem would be to fill this niche and create and acquire media aimed primarily at male audiences. With this goal in mind, Asper soon added the Pursuit Channel, a hunting and outdoor network; Edge Sports, a channel aimed at extreme sports fans; and the American combat sports channel, My Combat Channel.[34]

Asper was just getting started building his new media empire when in 2014 he took what might be his

the number of segments it is targeting to include teenagers and university students. Recent advertisements for the company feature teenagers, rock bands, and youth. The company's new message is that BlackBerry is for everyone.

Niche marketing is a narrow market segment that focuses efforts on one small, well-defined segment that has a unique, specific set of needs. To cater to ice cream "addicts" and people who crave new, exotic flavours, several companies are selling ice cream on the Internet. This niche represents only a fraction of the $20.3 billion per year ice cream business, but online sales at some of the biggest makers increased 30 percent in just one year. Some of the firms focusing on this market are IceCreamSource.com, Nuts About Ice Cream, and Graeter's.[31] Another

example is HTT Technologies Inc., a car manufacturing company based in Saint-Eustache, Quebec that builds the Pléthore—a super high-end car aimed at the luxury market. The car currently retails for a special promotional price of $450,000, but HTT plans on raising the price to $798,000, typical for cars in this marketplace.[37]

For a firm to successfully use a concentration or multi-segment approach to market segmentation, several requirements must be met:

1. Consumers' needs for the product must be heterogeneous.

2. The segments must be identifiable and divisible.

3. The total market must be divided in a way that allows estimated sales potential, cost, and profits of the segments to be compared.

biggest risk and started the FNTSY Sports Network. The cable and online outlet is aimed specifically at men who participate in the growing $4 billion fantasy sports industry. The television channel won't actually show any sports but it will provide information and analysis on players, games, and leagues. Fantasy sports is a growing market, and active fantasy sports players are normally in a number of leagues, enter daily contests, and spend considerable time playing fantasy sports. In fact, some participants in fantasy sports are doing it professionally, taking advantage of the many daily contests and leagues they can enter to earn a living. Asper says, "The one thing that convinced me to do this is watching my staff and never being sure if they are working when they have their computers on or if they checking fantasy sites, because they are all doing it."[35] Yet some business analysts have expressed concerned about Asper's gamble on fantasy sports. They maintain that there are not enough dedicated fantasy sports participants to sustain a 24-hour, seven day a week channel, and doubt that Asper will be able to generate enough advertising revenue to make money. Asper counters that channels that focus on a specific target market with focused programming are exactly what consumers and advertisers want. "People thought 'How can there be an entire channel devoted to golf?' but now the Golf Channel is in 82 million homes. It's an obvious trend and we're trying to capture it. . . . That's where sports channels are going. The whole world is going to a channel for every sport."[36] Asper's ambitious plans of creating specialized programming for men doesn't appear to be slowing down. He recently announced he would be starting a Canadian version of MATV, a motor sports channel.

DISCUSSION QUESTIONS:

1. What are the pros and cons of creating an entire media group aimed specifically at men? Will Asper's company succeed? Why or why not?

2. Asper appears to be creating a media group with a very traditional, if not stereotypical, view of male audiences with a focus on combat sports, hunting, fishing, race cars, and fantasy sports. Do you think enough males are still interested in these pursuits to support independent 24-hour channels? Why or why not?

3. Women are also playing fantasy sports and watching and participating in extreme sports, auto racing, combat sports, and hunting and fishing. Based on this information, should Asper consider changing his message to advertisers that his media company is targeted primarily at men? Why or why not? What would be the advantages and disadvantages of changing his message to advertisers?

4. Assume that you are a corporate marketing expert, and Asper has asked you to change his message to advertisers to make it more inclusive. Develop a new message, which Asper can use, to convince businesses to advertise on his speciality channels.

5. Some critics point out that Asper's focus on males is almost borderline unethical as it treats both men and women in a very stereotypical fashion. Do you think Asper's approach is ethical or unethical? Why?

6. Many media companies, especially those with a television and radio focus, have failed in recent years due the high costs of creating content and the increased time people are spending online. Do you think Asper's company will be successful? Why or why not?

4. At least one segment must have enough profit potential to justify developing and maintaining a special marketing strategy.

5. The firm must be able to reach the chosen market segment with a particular market strategy.

Bases for Segmenting Markets. Companies segment markets on the basis of several variables:

1. *Demographic*—age, sex, race, ethnicity, income, education, occupation, family size, religion, social class. These characteristics are often closely related to customers' product needs and purchasing behaviour, and they can be readily measured. Some demographers, such as Canada's David Foot, author of *Boom Bust & Echo*, argue that simple demographics can

explain upwards of two-thirds of consumer decisions. Foot states that if you know the number of people in each age category, you can make reliable decisions about what products will be popular now and in the future.[38] For example, baby boomers, or people born between 1946 and 1966, make up approximately 33 percent of Canada's population and are responsible for the recent rise in spending on cosmetic surgery and nostalgia products such as the Dodge Dart. The next-largest group of people in Canada is known as the Echo generation, or Millennials, and they are the children of baby boomers. This group born between 1980 and 2004 is responsible for a renewed interest in child care and kindergarten as they are starting to have their own children.[39]

Yu Yiping Wallace and Wang Jian

Business: Tibet 5100 Water Resources

Founded: 2006, in Wanchai, Hong Kong

Success: While many Chinese bottled water companies have trouble competing against foreign brands, Tibet 5100 Water Resources achieved profitability in two years.

Bottled water is taking off in China. For a long time, foreign bottled water brands such as Evian dominated the market, but domestic bottled water manufacturers are ready to challenge them. One such Chinese company is Tibet 5100 Water Resources. The water that Tibet 5100 sells is high-quality mineral water from a glacial water source in Tibet. Due to the prestige associated with its water, Tibet 5100 prices its water at a 500 percent premium over other domestic water brands. The price may be high, but the increase in consumers' disposable income and the demand for quality water (most water sources in China are polluted) enabled Tibet 5100 to become profitable in two years. Due

to its success, Tibet 5100 went public and plans to use the money to try and gain market share from competitors. Its high-end, "pristine" water as well as its relationships with large customers such as China Railway Express and Air China may make Tibet 5100's lofty goals possible.[40]

© epa european pressphoto agency b.v./Alamy Stock Photo

2. *Geographic*—climate, terrain, natural resources, population density, subcultural values. These influence consumers' needs and product usage. Climate, for example, influences consumers' purchases of clothing, automobiles, heating and air conditioning equipment, and leisure activity equipment.

3. *Psychographic*—personality characteristics, motives, lifestyles. For example, Canadian smoothie operator Booster Juice presents its products in bright glasses with illustrations of healthy fruit to appeal to customers who want not only to eat healthy but to be seen eating healthy.

4. *Behaviouristic*—some characteristic of the consumer's behaviour toward the product. These characteristics commonly involve some aspect of product use. The three major issues in this category are what benefits consumers are seeking, consumers' rate of use, and how they use and purchase products.

Figure II.3 The Marketing Mix: Product, Price, Promotion, and Distribution

Marketing Environment

marketing mix the four marketing activities—product, price, promotion, and distribution—that the firm can control to achieve specific goals within a dynamic marketing environment

Developing a Marketing Mix

The second step in developing a marketing strategy is to create and maintain a satisfying marketing mix. The **marketing mix** refers to four marketing activities—product, price, distribution, and promotion—that the firm can control to achieve specific goals within a dynamic marketing environment (Figure 11.3). The buyer or the target market is the central focus of all marketing activities.

Product. A product—whether a good, a service, an idea, or some combination—is a complex mix of tangible and intangible attributes that provide satisfaction and benefits. A *good* is a physical entity you can touch. A Porsche Cayenne, Lululemon pants, Rona lumber, and a kitten available for adoption at an animal shelter are examples of goods. A *service* is the application of human and mechanical efforts to people or objects to provide intangible benefits to customers. Air travel on WestJet or Air Canada, haircuts at SuperCuts, banking at CIBC, and/or insurance from Manulife are examples of services.

A product has emotional and psychological as well as physical characteristics and includes everything that the buyer receives from an exchange. This definition includes supporting services such as installation, guarantees, product information, and promises of repair. Products usually have both favourable and unfavourable attributes; therefore, almost every purchase or exchange involves trade-offs as consumers try to maximize their benefits and satisfaction and minimize unfavourable attributes. For example, a consumer trying to choose between a BlackBerry and an iPhone may have to trade off the superior e-mail service offered by a BlackBerry in order to purchase the iPhone, which offers more apps and a better Web browser.

Products are among a firm's most visible contacts with consumers. If they do not meet consumer needs and expectations, sales will be difficult, and product life spans will be brief. The product is an important variable—often the central focus—of the marketing mix; the other variables (price, promotion, and distribution) must be coordinated with product decisions.

Price. Almost anything can be assessed by a **price**, a value placed on an object exchanged between a buyer and a seller. Although the seller usually establishes the price, it may be negotiated between buyer and seller. The buyer usually exchanges purchasing power—income, credit, wealth—for the satisfaction or utility associated with a product. Because financial price is the measure of value commonly used in an exchange, it quantifies value and is the basis of most market exchanges.

> **price** a value placed on an object exchanged between a buyer and a seller

Marketers view price as much more than a means of assessing value, however. It is a key element of the marketing mix because it relates directly to the generation of revenue and profits. Prices can also be changed quickly to stimulate demand or respond to competitors'

Consider the Following: RBC's Youth Marketing Strategy

As stated above, marketing strategy consists of selecting a target market and designing your marketing mix or your products, price, place, and promotion to appeal to your targeted market and create value compared to your competitors. RBC, Canada's largest bank, obviously has many different target markets, which results in the bank managing different marketing mixes. One key target market for the bank is university students and recent graduates. The group is particularly important as they are just starting to form relationships with companies and the bank realizes that if it captures a young customer's business now it may be able to retain the customer for a lifetime. To achieve this result, RBC tries to differentiate itself from the other banks by creating a superior "student focused" marketing mix.

While all the banks in Canada are offering student banking packages, student lines of credit, credit cards for students, and so forth, RBC is attempting to differentiate itself first and foremost by using promotions that appeal to youth. The bank spent upwards of $120 million to sponsor the 2010 Olympics, including the "Own the Podium" campaign, which consisted of directing money to athletes who had the best chance to capture an Olympic medal, and the "Torch Relay," a 45,000-kilometre trip across the country that stopped in cities and towns and featured youth-focused entertainment. RBC has followed up that promotion with a commitment to the "Road to Excellence" program, which replaced "Own the Podium." Royal Bank has now committed to being the Premier National Partner of the Canadian Olympic Committee through 2016 and is proving additional support for the Paralympic teams.[41]

In addition, RBC is considered the social media leader among the big banks in Canada. RBC has invested heavily in social media including Twitter, Facebook, blogs, avatars, and online competitions and communities to attract young clients. For example, a recent online contest focused on recent university graduates who were asked to provide the best advice they could to new university students.[42]

DISCUSSION QUESTIONS

1. What markets is RBC targeting with social media?
2. Are there other things RBC could be doing with its marketing mix to appeal to the youth market?
3. Do you think RBC's investment in the Olympics and the Torch Relay was a good idea? Will it improve the bank's market share?
4. Will being a leader in social media translate into more young clients for the bank?

Consider the Following: Canada: A Tale of Two Segments

Marketers know that if they are going to be successful in Canada, their goods should appeal to one of two market segments—baby boomers, or their children (better known as the Millennial generation). Baby boomers were born between 1946 and 1966, represent approximately one-third of Canada's population, and, as a group, are quite wealthy. Boomers entered the workforce when there were many jobs. They have often been described as materialistic in nature and consider their time to be very valuable. Businesses that appeal to this group include Nurse Next Door, a Vancouver-based home care company for seniors that boomers hire to help with their aging parents, and Medicard Finance Inc., an Ontario-based company that offers loans and lines of credit to boomers who are interested in cosmetic surgery.

From a marketer's perspective, the best innovation or creation by the baby boomers may be the Millennial generation. This group is the second-largest segment in the population and represents people born from 1980 to 2004. The well-educated Echo generation is interested in the environment and technology and expect to be successful, much like their parents. This generation is starting to buy their first homes, get married, and have children. The result—many products and services that fell out of favour as the baby boomers aged will become popular again.[43]

DISCUSSION QUESTIONS

1. What other products or industries should do well as baby boomers continue to age?

2. What do you think are the best ways to promote products or services to baby boomers?

3. What other products or industries should do well as the Millennial generation starts to have families?

4. What do you think are the best ways to promote products or services to the Millennial generation?

5. Do some research and determine the size of the baby boomer and Millennial segments.

6. Do you think companies would be wise to consider marketing their products to other groups? Why or why not? What products or industries are aimed at other groups?

actions. For example, WestJet will usually drop its prices quickly in response to similar price drops by Air Canada, and Tim Hortons introduced an English muffin version of its breakfast sandwich, priced lower than McDonald's Egg McMuffin, to generate sales. Recently, the big Canadian banks have started using pricing as a way to generate more sales. BMO has twice offered five-year mortgage rates at 2.99 percent and other banks have dropped their mortgage rates as a result. Former Finance Minister, the late Jim Flaherty, actually urged the banks to be cautious about such low interest rates as he was fearful consumers may borrow beyond their means and wouldn't be able to repay their mortgage if and when interest rates rise.[44]

Place/Distribution. **Place/distribution** is making products available to customers in the location and the quantities desired. The Internet and online sales have greatly impacted the place/distribution category as more and more shoppers are looking to make purchases and receive services online. For example, a number of banks, including CIBC, have recently introduced a smartphone app for online banking service. The app was introduced to appeal to the vast number of youth who want to bank over their smartphone. Almost every product and service can now be purchased on the

place/distribution making products available to customers in the quantities desired

Internet, including airline tickets from Air Canada and WestJet and sporting goods from SportChek.[45] Via Vegan Ltd., a Montreal-based designer of women's and men's handbags made out of recycled plastic bottles, has used exporting to reach consumers throughout the world as the environmentally friendly nature of the product has resulted in global demand. The company sells handbags in such high-end department stores as Saks Fifth Avenue in the United States and Selfridges & Co. in the United Kingdom.[46] In fact, global distribution is becoming increasingly important to Canadian companies. The top 71 exporters identified by *Profit* magazine as the top 100 growth companies sold $17 billion abroad last year.[47]

> "Global distribution is becoming increasingly important to Canadian companies. The top 71 exporters identified by *Profit* magazine as the top 100 growth companies sold $17 billion abroad last year."

In addition to making products available in the locations and quantities customers want, place also refers to creating a location that consumers find desirable. For example, Dollarama, a Quebec-based chain, became a billion-dollar retailer by offering consumers not just

594-plus locations to shop at, but by creating a location that customers wanted to visit. Dollarama's stores are organized, clean, and attractive, unlike many mom-and-pop dollar stores, which are often characterized by their unkempt aisles. Some retailers are now opting to build smaller stores as a way to reduce overhead, focus on items that consumers want, and create a more intimate shopping experience. Rona has recently announced the creation of 11 smaller satellite stores that, according to the company, will have a neighbourhood feel to them. Best Buy is testing 5,000-square-foot stores, one-fifth the size of the average Best Buy, offering 1,000 of its best-selling items. The store will also have computer kiosks where customers can access the company's other 59,000 products for delivery to the store or their home.[48] Fast-food giant McDonald's has expanded distribution by opening restaurants in Walmart stores, and Starbucks is selling its specialty coffee in Targets throughout the U.S. This practice permits the food and coffee giants to share costs with their partners and to reach more customers when and where hunger strikes.[49]

Intermediaries, usually wholesalers and retailers, perform many of the activities required to move products efficiently from producers to consumers or industrial buyers. These activities involve transporting, warehousing, materials handling, and inventory control, as well as packaging and communication. For example, Dr. Abdullah Kirumira, founder of Nova Scotia–based biomedical company BioMedical Diagnostic Inc., which developed the world's first rapid HIV test and "lab in a box" diagnostic tools, notes that marketing and distribution were never his strengths. BioMedical relies on a number of distributors to transport and sell his products throughout the world, which allows him to focus on the development of new drugs and medical applications.[50]

Critics who suggest that eliminating wholesalers and other middlemen would result in lower prices for consumers do not recognize that eliminating intermediaries would not do away with the need for their services. Other institutions would have to perform those services, and consumers would still have to pay for them. For example, Mississauga-based Solutions 2 GO Inc. has achieved approximately $750 million in annual sales by relieving video game manufacturers of the task of getting their games onto the shelves of thousands of stores all on the same day. The company serves as a master distributor for many major game manufacturers and some of its top sellers include New Super Mario Brothers, Call of Duty: Modern Warfare 2, and Final Fantasy XIII. In addition, in the absence of wholesalers, all producers would have to deal directly with retailers or customers, keeping voluminous records and hiring people to deal with customers.[51]

promotion a persuasive form of communication that attempts to expedite a marketing exchange by influencing individuals, groups, and organizations to accept goods, services, and ideas

Promotion. **Promotion** is a persuasive form of communication that attempts to expedite a marketing exchange by influencing individuals, groups, and organizations to accept goods, services, and ideas. Promotion includes advertising, personal selling, social media, publicity, and sales promotion, all of which we will look at more closely in Chapter 12. One aspect of promotion that has been growing rapidly in recent years is the use of non-traditional marketing to achieve corporate goals. Lululemon, for example, once offered customers free clothing if they would wait in line naked at a store's grand opening. The result was national media coverage of the store's opening and extended coverage in the media about the corporation's edgy promotions.[52] Another example is Tim Hortons' successful Roll Up the Rim to Win contest. The contest has been running for over 20 years and still results in increased sales and publicity for the company.

The aim of promotion is to communicate directly or indirectly with individuals, groups, and organizations to facilitate exchanges. When marketers use advertising and other forms of promotion, they must effectively manage their promotional resources and understand product and target-market characteristics to ensure that these promotional activities contribute to the firm's objectives. For example, Tim Hortons is using television advertising to appeal to Canadians across the country who want a fresh cup of coffee in a friendly atmosphere. Tim Hortons' advertisements highlight the fact that every 20 minutes there is a new pot of coffee being brewed. Also, as previously noted, both CIBC with its smartphone app and RBC with its reliance on social media are attempting to reach the under-30 market segment with their products and services.

> **"The aim of promotion is to communicate directly or indirectly with individuals, groups, and organizations to facilitate exchanges."**

Marketing Research and Information Systems

LO5 Investigate how marketers conduct marketing research and study buying behaviour.

Before marketers can develop a marketing mix, they must collect in-depth, up-to-date information about customer needs. **Marketing research** is a systematic, objective process of getting information about potential customers to guide marketing decisions. For example, when Simple Audiobook, an Oakville, Ontario company, was contemplating whether

marketing research a systematic, objective process of getting information about potential customers to guide marketing decisions

to enter the United States market, the company relied on market research to determine if the strategy made sense. CEO Sean Neville says that firms can't guess if there is a market—they need to do research and determine if a market exists, the size of that market, and if customers will purchase the company's product.[53] Janet and Greta Podleski, authors of two best-selling Canadian cookbooks, *Looneyspoons* and *Crazy Plates*, along with partner David Chilton, discovered the dangers of not doing any market research. They decided to turn some of their favourite recipes into frozen dinners, but were initially quite unsuccessful. Chilton said that almost all of the errors came because they didn't properly research the market. They were making a product for families of four or five priced between $13 and $14—what they found out later is that most people want frozen dinners to feed one or two people and they want to pay much less for them.[54] Since the group had produced a product no one wanted, they were left to repurchase the product from store shelves and re-enter the marketplace only after conducting the necessary market research.

Market research might include data about the age, income, ethnicity, gender, and educational level of people in the target market; their preferences for product features; their attitudes toward competitors' products; and the frequency with which they use the product. For example, Tim Hortons' market research revealed customers wanted larger cups of coffee. As a direct result, the stores are now selling extra-large 24-ounce cups.[55] Toyota's marketing research about Generation Y drivers (born between 1977 and 1994) found that they practically live in their cars, and many even keep a change of clothes handy in their vehicles. As a result of this research, Toyota designed its Scion as a "home on wheels" with a 15-volt outlet for plugging in a computer, reclining front seats for napping, and a powerful audio system for listening to MP3 music files, all for a $12,500 price tag.[56] Les Mandelbaum, founder of Umbra, a Toronto-based company that is known as one of the world's top designers of products, states that Umbra is very disciplined when it comes to entering the marketplace with new products and spends considerable time analyzing market research including what customers want, what products are already in stores, and what competitors are offering.[57]

Marketing research is vital because the marketing concept cannot be implemented without information about customers. As evident in this chapter's discussion about the revival at The Bay, market research is essential to making decisions for companies. As discussed above, The Bay's senior executives spent several months reviewing data from thousands of interviews prior to making decisions about target markets and store layout. Canadian Tire uses the massive amount of customer information it gathers when customers use their Canadian Tire card to assist in making decisions on a variety of issues including prices, new product ideas, store layout, and promotional campaigns.

The market research process consists of the following steps:

1. *Define the problem or objective.* Objectives could include whether potential customers will buy a product or what price they are willing to pay for a service.

2. *Collect data.* Researchers will normally start their search for information from pre-existing sources known as secondary sources or secondary data. **Secondary data** are compiled inside or outside the organization for some purpose other than changing the current situation. Marketers typically use information compiled by Statistics Canada, business development centres, and other government agencies; databases created by marketing research firms; as well as sales and other internal reports to gain information about customers. To stay on top of consumer demands and emerging trends Somerset Entertainment Ltd., a Toronto-based music company, hires marketers to read the latest entertainment publications and report back to management. Jason Abbott, founder of Winnipeg-based tour company The Toban Experience, used secondary sources to determine if a market existed for a tour company in his region and if there were any competitors. Abbott relied on secondary data to determine that 6,000 visitors travel through Winnipeg in the summer and spring and no other tour companies were operating in his market.[58]

secondary data information that is compiled inside or outside an organization for some purpose other than changing the current situation

primary data marketing information that is observed, recorded, or collected directly from respondents

If there is not enough secondary information available, then marketers will often turn to primary research, or the collection of new data that is specific to the problem at hand. **Primary data** is new data or new information. Primary data is usually collected either by observation, where companies watch what consumers do or how consumers react to certain situations; surveys, where people complete a questionnaire; personal interviews; or focus groups, where groups of consumers come together to discuss a product, service, or business. Examples of observation include the use of "mystery shoppers" to visit their retail establishments and report on whether the stores were adhering to the company's standards of service. For example, Tell Us About Us Inc. (TUAU), which was profiled in Chapter 5, is a Winnipeg-based full-service customer feedback company. TUAU offers companies numerous methods, including social media monitoring, surveys, and secret shoppers, to determine if standards are being met and if consumers are happy and/or would like additional products or services. The province of Nova Scotia used focus groups as part of its effort to develop a formal marketing campaign. Among other things, focus groups suggested the province promote its friendly atmosphere and natural beauty. As noted above, The Bay has used interviews as part of its marketing research efforts and Shoppers Drug Mart has used surveys.

3. *Analyze the research data.* Data results must then be analyzed and interpreted. Researchers may use a number of software and/or online diagnostic tools to generate different alternatives to a problem.

4. *Choose the best options.* The final step in the research process is determining which alternatives exist and deciding what recommendations to make. For example, when Eryn Green and Tamar Wagman started Sweetpea Baby Food, a Toronto-based fresh-frozen baby food company, they used market research to ensure there was a market for their product. They started with a objective to determine if a market did exist for gourmet baby food. The pair collected data from secondary sources, including Statistics Canada, to determine that while birth rates are declining, the number of mothers in their target group (aged 30–35) is rising. The company founders than used primary research and interviewed 50 new moms to see if there was an actual demand for their product. Green and Wagman then analyzed the data and concluded a large market did exist for their business.[59]

A marketing information system (MIS) is a framework for accessing information about customers from sources both inside and outside the organization. Inside the organization, there is a continuous flow of information about prices, sales, and expenses. Outside the organization, data are readily available through private or public reports and census statistics, as well as from many other sources. Computer networking technology provides a framework for companies to connect to useful databases and customers with instantaneous information about product acceptance, sales performance, and buying behaviour. This information is important to planning and marketing strategy development.

The marketing of products and collecting of data about buying behaviour—information on what people actually buy and how they buy it—represents the marketing research of the future. New information technologies are changing the way businesses learn about their customers and market their products. Interactive multimedia research, or *virtual testing*, combines sight, sound, and animation to facilitate the testing of concepts as well as packaging and design features for consumer products. Computerization offers a greater degree of flexibility, shortens the staff time involved in data gathering, and cuts marketing research costs. The evolving development of telecommunications and computer technologies is allowing marketing researchers quick and easy access to a growing number of online services and a vast database of potential respondents. Online research is set to grow from $1.3 billion to $4 billion in the next few

© Linqong/Dreamstime.com

Market research can lead to a whole new market for your product. BMW targets a lower-income consumer than its typical high-end one by selling "certified" used BMWs at a lower cost, but still with the BMW brand recognition and expectation.

years, according to a new report by Cambiar and GMI.[60] Many companies have created private online communities and research panels that bring consumer feedback into the companies 24 hours a day.

Look-Look.com is an online, real-time service that provides accurate and reliable information, research, and news about trend-setting youths aged 14 to 30. With this age group spending an estimated $140 billion a year, many companies are willing to shell out an annual subscription fee of about $20,000 for access to these valuable data. Look-Look pays more than 35,000 hand-picked, pre-screened young people from all over the world to e-mail the company information about their styles, trends, opinions, and ideas.[61]

Other companies are finding that quicker, less-expensive online market research is helping them develop products faster and with greater assurance that the products will be successful. The CEO of Stonyfield Farm (maker of higher-priced yogurt) is convinced that Web feedback saved his company from a multimillion-dollar mistake. The online responses from 105 women caused the company to scrap the name originally planned for its new yogurt from YoFemme (which the respondents did not like) to YoSelf (to which the respondents voted yes).[62]

In addition to online market research, and as discussed above, companies are tracking website use, online feedback via blogs, communities, and Facebook and Twitter posts to see how customers are responding to products or messages. This type of activity has resulted in the development of new companies such as Fredericton, New Brunswick–based Radian6, which allows companies to listen to social media by tracking and preparing comprehensive reports about what is being said about the company online, measuring what people are saying about their business and competitors, and analyzing the data to assist companies in making marketing decisions.

Buying Behaviour

Carrying out the marketing concept is impossible unless marketers know what, where, when, and how consumers buy; marketing research into the factors that influence buying behaviour helps marketers develop effective marketing strategies. **Buying behaviour** refers to the decision processes and actions of people who purchase and use products. It includes the behaviour of both consumers purchasing products for personal or household use and organizations buying products for business use. Marketers analyze buying behaviour because a firm's marketing strategy should be guided by an understanding of buyers. People view pets as part of their families, and they want their pets to have the best of everything. Iams, which markets the Iams and Eukanuba pet food brands, recognized this trend and shifted its focus. Today, it markets high-quality pet food, fancy pet treats, sauces, and other items that allow pet lovers to spoil their pets.[63]

Both psychological and social variables are important to an understanding of buying behaviour.

© The Advertising Archives/Alamy Stock Photo

Polo appeals to people who want to express social roles or identify with a reference group.

Psychological Variables of Buying Behaviour

Psychological factors include the following:

- **Perception** is the process by which a person selects, organizes, and interprets information received from the senses, as when hearing an advertisement on the radio or touching a product to better understand it.
- *Motivation*, as we said in Chapter 9, is an inner drive that directs a person's behaviour toward goals. A customer's behaviour is influenced by a set of motives rather than by a single motive. A buyer of a home computer, for example, may be motivated by ease of use, ability to communicate with the office, and price.
- **Learning** brings about changes in a person's behaviour based on information and experience. If a person's actions result in a reward, he or she is likely to behave the same way in similar situations. If a person's actions bring about a negative result, however—such as feeling ill after eating at a certain restaurant—he or she will probably not repeat that action.

- **Attitude** is knowledge and positive or negative feelings about something. For example, a person who feels strongly about protecting the environment may refuse to buy products that harm the earth and its inhabitants.

- **Personality** refers to the organization of an individual's distinguishing character traits, attitudes, or habits. Although market research on the relationship between personality and buying behaviour has been inconclusive, some marketers believe that the type of car or clothing a person buys reflects his or her personality.

Social Variables of Buying Behaviour

Social factors include **social roles**, which are a set of expectations for individuals based on some position they occupy. A person may have many roles: mother, wife, student, executive. Each of these roles can influence buying behaviour. Consider a woman choosing an automobile. Her father advises her to buy a safe, gasoline-efficient car, such as a Volvo. Her teenaged daughter wants her to buy a cool car, such as a Honda Civic; her young son wants her to buy a Ford Explorer to take on camping trips. Some of her colleagues at work say she should buy a hybrid Prius to help the environment. Thus, in choosing which car to buy, the woman's buying behaviour may

attitude knowledge and positive or negative feelings about something

personality the organization of an individual's distinguishing character traits, attitudes, or habits

social roles a set of expectations for individuals based on some position they occupy

buying behaviour the decision processes and actions of people who purchase and use products

perception the process by which a person selects, organizes, and interprets information received from his or her senses

learning changes in a person's behaviour based on information and experience

Successful company marketers take the time to study and understand what they call consumer buying behaviour—in other words, the behaviour of customers buying a company's products for personal or household uses. Marketers pay attention to this behaviour because how customers respond to a company's marketing strategies affects that company's success. They also aim to please customers and undertake research to discover what a company can do to satisfy its customers and keep them coming back. When marketers have a solid grasp on buying behaviour, they can better predict how customers will react to marketing campaigns. A new strategy being used by large companies such as RBC, TD Canada Trust, Johnson & Johnson, Pfizer, and Procter & Gamble is the use of online software to create large-scale focus groups. Companies that sell this software aim to help marketers listen to what their customers want rather than designing marketing campaigns based on generic strategies.

For years, companies have brought people together for traditional, face-to-face focus groups. In other words, a small group of people was brought together in a room to discuss products while people from the company listened (often from another room) to what they had to say. The advantage to the new, large-scale focus groups is that companies can reach a much larger audience—therefore, getting a much wider range of ideas and opinions. Perhaps this may create a more accurate picture of what the general public at large is looking for from a company. For example, for years Lego had been producing the same Lego sets based on feedback from traditional focus groups. The company created an online focus group involving 10,000 people—all Lego customers were invited via e-mail to participate in an online contest regarding new products—and the result was essentially brainstorming in cyberspace and customers suggesting departures from Lego's traditional toys.

Here is how this software works: In the case of Lego, customers who had received e-mail invitations were part of an online "popularity contest" regarding new-product suggestions. Customers were shown lists of six proposed products at a time. They were asked to rank the toys they liked and, if they chose, offer their own ideas. The customer ideas were then filtered into the mix and sent to other customers to rank against Lego's proposed toys. The software filters the selections shown to customers—those receiving the most votes early on most often appear later, and over time, the most popular ideas rise to the forefront.

Although there are many challenges regarding this new software and its uses (for example, some suggest online research may be skewed toward Internet users), online focus groups are much less expensive than the traditional version. At least for now, this new research method may be a good way to understand more about buying behaviour.[64]

DISCUSSION QUESTIONS

1. How can technology be used to determine consumer beliefs and opinions?

2. Compare face-to-face focus groups with online discussions for understanding consumer behaviour.

3. What are the possible biases from using online research to assess consumer beliefs, opinions, and behaviour?

---

reference groups groups with whom buyers identify and whose values or attitudes they adopt

social classes a ranking of people into higher or lower positions of respect

be affected by the opinions and experiences of her family and friends and by her roles as mother, daughter, and employee.

Other social factors include reference groups, social classes, and culture.

- **Reference groups** include families, professional groups, civic organizations, and other groups with whom buyers identify and whose values or attitudes they adopt. A person may use a reference group as a point of comparison or a source of information. A person new to a community may ask other group members to recommend a family doctor, for example.

- **Social classes** are determined by ranking people into higher or lower positions of respect. Criteria vary from one society to another. People within a particular social class may develop common patterns of behaviour. People in the upper-middle class, for example, might buy a Lexus or a Cadillac as a symbol of their social class.

- **Culture** is the integrated, accepted pattern of human behaviour, including thought, speech, beliefs, actions, and artifacts. Culture determines what people wear and eat and where they live and travel. For example, many Atlantic Canadians restrict travel to that particular region of the country because they are less likely to take longer vacations than other groups of Canadians; people in Quebec are more prone to eat baked beans for breakfast; and people in Alberta are more prone to purchase trucks.

culture the integrated, accepted pattern of human behaviour, including thought, speech, beliefs, actions, and artifacts

If you want recommendations on a business, Yelp may be just what you need. Founded by Jeremy Stoppelman and Russel Simmons, Yelp.com is a website on which consumers can rate and review businesses. Approximately 142 million users visit the site monthly, with roughly 79.5 million doing so from a mobile device. Consumers love this site and other online review sites as they provide people with objective third-party opinions. During her stint as marketing director for Yelp Canada, Crystal Henrickson stated that businesses have to be concerned about online review sites as almost 80 percent of regular Internet users consult the Web before making a purchase decision, and the vast majority of all searches on Yelp come from mobile apps. Mobile users are normally in the process of making a purchase decision and not just conducting research, so their impact on a business could be immediate.

Yet while consumers may love Yelp, the site has a love-hate relationship with many business owners. On the one hand, businesses with loyal customers who post positive reviews on Yelp appreciate the viral nature of the site. A positive review can influence a range of potential customers. For example, Harvard Business School professor Michael Luca recently conducted a study and determined that a one-star increase in Yelp can positively impact revenue. On the other hand, Yelp makes it easy for consumers to post negative reviews. All a business owner can do is respond either publicly on the site or privately via e-mail to a reviewer. A common complaint from business owners is that responding to complaints can take a significant amount of time. Henrickson's advice is to take the time to respond to consumer comments, as a business would almost always respond to a customer complaining in person. She says a customer complaining online is no different than a complaint in person.

Yelp earns money by selling ad space on the site to represented businesses, but according to co-founder Stoppelman, this does not allow business owners any greater freedom to control review content. What it does give them is the ability to eliminate advertisements of other companies on their pages, the possibility for their ads to appear on other pages, and the opportunity to post photo and video content.

Despite Stoppleman's assurances, businesses have accused Yelp of manipulating reviews either to gain more advertising customers or to punish companies that refuse to advertise through Yelp's paid system. To combat complaints, Yelp has made filtered reviews visible, although they are clearly marked as filtered. Stoppelman continues to support the company's algorithm and claims that Yelp is striving for greater transparency. Whether or not Yelp's actions serve to pacify its detractors, companies are increasingly realizing that the power structure between business and consumer is changing—often in the consumer's favour.[65]

DISCUSSION QUESTIONS

1. What is the benefit of Yelp to consumers?

2. What challenges face businesses that are evaluated on Yelp?

3. Do you think businesses should take the time to respond to customer feedback on Yelp? What are the pros and cons of this strategy?

4. How does Yelp contribute to improving competition and the quality of products?

Understanding Buying Behaviour

Although marketers try to understand buying behaviour, it is extremely difficult to explain exactly why a buyer purchases a particular product. The tools and techniques for analyzing consumers are not exact. Marketers may not be able to determine accurately what is highly satisfying to buyers, but they know that trying to understand consumer wants and needs is the best way to satisfy them. In an attempt to better understand consumer behaviour, Procter & Gamble sent video crews into about 80 households all around the world. The company, maker of Tide, Crest, Pampers, and many other consumer products, hoped to gain insights into the lifestyles and habits of young couples, families with children, and empty nesters. Participants were recorded over a four-day period

and were paid about $200 to $250 a day. The behaviours caught on video may lead the company to develop new products or change existing ones to better meet consumers' needs and give the company a competitive advantage over its rivals.[66]

The Marketing Environment

LO6 Summarize the environmental forces that influence marketing decisions.

A number of external forces directly or indirectly influence the development of marketing strategies; the following political, legal, regulatory, social, competitive, economic, and technological forces comprise the marketing environment:

- *Political, legal, and regulatory forces*—laws and regulators' interpretation of laws; law enforcement and regulatory activities; regulatory bodies, legislators and legislation, and political actions of interest groups. Specific laws, for example, require that advertisements be truthful and that all health claims be documented. Changing laws can greatly impact a business. For example, in Nova Scotia, the government announced that smoking would be permitted only in bars and restaurants that have a special smoking room. Many businesses spent thousands of dollars building these rooms only to have the government ban smoking altogether a short time later.

- *Social forces*—the public's opinions and attitudes toward issues such as living standards, ethics, the environment, lifestyles, and quality of life. For example, Ontario-based Crystal Head Vodka attempted to sell its vodka in a clear, skull-shaped bottle. The response from the Liquor Control Board of Ontario was to ban the booze as it deemed that the message was not appropriate, reflecting society's changing opinion about liquor consumption. Other examples include social concerns that have led marketers to design and market safer toys for children.

- *Competitive and economic forces*—competitive relationships, unemployment, purchasing power, and general economic conditions (prosperity, recession, depression, recovery, product shortages, and inflation).

- *Technological forces*—computers and other technological advances that improve distribution, promotion, and new-product development.

Marketing environment forces can change quickly and radically, which is one reason that marketing requires creativity and a customer focus. For example, *Rolling Stone* magazine did a business analysis before entering the Chinese market. Unfortunately, after a successful debut, the Chinese government had concerns about its licence to publish in China. The success of *Rolling Stone* concerned other lifestyle and music magazines, and they informed the authorities that the licence was not appropriate.[67]

Because such environmental forces are interconnected, changes in one may cause changes in others. Consider that because of evidence linking children's consumption of soft drinks and fast foods to health issues such as obesity, diabetes, and osteoporosis, marketers of such products have experienced negative publicity and calls for legislation regulating the

GOING GREEN | Monsanto Faces Threats from New Superweeds

Superweeds are bad news for Monsanto, one of the world's leading agricultural products companies. Monsanto's Roundup is the best-selling herbicide in the nation. However, because of the wide-scale use of Roundup, superweeds—weeds that are resistant to herbicides and are therefore harder to control—are becoming a major challenge for farmers. When first introduced, Roundup was heralded for its remarkable ability to ward off weeds. Even when Roundup resistance first became a problem less than a decade ago, Monsanto officials claimed that resistance was rare and "manageable." Today, despite continued reassurance from Monsanto, this is no longer the case. Superweeds are increasing, with 11 species now resistant to the herbicide.

Competitors such as Dow Chemical and Syngenta are jumping at the chance to grab market share from Monsanto. They have begun promoting older herbicides and herbicide mixtures to combat superweeds. However, scientists caution that even mixing herbicides can eventually lead to resistance. The problem is not the herbicides themselves, but the way they are used. For many years, farmers and scientists have known that crop rotation prevents pests from

developing resistance to certain chemicals. However, because Roundup was so effective, many farmers would rotate one Roundup Ready (seeds that are genetically engineered to resist the herbicide) crop with another. Therefore, in order to prevent future resistance, many farmers and companies will have to change their tactics. To help in this endeavour, Monsanto has the responsibility to promote and design its products in a way that will better consider their long-term impact on the environment.[68]

DISCUSSION QUESTIONS

1. Why are superweeds becoming a problem for Monsanto?

2. How are competitors capitalizing on Roundup-resistant superweeds?

3. What are some of the reasons weeds have become resistant to Roundup herbicide?

Figure 11.4 The Marketing Mix and the Marketing Environment

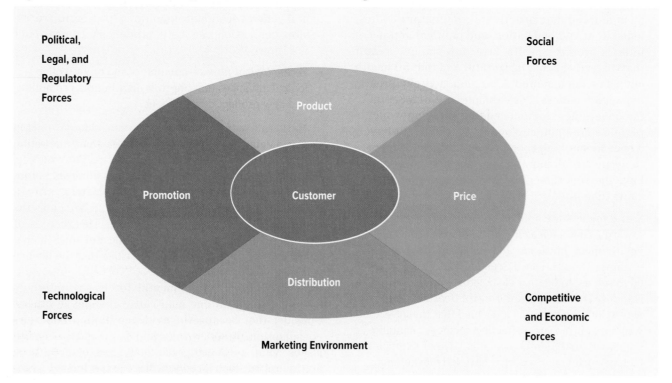

sale of soft drinks in public schools. When Morgan Spurlock saw an evening news story about two teenagers who unsuccessfully sued McDonald's for their poor health, he decided to make the movie *Super Size Me.* As director, he went on a supersized diet of fast food and gained 25 pounds, suffered from depression, and experienced heart pain.[69] Some companies have responded to these concerns by reformulating products to make them healthier. Kellogg Company is reformulating many of its popular child-targeted products (which account for 50 percent of its products) to make them more healthy. The goal is to cut sugar and fat to help fight childhood obesity. If brands such as Pop-Tarts, Froot Loops, Apple Jacks, or other products cannot be made more healthy while maintaining their

same taste, the products will not be marketed to children under 12.[70] The fast-food industry's frantic race to cook up the first "better-for-you" french fry appears to have been won by Wendy's. The number-three fast-food chain announced that it will dump cooking oil for a blend of non-hydrogenated corn and soy oil containing nearly no artery-clogging trans fats.[71]

Although the forces in the marketing environment are sometimes called *uncontrollables,* they are not totally so. A marketing manager can influence some environmental variables. For example, businesses can lobby legislators to dissuade them from passing unfavourable legislation. Figure 11.4 shows the variables in the marketing environment that affect the marketing mix and the buyer.

TEAM EXERCISE

Form groups and assign the responsibility of finding examples of companies that excel in one dimension of the marketing mix (price, product, promotion, and distribution). Provide several company and product examples, and defend why this would be an exemplary case. Present your research to the class.

LEARNING OBJECTIVES SUMMARY

LO1 Define marketing and describe the exchange process.

Marketing is a group of activities designed to expedite transactions by creating, distributing, pricing, and promoting goods, services, and ideas. Marketing facilitates the exchange, the act of giving up one thing in return for something else. The central focus of marketing is to satisfy needs.

LO2 Specify the functions of marketing.

Marketing includes many varied and interrelated activities: buying, selling, transporting, storing, grading, financing, marketing research, and risk taking.

LO3 Explain the marketing concept and its implications for developing marketing strategies.

The marketing concept is the idea that an organization should try to satisfy customers' needs through coordinated activities that also allow it to achieve its goals. If a company does not implement the marketing concept, by providing products that consumers need and want while achieving its own objectives, it will not survive.

LO4 Examine the development of a marketing strategy, including market segmentation and marketing mix.

A marketing strategy is a plan of action for creating a marketing mix (product, price, promotion, distribution) for a specific target market (a specific group of consumers on whose needs and wants a company focuses its marketing efforts). Some firms use a total-market approach, designating everyone as the target market. Most firms divide the total market into segments of people who have relatively similar product needs. A company using a concentration approach develops one marketing strategy for a single market segment, whereas a multi-segment approach aims marketing efforts at two or more segments, developing a different marketing strategy for each.

LO5 Investigate how marketers conduct marketing research and study buying behaviour.

Carrying out the marketing concept is impossible unless marketers know what, where, when, and how consumers buy. Marketing research into the factors that influence buying behaviour helps marketers develop effective marketing strategies. Marketing research is a systematic, objective process of getting information about potential customers to guide marketing decisions. Buying behaviour is the decision processes and actions of people who purchase and use products.

LO6 Summarize the environmental forces that influence marketing decisions.

There are several forces that influence marketing activities: political, legal, regulatory, social, competitive, economic, and technological.

KEY TERMS

attitude
buying behaviour
concentration approach
culture
exchange
learning
market
market segment
market segmentation
marketing
marketing concept
marketing mix
marketing orientation
marketing research

marketing strategy
multi-segment approach
perception
personality
place/distribution
price
primary data
promotion
reference groups
secondary data
social classes
social roles
target market
total-market approach

1. Why is Spin Master Toys successful?

2. What are some of the advantages of non-traditional marketing? What are some of the potential pitfalls?

3. Would non-traditional marketing work in all industries? Why or why not?

4. What are the advantages and disadvantages of switching from a toy company to a children's entertainment company?

SO YOU WANT A JOB *in Marketing*

You probably did not think as a child how great it would be to grow up and become a marketer. That's because often marketing is associated with sales jobs, but opportunities in marketing, public relations, product management, advertising, e-marketing, and customer relationship management and beyond represent almost one-third of all jobs in today's business world. To enter any job in the marketing field, you must balance an awareness of customer needs with business knowledge while mixing in creativity and the ability to obtain useful information to make smart business decisions.

Marketing starts with understanding the customer. Marketing research is a vital aspect in marketing decision making and presents many job opportunities. Market researchers survey customers to determine their habits, preferences, and aspirations. Activities include concept testing, product testing, package testing, test-market research, and new-product research. Salaries vary, depending on the nature and level of the position as well as the type, size, and location of the firm. An entry-level market analyst may make between $24,000 and $50,000, while a market research director may earn from $75,000 to $200,000 or more.

One of the most dynamic areas in marketing is direct marketing, where a seller solicits a response from a consumer using direct communication methods such as telephone, online communications, direct mail, or catalogues. Jobs in direct marketing include buyers, catalogue managers, research/mail-list managers, or order fulfillment managers. Most positions in direct marketing involve planning and market analysis. Some require the use of databases to sort and analyze customer information and sales history.

Use of the Internet for retail sales is growing, and the Internet continues to be very useful for business-to-business sales. E-marketing offers many career opportunities including customer relationship management (CRM). CRM helps companies market to customers through relationships, maintaining customer loyalty. Information technology plays a huge role in such marketing jobs, as you need to combine technical skills and marketing knowledge to effectively communicate with customers. Job titles include e-marketing manager, customer relationship manager, and e-services manager. A CRM customer service manager may receive a salary in the $40,000 to $45,000 range, and experienced individuals in charge of online product offerings may earn up to $100,000.

A job in any of these marketing fields will require a strong sense of the current trends in business and marketing. Customer service is vital to many aspects of marketing so the ability to work with customers and to communicate their needs and wants is important. Marketing is everywhere from the corner grocery or local non-profit organization to the largest multinational corporation, making it a shrewd choice for an ambitious and creative person. We will provide additional job opportunities in marketing in Chapter 12.

BUILD YOUR BUSINESS PLAN

Customer-Driven Marketing

The first step is to develop a marketing strategy for your product or service. Who will be the target market you will specifically try to reach? What group(s) of people has the need, ability, and willingness to purchase this product? How will you segment customers within your target market? Segmenting by demographic and geographic variables are often the easiest segmentation strategies to attempt. Remember that you would like to have the customers in your segment be as homogeneous and accessible as possible. You might target several segments if you feel your product or service has broad appeal.

The second step in your marketing strategy is to develop the marketing mix for your product or service. Whether you are dealing with an established product or you are creating your own product or service, you need to think about what differential advantage your product offers. What makes it unique? How should it be priced? Should the product be priced below, above, or at the market? How will you distribute the product? And last but certainly not least, you need to think about the promotional strategy for your product.

What about the uncontrollable variables you need to be aware of? Is your product something that can constantly be technologically advanced? Is your product a luxury that will not be considered by consumers when the economy is in a downturn?

For years, when the 4Ps were discussed, "place," which represents the place where items were sold, rarely changed. Food items were sold in grocery stores, computers in small computer boutiques, music and musical instruments in music stores, clothing in department stores, and so forth. This all changed with the emergence of supercentre department stores, discounters, and ultimately the Internet, as suddenly products had no traditional "place" of sale. Originally, items such as books and computers were products deemed perfect for department stores, discount locations, and eventually online sales as they were mostly straightforward purchases involving little emotion. Naysayers, however, noted that specialty goods such as wedding gowns and engagement rings had too much emotional involvement ever to be sold in non-traditional locations. Most women have been planning their wedding day their whole lives, with a lot of thought going into big-ticket items such as the wedding dress and engagement ring. Even into adulthood, many women continue to dream of wearing their fairy-tale gown and beautiful rings. Consumed by the vision of a magical, designer-made dress, many women are willing to spend thousands of dollars to purchase it, and many grooms and couples will spend countless hours and dollars on an engagement ring. In fact, the cost of the average wedding in Canada now exceeds $31,000, and not everyone can afford such luxury. Increasingly, however, alternatives do exist; more companies, including some online entrants, are seeking to take advantage of a large segment of the market that cannot afford this level of extravagance by offering lower-cost, yet stylish gowns and rings.

In the past 60 years, the bridal industry has reinvented itself numerous times. In the 1950s, most women purchased their wedding dresses in department stores. Then in the 1960s, small, exclusive, boutique-style wedding shops offering more expensive selections began popping up. Finally, in the 1990s, David's Bridal entered the market, offering affordable gowns ranging from $99 to $1,000. Today, David's Bridal maintains about 30 percent of the wedding dress market. Recognizing this company's success, a number of well-known apparel retailers also now produce low-cost wedding dresses: JC Penney offers a popular wedding gown style for $179.99; Ann Taylor has gowns for $600 to $1,200; and Target features an entire line of Isaac Mizrahi gowns all for under $160. New entrants to the market have also emerged on the Internet as many e-tailers such as TBDress.com offer wedding dresses at even deeper discounts, while other sites such as NearlyNewlywed.com, OnceWed.com, and Tradesy.com sell used wedding dresses to brides.

Wedding savings don't end with the dress. More couples are using the Internet to cut costs on what is often the most expensive wedding product—the engagement ring. BlueNile.com is the world's largest online retailer of diamonds, with global sales in excess of $480 million and strong revenue growth.[72] The company boasts that buying a diamond should be a simple process, offers customers deep discounts compared to bricks-and-mortar stores, and provides shoppers with online videos, FAQs, and chat features to assist in the process. A recent study by the Wakefield Research concluded that consumers are overpaying by as much as 72 percent when they purchase rings from a traditional bricks-and-mortar retailer.[73] One of the primary reasons BlueNile can sell rings at such a discount is that it does not take possession of the rings until it actually sells them. BlueNile has established relationships with diamond wholesalers throughout the world who will ship the diamonds to BlueNile on demand. While traditionalists may have a problem with not being able to see the diamond before buying it, customers do not. In fact, the average engagement ring sold at BlueNile is $5,500, which is almost twice the industry average, and BlueNile boasts that it sells $20,000 to $50,000 rings daily.[74] Other online retailers of wedding rings have popped up, including DiamondPriceGuru.com and Ice.com, that are hoping to duplicate BlueNile's success.

The wedding industry has grown by leaps and bounds, and lower-priced alternatives, especially online retailers, are starting to reshape what has been a very traditional industry, with consumers benefiting from increased competition and lower prices.

DISCUSSION QUESTIONS

1. Are you surprised that people will purchase wedding dresses and engagement rings from discount or online companies? Would you do this? Why or why not?

2. Wedding dresses and engagement rings were thought to be emotional purchases. Is this still true as discount, department, and online stores have become so successful in selling these products?

3. What are some of the reasons that David's Bridal and BlueNile have been so successful?

4. Online retailers such as BlueNile are often blamed for putting small local stores out of business. Do you think this could be true? Why or why not?

5. Visit BlueNile's website and try out some of the custom apps. After visiting the site and browsing its merchandise, do you feel you are more or less likely to purchase a ring online?

DESTINATION CEO

Everyone in Canada has heard of **Tobias Lütke** and his company Shopify . . . haven't they? Lütke is one of Canada's most successful Internet entrepreneurs: His Ottawa-based company Shopify was recently valued at $1.9 billion,[1] and one of his largest competitors, Amazon.com, actually stopped trying to compete with him and instead urged its users to use Shopify's products instead.[2] But wait, Shopify is not a consumer company, and while its customers and investors may have heard of Lütke, most Canadians are unaware of the entrepreneur and the company that has grown to be a global leader. In fact, the *Globe and Mail* recently named Lütke CEO of the year, and introduced him in a feature story aptly titled, "Our Canadian CEO of the year you've probably never heard of."[3]

So what exactly is Shopify and who is Lütke? Shopify is an online business that offers other companies a simple platform to create online stores and websites. Users of Shopify, and there are 200,000 of them, including Tesla Motors, Gatorade, General Electric, Pixar, and Penny Arcade, love the fact that they can design a great feature-rich online store using simple, easy-to-use software.[4] Shopify makes money by either taking a small transaction fee for each online purchase and/or by charging a subscription fee to users. While Shopify has some large customers, the software was originally designed to allow micro, small, and medium-sized businesses to create a professional web-based store to compete with larger firms.[5]

Helping smaller firms compete with large ones is what Lütke, a German immigrant, imagined when he first wrote the software for Shopify. At the time, Lütke was operating a snowboard company with an online Yahoo! store and was increasingly frustrated with the lack of features available to small companies trying to compete with larger competitors. Lütke says, "We did a lot of online retail using Yahoo! stores, but it wasn't very good." Lütke goes on to state that "to make a long story short, after trying a series of existing online store software packages I got so disgusted with the quality of the whole lot, that I wanted to do something to spite them."[6] Soon after creating the original software for Shopify, Lütke realized he may be able to make more money selling his software than snowboards and decided to pursue the venture full-time.

After creating the Shopify software, Lütke then made a very important business decision: He opted to immediately charge users for his software. At that time, most Internet companies were trying to grab market share and would offer their products or services for free. Many firms would start to charge customers only after establishing loyal users, and sometimes customers would balk at paying for products or services they were originally receiving for free. Lütke disagreed with the concept of giving his product away, and charging money up front provided Shopify with much-needed capital. Lütke says, "Most companies, particularly start-ups, don't charge any money and just try to grab as much land as possible (market share). . . . I think it's wrong to offer a product for free. . . . I like making a product people really like and charging money for it."[7]

Shopify's growth has been phenomenal since Lütke started the firm. Year-over-year revenue has increased by over 100 percent a year as more and more firms embrace Shopify's user-friendly and feature-rich product. Online reviews of Shopify, such as those found on ecommerce-platforms. com and websitebuilderexpert.com, praise the software's features, ease of use, and support.[8]

Lütke's company appears poised for even further growth as online and particularly mobile shopping grow exponentially. In 2014, 60 percent of online shoppers accessed Shopify-supported stores using mobile technology, with mobile sales accounting for roughly $2.8 billion of the $8 billion spent on Shopify sites.[9] Still, Lütke, true to the company's origins, states while he is happy with the growth, his biggest source of pride remains the small companies that establish an online presence, helped by Shopify. "We are broadening the number of people who can build these businesses," he says. "It's gratifying looking at the newbies, people who just started their business this year, and seeing how well they did."[10]

Introduction

Creating an effective marketing strategy is important. Getting just the right mix of product, price, promotion, and distribution is critical if a business is to satisfy its target customers and achieve its own objectives (implement the marketing concept).

In Chapter 11, we introduced the concept of marketing and the various activities important in developing a marketing strategy. In this chapter, we'll take a closer look at the four dimensions of the marketing mix—product, price, distribution, and promotion—used to develop the marketing strategy. The focus of these marketing mix elements is a marketing strategy that builds customer relationships and satisfaction.

The Marketing Mix

The key to developing a marketing strategy is maintaining the right marketing mix that satisfies the target market and creates long-term relationships with customers. To develop meaningful customer relationships, marketers have to develop and manage the dimensions of the marketing mix to give their firm an advantage over competitors. Successful companies offer at least one dimension of value that surpasses all competitors in the marketplace in meeting customer expectations. However, this does not mean that a company can ignore the other dimensions of the marketing mix; it must maintain acceptable and—if possible—distinguishable differences in the other dimensions as well.

> "The key to developing a marketing strategy is maintaining the right marketing mix that satisfies the target market and creates long-term relationships with customers."

Tim Hortons, for example, is known for always having fresh coffee. Rogers Communications and Bell Canada are well known for their product bundles that allow consumers to save money by purchasing their smartphone, home phone, Internet, and TV programming as one package. Bombay Canada is well known for its home décor and mahogany furniture. Domino's Pizza is recognized for its superiority in distribution after developing the largest home-delivery pizza company in the world and its innovative product introductions.

Product Strategy

LO1   Describe the role of product in the marketing mix, including how products are developed, classified, and identified.

As mentioned previously, the term *product* refers to goods, services, and ideas. Because the product is often the most visible of the marketing mix dimensions, managing product decisions is crucial. In this section, we'll consider product development, classification, mix, life cycle, and identification.

Developing New Products

Each year thousands of products are introduced, but few of them succeed. For example, some estimate that BlackBerry lost roughly $1.5 billion trying to develop a tablet computer to compete with Apple's iPad.[11] Umbra, a Toronto-based leader in original designs for the home, sells its products through 25,000 retailers in more than 75 countries. Umbra's co-founder and chairman Les Mandelbaum notes that while developing products is a key to the company's success, there are many failures that occur on the way to developing a successful product. The company operated for ten years prior to developing its first breakthrough product, which was a swing-top plastic trash can. Mandelbaum says he came up with the idea after purchasing a similar toy-sized trash can in a children's shop in Paris. He states that when he brought the product back to Canada, his staff doubted it would ever result in a profitable product for the company, but he pushed forward anyway.[12] Even though new product development can be risky, companies can build a competitive advantage by developing new products. For example, Apple has built a very profitable company by developing the iPod, iPhone, and iPad. Readers should recognize that some success in developing new products does not result in success every time. BlackBerry had built a dominant position in the market by developing what amounted to the world's first smartphone. Recently, the company has failed to deliver products customers want, such as smartphones with advanced browsers and game capabilities, and as a result, the company has fallen on hard times. Even

© PG Pictures/Alamy

Apple, the global technology company, that has made billions by developing iPhones and iPads, is not always successful with its product development. The Apple Watch has yet to catch on with consumers as early sales were disappointing. Do you think the Apple Watch will ultimately succeed?

Apple has developed products that have not succeeded commercially, such as Apple TV, and sales results from the Apple Watch have been less than stellar.[13] Worldwide giant Nortel Networks declared bankruptcy in 2009, despite being the Canadian leader in investing in new technologies during the previous ten years.[14] Coca-Cola has, in recent years, created or acquired thousands of new products, including Glacéau, a maker of vitamin water. New products include Enviga green tea, Vault and Vault Zero energy soda, Full Throttle, and many variations and flavours of Dasani water.[15] A firm can take considerable time to get a product ready for the market: It took more than 20 years for the first photocopier, for example. General Motors has trimmed the time required to develop and introduce a new vehicle model from four years to 18 months. The automaker released 29 new models, many with innovative designs, over a 16-month period.[16] The one-time leader in the automobile industry is hoping innovation, particularly in the area of hybrid technology, will restore the company to greatness. In 2011–12, the company introduced a hybrid called the Volt that runs only on battery power. *Profit* columnist Rick Spence notes that senior management must

DID YOU KNOW?

Apple spent $2 billion on research and development in the first quarter of 2015 alone.[17]

employ and support innovators if a company hopes to develop new products and processes. Before introducing a new product, a business must follow a multistep process: idea development, the screening of new ideas, business analysis, product development, test marketing, and commercialization.

Idea Development. New ideas can come from marketing research, engineers, and outside sources such as advertising agencies and management consultants. Microsoft has a separate division—Microsoft Research— where scientists devise the technology of the future. The division has more than 700 full-time employees who work in a university-like research atmosphere. Research teams then present their ideas to Microsoft engineers who are developing specific products.[18] As stated in Chapter 11, ideas sometimes come from customers too. For example, in preparation for the 2010 Winter Olympic Games in Vancouver, Speed Skating Canada relied heavily on feedback from skaters (customers) to develop new skating suits designed to reduce wind traction and improve race times.[19] Kevin Halliday relied on feedback from customers when he started his Calgary-based company, Spindle, Stairs and Railings. Halliday, who had years of experience in the industry, had heard from customers that staircases can be decorative centrepieces in a home. Halliday went on to develop a process of manufacturing winding decorative staircases for smaller homes.[20] Ideas can also come from observing trends in the marketplace and paying attention to what competitors are doing. Oded Shenkar, a business expert, notes that many successful entrepreneurs and companies copy ideas from others, including such giants as Walmart and Procter & Gamble. Shenkar states that while many business and aspiring entrepreneurs think they have to come up with a truly original idea in order to be successful, this is not the case. In fact, copying effectively can also be a good strategy.[21] Other sources for new products are brainstorming and intracompany incentives or rewards for good ideas. New ideas can even create a company. As discussed in Chapter 4, David Reynolds of Halifax developed the idea for QuickSnap, a shoe-fastening device, while waiting impatiently for his friend to tie his shoes. Reynolds, a university student at the time, went on to develop and grow the product into a successful business.

New Idea Screening. The next step in developing a new product is idea screening. In this phase, a marketing manager should look at the organization's resources and objectives and assess the firm's ability to produce and market the product. Important aspects to be considered at this stage are consumer desires, the competition, technological changes, social trends, and political, economic, and environmental considerations. Basically, there are two reasons new products succeed: They are able to meet a need or solve a problem better than products already available, or they add variety to the product selection currently on the market. For example, Goodyear has developed a tire that will self-inflate as soon as the air pressure in the tire starts to drop. The tire passed through the screening stage as Goodyear obviously has experience manufacturing and marketing innovative tires, and management felt there would be a demand for such a product.[22] *Dragons' Den*, a show in which entrepreneurs pitch businesses as well as inventions, usually showcases a number of products that shouldn't have gotten past the screening stage. In recent telecasts, entrepreneurs brought forward fully developed products such as Logo Locs, a hair extension with a button designed for advertisements. Another entrepreneur presented a harness to attach a phone to a shirt.[23] If these entrepreneurs had screened their ideas, they would have realized that neither invention was desired by consumers, solved a problem, or improved a current product.

Bringing together a team of knowledgeable people, including design, engineering, marketing, and customers, is a great way to screen ideas. Using the Internet to encourage collaboration is the next sea of innovation for marketers to screen ideas.[24] After many ideas were screened, Heinz Ketchup introduced kid-targeted Silly Squirts with three cool drawing nozzles to keep kids amused and entertained at dinner. In addition, Easy Squeeze upside-down bottles added to convenience.[25] Most new-product ideas are rejected during screening because they seem inappropriate or impractical for the organization, but many, which go on to fail, still make it to market. Indeed, GfK Custom Research has established a collection, nicknamed the Museum of Product Failures, just outside Ann Arbor, Michigan. While not open to the public, companies considering a product idea can visit—for a $5,000 entrance fee—this massive physical database of products as a stark reminder of the consequences of poor market research.[26]

Business Analysis. Business analysis is a basic assessment of a product's compatibility in the marketplace and its potential profitability. Both the size of the market and competing products are often studied at this point. The most important question relates to market demand: How will the product affect the firm's sales, costs, and profits?

Product Development. If a product survives the first three steps, it is developed into a prototype that should reveal the intangible attributes it possesses as perceived by the consumer. Product development is often expensive, and few product ideas make it to this stage. New product research and development costs vary. Adding a new colour to an existing item may cost $100,000 to $200,000, but launching a completely new product can cost millions of dollars. For example, Andrew Scott of Vancouver spent over $1 million developing a replacement for traditional parking meters. Scott's parking meters enable remote monitoring by parking enforcement, six locking points to detect theft, full-colour graphic screens, and a wide variety of payment options including coins, bank cards, and credit cards.[27] The

Coca-Cola Co. reduced the time and cost of product development research by 50 percent when it created an online panel of 100 teenagers and asked them how to remake its Powerade sports drink.[28] During product development, various elements of the marketing mix must be developed for testing. Copyrights, tentative advertising copy, packaging, labelling, and descriptions of a target market are integrated to develop an overall marketing strategy.

Test Marketing. **Test marketing** is a trial mini-launch of a product in limited areas that represent the potential market. It allows a complete test of the marketing strategy in a natural environment, giving the organization an opportunity to discover weaknesses and eliminate them before the product is fully launched. For example, when Tim Hortons was considering introducing steeped tea, the company first tried the product in Atlantic Canada to determine what the public reaction would be to the product. Recently, when Tim Hortons was considering increasing the size of its coffee cups, it tested the concept in two Ontario markets, Sudbury and Kingston, to gauge customer reaction.[29] Imperial Tobacco Canada ran similar testing marketing for a type of smokeless tobacco called Snus.[30] The company first introduced the powdered tobacco product at 230 retail outlets in Edmonton to determine whether it might be successful with consumers across the country. Best Buy has recently started selling used games in Canada to determine if the strategy will work. Consider Seasons 52, the latest concept restaurant developed by Darden Restaurants Inc., the world's largest casual dining company with such well-known restaurants as Red Lobster and Olive Garden. Seasons 52 boasts a seasonally inspired menu with the freshest goods available served in a casual atmosphere. Seasons 52 targets those who are striving to live fit, active lives and are concerned about the quality and nutrition of their food. All menu items at Seasons 52 have fewer than 475 calories (significantly lower than competing restaurants), are nutritionally balanced, and are not fried. Darden is test-marketing this restaurant concept in Florida and Georgia to experiment with variations in menu, advertising, and pricing and to measure the extent of brand awareness, brand switching, and repeat purchases resulting from these alterations in this concept restaurant.[31] ACNielsen assists companies in test-marketing their products. Figure 12.1 shows the permanent U.S. sites as well as custom locations for test marketing.

Commercialization. **Commercialization** is the full introduction of a complete marketing strategy and the launch of the product for commercial success. During commercialization, the firm gears up for full-scale production, distribution, and promotion. When Research In Motion introduced BlackBerry Storm, it spent millions

> **test marketing** a trial mini-launch of a product in limited areas that represent the potential market
>
> **commercialization** the full introduction of a complete marketing strategy and the launch of the product for commercial success

Figure 12.1 ACNielsen Market Decisions

**Market Decisions
Test Market Locations**

Portland

Boise

Peoria

Colorado Springs

Evansville

Lexington

Charleston

Tucson

◆ Permanent Test Markets ("Data Markets")

★ Additional "Custom" Test Markets

Source: "Test Marketing," ACNielsen (n.d.), www.acnielsen.com/services/testing/testl.htm (accessed June 5, 2004). Reprinted with permission of ACNielsen Market Decisions.

on production, distribution, advertising, and publicity for the product. The original product did not catch on with consumers and was replaced by the Storm2 a short time later. A more successful example of a product launch may be Procter & Gamble's introduction of the Fusion razor, when it used its large distribution and retail network and spent more than $6 million for just two Super Bowl ads for the five-blade product. It blanketed stores with 180,000 displays in the first week, coverage that it took a year to achieve with the Mach3 razor in 1998. The Fusion razor commands 30 percent higher prices than Mach3 products, which—at a time when Procter & Gamble cannot increase the prices on Tide or Crest—will boost earnings by $120 million and increase market share to 15 percent.[32] It's often not until commercialization that companies will know if a product is going to be successful. New products released in 2015–16 included wireless air buds, hoverboards, and a number of virtual reality headsets. Only time will tell if these products will be successful even though the companies have spent countless hours and millions of dollars ensuring that consumers will want to buy them.[33]

Virtual reality headsets are slated to be the next big thing in technology and gaming. Yet only time will tell if people will be willing to buy and wear the devices.

© Digital Archive Japan/Alamy

© hurricanehank/Shutterstock

Hoverboards started being sold in late 2015 and into 2016. Would you purchase one of these?

© Waxart/Dreamstime

Milk is a convenience product. It is bought frequently by consumers for relatively quick consumption without their conducting a lengthy search.

Classifying Products

Products are usually classified as either consumer products or business products. **Consumer products** are for household or family use; they are not intended for any purpose other than daily living. They can be further classified as convenience products, shopping products, and specialty products on the basis of consumers' buying behaviour and intentions.

consumer products products intended for household or family use

- *Convenience products*, such as eggs, milk, bread, and newspapers, are bought frequently, without a lengthy search, and often for immediate consumption. Consumers spend virtually no time planning where to purchase these products and usually accept whatever brand is available.

- *Shopping products*, such as furniture, audio equipment, clothing, and sporting goods, are purchased after the consumer has compared competitive products and "shopped around." Price, product features, quality, style, service, and image all influence the decision to buy.

- *Specialty products*, such as ethnic foods, designer clothing and shoes, art, and antiques, require even greater research and shopping effort. Consumers know what they want and go out of their way to find it; they are not willing to accept a substitute.

Business products are used directly or indirectly in the operation or manufacturing processes of businesses. They are usually purchased for the operation of an organization or the production of other products; thus, their purchase is tied to specific goals and objectives. They too can be further classified:

business products products that are used directly or indirectly in the operation or manufacturing processes of businesses

- *Raw materials* are natural products taken from the earth or from the oceans, and recycled solid waste. Iron ore, bauxite, lumber, cotton, and fruits and vegetables are examples.

- *Major equipment* covers large, expensive items used in production. Examples include earth-moving equipment, stamping machines, and robotic equipment used on auto assembly lines.

- *Accessory equipment* includes items used for production, office, or management purposes, which usually do not become part of the final product. Computers, fax machines, calculators, and hand tools are examples.

- *Component parts* are finished items, ready to be assembled into the company's final products. Tires, window glass, batteries, and spark plugs are component parts of automobiles.

- *Processed materials* are things used directly in production or management operations but not readily identifiable as component parts. Varnish, for example, is a processed material for a furniture manufacturer.

- *Supplies* include materials that make production, management, and other operations possible, such as paper, pencils, paint, cleaning supplies, and so on.

- *Industrial services* include financial, legal, marketing research, security, janitorial, and exterminating services. Purchasers decide whether to provide these services internally or to acquire them from an outside supplier.

Levi Strauss & Co. has long been known for its 501s and affordable prices. Recently, the company delved into the premium denim market, dominated by brands such as Earl Jeans, 7 for All Mankind, Citizens for Humanity, and True Religion, by launching its Premium collection. Now, in an attempt to break into yet another hot market, Levi's is going green.

According to the research group Mintel, about 35 million people in the United States regularly purchase "green" products. Consumers are increasingly willing to pay more for earth-friendly products and services. As a result, companies are going to great lengths to prove that they are part of the green movement. Many are switching to earth-friendly packaging or new production methods that conserve energy. Levi's is producing 100 percent organic cotton jeans.

These new jeans, priced at $250 a pair, are made with 100 percent organic cotton, natural dyes, tags composed of recycled paper and soy ink, and recycled rivets. The company is also releasing less expensive lines composed partly of organic and recycled materials.

Although many of us might be willing to switch to green jeans, we may wonder at the price and find it prohibitive. Why is going green sometimes so expensive? In the case of Levi's jeans, it's the organic cotton. The demand for organic cotton is currently much greater than the supply, making it expensive. For cotton to be certified organic, it cannot be genetically modified and must be pesticide and fungicide free. In 2005, more than 50 percent of cotton in the United States was genetically modified. Many companies are turning to farmers overseas, but certification for these farmers can be a challenge. As of 2007, certified organic cotton composed less than 1 percent of the world's cotton supply. For now, Levi's can only produce a limited number of green jeans, hence the high price.

However, the very issue that drives up prices can be used as a marketing strategy to gain customers. Many people are willing to pay more to support farmers committed to harvesting through organic methods. In fact, at the recent Cannes Lions International Advertising Festival, "eco-marketing" was an extremely popular topic. Consumers are excited about green products and services, and companies are spending big bucks to promote their stances on going green. According to TNS Media Intelligence, marketers spent $18 million on green-focused television advertising in a three-month time span.

While going green may seem to some like a current fad, indicators point to a prolonged increase in demand for such products. According to the Organic Trade Association, Canadian organic retail sales have grown every year since 1990. It seems that companies can only benefit from a continued investment in eco-friendly items, and Levi's appears committed to incorporating organic cotton and other eco-friendly materials into its product lines.[34]

DISCUSSION QUESTIONS

1. Why can companies charge a premium price for green products?

2. What else might Levi's do to increase its offering of moderately priced green products?

3. How much more would you be willing to pay for environmentally friendly clothing such as Levi's new green jeans?

Product Line and Product Mix

Product relationships within an organization are of key importance. A **product line** is a group of closely related products that are treated as a unit because of similar marketing strategy. At Colgate-Palmolive, for example, the oral-care product line includes Colgate toothpaste, toothbrushes, and dental floss. A **product mix** is all the products offered by an organization. For example, a product line at Lulelemon could be all of the company's yoga gear while its product

product line
a group of closely related products that are treated as a unit because of similar marketing strategy, production, or end-use considerations

product mix all the products offered by an organization

© Radu Bercan/Shutterstock.com

Apple's product mix and its many product lines are visible on the company's website.

Figure 12.2 Colgate-Palmolive's Product Mix and Product Lines

Product Mix			
Oral Care	**Personal Care**	**Household Care**	**Pet Nutrition**
Toothpaste	Men's antiperspirant/deodorant	Dishwashing	Science diet
Toothbrushes	Women's antiperspirant/deodorant	Fabric conditioner	Prescription diet
Kids' products	Bar soap	Household cleaners	
Whitening products	Body wash	Institutional products	
Over the counter	Liquid hand wash		
From the dentist	Toiletries for men		

(Product Lines — vertical axis label)

Based on Colgate Products, http://www.colgate.com/app/Colgate/US/Corp/Consumers/HomePage.cvsp (accessed June 17, 2007).

> "During the *decline stage*, sales continue to fall rapidly. Profits also decline and may even become losses as prices are cut and necessary marketing expenditures are made."

mix would be its full range of products—clothing, equipment, and accessories. Figure 12.2 displays a sampling of the product mix and product lines of the Colgate-Palmolive Company.

Product Life Cycle

Like people, products are born, grow, mature, and eventually die. Some products have very long lives. Ivory Soap was introduced in 1879 and is still popular. In contrast, a new computer chip is usually outdated within a year because of technological breakthroughs and rapid changes in the computer industry. There are four stages in the life cycle of a product: introduction, growth, maturity, and decline (Figure 12.3). The stage a product is in helps determine marketing strategy.

In the *introductory stage*, consumer awareness and acceptance of the product are limited, sales are zero, and profits are negative. Profits are negative because the firm has spent money on research, development, and marketing to launch the product. During the introductory stage, marketers focus on making consumers aware of the product and its benefits. When Procter & Gamble introduced the Tide Stainbrush to reach the 70 percent of consumers who pre-treat stains when doing laundry, it employed press releases as well as television and magazine advertising to make consumers aware of the new product.[35] Sales accelerate as the product enters the growth stage of the life cycle.

In the *growth stage*, sales increase rapidly and profits peak, then start to decline. One reason profits start to decline during the growth stage is that new companies enter the market, driving prices down and increasing marketing expenses. Consider Apple's iPod, the most popular digital music player with more than 74 percent of the music player market. It sold 32 million iPods in 2005, and its iTunes music store has 83 percent of the North American market share for legal music downloads. iTunes has more than 20 million unique visitors a month.[36] During the growth stage, the firm tries to strengthen its position in the market by emphasizing the product's benefits and identifying market segments that want these benefits.

Sales continue to increase at the beginning of the *maturity stage*, but then the sales curve peaks and starts to decline while profits continue to decline. This stage is characterized by severe competition and heavy expenditures. Automobiles are an example of a mature product; intense competition in the auto industry requires Toyota, GM, and other automakers to spend huge sums to make their products stand out in a crowded marketplace.

During the *decline stage*, sales continue to fall rapidly. Profits also decline and may even become losses as prices are cut and necessary marketing expenditures are made. As profits drop, firms may eliminate certain models or items. To reduce expenses and squeeze out any remaining profits, marketing expenditures may be cut back, even though such cutbacks accelerate the sales decline. Finally, plans must be made for phasing out the product and introducing new ones to take its place. Unfortunately for Mattel, the Barbie doll has seen her status and sales slide as she has been replaced on retail shelves with more edgy products such as Bratz. Barbie became vulnerable to competition from Bratz and other toys and to the growth of toy sales in stores such as Walmart when they chose to allocate shelf space to products they considered more profitable.[37] CanJet airlines, founded in Halifax, Nova Scotia, was pulled from the market after two years after its owner decided the marketplace would not sustain the airline. The company later re-emerged specializing in charter flights and southern destinations.

Figure 12.3 Product Life Cycle

Introduction	Growth	Maturity	Decline
3D television	DVRs	Flat-screen televisions	AM/FM radios
YouTube movies	Blu-ray players	Laptop computers	VCRs
Electric cars	Tablet computers	Chevrolet Corvette	Desktop computers

Although Disney had high hopes for developing a theme park in Hong Kong, it was soon disappointed. Attendance at Hong Kong Disneyland was below expectations, costing Disney millions of dollars. Although attendance has risen in recent years, Hong Kong Disneyland still faced 2011 losses of more than $30 million. The company plans to open a bigger $4.4 billion resort on the Chinese mainland in Shanghai. Although this new venture might be successful, it could also further cannibalize Hong Kong Disneyland sales. Disney theme parks face many challenges as the company tries to adapt to different cultures.

Ironically, there is one business niche in China where Disney appears to be thriving: English education. In 2008, the Walt Disney Company launched Disney English in China. Learning English early in China is big business, and the growing private education sector is a $3.7 billion market. Chinese parents are determined that their children learn English early as a component of future academic and job success. Disney English caters to children aged 2 through 6 and to grade-school children. Its locations have tripled to 22 in a one-year period. Lessons, books, songs, exercises, and more are based on Disney stories and characters, fully immersing

children in all things Disney. The program is expensive for the average Chinese citizen, but many parents are willing to pay.

Disney claims its schools in China were created solely to teach English, saying that it saw an opportunity to use its characters to motivate learning. However, it also has the unique marketing opportunity to make both parents and children aware of Disney offerings. Many parents and children appear happy with the program, which could cause them to view Disney favourably in the future. One has to wonder whether these favourable relationships with Disney English participants will help to increase demand for its Hong Kong and Shanghai theme parks.[36]

DISCUSSION QUESTIONS

1. Why do you think Disney has decided to open up a larger park in Shanghai?

2. Why has Disney English been such a successful program?

3. How might the Disney English program indirectly market the theme parks?

Identifying Products

Branding, packaging, and labelling can be used to identify or distinguish one product from others. As a result, they are key marketing activities that help position a product appropriately for its target market.

Branding. **Branding** is the process of naming and identifying products. A *brand* is a name, term, symbol, design, or combination of these that identifies a product and distinguishes it from other products. Consider that Tim Hortons, Google, and iPhone are brand names that are used to identify entire product categories, much like Xerox has become synonymous with photocopying and Kleenex with tissues. Protecting a brand name is important in maintaining a brand identity.[38]

Recently a Cape Breton, Nova Scotia–based company, Glenora Distilleries, makers of Glen Breton Whisky, has emerged from a nine-year fight over the right to use the word "Glen" in its brand and on its labels. The Scotch Whisky Association claimed that the use of the name was leading consumers to believe the product was manufactured in Scotland. Throughout the legal proceedings, the Association stated it was protecting the Scottish brand

> **branding** the process of naming and identifying products

and reputation as the premier manufacturer of whisky and scotch in the world. Lauchie MacLean, owner of Glenora, argued that the company name is derived from the company's home community—Glenville, Cape Breton. After a lengthy dispute, the Supreme Court of Canada found that MacLean could continue to use the name "Glen," which prompted the company to release a new product aptly called "The Battle of Glen."[39]

A new trend has emerged in marketing where the CEO or founder of the firm actually becomes the brand or unique feature that distinguishes the company from its competitors. Heather Reisman from Indigo/Chapters and Galen Weston Jr. from President's Choice and Loblaws are two Canadian examples. While this strategy appears to be becoming more popular, challenges exist if the CEO leaves the company or fails to live up to the brand image, as was the case with Martha Stewart in the U.S. who actually spent time in prison.

Students should realize that successful brands can on their own become very valuable and sometimes be worth more than the products that they represent. For example, Polaroid, a brand that was once synonymous with instant cameras, is making a comeback with Lady Gaga as the firm's creative director. The company, which was bought by private investors including Toronto-based Hilco Consumer

© Jason Ip/Dreamstime

Polaroid is making a comeback with Lady Gaga as the firm's creative director. The company, which was bought by private investors including Toronto-based Hilco Consumer Capital, is returning to the photo business and even selling some its classic instant cameras.

Table 12.2 The Ten Most Valuable Brands in Canada–2014[42]

Rank	Brand	Brand Value (C$ million)
1.	Toronto-Dominion Bank (TD)	$10.7
2.	Royal Bank of Canada	10.5
3.	Thomson Reuters	8.3
4.	Scotiabank	7.7
5.	Tim Hortons	3.9
6.	Bell	3.3
7.	Shoppers Drug Mart	3.2
8.	Rogers	3.2
9.	Lululemon	2.9
10.	Telus	2.9

Capital, is returning to the photo business with a slew of new products, including some of its classic instant cameras.[40]

Brand equity refers to the awareness, loyalty, perceived quality, image, and emotions that people feel toward certain brands. Brands that are well established enjoy brand equity, which is the degree to which customers are committed to future purchases of the brand. The world's ten most valuable brands are shown in Table 12.1 and the ten most valuable brands in Canada are displayed in Table 12.2. The brand name is the part of the brand that can be spoken and consists of letters, words, and numbers—such as WD-40 lubricant. A *brand mark* is the part of the brand that is a distinctive design, such as the silver star on the hood of a Mercedes or the McDonald's golden arches logo. A **trademark** is a brand that is registered with the Canadian Intellectual Property Office,

trademark a brand that is registered with the Canadian Intellectual Property Office and is thus legally protected from use by any other firm

and is thus legally protected from use by any other firm. Examples of well-known trademarks include the National Hockey League's logo and the Stanley Cup and the Nike swoosh.

Two major categories of brands are manufacturer brands and private distributor brands. **Manufacturer brands** are brands initiated and owned by the manufacturer to identify products from the point of production to the point of purchase. Bell, Bombardier, Canadian Tire, and Petro-Canada are examples. **Private distributor brands**, which may be less expensive than manufacturer brands, are owned and controlled by a wholesaler or retailer, such as Kenmore appliances (Sears) and President's Choice grocery products (Loblaws). While private-label brands were once considered cheaper and of poorer quality, such as Walmart's Ol' Roy dog food, many private-label brands are increasing quality and image and competing with national brands. For example, many President's Choice products are considered to be on par with or superior to branded products. The brand was launched by former Loblaws president Dave Nichol, and his first major success was *The Decadent*, a chocolate chip cookie made with butter and President's Choice–brand *Decadent* chocolate chips, which became Canada's best-selling cookie. Sobeys, in response to President's Choice, re-launched its own private brand, which was originally called *Sobeys*, changing the name to *Our Best* then to *Our Compliments* brand and finally today to *Compliments* or *Sensations by Compliments* for premium products.[43]

manufacturer brands brands initiated and owned by the manufacturer to identify products from the point of production to the point of purchase

private distributor brands brands, which may cost less than manufacturer brands, that are owned and controlled by a wholesaler or retailer

Table 12.1 The Ten Most Valuable Brands in the World–2015[41]

Rank	Brand	Brand Value (US$ million)
1	Apple	$170
2	Google	120
3	Coca-Cola	78
4	Microsoft	67
5	IBM	65
6	Toyota	49
7	Samsung	45
8	General Electric (GE)	42
9	McDonald's	39
10	Amazon	37

Generic products like these appeal to consumers who are less concerned about quality and consistency, but want lower prices.

© Cathy Melloan/PhotoEdit

© Jonathan Hayward/CP Images

Coca-Cola's bottle was changed for the 2010 Winter Olympic Games into a canvas for Aboriginal art.

Another type of brand that has developed is **generic products**—products with no brand name at all. They often come in plain, simple packages that carry only the generic name of the product—peanut butter, tomato juice, aspirin, dog food, and so on. They appeal to consumers who may be willing to sacrifice quality or product consistency to get a lower price.

Companies use two basic approaches to branding multiple products. In one, a company gives each product within its complete product mix its own brand name. Warner-Lambert, for example, sells many well-known consumer products—Dentyne, Chiclets, Listerine, Halls, Rolaids, and Trident—each individually branded. This branding policy ensures that the name of one product does not affect the names of others, and different brands can be targeted at different segments of the same market, increasing the company's market share (its percentage of the sales for the total market for a product). Another approach to branding is to develop a family of brands with each of the firm's products carrying the same name or at least part of the name. Gillette, Sara Lee, and Dell use this approach.

Packaging. The **packaging**, or external container that holds and describes the product, influences consumers' attitudes and their buying decisions. A survey of over 1,200 consumers found that 40 percent are willing to try a new product based on its packaging.[44] It is estimated that consumers' eyes linger only 2.5 seconds on each product on an average shopping trip; therefore, product packaging should be designed to attract and hold consumers' attention.

A package can perform several functions, including protection, economy, convenience, and promotion. Beverage manufacturers have been redesigning their bottles to make them more convenient for consumers and to promote them to certain markets. Scientists videotaped people drinking from different types of bottles and made plaster casts of their hands. They found that the average gulp is 190.45 mL (6.44 ounces) and that half the population would rather suck liquid through a pop-up top than drink it. Packaging also helps create an overall brand image. Coca-Cola's iconic bottle was transformed for the 2010 Winter Olympic Games in Vancouver into a canvas for Aboriginal art. In this way, the corporation was able to connect with Canadians, and the bottles have become collector's items.[45] Coke engaged in a similar practice for the 2006 World Cup by transforming its bottles into the shape of a soccer ball. The soccer ball–shaped bottle was used in association with World Cup meals at McDonald's 1,300 German outlets, and featured pictures of six soccer stars from leading national teams.[46]

Labelling. **Labelling**, the presentation of important information on the package, is closely associated with packaging. The content of labelling, often required by law, may include ingredients or content, nutrition facts (calories, fat, etc.), care instructions, suggestions for use (such as recipes), the manufacturer's address and toll-free number, website, and other useful information. In Canada, all labels must be bilingual. McDonald's introduced packaging that lets consumers know the nutritional value of Big Macs as well as other products. It was the first fast-food chain to adopt the initiative.[47] This information can have a strong impact on sales. The labels of many products, particularly food and drugs, must carry warnings, instructions, certifications, or manufacturers' identifications.

Product Quality. **Quality** reflects the degree to which a good, service, or idea meets the demands and requirements of customers. Quality products are often referred to as reliable, durable, easily maintained, easily used, a good value, or a trusted brand name. The

generic products products with no brand name that often come in simple packages and carry only their generic name

packaging the external container that holds and describes the product

labelling the presentation of important information on a package

quality the degree to which a good, service, or idea meets the demands and requirements of customers

level of quality is the amount of quality that a product possesses, and the consistency of quality depends on the product maintaining the same level of quality over time.

Quality of service is difficult to gauge because it depends on customers' perceptions of how well the service meets or exceeds their expectations. In other words, service quality is judged by consumers, not the service providers. A bank may define service quality as employing friendly and knowledgeable employees, but the bank's customers may be more concerned with waiting time, ATM access, security, and statement accuracy. Similarly, an airline traveller considers on-time arrival, on-board food service, and satisfaction with the ticketing and boarding process. J.D. Power, a global market information service firm, ranks customer satisfaction in many Canadian and worldwide industries.

The quality of services provided by businesses on the Internet can be gauged by consumers on such sites as ConsumerReports.org and BBBOnline. The subscription service offered by ConsumerReports.org provides consumers with a view of e-commerce sites' business, security, and privacy policies. BBBOnline is dedicated to promoting responsibility online. The Web Credibility Project focuses on how health, travel, advocacy, news, and shopping sites disclose business relationships with the companies and products they cover or sell, especially when such relationships pose a potential conflict of interest.[48]

Pricing Strategy

LO2 Define price and discuss its importance in the marketing mix, including various pricing strategies a firm might employ.

In Chapter 11, we defined *price* as the value placed on an object exchanged between a buyer and a seller. Buyers' interest in price stems from their expectations about the usefulness of a product or the satisfaction they may derive from it. Because buyers have limited resources, they must allocate those resources to obtain the products they most desire. They must decide whether the benefits gained in an exchange are worth the buying power sacrificed. Almost anything of value can be assessed by a price. Many factors may influence the evaluation of value, including time constraints, price levels, perceived quality, and motivations to use available information about prices.[49] Indeed, consumers vary in their response to price: Some focus solely on the lowest price, while others consider quality or the prestige associated with a product and its price. Two of Canada's retail success stories have used very opposing strategies when setting prices for their items. Dollarama has risen to become the largest dollar store in Canada based on its low-price policy, while Birks, a high-end jewellery store that has been in business in Canada in one form or another since

1879, is known to charge premium prices for many of its prestigious items.

Price is a key element in the marketing mix because it relates directly to the generation of revenue and profits. Sobeys, for example, has generated more revenue from its premium private-label brand *Sensations by Compliments* by charging more for those items than for its regular private-label goods—*Compliments*. McDonald's has increased profits with upscale items such as its higher-priced Cobb salad.[50] In large part, the ability to set a price depends on the supply of and demand for a product. For most products, the quantity demanded goes up as the price goes down, and as the price goes up, the quantity demanded goes down. This has been evident in the price of oil and gas in Canada in recent years. When the price per litre has fallen below one dollar, consumers have been much more willing to purchase gas than when the price exceeds one dollar per litre. The change in gas prices has also impacted the sale of other items, such as the sales decline of larger, less fuel-efficient sport utility vehicles, especially when the price of gas rose in recent years and topped $1.20 per litre. Of course, price also depends on the cost to manufacture a good or provide a service or idea.

Changes in buyers' needs, variations in the effectiveness of other marketing mix variables, the presence of substitutes, and dynamic environmental factors can influence demand. A firm may temporarily sell products below cost to match competition, to generate cash flow, or even to increase market share, but in the long run it cannot survive by selling its products below cost. For example, many small independent stores in Halifax sold milk well below cost during the early part of 2012 to increase sales of other more profitable items. Sobeys executives have stated that they are not worried about this trend as the practice is not sustainable in the long term.[51]

Price is probably the most flexible variable in the marketing mix. Although it may take years to develop a product, establish channels of distribution, and design and implement promotion, a product's price may be set and changed in a few minutes. Under certain circumstances, of course, the price may not be so flexible, especially if government regulations prevent dealers from controlling prices.

Pricing Objectives

Pricing objectives specify the role of price in an organization's marketing mix and strategy. They usually are influenced not only by marketing mix decisions but also by finance, accounting, and production factors. Maximizing profits and sales, boosting market share, maintaining the status quo, and survival are four common pricing objectives.

Specific Pricing Strategies

Pricing strategies provide guidelines for achieving the company's pricing objectives and overall marketing strategy. They specify how price will be used as a variable in the marketing mix. Significant pricing strategies relate to price lining, pricing new products, psychological pricing, and price discounting.

Price Lining.   Price lining occurs when a company sells [*maximise profit/sales*] multiple products in the same product category. For example, Peoples Jewellers sells three different one-carat diamond rings and has labelled them as good, better, and best. Research indicates people are willing to move up one product/price category if the price difference is not perceived as significant. So if a ring labelled as "good" is priced at $2,000 and cost Peoples $1,200, the company would make $800. But a ring labelled as "better" could sell for $2,500 and cost People's $1,500, resulting in a $1,000 profit. Peoples knows that by creating these labels, consumers will be inclined to jump to the better product description, and as a result Peoples will make more money by selling the ring that is priced slightly higher. As discussed below, Tim Hortons uses a type of product line pricing in its coffee sales to generate additional sales volume and more revenue per cup of coffee sold.

Pricing New Products.   Setting the price for a new product is critical: The right price leads to profitability; the wrong price may kill the product. In general, there are two basic strategies to setting the base price for a new product. **Price skimming** is charging the highest possible price that buyers who want the product will pay and gradually lowering it over time. For example, when the new gaming console Xbox One was introduced into the marketplace, it was priced at $699. Over time, Microsoft gradually lowered the price to appeal to more consumers and to maintain sales. This strategy allows companies to generate much-needed revenue to help offset the costs of research and development. Conversely, a **penetration price** is a low price designed to help a product enter the market and gain market share rapidly. [*boosting market share*] For example, many discount real estate brokers have started to emerge in Canada in recent years. Many of these, such as PropertyGuys.com, have been charging much lower fees than traditional real estate agents as a way to break into the market. The discount brokers have been dealing with strong resistance from traditional real estate agents who can charge thousands more than discount real estate companies. Examples other than real estate also exist. When Industrias Añaños introduced Kola Real to capitalize on limited supplies of Coca-Cola and Pepsi in Peru, it set an ultra-low penetration price to appeal to the poor who predominate in the region. Kola Real quickly secured one-fifth of the Peruvian market and has since made significant gains in Ecuador, Venezuela, and Mexico, forcing larger soft-drink marketers to cut prices.[53] Penetration pricing is less flexible than price skimming; it is more difficult to raise a penetration price than to lower a skimming price.

price skimming charging the highest possible price that buyers who want the product will pay

penetration price a low price designed to help a product enter the market and gain market share rapidly

© Keith Homan / Shutterstock.com

The creators of the Xbox One visual novels use a price skimming strategy. They set the price high when the unit is first introduced, then lower the price significantly to maintain sales.

Penetration pricing is used most often when marketers suspect that competitors will enter the market shortly after the product has been introduced.

Psychological Pricing.   **Psychological pricing** encourages purchases based on emotional rather than rational responses to the price. For example, the assumption behind *even/odd pricing* is that people will buy more of a product for $9.99 than $10 because it seems to be a bargain at the odd price. The assumption behind *symbolic/prestige pricing* is that high prices connote high quality. Thus the prices of certain fragrances are set artificially high to give the impression of superior quality. Some over-the-counter drugs are priced high because consumers associate a drug's price with potency.

psychological pricing encouraging purchases based on emotional rather than rational responses to the price

discounts temporary price reductions, often employed to boost sales

Price Discounting.   Temporary price reductions, or **discounts**, are often employed to boost sales. Although there are many types, quantity, seasonal, and promotional discounts are among the most widely used. Quantity discounts reflect the economies of purchasing in large volume. Seasonal discounts to buyers who purchase goods or services out of season help even out production capacity. Promotional discounts attempt to improve sales by advertising price reductions on selected products to increase customer interest. Often promotional pricing is geared to increased profits. On the other hand, many companies such as Walmart, Home Depot, and Toys 'R' Us have shunned promotional price discounts and, with everyday low pricing, are focusing more on relationships with customers. Polo killed its Polo jeans brand because the price of this product hurt its luxury image.[54] In the airline industry, lower-cost airlines like WestJet and Air Canada Rouge are competing head-to-head with the major airlines by offering sharply discounted fares. Additionally, websites like iTravel.com, Expedia.ca, Priceline.com, Orbitz.com, and Travelocity.com help flyers find the lowest fares quickly, forcing airlines to become even more price competitive.

Distribution Strategy

LO3 Identify factors affecting distribution decisions, such as marketing channels and intensity of market coverage.

The best products in the world will not be successful unless companies make them available where and when customers want to buy them. In this section, we will explore dimensions of distribution strategy, including the channels through which products are distributed, the intensity of market coverage, and the physical handling of products during distribution.

Marketing Channels

A **marketing channel**, or channel of distribution, is a group of organizations that moves products from their producer to customers. Marketing channels make products available to buyers when and where they desire to purchase them. Organizations that bridge the gap between a product's manufacturer and the ultimate consumer are called *middlemen*, or intermediaries. They create time, place, and ownership utility. Two intermediary organizations are retailers and wholesalers.

Retailers buy products from manufacturers (or other intermediaries) and sell them to consumers for home and

marketing channel a group of organizations that moves products from their producer to customers; also called a channel of distribution

retailers intermediaries who buy products from manufacturers (or other intermediaries) and sell them to consumers for home and household use rather than for resale or for use in producing other products

Table 12.3 General Merchandise Retailers

Type of Retailer	Description	Examples
Department store	Large organization offering wide product mix and organized into separate departments	Hudson's Bay Sears
Discount store	Self-service, general merchandise store offering brand name and private brand products at low prices	Dollarama
Supermarket	Self-service store offering complete line of food products and some non-food products	Sobeys Loblaws
Superstore	Giant outlet offering all food and non-food products found in supermarkets, as well as most routinely purchased products	Walmart Real Canadian Superstores
Warehouse club	Large-scale, members-only establishments combining cash-and-carry wholesaling with discount retailing	Costco
Warehouse showroom	Facility in a large, low-cost building with large on-premises inventories and minimum service	Ikea
Catalogue showroom	Type of warehouse showroom where consumers shop from a catalogue and products are stored out of buyers' reach and provided in manufacturer's carton	Sears Catalogue

Source: William M. Pride and O. C. Ferrell, *Marketing: Concepts and Strategies, 2008*, p. 428. Copyright 2008 by Houghton Mifflin Company. Reprinted with permission.

household use rather than for resale or for use in producing other products. Hudson's Bay, for example, buys products from Spin Master Toys and resells them to consumers. Retailing usually occurs in a store, but the Internet, vending machines, mail-order catalogues, and entertainment, such as going to a Montreal Canadiens hockey game, also provide opportunities for retailing. With more than 20 million Canadians accessing the Internet, consumers spent an estimated at $29.3 billion in 2015, and with more and more people engaging in online and mobile shopping, the amount is expected to grow to almost $50 billion by 2019.[56] By bringing together an assortment of products from competing producers, retailers create utility. Traditional retailers arrange for products to be moved from producers to a convenient retail establishment (place utility). They maintain hours of operation for their retail stores to make merchandise available when consumers want it (time utility). They also assume the risk of ownership of inventories (ownership utility). New online retailers have altered the landscape as they do not have all the costs associated with operating a retail location and can offer consumers access to products 24 hours a day. However, Internet retailing has given rise to a new term, "showrooming." This is where consumers visit a traditional merchant location to see and touch a product and then purchase it at a savings online. Many traditional retailers, such as Canadian Tire and SportChek, have created online shopping sites to retain customers and compete with online-only retailers. One of the best-known online-only, or cyber, merchants is Amazon. Amazon offers millions of products from which to choose, all from the privacy and convenience of the purchaser's home. In some cases, Web merchants offer wide selections, ultra-convenience, superior service, knowledge, and the best products. More detail on the Internet's effect on marketing is presented in Chapter 13.

Table 12.3 describes various types of general merchandise retailers.

Today, competition between retailers in Canada has never been more intense due to the growth in online retailers, Target entering the Canadian market, and upscale retailer Nordstrom following behind. Furthermore, competition between different types of stores is changing the nature of retailing. Supermarkets compete with specialty food stores, wholesale clubs, and discount stores. Department stores compete with nearly every other type of store including specialty stores, off-price chains, category killers, discount stores, and online retailers.

> **"Internet retailing has given rise to a new term, 'showrooming.' This is where** consumers visit a traditional merchant location to see and touch a product **and then purchase it at a savings online."**

Wholesalers are intermediaries who buy from producers or from other wholesalers and sell to retailers. They usually do not sell in significant quantities to ultimate consumers. Wholesalers perform the functions listed in Table 12.4.

Wholesalers are extremely important because of the marketing activities they perform, particularly for consumer products. Although it is true that wholesalers can be eliminated, their functions must be passed on to some other entity, such as the producer, another intermediary, or even the customer. Wholesalers help consumers and retailers by buying in large quantities, then selling to retailers in smaller quantities. By stocking an assortment of products, wholesalers match products to demand.

wholesalers intermediaries who buy from producers or from other wholesalers and sell to retailers

> **"Although it is true that** wholesalers can be eliminated, **their functions must be** passed on to some other entity, **such as the producer, another intermediary, or even the customer."**

Table 12.4 Major Wholesaling Functions

Supply Chain Management	Creating Long-Term Partnerships Among Channel Members
Promotion	Providing a sales force, advertising, sales promotion, and publicity
Warehousing, shipping, and product handling	Receiving, storing, and stockkeeping
	Packaging
	Shipping outgoing orders
	Materials handling
	Arranging and making local and long-distance shipments
Inventory control and data processing	Processing orders
	Controlling physical inventory
	Recording transactions
	Tracking sales data for financial analysis
Risk taking	Assuming responsibility for theft, product obsolescence, and excess inventories
Financing and budgeting	Extending credit
	Making capital investments
	Forecasting cash flow
Marketing research and information systems	Providing information about market
	Conducting research studies
	Managing computer networks to facilitate exchanges and relationships

Source: William M. Pride and O. C. Ferrell, *Marketing: Concepts and Strategies, 2008*, p. 389. Copyright 2008 by Houghton Mifflin Company. Reprinted with permission.

Supply Chain Management. In an effort to improve distribution channel relationships among manufacturers and other channel intermediaries, supply chain management creates alliances between channel members. In Chapter 8, we defined *supply chain management* as connecting and integrating all parties or members of the distribution system to satisfy customers. It involves long-term partnerships among marketing channel members working together to reduce costs, waste, and unnecessary movement in the entire marketing channel in order to satisfy customers.[57] It goes beyond traditional channel members (producers, wholesalers, retailers, customers) to include *all* organizations involved in moving products from the producer to the ultimate customer. In a survey of business managers, a disruption in the supply chain was viewed as the number-one crisis that could decrease revenue.[58]

The focus shifts from one of selling to the next level in the channel to one of selling products *through* the channel to a satisfied ultimate customer. Information, once provided on a guarded, "as needed" basis, is now open, honest, and ongoing. Perhaps most importantly, the points of contact in the relationship expand from one-on-one at the salesperson–buyer level to multiple interfaces at all levels and in all functional areas of the various organizations.

Channels for Consumer Products. Typical marketing channels for consumer products are shown in Figure 12.4. In Channel A, the product moves from the producer directly to the consumer. Farmers who sell their fruit and vegetables to consumers at roadside stands use a direct-from-producer-to-consumer marketing channel.

In Channel B, the product goes from producer to retailer to consumer. This type of channel is used for products such as textbooks, automobiles, and appliances. In Channel C, the product is handled by a wholesaler and a retailer before it reaches the consumer. Producer-to-wholesaler-to-retailer-to-consumer marketing channels distribute a wide range of products including refrigerators, televisions, soft drinks, cigarettes, clocks, watches, and office products. In Channel D, the product goes to an agent, a wholesaler, and a retailer before going to the consumer. This long channel of distribution is especially useful for convenience products. Candy and some produce are often sold by agents who bring buyers and sellers together.

Services are usually distributed through direct marketing channels because they are generally produced *and*

Figure 12.4 Marketing Channels for Consumer Products

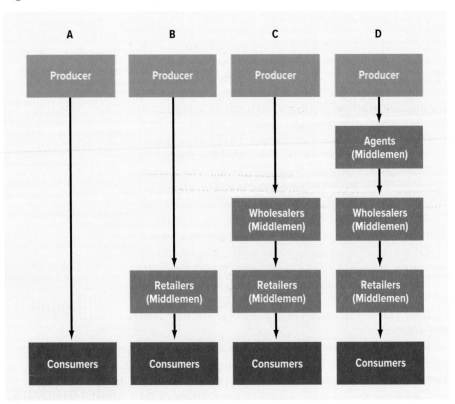

consumed simultaneously. For example, you cannot take a haircut home for later use. Many services require the customer's presence and participation: The sick patient must visit the physician to receive treatment; the child must be at the daycare centre to receive care; the tourist must be present to sightsee and consume tourism services.

Channels for Business Products. In contrast to consumer goods, more than half of all business products, especially expensive equipment or technically complex products, are sold through direct marketing channels. Business customers like to communicate directly with producers of such products to gain the technical assistance and personal assurances that only the producer can offer. For this reason, business buyers prefer to purchase expensive and highly complex mainframe computers directly from Dell, HP, and other mainframe producers. Other business products may be distributed through channels employing wholesaling intermediaries such as industrial distributors and/or manufacturer's agents.

Intensity of Market Coverage

A major distribution decision is how widely to distribute a product—that is, how many and what type of outlets should carry it. The intensity of market coverage depends on buyer behaviour, as well as the nature of the target market and the competition. Wholesalers and retailers provide various intensities of market coverage and must be selected carefully to ensure success. Market coverage may be intensive, selective, or exclusive.

Intensive distribution makes a product available in as many outlets as possible. Because availability is important to purchasers of convenience products such as bread, milk, gasoline, soft drinks, and chewing gum, a nearby location with a minimum of time spent searching and waiting in line is most important to the consumer. To saturate markets intensively, wholesalers and many varied retailers try to make the product available at every location where a consumer might desire to purchase it. For example, to market its one-time-use Max cameras, Eastman Kodak rolled out 10,000 climate-controlled, Internet-connected vending machines. The machines allow credit card transactions and are refrigerated to protect the film. The vending machine's Internet connection allows Kodak to know who bought each camera, where customers live, the specific location of the machine, and the machine's inventory level. The machines are found at zoos, stadiums, parks, hotels, and resorts—all places where consumers typically desire a single-use camera.[59]

Selective distribution uses only a small number of all available outlets to expose products. It is used

Top to bottom: © Jeff Greenberg/Alamy, © Lars Niki

Most consumer packaged goods companies, such as Pepsi, strive for intensive distribution—they want to be everywhere. But many cosmetics firms use an exclusive distribution strategy by limiting their distribution to a few select, higher-end retailers in each region.

most often for products that consumers buy only after shopping and comparing price, quality, and style. Many products sold on a selective basis require salesperson assistance, technical advice, warranties, or repair service to maintain consumer satisfaction. Typical products include automobiles, major appliances, clothes, and furniture.

Exclusive distribution exists when a manufacturer gives an intermediary the sole right to sell a product in a defined geographic territory. Such exclusivity provides an incentive for a dealer to handle a product that has a limited market. Exclusive distribution is the opposite of intensive distribution in that products are purchased and consumed over a long period of time, and service or information is required to develop a satisfactory sales relationship. Products distributed on an exclusive basis include high-quality musical instruments, yachts, airplanes, and high-fashion leather goods.

intensive distribution a form of market coverage whereby a product is made available in as many outlets as possible

selective distribution a form of market coverage whereby only a small number of all available outlets are used to expose products

exclusive distribution the awarding by a manufacturer to an intermediary of the sole right to sell a product in a defined geographic territory

Physical Distribution

Physical distribution includes all the activities necessary to move products from producers to customers—inventory control, transportation, warehousing, and materials handling. Physical distribution creates time and place utility by making products available when they are wanted, with adequate service and at minimum cost. Walter Hachborn, president of Home Hardware, says that the firm's distribution system is one characteristic that allows it to compete against much larger firms such as Home Depot and RONA. "We have four warehouses across Canada. We likely have one of the most efficient hardware packing and shipping operations in the world."[60] Both goods and services require physical distribution. Many physical distribution activities are part of supply chain management, which we discussed in Chapter 8; we'll take a brief look at a few more now.

physical distribution
all the activities necessary to move products from producers to customers—inventory control, transportation, warehousing, and materials handling

transportation
the shipment of products to buyers

Transportation. **Transportation**, the shipment of products to buyers, creates time and place utility for products, and thus is a key element in the flow of goods and services from producer to consumer. The five major modes of transportation used to move products between cities in Canada are railways, motor vehicles, inland waterways, pipelines, and airways.

Railroads offer the least expensive transportation for many products. Heavy commodities, foodstuffs, raw materials, and coal are examples of products carried by railroads. Trucks have greater flexibility than railroads because they can reach more locations. Trucks handle freight quickly and economically, offer door-to-door service, and are more flexible in their packaging requirements than are ships or airplanes. Air transport offers speed and a high degree of dependability but is the most expensive means of transportation; shipping is the least expensive and slowest form. Pipelines are used to transport petroleum, natural gas, semi-liquid coal, wood chips, and certain chemicals. Many products can be moved most efficiently by using more than one mode of transportation.

Factors affecting the selection of a mode of transportation include cost, capability to handle the product, reliability, and availability, and, as suggested, selecting transportation modes requires trade-offs. Unique characteristics of the product and consumer desires often determine the mode selected.

Warehousing. **Warehousing** is the design and operation of facilities to receive, store, and ship products. A warehouse facility receives, identifies, sorts, and dispatches goods to storage; stores them; recalls, selects, or picks goods; assembles the shipment; and finally, dispatches the shipment.

warehousing the design and operation of facilities to receive, store, and ship products

Companies often own and operate their own private warehouses that store, handle, and move their own products. They can also rent storage and related physical distribution services from public warehouses. Regardless of whether a private or a public warehouse is used, warehousing is important because it makes products available for shipment to match demand at different geographic locations.

ENTREPRENEURSHIP IN ACTION | Online Garage Sale App Competes with Kijiji and Craigslist

Carl Mercier and Tami Zuckerman

Business: VarageSale

Founded: 2012

Success: VarageSale, which started as a home-based business in Montreal, has over a million members in four different countries and recently raised $34 million in venture capital from Sequoia Capital and Lightspeed Venture Partners.[61]

Tami Zuckerman was trying to sell used items online and was frustrated with the lack of a user-friendly app. Zuckerman noted that the apps and online sites such as Kijiji were difficult to use, and rather than sell or buy items from people in your community, you were often left dealing with anonymous strangers. At her request, her husband Carl Mercier, a programmer, created varagesale.com, a site similar to Kijiji and Craigslist but with some significant differences. First and foremost, the app was built to work seamlessly with mobile devices, thus making the buying and selling of goods easier. The second significant difference is that users had to be approved prior to joining the site by submitting their real names and addresses. VarageSale then assigns participants to online communities based on their geographic location. The end result is people are often buying and selling goods from their neighbours rather than strangers, making the process safer.[62] The ideas has taken off, and VarageSale now has over one million registered users and recently received $34 million in funding to fuel growth.[63]

Materials Handling. **Materials handling** is the physical handling and movement of products in warehousing and transportation. Handling processes may vary significantly due to product characteristics. Efficient materials-handling procedures increase a warehouse's useful capacity and improve customer service. Well-coordinated loading and movement systems increase efficiency and reduce costs.

materials handling the physical handling and movement of products in warehousing and transportation

Importance of Distribution in a Marketing Strategy

Distribution decisions are among the least flexible marketing mix decisions. Products can be changed over time; prices can be changed quickly; and promotion is usually changed regularly. But distribution decisions often commit resources and establish contractual relationships that are difficult if not impossible to change. As a company attempts to expand into new markets, it may require a complete change in distribution. Moreover, if a firm does not manage its marketing channel in the most efficient manner and provide the best service, then a new competitor will evolve to create a more effective distribution system.

Promotion Strategy

LO4 Specify the activities involved in promotion, as well as promotional strategies and promotional positioning.

The role of promotion is to communicate with individuals, groups, and organizations to facilitate an exchange directly or indirectly. It encourages marketing exchanges by attempting to persuade individuals, groups, and organizations to accept goods, services, and ideas. Promotion is used not only to sell products but also to influence opinions and attitudes toward an organization, person, or cause. The province of Prince Edward Island, for example, has successfully used promotion to educate potential tourists about beautiful beaches and golf courses on the island. The provincial tourism board and the Atlantic Canada Opportunities Agency spent $1 million to bring popular daytime television personalities Regis Philbin and Kelly Ripa to host their show *Live!* from the island for three days. On day one of the show, Prince Edward Island skyrocketed to the number two spot on Google search in the United States.[64] Most people probably equate promotion with advertising, but it also includes personal selling, publicity, and sales promotion. The role that these elements play in a marketing strategy is extremely important.

The Promotion Mix

Advertising, personal selling, publicity, and sales promotion are collectively known as the promotion mix because a strong promotion program results from the careful selection and blending of these elements. The process of coordinating the promotion mix elements and synchronizing promotion as a unified effort is called **integrated marketing communications**. When planning promotional activities, an integrated marketing communications approach results in the desired message for customers. Different elements of the promotion mix are coordinated to play their appropriate roles in delivery of the message on a consistent basis. For example, RBC uses TV commercials, social media, Internet marketing, and publicity to reach its target market. The main components of a promotional campaign include:

integrated marketing communications coordinating the promotion mix elements and synchronizing promotion as a unified effort

advertising a paid form of non-personal communication transmitted through a mass medium, such as television commercials or magazine advertisements

1. *Determine objectives.* What are you hoping to accomplish? Objectives must be quantifiable so that they are measurable. Examples include "Increase sales by 2 percent," "Generate 20 leads," "Increase website traffic," and so on.

2. *Define customers.* Whom are you targeting? Are you targeting new customers, current customers, frequent shoppers, holiday shoppers, or some other group?

3. *Determine benchmarks.* Establish measures/controls to measure the effectiveness of a promotion, such as the number of website hits, sales figures, information requests, and so on.

4. *Get the message out.* Determine the method including what you will say to your audience and medium to use: the Internet, TV, radio, direct mail, or some other.

5. *Implement the plan.*

6. *Evaluate the plan.* Look at the controls that you have established and determine if the plan has been successful.

Advertising. Perhaps the best-known form of promotion, **advertising** is a paid form of non-personal communication transmitted through a mass medium, such as television commercials, magazine advertisements, or online ads. Commercials featuring celebrities, customers, or unique creations (baby animals for Telus or the Tim Hortons commercials with Sidney Crosby) serve to grab viewers' attention and pique their interest in a product. Advertisers are doing more and more to make their advertising stand out. Examples include Red Bull with the tag line "Red Bull Gives You Wings," and Molson beer and Coca-Cola, which rely on making emotional appeals to

© Foto by M/Shutterstock.com

To convince consumers that the S60 model is both safe and sporty, Volvo used an integrated marketing communication program that included print and broadcast advertising as well as new communication technologies such as social media.

Canadians by using advertisements that highlight national pride and hockey. During the NHL lockout, both Bauer with its "Own the Moment" advertisements and Nike's "Hockey is Ours" marketing campaign, which went viral, used emotional pitches to connect to viewers. Table 12.5 shows companies that spent between $2 billion and $4 billion on ads in North America in one year.

An **advertising campaign** involves designing a series of advertisements and placing them in various media to reach a particular target audience. The basic content and form of an advertising campaign are a function of several factors. A product's features, uses, and benefits affect the content of the campaign message and individual ads. Characteristics of the people in the target audience—gender, age, education, race, income, occupation, lifestyle, and

advertising campaign
designing a series of advertisements and placing them in various media to reach a particular target market

Table 12.5 Top Ten Leading North American Advertisers

Organization	Advertising Expenditures ($ Millions)
1. General Motors	3,997
2. Procter & Gamble	3,920
3. Time Warner	3,283
4. Pfizer	2,957
5. SBC Communications	2,687
6. DaimlerChrysler	2,462
7. Ford Motor Co.	2,458
8. Walt Disney Co.	2,242
9. Verizon Communications	2,197
10. Johnson & Johnson	2,176

Source: "Fact Pack," 4th Annual Guide to Advertising Marketing, a supplement to Advertising Age, p. 8.

other attributes—influence both content and form. When Procter & Gamble promotes Crest toothpaste to children, the company emphasizes daily brushing and cavity control, whereas it promotes tartar control and whiter teeth when marketing to adults. To communicate effectively, advertisers use words, symbols, and illustrations that are meaningful, familiar, and attractive to people in the target audience.

An advertising campaign's objectives and platform also affect the content and form of its messages. If a firm's advertising objectives involve large sales increases, the message may include hard-hitting, high-impact language and symbols. When campaign objectives aim at increasing brand awareness, the message may use much repetition of the brand name and words and illustrations associated with it. Thus, the advertising platform is the foundation on which campaign messages are built.

Advertising media are the vehicles or forms of communication used to reach a desired audience. Print media include newspapers, magazines, direct mail, and billboards, and electronic media include television, radio, and cyber ads. Newspapers, television, and direct mail are the most widely used advertising media. According to a recent article in the Globe and Mail, advertising spending is on the rise in Canada, reaching $114 billion in 2015.[65]

Choice of media influences the content and form of the message. Effective outdoor displays and short broadcast spot announcements require concise, simple messages. Magazine and newspaper advertisements can include considerable detail and long explanations. For example, Oreck Canada, a Winnipeg-based distributor of air purifiers and vacuums, uses 2- and 30-minute infomercials to sell its products. The company attributes much of its 820 percent, five-year revenue growth to this form of promotion, which first informs consumers about these superior products and then effectively closes the sale.[66] Because several kinds of media offer geographic selectivity, a precise message can be tailored to a particular geographic section of the target audience. For example, a company advertising in *Maclean's* might decide to use one message in Ontario and another in the rest of the nation. A company may also choose to advertise in only one region. Such geographic selectivity lets a firm use the same message in different regions at different times.

"Choice of media influences the content and form of the message."

Online Marketing and Social Media. The use of online advertising is increasing as companies are attracted to its wide reach and ability to interact with customers. Businesses are also aware that Canadians are spending more time online than citizens in other countries in the world. For example, recent research revealed that Canadians are spending an average of 36.3 hours online a month, visiting on average 80 websites. Interestingly much of their time

© Tribune Content Agency LLC / Alamy Stock Photo

Companies are spending hundreds of millions of dollars sponsoring the Olympics with the hope of building emotional ties with consumers. Do you think this strategy works?

is spent on social media where Canadians spent on average the equivalent of 10,000 minutes on Facebook alone.[67] In addition to spending more time online, Canadians are following, if not leading, the global trend of accessing the Internet, especially social media sites, using mobile devices such as smartphones and tablets.[68]

"New technology, such as *behavioural tracking,* is allowing companies to track user information including demographics, location, and search terms to tailor online advertisements and target their online messages to be more effective and appealing."

Consider the Following: Sponsoring the Olympics—A Golden Promotional Strategy?

Minutes after Sidney Crosby scored the game-winning goal to capture the 2010 Olympic Gold Medal for Canada in men's hockey, a Coke commercial ran ending with the words, ". . . now they know it's our game." A scan of the audience at the championship game showed thousands of people, including many Canadian Olympic champions, cheering while they were wearing Olympic clothing branded and sold by The Bay. A short time later, television commercials by RBC, Bell, RONA, McDonald's, Loblaws, Petro-Canada, and GM appeared highlighting their support of Canada's Olympic efforts. If you were to ask Canadians on the day after the games closed who supported the 2010 Olympic Games, most would be able to name some if not all of these companies.

The major question that many executives of these companies will be asking themselves one, three, and likely several years later is whether their $100 million-plus investment was worth the money spent. Top games sponsors such as Bell Canada contributed $200 million to the games, and RBC originally committed $110 million but then increased the amount when it was given the opportunity to sponsor the Olympic Torch Relay. What executives may not want to hear is that *Forbes* magazine concluded that companies that sponsored the 2008 Summer Olympic Games in Beijing saw little long-term effect on brand loyalty. Yet others, including RBC chief brand manager Jim Little, differ: "The bank has built a huge list of potential clients, and internal surveys show branch staff feel a new sense of pride and involvement in their bank." Senior managers at The Bay are also telling a much different story. The oldest retailer in Canada, which is trying to write a comeback story of its own, has sold out of almost all of its Olympic

clothing, and has created a buzz around the company for the first time in years. Chris Staples, president of Rethink Communications in Vancouver, notes, "This is the first instance of cool stuff at The Bay that I can remember." Furthermore, a report by Charlton Strategic Research indicates that people who bought Olympic goods at The Bay are now more likely to consider making another purchase at the store. The Bay has reported that sales of Olympic apparel have exceeded expectations by 40 to 50 percent and customer numbers have doubled.

The question remains, however: Are The Bay and RBC exceptions to the rule that investing in the Olympics does not make sense, as found by *Forbes* magazine, or is the investment worth the money? In its extensive reporting on the Olympics, the *Globe and Mail* has concluded that The Bay and RBC are obvious short-term winners but have also pegged Loblaws, GM, and Petro-Canada, firms which spent $100 million plus on the 2010 games, as businesses that may have been better off investing their money elsewhere.[69]

DISCUSSION QUESTIONS

1. Do you think it was a worthwhile investment to sponsor the Olympic Games?

2. Think back to the recent Olympic Games—did any of the companies benefit after the torch went out?

3. Besides increased sales, what other benefits would a firm earn by investing in the Olympic Games?

4. If you were the CEO of a large company, would you invest in the Olympics? Why or why not?

Because Chapter 13 discusses the use of social media and digital marketing in greater detail, the coverage here will be condensed. Prior to reading Chapter 13, readers should recognize that the Internet and social media have become a vital part of most companies' integrated marketing communication plan. Online marketing is growing at a phenomenal rate in Canada, especially since consumers not only are accessing the Internet through computers but also are using smartphones and tablets to stay online when on the move. For example, 73 percent of people always have their mobile device with them, they look at their device on average 150 to 200 times a day, and they spend roughly two hours a day using their mobile device.[70] Additionally, new technology, such as *behavioural tracking*, is allowing companies to track user information including demographics, location, and search terms to tailor online advertisements and target their online messages to be more effective and appealing.

Following are some ways in which companies increase their online marketing presence:

- *Company websites:* Websites allow companies to provide stakeholders with a significant amount of information, including their entire marketing mix; provide an opportunity for people to make direct purchases; and present significant company information. The sites also allow businesses the chance to interact and communicate with customers using a variety of channels, including e-mails, reviews, and so forth. A good example of website development and operation is the Chapters/Indigo online bookstore (ChaptersIndigo.ca). The site was developed to keep current customers returning and to provide easy navigation for new visitors. The site stores customer account information to allow for easy processing of payment, provides customer reviews of text, and allows for the tracking of shipping information. In addition, the site contains a search function that allows new users to easily find what they are looking for, provides graphics so that consumers can ensure they are ordering the right material, and allows for immediate feedback so that consumers know whether their order or question has been received. The site is coordinated in both content and graphics with the other marketing divisions of the company, with the front page of the site updated on a weekly basis to draw people in and give them another reason to come back. Some companies also set up special websites to promote specials at their business or to engage consumers. When CBC was looking for a new *Hockey Night in Canada* theme song, it set up a special website that allowed visitors to pitch their ideas and to review other entrants.

- *Working with search engines (search engine optimization):* Companies want to be sure that their site will not only appear on the results page when consumers use popular search engines such as Google or Yahoo, but also that they appear in the first few results. This is referred to as *search engine optimization (SEO)*, where companies design websites using title tags (also referred to as *metatags*) that explain the intent of the website, have content pages that use words that relate to the purpose of the site, clearly link all documents, use appropriate external links, update content frequently, and have lots of pages.

- *Pay-per-click (PPC) advertising:* Businesses are now making significant use of PPC advertising. This advertising method allows firms to bid on key words or phrases relevant to their target market. Then, when a consumer enters the phrase or word in the search engine, the company will appear under the results section and their ads will appear on the side of the viewer's screen. The largest PPC advertisers are Google AdWords, Yahoo! Search Marketing, and Microsoft adCenter. For example, Prollenium Medical Technologies, an Aurora, Ontario–based manufacturer of cosmetics, purchased specific search terms using Yahoo! and Google AdWorks. The investment has paid off as the company's $2,000 per month investment has resulted in an increase from 1,000 monthly visitors to 50,000, and PPC now drives 90 percent of the company's sales.[71] The other popular form of PPC advertising is when companies place ads on websites but only have to pay for them when their ad is clicked.

- *Social media websites:* Social media sites such as Facebook, LinkedIn, and Pinterest are online communities where people can create and share information. As noted above, Canadians are spending a significant amount of time on these sites, and they are becoming increasingly important to businesses. Facebook is the third-most visited site in Canada, and worldwide boasts over 1.591 billion monthly users, of which more than 70 percent visit the site daily.[72,73] Facebook allows companies to create profiles, join online communities, send out flyers, share videos, post pictures, write blogs, encourage people to comment on their wall (bulletin board), join or create discussion groups, and advertise with banner and interactive advertisements.[74] For example, TD Bank's Facebook page alerts customers about company news and also answers customer questions posted to its wall. After the earthquake disaster in Haiti, the bank posted and e-mailed all its Facebook friends describing what the bank was doing to help.

  Facebook's targeted ads are becoming increasingly popular with businesses both large and small as they allow firms to target groups of people who are likely to be interested in their products or services. Facebook compiles data on its users, including interests, likes, and web-browsing history, and then allows companies to target groups of people who share similar interests. For example, if you have liked baby products, searched out baby information, and viewed baby-centric pages, chances are Facebook would place you in a group of people who are interested in baby products. So companies that sell baby products, such as Pampers, would buy advertising space from Facebook but the ads would appear only to groups of people who have been classified as interested in babies and baby products. Terre Bleu

© Ingram Publishing

Terre Bleu Lavender Farm used Facebook to double its visitors and triple its annual sales.

Lavender Farm, a Milton, Ontario–based tourist destination, doubled its number of visitors and tripled sales year over year using Facebook targeted ads. Ian Baird, CEO of Terre Bleu Lavender Farm, says Facebook gave him confidence to start the business, and its use helped the company stay in touch with the customers from opening day on: "Ours has been an ongoing campaign with Facebook. We used Facebook to build momentum for our farm business even before we opened, thereby creating a pre-demand for when we actually opened the farm to the public. It gave us far more confidence to invest in the business as we built the farm and helped us launch with keen customers searching us out right from day one."[75]

Facebook is also engaged in significant efforts to attract more users to its site and increase its attractiveness to businesses. Facebook is investing a substantial amount of money into Facebook Search, which allows users to search for information on the social media site. Facebook's search, unlike Google, is built to give you results directly for your search term and also results based on the context. Facebook has also created Instant Articles, an online platform that allows businesses to create professional articles and videos to distribute through various social media channels.

LinkedIn is often described as a professional Facebook site where professionals can post their résumé, network, and gather information. LinkedIn is often used by professional companies to make and maintain initial contacts with clients and to source opportunities.

Pinterest is the fastest-growing and third-largest social media website in North America. Pinterest allows users to save and manage images and video content called *pins* to an online bulletin board known as a *pinboard*. Pinboards can be themed to allow users to easily manage pins, to share their content, and to search for similar content or pins posted by other users. Users can also pin content they find on the Internet and easily upload it to their pinboard. Businesses are particularly interested in Pinterest as it allows users to create their own business page, run contests, and engage with consumers. Victoria's Secret and AMC Theatres are using Pinterest to promote their businesses and actively engage with consumers.

© Pressureua / Dreamstime.com

Social media sites have become increasingly important to companies in connecting with consumers.

- *Twitter/Tumblr/Blogs:* These are websites where people can voice their opinion on any issue that they see fit to post. Twitter is a special blogger website that limits people to messages, or "tweets," of 140 characters in length and is frequently in the top ten monthly visited websites by Canadians.[76] Tumblr, much like Twitter, is a social blogging site, though the features in Tumblr are much more advanced. Users do not have any word limits, can easily upload photos, and can manage their information using an online dashboard. Twitter, Tumblr, and other similar blogging sites allow companies to communicate with key stakeholders. Jim Estill, CEO of Symex Canada, notes that he produces a blog to stay in touch with key stakeholders.[77] Michael Jagger, president of Vancouver-based Provident Security and Event Management Corp., dedicates four hours a week to his blog and states that it is part of the company's overall marketing strategy.[78] Jagger feels that his blog allows him to build closer bonds with current customers and generate new sales. David Mandelstam, president and CEO of Markham, Ontario–based Sangoma Technologies Inc., a manufacturer of telephone hardware, takes a different approach to using blogs. His firm identified the most popular blogs on technology and sends the bloggers press releases a few days prior to releasing them to the public. Mandelstam notes that the practice costs very little and the payoff is significant. For example, on days when his firm is mentioned by a blogger it is not uncommon for the company to be contacted by four or five prospective customers and/or potential investors.[79] The advantages of blogging include low costs, ability to reach wide audiences, and ability to reach customers on a personal level.

- *YouTube:* YouTube is the second-most visited site in Canada, and it enables people and companies to share videos with millions of daily visitors. The sites allow participants to load video clips onto their websites and display them for the public to see. The videos can act as mini-commercials or infomercials for a product or service, or can be used to attract prospective employees or as a means to generate PR for your company. For example, Toronto-based I Love Rewards has a four-minute employee recruitment video on YouTube.

- *Direct e-mail to customers:* E-mail marketing has an almost unlimited number of uses and can be used to welcome customers (such as the e-mails sent to new clients from RBC CEO Gordon Nixon), encourage people to visit your website (such as the e-mails that David Reynolds sends out from his Halifax office for QuickSnap), and encourage people to buy a product or service (such as the e-mails sent out to past customers by Delta Hotels). In addition, e-mails can convert leads, provide additional information, and/or be used as a mechanism to send videos, blogs, newsletters, and podcasts. E-mails can also be used to supplement other forms of marketing, and research indicates that including e-mail as part of a direct mail campaign increases response rates by 40 percent; when used in conjunction with telemarketing the response rate jumps by 76 percent.[80] It should be noted that e-mail marketing is not spamming, a practice where companies send out e-mails to random lists of people. Rather, it is permission-based marketing.

- *Advertainments:* Advertainments are 6- to 11-minute made-for-the-Web ads. Produced, posted, and promoted by Ford, BMW, Diet Coke, and Absolut vodka, the movies feature a product as the star. One BMW movie features a man who drives difficult passengers (in one film, Madonna stars as a difficult, foul-mouthed celebrity) around in flashy BMWs and gives them the ride of their lives. The Ford advertainments feature a Ford vehicle in three different scenarios— the promise of a Ford Focus to a teenager if he can make the team; a shirtless teen boy lying on a Ford Focus, smoking and eyeing a nearby teen girl; and a young man who drives around in a Ford trying to save his goldfish.[81]

- *Banner advertisements:* Banner ads are interactive display advertising for the Internet. Just use the Internet and you will see examples of banner advertising by numerous Canadian companies such as Porter Airlines, EastLink, and many of Canada's banks. Banner ad placement has become more effective as companies are using information on consumers' Web usage to create personalized ads that people will find more appealing.

- *Online classified advertising sites:* Sites such as eBay, Kijiji, Backpage, and Craigslist are frequently used by businesses to promote and sell their products and services. eBay is one of the most commonly visited sites in the world, and many small businesses use the site for its global reach. eBay allows businesses to sell individual products as well as maintain a virtual storefront. Canadian eBay Entrepreneur of the Year in 2012, Gatineau's Jean-Francois Lapointe, successfully sells more than $1 million worth of bicycle parts on an annual basis using his digital storefront, Bhdbikestore.[82] Kijiji has become the ninth-most visited site in Canada and businesses are using the site to advertise products and services through individual postings or banner advertisements.[83] Car companies, real estate agents, and landscaping companies are frequent users of Kijiji as they find it to be highly effective in reaching consumers. For example, Chris Neville owns a landscaping business in Nova Scotia and states, "Kijiji is actually my most effective form of advertsing. I use Facebook and other forms of social media but most calls for our services come as a direct result from Kijiji."[84] Craigslist and Backpage work similarly to Kijiji and many companies are promoting their products and services using multiple sites.

- *Online games:* Many companies are delivering promotional messages during game play or sponsoring games as a way to communicate with consumers.

- *Podcasts:* These online broadcasts use audio and/or video clips that can be downloaded on a wireless device such as an iPod, an MP3 player, or a BlackBerry. Podcasts are increasing in popularity and offer businesses many of the same benefits as posting clips on YouTube or Facebook.

- Other methods of using the Internet for marketing include deal-of-the day websites such as Groupon (see below); affiliate programs where companies post information or links on other companies' sites and do the same in turn; Webinars, which are Web-based seminars where you can engage in a full sales pitch with a customer regardless of their location; online newsletters; contributing to online bulletin boards/message boards; and posting to live online chat rooms.

Mobile Marketing. **Mobile marketing** is the use of a mobile device to communicate marketing messages. Given the growth in mobile device usage, especially globally, mobile marketing is expected to grow significantly in coming years. While mobile devices, in particular their Web browsers, can be used for many of the activities discussed above, such as searching the Internet and using social media, this section of the chapter is going to discuss mobile marketing methods that can be used primarily on mobile devices. The most common mobile marketing methods are as follows:

mobile marketing using a mobile device to communicate marketing messages

- *Apps or applications:* Companies are now creating applications, or as they are better known, "apps," to be used on smartphones and mobile devices. Given that Canadians are spending more time using apps than watching television one can expect the importance of apps to grow steadily in the next few years.[85] For example, Yellow Pages offers apps for both the iPhone and BlackBerry where customers can look up addresses, read reviews, and even receive information on discounts. The Score has been a first mover in apps marketing. Their app allows viewers to receive stats, blogs, sports headlines, and real-time updates. CIBC, the first Canadian bank to develop an app, allows customers to complete most of their daily banking on their smartphone and ties into the smartphone's GPS capabilities to assist customers in finding the nearest bank. The use of apps are certainly not limited to large businesses however. Checkout 51, is a Canadian coupon app that was created by young entrepreneurs Noah Godfrey, Pema Hegan and Andrew McGrath. The app provides consumers with online coupons that are updated on a regular basis. Rather than redeem the coupons in stores, consumers take a picture of the receipt showing they bought the item and submit the image through their mobile device. When consumers accumulate at least $20 in savings, they can request a cheque.[86]

- *Text/SMS/MMS messages:* Many companies use smartphones to send quick messages to potential customers. For example, at a recent Youth World Beach Volleyball Championship in Halifax, one of the alcoholic beverage sponsors used text messages to alert people about drink specials and opportunities to win prizes. As text messages are normally read within four minutes of receipt, customers are likely to receive them and respond. MMS messaging is also used to send pictures and videos to further engage consumers.

- *QR codes:* These are block bar codes that link print and other forms of media advertising to websites using a mobile device that scans and reads the code. QR codes have become increasingly popular as companies can add them to virtually any form of advertising, and consumers can use them to link to additional information. One recent study found that 6.2 percent (or 14 million) of mobile users in the U.S. clicked on a QR code in one month alone. The advertisements with the highest click rates are most often printed in magazines and newspapers.[87] Store owners are also using them at the entrance of their stores to entice people in by offering coupons, links to food items, and additional information that consumers will find attractive.

- *Proximity/location-based marketing:* Software embedded or downloaded in a mobile device can allow companies to send out real-time advertising and communication to potential customers when they are in close proximity to a business. For example, restaurants located on Spring Garden Road in Halifax, Nova Scotia, would be able to send ads, menus, and/or coupons to potential customers—pedestrians walking in the area—via their mobile device. For example, skin care retailer Kiehls, with locations throughout North America, recently engaged in a proximity-based mobile marketing campaign. Kiehls first ran in-store and online promotions

© Vincenzo Lombardo/Getty Images

Businesses are using QR codes like this one to allow consumers to link to additional corporate or product information.

motivating consumers to opt into receiving text messages from the company. The company then sent both SMS and MMS text messages to customers based on their proximity to stores. The result was 73 percent of customers who received messages made a purchase as a direct result of the campaign.[88]

Personal Selling. Personal selling is direct, two-way communication with buyers and potential buyers. For many products—especially large, expensive ones with specialized uses, such as cars, appliances, and houses—interaction between a salesperson and the customer is probably the most important promotional tool. Robert Herjavec, founder of The Herjavec Group and former panelist on *Dragons' Den*, states that the key to building successful firms is to develop a culture that focuses on sales. Herjavec's IT company has amassed millions in sales by having all employees, whether they be front-line workers or salespeople, focus on sales.[89]

personal selling direct, two-way communication with buyers and potential buyers

Personal selling is the most flexible of the promotional methods because it gives marketers the greatest opportunity to communicate specific information that might trigger a purchase. Only personal selling can zero in on a prospect and attempt to persuade that person to make a purchase. Although personal selling has a lot of advantages, it is one of the most costly forms of promotion. A sales call on an industrial customer can cost as much as $200 or $300. One Canadian firm that has mastered personal selling is Rebecca MacDonald's Energy Saving Plus Income Fund. The company allows people to lock in the price of natural gas for five years at a time using door-to-door salespeople who specialize in cold calls. MacDonald notes that training salespeople is a key to long-term success.[90]

There are three distinct categories of salespersons: order takers (for example, retail sales clerks and route salespeople), creative salespersons (for example, automobile, furniture, and insurance salespeople), and support salespersons (for example, customer educators and goodwill builders who usually do not take orders). For most of these salespeople, personal selling is a six-step process:

1. *Prospecting:* Identifying potential buyers of the product.

2. *Approaching:* Using a referral or calling on a customer without prior notice to determine interest in the product.

3. *Presenting:* Getting the prospect's attention with a product demonstration.

4. *Handling objections:* Countering reasons for not buying the product.

5. *Closing:* Asking the prospect to buy the product.

6. *Following up:* Checking customer satisfaction with the purchased product.

© mobil11 / Shutterstock.com

Red Bull has successfully used entertaining content marketing to create traffic to its website.

Content Marketing. One of the emerging trends in marketing is the creation of valuable content by companies to attract consumers to their products and further build a company's brand. Rather than focus on selling a product, the company creates either valuable or entertaining content which brings consumers back to their website on a regular basis. Content marketing campaigns have been used to 1) improve brand awareness, 2) increase traffic to a website, 3) increase the number of registered users for a website, and 4) create sales. Mint.com, an online provider of financial information for young people, effectively used content marketing to build its business. When the site was first created, it sold no products, instead publishing articles such as "How to Pay Off Your Student Loans" that site visitors found interesting. Later on, when Mint started to introduce products, it already had loyal visitors to the site who trusted the brand. Mint was ultimately so successful that Intuit eventually bought the company for $170 million.[91] Red Bull is another example of a company (see below) that embraces content marketing. Rather than creating educational information, Red Bull creates engaging and entertaining information that keeps users coming back time and time again.

Consider the Following: Examining Red Bull's Marketing Prowess

Red Bull is not meant to taste good, but to provide energy and enhance endurance. At least this was the intention of Austrian founder Dietrich Mateschitz. Indeed, while Red Bull has frequently been compared to cough syrup in tests of the product, the drink is beloved for its intense caffeine boost. Red Bull markets its $2 drink to those wanting to think and perform at top capacity. With the slogan "Red Bull gives you wings," the drink has enough caffeine to equal one cup of strong coffee and contains an amino acid called taurine. Taurine occurs naturally in meat, eggs, and human breast milk but is a questionable additive. To date, evidence of its short- and long-term impacts remain inconclusive.

Despite being dubbed "speed in a can" and "liquid cocaine," Red Bull pulled in more than $5 billion in a recent year. Its red and blue can and distinctive logo infiltrate our lives, but when and where we see them is what sets Red Bull apart. Because Red Bull is marketed as a performance enhancer, the company focuses on extreme sports and its athletes. The company's stable of roughly 500 sponsored athletes promotes the brand far more effectively than commercials and other traditional methods. For example, Red Bull offers thousands of YouTube videos of extreme sports, some of which have received millions of views. While the videos do not distinctly urge consumers to buy the product, the brand is always present. The product is rarely talked about, but the plug is always there visually. The company's online content includes shows, films, and games; it also runs a magazine called the *Red Bulletin* (published by the Red Bull Media House). Rebecca Lieb, a marketing analyst, praised Red Bull's content marketing strategy as one of the best in the industry. "Look, Red Bull has introduced its content marketing around and about the product, but it is never directly correlated to the drink itself," Lieb says. "Nobody is going to go to a website and spend 45 minutes looking at video about a drink. But Red Bull has aligned its brand unequivocally and consistently with extreme sports and action. They are number-one at creating content so engaging that consumers will spend hours with it, or at least significant minutes."[92]

DISCUSSION QUESTIONS

1. You have likely seen either intentionally or unintentionally some of Red Bull's content marketing. Were you aware that their sponsorships, online presence, and advertising were part of a content marketing strategy? What is your opinion of the company's marketing efforts?

2. What do you think are the pros and cons of content marketing?

3. Red Bull's marketing, both traditional and content-based, has become popular with people in their teens and even children. Given some of the controversy surrounding energy drinks, is it ethical for Red Bull to create videos and ads that young teens and children find appealing? Why or why not?

4. Think about your school or place of business. How could it create a content marketing campaign that would build its brand. What content could it promote and how would it distribute it to consumers?

Guerrilla Marketing. Guerrilla marketing is pursuing traditional marketing through unconventional means. Essentially, guerrilla marketing consists of attracting consumer attention to a company using unique and/or creative methods. For example, Montreal-based Lezza Distribution Inc., a high-end manufacturer of countertops and flooring surfaces, is known for its risky marketing efforts. At a recent trade show, the company had barely clothed male models serving drinks, and it has recently started hosting an annual "Seven Sins" party where there are half-naked models and strip poker. Company president Mark Hanna says, "Parties give us a chance to showcase our core values of passion, risk, and creativity and they give us a cool factor that distinguishes us from our competitors."[93] Other examples include Atlantic Lotto's introduction of the Lotto Max game. The company placed large balls onto smashed cars with the words Lotto Max printed on the balls. Other methods include contests or raffles like "Roll Up the Rim to Win"; sample giveaways—a strategy successfully used by Swiss Medica Inc., a Mississauga-based company that develops over-the-counter health food products, to compete with much larger drug companies; public demonstrations such as the ones used by Sweetpea, which used new moms as product ambassadors in Vancouver, Calgary, and Montreal to demonstrate organic frozen baby food products at local events; speaking at public events; and so forth. The difference between guerrilla marketing and publicity, which is discussed below, is that guerrilla marketing focuses on creating sales and creating awareness.

Publicity. **Publicity** is non-personal communication transmitted through the mass media. Publicity can be free or sometimes paid for directly by the firm. As already discussed, Prince Edward Island paid *Live! With Regis and Kelly* to come to the island and tape three episodes. The investment resulted in strong interest from potential tourists. Sometimes, firms won't pay the media cost for publicity, nor will they be identified as the originator of the message; instead, the message is presented in news story form. Obviously, a company can benefit from publicity by releasing to news sources newsworthy messages about the firm and its involvement with the public. Many companies have *public relations* departments to try to gain favourable publicity and minimize negative publicity for the firm.

> **publicity** non-personal communication transmitted through the mass media but not paid for directly by the firm

Although advertising and publicity are both carried by the mass media, they differ in several major ways. Advertising messages tend to be informative, persuasive, or both; publicity is mainly informative. Advertising is often designed to have an immediate impact or to provide specific information to persuade a person to act; publicity describes what a firm is doing, what products it is launching, or other newsworthy information, but seldom calls for action although action is sometimes implied or is seen by businesses and consumers as the next logical step. For example, Spin Master Toys, Canada's largest private toy company, originally did no advertising at all and relied on PR to increase brand awareness and sell products. When advertising is used, the organization must pay for media time and select the media that will best reach target audiences—this is not always the case with publicity. The mass media often willingly carry publicity because they believe it has general public interest. Advertising can be repeated a number of times; most publicity appears in the mass media once and is not repeated. One of the keys to success in generating positive PR is to create value for all participants.

Advertising, personal selling, and sales promotion are especially useful for influencing an exchange directly. Publicity is extremely important when communication focuses on a company's activities and products and is directed at interest groups, current and potential investors, regulatory agencies, and society in general. Yet, as noted above, companies do expect advertising to result in an increase in sales. Brian Scudamore, CEO of Vancouver-based 1-800-GOT-JUNK?, spent a considerable amount of time and effort getting the company onto the *Oprah* show. While this would be considered publicity, Scudamore knew that the spot would generate sales to customers and increase interest among entrepreneurs who might want to purchase a franchise. In fact, in the days after the spot on *Oprah* aired, the firm received 3,000 calls from customers—up 300 percent from usual—and 500 franchise inquiries.[94]

Linda Hipp, owner of Lija Style Inc., based in British Columbia, has been using PR since 2003. Hipp relies on PR to jumpstart sales in new markets rather than spending money on traditional advertising or a sales staff. Prior to entering a market, she blitzes local newspapers and magazines where she almost always generates some publicity with fashion writers. She then passes out free clothes to opinion leaders in the community (ambassador program) in hopes that they will promote the clothes to their colleagues and friends. Only when she establishes her company in the local market does Hipp advertise and hire a salesperson.[95]

Examples of good public relations include the following:

- Develop a press kit
- Write articles for a newspaper, newsletter, or community guide
- Write letters to the editor
- Participate in discussions either online or through traditional mediums
- Host events
- Offer services as a guest speaker

One of the keys to success in generating positive PR is to create value for all participants. Just going to a newspaper and announcing the grand opening of a store or an expansion may not be enough. Furthermore, you do not have to spend a great deal of money to generate positive PR. Publishers are interested in business events and/or ideas that are interesting to their readers.

Consider the Following: Lululemon's Unconventional Marketing

Dennis Wilson founded Vancouver-based Lululemon in 1998 as yoga began to increase in popularity across North America. Wilson opened his first store with the goal of producing products that encourage people to be active and stress free. The first store opened in Vancouver and sales immediately exceeded expectations, fuelled by the popularity of the products and growth in yoga. Today the company operates over 160 stores and sells not only yoga attire but also sports apparel.

A hallmark of the company's success is its unique promotional campaigns, which range from providing local yoga instructors with free clothing, to having customers receive discounts for engaging in wacky activities such as shopping with barely anything on. The company also relies heavily on the Internet and buzz from social media to promote its products. Former CEO Christine Day describes the company's marketing as selling in the moment without the aid of large promotions as, "Our number one goal is to sell to customers where they are at. . . . We don't do gift-giving and we don't do, like, special promotions, discounts, whatever. That's not our MO, and we don't do big." The company also doesn't engage in market research. Rather, it relies on employees to gather information on customers and Lululemon pays close attention to customer feedback on chalkboards in stores. Unconventional marketing appears to be working as Interbrand recently concluded that Lululemon was the fastest-growing brand of the year as it has increased in value 292 percent to $3.24 billion.[96] Much like anything in life, if you do things unconventionally you are going to get some negative feedback, and Lululemon is no exception.[97] For example, during the 2010 Vancouver Olympic games, Lululemon received some negative reaction to its "Cool Sporting Event That Takes Place in British Columbia Between 2009 & 2011 Edition" promotional campaign for its *Cheer Gear*, which included mitts, toques, and jackets. The company did not sponsor the games and is technically not allowed to use the word *Olympic* in its

© Eric Broder Van Dyke/Shutterstock.com

Lululemon has built a brand by engaging in non-conventional sales techniques.

promotional efforts. Officials at the 2010 Vancouver games felt that while Lulelemon did not break the law, the company did not follow its spirit, noting the games would not be possible without official sponsors and many paid over $100 million to be associated with the 2010 games.[98]

DISCUSSION QUESTIONS

1. What are the pros and cons of using unconventional marketing campaigns?

2. Do you think customers know that their feedback to employees and on in-store chalkboards is impacting company decisions? Would they appreciate this or feel that to some extent their privacy is being violated?

3. Do you think Lulelemon should have produced and sold *Cheer Gear*? Why or why not?

4. What are the long-term consequences to the Olympics if companies produce and sell merchandise without paying any sponsorship dollars?

Sales Promotion. **Sales promotion** involves direct inducements offering added value or some other incentive for buyers to enter into an exchange. The major tools of sales promotion are store displays, premiums, samples and demonstrations, coupons, contests and sweepstakes, refunds, and trade shows. Distribution of coupons increased 10 percent in recent years to more than 3.2 billion coupons, which save Canadians approximately $120 million a year.

sales promotion direct inducements offering added value or some other incentive for buyers to enter into an exchange

About 88 percent of these coupons were distributed via weekend newspapers.[99] Recently, online deal-of-the day websites, such as Groupon, have been promoting coupons, that will be redeemable only if sales targets are achieved. Consumers who want to purchase the deal will often share information about the coupon with their friends using social media. Companies are taking advantage of these deal-of-the-day sites as they often expose their business to new customers and lower customer acquisition costs. Additionally, businesses don't pay an upfront fee to participate and they can limit how many coupons are sold. One of the challenges of deal-of-the-day sites is the deep discounts companies are expected to offer consumers in order to participate. The normal discount on Groupon is 50 percent off the purchase price, so a $100 lawn care service would be sold for $50. Groupon normally charges 50 percent of the deal's sale price, meaning in this example they would charge the business $25, leaving the business to perform $100 worth of service for $25.

Sales promotion stimulates customer purchasing and increases dealer effectiveness in selling products. It is used to enhance and supplement other forms of promotion. Test drives allow salespersons to demonstrate vehicles, which can help purchase decisions. Sampling a product may also encourage consumers to buy. PepsiCo, for example, used sampling to promote its Sierra Mist soft drink to reach more than 5 million potential consumers at well-travelled sites such as Times Square and Penn Station.[100] In a given year, almost three-fourths of consumer product companies may use sampling.

Sales promotions are generally easier to measure and less expensive than advertising. Although less than 2 percent of the 3.2 billion coupons distributed annually are redeemed, offering them in weekend paper inserts is cheaper than producing a television commercial.

Promotion Strategies: To Push or to Pull

In developing a promotion mix, organizations must decide whether to fashion a mix that pushes or pulls the product (Figure 12.5). A **push strategy** attempts to motivate intermediaries to push the product down to their customers. When a push strategy is used, the company attempts to motivate wholesalers and retailers to make the product available to their customers. Sales personnel may be used to persuade intermediaries to offer the product, distribute promotional materials, and offer special promotional incentives for those who agree to carry the product. A great example of using successful push strategies comes from Jewel Pop, a Dartmouth, Nova Scotia–based jewellery company that recently reached $3 million in sales. Company founder and president Robert Smith developed a Kameleon jewellery line where beads and silver rings are interchangeable, allowing customers to intermingle and colour-coordinate their outfits and jewellery. After taking samples of the

push strategy an attempt to motivate intermediaries to push the product down to their customers

product to an Atlanta gift show, Smith found a number of retailers that were willing to sell the product. But Smith, who has years of experience in the jewellery industry, knows that retailers may offer to sell a product but not push it onto the customers. Smith then devised an incentive plan providing retailers with exclusive territories, free shipping, and other bonuses to push the unique jewellery onto their customers. The strategy is working as Smith notes that some independent retailers are selling in excess of $100,000 a year in jewellery and he hopes to reach $100 million in sales in the next five to six years.[101] On a much larger scale, BlackBerry owes much of its success to its ability to create relationships with national carriers and dealers who in turn push the product onto their customers. BlackBerry provides carriers with unique designs that they can call their own and assists in managing traffic and security on the carrier's network to keep it from overflowing. Chrysler manufacturing plants operate on a push system. They assemble cars according to forecasts of sales demand. Dealers then sell to buyers with the help of incentives and other promotions.[102]

A **pull strategy** uses promotion to create consumer demand for a product so that consumers exert pressure on marketing channel members to make it available. For example, when the Coca-Cola Company launched its new hybrid energy soda VAULT, the company gave away samples throughout the United States via sampling teams in VAULT-branded International CXTs, the world's largest production pickup trucks. They distributed ice-cold VAULT at concerts and targeted retail outlets, sporting events, and other locations.[103] Such sampling prior to a product roll-out

pull strategy the use of promotion to create consumer demand for a product so that consumers exert pressure on marketing channel members to make it available

Figure 12.5 Push and Pull Strategies

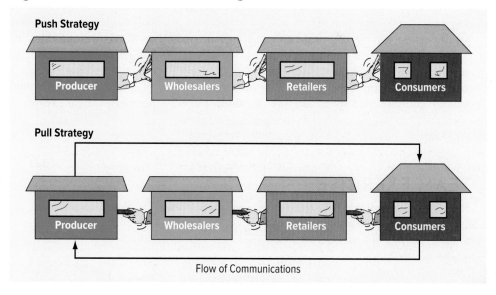

Flow of Communications

encourages consumers to request the product from their favourite retailer.

A company can use either strategy, or it can use a variation or combination of the two. The exclusive use of advertising indicates a pull strategy. Personal selling to marketing channel members indicates a push strategy. The allocation of promotional resources to various marketing mix elements probably determines which strategy a marketer uses.

Objectives of Promotion

The marketing mix a company uses depends on its objectives. It is important to recognize that promotion is only one element of the marketing strategy and must be tied carefully to the goals of the firm, its overall marketing objectives, and the other elements of the marketing strategy. Firms use promotion for many reasons, but typical objectives are to stimulate demand, to stabilize sales, and to inform, remind, and reinforce customers. For example, Tim Hortons will advertise in Canada to stimulate demand at certain times of the year, but it will also advertise to remind consumers and Canadians that Tim Hortons is a national brand in the country.

Increasing demand for a product is probably the most typical promotional objective. Stimulating demand, often through advertising and sales promotion, is particularly important when a firm is using a pull strategy.

Another goal of promotion is to stabilize sales by maintaining the status quo—that is, the current sales level of the product. During periods of slack or decreasing sales, contests, prizes, vacations, and other sales promotions are sometimes offered to customers to maintain sales goals. Advertising is often used to stabilize sales by making customers aware of slack use periods. For example, both Air Canada and WestJet use Internet advertising to promote air travel and vacation specials during slow times of the year. During the 2014 Olympics, Air Canada announced a new special the day after any Canadian gold medal—most of which were aimed at increasing sales during traditionally slow periods.

An important role of any promotional program is to inform potential buyers about the organization and its products. A major portion of advertising in Canada, particularly in daily newspapers, is informational. Providing information about the availability, price,

technology, and features of a product is very important in encouraging a buyer to move toward a purchase decision. Nearly all forms of promotion involve an attempt to help consumers learn more about a product and a company.

Promotion is also used to remind consumers that an established organization is still around and sells certain products that have uses and benefits. Often advertising reminds customers that they may need to use a product more frequently or in certain situations. Canadian Tire, for example, has used a variety of promotions reminding car owners that they need to change their oil every 5,000 kilometres to ensure proper performance of their cars.

Reinforcement promotion attempts to assure current users of the product that they have made the right choice and tells them how to get the most satisfaction from the product. Also, a company could release publicity statements through the news media about a new use for a product. Additionally, firms can have salespeople communicate with current and potential customers about the proper use and maintenance of a product—all in the hope of developing a repeat customer.

Promotional Positioning

Promotional positioning uses promotion to create and maintain an image of a product in buyers' minds. It is a natural result of market segmentation. In both promotional positioning and market segmentation, the firm targets a given product or brand at a portion of the total market.

> **promotional positioning**
> the use of promotion to create and maintain an image of a product in buyers' minds

A promotional strategy helps differentiate the product and make it appeal to a particular market segment. For example, VIA Rail advertises ease of boarding and comfort to appeal to consumers who want the freedom to move about as they travel and others who do not want the long security check-ins that are common at airports. Volvo heavily promotes the safety and crashworthiness of Volvo automobiles in its advertising. Volkswagen has done the same thing with its edgy ads showing car crashes. Promotion can be used to change or reinforce an image. Effective promotion influences customers and persuades them to buy.

TEAM EXERCISE

Form groups and search for examples of convenience products, shopping products, specialty products, and business products. How are these products marketed? Provide examples of any ads that you can find to show examples of the promotional strategies for these products. Report your findings to the class.

LEARNING OBJECTIVES SUMMARY

LO1 Describe the role of product in the marketing mix, including how products are developed, classified, and identified.

Products (goods, services, ideas) are among a firm's most visible contacts with consumers and must meet consumers' needs and expectations to ensure success. New product development is a multi-step process: idea development, the screening of new ideas, business analysis, product development, test marketing, and commercialization. Products are usually classified as either consumer or industrial products. Consumer products can be further classified as convenience, shopping, or specialty products. The industrial product classifications are raw materials, major equipment, accessory equipment, component parts, processed materials, supplies and industrial services. Products also can be classified by the stage of the product life cycle (introduction, growth, maturity and decline). Identifying products includes branding (the process of naming and identifying products); packaging (the product's container); and labelling (information, such as content and warnings, on the package).

LO2 Define price and discuss its importance in the marketing mix, including various pricing strategies a firm might employ.

Price is the value placed on an object exchanged between a buyer and a seller, and is probably the most flexible variable of the marketing mix. Pricing objectives include survival, maximization of profits and sales volume, and maintaining the status quo. When a firm introduces a new product, it may use price skimming or penetration pricing. Psychological pricing and price discounting are other strategies.

LO3 Identify factors affecting distribution decisions, such as marketing channels and intensity of market coverage.

Making products available to customers is facilitated by intermediaries who bridge the gap between the producer of the product and its ultimate user. A marketing channel is a group of marketing organizations that direct the flow of products from producers to consumers. Market coverage relates to the number and variety of outlets that make products available to the customers; it may be intensive, selective, or exclusive. Physical distribution is all the activities necessary to move products from producers to consumers, including inventory planning and control, transportation, warehousing, and materials handling.

LO4 Specify the activities involved in promotion, as well as promotional strategies and promotional positioning.

Promotion encourages marketing exchanges by persuading individuals, groups and organizations to accept advertising (a paid form of non-personal communication transmitted through a mass medium); personal selling (direct, two-way communication with buyers and potential buyers); publicity (non-personal communication transmitted through mass media but not paid for directly by the firm); and sales promotion (direct inducements offering added value or some other incentive for buyers to enter into an exchange). A push strategy attempts to motivate intermediaries to push the product down to their customers, whereas a pull strategy tries to create consumer demand for a product so that consumers exert pressure on marketing channel members to make the product available. Typical promotion objectives are to stimulate demand, stabilize sales, and inform, remind, and reinforce customers. Promotional positioning is the use of promotion to create and maintain in the buyer's mind an image of the product.

KEY TERMS

advertising
advertising campaign
branding
business products
commercialization
consumer products
discounts
exclusive distribution

generic products
integrated marketing communications
intensive distribution
labelling
manufacturer brands
marketing channel
materials handling
mobile marketing

packaging
penetration price
personal selling
physical distribution
price skimming
private distributor brands
product line
product mix
promotional positioning
psychological pricing
publicity

pull strategy
push strategy
quality
retailers
sales promotion
selective distribution
test marketing
trademark
transportation
warehousing
wholesalers

DESTINATION CEO DISCUSSION QUESTIONS

1. Have you heard of Shopify? Were you surprised to learn that a Canadian company was powering so many online stores and websites? Should Shopify promote its brand to the average consumer? Why or why not?

2. Tobias Lütke decided to charge for his product rather than allow companies to initially access Shopify for free. Most Internet companies normally offer their product for free or on a trial basis prior to charging a fee. What are the pros and cons of charging for a product right away?

3. Lütke's business is increasingly attracting larger companies that have highly specialized needs. This raises the possibility that Shopify could move away from its roots of helping small firms sell online? What are the pros and cons of such a change?

SO YOU WANT TO BE *a Marketing Manager*

Many jobs in marketing are closely tied to the marketing mix functions: distribution, product, promotion, and price. Often the job titles could be sales manager, distribution or supply chain manager, advertising account executive, or store manager.

A distribution manager arranges for transportation of goods within firms and through marketing channels. Transportation can be costly, and time is always an important factor, so minimizing their effects is vital to the success of a firm. Distribution managers must choose one or a combination of transportation modes from a vast array of options, taking into account local, federal, and international regulations for different freight classifications; the weight, size, and fragility of products to be shipped; time schedules; and loss and damage ratios. Manufacturing firms are the largest employers of distribution managers.

A product manager is responsible for the success or failure of a product line. This requires a general knowledge of advertising, transportation modes, inventory control, selling and sales management, promotion, marketing research, packaging, and pricing. Frequently, several years of selling and sales management experience are prerequisites for such a position as well as college training in business administration. Being a product manager can be rewarding both financially and psychologically.

Some of the most creative roles in the business world are in the area of advertising. Advertising pervades our daily lives, as businesses and other organizations try to grab our attention and tell us about what they have to offer. Copywriters, artists, and account executives in advertising must have creativity, imagination, artistic talent, and expertise in expression and persuasion. Advertising is an area of business in which a wide variety of educational backgrounds may be useful, from degrees in advertising itself, to journalism or liberal arts degrees. Common entry-level positions in an advertising agency are found in the traffic department, account service (account coordinator), or the media department (media assistant). Advertising jobs are also available in many manufacturing or retail firms, nonprofit organizations, banks, professional associations, utility companies, and other arenas outside of an advertising agency.

Although a career in retailing may begin in sales, there is much more to retailing than simply selling. Many retail personnel occupy management positions, focusing on selecting and ordering merchandise, promotional activities, inventory control, customer credit operations, accounting, personnel, and store security. Many specific examples of retailing jobs can be found in large department stores. A section manager coordinates inventory and promotions and interacts with buyers, salespeople, and consumers. The buyer's job is fast-paced, often involving much travel and pressure. Buyers must be open-minded and forward-looking in their hunt for new, potentially successful items. Regional managers coordinate the activities of several retail stores within a specific geographic area, usually monitoring and supporting sales, promotions, and general procedures. Retail management can be exciting and challenging. Growth in retailing is expected to accompany the growth in population and is likely to create substantial opportunities in the coming years.

While a career in marketing can be very rewarding, marketers today agree that the job is getting tougher. Many advertising and marketing executives say the job has gotten much more demanding in the past ten years, viewing their number-one challenge as balancing work and personal obligations. Other challenges include staying current on industry trends or technologies, keeping motivated/inspired on the job, and measuring success. If you are up to the challenge, you may find that a career in marketing is just right for you to utilize your business knowledge while exercising your creative side as well.

BUILD YOUR BUSINESS PLAN

Dimensions of Marketing Strategy

If you think your product/business is truly new to or unique to the market, you need to substantiate your claim. After a thorough exploration on the Web, you want to make sure there has not been a similar business/service recently launched in your community. Check with your chamber of commerce or economic development office, which might be able to provide you with a history of recent business failures. If you are not confident about the ability or willingness of customers to try your new product or service, collecting your own primary data to ascertain demand is highly advisable.

The decision of where to initially set your prices is a critical one. If there are currently similar products in the market, you need to be aware of competitors' prices before you determine yours. If your product/service is new to the

market, you can price it high (market skimming strategy) as long as you realize that the high price will probably attract competitors to the market more quickly (they will think they can make the same product for less), which will force you to drop your prices sooner than you would like. Another strategy to consider is market penetration pricing, a strategy that sets prices lower and discourages competition from entering the market as quickly. Whatever strategy you decide to use, don't forget to examine your product/service's elasticity.

At this time, you need to start thinking about how to promote your product. Why do you feel your product/service is different or new to the market? How do you want to position your product/service so customers view it favourably? Remember that this is all occurring *within the consumer's mind.*

CASE | Finding the Real Green Products

What makes a green product green? This question is actually quite complicated. The growing popularity of eco-friendly products is encouraging businesses to create and sell more green items. Nancy Wright, vice-president of Vancouver's Globe Foundation, states that the green industry in Canada is flourishing as 70 percent of consumers say they are willing to spend up to 20 percent more for environmentally friendly items. She describes sales of "green" products and services as flourishing. However, some businesses are cutting corners by touting their products as green when they really aren't—a form of misconduct known as *greenwashing.* Greenwashers make

unjustifiable green claims about their products to appeal to the eco-friendly consumer. In fact, a recent study by Terra Choice Environmental Marketing found that 99.9 percent of so-called green products make false, misleading, or unsubstantiated claims. As a result, 40 percent of consumers claim that they don't know how to ensure that a company is really eco-friendly.

One common way that companies engage in greenwashing is by sustainably sourcing one product ingredient while the other ingredients remain unsustainable. This might be akin to a company claiming that its product is green since one of the ingredients is organic cotton, while simultaneously glossing over the fact that the product also consists of non-recyclable plastics or chemicals. Unfortunately, the subjective nature of greenwashing makes it harder to detect, as consumers themselves differ on what is green and what is greenwashing. For instance, the Fur Council of Canada (FCC) launched its "Fur is Green" campaign a few years ago, advocating that fur is a green product and industry that does more good for society than harm. The Fur Council of Canada maintains a website, www.FurIsGreen.com, that states, "fur is [a] natural, renewable resource . . . in nature, each plant and animal species generally produces more offspring than the land can support to maturity. Like other species, we live by making use of part of this surplus that nature creates." As a result of the campaign, companies like Canada Goose added a "Green" label to their clothing. Others, including animal rights advocates, were shocked that people would consider the fur industry to be green or eco-friendly. Other examples include the number of consumers who posted on social media sites that they felt misled by Cascade Farm's logo of a small idyllic farm after they discovered that the brand is actually owned by General Mills. Others are unconcerned as long as the brand's organic claims are true. The topic of greenwashing has become so pervasive that it is prompting government intervention. Canada's Competition Bureau, along with the Canadian Standards Association, has established standards to cut down on greenwashing, with set guidelines that prohibit vague or misleading environmental claims on products and services. Critics of the Competition Bureau note that these are not laws, only guidelines, and there is nothing to legally prevent a company from claiming a product is green. For now, consumers must investigate green claims for themselves. Such an investigation could include looking for third-party certification of a product's "greenness," paying attention to ingredient lists, and looking for information on trustworthy websites. However, until more stringent guidelines are created, the term *green* is likely to remain steeped in subjectivity.[104]

DISCUSSION QUESTIONS

1. Are you more inclined to purchase products because they are labelled as "green"? Would you pay more for such products? Why or why not?

2. Do you feel confident that you can determine if a product is really "green"?

3. Do you think the fur industry is a "green" industry? Why or why not?

4. Are you concerned whether Cascade Farms, owned by General Mills, is making valid organic claims?

5. What will happen to companies and their products if consumers find their green claims to be false?

Groupon Masters Promotion to Become a Popular Daily Deal Site

In 2008, a start-up company called Groupon launched an innovative business model. The model works in the following way: Groupon partners with businesses to offer subscribers daily deals. These deals are provided through the Groupon website, e-mail, and mobile devices. Groupon deals are similar to coupons, but with one major catch. A certain number of people (a group) must agree to purchase the deal. If enough people purchase, then the deal becomes available to everyone. If not enough people purchase, then no one receives that particular deal. In this way, Groupon has made the idea of coupons or deals into a social process.

The model quickly caught on with consumers. In many ways, Groupon lowers the risk for consumers when purchasing a new product because the product or activity costs less than its regular price. This encourages consumers to try out new activities such as skydiving or dining at a certain restaurant. Groupon also alerts consumers about deals that they were not aware of beforehand. Making consumers aware of products is one of the major purposes of promotion.

When it first started promoting Groupon deals, the company used social media sites such as Twitter and Facebook.

One of the advantages of this type of advertising is the chance for an Internet ad or posting to go viral. With just a simple click of a button, an Internet user can inform his or her friends about the deal, spreading awareness of the company or product. This word-of-mouth marketing has been proven to be one of the most effective and trusted forms of promotion.

The benefit for businesses is the possibility of attracting repeat customers. By offering deals through the Groupon site, businesses are able to get consumers into the store. If consumers have a good experience, then they might return or tell their friends about the business. Groupon therefore acts as a type of conduit that brings consumers and businesses together. Bo Hurd, national sales manager/business development, describes how this works for businesses. "We're going get the word out there, and then we're actually going to have these people decide that they want to come in and try your services. And then it's up to you to actually convert them into long-term, full-paying customers."

Because Groupon depends on businesses as much as consumers, they must get businesses to agree to offer deals through its site. Groupon engages heavily in public relations to make its name known among companies. Personal selling is also very important to Groupon's promotion mix. Groupon's sales force uses phone calls and e-mails to contact businesses in the major cities in which it does business. Because it wants to offer the best deals, Groupon will generate leads by looking at review websites such as Yelp and Citysearch. By looking at how consumers rate certain businesses, Groupon can get a better idea of which businesses to target.

The introduction of rival deal sites such as Google Offers and Living Social is requiring Groupon to continue innovating. The firm has begun to invest in new product offerings, such as Groupon Now!, which is a mobile app that provides time-specific deals to consumers based on their location at a particular moment. Each new product that Groupon introduces requires adaptations to the promotion mix. For instance, promoting Groupon Now! to businesses resulted in some challenges. At first, there were two separate sales teams: one for Groupon's daily deal service and another for Groupon Now! The problem was that both sales teams would call up the same business, essentially duplicating the sales calls and making the business feel overwhelmed. As a result, Groupon changed its structure so that now one sales representative will offer both products during the sales call. Because promotion is an easier variable to modify than distribution or product, Groupon was able to adapt part of its promotion mix to increase its effectiveness.

Groupon's ability to master different forms of promotion has contributed to its success as a company. Going forward, it will need to continue to communicate its value, particularly of its new products, to both businesses and consumers.[105]

DISCUSSION QUESTIONS

1. How has Groupon effectively used personal selling, advertising, and public relations to market its products and services?

2. Is there a difference in how Groupon markets itself to consumers versus how it markets itself to businesses? If so, describe these differences.

3. Groupon had to adapt the personal selling component of the promotion mix. Why is it sometimes necessary for businesses to adapt the promotion mix?

Arlene Dickinson

Arlene Dickinson is living proof that the Canadian dream is possible.

Dickinson, a former star of CBC's *Dragons' Den*, is also the owner of Venture Communications, one of the largest marketing and communications companies in the country. She also has an ownership stake in over 50 businesses, and has won numerous business awards, including being recognized as one of Canada's Most Powerful Women, Top 100 Hall of Fame, and *PROFIT* and *Chatelaine* magazines' Top 100 Business Owners. She was awarded the Pinnacle Award for Entrepreneurial Excellence, Ad Rodeo's Lifetime Achievement Award, and McGill University's Management Achievement Award. She was even recognized as Global Television's Woman of Vision. Today, Dickinson's net worth is estimated to be in excess of $80 million.

Dickinson immigrated to Canada with her parents who, by the time they arrived here from South Africa, only had $50 left to support the family of five. Dickinson's family struggled so much during their early years in Canada that her mother had to sell her engagement ring as their car broke down moving from Edmonton to Calgary and the family had no money to fix the car or buy a replacement. Things improved in Calgary, and Dickinson graduated from high school at the age of 16, but didn't have an interest in pursuing anything that resembled a career. Her main goal was to have a family, which started when she married at the young age of 19. Dickinson soon became a working mother, paying her husband's way through teacher's college. The marriage was very rocky, and Dickinson divorced her husband at the age at 27, leaving her with four children and no job. At this point, Dickinson had her first break when she was offered a job selling advertising for a TV station. While she had no experience in sales, she excelled at the position and spent 18 months working on what she assumed was a new career. Unfortunately, the station went through a cost-cutting program and Dickinson lost her job. One of Dickinson's co-workers had recently started a company called Venture Communications and he inquired if Dickinson would like to become a partner. According to Dickinson, becoming a partner meant working for no pay and hoping that the company became successful. Dickinson says, "I joined the company with no income and we barely scraped by the first few years living off credit cards and whatever money I could scrape together."

The partners eventually received a break. Bob Morrisette wanted a national campaign to be developed for hair salons across the country and asked Venture if they could come to Vancouver and present their ideas to 1,200 hairdressers. Describing the situation, Dickinson says, "...they (Bob Morrisette) could not pay us for the proposal...we couldn't afford to fly to Vancouver or even stay at a hotel. We flew out using points and had to sleep on a friend's boat." The day of the presentation, Dickinson's hair dryer actually stopped working and she arrived to present before 1,200 hairdressers with her hair windblown and a mess; in Dickinson's words, "I looked like Orphan Annie." But the partners did something right as the hairdressers loved their presentation and Venture Communications received its first large contract. The firm continued to grow, and in 1998 Dickinson took over as owner of the company. Today, Venture Communications is one of the largest marketing and communications firms

LEARNING OBJECTIVES

After reading this chapter, you will be able to:

LO1 Define digital media and digital marketing and recognize their increasing value in strategic planning.

LO2 Understand the characteristics of digital media and how they differentiate these methods from traditional marketing activities.

LO3 Demonstrate the role of digital marketing and social networking in today's business environment.

LO4 Show how digital media affect the marketing mix.

LO5 Define social networking and illustrate how businesses can use different types of social networking media.

LO6 Identify legal and ethical considerations in digital media.

in Canada, with estimated annual gross sales in excess of $45 million.

While on *Dragons' Den*, Dickinson founded Arlene Dickinson Enterprises, which is a venture capital firm committed to supporting entrepreneurship. Shortly afterwards, Dickenson founded YouInc.com, a website committed to promoting entrepreneurship as a lifestyle. Visitors to YouInc.com can read articles on social media promotions, share their entrepreneurship successes, and even pose questions to informal focus groups to get feedback from other entrepreneurs.

While Dickinson is considered an expert in digital media, she believes in doing business a little differently than what you may think. In today's digital world, Dickinson still wants to meet clients face-to-face; she wants to talk to them and understand not only what story they are trying to convey in their marketing plan but also their personal and business story. Dickinson states, "You still have to build relationships; you have to get to know people. E-mail is great for content but if you want to emotionally connect with clients you have to meet them. By connecting with people you can become a better storyteller and do a better job." Dickinson also believes in being nice. On *Dragons' Den*, Arlene is known to be the socially responsible and supportive Dragon. She frequently invests in companies that are developing environmentally friendly businesses and states that the way people conduct business is changing for the better. As Dickinson says, "You can be successful and nice."[1]

Introduction[2]

The Internet and information technology have dramatically changed the environment for business. Marketers' new ability to convert all types of communications into digital media has created efficient, inexpensive ways of connecting businesses and consumers and has improved the flow and the usefulness of information. Businesses have the information they need to make more informed decisions, and consumers have access to a greater variety of products and more information about choices and quality.

The defining characteristic of information technology in the twenty-first century is accelerating change. New systems and applications advance so rapidly that it is almost impossible to keep up with the latest developments. Start-up companies emerge that quickly overtake existing approaches to digital media. When Google first arrived on the scene, a number of search engines were fighting for dominance, including Excite, Infoseek, Lycos, and WebCrawler. With its fast, easy-to-use search engine, Google became number one and is now challenging many industries, including advertising, newspapers, mobile phones, and book publishing. Despite its victory, Google is constantly being challenged itself by competitors like Yahoo! and Baidu. The Chinese search engine Baidu represents a particular threat as it is the fifth-largest "pure-play" Internet company (after Google, Amazon, Tencent, and eBay) and has the majority of the Chinese Internet market. Google is also being challenged by social networks, which most observers believe will dominate digital communication in the future.[3] Today, people spend more time on social networking sites, such as Facebook, than they spend on e-mail. Facebook, in an attempt to compete directly against Google in search has actually launched Facebook Search (http://search.fb.com), which allows users to find information from social networks. Facebook's search engine not only searches for keywords but will also give you results based on the context of your search items, which is something Google does not do.

In this chapter we first provide some key definitions related to digital marketing and social networking. Next we discuss using digital media in business and marketing. We look at marketing mix considerations when using digital media and pay special attention to social networking. Then we focus on digital marketing strategies—particularly new communication channels like social networks—and consider how consumers are changing their information searches and consumption behaviour to fit emerging technologies and trends. Finally, we examine the legal and social issues associated with information technology, digital media, and e-business.

What Is Digital Marketing?

LO1 Define digital media and digital marketing and recognize their increasing value in strategic planning.

Let's start with a clear understanding of our focus in this chapter. First, we can distinguish **e-business** from traditional business by noting that conducting e-business means carrying out the goals of business through the use of the Internet. **Digital media** are electronic media that function using digital codes—when we refer to digital media, we mean media available via computers and other digital devices, including mobile and wireless ones like cellphones and smartphones.

Digital marketing uses all digital media, including the Internet and mobile and interactive channels, to develop communication and exchanges with customers. *Digital marketing* is a term we will use often because we are interested in all types of digital communications, regardless of the electronic channel that transmits the data.

e-business carrying out the goals of business through utilization of the Internet

digital media electronic media that function using digital codes via computers, cellular phones, smartphones, and other digital devices that have been released in recent years

Growth and Benefits of Digital Communication

LO2 Understand the characteristics of digital media and how they differentiate these methods from traditional marketing activities.

The Internet has created tremendous opportunities for businesses to forge relationships with consumers and business customers, target markets more precisely, and even reach previously inaccessible markets at home and around the world. The Internet also facilitates business transactions, allowing companies to network with manufacturers, wholesalers, retailers, suppliers, and outsource firms to serve customers more quickly and more efficiently. The telecommunication opportunities created by the Internet have set the stage for digital marketing's development and growth.

Digital communication offers a completely new dimension in connecting with others. Some of the characteristics that distinguish digital from traditional communication are addressability, interactivity, accessibility, connectivity, and control. Let's look at what these mean and how they enhance marketing.

The ability of a business to identify customers before they make a purchase is **addressability**. Digital media make it possible for visitors on a website like Amazon.ca and Chapters. Indigo.ca to provide information about their needs and wants before they buy. A social network such as Facebook lets users create a profile to keep in touch or to build a network of identified contacts, including friends, colleagues, and businesses. Companies such as Porter Airlines, Canada's third-largest airline, use social networks such as Facebook to announce new promotions, share company news, collect customer feedback, and answer questions. Porter uses Twitter primarily to answer questions from customers and YouTube to share videos about the company.

Interactivity allows customers to express their needs and wants directly to the firm in response to its communications. In traditional one-way forms of communication, such as television advertising, the customer must contact the company by phone or other means. Interactivity relies on digital media

that can make a conversation between the firm and the customer happen without any delay; thus, real relationships become possible. Digital media such as blogs and social networks allow marketers to engage with customers, shape their expectations and perceptions, and benefit from broader market reach at lower cost. As mentioned above, Porter Airlines uses social media sites to communicate with customers in real time. Customers can ask questions about promotions, flight times, and so forth, and Porter will respond. Other customers who may not be directly involved in the interaction can also read and benefit from the information. Ken Tencer, a branding and innovation expert, states that conversations with customers are better than a strong communication strategy. Tencer uses the example of Fluevog, a Vancouver-based specialty shoe and accessory store with 14 North American locations. According to Tencer, Fluevog's website and digital strategy have been successful because the company engages the customers and asks them to participate in a conversation about products and the brand.[5]

Accessibility allows consumers to find information about competing products, prices, and reviews and become more informed about a firm and the relative value of its products. Mobile devices—including smartphones and mobile computing devices like the iPad—allow customers to leave their desktops and access digital networks from anywhere. Thanks to the popularity of the iPhone, businesses and their customers can stay in constant touch. Benjamin Moore & Co. has an iPhone app (application) that allows customers to match anything, such as their own home-decorating colour samples and photographs, with shades of Benjamin Moore paint. Many companies are adopting a digital media philosophy of open communication with customers; for example, a firm can go to a site such as GeniusRocket.com, a marketing firm that provides customized services linking businesses with customers, to request ideas for new products.

Connectivity keeps customers, employees, and businesses connected with each other. It involves the use of digital networks to provide linkages between information providers and users. Social networking is a key form of connectivity made easier on a global scale by Facebook, LinkedIn, Twitter, Tumblr, Pinterest, and other networking sites. Facebook has a larger audience than any television network that has ever existed. Firms can also target precise markets through local social networking sites such as Orkut, a Google-owned service operating in India and Brazil.

> **DID YOU KNOW?**
>
> The average Canadian sits in front of a computer for 45.3 hours a month, taking in content from some 98 websites.[4]

digital marketing uses all digital media, including the Internet and mobile and interactive channels, to develop communication and exchanges with customers

addressability the ability of a business to identify customers before they make purchases

interactivity allows customers to express their needs and wants directly to the firm in response to its communications

accessibility allows consumers to find information about competing products, prices, and reviews and become more informed about a firm and the relative value of its products

connectivity the use of digital networks to provide linkages between information providers and users

© Robseguin/Dreamstime.com

Porter uses Facebook, Twitter, and YouTube in its digital marketing strategy. Porter's online strategy has been successful as it actively encourages consumers to ask questions and engage in conversations with the company.

control consumers' ability to regulate the information they receive via the Internet, and the rate and sequence of their exposure to that information

Control refers to consumers' ability to regulate the information they receive via the Internet, and the rate and sequence of their exposure to that information. Consumers choose the websites they view, the blogs they follow, and the social networking sites to which they belong. This trend toward a consumer-controlled market requires marketers to approach their jobs in a different way than they did in traditional marketing.

Using Digital Media in Business

LO3 Demonstrate the role of digital marketing and social networking in today's business environment.

The phenomenal growth of digital media has provided new ways of conducting business. Given almost instant communication with precisely defined consumer groups, firms can use real-time exchanges to stimulate interactive communication, forge closer relationships, and learn more accurately about consumer and supplier needs. Consider that Amazon, one of the most successful e-businesses, ranked 29th on the *Fortune* 500 list of America's largest corporations.[6] Amazon is a true global e-business, and was one of the early success stories in the industry, getting 50 percent of its revenue from international sales.[7] Many of you may not remember a world before Amazon because it has completely transformed how many people shop. Previously, consumers had to travel store to store in order to find goods and compare prices.

Because it is fast and inexpensive, digital communication is making it easier for businesses to conduct marketing research, provide and obtain price and product information, and advertise, as well as to fulfill their business goals by selling goods and services online. Even the government engages in digital marketing activities—marketing everything from bonds and other financial instruments to oil-drilling leases and surplus equipment. Lululemon uses social media—including over 1.4 million Facebook fans, 818,000 Twitter followers, almost 120,000 LinkedIn followers, hundreds of videos on YouTube, and additional presence on Tumblr, Foursquare, Instagram, Zite, and Pinterest—to create links with customers, get immediate feedback on products, and promote both products and its brand. By getting feedback online, the company can save significant time and money in determining what products are likely to appeal to different segments of the marketplace.

New businesses and even industries are evolving that would not exist without digital media. YouTube is a video website that lets consumers watch a broad collection of videos, anytime and from anywhere. In the U.S., Hulu has emerged as a site that allows users to watch videos from 260 content partners—anywhere and anytime. The company has partnered with several companies to advertise on their sites, including Johnson & Johnson and Best Buy.[8] Rumours persist that Hulu is coming to Canada in 2016 but nothing has been announced as of yet.

The reality, however, is that Internet markets are more similar to traditional markets than they are different. Thus, successful e-business strategies, like traditional business strategies, focus on creating products that customers need or want, not merely developing a brand name or reducing the costs associated with online transactions. Instead of changing all industries, e-business has had much more impact in certain industries where the cost of business and customer transactions has been very high. For example, investment trading is less expensive online because customers can buy and sell investments, such as stocks and mutual funds, on their own. Firms such as TD

© Wavebreakmedia Ltd/Getty Images

Yoga retailer Lululemon has amassed millions of social media followers. The company uses Facebook, Twitter, and other sites to promote yoga clothes and a fit lifestyle.

Waterhouse, the biggest online brokerage firm, have been innovators in promoting online trading. As a result, traditional brokers such as Nesbitt Burns have had to follow with online trading for their customers.

Because the Internet lowers the cost of communication, it can contribute significantly to any industry or activity that depends on the flow of digital information, such as entertainment, health care, government services, education, and computer services like software development. The publishing industry is transitioning away from print newspapers, magazines, and books as more consumers purchase e-readers, like the Kobo or iPad, or read the news online. For example, *Fifty Shades of Grey* has been downloaded millions of times over the past few years. Even your textbook is available electronically. Because publishers save money on paper, ink, and shipping, many times electronic versions of books are cheaper than their paper counterparts.

Digital media can also improve communication within and between businesses. In the future, most significant gains will come from productivity improvements within businesses. Communication is a key business function, and improving the speed and clarity of communication can help businesses save time and improve employee problem-solving abilities. Digital media can be a communications backbone that helps to store knowledge, information, and records in management information systems so co-workers can access it when faced with a problem to solve. A well-designed management information system that utilizes digital technology can, therefore, help reduce confusion, improve organization and efficiency, and facilitate clear communication. Given the crucial role of communication and information in business, the long-term impact of digital media on economic growth is substantial, and it will inevitably grow over time.

Firms also need to control access to their digital communication systems to ensure worker productivity. This can be a challenge. For example, in companies across Canada and the United States, employees are surfing the Internet for as much as an hour during each workday. Many firms are trying to curb this practice by limiting employees' access to instant messaging services, streaming music, and websites with adult content.[9] Digital communication offers a completely new dimension in connecting with others.

Digital Media and the Marketing Mix

LO4 Show how digital media affect the marketing mix.

While digital marketing shares some similarities with conventional marketing techniques, a few valuable differences stand out. First, digital media make customer communications faster and interactive. Second, digital

media help companies reach new target markets more easily, affordably, and quickly than ever before. Finally, digital media help marketers utilize new resources in seeking out and communicating with customers. One of the most important benefits of digital marketing is the ability of marketers and customers to easily share information. Through websites, social networks, and other digital media, consumers can learn about everything they consume and use in their lives, ask questions, voice complaints, indicate preferences, and otherwise communicate about their needs and desires. Many marketers use e-mail, mobile phones, social networking, wikis, video sharing, podcasts, blogs, videoconferencing, and other technologies to coordinate activities and communicate with employees, customers, and suppliers. Twitter, considered both a social network and a micro blog, illustrates how these digital technologies can combine to create new communication opportunities.

Nielsen Marketing Research revealed that consumers now spend more time on social networking sites than they do on e-mail, and social network use is still growing. In Canada, it is estimated that 20 million people or 57 percent of the Canadian population will be using social media by the end of 2016, with roughly 18.5 million having a Facebook account.[10] Globally, researchers disagree on which country's citizens spend the most time using social networks, but Australians, British, Italians, Americans, and Canadians are considered heavy users of social media.[11] With digital media, even small businesses can reach new markets through these inexpensive communication channels. For example, FreshBooks, a Toronto-based accounting service for small companies, has expanded to reach five million users in 120 countries. FreshBooks uses social media to communicate with customers and promote its products and services. Bricks-and-mortar companies like Canadian Tire and Best Buy utilize online catalogues and

© Alberto Pomares/Getty Images

Amazingly, almost 60 percent of Canadians visit a social media/ networking site once a week.

company websites and blogs to supplement their retail stores. Internet companies like Amazon and BlueNile, which lack physical stores, let customers post reviews of their purchases on their websites, creating company-sponsored communities.

One aspect of marketing that has not changed with digital media is the importance of achieving the right marketing mix. Product, distribution, promotion, and pricing are as important as ever for successful online marketing strategies. More than 40 percent of the world's population now uses the Internet.[12] That means it is essential for businesses large and small to use digital media effectively, not only to grab or maintain market share but also to streamline their organizations and offer customers entirely new benefits and convenience. Let's look at how businesses are using digital media to create effective marketing strategies on the Web.

Product Considerations. Like traditional marketers, digital marketers must anticipate consumer needs and preferences, tailor their products and services to meet these needs, and continually upgrade them to remain competitive. The connectivity created by digital media provides the opportunity for adding services and can enhance product benefits. Some products—such as online games, applications, and virtual worlds—are available only via digital media. Netflix offers a much wider array of movies and games than the average movie rental stores, along with a one-month free trial, and of course no late fees. Netflix also prides itself on its recommendation engine, which recommends movies for users based on their previous viewing history and how they rate movies they have seen. As Netflix demonstrates, the Internet can make it much easier to anticipate consumer needs. However, fierce competition makes quality product and service offerings more important than ever.[13]

Distribution Considerations. The Internet is a new distribution channel for making products available at the right time, at the right place, and in the right quantities. Marketers' ability to process orders electronically and increase the speed of communication via the Internet reduces inefficiencies, costs, and redundancies while increasing speed throughout the marketing channel. Shipping times and costs have become an important consideration in attracting customers, prompting many companies to offer consumers low shipping costs or next-day delivery. For example, Coastal Contacts, which operates as Clearly Contacts in Canada, is successfully taking customers away from traditional optometrists and eyeglass retailers. The company, which was founded in 2000, was expected to have revenue in excess of $250 million in recent years.[14] Coastal Contacts is thriving as it sells contacts and glasses at a cheaper price than traditional retailers and is often considered

---

ENTREPRENEURSHIP IN ACTION | Etsy: The Site for the Creative Entrepreneur

Robert Kalin, Chris Maguire, and Haim Schoppik

Business: Etsy

Founded: 2005

Success: Etsy has 54 million members and 22.6 million shoppers who spent $1.93 billion in 2015 shopping on Etsy.[15] Humpty Dumpty mugs, T-shirts featuring texting zombies, and pet beds made from suitcases—all have been listed for sale on Etsy, the digital marketing website for handmade, vintage, and do-it-yourself products. The company is popular with artists and small businesses and reached profitability in just four years. Etsy allows entrepreneurs a central site to distribute handmade creations at a fraction of the cost of setting up a traditional website or selling the goods in retail locations. Etsy also allows business owners access to thousands of daily visitors who come to a central site to see what is new, unique, and/or unusual. Co-founder Rob Kalin expresses Etsy's goal of "restoring community and culture to our commerce." Etsy therefore refuses manufactured goods on its website—all products must be handmade. Etsy charges 20 cents to list a seller's product on its website for four months along with 3.5 percent on each sale. Sellers can also advertise their products on the website for a fee.

Despite its initial success, Etsy faces many challenges. Some analysts believe Etsy's insistence on only handmade goods might limit its growth.

Etsy allows home-based business owners a central website with millions of users to sell their homemade products.

more convenient by consumers. Rather than visit a retailer, consumers can order contacts or glasses online and have them arrive at their home within 48 hours. Coastal has also established an automatic refill program where contact lenses are shipped automatically at a predetermined time.

Costco Canada is attempting to take market share away from e-marketers like Amazon by reducing delivery time and creating a "site to store" system so consumers can get a product shipped to their house or, for faster delivery, to a store. This offer has the increased benefit of getting customers into the store, where they might make add-on purchases. Walmart is trying a similar strategy in the U.S. where it is not charging consumers shipping costs if items are delivered to stores. Walmart has even tested a new distribution concept to complement store pick-ups: a drive-through window that allows customers to pick up the products they ordered through Walmart's website. Through even more sophisticated distribution systems, Walmart hopes to overtake online retailers to become the biggest online merchant.[16]

Promotion Considerations. Perhaps one of the best ways businesses can utilize digital media is for promotion purposes—whether they are increasing brand awareness, connecting with consumers, or taking advantage of social networks or virtual worlds (discussed later) to form relationships and generate positive publicity or "buzz" about their products. Thanks to online promotion, consumers can be more informed than ever, including reading customer-generated content before making purchasing decisions. Consumer consumption patterns are radically changing, and marketers must adapt their promotional efforts to meet them. For example, more and more travellers are using the Internet to purchase flights and to compare prices when planning a trip. WestJet has gone to great lengths to make it easy for consumers to buy airline tickets online using its website, and it relies on digital marketing to promote sales and special events, and to stay connected with customers.

These effects are not limited to the Western world. In a revolutionary shift in China, where online shopping had not been widely adopted by consumers, businesses are now realizing the benefits of marketing online. One of the first adopters of Internet selling was the Chinese company Taobao, a consumer auction site that also features sections for Chinese brands and retailers. Taobao provides online promotion of retailers and products featured on its site. The majority of online sales in China take place on Taobao.[17] Consumer trends like these demonstrate that the shift to digital media promotion is well under way worldwide.

Pricing Considerations. Price is the most flexible element of the marketing mix. Digital marketing can enhance the value of products by providing extra benefits such as service, information, and convenience. Through digital media, discounts and other promotions can be quickly communicated. As consumers have become better informed about their options, the demand for low-priced products has grown, leading to the creation of deal sites where consumers can directly compare prices. Expedia, for instance, provides consumers with a wealth of travel information about everything from flights to hotels, which lets them compare benefits and prices. Many marketers offer buying incentives like online coupons or free samples to generate consumer demand for their products.

Social Networking

A **social network** is "a Web-based meeting place for friends, family, co-workers, and peers that lets users create a profile and connect with other users for purposes that range from getting acquainted, to keeping in touch, to building a work-related network."[18] Social networks are a valued part of marketing because they are changing the way consumers communicate with

> **social network** a Web-based meeting place for friends, family, co-workers, and peers that lets users create a profile and connect with other users for a wide range of purposes

| Mobovivo Allows Consumers Legal Access to TV and Movies on Mobile Devices

Trevor Doerksen

Business: Mobovivo

Founded: 1999

Success: Trevor Doerksen's company offered legal downloads of TV shows for iPods faster than Apple.

Mobovivo is a Canadian-based company that enables video content producers (think TV and movies) to distribute their shows on mobile devices. The company, founded by Trevor Doerksen, managed to be the first legal provider of TV shows to the iPod in 2006, beating even Apple. The company has grown using strategic partnerships with content providers such as the BBC Worldwide and Cinram. The partnership with the BBC allows Mobovivo to distribute such hit shows as *The Tudors*, while its alliance with Cinram, a company which takes content and places it on DVDs and Blu-Ray discs for production studios, will have Mobovivo enable all its discs for mobile devices such as smartphones and tablets.[19]

each other and with firms. Sites such as Facebook, Instagram, Twitter, LinkedIn, Tumblr and Pinterest have emerged as opportunities for marketers to build communities, provide product information, and learn about consumer needs. By the time you read this, it is possible there will be new social network sites that continue to advance digital communication and opportunities for marketers.

You might be surprised to know that social networks have existed in some form or other for 40 years. The precursors of today's social networks began in the 1970s as online bulletin boards that allowed users with common interests to interact with one another. The first modern social network was Six Degrees, launched in 1997. This system permitted users to create a profile and connect with friends—the core attributes of today's networks.[20] Although Six Degrees eventually shut down for lack of interest, the seed of networking had been planted.[21] Other social networks followed, with each new generation becoming increasingly sophisticated. Today's sites offer a multitude of consumer benefits, including the ability to download music, games, and applications; upload photos and videos; join groups; find and chat with friends; comment on friends' posts; and post and update status messages. Table 13.1 lists some popular social networks in different countries.

> ## "Social networks are a valued part of marketing because they are changing the way consumers communicate with each other and with firms."

Table 13.1 Popular Social Networking Sites in Different Countries

South Korea	Cyworld
Netherlands	Hyves
Japan	Mixi
Brazil	Orkut
China	QZone
France	SkyRock
Germany	StudiVZ
Spain	Tuenti
Russia	Vkontakte
United Kingdom	Bebo
United States	Facebook

Source: "Nine Extremely Successful Non-English Social Networking Sites," Pingdom, September 9, 2009, http://royal.pingdom.com/2009/09/09/nine-extremely-successful-non-english-social-networking-sites/ (accessed March 25, 2010); Sorav Jain, "40 Most Popular Social Networking Sites of the World," Social Media Today, http://socialmediatoday.com/index.php?q=soravjain/195917/40-most-popular-social-networking-sites-world (accessed January 17, 2011).

As the number of social network users increases, interactive marketers are finding opportunities to reach out to consumers in new target markets. MeetMe.com is a social networking site that offers teenagers a forum in which to write about particular subjects important to them, including sensitive topics facing today's younger generation. Its popularity with teenagers is rising; the site's traffic has increased 36 percent annually, with most users coming from North America. For advertisers, the site is an opportunity to connect with teens and young adults, a demographic that is difficult to reach with traditional marketing. Advertisers from Nikon and Paramount Pictures both made deals to advertise through MeetMe.com.[22] We'll have more to say about how marketers utilize social networks later in this chapter.

An important question relates to how social media sites are adding value to the economy. Marketers at companies like Lululemon and Ford Canada, for instance, are using social media to promote products and build consumer relationships. Most corporations are supporting Facebook pages and Yammer accounts for employees to communicate across departments and divisions. Professionals such as professors, doctors, and engineers also share ideas on a regular basis. Even staffing organizations use social media, bypassing traditional e-mail and telephone channels. While billions of dollars in investments are being funnelled into social media, it may be too early to assess the exact economic contribution of social media to the entire economy.[23]

Types of Consumer-Generated Marketing and Digital Media

LO5 Define social networking and illustrate how businesses can use different types of social networking media.

While digital marketing has generated exciting opportunities for companies to interact with their customers, digital media are also more consumer-driven than traditional media. Internet users are creating and reading consumer-generated content as never before and are having a profound effect on marketing in the process.

Two factors have sparked the rise of consumer-generated information:

1. The increased tendency of consumers to publish their own thoughts, opinions, reviews, and product discussions through blogs or digital media.

2. Consumers' tendencies to trust other consumers over corporations. Consumers often rely on the recommendations of friends, family, and fellow consumers when making purchasing decisions.

Marketers who know where online users are likely to express their thoughts and opinions can use these forums to interact with them, address problems, and promote their companies. Types of digital media in which Internet users are likely to participate include blogs, wikis, video- and photo-sharing sites, podcasts, social networking sites, virtual reality sites, and mobile applications. Let's look a little more closely at each.

Blogs and Wikis

Today's marketers must recognize that the impact of consumer-generated material like blogs and wikis and their significance to online consumers have increased a great deal. A **blog** (short for Web log) is a Web-based journal in which writers can editorialize and interact with other Internet users. Two-thirds of Internet users read blogs, and more than half of bloggers say they blog about topics and brands about which they feel strongly.[24] The blogging phenomenon is not limited to North America. In South Korea, for example, more than two-thirds of the online population

> **blog** a Web-based journal in which a writer can editorialize and interact with other Internet users

creates blogs or similar material.[25] Blogs have also grown significantly from their origin as shorter, less interactive sources of information. For example, popular Canadian travel blog www.departful.com features full length articles on travelling, videos, and beautiful pictures.

Blogs give consumers power, sometimes more than companies would like. Bloggers can post whatever they like about a company or its products, whether their opinions are positive or negative, true or false. When a Korean Dunkin' Donuts worker created a blog alleging that a company factory had unsanitary conditions, the company forced him to delete the blog. However, readers had already created copies of it and spread it across the Internet after the original's removal.[27] In other cases, a positive review of a product or service posted on a popular blog can result in large increases in sales. Thus, blogs can represent a potent threat or opportunity to marketers.

Rather than trying to eliminate blogs that cast their companies in a negative light, some firms are using their own blogs, or employee blogs, to answer consumer concerns or defend their corporate reputations. For example, when Electronic Arts' SimCity game failed to work properly, the company used blogs to respond to consumer complaints and questions. Electronic Arts also used blogs to highlight some of the company's news and promotions.[28] As blogging changes the face of media, smart companies are using it to build enthusiasm for their products and create relationships with consumers. As noted in Chapter 12, many CEOs, such as Jim Estill, CEO of Symex Canada, are using blogs to reach out and connect with consumers and provide information that customers find relevant and interesting.

A **wiki** is a website where users can add to or edit the content of posted articles. One of the best known is Wikipedia, an online encyclopedia with over 17 million entries in over 250 languages on nearly every subject imaginable (*Encyclopedia Britannica* only has 120,000 entries).[29] Wikipedia is one of the ten most popular sites on the Web, and because much of its content can be edited by anyone, it is easy for online consumers to add detail and supporting evidence and to correct inaccuracies in content. Wikipedia used to be completely open to editing, but in order to stop vandalism, the site had to make some topics off-limits, now editable only by a small group of experts.

> **wiki** software that creates an interface that enables users to add or edit the content of some types of websites

Like all digital media, wikis have advantages and disadvantages for companies. Wikis about controversial companies like Walmart and Nike often contain negative publicity, such as about workers' rights violations. However, monitoring relevant wikis can provide companies with a better idea of how consumers feel about the company or brand. Some companies have also begun to use wikis as internal tools for teams working on projects that require a great deal of documentation.[30] There is too much at stake financially for marketers to ignore wikis and blogs. Despite this fact, less than one-fifth of *Fortune* 500 companies have a blog.[31] Marketers who want to form better customer relationships and promote their company's products must not underestimate the power of these two media outlets.

> ## DID YOU KNOW?
> Searching is the most popular online activity.[26]

Video Sharing

Video-sharing sites allow virtually anybody to upload videos, from professional marketers at *Fortune* 500 corporations to the average Internet user. Businesses are using video-sharing sites to post advertisements prior to videos playing, to create and share entertaining and/or educational content, and to interact with consumers. Some of the most popular video-sharing sites include YouTube, Vine, Video, Yahoo!, Metacafe, and Hulu. Video-sharing sites give companies the opportunity to upload ads and informational videos about their products. YouTube use in Canada and globally is significant, and YouTube has recently released the following statistics about traffic to its site:[32]

- YouTube is the second most visited site in Canada.

- One billion unique users visit the site monthly.

- YouTube and YouTube mobile on its own reach more people aged 18 to 49 than cable TV.

- YouTube is localized in 56 countries and across 61 languages.

- The average mobile visitor spends over 40 minutes per visit watching video.
- Over 6 billion hours of video are watched each month on YouTube.[33]

Video-sharing sites are increasingly being used as a low-cost promotional method to educate and entertain potential consumers. Almost all major North American companies make use of YouTube. For example, Supercell, makers of the popular online game Clash of Clans, uses YouTube to promote its online games using ads and content. Its online ad, featuring Liam Neeson, was the most viewed ad in Canada in 2015 with more than 82 million views.[34] Many small organizations are using the video-sharing site as well. For example, many schools—such as Mount Saint Vincent University with 4,500 students—are using YouTube to create promotional videos about student experiences and to showcase campus events on the Internet. Ontario-based Roger Neilson's Hockey Camp is using YouTube to advertise annual hockey camps and highlight some of the instruction that occurs in its programs. Global pop sensation Justin Bieber actually owes a lot of his fame and fortune to YouTube and other social media sites. After finishing second in a local singing contest, Bieber started posting videos on both YouTube and Myspace. This eventually led to his being noticed by his first music contact.

A few videos become viral at any given time, and although many of these gain popularity because they are unusual in some way, others reach viral status because people find them entertaining. **Viral marketing** occurs when a message gets sent from person to person to person. It can be an extremely effective tool for marketers—particularly on the Internet, where one click can send a message to dozens or hundreds of people simultaneously. However, viral marketing often requires marketers to develop an offbeat sense of humour and creativity in order to catch the viewer's attention—something with which some marketers may not be comfortable. For instance, April Fool's Day has become a day when Canadian companies try to generate some added attention to their company and products by offering some offbeat ads and often fake products. Recently, WestJet, Lululemon, and Boston Pizza all offered gag products on April Fool's Day in Canada. WestJet used April Fool's Day to promote a "new policy" where any animal including pet bears are allowed on airplanes; Lululemon introduced the mock product Lululeather, including Cowabunga leather yoga pants; and Boston Pizza announced that it was banning all buns from the store and creating new products with pizza dough such as pizza salad, pizza beer, and pizza cake. Such campaigns can be successful as WestJet's gag "Child-Free Cabins" promotion video had 600,000 hits on YouTube and boosted the company's rank in search engines. Other times, when consumers do not know they are being tricked, the gag can backfire. While most of Lululemon's loyal followers recognized leather yoga pants were an April Fool's Day prank, the company did such a good job making the announcements that some consumers thought the product was in fact real and expressed displeasure with the company on its website.[35] Companies such as IBM have created an entire video series to generate publicity for the company. IBM's six videos, called "The Art of the Sale," present three attributes of the company's mainframe computer in a humorous format reminiscent of episodes of *The Office*. Though some wrote off the videos as a forced attempt at humorous marketing, they received hundreds of thousands of hits on YouTube.[36]

Businesses have also begun to utilize consumer-generated video content, saving money they would have spent on hiring advertising firms to develop professional advertising campaigns. For example, many universities and colleges throughout Canada are creating their own content with students and staff, and running video contests to promote their school or a particular field of academic study. The Ontario government has recently started using a similar strategy asking people to create their own videos stressing job safety in the "It's Your Job" video contest.[37] Perhaps the most successful campaign

viral marketing a marketing tool that uses the Internet, particularly social networking and video-sharing sites, to spread a message and create brand awareness

© Yeamake/Shutterstock.com

Supercell, makers of Clash of Clans, created the most popular YouTube video in Canada in 2015. Its video, featuring Lian Neeson, was viewed over 82 million times.

© Debby Wong/Shutterstock.com

Justin Bieber's singing career actually started on YouTube with videos he created himself. Bieber's videos were eventually discovered and he has gone on to sing numerous number one hits and star in his own movie.

in recent years is Frito Lay's "Crash the Super Bowl" contest, where the company invites customers to create ads, which may be selected for broadcast during the football game. The most recent winner created an ad featuring dogs trying to get into a supermarket to buy bags of Doritos. The advertisement was widely considered to be the best commercial played during the Super Bowl and created significant attention from social and mainstream media.[38] Marketers believe consumer videos appear more authentic and create enthusiasm for the product among consumer participants.

Google is so confident that video-sharing sites will revolutionize online marketing that it purchased YouTube for $1.65 billion in 2006.[39] If Google is correct in its predictions, then online videos clips—both corporate-sponsored and consumer-generated—are likely to revolutionize the marketing industry.

Photo Sharing

Photo-sharing sites allow users to upload and share their photos and short videos with the world. Well-known photo-sharing sites include Instagram, SmugMug, Webshots, Photobucket, and Flickr. Flickr is owned by Yahoo! and once was the most popular photo-sharing

site on the Internet. A Flickr user can upload images, edit them, classify the images, create photo albums, and share photos with friends without having to e-mail bulky image files or send photos through the mail. Flickr is still popular, and the site experiences thousands of new image uploads every minute. Most users have free accounts that allow them to upload two videos and 100 MB of photos per month, but for around $25 a year, users can open an unlimited Pro account.[40] Photo sharing represents an opportunity for companies to market themselves visually by displaying snapshots of company events, company staff, and/or company products. Companies can direct viewers to their photostreams (their sets of photographs) by marking their pictures with the appropriate keywords, or tags.[41] Tags are essential for marketing on Flickr as they help direct traffic to the corporate photostreams.

Many businesses with pictures on Flickr have a link connecting their Flickr photostreams to their corporate websites.[42] Suncor Energy, for example, a Canadian oil and gas company, uses Flickr to showcase its work and important events. One of Flickr's rivals is Picasa Web Albums, a Google photo-sharing site that developed out of Google's photo-editing program Picasa. The program has grown rapidly and is growing in popularity, as it provides more features than Flickr and other major photo-sharing websites. Picasa Web Albums is free, and generates revenues through ads shown on the site. If users want to use more than 1 GB of storage space, they can rent additional space up to 16 TB.

Flickr has recently been surpassed in popularity by two new photo-sharing sites that have a much stronger social networking element to them. Pinterest (see below) is actually now the third-largest social media site in the world. Instagram, which has 100 million monthly users, allows people to post photos onto its site using their smartphones as the primary camera and to share the photos using other social networking sites. Instagram is especially popular among people under the age of 24 and has very few users older than 35. Many younger celebrities frequently use Instagram to post pictures of their daily routine, including Canadian star Justin Bieber. Businesses have been using Instagram to post pictures of their products to get customer feedback or to tell a story about their brand. Pinterest is described below and the focus is not just on posting business or personal pictures, but on building pinboards with similar content. Pinterest's users are predominantly female and cover a much broader demographic compared to Instagram. Pinterest has less peer-to-peer communication compared to Instagram but offers businesses more peer-to-social network communication.

As one Web marketer puts it, companies that use photo sharing "add a personal touch to their businesses."[43] Although it is too early to gauge the effects of marketing through photo-sharing sites, more and more marketers will likely use the sites as an inexpensive way to reach their audience.

Consider the Following: Going Viral

As social media increases in importance, more and more companies are relying on the public to create a buzz for their products and/or their online promotions. Companies are often hoping that their online advertisements will "go viral," meaning that the public will become so interested in an ad campaign or product that they will share it within their own online social networks, thus spreading the company's brand, products, or advertisement to thousands if not millions of computers. As discussed in Chapter 12, both Bauer's "Own the Moment" and Nike's "Hockey is Ours" campaigns went viral, as the ads connected with Canadians during the NHL lockout. Other Canadian examples include Mike Evans and Nick de Pencier's healthy-living YouTube video, which has been seen by over two million North Americans and shared throughout the globe. Old Spice had a viral hit on its hands with the "Old Spice Guy" advertisements. The ads, which were originally intended only for TV use, resonated with viewers and became a YouTube sensation. Old Spice supported the campaign by releasing hundreds of videos on YouTube and has the actor in the commercials answering questions using the popular video-sharing network and Twitter. The campaign has spread like wildfire on the Internet as consumers are using Facebook, Twitter, and other social media sites to promote the advertisements to their networks. Groupon relying on social media and going viral as a business model. The company is an online social buying website where people sign up to receive e-mails promoting "deals of the day." Interested consumers agree to purchase the product using their credit card but no sales occur until a minimum number of buyers are reached and the deal is unlocked. If the minimum number of buyers is not reached, then the deal is withdrawn. Since customers want the deal, they usually share it with their social networks using Facebook, Twitter, and YouTube. Participating companies like the concept as they acquire customers at low cost and increase the number of people who know about their company. Consumers like the idea as they get to purchase products at substantial savings. Groupon's biggest challenge may not be getting customers and companies to participate, but dealing with competitors such as Living Social and other daily deal sites. While Groupon operates as a traditional deal of the day coupon, Living Social actually allows users to get their product for free. Once you purchase a coupon on Living Social, you are given a link to share; if three people buy through your link, then the deal is free.[44]

DISCUSSION QUESTIONS

1. Do you think companies' sales benefit from viral ads such as the ones discussed above and throughout this chapter? Why or why not?

2. Do you think advertising with a strong emotional appeal is effective?

3. Given that firms are intentionally trying to generate viral campaigns such as creating mock ads on April Fool's Day, do you think consumers will eventually grow tired of such campaigns?

4. Given the increasing number of "deal of the day" coupon sites, do you think they will lose their effectiveness as an advertising tool?

5. Companies who participate in "deal of the day" sites often have to perform services or offer products well below costs. For example, restaurants which offer coupons for $100 worth of food for $50 normally only receive $25 after paying all the fees to the coupon site. Do you think this is a worthwhile investment for the restaurant? Why or why not?

Podcasting

A **podcast** is made up of audio or video files that can be downloaded from the Internet via a subscription and automatically deliver new content to listening devices or personal computers. Podcasting offers the benefit of convenience, giving users the ability to listen to or view content when and where they choose.

podcast an audio or video file that can be downloaded from the Internet with a subscription and automatically deliver new content to listening devices or personal computers

Podcasting is rapidly gaining in popularity. Dozens of online programs, such as Apple's iPodderX and Podcast Studio or Android's dPod, offer podcasting services. Other companies, such as Yodio, combine podcasting with photos to create customized online greeting card–style messages. It is estimated that by 2016, more than 53 million North American consumers will be downloading podcasts every month.[45] Most current podcast users are between 18 and 29 years of age, making podcasts a good marketing tool for reaching this demographic.[46]

> **"Podcasting offers the benefit of convenience, giving users the ability to listen to or view content when and where they choose."**

As podcasting continues to catch on, radio stations and television networks like CBC Radio, NPR, MSNBC, and PBS are creating podcasts of their shows to profit from this growing trend. Many companies hope to use podcasts to create brand awareness, promote their products, and encourage customer loyalty.

Social Networks

Social media use has become an integral part of daily Canadian life; in fact, 59 percent of Canadians use Facebook, 30 percent LinkedIn, 25 percent Twitter, and 16 percent Instagram. Most Canadians visit their social media environment of choice numerous times a day and spend a significant amount of their online time on social networks.[47] Canadians are not alone though, as two-thirds of Americans visit social media networks or blogs.[48] One in three South Korean and one in five Japanese Internet users participate in social networks.[49] As social networks evolve, both marketers and the owners of social networking sites are realizing the opportunities such networks offer—an influx of advertising dollars for site owners and a large reach for the advertiser. As a result, marketers have begun investigating and experimenting with promotion on social networks. Some of the most prominent sites are highlighted below.

Facebook. In April 2008, the social networking site Facebook surpassed Myspace in its number of members, becoming the most popular social networking site in the world.[51] It is estimated that 59 percent of Canadians use Facebook, and they visit the site on average nine times a week. While the site is popular with young people as 75 percent of them frequent Facebook, the site is also

---

Consider the Following: Pinterest Successfully Combines Social Networking and Photo Sharing to Overtake Flickr

As discussed in Chapter 12, Pinterest is the fastest-growing, and third-largest, social media website in North America. In a very short time, the company has overtaken Flickr as the number one photo-sharing site by combining photo sharing with elements of social media.

Pinterest allows users to manage pictures and videos named pins to an online bulletin board known as a pinboard. Themed pinboards allow users to easily manage pins, to share their content, and to search pins posted by other users. Users can also pin content they find on the Internet and easily upload it to their pinboard. Pinboard users take great pride in creating attractive pinboards to share.

According to experts, Pinterest's success can be attributed to many subtle differences compared to traditional photo-sharing sites. Pinterest is, first and foremost, free, and its focus is on social networking. The site refers to users as friends and lets you know when friends are logged on to Twitter and Facebook. Additionally, the company allows you to follow others, comment on their pinboard, and quickly load embedded photos to an attractive website. These subtle differences stand out when compared to Flickr, the previous leader in the online photo-sharing industry. Flickr, while allowing for some free sharing of photos, charges for a premium account, does not alert you when contacts are online, and, while having a social network element, has stayed fairly rigid in its business model. Charlotte Henry, an online journalist, says Pinterest has clearly won the battle for online photo sharing. "In terms of advertising and building an online presence, the choice is simple. The ability to categorize images, the deep social interaction, not to mention the attractive interface, make Pinterest the clear winner. You can really build a brand image on Pinterest, and display your products. Flickr remains important to photographers, but has been overtaken by Pinterest by almost every other kind of user."[50]

DISCUSSION QUESTIONS

1. Why do you think Pinterest has replaced Flickr as the number one photo-sharing site?

2. Do you think Flickr charging for a premium account has hindered its ability to grow?

3. Flickr has recently added some additional social networking elements to its website. Do you think it will be able to re-establish itself as the leader in photo sharing?

4. Given what you have learned about Pinterest, Flickr, and Instagram, which photo-sharing site would you recommend for a company to use if it were trying to appeal to young women between the ages of 25 and 40 with a new product? Why?

popular with professionals, at 75 percent of Canadians who earn between $80,000 and $100,000 also use the social network.[52] Facebook users create profiles, which they can make public or private, and then search the network for people with whom to connect. Users often must be a "friend" of the person whose profile they are trying to view before they can see that user's personal information. Facebook appeals to a broad demographic, attracting parents and grandparents as well as teens and college and university students.[53] In fact, the fastest-growing group on Facebook is women 55 and over.[54] As discussed in Chapter 12, many marketers are turning to Facebook to market products, interact with consumers, and gain publicity. It is possible for a consumer to become a "fan" of a major company like Starbucks by clicking on the "Like" icon on the coffee retailer's Facebook page. Companies are also using Facebook to generate awareness about themselves and encourage repeat visits. Many companies, such as RBC and CBC, have online contests to keep people coming back to their social media sites. CBC, for example, held a national contest that was heavily promoted on social media sites including Facebook to come up with a new theme song for *Hockey Night in Canada*.[55] Facebook, like other social networking sites, is also allowing companies to sell goods directly to users; this is known as F-commerce when talking purely about Facebook and as social commerce when discussing this new emerging trend. As noted in Chapter 12, Facebook is also well known for its targeted advertisements. Facebook compiles information about users, including what they like or search on Facebook along with their other Web browsing history, to identify groups of consumers with similar interests. Facebook then allows companies to post advertising specific to this group. For example, the Stratford Festival, an Ontario-based theatre group, successfully used targeted Facebook ads to post a one-day coupon aimed at increasing ticket sales from new and lapsed patrons. As a result, Stratford sold three times its normal ticket sales. Stratford's social media coordinator, Aaron George says,

"Many marketers are turning to Facebook to market products, interact with consumers, and gain publicity."

DID YOU KNOW?

In a recent global survey on the effectiveness of social marketing, researchers determined that:

- 54% of those polled think social marketing has been very successful at increasing brand/product awareness.

- 49% were very successful at using social marketing to increase customer engagement.

- 39% found social marketing efforts effective for lead generation.

- 34% successfully used social marketing to increase website traffic.

- 26% were very successful in increasing direct sales revenue for their company through social marketing.[58]

"Using Facebook as a media tool has definitely been beneficial for us. It's given us the reach of television with the targeting capabilities of a direct mail campaign. It allows us to target lapsed patrons or reach those who came to a performance a few years ago, and gave us a great return on ad spend. Facebook Ads have helped us strengthen our digital brand presence, increase ticket sales, and cultivate new audiences."[56]

Social networking sites are also useful for small businesses. Ela restaurant in Halifax, Nova Scotia, uses interactive marketing on a social networking outlet to drum up more business. The company provides users with coupons, special seating, and updates on new menu items on Facebook and other social media sites.[57] Some small businesses are actually abandoning traditional websites and just maintain a Facebook page.

Other companies that have utilized relationship marketing to help consumers feel more connected to their products are Pepsi and the Walt Disney Co. The Pepsi Refresh Project (PRP) invites consumers to suggest local charities that are making a positive impact. Consumers vote for their favourites, and Pepsi donates money to the winning causes. The company utilized Facebook, Twitter, and blogging to spread the word about PRP.[59] The Walt Disney Co. has created many different Facebook pages, which have succeeded in generating over 100 million Facebook fans. Some of its success is attributed to the Disney Pages promotion tab on its main Disney Facebook page. The tab allows users to access promotional content without having to navigate away from Facebook. In many ways, Facebook is becoming an e-commerce platform whereby companies can sell products through the site. DigiSynd, Disney's social media agency, was able to use a platform on Facebook called Disney Tickets Together that allowed fans to purchase tickets for movies like *Toy Story 3*. These new opportunities for businesses demonstrate the evolution of Facebook into a marketing destination.[60]

LinkedIn. LinkedIn is a social networking site geared toward professionals from all over the world. With 120 million professional members, including executives from all the *Fortune* 500 companies, it is the fourth-largest social networking site and logs several million visitors a month.[61] Roughly 30 percent of Canadians are on LinkedIn with the majority being aged 45 to 54.[62] A LinkedIn profile resembles a résumé. It contains information about past and current job experiences, qualifications, goals, and educational background. Like all social networking sites, it lets users locate and connect with other members and join groups, which are often professional organizations. LinkedIn facilitates job searches and allows companies to search the network for potential employees with the necessary skills. Scotiabank, Delta Hotels, Microsoft, Target, eBay, and Netflix have all used the LinkedIn network to recruit new employees.[63] Employees are also using LinkedIn to search for potential employers. Approximately 28 percent of college and university students have indicated that they plan to use LinkedIn to search for employment opportunities.[64] Although a professional networking site like LinkedIn seems more like a recruiting site than a marketing tool, companies do use it to familiarize users with their business. In addition to listing job openings, most company LinkedIn profiles also offer a link to the company website, some background on the business, links to news updates on company activities and products, and stock information. Procter & Gamble has a LinkedIn page that allows users to locate professionals, research careers, and get updates about the company. LinkedIn Groups—a feature on the site that highlights particular industries—is a useful tool for companies that want to describe their expertise and activities. Organizations can also build a group on LinkedIn based around their company or industry for no charge.[65] Smart marketers can use LinkedIn to reach professionals not only for recruiting purposes but also to spread information about and interest in the company.

Twitter. Twitter is a hybrid of a social networking site and a micro-blogging site that asks users one simple question: "What are you doing?" Members can post answers of up to 140 characters, which are then available for their registered "followers" to read. It sounds simple enough, but Twitter's effect on digital media has been immense. The site quickly progressed from a novelty to a social networking staple, attracting millions of viewers each month.[66] Globally, Twitter has 1.3 billion registered users, with 100 million daily active users who send millions of tweets every day.[67] In Canada, 25 percent of the population uses Twitter, and Canadian users visit the site five times a week.[68] The thrill of Twitter is that users get to tell the world about their daily lives in short messages, known as tweets. These tweets can be mundane, such as "I'm eating a sandwich," to interesting. Prime Minister Justin Trudeau is an active Twitter user, using the forum to make various announcements and often respond to questions. Halfway across the world, former Russian president Dmitry Medvedev actually had to rebuke one of his regional governors for tweeting during a government session on educational policy.[69] Twitter has quickly transformed from novelty to serious marketing tool, with the company announcing plans to generate revenue through sponsored tweets and working to make the service more user-friendly.[70] Although 140 characters may not seem like enough for companies to send an effective message, some have become experts at using Twitter in their marketing strategies. Starbucks Canada has used Twitter in marketing campaigns to promote new store openings, offer coupons, and respond to questions. Twitter and social networks were heavily used by Starbucks when it released its Blonde Roast coffee, which was aimed primarily at Canadians.[71] On a small scale, many local restaurants have turned to Twitter to share nightly specials, interact with customers, and book reservations. Restaurants such as Ryan Duffy's in Halifax use the social media site to promote specials and solicit consumer response.

Like other social networking tools, Twitter is also being used to build customer relationships. Media experts almost universally agree that the most effective use of Twitter involves creating conversation, not just pushing information onto followers. As discussed above, Porter Airlines is a service business that effectively uses Twitter to communicate with followers. Finally, companies are using Twitter to gain a competitive advantage. Microsoft's search engine Bing developed a partnership with Twitter in which Bing sorts the millions of tweets by relevance and the popularity of the person tweeting. By doing a Bing–Twitter search, Twitter fans can get the most important tweets in real time.[72] Firms also have a chance to utilize promoted tweets, promoted accounts, and promoted trends offered on the site. Marketers can pay Twitter to highlight advertisements or company brands to a wider array of users while they search for specific terms or topics.[73] The race is on among companies that want to use Twitter to gain a competitive edge.

Social Media Dashboards

Given the popularity of social networking/media sites, businesses—especially larger businesses—often attempt to maintain an active presence on all the sites. Posting and then managing responses to numerous social networking sites can be time consuming, and businesses often simultaneously monitor numerous websites. A recent emerging solution has been social media dashboards, which enable companies to submit information to a central location, and then software posts the information onto various social media sites. For example, RBC could enter information about a new promotion into a social media dashboard, and the dashboard would then distribute the information to RBC's various social networks such as Facebook, Twitter, Tumblr, and YouTube. The dashboard could then monitor the consumer feedback about the posting

By this point in your reading, it should be clear that social media monitoring has become quite important for businesses. Not only do companies want to share information on social media sites, but they want to learn what you are saying about their organizations. Social media dashboards (discussed below) are becoming increasingly common tools to monitor what people are saying about a company on the Internet. Still, other tools exist. For example, Google Alerts notifies a business if its name comes up anywhere online. As discussed above, Facebook tracks not only its users' activity on its site but other Web-browsing activity. Businesses such as New Brunswick–based Radian6 identify trends in online communities and assist businesses in dealing with complaints. Other software tools, such as KISSmetrics, have been developed to help businesses identify the behaviour of Web users. Users of

KISSmetrics can identify not only who is visiting their site but their actions as well. This information can be used to tailor offerings and improve sales. Since the company's inception, it has tracked the Web use of 4.5 billion people and their 36 billion interactions.[74]

DISCUSSION QUESTIONS

1. Do you think organizations should be able to track who visits their websites and their online behaviour?

2. Do you think it is a worthwhile investment for businesses to monitor and respond to social media discussions about their companies? Why or why not?

and summarize the information for RBC. As previously mentioned in the text, the most common social media dashboard is HootSuite, which is based in British Columbia. HootSuite is popular as it allows companies to post and manage information to multiple sites including Twitter, Facebook, LinkedIn, Google+, Foursquare, Myspace, WordPress, Mixi, Instagram, MailChimp, Reddit, Storify, Tumblr, Vimeo, and YouTube. HootSuite's major competitor, TweetDeck, only allows for companies to work with Twitter and Facebook.[75]

© Crystal Eye Studio/Shutterstock

Facebook, Google, and KISSmetrics are all tracking social media and Web-browsing activity. They then sell this information to corporations. Do you think this is ethical?

Virtual Worlds

Games and programs allowing viewers to develop avatars that exist in an online virtual world have exploded in popularity in the twenty-first century. Second Life is a social network with a twist. It is a virtual, three-dimensional game world created by users that features its own economy, its own lands, and residents of every shape and size. Internet users who participate in Second Life choose a fictional persona, called an *avatar*, to communicate with one another; purchase goods with virtual Linden dollars (convertible to real dollars at a rate of around 250 Linden dollars per $1); and even own virtual businesses. For entertainment purposes, residents can shop, attend concerts, or travel to virtual environments—all while spending real money. Farmville provides a similar virtual world experience, except it is limited to life on a farm.

Second Life has the most potential for marketers, given that avatars can purchase property, goods, and services. While the businesses in Second Life are virtual ones, real-world marketers and organizations have been eager to capitalize on the site's popularity. Second Life allows businesses to reach consumers in ways that are creative and fun. For instance, to connect with consumers and build brand loyalty, car companies like Toyota and General Motors began selling virtual cars to Second Life residents.[76] Other businesses are looking toward Second Life to familiarize consumers with their products and services. For instance, large corporations such as Best Buy and H&R Block offer support services on Second Life.

Second Life has become so popular that even professors are using it as a way to connect with their students. Ulrike Schultze is a business professor at Southern Methodist University. Students can choose to attend her real-world class, the virtual one, or both. Schultze sees virtual worlds as the next step in communications and feels that they are a great way to connect with young people who are accustomed to being wired for most of their waking hours.[77] Schultze sees opportunities for businesses in virtual environments, not only to promote and sell products but also to engage in virtual teamwork between physically distant employees and in role-playing exercises. Prestigious universities like the University of Texas, Harvard Law School, Bowling Green State University, and the University of California at Davis all have virtual classrooms in Second Life.

Companies are also using Second Life to encourage residents to participate in company activities. CNN created a virtual news hub and began encouraging residents to submit stories that occur in this virtual world.[78] Such firms are not only creating brand loyalty by connecting with Second Life residents but also using consumer knowledge and money to earn virtual and real-world profits. Although the presence of real-world companies in virtual worlds is still in the experimental stages, virtual worlds like Second Life offer a novel way for marketers to interact with consumers.

Mobile Marketing

Digital marketing is becoming increasingly sophisticated as consumers are beginning to utilize mobile devices such as smartphones as a highly functional communication method. The iPhone and Android phone have changed the way consumers communicate, and a growing number of travellers are using their smartphones to find online maps, travel guides, and taxis. In industries such as hotels, airlines, and car rental agencies, mobile phones have become a primary method for booking reservations and communicating about services. They can act as airline boarding passes, GPS devices, and even hotel room keys. Travel companies are collecting personal information so they can send consumers relevant updates about travel opportunities. Farelogix, a travel software company, is working with a number of airlines to introduce features that allow airlines to sell services such as priority boarding. While airlines already make these services available on their websites, they also want to communicate with travellers who experience unexpected changes on their trips. Other marketing uses of mobile phones include sending shoppers timely messages related to discounts and shopping opportunities.[79]

"New businesses and even industries are evolving that would not exist without digital media."

© Chimeandsense/Dreamstime.com

The use of mobile marketing is growing as more and more people are replacing their desktop with a mobile device.

Marketing over mobile devices has been made possible largely by mobile applications, or apps—programs that can be loaded onto certain mobile devices to allow users to perform a variety of functions, from playing games to comparing product prices from different stores. The latter is becoming particularly useful for consumers. The smartphone's ability to find retailers and entertainment and to organize an itinerary is changing the nature of consumer and business relationships. Large hotel chains, such as Delta Hotels, are increasingly using iPhone apps that allow guests to check in early, order room service so food is waiting for them when they arrive, and even specify bed and pillow types.

The most important feature of apps is the convenience and cost savings they offer the consumer. To remain competitive, companies are beginning to use mobile marketing to offer additional customer incentives, with some success. Jiffy Lube offered coupons for one of its franchises over mobile devices. The company estimated that 50 percent of the new customers who came to the franchise did so as a result of its mobile marketing.[80]

Another application that marketers are finding useful is the QR scanning app. You might have noticed that black-and-white squares have begun appearing on magazines, posters, storefront displays, and more. These are QR codes, and they contain messages not visible to the naked eye. To read these messages, smartphone users must download a QR scanning application. When they come across a QR code, they simply open their smartphone and scan the black-and-white square. The QR scanning app will recognize the code and open up the link, video, or image on the phone's screen. Marketers are using QR codes to market their companies and offer consumer discounts. As more people adopt smartphones, these apps are likely to add a whole new layer to digital marketing.[81]

Mobile payments are also gaining traction, and companies like Google are working to capitalize on this opportunity.[82] Google Wallet is a mobile app that stores credit card information on the smartphone. When the shopper is ready to check out, he or she can tap the phone at the point of sale for the transaction to be registered.[83] The success of mobile payments in revolutionizing the shopping experience will largely depend upon retailers to adopt this payment system, but companies such as Starbucks are already jumping at the opportunity. An estimated 70 percent of consumers will own smartphones by 2015, so businesses cannot afford to miss out on the chance to profit from these new trends.[84]

Widgets are small bits of software on a website, desktop, or mobile device that enables users "to interface with the application and operating system." Marketers might use widgets to display news headlines, clocks, or games on their Web pages.[85] Widgets have been used by companies such as A&E television network as a form of viral marketing—users can download the widget and send it to their friends with a click of a button.[86] Widgets downloaded to a user's desktop can update the user on the latest company or product information, enhancing relationship marketing between companies and their fans. For instance, Krispy Kreme® Doughnuts developed a widget that will alert users when their Original Glazed® doughnuts are hot off the oven at their favourite Krispy Kreme shop.[87] Widgets are an innovative digital marketing tool to personalize Web pages, alert users to the latest company information, and spread awareness of the company's products.

As previously discussed in Chapter 12, the major uses of mobile marketing by firms both large and small include:

- *SMS messages:* SMS messages are text messages of 160 words or less. SMS messages have been an effective way to send coupons to prospective customers.[88]

- *Multimedia messages:* Multimedia messaging takes SMS messaging a step further by allowing companies to send video, audio, photos, and other types of media over mobile devices. Motorola's House of Blues multimedia campaign allowed users to receive access to discounts, tickets, music, and other digital content on their mobile phones.[89]

- *Mobile advertisements:* Mobile advertisements are visual advertisements that appear on mobile devices. Companies might choose to advertise through search engines, websites, or even games accessed on mobile devices. Orville Redenbacher has used mobile advertisements to promote its healthy snacks.[90]

- *Mobile websites:* Mobile websites are websites designed for mobile devices. Mobile devices constitute one-third of Web traffic.[91]

- *Location-based networks:* Location-based networks are built for mobile devices. One of the most popular location-based networks is Foursquare, which lets users check in and share their location with others. Businesses such as Walgreen's and Chili's Grill & Bar have partnered with Foursquare to offer incentives to consumers who check in at their venues.[92]

- *Mobile applications:* Mobile applications (known as apps) are software programs that run on mobile devices and give users access to certain content.[93] Businesses release apps to help consumers access more information about their company or to provide incentives. Apps are discussed in further detail in the next section.

Using Digital Media to Reach Consumers

We've seen that customer-generated communications and digital media connect consumers. These connections let consumers share information and experiences without company interference so they get more of the "real story" on a product or company feature. In many ways, these media take some of the professional marketer's power to control and dispense information and place it in the hands of the consumer.

However, this shift does not have to spell doom for marketers, who can choose to utilize the power of the consumer and Internet technology to their advantage. While consumers use digital media to access more product information, marketers can use the same sites to get better and more targeted information about the consumer— often more than they could gather through traditional marketing venues. Marketers increasingly use consumer-generated content to aid their own marketing efforts, even going so far as to incorporate Internet bloggers in their publicity campaigns. Finally, marketers are using the Internet to track the success of their online marketing campaigns, creating an entirely new way of gathering marketing research.

Although support for the green movement is growing, most consumers want to know how going green can save them money. Until recently, acquiring this information was difficult for the average consumer. Now the explosive growth of mobile applications (apps) is creating a solution to this problem. These "green" apps enable users to save money and/or locate green products by making small changes in their everyday lives. For instance, zerogate's MeterRead iPhone app allows users to monitor their energy meters and then suggests ways that users could further reduce their energy usage. Founder Mark Barton claims that by adopting these suggestions, he was able to decrease his monthly energy bill by $50.

In addition to helping consumers save money, mobile apps can also help to combat greenwashing. Greenwashing occurs when marketers claim that a product is greener than it really is. Because there are very few guidelines on what constitutes a green product, consumers must often research products before they enter the store. One of the most popular green mobile apps, known as GoodGuide, is eliminating this problem.

Consumers with the app can use their phones to photograph product barcodes. The app will then provide information on the sustainability of the product while the consumer is still in the store.

Green apps have the potential to revolutionize the green movement, particularly as it meets consumer desires for cost savings and convenience. Perhaps best of all, many of the apps are relatively inexpensive, ranging from free to a few dollars.[94]

DISCUSSION QUESTIONS

1. What are some of the barriers preventing consumers from buying green products?

2. How can mobile apps help consumers to be more "green"?

3. What are some ways that mobile apps are combating greenwashing?

The challenge for digital media marketers is to constantly adapt to new technologies and changing consumer patterns. Unfortunately, the attrition rate for digital media channels is very high, with some dying off each year as new ones emerge. Social networks are no exception: the earliest ones, like Six Degrees, disappeared when they failed to catch on with the general public, and Friendster, though still active, has been far surpassed by newer networks. As time passes, digital media are becoming more sophisticated so as to reach consumers in more effective ways. Those that are not able to adapt and change eventually fail.

Mastering digital media presents a daunting task for businesses, particularly those used to more traditional means of marketing. For this reason, it is essential that marketers focus on the changing social behaviours of consumers, the ways in which they gather and use information, and the way the Internet is enabling them to get involved in the marketing process.

Charlene Li and Josh Bernoff of Forrester Research, a technology and market research company, emphasize the need for marketers to understand these changing relationships in the online media world. By grouping consumers into different segments based on how they utilize digital media, marketers can gain a better understanding of the online market and how best to proceed.[95] Table 13.2 shows six ways to group consumers based on their Internet activity (or lack thereof). The categories are not mutually exclusive; online consumers can participate in more than one at a time.

Creators are consumers who create their own media outlets, such as blogs, podcasts, consumer-generated videos, and wikis.[96] Consumer-generated media are increasingly important to online marketers as a conduit for addressing consumers directly. The second category, *critics*, consists of people who comment on blogs or post ratings and reviews. Because many online shoppers read ratings and reviews to aid their purchasing decisions, critics should be a primary component in a company's digital marketing strategy. *Collectors* are the most recently recognized category. They collect information and organize content generated by critics and creators.[97] Because collectors are active members of the online community, a company story or site that catches the eye of a collector is likely to be posted, discussed on collector sites, and made available to other online users looking for information.

Joiners include all who become users of Twitter, Facebook, LinkedIn, Pinterest, Tumblr, or other social networking sites. It is not unusual for consumers to be members of several social networking sites at once. Joiners use these sites to connect and network with other users, but as we've seen, marketers too can take significant advantage of these sites to connect with consumers and form customer

Table 13.2 Social Technographics

Creators	• Publish a blog
	• Publish your own Web pages
	• Upload video you created
	• Upload audio/music you created
	• Write articles or stories and post them
Critics	• Post ratings/reviews of products or services
	• Comment on someone else's blog
	• Contribute to online forums
	• Contribute to/edit articles in a wiki
Collectors	• Use RSS feeds
	• Add tags to Web pages or photos
	• "Vote" for websites online
Joiners	• Maintain profile on a social networking site
	• Visit social networking sites
Spectators	• Read blogs
	• Watch video from other users
	• Listen to podcasts
	• Read online forums
	• Read customer ratings/reviews
Inactives	• None of the activities

Source: Charlene Li and Josh Bernoff, *Groundswell* (Boston: Harvard Business Press, 2008), p. 43.

relationships.[98] The last two segments are spectators and inactives. *Spectators,* who read online information but do not join groups or post anywhere, are the largest group in most countries. *Inactives* are online users who do not participate in any digital online media, but their numbers are dwindling.

Marketers who want to capitalize on social and digital media marketing need to consider what proportion of online consumers are creating, rating, collecting, joining, or simply reading online materials. As in traditional marketing efforts, they need to know their target market. For instance, where spectators make up the majority of the online population, companies should post their own corporate messages through blogs and websites promoting their organizations.

Using Digital Media to Learn About Consumers

Marketing research and information systems can use digital media and social networking sites to gather useful information about consumers and their preferences.

Sites such as Twitter, Facebook, LinkedIn, Pinterest, and Tumblr can be good substitutes for focus groups. Online surveys can serve as an alternative to mail, telephone, or personal interviews.

Crowdsourcing describes how marketers use digital media to find out the opinions or needs of the crowd (or potential markets). Communities of interested consumers join sites like threadless.com, which designs T-shirts, or crowdspring.com, which creates logos and print and Web designs. These companies give interested consumers opportunities to contribute and give feedback on product ideas. Crowdsourcing lets companies gather and utilize consumers' ideas in an interactive way when creating new products. There are even sites that crowdsource entire advertising campaigns, like victorsandspoils.com. Mobile phone brand LG offered the public more than $80,000 for ideas about what the mobile phone should look like in two, five, or ten years. Barilla, the Italian pasta brand, gets consumers involved in designing new pasta for little expense—far less than the cost of banner ads on websites. The Ottawa-based company Ideavibes has built a crowdsourcing app that will allow companies to engage with consumers in crowdsourcing campaigns. Ideavibes states, "Crowdsourcing can lead to the creation of cool products, which are customer focused and easy to use."[99] Chaordix is another Canadian company that is enabling businesses to use crowdsourcing. The company has built a platform using feedback from a 50,000-member crowd. The platform allows companies to engage crowds online in a user-friendly environment.

There is no end to the opportunities to gain information, insights, and new-product ideas from consumers. For instance, Rupert Barksfield developed the Multi-Pet Feeder to end pet feeding-time frenzy when one greedy pet eats the other pet's food. Barksfield paid $99 to post a concept and some drawings at quirky.com, and 30,000 people passed judgment on his idea.[100] Consumer feedback is an important part of the digital media equation. Some of the oldest forms of digital media are online forums, where participants post and respond to messages and discuss specific topics. About one-fifth of U.S. and Japanese Internet users participate in discussion forums, whose topics can range from consumer products to movies. Ratings and reviews have become exceptionally popular; 25 percent of the U.S. online population reads this type of consumer-generated feedback.[101] Retailers such as Amazon, Netflix, and Priceline allow consumers to post comments on their sites about the books, movies, and travel arrangements they sell. Today, most online shoppers search the Internet for ratings and reviews before making major purchase decisions.

While consumer-generated content about a firm can be either positive or negative, digital media forums do

DID YOU KNOW?

About three-quarters of people shopping on the Web read online ratings and reviews before making a purchasing decision.[102]

allow businesses to closely monitor what their customers are saying. In the case of negative feedback, businesses can communicate with consumers to address problems or complaints much more easily than through traditional communication channels. Hotels and resorts, for example, have begun monitoring social media sites to see what their guests are saying about them. In some cases, guests who have complained about their rooms using digital media have found themselves upgraded to better rooms that very night.[103] Yet despite the ease and obvious importance of online feedback, many companies do not yet take full advantage of the digital tools at their disposal.

Legal and Social Issues in Internet Marketing

LO6 Identify legal and ethical considerations in digital media.

The extraordinary growth of information technology, the Internet, and e-business has generated many legal and social issues for consumers and businesses. These issues include privacy concerns, the risk of identity theft and online fraud, and the need to protect intellectual property. The major issues related to digital media are privacy, identify theft, online fraud, and intellectual property, which are discussed below.

Privacy

Businesses have long tracked consumers' shopping habits with little controversy. However, observing the contents of a consumer's shopping cart or the process a consumer goes through when choosing a box of cereal generally does not result in the collection of specific, personally identifying data. Although using credit cards, shopping cards, and coupons forces consumers to give up a certain degree of anonymity in the traditional shopping process, they can still choose to remain anonymous by paying cash. Shopping on the Internet, however, allows businesses to track them on a far more personal level, from the contents of their online purchases to the websites they favour. Current technology has made it possible for marketers to amass vast quantities of personal information, often without consumers' knowledge, and to share and sell this information to interested third parties.

How is personal information collected on the Web? Many sites follow users online by storing a *cookie*, or an identifying string of text, on users' computers. Cookies permit website operators to track how often a user visits the site, what he or she looks at while there, and in what sequence. They also allow website visitors to customize services, such as virtual shopping carts, as well as the particular content they see when they log onto a Web page. Users have the option of turning off cookies on their machines, but nevertheless the potential for misuse has left many consumers uncomfortable with this technology. The European Union even passed a law that requires companies to get users' consent before using cookies to track their information. Because of this law, Yahoo Inc. allows Internet users in the United Kingdom to choose whether to opt out of having their Internet habits tracked.[104] Some companies have become even more creative when tracking users. Aaron's, a rent-to-own store, has recently gotten into hot water for installing software in laptops that enables the company to use the computer's webcam to see what its customers are doing. The software, called PC Rental Agent, has been the subject of a number of consumer complaints as it has been used to capture pictures and video of people in very intimate moments, including playing with their children and in some cases having sex.

Even information that consumers willingly post can be used improperly. Facebook in particular has been criticized over the last few years for the mishandling of user information. In 2010, an online security consultant collected public user information from over 100 million

---

Consider the Following: Viewpoints Network Helps Manage Brands Online

As more companies turn toward social media to promote their products, Viewpoints Network is there to help. Founded by entrepreneur Matt Moog in 2006, Viewpoints Network consists of a product-review website (the second-largest) and a software suite to help companies use social media to create effective marketing campaigns. Clients include such well-known companies as Procter & Gamble, Sears, and Kraft.

Viewpoints Network utilizes the power of viral marketing with over a million members registered on its website.

When a company hires Viewpoints Network to promote a brand, Viewpoints Network invites members, specifically opinion leaders, to try the product. Members then write product reviews and share them with their friends on sites like Twitter and Facebook. This represents a growing trend where consumers use the feedback of other consumers—many whom they've never met—in their purchasing decisions. According to founder Matt Moog, this will require a significant change in marketing: the incorporation of the consumer into the marketing mix.[105]

© Simon Jarratt/Corbis

Businesses may be taking online monitoring to a whole new level. PC Rental Agent is software installed on people's laptops that enables the rental agent to capture pictures and video of users.

Facebook users and placed it in a file for companies to download. This type of "scraping"—where companies offer to collect personal information from social networking sites and other online forums—is becoming increasingly common. Since Internet privacy issues have become such a problem, governments in both Canada and the U.S. are proposing bills to address the issue. One proposed law, called the "do not track" law, has been supported by several elected officials in both countries. The "do not track" bill would be an online equivalent of the "do not call" bill for telephones, allowing users to opt out of having their information tracked.[106]

Laws or regulation could pose a significant threat to Web advertisers, who use consumer information to better target advertisements. Such regulations could harm search engines and social networking sites as well. According to Facebook, 80 percent of the world's 100 largest advertisers are on Facebook. As a result of this threat, Google, Facebook, and other Web-based companies are increasing their lobbying efforts to ward off regulation that may be potentially damaging. In one year, Google spent approximately $4 million on lobbying efforts. Self-regulation is another option some Web advertisers are pursuing.[107] On the other hand, certain advertising agencies, networks, and industry trade groups have made the decision to work with Internet-browser makers to create a "do-not-track" system. This represents a major shift for these advertising groups, which until recently have largely opposed such a system. However, although Microsoft and Mozilla have both integrated "do-not-track" features into their browsers, advertisers have a choice as to whether they will respect users' do-not-track requests.[108] Several non-profit organizations have stepped in to help companies develop privacy policies. Among the best known are TRUSTe and the Better Business Bureau Online. TRUSTe is a non-profit organization devoted to promoting global trust in Internet technology. Companies that agree to abide by TRUSTe's privacy standards may display a "trustmark" on their websites; thousands of websites currently do so.[109] The BBBOnline program provides verification, monitoring and review, consumer dispute resolution, a compliance seal, enforcement mechanisms, and an educational component. It is managed by the Council of Better Business Bureaus, an organization with considerable experience in conducting self-regulation and dispute-resolution programs.[110] The hope among online marketers is that widespread adoption of these privacy policies may prevent regulation that could make it more difficult to advertise effectively online.

Identity Theft

Identity theft occurs when criminals obtain personal information that allows them to impersonate someone else in order to use the person's credit to access financial accounts and make purchases. Many of these breaches occur at banks, universities, and other businesses that contain sensitive consumer information.[111] This requires organizations to implement increased security measures to prevent database theft and while these usually work, problems do still occur. For example, in 2013, the Canadian government announced it lost a portable hard drive containing the personal information of over 500,000 people who took out student loans. The lost drive included vast amounts of information including names, Social Insurance Numbers, dates of birth, addresses, and other personal information. The most common complaints about identity theft relate to credit card fraud, followed by utility fraud, bank fraud, employment-related fraud, government document fraud, and loan fraud.[112]

identity theft when criminals obtain personal information that allows them to impersonate someone else in order to use their credit to access financial accounts and make purchases

The Internet's relative anonymity and speed make possible both legal and illegal access to databases storing Social Insurance Numbers, driver's licence numbers, dates of birth, mothers' maiden names, and other information that can be used to establish a credit card or bank account in another person's name in order to make fraudulent transactions. One growing scam used to initiate identity theft fraud is the practice of *phishing*, whereby con artists counterfeit a well-known website and send out e-mails directing victims to it. There visitors find instructions to reveal sensitive information such as their credit card numbers. Phishing scams have faked websites for PayPal, AOL, and the U.S. Federal Deposit Insurance Corporation.

Some identity theft problems are resolved quickly, while other cases take weeks and hundreds of dollars before a victim's bank balances and credit standings are restored.

Online Fraud

Online fraud includes any attempt to conduct fraudulent activities online, such as by deceiving consumers into releasing personal information. It is becoming a major source of frustration among users of social networking sites, because

online fraud any attempt to conduct fraudulent activities online

cybercriminals are finding new ways to use sites like Facebook and Twitter to commit fraudulent activities. For instance, they will create profiles under a company's name to either damage the company's reputation (particularly larger, more controversial companies) or lure that company's customers into releasing personal information the perpetrators can use for monetary gain.

Another tactic is to copy a blog entry from a reputable company and repost it with a link that connects the user to the criminal's own fraudulent site, where he or she attempts to sell the user goods (under the reputable company's name) or collect personal information. For instance, a fraudster may repost a blog written by a professional sport organization with a fraudulent link that connects users to a site that sells unlicensed sporting goods.[113] Criminals may also use social networking sites to pose as charitable institutions. After the 2010 earthquake in Haiti, fraudsters set up fake accounts to scam Facebook users into donating money for the fraudsters' own financial gain.[114] Despite any number of safeguards, the best protection for consumers is to be careful when they divulge information online. The surest way to stay out of trouble is never to give out personal information, like a Social Insurance Number or credit card number, unless it is a site you trust and that you know is legitimate.

Intellectual Property

In addition to protecting personal privacy, Internet users and others want to protect their rights to property they may create, including songs, movies, books, and software. Such intellectual property consists of the ideas and creative materials developed to solve problems, carry out applications, and educate and entertain others.

Although intellectual property is generally protected by patents and copyrights, each year losses from the illegal copying of computer programs, music, movies, compact discs, and books reaches billions of dollars in North America. This has become a particular problem with digital media sites. Chinese search engine Baidu has been accused of offering an MP3 service that allows users to download proprietary songs for free. The recording industry sued Baidu in 2005 for Internet piracy, but the Chinese government sided with Baidu.[115] Another example is YouTube, which has faced lawsuits over its users' possible infringement of other companies' copyrights. In one case, Viacom Inc. sued YouTube's owner, Google, claiming Google had violated its copyrights by allowing users to post protected film clips on YouTube.[116] Although YouTube is responsible for the video content shown on its sites, it can be difficult for Google to monitor and remove all the videos that may contain copyrighted content, given the many millions of clips that are loaded onto YouTube daily.

Illegal sharing of content is another major intellectual property problem. Some consumers rationalize the pirating of software, videogames, movies, and music for a number of reasons. First, many feel they just don't have the money to pay for what they want. Second, because their friends engage in piracy and swap digital content, some users feel influenced to engage in this activity. Others enjoy the thrill of getting away with something with a low risk of consequences. And finally, some people feel being tech-savvy allows them to take advantage of the opportunity to pirate content.[117] There are also a number of consumers who simply do not feel they are doing anything wrong when they share or download software. As discussed in Chapter 2, Gary Fung, founder of Vancouver-based isoHunt, does not think there is anything wrong with sharing TV shows, films, and so forth and has made millions selling advertising to his website. The U.S. courts do not agree with Mr. Fung and have levied a $150 million fine against his company. Fung's argument is that his site, much like Google, is a search engine that organizes data. What users do with that data is not for him to control and when asked to remove a movie or TV show due to copyright he complies.

"Developing a strategic understanding of how digital marketing can make business more efficient and productive is increasingly necessary."

The software industry loses over $50 billion globally each year due to theft and illegal use of software products, according to the Business Software Alliance.[118] About 90 percent of illegal software copying is actually done by businesses. For example, a firm may obtain a licence to install a specific application on 100 of its computers but actually installs it on 300. In some cases, software is illegally made available through the Internet by companies that have taken the software from the producer and set up their own distribution system. Both the Canadian and U.S. governments are pursuing tougher laws against online piracy.

© Perry Mastrovito/Creatas/PictureQuest

Even the government is prone to mistakes in managing people's information as is evident in the 2013 announcement that Canada lost a file containing personal information about 500,000 Canadians.

Digital Media's Impact on Marketing

To be successful in business, you need to know much more than how to use a social networking site to communicate with friends. Developing a strategic understanding of how digital marketing can make business more efficient and productive is increasingly necessary. If you are thinking of becoming an entrepreneur, then the digital world can open doors to new resources and customers. Smart phones, mobile broadband, and webcams are among the tools that can make the most of the online business world, creating greater efficiency at less cost. For example, rather than using traditional phone lines, Skype helps people make and receive calls via the Internet and provides free video calling and text messaging for a fraction of the cost of a land line.[119] It is up to businesses and entrepreneurs to develop strategies that achieve business success using existing and future technology, software, and networking opportunities.

Traditional businesses accustomed to using print media can find the transition to digital challenging. New media may require employees with new skills or additional training for current employees. There is often a gap between technical knowledge of how to develop sites and how to develop effective digital marketing strategies to enhance business success. Determining the correct blend of traditional and new media requires careful consideration; the mix will vary depending on the business, its size, and its target market. Future career opportunities will require skills in both traditional and digital media areas so that marketers properly understand and implement marketing strategies that help businesses achieve a competitive advantage.

TEAM EXERCISE

Develop a digital marketing promotion for a local sports team. Use Twitter, Facebook, and other social networking media to promote ticket sales for next season's schedule. In your plan, provide specific details and ideas for the content you would use on the sites. Also, describe how you would encourage fans and potential fans to go to your site. How would you use digital media to motivate sports fans to purchase tickets and merchandise and attend games?

LEARNING OBJECTIVES SUMMARY

LO1 Define digital media and digital marketing and recognize their increasing value in strategic planning.

Digital media are electronic media that function using digital codes via computers, cellular phones, smartphones, and other digital devices that have been released in recent years. Digital marketing uses all digital media, including the Internet and mobile and interactive channels, to develop communication and exchanges with customers.

Because both have impacted strategic planning by allowing for instant communication with precisely defined consumer groups, firms can use real-time exchanges to stimulate interactive communication, forge closer relationships, and learn more accurately about consumer and supplier needs. Thus, firms who use digital media and digital marketing should have a better understanding of consumers, be able to communicate with them more efficiently, and be able to manage their marketing mix to appeal to a broad range of people.

LO2 Understand the characteristics of digital media and how they differentiate these methods from traditional marketing activities.

While digital marketing shares some similarities with conventional marketing techniques, a few valuable differences stand out. First, digital media make customer communications faster and interactive. Second, digital media help companies reach new target markets more easily, affordably, and quickly than ever before. Finally, digital media help marketers utilize new resources in seeking out and communicating with customers.

LO3 Demonstrate the role of digital marketing and social networking in today's business environment.

One of the most important benefits of digital marketing is the ability of marketers and customers to easily share information. Through websites, social networks, and other digital media, consumers can learn about everything they consume and use in their lives, ask questions, voice complaints, indicate preferences, and otherwise communicate about their needs and desires. Many marketers use e-mail, mobile phones, social networking, wikis, video sharing, podcasts, blogs, videoconferencing, and other technologies to coordinate activities and communicate with employees, customers, and suppliers. Twitter, considered both a social network and a micro blog, illustrates how these digital technologies can combine to create new communication opportunities.

LO4 Show how digital media affect the marketing mix.

Product Considerations. Like traditional marketers, digital marketers must anticipate consumer needs and preferences, tailor their products and services to meet these needs, and continually upgrade them to remain competitive. The connectivity created by digital media provide the opportunity for adding services and enhancing product benefits.

Distribution/Place. The Internet is a new distribution channel for making products available at the right time, at the right place, and in the right quantities. Marketers' ability to process orders electronically and increase the speed of communication via the Internet reduces inefficiencies, costs, and redundancies while increasing speed throughout the marketing channel. Shipping times and costs have become an important consideration in attracting customers, prompting many companies to offer consumers low shipping costs or next-day delivery.

Promotion Considerations. Perhaps one of the best ways businesses can utilize digital media is for promotion purposes—whether they are increasing brand awareness, connecting with consumers, or taking advantage of social networks or virtual worlds to form relationships and generate positive publicity or "buzz" about their products. Thanks to online promotion, consumers can be more informed than ever, including reading customer-generated content before making purchasing decisions. Consumer consumption patterns are radically changing, and marketers must adapt their promotional efforts to meet them.

Pricing Considerations. Price is the most flexible element of the marketing mix. Digital marketing can enhance the value of products by providing extra benefits such as service, information, and convenience. Through digital media, discounts and other promotions can be quickly communicated.

LO5 Define social networking and illustrate how businesses can use different types of social networking media.

A social network is "a Web-based meeting place for friends, family, co-workers, and peers that lets users create a profile and connect with other users for purposes that range from getting acquainted, to keeping in touch, to building a work-related network." Social networks are a valued part of marketing because they are changing the way consumers communicate with each other and with firms. Sites such as Facebook, Instagram, Twitter, and LinkedIn have emerged as opportunities for marketers to build communities, provide product information, and learn about consumer needs. By the time you read this, it is possible there will be new social network sites that continue to advance digital communication and opportunities for marketers. The uses of social networking are widespread. Companies can use blogs to answer questions, YouTube to post videos, and social network sites such as Facebook to communicate with customers.

LO6 Identify legal and ethical considerations in digital media.

The major issues related to legal and ethical concerns are privacy, identity theft, online fraud, and intellectual property.

KEY TERMS

accessibility
addressability
blog
connectivity
control
digital marketing
digital media
e-business

identity theft
interactivity
online fraud
podcast
social network
viral marketing
wiki

[Handwritten notes:]
1) Identify your focus chapters and or questions
2) choose the one most comfortable with
3) Link text book with slides this will help to shape ur understand around what they r look for sma they team using the slides.

DESTINATION CEO DISCUSSION QUESTIONS

1. Do you think Arlene Dickinson's approach of getting to know people personally is becoming more difficult in today's business world?

2. Do you think it is essential to get to know people's stories, both business and personal, to serve them successfully in a marketing and communication campaign? Why or why not?

3. Dickinson works for businesses that are heavily reliant on social media and frequently track website usage of consumers. Does this information change your opinion of her, especially given her belief that she acts in a socially responsible manner?

4. Dickinson's company represents businesses that have been charged with harming the environment in Canada's oil sands. Can you be personally ethical if you work for firms in questionable industries?

SO YOU WANT TO BE *a Digital Marketer*

The business world has grown increasingly dependent on digital marketing to maintain communication with stakeholders. Reaching customers is often a major concern, but digital marketing can also be used to communicate with suppliers, concerned community members, and special interest groups about issues related to sustainability, safety practices, and philanthropic activities. Many types of jobs exist: account executive directors of social media and directors of marketing for digital products, as well as digital advertisers, online marketers, global digital marketers, and brand managers are prominently listed on career opportunity websites.

Entrepreneurs are taking advantage of the low cost of digital marketing, building social networking sites to help market their products. In fact, some small businesses such as specialty publishing, personal health and beauty, and other specialty products can use digital marketing as the primary channel for reaching consumers. Many small businesses are posting signs outside their stores with statements such as "Follow us on Twitter" or "Check out our Facebook page."

To utilize digital marketing, especially social networking, requires more than information technology skills related to constructing websites, graphics, videos, podcasts, and so on. Most importantly, one must be able to determine how digital media can be used in implementing a marketing strategy. All marketing starts with identifying a target market and developing a marketing mix to satisfy customers. Digital marketing is just another way to reach customers, provide information, and develop relationships. Therefore, your opportunity for a career in this field is greatly based on understanding the messages, desired level of interactivity, and connectivity that helps achieve marketing objectives.

As social media use skyrockets, digital marketing professionals will be in demand. The experience of many businesses and research indicate digital marketing is a powerful way to increase brand exposure and generate traffic. In fact, a study conducted on Social Media Examiner found that 85 percent of marketers surveyed believe generating exposure for their business is their number-one advantage in Internet marketing. As consumers use social networking for their personal communication, they will be more open to obtaining information about products through this channel. Digital marketing could be the fastest-growing opportunity in business.

To prepare yourself for a digital marketing career, learn not only the technical aspects, but also how social media can be used to maximize marketing performance. A glance at careerbuilder.com indicates that management positions such as account manager, digital marketing manager, and digital product manager can pay from $60,000 to $170,000 or more per year.

BUILD YOUR BUSINESS PLAN

Digital Marketing and Social Networking

As you are building your business plan, one thing that is virtually certain is that you will need a digital marketing strategy. Digital marketing including social networking sites allows businesses to engage with more consumers, establish a two-way communication relationship with customers, and ultimately should enable a business to be more successful.

The question many new businesses face is not whether they should use online marketing tools, but what tools are most appropriate for their business. As discussed throughout the chapter, there are a number of different online techniques a business can use, and each involves an investment of time and sometimes money. Given that new businesses often have a shortage of both, it is crucial that as an entrepreneur you develop a clear strategy for digital marketing. A successful way to do this is to evaluate each marketing tool in a table or spreadsheet as they relate to your business. Create a table where you assess and highlight the user demographics of the various sites—Facebook, Twitter, and so forth—and how you may use the site in your business. You can start to think about which tools you will use, and which tools would likely not work best for your business. You could then extend the table further and state specifically how you could incorporate these digital marketing sites into your company's overall marketing plan. After completing this analysis you should have a sense of what digital marketing tools would work best with your prospective business.

As Facebook and other social media sites have gained popularity and expanded, managing their use at work has become an increasingly hot topic. Studies on the use of social media in the workplace conflict over how much it inhibits productivity. Should employees be allowed to access social media at work? Many offices have banned access to the site. The results are as mixed as the research. The 2011 National Business Ethics Survey® revealed that 11 percent of employees who engage in social networking are "active" social networkers who spend 30 percent or more of the work day on social networking sites. Many managers are conflicted as to whether this constitutes enough of a problem to be banned outright.

Another study conducted by Nucleus Research (an IT research company) revealed a 1.5 percent loss of productivity for businesses allowing social media access. It found that 77 percent of Facebook users used the site during work for as much as two hours a day; 87 percent of those surveyed admitted they were using social media sites to waste time. NBES also found that active social networkers were more likely to find certain questionable behaviours to be acceptable, such as criticizing the company or its managers on social networking sites. Procter & Gamble realized that many of its employees were using social networking sites for non-work purposes. Its investigations revealed that employees across the company were watching an average of 50,000 five-minute YouTube videos and listening to 4,000 hours of music on Pandora daily.

However, an outright ban could cause problems. Some younger employees have expressed that they do not want to work for companies without social media access; they view restricting or eliminating access like removing a benefit. Employees at companies with an outright ban often resent the lack of trust associated with such a move and feel that management is censoring their activities. Additionally, Procter & Gamble uses YouTube and Facebook extensively for marketing purposes. Banning these sites would disrupt the firm's marketing efforts.

An Australian study indicates that employees taking time out to pursue Facebook and other social media were actually 9 percent more productive than those who did not. Brent Coker, the study's author and University of Melbourne faculty member, says people are more productive when they take time to "zone out" throughout the work day. Doing so can improve concentration. Coker's study focused on those using less than 20 percent of the workday on such breaks, which is less than the amount of time "active" social networkers spend on these sites.

Some companies actually encourage employees to use social networking as part of their integrated marketing strategy. For example, Patrick Hoover Law Offices charges employees with the responsibility to use social media in ways that the employees believe can benefit the company. Although this does potentially allow employees to use social media for personal purposes rather than for work, this tactic has been effective in getting new clients and publicizing the organization. By trusting its employees and giving them leeway to use social media in ways they see fit, Patrick Hoover Law Offices has taken a potential problem and reworked it to its own advantage.

Despite the benefits that companies like Patrick Hoover Law Offices have received from allowing their employees to use social media, many companies have gone ahead with social media bans. For example, Procter & Gamble has restricted the use of Netflix and Pandora, but not Facebook or YouTube. Companies all need to ask, "Can management use social media to benefit the company?" If so, it may be more advantageous to take the risks of employees using social media for personal use if they can also be encouraged to use social networks to publicize their organizations, connect with customers, and view consumer comments or complaints. By restricting social media use, companies may be forfeiting an effective marketing tool.

DISCUSSION QUESTIONS

1. Why do you think results are so mixed on the use of social networking in the workplace?

2. What are some possible upsides to utilizing social media as part of an integrated marketing strategy, especially in digital marketing?

3. What are the downsides to restricting employee access to social networking sites?

DESTINATION CEO

Jack Dorsey grew up in Missouri and later studied at New York University. He then moved to California where he started a company to dispatch couriers, taxis, and emergency services using the Internet. He co-founded Twitter, Inc. in 2006, alongside Biz Stone and Evan Williams. Now, Dorsey is entering into new territory: the banking industry. Specifically, Dorsey has created a product called Square that he hopes will replace traditional credit card readers. Square is a small credit card swiper that merchants plug into their smartphones. After swiping the card, customers sign on the phone's screen, and within one minute, the transaction is complete. Square also tracks all sales conducted through its readers, creating a useful database.

Dorsey created Square after recognizing the massive unmet demand from less traditional merchants—such as artists—who do not own credit card readers. Square also reduces the number of organizations and fees involved with traditional credit card transactions, charging merchants a flat 2.75 percent and 15 cents for each transaction. *Time* was so impressed with Square that it nominated the product as one of the 50 best inventions of 2013. Despite its promising start, opportunities for credit card fraud will require Square to proactively take measures to ensure safe, convenient transactions.

Dorsey was ousted from Twitter in 2014, but returned as permanent CEO of the company in 2015, while still juggling his obligations as CEO of Square Inc. Each day, he spends eight to ten hours at Twitter where he guides decisions on product development and helps think through how to build out the business. Then he walks a few blocks over to the mobile payments company Square where he spends another eight to ten hours working with his team to design and build a next-generation payments system. No problem, says Dorsey: "Most people have major positions at companies and they're also raising families. They have two-year-olds. I have it easy," he says, noting as he often does that he is single and lives just a few blocks from the office.[1]

Introduction

Accounting, the financial "language" that organizations use to record, measure, and interpret all of their financial transactions and records, is very important in business. All businesses—from a small family farm to a giant corporation—use the language of accounting to make sure they use their money wisely and to plan for the future. Non-business organizations such as charities and governments also use accounting to demonstrate to donors and taxpayers how well they are using their funds and meeting their stated objectives.

This chapter explores the role of accounting in business and its importance in making business decisions. First, we discuss the uses of accounting information and the accounting process. Then, we briefly look at some simple financial statements and accounting tools that are useful in analyzing organizations worldwide.

The Nature of Accounting

LO1 Define accounting and describe the different uses of accounting information.

Simply stated, **accounting** is the recording, measurement, and interpretation of financial information. Large numbers of people and institutions, both within and outside businesses, use accounting tools to evaluate organizational operations. The Accounting Standards Board (AcSB) is the body with the authority to establish accounting standards for use by all Canadian companies outside the public sector.[2] These rules are called *generally accepted accounting principles*, or *GAAP*. GAAP is a framework that includes a common set of rules and a standard format for public companies to use when they prepare their reports. Public companies must follow the principles and rules set out in the International Financial Reporting Standards (IFRS). International Financial Reporting Standards (IFRS) are a single set of high-quality, understandable, and enforceable global standards.[3] Private companies follow *accounting standards for private enterprises* (ASPE), and non-for-profit organizations follow *accounting standards for not-for-profit organizations* (ASNPO).

To better understand the importance of accounting, we must first understand who prepares accounting information and how it is used.

© Tupungato/Shutterstock.com

KPMG is part of the "Big Four," or the four largest international accounting firms. The other three are PricewaterhouseCoopers, Ernst & Young, and Deloitte Touche Tohmatsu.

> **DID YOU KNOW?**
>
> More than one in ten global executives reported their company as having experienced a significant fraud in the past two years.[4]

money managers who can successfully hide illegal or misleading accounting practices for a while, eventually they are exposed. After the accounting scandals of Enron and Worldcom in the early 2000s, the U.S. Congress passed the *Sarbanes-Oxley Act*, which required firms to be more rigorous in their accounting and reporting practices. Canadian regulators favoured a more gradual approach, such as Bill 198 in Ontario. This allowed Canadian participants to better reflect the fundamental differences between the Canadian and U.S. capital

Accountants

Many of the functions of accounting are carried out by public or private accountants.

Large corporations, government agencies, and other organizations may employ their own **accountant** to prepare and analyze their financial statements. With titles such as controller, treasurer, or tax auditor, accountants are deeply involved in many of the most important financial decisions of the organizations for which they work. Accountants can be chartered professional accountants (CPAs) by completing the CPA certification program.

Other accountants are either self-employed or members of large public accounting firms such as Ernst & Young, KPMG, Deloitte, and PricewaterhouseCoopers, together referred to as "the Big Four." In addition, many CPAs work for one of the second-tier accounting firms that are much smaller than the Big Four firms, as illustrated in Table 14.1.

While there will always be companies and individual

accounting the recording, measurement, and interpretation of financial information

accountant a professional employed by large corporations, government agencies, and other organizations to prepare and analyze their financial statements

Table 14.1 Leading Accounting Firms

Company	2013 Revenues ('000)	Number of Offices
"Top ten Firms"		
Deloitte LLP	$1,776,000	55
PricewaterhouseCoopers LLP	$1,211,200	25
KPMG LLP	$1,203,102	37
Ernst & Young LLP	$968,000	17
Grant Thornton Canada	$582,000	135
MNP LLP	$487,000	58
BDO Canada LLP	$465,000	111
Collins Barrow	$177,570	41
Richter	$80,289	2
Mallette	$63,982	24

Adapted from "Canada's Accounting Top 30," *The Bottom Line*, April 2014, http://www.thebottomlinenews.ca/documents/canadas_accounting_top_30.pdf (accessed September 28, 2016).

markets.[5] Only five years after the passage of the *Sarbanes-Oxley Act*, the world experienced a financial crisis starting in 2008—part of which was due to excessive risk taking and inappropriate accounting practices. Many U.S. banks developed questionable lending practices and investments based on subprime mortgages made to individuals who had poor credit. When housing prices declined and people suddenly found that they owed more on their mortgages than their homes were worth, they began to default. The global financial crisis that resulted led to a series of significant regulatory changes to international banking rules, which are designed to reduce the risk of another financial crisis occurring. While these rules are set internationally, Canadian regulators have implemented them.[6]

A growing area for public accountants is *forensic accounting*, which involves analyzing financial documents in search of fraudulent entries or financial misconduct. Functioning as much like detectives as accountants, forensic accountants have been used since the 1930s. In the wake of the accounting scandals of the early 2000s, many auditing firms are rapidly adding or expanding forensic or fraud-detection services. Additionally, many forensic accountants root out evidence of "cooked books" for federal agencies like the RCMP. The Association of Certified Fraud Examiners, which certifies accounting professionals as *certified fraud examiners (CFEs)*, has grown to more than 80,000 members, with chapters in Canada and around the world.[7]

Accounting or Bookkeeping?

The terms *accounting* and *bookkeeping* are often mistakenly used interchangeably. Much narrower and far more mechanical than accounting, bookkeeping is typically limited to the routine, day-to-day recording of business transactions. Bookkeepers are responsible for obtaining and recording the information that accountants require to analyze a firm's financial position. They generally require less training than accountants. Accountants, on the other hand, usually complete course work beyond their basic four- or five-year accounting degrees. This additional training allows accountants not only to record financial information but also to understand, interpret, and even develop the sophisticated accounting systems necessary to classify and analyze complex financial information.

The Uses of Accounting Information

Accountants summarize the information from a firm's business transactions in various financial statements (which we'll look at in a later section of this chapter) for a variety of stakeholders, including managers, investors, creditors, and government agencies. Many business failures may be directly linked to ignorance of the information "hidden" inside these financial statements. Likewise, most business successes can be traced to informed managers who understand the consequences of their decisions. While maintaining and even increasing short-run profits is desirable, the failure to plan sufficiently for the future can easily lead an otherwise successful company to insolvency and bankruptcy court.

Basically, managers and owners use financial statements (1) to aid in internal planning and control, and (2) for external purposes such as reporting to the Canada Revenue Agency shareholders, creditors, customers, employees, and other interested parties. Figure 14.1 shows some of the users of the accounting information generated by a typical corporation.

Internal Uses. **Managerial accounting** refers to the internal use of accounting statements by managers in planning and directing the organization's activities. Perhaps management's greatest single concern is **cash flow**, the movement of money through an organization over a daily, weekly, monthly, or yearly basis. Obviously, for any business to succeed, it needs to generate enough cash to pay its bills as they fall due. However, it is not at all unusual for highly successful and rapidly growing

managerial accounting the internal use of accounting statements by managers in planning and directing the organization's activities

cash flow the movement of money through an organization over a daily, weekly, monthly, or yearly basis

Figure 14.1 The Users of Accounting Information

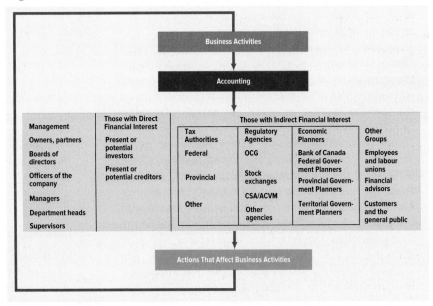

Source: Adapted from Belverd E. Needles, Henry R. Anderson, and James C. Caldwell, *Principles of Accounting*, 4th edition. Copyright © 1990 by Houghton Mifflin Company. Reprinted with permission.

companies to struggle to make payments to employees, suppliers, and lenders because of an inadequate cash flow. One common reason for a so-called cash crunch, or shortfall, is poor managerial planning.

budget an internal financial plan that forecasts expenses and income over a set period of time

Managerial accountants also help prepare an organization's **budget**, an internal financial plan that forecasts expenses and income over a set period of time. It is not unusual for an organization to prepare separate daily, weekly, monthly, and yearly budgets. Think of a budget as a financial map, showing how the company expects to move from Point A to Point B over a specific period of time. While most companies prepare *master budgets* for the entire firm, many also prepare budgets for smaller segments of the organization such as divisions, departments, product lines, or projects. "Top-down" master budgets begin at the top and filter down to the individual department level, while "bottom-up" budgets start at the department or project level and are combined at the chief executive's office. Generally, the larger and more rapidly growing an organization, the

greater will be the likelihood that it will build its master budget from the ground up.

Regardless of focus, the major value of a budget lies in its breakdown of cash inflows and outflows. Expected operating expenses (cash outflows such as wages, materials costs, and taxes) and operating revenues (cash inflows in the form of payments from customers) over a set period of time are carefully forecasted and subsequently compared with actual results. Deviations between the two serve as a "trip wire" or "feedback loop" to launch more detailed financial analyses in an effort to pinpoint trouble spots and opportunities.

External Uses. Managers also use accounting statements to report the business's financial performance to outsiders. Such statements are used for filing income taxes, obtaining credit from lenders, and reporting results to the firm's shareholders. They become the basis for the information provided in the official corporate **annual report**, a summary of the firm's financial

annual report summary of a firm's financial information, products, and growth plans for owners and potential investors

---

GOING GREEN | Accounting Goes Green

Accounting and sustainability may seem like an unusual combination. After all, the purpose of the accounting profession is handling and reporting financial information, not adopting green practices. However, an increasing emphasis on sustainability has prompted the Canadian Institute of Chartered Accountants, the Chartered Institute of Management Accountants, the American Institute of CPAs (AICPA), and other global organizations to rethink the importance of sustainability to the financial profession.

Studies by these organizations have determined that at least one-third of smaller companies are incorporating sustainability strategies into their businesses, with another quarter indicating that they intend to do the same in the next few years. For instance, organizations such as French firm Esker have begun adopting cloud-based hiring tools to replace traditional paper résumés. For such practices to succeed, managers from all levels of the organization must support these initiatives, particularly company accountants and finance executives. These finance professionals are essential to the process because they are the ones who are in the best position to understand the "big picture." Although sustainability is important, businesses must still succeed financially if they want to survive. Therefore, it is up to financial professionals—who have in-depth knowledge of the company's financial information—to

find ways to use sustainability initiatives to improve operations.

Accounting organizations have created recommendations for finance professionals to determine which sustainable strategies to adopt. For instance, finance professionals must link sustainability to profit and find out which initiatives would cut costs and increase efficiency. They must create metrics to measure the success of these initiatives and determine whether changes are needed. Additionally, these organizations recommend that accountants incorporate the company's sustainability efforts into "mainstream reporting" for stakeholders.[8]

DISCUSSION QUESTIONS

1. Why should accountants be involved in a company's decision to incorporate greener business practices?

2. Describe some of the recommendations that accounting organizations have developed regarding sustainability strategies.

3. What could happen if companies arbitrarily adopted sustainability strategies without assessing their impact?

information, products, and growth plans for owners and potential investors. While frequently presented between slick, glossy covers prepared by major advertising firms, the single most important component of an annual report is the signature of a certified public accountant attesting that the required financial statements are an accurate reflection of the underlying financial condition of the firm. Financial statements meeting these conditions are termed *audited*. The primary external users of audited accounting information are government agencies, shareholders and potential investors, and lenders, suppliers, and employees.

During the global financial crisis, it turns out that Greece had been engaging in deceptive accounting practices, with the help of U.S. investment banks. Greece was using financial techniques that hid massive amounts of debt from its public balance sheets. Eventually, the markets figured out that the country might not be able to pay off its creditors. The European Union and the International Monetary Fund came up with a plan to give Greece some credit relief, but tied to this was the message to "get your financial house in order." By the middle of 2012, the European problem was often referred to as the PIGS. This referred to Portugal, Italy, Ireland, Greece, and Spain—all of which were having debt problems. The PIGS have caused cracks in the European Monetary Union. While Germany demanded austerity, others wanted more growth-oriented strategies. Clearly, the financial crisis will have some lasting effects that need clear accounting solutions.[9]

Financial statements evaluate the return on shareholders' investment and the overall quality of the firm's management team. A corporation's shareholders use financial statements to evaluate the return on their investment and the overall quality of the firm's management team. As a result, poor financial statements often result in changes in top management. Potential investors study the financial statements in a firm's annual report to determine whether the company meets their investment requirements

and whether the returns from a given firm are likely to compare favourably with other similar companies.

"A corporation's shareholders use financial statements to evaluate the return on their investment and the overall quality of the firm's management team."

Banks and other lenders look at financial statements to determine a company's ability to meet current and future debt obligations if a loan or credit is granted. To determine this ability, a short-term lender examines a firm's cash flow to assess its ability to repay a loan quickly with cash generated from sales. A long-term lender is more interested in the company's profitability and indebtedness to other lenders.

Labour unions and employees use financial statements to establish reasonable expectations for salary and other benefit requests. Just as firms experiencing record profits are likely to face added pressure to increase employee wages, so too are employees unlikely to grant employers wage and benefit concessions without considerable evidence of financial distress.

The Accounting Process

LO2 Demonstrate the accounting process.

Many view accounting as a primary business language. It is of little use, however, unless you know how to "speak" it. Fortunately, the fundamentals—the accounting equation and the double-entry bookkeeping system—are not difficult to learn. These two concepts serve as the starting point for all currently accepted accounting principles.

"Many view accounting as a primary business language."

The Accounting Equation

Accountants are concerned with reporting an organization's assets, liabilities, and owners' equity. To help illustrate these concepts, consider a hypothetical flower shop called Anna's Flowers, owned by Anna Rodriguez. A firm's economic resources, or items of value that it owns, represent its **assets**—cash, inventory, land, equipment, buildings, and other tangible and intangible things. The assets of Anna's Flowers include counters, refrigerated display cases, flowers, decorations, vases, cards, and other gifts,

assets a firm's economic resources, or items of value that it owns, such as cash, inventory, land, equipment, buildings, and other tangible and intangible things

© pandpstock001/iStockphoto/Getty Images

The annual report is a summary of the firm's financial information, products, and growth plans for owners and potential investors. Many investors look at a firm's annual report to determine how well the company is doing financially.

liabilities debts that a firm owes to others

owners' equity equals assets minus liabilities and reflects historical values

accounting equation assets equal liabilities plus owners' equity

double-entry bookkeeping a system of recording and classifying business transactions that maintains the balance of the accounting equation

as well as something known as "goodwill," which in this case is Anna's reputation for preparing and delivering beautiful floral arrangements on a timely basis. **Liabilities**, on the other hand, are debts the firm owes to others. Among the liabilities of Anna's Flowers are a loan from the Business Development Bank of Canada and money owed to flower suppliers and other creditors for items purchased. The **owners' equity** category contains all of the money that has ever been contributed to the company that never has to be paid back. The funds can come from investors who have given money or assets to the company, or it can come from past profitable operations. In the case of Anna's Flowers, if Anna were to sell off, or liquidate, her business, any money left over after selling all the shop's assets and paying off its liabilities would comprise her owner's equity. The relationship between assets, liabilities, and owners' equity is a fundamental concept in accounting and is known as the **accounting equation**:

$$Assets = Liabilities + Owners'\ equity$$

Double-Entry Bookkeeping

Double-entry bookkeeping is a system of recording and classifying business transactions in separate accounts in order to maintain the balance of the accounting equation. Returning to Anna's Flowers, suppose Anna buys $325 worth of roses on credit from the Antique Rose Emporium to fill a wedding order. When she records this transaction, she will list the $325 as a liability or a debt to a supplier. At the same time, however, she will also record $325 worth

© Pavel L Photo and Video/Shutterstock

A firm's assets include tangible items, as in the case of this restaurant's service tables, equipment, and even the atmosphere created by the wall's artwork.

of roses as an asset in an account known as *inventory*. Because the assets and liabilities are on different sides of the accounting equation, Anna's accounts increase in total size (by $325) but remain in balance:

$$Assets = Liabilities + Owners'\ equity$$
$$\$325 = \$325$$

Thus, to keep the accounting equation in balance, each business transaction must be recorded in two separate accounts.

In the final analysis, all business transactions are classified as either assets, liabilities, or owners' equity. However, most organizations further break down these three accounts to provide more specific information about a transaction. For example, assets may be broken down into specific categories such as cash, inventory, and equipment, while liabilities may include bank loans, supplier credit, and other debts.

Figure 14.2 shows how Anna used the double-entry bookkeeping system to account for all of the transactions that took place in her first month of business. These transactions include her initial investment of $2,500, the loan from the Small Business Administration, purchases of equipment and inventory, and the purchase of roses on credit. In her first month of business, Anna generated revenues of $2,000 by selling $1,500 worth of inventory. Thus, she deducts, or (in accounting notation that is appropriate for assets) *credits*, $1,500 from inventory and adds, or *debits*, $2,000 to the cash account. The difference between Anna's $2,000 cash inflow and her $1,500 outflow is represented by a credit to owners' equity, because it is money that belongs to her as the owner of the flower shop.

The Accounting Cycle

In any accounting system, financial data typically pass through a four-step procedure sometimes called the **accounting cycle**. The steps include examining source documents, recording transactions in an accounting journal, posting recorded transactions, and preparing financial statements. Figure 14.3 shows how Anna works through them. Traditionally, all of these steps were performed using paper, pencils, and erasers (lots of erasers!), but today the process is often fully computerized.

Step One: Examine Source Documents. Like all good managers, Anna Rodriguez begins the accounting cycle by gathering and examining source documents— cheques, credit-card receipts, sales slips, and other related evidence concerning specific transactions.

accounting cycle the four-step procedure of an accounting system: examining source documents, recording transactions in an accounting journal, posting recorded transactions, and preparing financial statements

journal a time-ordered list of account transactions

Step Two: Record Transactions. Next, Anna records each financial transaction in a **journal**, which is

Figure 14.2 The Accounting Equation and Double-Entry Bookkeeping for Anna's Flowers

	Assets			= Liabilities		+ Owners' Equity
	Cash	Equipment	Inventory	Debts to suppliers	Loans	Equity
Cash invested by Anna	$2,500.00					$2,500.00
Loan from SBA	$5,000.00				$5,000.00	
Purchase of furnishings	–$3,000.00	$3,000.00				
Purchase of inventory	–$2,000.00		$2,000.00			
Purchase of roses			$325.00	$325.00		
First month sales	$2,000.00		–$1,500.00			$500.00
Totals	$4,500.00	$3,000.00	$825.00	$325.00	$5,000.00	$3,000.00

$8,325 = $5,325 + $3,000

$8,325 Assets = $8,325 Liabilities + Owners' Equity

ledger a book or computer file with separate sections for each account

basically just a time-ordered list of account transactions. While most businesses keep a general journal in which all transactions are recorded, some classify transactions into specialized journals for specific types of transaction accounts.

Step Three: Post Transactions. Anna next transfers the information from her journal into a **ledger**, a book or computer program with separate files for each account. This process is known as *posting.* At the end of the accounting period (usually yearly, but occasionally quarterly or monthly), Anna prepares a *trial balance,* a summary of the balances of all the accounts in the general ledger. If, upon totalling, the trial balance doesn't balance (that is, the accounting equation is not in balance), Anna or her accountant must look for mistakes (typically an error in one or more of the ledger entries) and correct them. If the trial balance is correct, the accountant can then begin to prepare the financial statements.

connect Need help understanding this concept? Check out an informational video! Log into Connect, go to Resources, and click on the Videos page.

Step Four: Prepare Financial Statements. The information from the trial balance is also used to prepare the company's financial statements. In the case of public corporations and certain other organizations, a CPA must *attest,* or certify, that the organization followed generally accepted accounting principles in preparing the financial statements. When these statements have been completed, the organization's books are "closed," and the accounting cycle begins anew for the next accounting period.

Financial Statements

The end results of the accounting process are a series of financial statements. The income statement, the balance sheet, and the statement of cash flows are the best-known examples of financial statements. These statements are provided to shareholders and potential investors in a firm's annual report as well as to other relevant outsiders such as creditors, government agencies, and the Canada Revenue Agency.

It is important to recognize that not all financial statements follow precisely the same format. The fact that different organizations generate income in different ways suggests that when it comes to financial statements, one size definitely does not fit all. Manufacturing firms, service providers, and non-profit organizations each use a different set of accounting principles or rules upon which the public accounting profession has agreed. As we have already mentioned, these are sometimes referred to as generally accepted accounting principles (or GAAP). Each country has a different set of rules that the businesses within that country are required to use for their accounting process and financial statements; however, many countries (including Canada) have adopted International Financial Reporting Standards (IFRS) for listed or large companies so that statutory reporting is comparable across international jurisdictions. Still, as is the case in many other disciplines, certain concepts have

Figure 14.3 The Accounting Process for Anna's Flowers

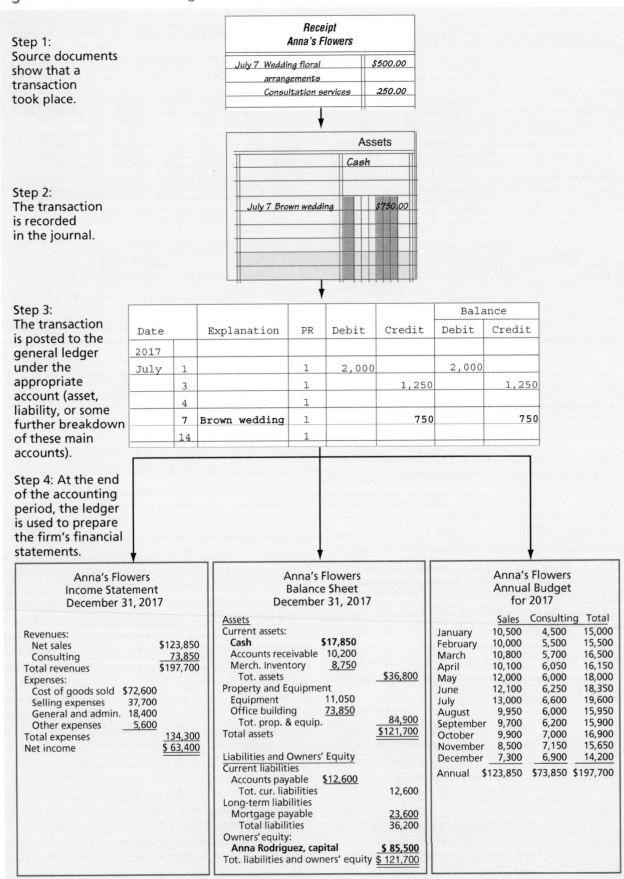

Step 1: Source documents show that a transaction took place.

Receipt Anna's Flowers	
July 7 Wedding floral arrangements	$500.00
Consultation services	250.00

Step 2: The transaction is recorded in the journal.

Assets

Cash

| July 7 Brown wedding | $750.00 |

Step 3: The transaction is posted to the general ledger under the appropriate account (asset, liability, or some further breakdown of these main accounts).

Date		Explanation	PR	Debit	Credit	Balance Debit	Balance Credit
2017							
July	1		1	2,000		2,000	
	3		1		1,250		1,250
	4		1				
	7	Brown wedding	1		750		750
	14		1				

Step 4: At the end of the accounting period, the ledger is used to prepare the firm's financial statements.

Anna's Flowers
Income Statement
December 31, 2017

Revenues:		
Net sales		$123,850
Consulting		73,850
Total revenues		$197,700
Expenses:		
Cost of goods sold	$72,600	
Selling expenses	37,700	
General and admin.	18,400	
Other expenses	5,600	
Total expenses		134,300
Net income		$ 63,400

Anna's Flowers
Balance Sheet
December 31, 2017

Assets
Current assets:

Cash	**$17,850**	
Accounts receivable	10,200	
Merch. Inventory	8,750	
Tot. assets		$36,800
Property and Equipment		
Equipment	11,050	
Office building	73,850	
Tot. prop. & equip.		84,900
Total assets		$121,700

Liabilities and Owners' Equity
Current liabilities

Accounts payable	$12,600	
Tot. cur. liabilities		12,600
Long-term liabilities		
Mortgage payable		23,600
Total liabilities		36,200
Owners' equity:		
Anna Rodriguez, capital		**$ 85,500**
Tot. liabilities and owners' equity		$ 121,700

Anna's Flowers
Annual Budget
for 2017

	Sales	Consulting	Total
January	10,500	4,500	15,000
February	10,000	5,500	15,500
March	10,800	5,700	16,500
April	10,100	6,050	16,150
May	12,000	6,000	18,000
June	12,100	6,250	18,350
July	13,000	6,600	19,600
August	9,950	6,000	15,950
September	9,700	6,200	15,900
October	9,900	7,000	16,900
November	8,500	7,150	15,650
December	7,300	6,900	14,200
Annual	$123,850	$73,850	$197,700

more than one name. For example, *sales* and *revenues* are often interchanged, as are *profits*, *income*, and *earnings*. Table 14.2 lists a few common equivalent terms that should help you decipher their meaning in accounting statements.

The Income Statement

LO3 Examine the various components of an income statement to evaluate a firm's "bottom line."

The question, "What's the bottom line?" derives from the income statement, where the bottom line shows the overall profit or loss of the company after taxes. Thus, the **income statement** is a financial report that shows an organization's profitability over a period of time, be that a month, quarter, or year. By its very design, the income statement offers one of the clearest possible pictures of the company's overall revenues and the costs incurred in generating those revenues. Other names for the income statement include profit and loss (P&L) statement or operating statement. A sample income statement with line-by-line explanations is presented in Table 14.3, while Table 14.4 presents the income statement of Starbucks. The income statement indicates the firm's profitability or income (the bottom line), which is derived by subtracting the firm's expenses from its revenues.

income statement a financial report that shows an organization's profitability over a period of time—month, quarter, or year

Revenue. **Revenue** is the total amount of money received (or promised) from the sale of goods or services, as well as from other business activities such as the rental of property and investments. Non-business entities typically obtain revenues through donations from individuals and/or grants from governments and private foundations. One of the controversies in accounting has been when a business should recognize revenue. For instance, should an organization book revenue during a project or after the project is completed? Differences in revenue recognition have caused similar organizations to book different accounting results. A proposed rule states that firms should book revenue when "it satisfie[s] a performance obligation by transferring a promised good or service to a customer."[10] Starbucks' income statement (see Table 14.4) shows three sources of revenue: retail sales, licensing, and consumer processed goods (CPG), food service, and other.

revenue the total amount of money received from the sale of goods or services, as well as from related business activities

cost of goods sold the amount of money a firm spent to buy or produce the products it sold during the period to which the income statement applies

gross income (or profit) revenues minus the cost of goods sold required to generate the revenues

expenses the costs incurred in the day-to-day operations of an organization

For most manufacturing and retail concerns, the next major item included in the income statement is the **cost of goods sold**, the amount of money the firm spent (or promised to spend) to buy and/or produce the products it sold during the accounting period. This figure may be calculated as follows:

$$\text{Cost of goods sold} = \text{Beginning inventory} + \text{Interim purchases} - \text{Ending inventory}$$

Let's say that Anna's Flowers began an accounting period with an inventory of goods for which it paid $5,000. During the period, Anna bought another $4,000 worth of goods, giving the shop a total inventory available for sale of $9,000. If, at the end of the accounting period, Anna's inventory was worth $5,500, the cost of goods sold during the period would have been $3,500 ($5,000 + $4,000 − $5,500 = 3,500). If Anna had total revenues of $10,000 over the same period of time, subtracting the cost of goods sold ($3,500) from the total revenues of $10,000 yields the store's **gross income (or profit)** (revenues minus the cost of goods sold required to generate the revenues): $6,500. The same process occurs at Starbucks. As indicated in Table 14.4, the cost of goods sold was more than $6.9 million in 2014. Notice that Starbucks calls it cost of sales, rather than cost of goods sold. This is because Starbucks buys raw materials and supplies and produces drinks.

Expenses. **Expenses** are the costs incurred in the day-to-day operations of an organization. Three common expense accounts shown on income statements are (1) selling, general, and administrative expenses; (2) research,

Table 14.2 Equivalent Terms in Accounting

Term	Equivalent Term
Revenues	Sales
	Goods or services sold
Gross profit	Gross income
	Gross earnings
Operating income	Operating profit
	Earnings before interest and taxes (EBIT)
	Income before interest and taxes (IBIT)
Income before taxes (IBT)	Earnings before taxes (EBT)
	Profit before taxes (PBT)
Net income (NI)	Earnings after taxes (EAT)
	Profit after taxes (PAT)
Income available to common shareholders	Earnings available to common shareholders

Table 14.3 Sample Income Statement

Company Name for the Year Ended December 31

The following presents an income statement in word form with all the terms defined and explained.

Revenues (sales)	Total dollar amount of products sold (includes income from other business services such as rental-lease income and interest income).
Less: Cost of goods sold	The cost of producing the goods and services, including the cost of labour and raw materials as well as other expenses associated with production.
Gross profit	The income available after paying all expenses of production.
Less: Selling and administrative expense	The cost of promoting, advertising, and selling products as well as the overhead costs of managing the company. This includes the cost of management and corporate staff. One non-cash expense included in this category is depreciation, which approximates the decline in the value of plant and equipment assets due to use over time. In most accounting statements, depreciation is not separated from selling and administrative expenses. However, financial analysts usually create statements that include this expense.
Income before interest and taxes (operating income or EBIT)	This line represents all income left over after operating expenses have been deducted. This is sometimes referred to as operating income since it represents all income after the expenses of operations have been accounted for. Occasionally, this is referred to as EBIT, or earnings before interest and taxes.
Less: Interest expense	Interest expense arises as a cost of borrowing money. This is a financial expense rather than an operating expense and is listed separately. As the amount of debt and the cost of debt increase, so will the interest expense. This covers the cost of both short-term and long-term borrowing.
Income before taxes (earnings before taxes—EBT)	The firm will pay a tax on this amount. This is what is left of revenues after subtracting all operating costs, depreciation costs, and interest costs.
Less: Taxes	The tax rate is specified in the federal tax code.
Net income	This is the amount of income left after taxes. The firm may decide to retain all or a portion of the income for reinvestment in new assets. Whatever it decides not to keep, it will usually pay out in dividends to its shareholders.
Less: Preferred dividends	If the company has preferred shareholders, they are first in line for dividends. That is one reason why their stock is called "preferred."
Income to common shareholders	This is the income left for the common shareholders. If the company has a good year, there may be a lot of income available for dividends. If the company has a bad year, income could be negative. The common shareholders are the ultimate owners and risk takers. They have the potential for very good or very poor returns since they get whatever is left after all other expenses.
Earnings per share	Earnings per share is found by taking the income available to the common shareholders and dividing by the number of shares of common stock outstanding. This is income generated by the company for each share of common stock.

development, and engineering expenses; and (3) interest expenses (remember that the costs directly attributable to selling goods or services are included in the cost of goods sold). Selling expenses include advertising and sales salaries. General and administrative expenses include salaries of executives and their staff and the costs of owning and maintaining the general office. Research and development costs include scientific, engineering, and marketing personnel and the equipment and information used to design and build prototypes and samples. Interest expenses include the direct costs of borrowing money.

The number and type of expense accounts vary from organization to organization. Included in the general and administrative category is a special type of expense known as **depreciation**, the

depreciation the process of spreading the costs of long-lived assets such as buildings and equipment over the total number of accounting periods in which they are expected to be used

process of spreading the costs of long-lived assets such as buildings and equipment over the total number of accounting periods in which they are expected to be used. Consider a manufacturer that purchases a $100,000 machine expected to last about ten years. Rather than showing an expense of $100,000 in the first year and no expense for that equipment over the next nine years, the manufacturer is allowed to report depreciation expenses of $10,000 per year in each of the next ten years because that better matches the cost of the machine to the years the machine is used. Each time this depreciation is "written off" as an expense, the book value of the machine is also reduced by $10,000. The fact that the equipment has a zero value on the firm's balance sheet when it is fully depreciated (in this case, after ten years) does not necessarily mean that it can no longer be used or is economically worthless. Indeed, in some industries, machines used every day have been reported as having no book value whatsoever for over 30 years.

Table 14.4 Starbucks Corporation Consolidated Statements of Earnings (in USD millions, except per share data)

Fiscal Year Ended	Sept 28, 2014	Sept 29, 2013	Sept 30, 2012
Net revenues:			
Company-operated stores	$12,977.9	$11,793.2	$10,534.5
Licensed stores	1,588.6	1,360.5	1,210.3
CPG, food service, and other	1,881.3	1,713.1	1,532.0
Total net revenues	16,447.8	14,866.8	13,276.8
Cost of sales including occupancy costs	6,858.8	6,382.3	5,813.3
Store operating expenses	4,638.2	4,286.1	3,918.1
Other operating expenses	457.3	431.8	407.2
Depreciation and amortization expenses	709.6	621.4	550.3
General and administrative expenses	991.3	937.9	801.2
Litigation charge/(credit)	(20.2)	2,784.10	
Total operating expenses	13,635.0	15,443.6	11,490.1
Income from equity investees	268.3	251.4	210.7
Operating income	3,081.1	(325.40)	1,997.4
Interest income and other, net	142.7	123.60	94.4
Interest expense	(64.1)	(28.1)	(32.7)
Earnings before income taxes	3,159.7	(229.9)	2,059.1
Income taxes	1,092.0	(238.7)	674.4
Net earnings including noncontrolling interests	2,067.7	8.8	1,384.7
Net earnings (loss) attributable to noncontrolling interests	(0.4)	0.5	0.9
Net earnings attributable to Starbucks	$2,068.1	$8.3	$1,383.8
Earnings per share—basic	$2.75	$0.01	$1.83
Earnings per share—diluted	$2.71	$0.01	$1.79
Weighted average shares outstanding:			
Basic	753.1	749.3	754.4
Diluted	763.10	762.3	773.0
Cash dividends declared per share	$1.10	$0.89	$0.72

Source: Data from Starbucks 2014 Annual Report, p. 45.

Net Income. **Net income** (or net earnings) is the total profit (or loss) after all expenses including taxes have been deducted from revenue. Generally, accountants divide profits into individual sections such as operating income and earnings before interest and taxes. Starbucks, for example, lists earnings before income taxes, net earnings, and earnings per share of outstanding stock (see Table 14.4). Like most companies, Starbucks presents not only the current year's results but also the

previous two years' income statements to permit comparison of performance from one period to another.

Temporary Nature of the Income Statement Accounts. Companies record their operational activities in the revenue and expense accounts during an accounting period. Gross profit, earnings before interest and taxes, and net income are the results of calculations made from the revenue and expense accounts; they are not actual accounts. At the end of each accounting period, the dollar amounts in all the revenue and expense accounts are moved into an account called "Retained Earnings," one of

Mark Zuckerberg, Eduardo Saverin, Dustin Moskovitz, Chris Hughes

Business: Facebook

Founded: 2004

Success: Facebook has become the largest social networking site in the world with an estimated market value of $1.04 billion.

When Mark Zuckerberg decided to exchange computer code writing for managing his start-up in 2006, nobody would have guessed that Facebook would become the biggest social network worldwide. In 2012, Facebook went public. At $38 a share, the social network had the third-largest public offering in U.S. history at $16 billion. However, it was not long before Facebook hit a snag.

Facebook's massive growth requires accurate accounting and financial growth forecasts. Everything seemed to go well with its initial public offering (IPO) on the opening day. Yet shortly after the launch, Facebook stock dropped 16 percent from its original price. Investors realized that analysts at Morgan Stanley and other firms had reduced Facebook's earnings estimates prior to the IPO launch. Knowledge of Facebook's decreased earnings projections would likely have reduced the value of Facebook's IPO, yet this information was not made widely available until after the launch. Investors filed a lawsuit against Facebook, Morgan Stanley, and other firms because they felt deceived into paying more for Facebook shares than they were worth. This debacle will likely teach all participants in the IPO the valuable lesson about the importance of transparency and disclosure in accounting.[11]

the owners' equity accounts. Revenues increase owners' equity, while expenses decrease it. The resulting change in the owners' equity account is exactly equal to the net income. This shifting of dollar values from the revenue and expense accounts allows the firm to begin the next accounting period with zero balances in those accounts. Zeroing out the balances enables a company to count how much it has sold and how many expenses have been incurred during a period of time. The basic accounting equation (assets = liabilities + owners' equity) will not balance until the revenue and expense account balances have been moved or "closed out" to the owners' equity account.

One final note about income statements: You may remember from Chapter 4 that corporations may choose to make cash payments called dividends to shareholders out of their net earnings. When a corporation elects to pay dividends, it decreases the cash account (in the assets category) as well as a capital account (in the owners' equity category). During any period of time, the owners' equity account may change because of the sale of stock (or contributions/withdrawals by owners), the net income or loss, or from the dividends paid.

The Balance Sheet

LO4 Interpret a company's balance sheet to determine its current financial position.

balance sheet a "snapshot" of an organization's financial position at a given moment

The second basic financial statement is the **balance sheet**, which presents a "snapshot" of an organization's financial position at a

given moment. As such, the balance sheet indicates what the organization owns or controls and the various sources of the funds used to pay for these assets, such as bank debt or owners' equity.

The balance sheet takes its name from its reliance on the accounting equation: Assets *must* equal liabilities plus owners' equity. Table 14.5 provides a sample balance sheet with line-by-line explanations. Unlike the income statement, the balance sheet does not represent the result of transactions completed over a specified accounting period. Instead, the balance sheet is, by definition, an accumulation of all financial transactions conducted by an organization since its founding. Following long-established traditions, items on the balance sheet are listed on the basis of their original cost less accumulated depreciation, rather than their present values.

> **"The balance sheet takes its name from its reliance on the accounting equation: Assets must equal liabilities plus owners' equity."**

Balance sheets are often presented in two different formats. The traditional balance sheet format placed the organization's assets on the left side and its liabilities and owners' equity on the right. More recently, a vertical format, with assets on top followed by liabilities and owners' equity, has gained wide acceptance. Starbucks' balance sheet for 2013 and 2014 is presented in Table 14.6. In the sections that follow, we'll briefly describe the basic items found on the balance sheet; we'll take a closer look at a number of these in Chapter 16.

Table 14.5 Sample Balance Sheet

The following presents a balance sheet in word form with each item defined or explained.

Assets	This is the major category for all physical, monetary, or intangible goods that have some dollar value.
Current assets	Assets that are either cash or are expected to be turned into cash within the next 12 months.
Cash	Cash or chequing accounts.
Marketable securities	Short-term investments in securities that can be converted to cash quickly (liquid assets).
Accounts receivable	Cash due from customers in payment for goods received. These arise from sales made on credit.
Inventory	Finished goods ready for sale, goods in the process of being finished, or raw materials used in the production of goods.
Prepaid expense	A future expense item that has already been paid, such as insurance premiums or rent.
Total current assets	The sum of the above accounts.
Fixed assets	Assets that are long term in nature and have a minimum life expectancy that exceeds one year.
Investments	Assets held as investments rather than assets owned for the production process. Most often, the assets include small ownership interests in other companies.
Gross property, plant, and equipment	Land, buildings, and other fixed assets listed at original cost.
Less: Accumulated depreciation	The accumulated expense deductions applied to all plant and equipment over their life. Land may not be depreciated. The total amount represents in general the decline in value as equipment gets older and wears out. The maximum amount that can be deducted is set by the Canada Revenue Agency (CRA) and varies by type of asset.
Net property, plant, and equipment	Gross property, plant, and equipment minus the accumulated depreciation. This amount reflects the book value of the fixed assets and not their value if sold.
Other assets	Any other asset that is long-term and does not fit into the above categories. It could be patents or trademarks.
Total assets	The sum of all the asset values.
Liabilities and Shareholders' Equity	This is the major category. Liabilities refer to all indebtedness and loans of both a long-term and short-term nature. Shareholders' equity refers to all money that has been contributed to the company over the life of the firm by the owners.
Current liabilities	Short-term debt expected to be paid off within the next 12 months.
Accounts payable	Money owed to suppliers for goods ordered. Firms usually have between 30 and 90 days to pay this account, depending on industry norms.
Wages payable	Money owed to employees for hours worked or salary. If workers receive cheques every two weeks, the amount owed should be no more than two weeks' pay.
Taxes payable	Firms are required to pay corporate taxes quarterly. This refers to taxes owed based on earnings estimates for the quarter.
Notes payable	Short-term loans from banks or other lenders.
Other current liabilities	The other short-term debts that do not fit into the above categories.
Total current liabilities	The sum of the above accounts.
Long-term liabilities	All long-term debt that will not be paid off in the next 12 months.
Long-term debt	Loans of more than one year from banks, pension funds, insurance companies, or other lenders. These loans often take the form of bonds, which are securities that may be bought and sold in bond markets.
Deferred income taxes	This is a liability owed to the government but not due within one year.
Other liabilities	Any other long-term debt that does not fit the above two categories.
Shareholders' equity	The following categories are the owners' investment in the company.
Common stock	The tangible evidence of ownership is a security called common stock. The par value is stated value and does not indicate the company's worth.
Capital in excess of par (a.k.a. contributed capital)	When shares of stock were sold to the owners, they were recorded at the price at the time of the original sale. If the price paid was $10 per share, the extra $9 per share would show up in this account at 100,000 shares times $9 per share, or $900,000.
Retained earnings	The total amount of earnings the company has made during its life and not paid out to its shareholders as dividends. This account represents the owners' reinvestment of earnings into company assets rather than payments of cash dividends. This account does not represent cash.
Total shareholders' equity	This is the sum of the above equity accounts representing the owners' total investment in the company.
Total liabilities and shareholders' equity	The total short-term and long-term debt of the company plus the owners' total investment. This combined amount *must* equal total assets.

Table 14.6 Starbucks Corporation Consolidated Balance Sheets (in USD millions, except per share data)

	Sep 28, 2014	Sep 29, 2013
ASSETS		
Current assets:		
Cash and cash equivalents	$1,708.4	$2,575.7
Short-term investments	135.40	658.1
Accounts receivable, net	631.0	561.4
Inventories	1,090.9	1,111.2
Prepaid expenses and other current assets	285.6	287.7
Deferred income taxes, net	317.4	277.3
Total current assets	4,168.7	5,471.4
Long-term investments—available-for-sale securities	318.4	58.3
Equity and cost investments	514.9	496.5
Property, plant and equipment, net	3,519.0	3,200.5
Other assets	198.9	185.3
Other intangible assets	273.5	274.8
Goodwill	856.2	862.9
TOTAL ASSETS	$10,752.9	$11,516.7
LIABILITIES AND EQUITY		
Current liabilities:		
Accounts payable	533.7	491.7
Accrued litigation charge		2,784.1
Accrued liabilities	1,514.4	1,269.3
Insurance reserves	196.1	178.5
Deferred revenue	794.5	653.7
Total current liabilities	3,038.7	5,377.3
Long-term debt	2,048.3	1,299.4
Other long-term liabilities	392.2	357.7
Total liabilities	5,479.2	7,034.4
Shareholders' equity:		
Common stock ($0.001 per value)—authorized, 1,200.0 shares; issued and outstanding, 744.8 and 742.6 shares, respectively (includes 3.4 common stock units in both periods)	0.7	0.8
Additional paid-in capital	39.4	282.1
Retained earnings	5,206.6	4,130.3
Accumulated other comprehensive income	25.3	67.0
Total shareholders' equity	5,272.0	4,480.2
Noncontrolling interests	1.7	2.1
Total equity	5,273.7	4,482.3
TOTAL LIABILITIES AND EQUITY	$10,752.9	$11,516.7

Source: Data from Starbucks 2014 Annual Report, p. 47

Assets. All asset accounts are listed in descending order of *liquidity*—that is, how quickly each could be turned into cash. **Current assets**, also called short-term assets, are those that are used or converted into cash within the course of a calendar year. Thus, cash is followed by temporary investments, accounts receivable, and inventory, in that order. **Accounts receivable** refers to money owed the company by its clients or customers who have promised to pay for the products at a later date. Accounts receivable usually includes an allowance for bad debts that management does not expect to collect. The bad-debts adjustment is normally based on historical collections experience and is deducted from the accounts receivable balance to present a more realistic view of the payments likely to be received in the future, called net receivables. Inventory may be held in the form of raw materials, work-in-progress, or finished goods ready for delivery.

Long-term or fixed assets represent a commitment of organizational funds of at least one year. Items classified as fixed include long-term investments, plant and equipment, and intangible assets, such as corporate "goodwill," or reputation, as well as patents and trademarks.

Liabilities. As seen in the accounting equation, total assets must be financed either through borrowing (liabilities) or through owner investments (owners' equity). **Current liabilities** include a firm's financial obligations to short-term creditors, which must be repaid within one year, while long-term liabilities have longer repayment

terms. **Accounts payable** represents amounts owed to suppliers for goods and services purchased with credit. For example, if you buy gas with a Shell credit card, the purchase represents an account payable for you (and an account receivable for Shell). Other liabilities include wages earned by employees but not yet paid and taxes owed to the government. Occasionally, these accounts are consolidated into an **accrued expenses** account, representing all unpaid financial obligations incurred by the organization.

Owners' Equity. Owners' equity includes the owners' contributions to the organization along with income earned by the organization and retained to finance continued growth and development. If the organization were to sell off all of its assets and pay off all of its liabilities, any remaining funds would belong to the owners. Not surprisingly, the accounts listed as owners' equity on a balance sheet may differ dramatically from company to company. As mentioned in Chapter 4, corporations sell stock to investors, who become the owners of the firm. Many corporations issue two, three, or even more different classes of common and preferred stock, each with different dividend payments and/or voting rights. Because each type of stock issued represents a different claim on the organization, each must be represented by a separate owners' equity account, called contributed capital.

The Statement of Cash Flow

LO5 Analyze the statement of cash flows to evaluate the increase and decrease in a company's cash balance.

The third primary financial statement is called the **statement of cash flows**, which explains how the company's cash changed from the beginning of the accounting period to the end. Cash, of course, is an asset shown on the balance sheet, which provides a snapshot of the firm's financial position at one point in time. However, many investors and other users of financial statements want more information about the cash flowing into and out of the firm than is provided on the balance sheet to better understand the company's financial health. The statement of cash flow takes the cash balance from one year's balance sheet and compares it to the next while providing detail about how the firm used the cash. Table 14.7 presents Starbucks' statement of cash flows.

This type of machinery would be considered a long-term asset on the balance sheet.

Table 14.7 Consolidated Statement of Cash Flows (in USD millions)

Consolidated Statement of Cash Flows (in millions)	Fiscal Year Ended		
	Sep 28, 2014	Sep 29, 2013	Sep 30, 2012
OPERATING ACTIVITIES:			
Net earnings including noncontrolling interests	$2,067.7	$8.8	$1,384.7
Adjustments to reconcile net earnings to net cash provided by operating activities:			
Depreciation and amortization	748.4	655.6	580.66
Litigation charge		2,784.1	
Deferred income taxes, net	10.2	67.7	61.1
Income earned from equity method investees	(182.7)	(171.8)	(136.0)
Distributions received from equity method investees	139.2	115.6	86.7
Gain resulting from sale of equity in joint ventures and certain retail operations	(70.2)	(80.1)	
Stock-based compensation	183.2	142.3	153.6
Excess tax benefit from exercise of stock options	(114.4)	(258.1)	(169.8)
Other	36.2	23.0	23.6
Cash provided/(used) by changes in operating assets and liabilities:			
Accounts receivable	(79.7)	(68.3)	(90.3)
Inventories	14.3	152.5	(273.3)
Accounts payable	60.4	88.7	(105.2)
Accrued litigation charge	(2,763.9)		
Income taxes payable, net	309.8	298.4	201.6
Accrued liabilities and insurance reserves	103.9	47.3	(8.1)
Deferred revenue	140.8	139.9	60.8
Prepaid expenses, other current assets and other assets	4.6	76.3	(19.7)
Net cash provided by operating activities	607.8	2,908.3	1,750.3
INVESTING ACTIVITIES:			
Purchase of investments	(1,652.5)	(785.9)	(1,748.6)
Sales of investments	1,454.8	60.2	
Maturities and calls of investments	456.1	980.0	1,796.4
Acquisitions, net of cash acquired		(610.4)	(129.1)
Additions to property, plant, and equipment	(1,160.9)	(1,151.2)	(856.2)
Proceeds from sale of property, plant, and equipment	103.9	108.0	
Other	(19.1)	(11.9)	(36.5)
Net cash used by investing activities	(817.7)	(1,411.2)	(974.0)
FINANCING ACTIVITIES:			
Proceeds from issuance of long-term debt	748.5	749.7	
Principal payments on long-term debt		(35.2)	
Payments on short-term borrowings			(30.8)
Proceeds from issuance of common stock	139.7	247.2	236.6
Excess tax benefit from exercise of stock options	114.4	258.1	169.8

Table 14.7 (Continued)

Consolidated Statement of Cash Flows (in millions)	Fiscal Year Ended		
	Sep 28, 2014	Sep 29, 2013	Sep 30, 2012
Cash dividends paid	(783.1)	(628.9)	(513.0)
Repurchase of common stock	(758.6)	(588.1)	(549.1)
Minimum tax withholdings on share-based awards	(77.3)	(121.4)	(58.5)
Other	(6.9)	10.4	(0.5)
Net cash used by financing activities	(623.3)	(108.2)	(745.5)
Effect of exchange rate changes on cash and cash equivalents	(34.1)	(1.8)	9.7
Net increase/(decrease) in cash and cash equivalents	(867.3)	1,387.1	40.5
CASH AND CASH EQUIVALENTS:			
Beginning of period	2,575.7	1,188.6	1,148.1
End of period	$1,708.4	$2,575.7	$1,188.6
SUPPLEMENTAL DISCLOSURE OF CASH FLOW INFORMATION:			
Cash paid during the period for:			
Interest, net of capitalized interest	$56.2	$34.4	$34.4
Income taxes, net of refunds	$766.3	$539.1	$416.9

The change in cash is explained through details in three categories: cash from (used for) operating activities, cash from (used for) investing activities, and cash from (used for) financing activities. *Cash from operating activities* is calculated by combining the changes in the revenue accounts, expense accounts, current asset accounts, and current liability accounts. This category of cash flows includes all the accounts on the balance sheet that relate to computing revenues and expenses for the accounting period. If this amount is a positive number, as it is for Starbucks, then the business is making extra cash that it can use to invest in increased long-term capacity or to pay off debts such as loans or bonds. A negative number may indicate a business that is still in a growing stage or one that is in a declining position with regards to operations. Negative cash flow is not always a bad thing, however. It may indicate that a business is growing, with a very negative cash flow indicating rapid growth.

Cash from investing activities is calculated from changes in the long-term or fixed asset accounts. If this amount is negative, as is the case with Starbucks, the company is purchasing long-term assets for future growth. A positive figure indicates a business that is selling off existing long-term assets and reducing its capacity for the future.

Finally, *cash from financing activities* is calculated from changes in the long-term liability accounts and the contributed capital accounts in owners' equity. If this amount is negative, the company is likely paying off long-term debt or returning contributed capital to investors. If this amount is positive, the company is either borrowing more money or raising money from investors by selling more shares of stock.

Ratio Analysis: Analyzing Financial Statements

LO6 Assess a company's financial position using its accounting statements and ratio analysis.

The income statement shows a company's profit or loss, while the balance sheet itemizes the value of its assets, liabilities, and owners' equity. Together, the two statements provide the means to answer two critical questions: (1) How much did the firm make or lose? and (2) How much is the firm currently worth based on historical values found on the balance sheet? **Ratio analysis**, calculations that measure an organization's financial health, brings the complex information from the income statement and balance sheet into sharper focus so that managers, lenders, owners, and other interested parties can measure and compare the organization's productivity, profitability, and financing mix with other similar entities.

ratio analysis calculations that measure an organization's financial health

As you know, a ratio is simply one number divided by another, with the result showing the relationship between the two numbers. Financial ratios are used to weigh and evaluate a firm's performance. Interestingly, an absolute value such as earnings of $70,000 or accounts receivable of $200,000 almost never provides as much useful information as a well-constructed ratio. Whether those numbers are good or bad depends on their relation to other numbers. If a company earned $70,000 on $700,000 in sales (a 10 percent return), such an earnings level might be quite satisfactory. The president of a company earning this same $70,000 on sales of $7 million (a 1 percent return), however, should probably start looking for another job!

Ratios by themselves are not very useful. It is the relationship of the calculated ratios to both prior organizational performance and the performance of the organization's "peers," as well as its stated goals, that really matters. Remember, while the profitability, asset utilization, liquidity, debt ratios, and per share data we'll look at here can be very useful, you will never see the forest by looking only at the trees.

Profitability Ratios

Profitability ratios measure how much operating income or net income an organization is able to generate relative to its assets, owners' equity, and sales. The numerator (top number) used in these examples is always the net income

profitability ratios ratios that measure the amount of operating income or net income an organization is able to generate relative to its assets, owners' equity, and sales

profit margin net income divided by sales

return on assets net income divided by assets

after taxes. Common profitability ratios include profit margin, return on assets, and return on equity. The following examples are based on the 2014 income statement and balance sheet for Starbucks, as shown in Tables 14.4 and 14.6. Except where specified, all data are expressed in millions of dollars.

The **profit margin**, computed by dividing net income by sales, shows the overall percentage profits earned by the company. It is based solely upon data obtained from the income statement. The higher the profit margin, the better the cost controls within the company and the higher the return on every dollar of revenue. Starbucks' profit margin is calculated as follows:

$$\text{Profit margin} = \frac{\text{Net income}}{\text{Sales}} = \frac{\$2,068.1}{\$16,447.8} = 12.57\%$$

Thus, for every $1 in sales, Starbucks generated profits after taxes of almost 13 cents.

Return on assets, net income divided by assets, shows how much income the firm produces for every dollar invested in assets. A company with a low return on assets is probably not using its assets very productively—a key managerial failing. By its construction, the return on assets calculation requires data from both the income statement and the balance sheet.

$$\text{Return on assets} = \frac{\text{Net income}}{\text{Assets}} = \frac{\$2,068.1}{\$10,752.9} = 19.23\%$$

In the case of Starbucks, every $1 of assets generated a return of close to 19 percent, or profits of 19.23 cents per dollar.

Shareholders are always concerned with how much money they will make on their investment, and they frequently use the return on equity ratio as one of their key performance measures.

Return on equity (also called return on investment [ROI]), calculated by dividing net income by owners' equity, shows how much income is generated by each $1 the owners have invested in the firm. Obviously, a low return on equity means low shareholder returns and may indicate a need for immediate managerial attention. Because some assets may have been financed with debt not contributed by the owners, the value of the owners' equity is usually considerably lower than the total value of the firm's assets. Starbucks' return on equity is calculated as follows:

return on equity net income divided by owners' equity; also called return on investment (ROI)

asset utilization ratios ratios that measure how well a firm uses its assets to generate each $1 of sales

receivables turnover sales divided by accounts receivable

$$\text{Return on equity} = \frac{\text{Net income}}{\text{Equity}} = \frac{\$2,068.1}{\$5,273.7} = 39.21\%$$

For every dollar invested by Starbucks stockholders, the company earned a 39.21 percent return, or 39.21 cents per dollar invested.

"Profitability ratios measure how much operating income or net income an organization is able to generate relative to its assets, owners' equity, and sales."

Asset Utilization Ratios

Asset utilization ratios measure how well a firm uses its assets to generate each $1 of sales. Obviously, companies using their assets more productively will have higher returns on assets than their less efficient competitors. Similarly, managers can use asset utilization ratios to pinpoint areas of inefficiency in their operations. These ratios (receivables turnover, inventory turnover, and total asset turnover) relate balance sheet assets to sales, which are found on the income statement.

The **receivables turnover**, sales divided by accounts receivable, indicates how many times a firm collects its accounts receivable in one year. It also demonstrates how quickly a firm is able to collect payments on its credit

If you've ever taken an accounting class, then you've probably heard of GAAP, or generally accepted accounting principles. GAAP are standardized rules used to ensure the clarity, consistency, and accuracy of financial statements for Canadian firms.

However, there is one problem with GAAP. As the world becomes increasingly globalized, multinational companies find it difficult to adhere to the different accounting standards of the countries in which they operate. Many countries have their own sets of generally accepted accounting principles that differ from Canadian GAAP. This situation also creates difficulty for investors. How can an investor compare a French company with a Canadian company when their accounting statements each use a different set of rules?

To eliminate this problem, about 120 countries have fully or partially adopted the International Financial Reporting Standards (IFRS). Support for IFRS adoption is strong. Another widely supported process is known as condorsement, which advocates assimilation of IFRS rules into GAAP over time.

Despite the widespread support for IFRS adoption, the standards have many critics. One criticism relates to the costs involved. Accountants have to be retrained, and some of the rules allowed under GAAP will have to be dropped altogether. Analysts predict that switching costs could be 1 percent of annual company revenues. Small companies that do not conduct business overseas argue that IFRS adoption would be too costly. Another argument is that IFRS is based more on guidelines than actual rules, which could result in less accurate financial statements and the potential for more lawsuits. Finally, opponents argue that there is no definitive proof that IFRS is any more beneficial than GAAP.[12]

DISCUSSION QUESTIONS

1. Why has it been difficult to compare financial statements of companies in different countries?

2. What would be some of the benefits of adopting International Financial Reporting Standards (IFRS) in Canada?

3. What are some potential disadvantages of adopting IFRS in the Canada?

---

sales. Obviously, no payments mean no profits. Starbucks collected its receivables a little more than 26 times per year. The reason the number is so high is that most of Starbucks' sales are for cash and not credit.

$$\text{Receivables turnover} = \frac{\text{Sales}}{\text{Receivables}} = \frac{\$16{,}447.8}{\$631} = 26.06 \times$$

inventory turnover sales divided by total inventory

total asset turnover sales divided by total assets

Inventory turnover, sales divided by total inventory, indicates how many times a firm sells and replaces its inventory over the course of a year. A high inventory turnover ratio may indicate great efficiency but may also suggest the possibility of lost sales due to insufficient stock levels. Starbucks' inventory turnover indicates that it replaced its inventory times 15.08 times last year, or slightly more than once a month.

$$\text{Inventory turnover} = \frac{\text{Sales}}{\text{Inventory}} = \frac{\$16{,}447.8}{1{,}090.9} = 15.08 \times$$

Total asset turnover, sales divided by total assets, measures how well an organization uses all of its assets in creating sales. It indicates whether a company is using its assets productively. Starbucks generated $1.53 in sales for every $1 in total corporate assets.

$$\text{Total asset turnover} = \frac{\text{Sales}}{\text{Total assets}} = \frac{\$16{,}447.8}{\$10{,}752.9} = 1.53 \times$$

Liquidity Ratios

Liquidity ratios compare current (short-term) assets to current liabilities to indicate the speed with which a company can turn its assets into cash to meet debts as they fall due. High liquidity ratios may satisfy a creditor's need for safety, but ratios that are too high may indicate that the organization is not using its current assets efficiently. Liquidity ratios are generally best examined in conjunction with asset utilization ratios because high turnover ratios imply that cash is flowing through an organization very quickly—a situation that dramatically reduces the need for the type of reserves measured by liquidity ratios.

liquidity ratios ratios that measure the speed with which a company can turn its assets into cash to meet short-term debt

current ratio current assets divided by current liabilities

The **current ratio** is calculated by dividing current assets by current liabilities. Starbucks's current ratio indicates that for every $1 of current liabilities, the firm had $1.37 of current assets on hand. This number improved from previous years, and indicates that Starbucks has increased its liquidity as it restructures its business. Current assets increased faster than current liabilities between 2013 and 2014 making for a much improved current ratio. Additionally, accounts receivable has increased over the same time period.

$$\text{Current ratio} = \frac{\text{Current assets}}{\text{Current liabilities}} = \frac{\$4,168.7}{\$3,038.7} = 1.37$$

quick ratio (acid test) a stringent measure of liquidity that eliminates inventory

debt utilization ratios ratios that measure how much debt an organization is using relative to other sources of capital, such as owners' equity

debt to total assets ratio a ratio indicating how much of the firm is financed by debt and how much by owners' equity

The **quick ratio (acid test)** is a far more stringent measure of liquidity because it eliminates inventory, the least liquid current asset. It measures how well an organization can meet its current obligations without resorting to the sale of its inventory. In 2014, Starbucks had $1.01 cents invested in current assets (after subtracting inventory) for every $1 of current liabilities, a decrease over previous years.

$$\text{Quick ratio} = \frac{(\text{Current assets} - \text{Inventories})}{\text{Current liabilities}}$$

$$= \frac{(\$4,168.7 - \$1,090.9)}{3,038.7} = 1.01 \times$$

Debt Utilization Ratios

Debt utilization ratios provide information about how much debt an organization is using relative to other sources of capital, such as owners' equity. Because the use of debt carries an interest charge that must be paid regularly regardless of profitability, debt financing is much riskier than equity. Unforeseen negative events such as recessions affect heavily indebted firms to a far greater extent than those financed exclusively with owners' equity. Because of this and other factors, the managers of most firms tend to keep debt-to-asset levels below 50 percent. However, firms in very stable and/or regulated industries, such as electric utilities, often are able to carry debt ratios well in excess of 50 percent with no ill effects.

The **debt to total assets ratio** indicates how much of the firm is financed by debt and how much by owners' equity. To find the value of Starbucks' total debt, you must add current liabilities to long-term debt and other liabilities.

$$\text{Debt to total assets} = \frac{\text{Total debt}}{\text{Total assets}} = \frac{\$5,479.20}{\$10,752.9} = 50.96\%$$

Thus, for every $1 of Starbucks' total assets, 51 percent is financed with debt. The remaining 49 percent is provided by owners' equity.

The **times interest earned ratio**, operating income divided by interest expense, is a measure of the safety margin a company has with respect to the interest payments it must make to its creditors. A low times interest earned ratio indicates that even a small decrease in earnings may lead the company into financial straits. Because Starbucks has more interest income than interest expense, it would appear that their times interest earned ratio is not able to be calculated by using the income statement. However, in the statement of cash flows in Table 14.7 on the second line from the bottom, we can see that Starbucks paid $56.2 million in interest expense, an amount that was covered nearly 48.07 times by income before interest and taxes. A lender would not have to worry about receiving interest payments.

$$\text{Times interest earned ratio} = \frac{\text{EBIT}}{\text{Interest}} = \frac{\$3,081.1}{64.10} = 48.07\%$$

Per Share Data

Investors may use **per share data** to compare the performance of one company with another on an equal, or per share, basis. Generally, the more shares of stock a company issues, the less income is available for each share.

Earnings per share is calculated by dividing net income or profit by the number of shares outstanding. This ratio is important because yearly changes in earnings per share, in combination with other economy wide factors, determine a company's overall stock price. When earnings go up, so does a company's stock price—and so does the wealth of its shareholders.

$$\text{Earnings per share} = \frac{\text{Net income}}{\text{Number of shares outstanding}}$$

$$= \frac{\$2,067.7}{763.1} = \$2.71$$

We can see from the income statement that Starbucks' basic earnings per share increased between 2012 and 2014. Notice that Starbucks lists diluted earnings per share, calculated here, of $1.79 per share in 2012 and $2.71 per share in 2014. You can see from the income statement that diluted earnings per share include more shares than the basic calculation; this is because diluted shares include potential shares that could be issued due to the exercise

times interest earned ratio operating income divided by interest expense

per share data data used by investors to compare the performance of one company with another on an equal, per share basis

earnings per share net income or profit divided by the number of stock shares outstanding

of stock options or the conversion of certain types of debt into common stock. Investors generally pay more attention to diluted earnings per share than basic earnings per share.

Dividends per share are paid by the corporation to the shareholders for each share owned. The payment is made from earnings after taxes by the corporation but is taxable income to the shareholder. Thus, dividends result in double taxation: The corporation pays tax once on its earnings, and the shareholder pays tax a second time on his or her dividend income. The dividend declared on the income statement is $1.10 per share.

dividends per share the actual cash received for each share owned

Industry Analysis

We have used McDonald's as a comparison to Starbucks because there are no real national and international coffee houses that compete with Starbucks on the same scale. While McDonald's is almost two and one-half times larger than Starbucks in terms of sales, they both have a national and international presence and, to some extent, compete for the consumer's dollars. In recent years, McDonald's has moved into Starbucks' market by putting McCafé coffee shops in many of its locations. Table 14.8 indicates that McDonald's dominates Starbucks in two out of three profitability categories.

Starbucks stumbled in 2007 as it overexpanded and lost focus. Howard Schultz, the founder, returned as CEO and successfully restructured the company. Investors rewarded the company's turnaround by pushing the stock price from a low of $8.12 in early 2009 to a high

© Scott Eells/Bloomberg via Getty Images

Many of Netflix's financial ratios were higher than the industry average. However, after the company raised the price on one of its most popular rental plans, the value of its stock price fell significantly. This could impact Netflix's future financial ratios.

of $39.52 in 2014. Both companies have little accounts receivables relative to the size of their sales, so the ratios are very high, indicating a lot of cash and credit card sales. McDonald's pushes off much of its inventory holding costs onto its suppliers, so it has much higher inventory turnover ratios. Both have current ratios that are reasonably solid given their level of profitability. The difference in the current ratios and the quick ratio is of little consequence to the financial analyst or lender because both companies have high times interest earned ratios. While McDonald's net income has grown more slowly in the past few years, its earnings per share dropped from $5.36 in 2012 to $4.82 in 2014. On the other hand, Starbucks' earnings per share in 2014 were $2.71. It dropped to $0.01 in 2013, and recovered to $1.36 in 2014. Both companies are in good financial health, and Starbucks is slowly regaining regained its past glow. One thing is for sure: If Starbucks could earn the same profit margin as McDonald's, it would improve its other profitability ratios and its stock price.

Importance of Integrity in Accounting

The financial crisis and the recession that followed provided another example of a failure in accounting reporting. Many firms attempted to exploit loopholes and manipulate accounting processes and statements. Banks and other financial institutions often held assets off their books by manipulating their accounts. In 2013, the examiner for the Lehman Brothers' bankruptcy found that the most common example of removing assets or liabilities from the books was entering into what is called a "repurchase agreement." In a repurchase agreement, assets are transferred to another entity with the contractual

Table 14.8 Industry Analysis, Year Ending 2014

	Starbucks	McDonald's
Profit margin	12.57	17.34
Return on assets	19.23	13.42
Return on equity	39.21	32.97
Receivables turnover	26.06	21.66
Inventory turnover	15.08	145.36
Total asset turnover	1.53	0.77
Current ratio	1.37	1.52
Quick ratio	1.01	1.20
Debt to total assets	50.96	2.04
Diluted earnings per share	2.71	4.82
Dividends per share	1.10	3.28

Source: Data calculated from 2014 annual reports and Morningstar (2016), retrieved January 17, 2016, from http://financials.morningstar.com/ratios/r.html?t=MCD.

promise of buying them back at a set price. In the case of Lehman Brothers and other companies, repurchase agreements were used as a method of "cooking the books" that allowed them to manipulate accounting statements so that their ratios looked better than they actually were. If the accountants, the SEC, and the bank regulators had been more careful, these types of transactions would have been discovered and corrected.

On the other hand, strong compliance to accounting principles creates trust among stakeholders. It is most important to remember that integrity in accounting processes requires ethical principles and compliance with both the spirit of the law and professional standards in the accounting profession. Transparency and accuracy in reporting revenue, income, and assets develops trust from investors and other stakeholders.

TEAM EXERCISE

You can look at websites such as Yahoo! Finance (http://finance.yahoo.com/), under the company's "key statistics" link, to find many of its financial ratios, such as return on assets and return on equity. Have each member of your team look up a different company, and explain why you think there are differences in the ratio analysis for these two ratios among the selected companies.

LEARNING OBJECTIVES SUMMARY

LO1   Define accounting and describe the different uses of accounting information.

Accounting is the language businesses and other organizations use to record, measure, and interpret financial transactions. Financial statements are used internally to judge and control an organization's performance and to plan and direct its future activities and measure goal attainment. External organizations such as lenders, governments, customers, suppliers, and the CRA are major consumers of the information generated by the accounting process.

LO2   Demonstrate the accounting process.

Assets are an organization's economic resources; liabilities are debts the organization owes to others; owners' equity is the difference between the value of an organization's assets and its liabilities. This principle can be expressed as the accounting equation: Assets = Liabilities + Owners' equity. The double-entry bookkeeping system is a system of recording and classifying business transactions in accounts that maintains the balance of the accounting equation. The accounting cycle involves examining source documents, recording transactions in a journal, posting transactions, and preparing financial statements on a continuous basis throughout the life of the organization.

LO3   Examine the various components of an income statement to evaluate a firm's "bottom line."

The income statement indicates a company's profitability over a specific period of time. It shows the "bottom line," the total profit (or loss) after all expenses (the costs incurred in the day-to-day operations of the organization) have been deducted from revenue (the total amount of money received from the sale of goods or services and other business activities). The statement of cash flow shows how much cash is moving through the firm and thus adds insight to a firm's "bottom line."

LO4   Interpret a company's balance sheet to determine its current financial position.

The balance sheet, which summarizes the firm's assets, liabilities, and owners' equity since its inception, portrays its financial position as of a particular point in time. Major classifications included in the balance sheet are current assets (assets that can be converted to cash within one calendar year), fixed assets (assets of greater than one year's duration), current liabilities (bills owed by the organization within one calendar year), long-term liabilities (bills due more than one year hence), and owners' equity (the net value of the owners' investment).

LO5   Analyze the statement of cash flows to evaluate the increase and decrease in a company's cash balance.

The statement of cash flows shows how the company's cash changed from the beginning of the accounting period to the end. Cash from operating activities includes all the accounts on the balance sheet that relate to computing revenues and expenses for the accounting period. Cash from investing activities is calculated from changes in the long-term or fixed asset accounts. Cash from financing activities is calculated from changes in the long-term liability accounts and the contributed capital accounts in owners' equity.

LO6 Assess a company's financial position using its accounting statements and ratio analysis.

Ratio analysis is a series of calculations that brings the complex information from the income statement and balance sheet into sharper focus so that managers, lenders, owners, and other interested parties can measure and compare the organization's productivity, profitability, and financing mix with other similar entities. Ratios may be classified in terms of profitability (dollars of return for each dollar of employed assets), asset utilization (how well the organization uses its assets to generate $1 in sales), liquidity (assessing organizational risk by comparing current assets to current liabilities), debt utilization (how much debt the organization is using relative to other sources of capital), and per share data (comparing the performance of one company with another on an equal basis).

Analyst can use the ratio analysis to measure & compare....

KEY TERMS

accountant
accounting
accounting cycle
accounting equation
accounts payable
accounts receivable
accrued expenses
annual report
asset utilization ratios
assets
balance sheet
budget
cash flow
cost of goods sold
current assets
current liabilities
current ratio
debt to total assets ratio
debt utilization ratios
depreciation
dividends per share
double-entry bookkeeping
earnings per share

expenses
gross income or profit
income statement
inventory turnover
journal
ledger
liabilities
liquidity ratios
managerial accounting
net income
owners' equity
per share data
profit margin
profitability ratios
quick ratio (acid test)
ratio analysis
receivables turnover
return on assets
return on equity
revenue
statement of cash flows
times interest earned ratio
total asset turnover

DESTINATION CEO DISCUSSION QUESTIONS

1. Why do you think Jack Dorsey was successful as an inventor?

2. What are the expansion opportunities for Square?

3. How does technology play a role in the success of Square?

SO YOU WANT TO BE *an Accountant*

Do you like numbers and finances? Are you detail oriented, a perfectionist, and highly accountable for your decisions? If so, accounting may be a good field for you. If you are interested in accounting, there are always job opportunities available no matter the state of the economy. Accounting is one of the most secure job options in business. Of course, becoming an accountant is not easy. You will need at least a bachelor's degree in accounting to get a job, and many positions require additional training. If you are really serious about getting into the accounting field, you will probably want to consider getting your master's in accounting and obtaining your accounting designation. The field of accounting can be complicated, and the extra training provided through a master's in accounting program will prove invaluable when you go out looking for a good job. Accounting is a volatile discipline affected by changes in legislative initiatives.

Accountants are needed in the public and the private sectors, in large and small firms, in for-profit and not-for-profit organizations. Accountants in firms are generally in charge of preparing and filing tax forms and financial reports. Public-sector accountants are responsible for checking the veracity of corporate and personal records in order to prepare tax filings. Basically, any organization that has to deal with money and/or taxes in some way or another will be in need of an accountant, either for in-house service or occasional contract work. The fact that accounting rules and tax filings tend to be complex virtually ensures that the demand for accountants will never decrease.[13]

Accounting rules and regulations are becoming increasingly complex, thereby not only requiring the skills of an accountant but also requiring more time and effort. With industry demand high and increasing, and the number of qualified accountants holding steady or even decreasing, accounting salaries continue to rise from what are already high levels when compared with other business degrees. One reason for this increase is that accountants are continually building upon their traditional reputation as having the best overall qualifications among the financial designations for leadership positions within public accounting, industry, government, and academia. As a result, they are valued highly by the market.[14]

BUILD YOUR BUSINESS PLAN

Accounting and Financial Statements

After you determine your initial *reasonable selling price*, you need to estimate your sales forecasts (in terms of units and dollars of sales) for the first year of operation. Remember to be conservative and set forecasts that are modest.

While customers may initially try your business, many businesses have seasonal patterns. A good budgeting/planning system allows managers to anticipate problems, coordinate activities of the business (so that subunits within the organization are all working toward the common goal of the organization), and control operations (know whether spending is "in line").

The first financial statement you need to prepare is the income statement. Beginning with your estimated sales revenue, determine what expenses will be necessary to generate that level of sales revenue. Refer to Table 14.3 to assist you with this process.

The second financial statement you need to create is your balance sheet. Your balance sheet is a snapshot of your financial position in a moment in time. Refer to Table 14.5 to assist you in listing your assets, liabilities, and owners' equity.

The last financial statement, the statement of cash flow, is the most important one to a bank. It is a measure of your ability to get and repay the loan from the bank. Referring to Table 14.7, be as realistic as possible as you are completing it. Allow yourself enough cash on hand to survive until the point at which the business starts to support itself.

Accountants play a key role in helping individuals and organizations manage their responsibilities to pay taxes. However, for years foreign giants such as Amazon.com Inc., Apple Inc. and Netflix Inc. have had an unfair edge when selling digital products. Companies argue that without a physical presence in Canada are deemed not to be "carrying on business" in the country, and are not required to collect sales tax when they sell digital supplies to Canadians.

"Digital supplies" fall in a sales-tax grey area when sold to Canadians from abroad—including popular purchases such as streaming or downloading music, movies and TV shows, e-books, mobile apps, video games and software, online advertising, and cloud computing. When Canadian-based customers buy digital music or movies from iTunes, they pay no tax because those products are distributed by Apple, incorporated in the U.S. When same customers buy e-books or apps from the company, however, those are distributed by Apple Canada Inc., incorporated years later north of the border, and sales tax is added to the price. Amazon.com charges no tax on its e-book sales.

The 2014 federal budget invited input on "ensuring the effective collection of sales tax on e-commerce sales to Canadians by foreign-based vendors," and whether to enforce mandatory collection, as the European Union and Norway already have. If the new laws are successful, various levels of governments could collect tens of millions of dollars each year. On the other hand, Web retailers maintain that this revenue will not come from the company's pockets, but from those of sellers and consumers.[15]

DISCUSSION QUESTIONS

1. Why have Internet retailers such as Amazon and eBay been able to avoid collecting sales taxes?

2. What reasons do companies provide for opposing the collection of sales taxes?

3. Do you think it is fair that Web retailers do not have to collect sales taxes?

CHAPTER 15 Money and the Financial System

LEARNING OBJECTIVES

After reading this chapter, you will be able to:

LO1 Define money, its functions, and its characteristics.

LO2 Describe various types of money.

LO3 Specify how the Bank of Canada manages the money supply and regulates the Canadian banking system.

LO4 Compare and contrast chartered banks, trust companies, and credit unions/ *caisses populaires*.

LO5 Distinguish among non-banking institutions such as insurance companies, pension funds, mutual funds, and finance companies.

LO6 Investigate the challenges ahead for the banking industry.

DESTINATION CEO

Stephen Poloz, much to the surprise of many in the financial world, was appointed head of the Bank of Canada. He replaced Mark Carney, who had been appointed as governor of the Bank of England. Born in Oshawa, Ontario, Poloz graduated from Queen's University in 1978 with a bachelor's degree in economics. He received a master's degree in economics in 1979 and a PhD in economics in 1982, both from the University of Western Ontario.

Mr. Poloz first joined the Bank of Canada in 1981 and occupied a range of increasingly senior positions, culminating in his appointment as chief of the Bank's research department in 1992. After his departure from the Bank in 1995, he spent four years at BCA Research, and joined the Export Development Canada (EDC) in 1999 as vice-president and chief economist. In January 2011, he was appointed president and chief executive officer of EDC, a position in which he served until his appointment as governor of the Bank of Canada. At the EDC, Poloz helped provide insurance, financial services, and consultation for Canadian investors looking to expand their business abroad, as well as international investors looking for direct investment opportunities in Canada. Also in this role, Poloz worked closely with the Canadian federal government, as well as with many Canadian financial institutions.[1]

Introduction

From Bay Street to Wall Street—both overseas and at home—money is the one tool used to measure personal and business income and wealth. Not surprisingly, **finance** is the study of money: how it's made, how it's lost, and how it's managed. This chapter introduces you to the role of money and the financial system in the economy. Of course, if you have a chequing account, automobile insurance, a student loan, or a credit card, you already have personal experience with some key players in the financial world.

finance the study of money; how it's made, how it's lost, and how it's managed

We begin our discussion with a definition of money and then explore some of the many forms money may take. Next, we examine the roles of the Bank of Canada and other major institutions in the financial system. Finally, we explore the future of the finance industry and some of the changes likely to occur over the course of the next several years.

Money in the Financial System

Strictly defined, **money** is anything generally accepted in exchange for goods and services. Materials as diverse as salt, cattle, fish, rocks, shells, and cloth, as well as precious metals such as gold, silver, and copper, have long been used by various cultures as money. Most of these materials were limited-supply commodities that had their own value to society (for example, salt can be used as a preservative or as jewellery). The supply of these commodities therefore determined the supply of "money" in that society. The next step was the development of "IOUs," or slips of paper that could be exchanged for a specified supply of the underlying commodity. "Gold" notes, for instance, could be exchanged for gold, and the money supply was tied to the amount of gold available. While paper money was first used in North America in 1685 (and even earlier in Europe), the concept of *fiat money*—a paper money not readily convertible to a precious metal such as gold—did not gain full acceptance until the Great Depression in the 1930s. Canada abandoned its gold-backed currency standard largely in response to the Great Depression and converted to a fiduciary, or fiat, monetary system. In Canada, paper money is really a government "note" or promise, worth the value specified on the note.

> **money** anything generally accepted in exchange for goods and services

Functions of Money

No matter what a particular society uses for money, its primary purpose is to enable a person or organization to transform a desire into an action. These desires may be for entertainment actions, such as party expenses; operating actions, such as paying for rent, utilities, or employees; investing actions, such as buying property or equipment; or financing actions, such as for starting or growing a business. Money serves three important functions: as a medium of exchange, a measure of value, and a store of value.

Medium of Exchange. Before fiat money, the trade of goods and services was accomplished through *bartering*—trading one good or service for another of similar value. As any school-age child knows, bartering can become quite inefficient—particularly in the case of complex, three-party transactions involving peanut butter sandwiches, baseball cards, and hair barrettes. There had to be a simpler way, and that was to decide on a single item—money—that can be freely converted to any other good upon agreement between parties.

For centuries, people on the Micronesian island of Yap have used giant round stones, like the ones shown here, for currency. The stones aren't moved, but their ownership can change.

Measure of Value. As a measure of value, money serves as a common standard for the value of goods and services. For example, $2 will buy a dozen large eggs and $25,000 will buy a nice car in Canada. In Japan, where the currency is known as the yen, these same transactions would cost about 185 yen and 2.3 million yen, respectively. Money, then, is a common denominator that allows people to compare the different goods and services that can be consumed on a particular income level. While a star athlete and a "burger-flipper" are paid vastly different wages, each uses money as a measure of the value of yearly earnings and purchases.

> "No matter what a particular society uses for money, its primary purpose is to enable a person or organization to transform a desire into an action."

Store of Value. As a store of value, money serves as a way to accumulate wealth (buying power) until it is needed. For example, a person making $500 per week who wants to buy a $500 computer could save $50 per week for each of the next ten weeks. Unfortunately, the value of stored money is directly dependent on the health of the economy. If, due to rapid inflation, all prices double in one year, then the purchasing power value of the money "stuffed in the mattress" would fall by half. On the other hand, deflation occurs when prices of goods fall. Deflation might seem like a good thing for consumers, but in many ways it can be just as problematic as inflation. Periods of major deflation often lead to decreases in wages and increases in debt burdens.[2] Deflation also tends to be an indicator of problems in the economy. When Ireland experienced deflation in 2009—the first time it had experienced deflation in 49 years—the country blamed it on decreasing mortgage interest rate costs.[3] Ireland was undergoing a serious deficit and required a bailout from the European commission, the International Monetary Fund, and the European Central Bank.[4]

Characteristics of Money

To be used as a medium of exchange, money must be acceptable, divisible, portable, stable in value, durable, and difficult to counterfeit.

Acceptability. To be effective, money must be readily acceptable for the purchase of goods and services and for the settlement of debts. Acceptability is probably the most important characteristic of money: If people do not trust the value of money, businesses will not accept it as a payment for goods and services, and consumers will have to find some other means of paying for their purchases.

Divisibility.   Given the widespread use of quarters, dimes, nickels, and pennies in Canada, it is no surprise that the principle of divisibility is an important one. With barter, the lack of divisibility often makes otherwise preferable trades impossible, as would be an attempt to trade a steer for a loaf of bread. For money to serve effectively as a measure of value, all items must be valued in terms of comparable units—dimes for a piece of bubble gum, quarters for laundry machines, and dollars (or dollars and coins) for everything else.

Portability.   Clearly, for money to function as a medium of exchange, it must be easily moved from one location to the next. Large coloured rocks could be used as money, but you couldn't carry them around in your wallet. Paper currency and metal coins, on the other hand, are capable of transferring vast purchasing power into small, easily carried (and hidden!) bundles. Eurodollars are U.S. dollars in circulation outside the United States. Currently, about $1.5 trillion of U.S. currency is in circulation, and the majority is held outside the United States.[5] Some countries, such as Panama, even use the U.S. dollar as their currency. Retailers in other countries often state prices in dollars and in their local currency.

Stability.   Money must be stable and maintain its declared face value. A $10 bill should purchase the same amount of goods or services from one day to the next. The principle of stability allows people who wish to postpone purchases and save their money to do so without fear that it will decline in value. As mentioned earlier, money declines in value during periods of inflation, when economic conditions cause prices to rise. Thus, the same amount of money buys fewer and fewer goods and services. In some countries, particularly in Latin America, people spend their money as fast as they can in order to keep it from losing any more of its value. Instability destroys confidence in a nation's money and its ability to store value and serve as an effective medium of exchange. Ultimately, people faced with spiralling price increases avoid the increasingly worthless paper money at all costs, storing all of their savings in the form of real assets such as gold and land.

Durability.   Money must be durable. The crisp new dollar bills you trade at the music store for the hottest new CD will make their way all around town for about 20 months before being replaced (see Table 15.1). Were the value of an old, faded bill to fall in line with the deterioration of its appearance, the principles of stability and universal acceptability

Table 15.1 The Life Expectancy of Paper Currency

Denomination of Bill	Life Expectancy (Years)
$ 5	1–2
$ 10	1–2
$ 20	2–4
$ 100	7–9

Based on Doug Hanchard, "Polymer to replace cotton in Canadian currency notes," *ZDNet*, March 9, 2010, http://www.zdnet.com/article/polymer-to-replace-cotton-in-canadian-currency-notes/ (accessed January 18, 2016).

would fail (but, no doubt, fewer bills would pass through the washer!). Although metal coins, due to their much longer useful life, would appear to be an ideal form of money, paper currency is far more portable than metal because of its light weight. Today, coins are used primarily to provide divisibility.

Difficulty to Counterfeit.   Finally, to remain stable and enjoy universal acceptance, it almost goes without saying that money must be very difficult to counterfeit—that is, to duplicate illegally. Every country takes steps to make counterfeiting difficult. Most use multicoloured money, and many use specially watermarked papers that are virtually impossible to duplicate. To thwart the problem of counterfeiting, the Bank of Canada has redesigned banknotes, most recently issuing the Polymer series, which uses innovative security features that can be seen in transparent areas on both sides of the notes.[6]

Although counterfeiting is not as much of an issue with coins, metal coins have their own problems. The value of certain coins is less than the money it costs to produce them. Due to the increased price of metals, many countries have removed the one-cent coin from circulation. Canada, for example, eliminated the one-cent coin with an estimated savings of $11 million a year.[7] Australia and New Zealand eliminated both the one-cent and two-cent coins. New Zealand has even stopped issuing the five-cent coin.[8]

© Vstock LLC/Getty Images

The Bank of Canada redesigns currency in order to stay ahead of counterfeiters and protect the public.

Types of Money

LO2   Describe various types of money.

While paper money and coins are the most visible types of money, the combined value of all of the printed bills and all of the minted coins is actually rather insignificant when compared with the value of money kept in chequing accounts, savings accounts, and other monetary forms.

You probably have a **chequing account** (also called a *demand deposit*), money stored in an account at a bank or other financial institution that can be withdrawn without advance notice. One way to withdraw funds from your account is by writing a *cheque*, a written order to a bank to pay the indicated individual or business the amount specified on the cheque from money already on deposit. As legal instruments, cheques serve as a substitute for currency and coins and are preferred for many transactions due to their lower risk of loss. If you lose a $100 bill, anyone who finds or steals it can spend it. If you lose a blank cheque, however, the risk of catastrophic loss is quite low. Not only does your bank have a sample of your signature on file to compare with a suspected forged signature, but you can render the cheque immediately worthless by means of a stop-payment order at your bank.

There are several types of chequing accounts, with different features available for different monthly fee levels or specific minimum account balances. Some chequing accounts earn interest (a small percentage of the amount deposited in the account that the bank pays to the depositor). The interest rate paid on such accounts varies with the interest rates available in the economy but is typically quite low (ranging between zero and a little over 1 percent).

Savings accounts (also known as *time deposits*) are accounts with funds that usually cannot be withdrawn without advance notice and/or have limits on the number of withdrawals per period. While seldom enforced, the "fine print" governing most savings accounts prohibits withdrawals without two or three days' notice. Savings accounts are not generally used for transactions or as a medium of exchange, but their funds can be moved to a chequing account or turned into cash.

Money market accounts are similar to interest-bearing chequing accounts, but with more restrictions. Generally, in exchange for slightly higher interest rates, the owner of a money market account can write only a limited number of cheques each month, and there may be a restriction on the minimum amount of each cheque.

Certificates of deposit (CDs) are savings accounts that guarantee a depositor a set interest rate over a specified interval of time as long as the funds are not withdrawn

---

chequing account money stored in an account at a bank or other financial institution that can be withdrawn without advance notice; also called a *demand deposit*

savings accounts accounts with funds that usually cannot be withdrawn without advance notice; also known as *time deposits*

money market accounts accounts that offer higher interest rates than standard bank rates but with greater restrictions

certificates of deposit (CDs) savings accounts that guarantee a depositor a set interest rate over a specified interval as long as the funds are not withdrawn before the end of the period—six months or one year, for example

before the end of the interval—six months, one year, or five years, for example. Money may be withdrawn from these accounts prematurely only after paying a substantial penalty. In general, the longer the term of the CD, the higher the interest rate it earns. As with all interest rates, the rate offered and fixed at the time the account is opened fluctuates according to economic conditions. Financial institutions issue CDs under a variety of names; for example, Deposit Receipts (DRs), Guaranteed Trust Certificates (GTCs), and Guaranteed Investment Certificates (GICs).

Credit cards allow you to promise to pay at a later date by using preapproved lines of credit granted by a bank or finance company. They are popular substitutes for cash payments because of their convenience, easy access to credit, and acceptance by merchants around the world. The institution that issues the credit card guarantees payment of a credit charge to merchants and assumes responsibility for collecting the money from the cardholders. Card issuers charge a transaction fee to the merchants for performing the credit check, guaranteeing the payment, and collecting the payment. The fee is typically between 2 and 5 percent, depending on the type of card. American Express fees are usually higher than Visa and MasterCard.

The original American Express cards require full payment at the end of each month, but American Express now offers credit cards similar to Visa and MasterCard that allow cardholders to make installment payments and carry a maximum balance. There is a minimum monthly payment with interest charged on the remaining balance. Some people pay off their credit cards monthly, while others make monthly payments. Charges for unpaid balances can run 18 percent or higher at an annual rate, making credit card debt one of the most expensive ways to borrow money.

Besides the major credit card companies, many stores—Sears, Hudson's Bay, and others—have their own branded credit cards. They use credit rating agencies to check the credit of the cardholders and they generally make money on the finance charges. Unlike the major credit cards discussed, these "private label" cards are generally accepted only at stores associated with the issuing company.

New credit card regulations came in force as of January 1, 2010. These regulations are important to all companies and cardholders. Without going into details, the regulations enhance consumers' access to clear information about key details, such as interest rates, fees, and penalty charges. They also strengthen consumers' rights by limiting certain business practices of financial institutions.[11]

A **debit card** looks like a credit card but works like a cheque. The use of a debit

© Teragram/Dreamstime.com

High interest rates on credit cards and the most recent recession have led many Canadians to reduce credit card balances.

card results in a direct, immediate, electronic payment from the cardholder's account to a merchant or other party. While they are convenient to carry and profitable for banks, they lack credit features, offer no purchase "grace period," and provide no hard "paper trail." Debit cards are gaining more acceptance with merchants, and consumers like debit cards because of the ease of getting cash from an increasing number of ATMs. Financial institutions also want consumers to use debit cards because they reduce the number of teller transactions and cheque processing costs.

"Two major credit cards— MasterCard and Visa—represent the vast majority of credit cards held in Canada."

Traveller's cheques, money orders, and cashier's cheques are other common forms of "near money." Although each is slightly different from the others, they all share a common characteristic: A financial institution, bank, credit company, or neighbourhood currency exchange issues them in exchange for cash and guarantees that the purchased note will be honoured and exchanged for cash when it is presented to the institution making the guarantee.

credit cards means of access to preapproved lines of credit granted by a bank or finance company

debit card a card that looks like a credit card but works like a cheque; using it results in a direct, immediate, electronic payment from the cardholder's chequing account to a merchant or third party

The Canadian Financial System

LO3 Specify how the Bank of Canada manages the money supply and regulates the Canadian banking system.

The Canadian financial system fuels our economy by storing money, fostering investment opportunities, and making loans for new businesses and business expansion as well as for homes, cars, and post-secondary educations. This amazingly complex system includes banking institutions, non-banking financial institutions such as finance companies, and systems that provide for the electronic transfer of funds throughout the world. Over the past 20 years, the rate at which money turns over, or changes hands, has increased exponentially. Different cultures place unique values on saving, spending, borrowing, and investing. The combination of this increased turnover rate and increasing interactions with people and organizations from other countries has created a complex money system. First, we need to meet the guardian of this complex system.

> "The Bank of Canada establishes and enforces banking rules that affect monetary policy and the overall level of the competition between different banks."

The Bank of Canada

The nation's central bank is the **Bank of Canada** (the Bank), a crown corporation of the federal government founded in 1934 "to promote the economic and financial welfare of Canada." The Bank of Canada tries to create a positive economic environment capable of sustaining low inflation, high levels of employment, and long-term economic growth. To this end, the Bank of Canada has four major responsibilities: (1) to conduct monetary policy; (2) to issue Canada's bank notes and be responsible for their design and security, distribution, and replacement; (3) to promote safe, sound, and efficient financial systems; and (4) to provide high-quality, effective, and efficient funds-management services for the federal government, the Bank, and other clients.

Monetary Policy. The Bank of Canada controls the amount of money available in the economy through **monetary policy**. Without this intervention, the supply of and demand for money might not balance. This could result in either rapid price increases (inflation), because of rapid growth in money supply, or economic recession and falling prices (deflation), because of too little growth in the money supply. In very rare cases (such as the depression of

the 1930s), Canada has suffered from deflation, where the actual purchasing power of the dollar increased as prices declined. To effectively control the supply of money in the economy, the Bank of Canada must have a good idea of how much money is in circulation at any given time. This has become increasingly challenging because of the global nature of our economy. Using several different measures of the money supply, the Bank of Canada establishes specific growth targets that, presumably, ensure a close balance between money supply and money demand. The Bank carries out monetary policy by influencing short-term interest rates. It does this by raising and lowering the target for the overnight rate. (The "overnight rate" is the interest rate at which major financial institutions, banks, credit unions, and similar credit-granting organizations borrow and lend one-day funds among themselves. This is different from the "bank rate," which is the midpoint of the range for the overnight rate.) There is generally a lag of 6 to 18 months before the effect of these changes shows up in economic activity. As with other central banks, notably those of the European Union and the United States, the Bank of Canada has other tools at its disposal to fine-tune money growth, including open market operations, desired reserves, the bank (discount) rate, and credit controls (see Table 15.2). **Open market operations** refer to decisions to buy or sell Treasury bills (short-term

Bank of Canada an independent agency of the federal government established in 1934 to regulate the nation's banking and financial industry

monetary policy means by which the Bank of Canada controls the amount of money available in the economy

open market operations decisions to buy or sell Treasury bills (short-term debt issued by the government) and other investments in the open market

Table 15.2 Tools for Regulating the Money Supply

Activity	Effect on the Money Supply and the Economy
Buy government securities	The money supply increases; economic activity increases.
Sell government securities	The money supply decreases; economic activity slows down.
Raise bank rate	Interest rates increase; the money supply decreases; economic activity slows down.
Lower bank rate	Interest rates decrease; the money supply increases; economic activity increases.
Increase reserves	Banks make fewer loans; the money supply declines; economic activity slows down.
Decrease reserves	Banks make more loans; the money supply increases; economic activity increases.
Relax credit controls	More people are encouraged to make major purchases, increasing economic activity.
Restrict credit controls	People are discouraged from making major purchases, decreasing economic activity.

debt issued by a government; also called T-bills) and other investments in the open market. The actual purchase or sale of the investments is performed by the Bank. This monetary tool, the most commonly employed of all operations, is performed almost daily in an effort to control the money supply.

When the Bank buys securities, it writes a cheque on its own account to the seller of the investments. When the seller of the investments (usually a large bank) deposits the cheque, the Bank transfers the balance from its account into the seller's account, thus increasing the supply of money in the economy and, hopefully, fuelling economic growth. The opposite occurs when the Bank sells investments. The buyer writes a cheque to the Bank, and when the funds are transferred out of the purchaser's account, the amount of money in circulation falls, slowing economic growth to a desired level.

The second major monetary policy tool is the requirement of **desired reserves**, the percentage of deposits that banking institutions must hold in reserve ("in the vault," as it were). Funds so held are not available for lending to businesses and consumers. For example, a bank holding $10 million in deposits with a 10 percent desired reserves requirement must have reserves of $1 million. If the Bank of Canada were to reduce the desired reserves requirement to, say, 5 percent, the financial institution would need to keep only $500,000 in reserves. It could then lend to customers the $500,000 difference between the old reserve level and the new lower reserve level, thus increasing the supply of money. Because desired reserves have such a powerful effect on the money supply, the Bank of Canada does not change them very often, relying instead on open market operations most of the time.

The third monetary policy tool, the **bank rate**, is the rate of interest the Bank charges to loan money to any banking institution to meet reserve requirements. The Bank is the lender of last resort for these banks. When a bank borrows from the Bank of Canada, the interest rates charged there are often higher than those charged on loans of comparable risk elsewhere in the economy. This added interest expense, when it exists, serves to discourage banking institutions from borrowing from the Bank. When the Bank wants to expand the money supply, it lowers the bank rate to encourage borrowing. Conversely, when the Bank wants to decrease the money supply, it raises the bank rate. Not surprisingly, economists watch changes in this sensitive interest rate as an indicator of the Bank of Canada's monetary policy.

desired reserves the percentage of deposits that banking institutions hold in reserve

bank rate the rate of interest the Bank of Canada charges to loan money to any banking institution to meet reserve requirements

credit controls the authority to establish and enforce credit rules for financial institutions and some private investors

© Sml/Dreamstime.com

One of the roles of the Bank of Canada is to use its policies to keep money flowing. Money is the lifeblood of the economy. If banks become too protective of their funds and stop lending money, the economy can grind to a halt.

Deposits / Duration (Time)

The final tool in the Bank's arsenal of weapons is **credit controls**—the authority to establish and enforce credit rules for financial institutions and some private investors. For example, the Bank can determine how large a down payment individuals and businesses must make on credit purchases of expensive items such as automobiles, and how much time they have to finish paying for the purchases. By raising and lowering minimum down payment amounts and payment periods, the Bank can stimulate or discourage credit purchases of "big ticket" items. The Bank also has the authority to set the minimum down payment investors must use for the credit purchases of stock. Buying stock with credit—"buying on margin"—is a popular investment strategy among individual speculators. By altering the margin requirement (commonly set at 50 percent of the price of the purchased stocks), the Bank can effectively control the total amount of credit borrowing in the stock market.

Bank Notes. Another responsibility of the Bank of Canada is for Canada's bank notes. The Bank of Canada is the country's sole bank note–issuing authority and is responsible for designing, producing, and distributing Canada's bank notes. The Bank of Canada must supply financial institutions with enough bank notes to satisfy public demand. Financial institutions get bank notes through the country's Bank Note Distribution System, and return notes that are considered unfit for further circulation to the Bank of Canada. These notes are verified on high-speed, note-processing equipment and then shredded.[12]

The Financial System. The Bank of Canada works to promote safe, sound, and efficient financial systems. A stable financial system is essential to the health of Canada's economy. The Bank of Canada works with other agencies and market participants to promote the safe and efficient operation of the system's key elements. The

Bank provides liquidity to the system; gives policy advice to the federal government on the design and development of the financial system; oversees major clearing and settlement systems; provides banking services to these systems and their participants; and collaborates with other domestic and international bodies involved in financial-stability issues.[13]

Funds Management Services. The Bank acts as the "fiscal agent" for the Government of Canada. As a government banker and treasury manager, the Bank manages the accounts of the Receiver General, through which almost all money collected and spent by the government flows. The Bank ensures that these accounts have enough cash to meet daily requirements and invests any surpluses in term deposits. The Bank also manages the government's foreign exchange reserves. These reserves promote stability in the Canadian-dollar foreign exchange market. The Bank also provides policy advice to the government on the efficient management of the government debt and sells the securities at auction to financial market distributors and dealers. The main goal of the Bank's debt-management activities is to help provide stable and low-cost funding to the government.[14]

Banking Institutions

LO4 Compare and contrast chartered banks, trust companies, and credit unions/*caisses populaires*.

Banking institutions accept money deposits from and make loans to individual consumers and businesses. Some of the most important banking institutions include chartered banks, trust companies, and credit unions/*caisses populaires*. Historically, these have all been separate institutions. However, new hybrid forms of banking institutions that perform two or more of these functions have emerged over the last two decades. The following banking institutions all have one thing in common: They are businesses whose objective is to earn money by managing, safeguarding, and lending money to others. Their sales revenues come from the fees and interest that they charge for providing these financial services.

Chartered Banks. The largest and oldest of all financial institutions are **chartered banks**, which perform a variety of financial services. They rely mainly on chequing and savings accounts as their major source of funds and use only a portion of these deposits to make loans to businesses and individuals. Because it is unlikely that all the depositors of any one bank will want to withdraw

chartered banks, the largest and oldest of all financial institutions, relying mainly on chequing and savings accounts as sources of funds for loans to businesses and individuals

"Banks are quite diversified **and offer a number of services.**"

all of their funds at the same time, a bank can safely loan out a large percentage of its deposits.

Today, banks are quite diversified and offer a number of services. Chartered banks make loans for virtually any conceivable legal purpose, from vacations to cars, from homes to post-secondary educations. Banks offer *home equity loans*, by which home owners can borrow against the appraised value of their already purchased homes. Banks also issue Visa and MasterCard credit cards and offer CDs and trusts (legal entities set up to hold and manage assets for a beneficiary). Many banks rent safe-deposit boxes in bank vaults to customers who want to store jewellery, legal documents, artwork, and other valuables. The banking industry in Canada includes domestic banks, foreign bank subsidiaries, and foreign bank branches. In total, these institutions manage almost $1.8 trillion in assets. The Office of the Superintendent of Financial Institutions, along with the Bank of Canada and the Canada Deposit Insurance Corporation, regulate and supervise federally registered financial institutions.[15] Table 15.3 gives an overview of the Canadian financial system.

Trust Companies. **Trust companies** act as fiduciaries or corporate trustees and operate under either provincial or federal legislation and conduct the same activities as a bank. Like a bank, they operate through a network of branches. However, because of its fiduciary role, a trust company can administer estates, trusts, pension plans, and agency contracts, which banks cannot do.[16] The *Bank Act* has allowed regulated

trust companies
corporations that act as a trustee and usually also provide banking services

Table 15.3 Overview of the Canadian Financial Services Sector

Sector	Number of Active Firms
Banks	82
Trust companies	44
Loan companies	18
Credit unions/*caisses populaires* (outside Quebec)	338
Life and health insurance companies	72
Property and casualty insurance companies	167
Mutual fund companies	423
Securities dealers	182
Finance and leasing companies	200

Sources: Office of the Superintendent of Financial Institutions, http://www.osfi-bsif.gc.ca/Eng/wt-ow/Pages/wwr-er.aspx; Credit Union Central of Canada, https://www.ccua.com/about/facts_and_figures; Investment Funds Institute of Canada, https://www.ific.ca/Content/Content.aspx?id=152; Investment Dealers Association of Canada, http://www.iiroc.ca/industry/Pages/Dealers-We-Regulate.aspx; Canadian Finance & Leasing Association, https://www.cfla-acfl.ca/information/about-cfla (all accessed January 18, 2016).

The World Bank, created in 1944 by delegates from across the world, raises money through donations, bond sales, and shareholder support. This money is then used to provide loans and other financial assistance to developing countries. The loans fund a variety of projects, including education, infrastructure, and public administration. Realizing that funding certain projects could negatively affect the environment, the World Bank adopted policies to assess the sustainability of proposed projects.

Despite these policies, environmental groups have accused the World Bank of funding projects that harm the environment. One project, the Sardar Sarovar Dam in India's River Narmada, was criticized for causing environmental degradation. Yet advocates for the dam argue that it provides irrigation and drinking water. The World Bank must juggle both the human and environmental impacts when determining which projects to fund. As the importance of sustainability grows, the World Bank has taken steps to curb climate change and support renewable energy initiatives. The World Bank partnered with the C40

Cities Climate Leadership Group to reduce global greenhouse gas emissions.

The bank has also increased its loans for renewable energy projects to almost 23 percent of energy loans, including $175 million for a geothermal project in Indonesia. Whether these actions will lead to significant change or whether they are merely window-dressing to reduce criticism remains to be seen.[17]

DISCUSSION QUESTIONS

1. Describe what the World Bank does. Why is it important?

2. Why is sustainability becoming a major issue for the World Bank?

3. Do you feel that the World Bank should make sustainability a priority?

---

federal financial institutions to own trust companies. As a result, and with the acquisition of Canada Trust by the Toronto Dominion Bank, trust companies are a small market segment.

Credit Unions and *Caisses Populaires*. A **credit union/ caisse populaire** (as it is known in Quebec) is a cooperative financial institution that is owned and controlled by its depositors, who usually have a common employer, profession, trade group, or religion. Because the credit union is tied to a common organization, the credit unions are operated democratically and owned by their depositors as members. The members are allowed to vote for directors and share in the credit union's profits in the form of higher interest rates on accounts and/ or lower loan rates. While credit unions were originally created to provide depositors with a short-term source of funds for low-interest consumer loans for items such as cars, home appliances, vacations, and post-secondary education, today they offer a wide range of financial services. Generally, the larger the credit union, the more sophisticated its financial service offerings will be. They are subject to provincial regulation and are usually small and locally oriented. This sector is almost exclusively regulated at the provincial level in Canada. However, the Credit Union Central of Canada is chartered and regulated by the federal government.[18]

credit union/*caisse populaire* a financial institution owned and controlled by its depositors, who usually have a common employer, profession, trade group, or religion

Insurance for Banking Institutions. The **Canada Deposit Insurance Corporation (CDIC)**, a federal Crown corporation that insures individual bank accounts, was established in 1967 and insures deposits in banks and trust and loan companies against loss in the event of member failure. It insures eligible deposits up to $100,000 per depositor in each member institution, which must pay premiums to cover CDIC's insurance obligations. Should a member bank fail, its depositors can recover all of their funds, up to $100,000. Deposits of credit unions and *caisses populaires* are protected under provincial stabilization funds and/or deposit insurance and guarantee corporations. Deposit insurance coverage ranges from $60,000 to unlimited coverage, with the amount varying by province.[19] When they were originally established, the federal government hoped that these insurance funds would make people feel secure about their savings so that they would not panic and withdraw their money when news of a bank failure was announced. During the Great Depression, many banks failed and their depositors lost everything. The fact that large numbers of major financial institutions failed in the 1980s and 1990s—without a single major banking panic—underscores the effectiveness of the current insurance system. While the future may yet bring unfortunate surprises, most depositors go to sleep every night without worrying about the safety of their savings.

Canada Deposit Insurance Corporation (CDIC) a federal Crown corporation that insures bank accounts

Non-banking Institutions

Non-bank financial institutions offer some financial services, such as short-term loans or investment products, but do not accept deposits. These include insurance companies, pension funds, mutual funds, brokerage firms, non-financial firms, and finance companies.

Diversified Firms. Recently, a growing number of traditionally non-financial firms have moved onto the financial field. These firms include manufacturing organizations, such as General Motors and General Electric, that traditionally confined their financial activities to financing their customers' purchases. GE was once so successful in the financial arena that its credit subsidiary accounted for more than 40 percent of the company's revenues and earnings. Unfortunately, GE Capital became a liability to GE during the financial crisis, and is in the process of recovery as GE cuts the size of its finance unit and writes off billions of dollars in bad loans.

Insurance Companies. **Insurance companies** are businesses that protect their clients against financial losses from certain specified risks (death, injury, disability, accident, fire, theft, and natural disasters, for example) in exchange for a fee, called a premium. Because insurance premiums flow into the companies regularly, but major insurance losses cannot be timed with great accuracy (although expected risks can be assessed with considerable precision), insurance companies generally have large amounts of excess funds. They typically invest these or make long-term loans, particularly to businesses in the form of commercial real estate loans.

Pension Funds. **Pension funds** are managed investment pools set aside by individuals, corporations, unions, and some non-profit organizations to provide retirement income for members. One type of pension fund is the *registered retirement savings plan (RRSP)*, which is established by individuals to provide for their personal retirement needs. RRSPs can be invested in a variety of financial assets, including shares, bonds, mutual funds, and low-risk financial "staples" such as Treasury securities. The choice is up to each person and is dictated solely by individual objectives and tolerance for risk. The interest earned by all of these investments may be deferred tax-free until retirement.

In 2009, the Canadian Minister of Finance announced the creation of a *tax-free savings account (TFSA)*. Investors may contribute up to a set amount per year (currently $5,500); the money and the contribution are considered an after-tax contribution. When the money is withdrawn at retirement, or at any other time, no tax is paid on the distribution. The TSFA is beneficial to young people who can allow a long time for their money to compound and who may be able to have their parents or grandparents fund the TSFA with gift money.

Most major corporations provide some kind of pension plan for their employees. Many of these are established with bank trust departments or life insurance companies. Money is deposited in a separate account in the name of each individual employee, and when the employee retires, the total amount in the account can be either withdrawn in one lump sum or taken as monthly cash payments over some defined time period (usually for the remaining life of the retiree).

All employed Canadians contribute to either the Canada Pension Plan or the Quebec Pension Plan through payroll deductions. The funds are managed separately from general tax dollars and all the monies generated are used to pay benefits to eligible plan members. The plans offer similar benefits including pensions after age 60, survivor benefits for spouses and dependants, and disability payments.

> "A growing number of traditionally non-financial firms have moved onto the financial field."

insurance companies businesses that protect their clients against financial losses from certain specified risks (death, accident, and theft, for example)

pension funds managed investment pools set aside by individuals, corporations, unions, and some non-profit organizations to provide retirement income for members

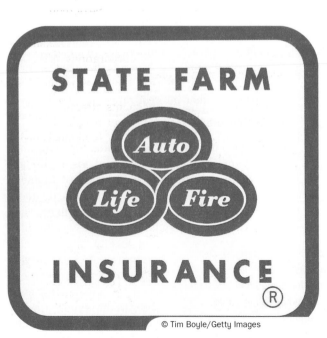

© Tim Boyle/Getty Images

State Farm Insurance allows users to input their information on its website to receive an auto insurance quote quickly and conveniently.

Jack Dorsey

Business: Square

Founded: 2009

Success: Square has already signed up thousands of users; it processed $66 million in credit card transactions in the first quarter of 2011 alone.

Twitter co-founder Jack Dorsey is entering into new territory: the banking industry. Specifically, Dorsey has created a product called Square that he hopes will replace traditional credit card readers. Square is a small credit card swiper that merchants plug into their smartphones. After swiping the card, customers sign on the phone's screen, and within one minute, the transaction is complete. Square also tracks all sales conducted through its readers, creating a useful database.

Dorsey created Square after recognizing the massive unmet demand from less traditional merchants—such as artists—who do not own credit card readers. Square also reduces the number of organizations and fees involved with traditional credit card transactions, charging merchants a flat 2.75 percent and 15 cents for each transaction. *Time* magazine was so impressed with Square that it nominated the product as one of the 50 best inventions of 2010. Despite its promising start, opportunities for credit card fraud will require Square to proactively take measures to ensure safe, convenient transactions.[20]

Mutual Funds. A **mutual fund** pools individual investor dollars and invests them in large numbers of well-diversified securities. Individual investors buy shares in a mutual fund in the hope of earning a high rate of return and in much the same way as people buy shares of stock. Because of the large numbers of people investing in any one mutual fund, the funds can afford to invest in hundreds (if not thousands) of securities at any one time, minimizing the risks of any single security that does not do well. Mutual funds provide professional financial management for people who lack the time and/or expertise to invest in particular securities, such as government bonds. While there are no hard-and-fast rules, investments in one or more mutual funds are one way for people to plan for financial independence at the time of retirement.

A special type of mutual fund called a *money market fund* invests specifically in short-term debt securities issued by governments and large corporations. Although they offer services such as cheque-writing privileges and reinvestment of interest income, money market funds differ from the money market accounts offered by banks primarily in that the former represent a pool of funds, while the latter are basically specialized, individual chequing accounts. Money market funds usually offer slightly higher rates of interest than bank money market accounts.

mutual fund an investment company that pools individual investor dollars and invests them in large numbers of well-diversified securities

brokerage firms firms that buy and sell stocks, bonds, and other securities for their customers and provide other financial services

Brokerage Firms. **Brokerage firms** buy and sell stocks, bonds, and other securities for their customers and provide other financial services. The largest of the brokerage firms (including RBC Dominion Securities) have developed so many specialized services that they may be considered financial networks—organizations capable of offering virtually all of the services an individual may require.

Most brokerage firms are really part of financial conglomerates that provide many different kinds of services besides buying and selling securities for clients.

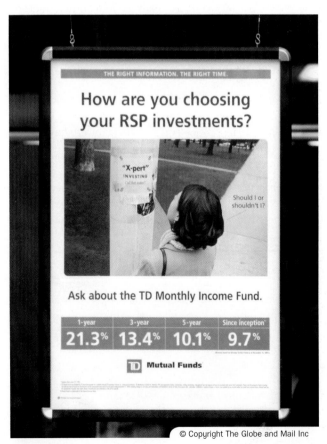

© Copyright The Globe and Mail Inc

Mutual funds are considered an excellent method for investing for retirement.

The investment banker underwrites new issues of securities for corporations, states, and municipalities that need to raise money in the capital markets. The new issue market is called a *primary market* because the sale of the securities is for the first time. After the first sale, the securities are traded in the *secondary markets* by brokers. The investment banker advises on the price of the new securities and generally guarantees the sale while overseeing the distribution of the securities through the selling brokerage houses. Investment bankers also act as dealers who make markets in securities. They do this by offering to sell the securities at an asked price (which is a higher rate) and buy the securities at a bid price (which is a lower rate)—the difference in the two prices represents the profit for the dealer.

Finance Companies. **Finance companies** are businesses that offer short-term loans at substantially higher rates of interest than banks. Commercial finance companies make loans to businesses, requiring their borrowers to pledge assets such as equipment, inventories, or unpaid accounts as collateral for the loans. Consumer finance companies make loans to individuals. Like commercial finance companies, these firms require some sort of personal collateral as security against the borrower's possible inability to repay the loans. Because of the high interest rates they charge and other factors, finance companies typically are the lender of last resort for individuals and businesses whose credit limits have been exhausted and/or those with poor credit ratings.

finance companies businesses that offer short-term loans at substantially higher rates of interest than banks

Electronic Banking

Since the advent of the computer age, a wide range of technological innovations have made it possible to move money all across the world electronically. Such "paperless" transactions have allowed financial institutions to reduce costs in what has been (and what appears to continue to be) a virtual competitive battlefield. **Electronic funds transfer (EFT)** is any movement of funds by means of an electronic terminal, telephone, computer, or magnetic tape. Such transactions order a particular financial institution to subtract money from one account and add it to another. The most commonly used forms of EFT are automated banking machines and home banking systems.

Automated Banking Machines. Probably the most familiar form of electronic banking is the **automated banking machine (ABM)**, which dispenses cash, accepts

electronic funds transfer (EFT) any movement of funds by means of an electronic terminal, telephone, computer, or magnetic tape

automated banking machine (ABM) the most familiar form of electronic banking, which dispenses cash, accepts deposits, and allows balance inquiries and cash transfers from one account to another

---

Consider the Following: Cost of Borrowing Poses a Threat to Brazilian Consumers

Debt is not necessarily a bad thing. Many companies borrow in order to finance projects, which can lead to greater profits. Consumers borrow to obtain objects that they value. The problem arises when businesses or individuals incur so much debt that they cannot pay it off. This is becoming a serious concern for consumers in Brazil.

The Brazilian economy has been booming in recent years, creating a growing middle class. With their newfound wealth, consumers are spending and using credit like never before. Unfortunately, many Brazilian consumers have little experience with credit, which is contributing to widespread consumer borrowing and a rising number of loan defaults. While retail sales rose 9 percent in one year—faster than GDP growth—the default rate on personal loans rose 22 percent in a six-month period.

Consumer spending has become such a problem that the central bank of Brazil has increased interest rates. However, some banks charge even higher rates than the central bank. Credit cards have an annual interest rate of 238 percent on average, whereas the cost of borrowing for personal loans is 85 percent for retailers and 47 percent for banks.

The ethics of charging such high interest rates are questionable. On the one hand, higher interest rates tend to deter spending. Additionally, inflation in Brazil has risen significantly, which in turn increases the cost of borrowing. On the other hand, the lack of knowledge that many Brazilian consumers have of credit puts them at a major disadvantage at understanding the financial dangers of too much debt.[21]

DISCUSSION QUESTIONS

1. Why are Brazilians having difficulty with borrowing and paying back debt?

2. Do you feel that it is ethical for banks to charge such high rates for borrowing?

3. What would you suggest as a way to reduce the debt problems that Brazilian consumers are facing?

© Royalty-Free/Corbis

Computers and handheld devices have made online banking extremely convenient. However, hackers have stolen millions from banking customers by tricking them into visiting websites and downloading malicious software that gives the hackers access to their passwords.

deposits, and allows balance inquiries and cash transfers from one account to another. ABMs provide 24-hour banking services—both at home (through a local bank) and far away (via worldwide ABM networks such as Cirrus and Plus). Rapid growth, driven by both strong consumer acceptance and lower transaction costs for banks (about half the cost of teller transactions), has led to the installation of hundreds of thousands of ABMs worldwide. Table 15.4 presents some interesting statistics about banks and technology.

Online Banking. Many banking activities may now be carried out on a computer at home or at work, or through wireless devices such as cellphones and PDAs anywhere there is a wireless "hot point." Consumers and small businesses can now make a bewildering array of financial transactions at home or on the go 24 hours a day. Functioning much like a vast network of personal ABMs, banks allow their customers to make sophisticated banking transactions, buy and sell stocks and bonds, and purchase products and airline tickets without ever leaving home or speaking to another human being. Many banks allow customers to log directly into their accounts to check balances, transfer money between accounts, view their account statements, and pay bills via home computer or other Internet-enabled devices. Computers and advanced telecommunications technology have revolutionized world commerce.

Future of Banking

LO6 Investigate the challenges ahead for the banking industry.

Rapid advances and innovations in technology are challenging the banking industry and requiring it to change. As we said earlier, more and more banks, both large and small, are offering electronic access to their financial services. ABM technology is rapidly changing, with machines now dispensing more than just cash. Online financial services, ABM technology, and bill presentation are just a few of the areas where rapidly changing technology is causing the banking industry to change as well.

The premise that banks will get bigger over the next ten years is uncertain. During 2007 and 2008, the financial markets collapsed under the weight of declining housing prices, subprime mortgages (mortgages with low-quality borrowers), and risky securities backed by these subprime mortgages. Because the value of bank assets declined dramatically, most large banks had a shrinking capital base; that is, the amount of debt in relation to their equity was so high that they were below the minimum required capital requirements. This was a financial environment where banks did not trust the counterparties to their loans and asset-backed securities. In this environment, the markets ceased to function in an orderly fashion. To keep the banking system from total collapse, central banks around the world created different programs, like the Troubled Asset Relief Program in the United States.

There have been very few bank failures in Canada, which is widely acknowledged as having one of the safest and soundest financial sectors in the world.[22] In response to technological innovation and globalization, the financial services sector has undergone rapid change. The sector is increasingly competitive as changes to federal laws and regulations have resulted in the entry of new domestic and foreign competitors in the Canadian market. The hunt will continue for other merger partners that will globally expand institutions' customer reach and the services they are able to offer.

Indeed, the recent trend toward ever bigger banks and other financial institutions is not happening by chance alone. Financial services may be an example of a "natural

Table 15.4 Bank Fact Sheet

Number of bank-owned ABMs in Canada	18,775
Number of online banking transactions completed with the six largest banks in Canada (2014)	698.2 million
Number of transactions logged at bank-owned ABMs in Canada (2014)	777 million
Amount six largest Canadian banks spent on technology in 2014	$9 billion
Amount six largest Canadian banks have spent on technology from 2005 to 2014	$64.9 billion

Source: Based on "Fast Facts About the Canadian Banking System," Canadian Bankers Association, March 14, 2016.

oligopoly," meaning that the industry may be best served by a few very large firms rather than a host of smaller ones. As the largest banks merge into even larger international entities, they will erase the relative competitive advantages now enjoyed by the largest banks. It is by no means implausible that the financial services industry in 2020 will be dominated by ten or so internationally oriented "megabanks."

TEAM EXERCISE

Mutual funds pool individual investor dollars and invest them in a number of different securities. Go to http://finance. yahoo.com/ and select some top-performing funds using criteria such as sector, style, or strategy. Assume that your group has $100,000 to invest in mutual funds. Select five funds in which to invest, representing a balanced (varied industries, risk, etc.) portfolio, and defend your selections.

LEARNING OBJECTIVES SUMMARY

LO1 Define money, its functions, and its characteristics.

Money is anything generally accepted as a means of payment for goods and services. Money serves as a medium of exchange, a measure of value, and a store of wealth. To serve effectively in these functions, money must be acceptable, divisible, portable, durable, stable in value, and difficult to counterfeit.

LO2 Describe various types of money.

Money may take the form of currency, chequing accounts, or other accounts. Chequing accounts are funds left in an account in a financial institution that can be withdrawn (usually by writing a cheque) without advance notice. Other types of accounts include savings accounts (funds left in an interest-earning account that usually cannot be withdrawn without advance notice), money market accounts (an interest-bearing chequing account that is invested in short-term debt instruments), certificates of deposit (deposits left in an institution for a specified period of time at a specified interest rate), credit cards (access to a preapproved line of credit granted by a bank or company), and debit cards (means of instant cash transfers between customer and merchant accounts), as well as traveller's cheques, money orders, and cashier's cheques.

LO3 Specify how the Bank of Canada manages the money supply and regulates the Canadian banking system.

The Bank of Canada regulates the Canadian financial system. The Bank manages the money supply indirectly through its influence on the target overnight rate. Increases in interest rates reduce the demand for loans and lead to debtors paying down existing debt. This results in slower growth or even a reduction in money supply. The Bank's other activities include the issuance of Canadian bank notes, provision of banking services for the federal government, and promotion of a safe financial system. Other central bank tools for the conduct of monetary policy are buying and selling government securities, raising or lowering the bank rate (the rate of interest at which banks may borrow cash reserves from the central bank), raising or lowering bank reserve requirements (the percentage of funds on deposit at a bank that must be held to cover expected depositor withdrawals), and adjusting down payment and repayment terms for credit purchases.

LO4 Compare and contrast chartered banks, trust companies, and credit unions/caisses populaires.

Chartered banks are federally regulated under the Bank Act. They take and hold deposits in accounts and make loans to individuals and businesses. Trust companies may be incorporated federally or provincially. Trust companies accept and hold deposits in accounts and make loans to individuals but are restricted in commercial lending. Only trust companies can offer trustee services. Credit unions/*caisses populaires* are provincially regulated co-operatives. Both offer deposit accounts and loan services to their members.

LO5 Distinguish among non-banking institutions such as insurance companies, pension funds, mutual funds, and finance companies.

Insurance companies are businesses that protect their clients against financial losses due to certain circumstances, in exchange for a fee. Pension funds are investments set aside by organizations or individuals to meet retirement needs. Mutual funds pool investors' money and invest in large numbers of different types of securities. Brokerage firms buy and sell stocks and bonds for investors. Finance companies make short-term loans at higher interest rates than do banks.

LO6 Investigate the challenges ahead for the banking industry.

Future changes in financial regulations are likely to result in fewer but larger banks and other financial institutions.

KEY TERMS

automated banking machine (ABM)
Bank of Canada
bank rate
brokerage firms
Canada Deposit Insurance Corporation (CDIC)
certificates of deposit (CDs)
chartered banks
chequing account
credit cards
credit controls
credit union/*caisse populaire*
debit card
desired reserves

electronic funds transfer (EFT)
finance
finance companies
insurance companies
monetary policy
money
money market accounts
mutual fund
open market operations
pension funds
savings accounts
trust companies

DESTINATION CEO DISCUSSION QUESTIONS

1. Discuss what prepared Mr. Poloz for his current position as Governor of the Bank of Canada.

2. Who was Mark Carney and what position is he in now?

3. How has his education helped Mr. Poloz?

SO YOU'RE INTERESTED IN *Financial Systems or Banking*

You think you might be interested in going into finance or banking, but it is so hard to tell when you are a full-time student. Classes that seem interesting when you take them might not translate into an interesting work experience after you graduate. A great way to see if you would excel at a career in finance is to get some experience in the industry. Internships, whether paid or unpaid, not only help you figure out what you might really want to do after you graduate but they are also a great way to build up your résumé, put your learning to use, and start generating connections within the field.

Internship opportunities are available, although you may need to do some research to find them. To start, talk to your program advisor and your professors about opportunities. Also, you can check company websites where you think you might like to work to see if they have any opportunities available. Municipal, provincial, or federal government offices often provide student internships as well. No matter where you end up interning, the real-life skills you pick up, as well as the résumé boost you get, will be helpful in finding a job after you graduate. When you graduate, chartered banks and other financial institutions offer major employment opportunities.

BUILD YOUR BUSINESS PLAN

Money and the Financial System

This chapter provides you with the opportunity to think about money and the financial system and just how many new businesses fail every year. In some industries, the failure rate is as high as 80 percent. One reason for such a high failure rate is the inability to manage the finances of the organization. From the start of the business, financial planning plays a key role. Try getting a loan without an accompanying budget/forecast of earnings and cash flow.

While obtaining a loan from a family member may be the easiest way to fund your business, it may cause more problems for you later on if you are unable to pay the money back as scheduled. Before heading to a lending officer at a bank, contact your local Small Business Enterprise Centre (SBEC) to see what assistance they might provide.

Is it time to ditch the bank for the credit union? Credit unions have several advantages over banks. Because they are non-profit institutions, and therefore do not have to pay shares or executive salaries, the money that credit unions earn goes back to members in the form of dividends. The lack of pressure to make a profit also allows credit unions to offer more attractive rates on items like GICs, mortgages, credit cards, and car loans.

Some consumers also feel that credit unions offer more quality services, such as taking the time to help customers set up financial plans. Additionally, most credit unions offer free chequing and lower penalty fees than banks. With 5.3 million members, credit unions are becoming a popular alternative to traditional banking. In Canada, one in three residents of British Columbia belong to a credit union; in Ontario, it is one in ten. According to a survey by the Canadian Federation of Independent Business (CFIB), credit unions ranked first when it comes to financing the business needs of small and medium-sized businesses.

Of course, credit unions have their downsides as well. Unlike banks, consumers must meet requirements to become members of credit unions, and in Canada, they must pay a small fee to join. Banks also offer more diverse products and services than many credit unions do. These downsides have led analysts to recommend that consumers carefully investigate financial institutions, be it bank or credit union, before investing. However, for those consumers who constantly get frustrated with their banks, credit unions might be the way to go.[23]

DISCUSSION QUESTIONS

1. What are the advantages of credit unions over banks?

2. What are the disadvantages of credit unions over banks?

3. Given a choice, would you rather deal with a bank or a credit union?

DESTINATION CEO

When **Prem Watsa**, chairman of the board of directors and CEO of Fairfax, arrived in Canada from India in 1972, he had $8 in his pocket and a $600 draft toward the first year's tuition for the MBA program at the University of Western Ontario. To pay his way he sold stationery and gifts door to door and peddled air conditioners in the summer. After graduating from Ivey, Watsa worked for Confederation Life, an insurance company. A decade after joining Confederation Life, Watsa and colleagues struck out to form the company that would eventually be called Fairfax. The name means "fair, friendly acquisitions," and through acquisitions he grew the company to assets of over $13 billion dollars and 9,000 employees.

Today, Fairfax owns insurance companies in Canada, the United States, Singapore, Hong Kong, Malaysia, Indonesia, and Brazil; a pet insurance company based in Toronto; and reinsurance companies in the United States, the United Kingdom, Poland, and Barbados. Much of Watsa's life has been influenced by his father, and the advice he passed to his son: "Work as hard as you can, as though everything depended on you. Pray as hard as you can, as though everything depended on God." Watsa also acknowledges that he has benefited from a good education.[1]

Introduction

While it's certainly true that money makes the world go 'round, financial management is the discipline that makes the world turn more smoothly. Indeed, without effective management of assets, liabilities, and owners' equity, all business organizations are doomed to fail—regardless of the quality and innovation of their products. Financial management is the field that addresses the issues of obtaining and managing the funds and resources necessary to run a business successfully. It is not limited to business organizations: All organizations, from the corner store to the local non-profit art museum, from giant corporations to county governments, must manage their resources effectively and efficiently if they are to achieve their objectives.

In this chapter, we look at both short- and long-term financial management. First, we discuss the management of short-term assets, which companies use to generate sales and conduct ordinary day-to-day business operations. Next, we turn our attention to the management of short-term liabilities, the sources of short-term funds used to finance the business. Then, we discuss the management of long-term assets such as plant and equipment, and the long-term liabilities such as stocks and bonds used to finance these important corporate assets. Finally, we look at the securities markets, where stocks and bonds are traded.

Managing Current Assets and Liabilities

LO1 Describe some common methods of managing current assets.

Managing short-term assets and liabilities involves managing the current assets and liabilities on the balance sheet (discussed in Chapter 14). Current assets are short-term resources such as cash, investments, accounts receivable, and inventory. Current liabilities are short-term debts such as accounts payable, accrued salaries, accrued taxes, and short-term bank loans. We use the terms *current* and *short-term* interchangeably because short-term assets and liabilities are usually replaced by new assets and liabilities within three or four months, and always within a year. Managing short-term assets and liabilities is sometimes called **working capital management** because short-term assets and liabilities continually flow through an organization and are thus said to be "working."

working capital management the managing of short-term assets and liabilities

Managing Current Assets

The chief goal of financial managers who focus on current assets and liabilities is to maximize the return to the business on cash, temporary investments of idle cash, accounts receivable, and inventory.

Managing Cash. A crucial element facing any financial manager is effectively managing the firm's cash flow. Remember that cash flow is the movement of money through an organization on a daily, weekly, monthly, or yearly basis. Ensuring that sufficient (but not excessive) funds are on hand to meet the company's obligations is one of the single most important facets of financial management.

Idle cash does not make money, and corporate chequing accounts typically do not earn interest. As a result, astute money managers try to keep just enough cash on hand, called **transaction balances**, to pay bills—such as employee wages, supplies, and utilities—as they fall due. To manage the firm's cash and ensure that enough cash flows through the organization quickly and efficiently, companies try to speed up cash collections from customers.

To facilitate collection, some companies have customers send their payments to a **lockbox**, which is simply an address for receiving payments, instead of directly to the company's main address. The manager of the lockbox, usually a commercial bank, collects payments directly from the lockbox several times a day and deposits them into the company's bank account. The bank can then start clearing the cheques and get the money into the company's chequing account much more quickly than if the payments had been submitted directly to the company. However, there is no free lunch: The costs associated with lockbox systems make them worthwhile only for those companies that receive thousands of cheques from customers each business day.

transaction balances cash kept on hand by a firm to pay normal daily expenses, such as employee wages and bills for supplies and utilities

lockbox an address, usually a commercial bank, at which a company receives payments in order to speed collections from customers

Large firms, such as HSBC Finance Corporation, frequently use electronic funds transfer to speed up collections. HSBC Finance Corporation's local offices deposit cheques received each business day into their local banks and, at the end of the day, HSBC Finance Corporation's corporate office initiates the transfer of all collected funds to its central bank for overnight investment. This technique is especially attractive for major international companies, which face slow and sometimes uncertain physical delivery of payments and/or less-than-efficient cheque-clearing procedures.

More and more companies are now using electronic funds transfer systems to pay and collect bills online. It is interesting that companies want to collect cash quickly but pay out cash slowly. When companies use electronic funds transfers between buyers and suppliers, the speed of collections and disbursements increases to one day. Only with the use of cheques can companies delay the payment of cash quickly and have a three- or four-day waiting period until the cheque is presented to their bank and the cash leaves their account.

Investing Idle Cash. As companies sell products, they generate cash on a daily basis, and sometimes cash comes in faster than it is needed to pay bills. Organizations often invest this "extra" cash, for periods as short as one day (overnight) or for as long as one year, until it is needed. Such temporary investments of cash are known as **marketable securities**. Examples include Treasury bills, Banker's Acceptances, commercial paper (corporate paper), and eurodollar loans. Table 16.1 summarizes a number of different marketable securities used by businesses and some sample interest rates on these investments. The safety rankings are relative. While all of the listed securities are very low risk, the Bank of Canada securities are the safest.

marketable securities temporary investment of "extra" cash by organizations for up to one year in Treasury bills, certificates of deposit, commercial paper, or eurodollar loans

Treasury bills (T-bills) short-term debt obligations the Canadian government sells to raise money

Many large companies invest idle cash in Government of Canada **Treasury bills (T-bills)**, which are short-term

Established green retailers such as Seventh Generation, Loblaw's PC GREEN, and Method, have driven market growth with new products, increased support, and expansion of distribution into more retail outlets. Method is a green company in more ways than one. Not only does it sell eco-friendly household supplies, but it also generates more than $100 million in annual revenues. Thanks to companies like Method, finance executives are beginning to realize the financial benefits of going green. At a time when the prices of commodities are rapidly fluctuating, finance executives are looking for ways to cut costs. Eco-friendly options such as decreasing energy use, using recycled materials, and reducing packaging are becoming viable methods for saving money and improving efficiency. A recent poll found that 40 percent of finance executives are increasing their facilities' efficiency through better energy management, while one-third are undertaking initiatives to increase the efficiency of their shipping, including the adoption of more fuel-efficient vehicles. Method, for instance, has significantly increased its use of biodiesel trucks, which are 13 percent more fuel efficient than traditional trucks.

Method aligns its environmental objectives with its cost-saving goals. The operations and finance departments routinely work together to look at what ingredients and processes would save money while also reducing Method's environmental impact. Sometimes, this requires the company to adopt additional costs in the short run in order to save money in the long term. Method's long-term perspective, efficient operations, and popularity with customers are catching on with competitors. It is estimated that eco-friendly household supplies make up 30 percent of household cleaning products. As green products and operational processes increase, Method already has a head start.[2]

DISCUSSION QUESTIONS

1. If greener operations cut company costs, how will this affect current assets and liabilities?

2. Why might Method decide to pursue greener business activities that are costly in the short run?

3. Do you think other household supply companies are beginning to realize how green products can improve their financial conditions?

Table 16.1 Short-Term Investment Possibilities for Idle Cash

Type of Security	Maturity	Issuer of Security	Interest Rate (on Jan. 13, 2016)	Safety Level
Treasury Bills	1 month	Bank of Canada	0.41	Excellent
Treasury Bills	3 months	Bank of Canada	0.40	Excellent
Commercial Paper	3 months	Corporations	0.84	Very Good
Certificates of Deposit	12 months	Chartered Banks	0.85	Very Good
Eurodollars	3 months	European Commercial Banks	0.70	Very Good

Sources: Adapted from "Interest Rates," Bank of Canada, http://www.bankofcanada.ca/rates/interest-rates; and "Selected Interest Rates," *Federal Reserve Statistical Release*, http://www.federalreserve.gov/releases/h15/update (both accessed January 18, 2016).

commercial certificates of deposit (CDs) certificates of deposit issued by commercial banks and brokerage companies, available in minimum amounts of $100,000, which may be traded prior to maturity

debt obligations the federal government sells to raise money. Auctioned biweekly by the Bank of Canada, T-bills carry maturities of one week to one year. T-bills are generally considered to be the safest of all investments and are called risk-free because the federal government will not default on its debt.

Commercial certificates of deposit (CDs) are issued by commercial banks and brokerage companies. They are available in minimum amounts of $100,000 but are typically in units of $1 million for large corporations investing excess cash. Unlike consumer CDs (discussed in Chapter 15), which must be held until maturity, commercial CDs may be traded prior to maturity. Should a cash shortage occur, the organization can simply sell the CD on the open market and obtain needed funds.

One of the most popular short-term investments for the largest business organizations is **commercial paper**—a written promise from one company to another to pay a specific amount of money. Because commercial paper is backed only by the name and reputation of the issuing company, sales of commercial

commercial paper a written promise from one company to another to pay a specific amount of money

paper are restricted to only the largest and most financially stable companies. As commercial paper is frequently bought and sold for durations of as short as one business day, many "players" in the market find themselves buying commercial paper with excess cash on one day and selling it to gain extra money the following day.

Some companies invest idle cash in international markets such as the **eurodollar market**, a market for trading U.S. dollars in foreign countries. Because the eurodollar market was originally developed by London banks, any dollar-denominated deposit in a non-U.S. bank is called a eurodollar deposit, regardless of whether the issuing bank is actually located in Europe, South America, or anyplace else. For example, if you travel overseas and deposit $1,000 in a German bank, you will have "created" a eurodollar deposit in the amount of $1,000. Since the U.S. dollar is accepted by most countries for international trade, these dollar deposits can be used by international companies to settle their accounts. The market created for trading such investments offers firms with extra dollars a chance to earn a slightly higher rate of return with just a little more risk than they would face by investing in Treasury bills.

eurodollar market a market for trading U.S. dollars in foreign countries

Maximizing Accounts Receivable. After cash and marketable securities, the balance sheet lists accounts receivable and inventory. Remember that accounts receivable are money owed to a business by credit customers. For example, if you charge your Shell gasoline purchases until you actually pay for them with cash or a cheque, they represent an account receivable to Shell. Many businesses make the vast majority of their sales on credit, so managing accounts receivable is an important task.

Each credit sale represents an account receivable for the company, the terms of which typically require customers to pay the full amount due within 30, 60, or even 90 days from the date of the sale. To encourage quick payment, some businesses offer some of their customers discounts of 1 to 2 percent if they pay off their balance within a specified period of time (usually between 10 and 30 days). On the other hand, late payment charges of between 1 and 1.5 percent serve to discourage slow payers from sitting on their bills forever. The larger the early payment discount offered, the faster customers will tend to pay their accounts. Unfortunately, while discounts increase cash flow, they also reduce profitability. Finding the right balance between the added advantages of early cash receipt and the disadvantages of reduced profits is no simple matter. Similarly, determining the optimal balance between the higher sales likely to result from extending credit to customers with less than sterling credit ratings and the higher bad-debt

© amana productions/Getty Images

The Canadian Bankers Association developed the YourMoney seminars as part of its commitment to improving financial literacy among Canadians.

losses likely to result from a more lenient credit policy is also challenging. Information on company credit ratings is provided by local credit bureaus, national credit-rating agencies such as Dun and Bradstreet, and industry trade groups.

Optimizing Inventory. While the inventory that a firm holds is controlled by both production needs and marketing considerations, the financial manager has to coordinate inventory purchases to manage cash flows. The object is to minimize the firm's investment in inventory without experiencing production cutbacks as a result of critical materials shortfalls or lost sales due to insufficient finished goods inventories. Every dollar invested in inventory is a dollar unavailable for investment in some other area of the organization. Optimal inventory levels are determined, in large part, by the method of production. If a firm attempts to produce its goods just in time to meet sales demand, the level of inventory will be relatively low. If, on the other hand, the firm produces materials in a constant, level pattern, inventory increases when sales decrease and decreases when sales increase. One way that companies are attempting to optimize inventory is through the use of radio frequency identification (RFID) technology. Companies such as Walmart are attempting to better manage their inventories by using RFID tags. An RFID tag, which contains a silicon chip and an antenna, allows a company to use radio waves to track and identify the products to which the tags are attached. These tags are primarily used to track inventory shipments from the manufacturer to the buyer's warehouses and then to the individual stores.

The automobile industry is an excellent example of an industry driven almost solely by inventory levels. Because it is inefficient to continually lay off workers in slow times and call them back in better times, Ford, General Motors, and Chrysler try to set and stick to quarterly production quotas. Automakers typically try to keep a 60-day supply of unsold cars. During particularly slow periods, however, it is not unusual for inventories to exceed 100 days of sales.

Although less publicized, inventory shortages can be as much of a drag on potential profits as too much inventory. Not having an item on hand may send the customer to a competitor—forever. Complex computer inventory models are frequently employed to determine the optimum level of inventory a firm should hold to support a given level of sales. Such models can indicate how and when parts inventories should be ordered so that they are available exactly when required—and not a day before. Developing and maintaining such an intricate production and inventory system is difficult, but it can often prove to be the difference between experiencing average profits and achieving spectacular ones.

Managing Current Liabilities

LO2 Identify some sources of short-term financing (current liabilities).

While having extra cash on hand is a delightful surprise, the opposite situation—a temporary cash shortfall—can be a crisis. The good news is that there are several potential sources of short-term funds. Suppliers often serve as an important source through credit sales practices. Also, banks, finance companies, and other organizations offer short-term funds through loans and other business operations.

Accounts Payable. Remember from Chapter 14 that accounts payable consist of money an organization owes to suppliers for goods and services. Just as accounts receivable must be actively managed to ensure proper cash collections, so too must accounts payable be managed to make the best use of this important liability.

The most widely used source of short-term financing, and therefore the most important account payable, is **trade credit**—credit extended by suppliers for the purchase of their goods and services. While varying in formality, depending on both the organizations involved and the value of the items purchased, most trade credit agreements offer discounts to organizations that pay their bills early. A supplier, for example, may offer trade terms of "1/10 net 30," meaning that the purchasing organization may take a 1 percent discount from the invoice amount if it makes payment by the 10th day after receiving the bill. Otherwise, the entire amount

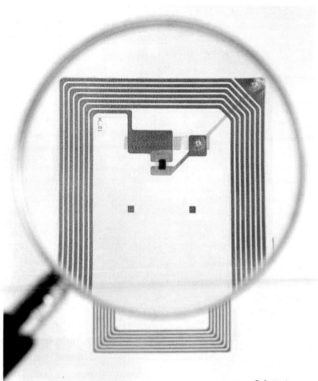

© Getty Images

Companies such as Walmart are attempting to better manage their inventories by using radio-frequency-identification (RFID) tags. An RFID tag, which contains a silicon chip and an antenna, allows a company to use radio waves to track and identify the products to which the tags are attached—even after the products have left the store.

is due within 30 days. For example, pretend that you are the financial manager in charge of payables. You owe Ajax Company $10,000, and it offers trade terms of 2/10 net 30. By paying the amount due within 10 days, you can save 2 percent of $10,000, or $200. Assume you place orders with Ajax once per month and have 12 bills of $10,000 each per year. By taking the discount every time, you will save 12 times $200, or $2,400, per year. Now assume you are the financial manager of Gigantic Corp., and it has monthly payables of $100 million per month. Two percent of $100 million is $2 million per month. Failure to take advantage of such trade discounts can, in many cases, add up to large opportunity losses over the span of a year.

Bank Loans. Virtually all organizations—large and small—obtain short-term funds for operations from banks. In most instances, the credit services granted these firms take the form of a line of credit or fixed dollar loan. A **line of credit** is an arrangement by which a bank agrees to lend a specified amount of money to the organization upon

trade credit credit extended by suppliers for the purchase of their goods and services

line of credit an arrangement by which a bank agrees to lend a specified amount of money to an organization upon request

Although thousands of companies failed during the most recent recession, Y Combinator and the companies it assists were among those thriving. Founder Paul Graham (famous in tech circles for creating Viaweb—sold to Yahoo! for $49 million) launched Y Combinator in 2005. His method is somewhat like a school for start-ups, and his funding somewhat like financial aid. Graham gathers entrepreneurs for three-month periods, during which time he provides them with small loans (typically under $20,000) to meet basic needs, allowing them to focus on developing their fledgling companies. In exchange, Y Combinator receives a 2 to 10 percent company stake.

Graham offers something more valuable than a simple loan—an experienced eye, solid advice, and a positive and creative environment. Y Combinator focuses on tech start-ups, with an emphasis on Web-based applications. Graham's experience allows him to help direct, or redirect, founders toward workable concepts attractive to larger investors. His business motto is "Make something people want." Graham also addresses running businesses, handling investors, and dealing with acquisitions. Y Combinator was rated number 11 in *Businessweek*'s list of top angel investors.

Small businesses like those funded by Y Combinator are making some *Fortune* 500 companies nervous.

For example, eBay, for all of its success, does not often update its auction system. This leaves room for a small start-up to gain market share if it can provide a superior service. These small companies are often less expensive and more flexible, making them better equipped to do well in a recession. Although Graham takes a risk with each start-up, graduates such as Scribd (which partnered with literary giants and received over $12 million in venture capital funding) and Omnisio (purchased by Google for more than $15 million) make it worthwhile. Some of the companies flourish—and when they do, Graham makes a substantial profit.[3]

DISCUSSION QUESTIONS

1. Why has Y Combinator succeeded while many other firms in the financial industry have failed?

2. What are the risks involved in creating a business like Y Combinator?

3. What are the rewards for Graham in taking a risk in small tech start-ups?

---

request—provided that the bank has the required funds to make the loan. In general, a business line of credit is very similar to a consumer credit card, with the exception that the preset credit limit can amount to millions of dollars.

In addition to credit lines, banks also make **secured loans**—loans backed by collateral that the bank can claim if the borrowers do not repay the loans—and **unsecured loans**—loans backed only by the borrowers' good reputation and previous credit rating. Both individuals and businesses build their credit rating from their history of borrowing and repaying borrowed funds on time and in full. The three national credit-rating services are Equifax, TransUnion, and Experian. A lack of credit history or a poor credit history can make it difficult to get loans from financial institutions. The *principal* is the amount of money borrowed; *interest* is a percentage of the principal that the bank charges for use of its money. As we mentioned in Chapter 15, banks also

secured loans loans backed by collateral that the bank can claim if the borrowers do not repay them

unsecured loans loans backed only by the borrowers' good reputation and previous credit rating

pay depositors interest on savings accounts and some chequing accounts. Thus, banks charge borrowers interest for loans and pay interest to depositors for the use of their money. In addition, these loans may include origination fees.

One of the complaints from borrowers during the financial crises was that banks weren't willing to lend. There were several causes. Banks were trying to rebuild their capital, and they didn't want to take the extra risk that lending offers in an economic recession. They were not sure how future loan losses would affect their capital. The banks' lack of lending caused problems for small businesses.

The **prime rate** is the interest rate commercial banks charge their best customers (usually large corporations) for short-term loans. While, for many years, loans at the prime rate represented funds at the lowest possible cost, the rapid development of the market for commercial paper has dramatically reduced the importance of commercial banks as a source of short-term loans. Today, most "prime" borrowers are actually small and medium-sized businesses.

prime rate the interest rate that commercial banks charge their best customers (usually large corporations) for short-term loans

© Comstock/Getty Images

Because both businesses and individuals want to keep their financing costs to a minimum, when interest rates drop, their investment in assets tends to increase.

The interest rates on commercial loans may be either fixed or variable. A variable, or floating-rate loan offers an advantage when interest rates are falling but represents a distinct disadvantage when interest rates are rising. Between 1999 and 2004, interest rates plummeted, and borrowers refinanced their loans with low-cost fixed-rate loans. Nowhere was this more visible than in the mortgage markets, where homeowners lined up to refinance their high-percentage home mortgages with lower-cost loans. Individuals and corporations have the same motivation: to minimize their borrowing costs.

Non-bank Liabilities. Banks are not the only source of short-term funds for businesses. Indeed, virtually all financial institutions, from insurance companies to pension funds, from money market funds to finance companies, make short-term loans to many organizations. The largest companies also actively engage in borrowing money from the eurodollar and commercial paper markets. As noted earlier, both of these funds' sources are typically slightly less expensive than bank loans.

In some instances, businesses actually sell their accounts receivable to a finance company known as a **factor**, which gives the selling organizations cash and assumes responsibility for collecting the accounts. For

factor a finance company to which businesses sell their accounts receivable—usually for a percentage of the total face value

example, a factor might pay $60,000 for receivables with a total face value of $100,000 (60 percent of the total). The factor profits if it can collect more than what it paid for the accounts. Because the selling organization's customers send their payments to a lockbox, they may have no idea that a factor has bought their receivables.

Additional non-bank liabilities that must be efficiently managed to ensure maximum profitability are taxes owed to the government and wages owed to employees. Clearly, businesses are responsible for many different types of taxes and similar payments, including federal, provincial, and municipal income taxes; property taxes; mineral rights taxes; unemployment insurance; CPP contributions; workers' compensation taxes; excise taxes; and even more! While the public tends to think that the only relevant taxes are on income and sales, many industries must pay other taxes that far exceed those levied against their income. Taxes and employees' wages represent debt obligations of the firm, which the financial manager must plan to meet as they fall due.

Managing Fixed Assets

LO3 Summarize the importance of long-term assets and capital budgeting.

Up to this point, we have focused on the short-term aspects of financial management. While most business failures are the result of poor short-term planning, successful ventures must also consider the long-term financial consequences of their actions. Managing the long-term assets and liabilities and the owners' equity portion of the balance sheet is important for the long-term health of the business.

Long-term (fixed) assets are expected to last for many years—production facilities (plants), offices, equipment, heavy machinery, furniture, automobiles, and so on. In today's

long-term (fixed) assets production facilities (plants), offices, and equipment—all of which are expected to last for many years

fast-paced world, companies need the most technologically advanced, modern facilities and equipment they can afford. Automobile, oil refining, and transportation companies are dependent on fixed assets.

Modern and high-tech equipment carries high price tags, and the financial arrangements required to support these investments are by no means trivial. Leasing is just one approach to financing. Obtaining major long-term financing can be challenging for even the most profitable organizations. For less successful firms, such challenges can prove nearly impossible. One approach is leasing assets such as equipment, machines, and buildings. In the case of leasing or not taking ownership but paying a fee for usage, potential long-term assets can be taken off the balance sheet as a debt. Still, the company has the asset and an obligation to pay money that is a contractual obligation. We'll take a closer look at long-term financing in a moment, but first let's address some issues associated with fixed assets, including capital budgeting, risk assessment, and the costs of financing fixed assets.

Capital Budgeting and Project Selection

One of the most important jobs performed by the financial manager is to decide what fixed assets, projects, and investments will earn profits for the firm beyond the costs necessary to fund them. The process of analyzing the needs of the business and selecting the assets that will maximize its value is called **capital budgeting**, and the capital budget is the amount of money budgeted for investment in such long-term assets. But capital budgeting does not end with the selection and purchase of a particular piece of land, equipment, or major investment. All assets and projects must be continually re-evaluated to ensure their compatibility with the organization's needs. If a particular asset does not live up to expectations, then management must determine why and take necessary corrective action. Budgeting is not an exact process, and managers must be flexible when new information is available.

> **capital budgeting** the process of analyzing the needs of the business and selecting the assets that will maximize its value

"All assets and projects must be continually re-evaluated to ensure their compatibility with the organization's needs."

Assessing Risk

Every investment carries some risk. Figure 16.1 ranks potential investment projects according to estimated risk. When considering investments overseas, risk assessments must include the political climate and economic stability of a region. The decision to introduce a product or build a manufacturing facility in England would be much less risky than a decision to build one in the Middle East, for example.

The longer a project or asset is expected to last, the greater its potential risk because it is hard to predict whether a piece of equipment will wear out or become obsolete in five or ten years. Predicting cash flows one year down the road is difficult, but projecting them over the span of a ten-year project is a gamble.

The level of a project's risk is also affected by the stability and competitive nature of the marketplace and the world economy as a whole. IBM's latest high-technology computer product is far more likely to become obsolete overnight than is a similar $10 million investment in a

Figure 16.1 Qualitative Assessment of Capital Budgeting Risk

© RosalreneBetancourt 5/Alamy Stock Photo

Although pharmaceutical manufacturers may want to undertake many projects, the costs involved require them to use capital budgeting to determine which projects will lead to the greatest profits. Allergan used capital budgeting to determine the potential profitability of its eye medication, Restasis.

manufacturing plant. Dramatic changes in the marketplace are not uncommon. Indeed, uncertainty created by the rapid devaluation of Asian currencies in the late 1990s wrecked a host of assumptions in literally hundreds of projects worldwide. Financial managers must constantly consider such issues when making long-term decisions about the purchase of fixed assets.

Pricing Long-Term Money

The ultimate profitability of any project depends not only on accurate assumptions of how much cash it will generate but also on its financing costs. Because a business must pay interest on money it borrows, the returns from any project must cover not only the costs of operating the project but also the interest expenses for the debt used to finance its construction. Unless an organization can effectively cover all of its costs—both financial and operating—it will eventually fail.

Clearly, only a limited supply of funds is available for investment in any given enterprise. The most efficient and profitable companies can attract the lowest-cost funds because they typically offer reasonable financial returns at very low relative risks. Newer and less prosperous firms must pay higher costs to attract capital because these companies tend to be quite risky. One of the strongest motivations for companies to manage their financial resources wisely is that they will, over time, be able to reduce the costs of their funds and in so doing increase their overall profitability.

In our free-enterprise economy, new firms tend to enter industries that offer the greatest potential rewards for success. However, as more and more companies enter an industry, competition intensifies, eventually driving profits down to average levels. The digital music player market of the early 2000s provides an excellent example of the changes in profitability that typically accompany increasing competition. The sign of a successful capital budgeting program is that the new products create higher than normal profits and drive sales and the stock price up. This has certainly been true for Apple when it made the decision to enter the electronics industry. In 2001, Apple introduced the first iPod. Since then, the iPod has undergone many enhancements in size, style, and different versions such as the small Nano. Sales of iPods have declined over time as iPhones took their place as music players. It was the iPod that made the iTunes Store possible, which has continued to grow at rates of 38 percent from 2011 to 2012 and 25 percent from 2012 to 2013. It now accounts for $16 billion in revenues. The iPhone, introduced in 2007, has now gone through many annual updates with the latest being the iPhone 7. During 2013, the iPhone sold 150 million units accounting for $91 billion in sales, up 100 percent since 2011. Finally, the iPad tablet was introduced in 2010 and is now the second biggest product after the iPhone, selling 71 million units and generating almost $32 billion in sales. Interestingly, Apple did not appear to be negatively affected by the recession. In fact, its sales grew from $42.9 billion in 2009 to $170.9 billion in 2013. It is on track to keep up its growth as it expands into China, India, and other emerging markets. An interesting development was that the ease of synchronization with all Apple computers caused an increase in the sale of iMacs and MacBooks.

Even with a well-planned capital budgeting program, it may be difficult for Apple to stay ahead of the competition because the Google Android platform is being used by Apple's competitors. This intense competition may make it difficult to continue market dominance for any extended period. However, Apple is now the most valuable company in the world, valued at $568 billion on June 10, 2014. On June 9, 2014, Apple split its stock seven for one, meaning that for every share you owned, you would get six more for a total of seven shares. There is no real gain involved because the stock price is divided by 7, so stockholders still have the same value, just more shares at a lower price. An investor who bought $1,000 of Apple stock in 2003 for $0.91 would have had Apple stock worth $103,700 on June 10, 2014. The problem is having the patience to continue to hold such a winner without taking some profits along the way.[4]

Maintaining market dominance is also difficult in the personal computer industry, particularly because tablet computers are taking away market share. With increasing

© The McGraw-Hill Companies, Inc./Jill Braaten, photographer

Apple stock trades at approximately 100 times what it did nearly ten years ago.

competition, prices have fallen dramatically since the 1990s. Even Dell, with its low-cost products, has moved into other markets such as servers in order to maintain growth in a maturing market. Weaker companies have failed, leaving the most efficient producers/marketers scrambling for market share. The expanded market for personal computers dramatically reduced the financial returns generated by each dollar invested in productive assets. The "glory days" of the personal computer industry—the time in which fortunes could be won and lost in the space of an average-sized garage—have long since passed into history. Personal computers have essentially become commodity items, and profit margins for companies in this industry have shrunk as the market matures.

Financing with Long-Term Liabilities

LO4 Specify how companies finance their operations and manage fixed assets with long-term liabilities, particularly bonds.

As we said earlier, long-term assets do not come cheap, and few companies have the cash on hand to open a new store across town, build a new manufacturing facility, research and develop a new life-saving drug, or launch a new product worldwide. To develop such fixed assets, companies need to raise low-cost, long-term funds to finance them. Two common choices for raising these funds are attracting new owners (*equity financing*), which we'll look at in a moment, and taking on long-term liabilities (*debt financing*), which we'll look at now.

long-term liabilities debts that will be repaid over a number of years, such as long-term loans and bond issues

Long-term liabilities are debts that will be repaid over a number of years, such as long-term bank loans and bond issues. These take many different forms, but in the end, the key word is *debt*.

Companies may raise money by borrowing it from commercial banks or other financial institutions in the form of lines of credit, short-term loans, or long-term loans. Many corporations acquire debt by borrowing money from pension funds, mutual funds, or life-insurance funds.

Companies that rely too heavily on debt can get into serious trouble should the economy falter; during these times, they may not earn enough operating income to make the required interest payments (remember the times interest earned ratio in Chapter 14). In severe cases, when the problem persists too long, creditors will not restructure loans but will instead sue for the interest and principal owed and force the company into bankruptcy.

Bonds: Corporate IOUs

Aside from loans, much long-term debt takes the form of **bonds**, which are debt instruments that larger companies sell to raise long-term funds. In essence, the buyers of bonds (bondholders) loan the issuer of the bonds cash in exchange for regular interest payments until the loan is repaid on or before the specified maturity date. The bond itself is a certificate, much like an IOU, that represents the company's debt to the bondholder. Bonds are issued by a wide variety of entities, including corporations; federal, provincial, and local governments; public utilities; and non-profit corporations. Most bondholders need not hold their bonds until maturity; rather, the existence of active secondary markets of brokers and dealers allows for the quick and efficient transfer of bonds from owner to owner.

bonds debt instruments that larger companies sell to raise long-term funds

The bond contract, or *indenture*, specifies all of the terms of the agreement between the bondholders and the issuing organization. The indenture, which can run more than 100 pages, specifies the basic terms of the bond, such as its face value, maturity date, and annual interest rate. Table 16.2 briefly explains how to determine these and more things about a bond from a bond quote, as it might appear in the *National Post*. The face value of the bond, its initial sales price, is typically $1,000. After this, however, the price of the bond on the open market will fluctuate along with changes in

Table 16.2 A Basic Bond Quote

Issuer (1)	Coupon (2)	Maturity Date (3)	Bid $ (4)	Yield % (5)
Loblaw	5.220	June 18/2020	113.61	1.98

(1) Issuer—the name or abbreviation of the name of the company issuing the bond; in this case, Loblaw.

(2) Coupon—the annual percentage rate specified on the bond certificate: Loblaw's is 5.22 percent so a $1,000 bond will earn $52.20 per year in interest.

(3) Maturity Date—the bond's maturity date; the year in which the issuer will repay bondholders the face value of each bond; 2020.

(4) Bid $—the closing price; 113.61 percent of $1,000 per value or $1,136.10 per bond.

(5) Yield %—yield to maturity; the percentage return based on the closing price; if you buy a bond with a $1,000 par value at today's closing price of 113.61 ($1,136.10) and receive $52.20 per year to maturity, your return will be 1.98 percent.

Source: Data from *Financial Post*, "Canadian Bonds," January 19, 2016, http://www.financialpost.com/markets/market-data/bonds-canadian.html.

the economy (particularly, changes in interest rates) and in the creditworthiness of the issuer. Bondholders receive the face value of the bond along with the final interest payment on the maturity date. The annual interest rate (often called the *coupon rate*) is the guaranteed percentage of face value that the company will pay to the bond owner every year. For example, a $1,000 bond with a coupon rate of 7 percent would pay $70 per year in interest. In most cases, bond indentures specify that interest payments be made every six months. In the preceding example, the $70 annual payment would be divided into two semiannual payments of $35.

In addition to the terms of interest payments and maturity date, the bond indenture typically covers other important areas, such as repayment methods, interest payment dates, procedures to be followed in case the organization fails to make the interest payments, conditions for the early repayment of the bonds, and any conditions requiring the pledging of assets as collateral.

Types of Bonds

Not surprisingly, there are a great many different types of bonds. Most are **unsecured bonds**, meaning that they are not backed by specific collateral; such bonds are termed *debentures*. **Secured bonds**, on the other hand, are backed by specific collateral that must be forfeited in the event that the issuing firm defaults. Whether secured or unsecured, bonds may be repaid in one lump sum or with many payments spread out over a period of time. **Serial bonds**, which are different from secured bonds, are actually a sequence of

A McGraw-Hill stock certificate.

unsecured bonds debentures, or bonds that are not backed by specific collateral

secured bonds bonds that are backed by specific collateral that must be forfeited in the event that the issuing firm defaults

serial bonds a sequence of small bond issues of progressively longer maturity

small bond issues of progressively longer maturity. The firm pays off each of the serial bonds as they mature. **Floating-rate bonds** do not have fixed interest payments; instead, the interest rate changes with current interest rates otherwise available in the economy.

In recent years, a special type of high-interest-rate bond has attracted considerable attention (usually negative) in the financial press. High-interest bonds, or **junk bonds** as they are popularly known, offer relatively high rates of interest because they have higher inherent risks. Historically, junk bonds have been associated with companies in poor financial health and/or start-up firms with limited track records. In the mid-1980s, however, junk bonds became a very attractive method of financing corporate mergers; they remain popular today with many

floating-rate bonds bonds with interest rates that change with current interest rates otherwise available in the economy

junk bonds a special type of high interest-rate bond that carries higher inherent risks

ENTREPRENEURSHIP IN ACTION | Studios Take Notice of Relativity Media

Ryan Kavanaugh

Business: Relativity Media

Founded: 2004, in California

Success: With its involvement in more than 200 films, Relativity Media LLC counts Universal and Sony among its clients.

Entrepreneur Ryan Kavanaugh has met many famous Hollywood celebrities since he started the studio Relativity Media, including director James Cameron and actor Christian Bale. Relativity Media is perhaps best known for its rise as the producer and/or financial backer of several hit movies such as *Salt*, *Despicable Me*,

and *Atonement*. The company has provided studios with nearly $8 billion in private-equity funding and has been involved with more than 200 films. However, because backing films is risky business (many expensive films ended up being flops), Relativity Media constantly looks for ways to reduce risk. One way is by using statistical tools to estimate a film's potential profitability. Another is similar to what many investors do—invest in a pool of diversified funds, or in this case, films, to reduce risk. At the same time, Relativity is seizing new opportunities for profit. It has recently acquired a stake in a Chinese production company to take advantage of the burgeoning Chinese film industry.[5]

investors as a result of their very high relative interest rates. But higher risks are associated with those higher returns (upward of 12 percent per year in some cases) and the average investor would be well-advised to heed those famous words: Look before you leap!

Financing with Owners' Equity

LO5 Discuss how corporations can use equity financing by issuing stock through an investment banker.

A second means of long-term financing is through equity. Remember from Chapter 14 that owners' equity refers to the owners' investment in an organization. Sole proprietors and partners own all or a part of their businesses outright, and their equity includes the money and assets they have brought into their ventures. Corporate owners, on the other hand, own stock or shares of their companies, which they hope will provide them with a return on their investment. Shareholders' equity includes common stock, preferred stock, and retained earnings.

"A second means of long-term financing is through equity."

Common stock (introduced in Chapter 4) is the single most important source of capital for most new companies. On the balance sheet, the common stock account is separated into two basic parts—common stock at par and capital in excess of par. The *par value* of a stock is simply the dollar amount printed on the stock certificate and has no relation to actual *market value*—the price at which the common stock is currently trading. The difference between a stock's par value and its offering price

is called *capital in excess of par*. Except in the case of some very low-priced stocks, the capital in excess of par account is significantly larger than the par value account. Table 16.3 briefly explains how to gather important information from a stock quote, as it might appear in financial newspapers.

Preferred stock was defined in Chapter 14 as corporate ownership that gives the shareholder preference in the distribution of the company's profits but not the voting and control rights accorded to common shareholders. Thus, the primary advantage of owning preferred stock is that it is a safer investment than common stock.

retained earnings earnings after expenses and taxes that are reinvested in the assets of the firm and belong to the owners in the form of equity

All businesses exist to earn profits for their owners. Without the possibility of profit, there can be no incentive to risk investors' capital and succeed. When a corporation has profits left over after paying all of its expenses and taxes, it has the choice of retaining all or a portion of its earnings and/or paying them out to its shareholders in the form of dividends. **Retained earnings** are reinvested in the assets of the firm and belong to the owners in the form of equity. Retained earnings are an important source of funds and are, in fact, the only long-term funds that the company can generate internally.

When the board of directors distributes some of a corporation's profits to the owners, it issues them as cash dividend payments. But not all firms pay dividends.

Many fast-growing firms retain all of their earnings because they can earn high rates of return on the earnings they reinvest. Companies with fewer growth opportunities typically

> Need help understanding this concept? Check out an informational video! Log into Connect, go to Resources, and click on the Videos page.

Table 16.3 A Basic Stock Quote

Stock (1)	Ticker (2)	Close (3)	Net Chg (4)	Volume (5)	Day High/Low (6)	% Yld (7)	52-Week High/Low (8)
Loblaw Companies Ltd	L	63.43	+$0.13	367,040	64.00/63.28	1.53	74.45/58.85

(1) Stock—the name of the issuing company.

(2) Ticker—the ticker tape symbol for the stock; for **Loblaw Companies Ltd**, L.

(3) Close—the last sale of the day; for **Loblaw**, $63.43.

(4) Net Change—the difference between the previous day's close and the close on the day being reported; **Loblaw** was up 13 cents.

(5) Volume—the number of shares traded on this day; for **Loblaw**, 367,040.

(6) Day High/Low—the highest and lowest prices, respectively, paid for the stock during the day; for **Loblaw**, the highest was $64.00 and the lowest price, $63.28.

(7) Percent Yield—the dividend return on one share of common stock; 1.53%.

(8) 52-Week High/Low—the highest and lowest prices, respectively, paid for the stock in the last year; for **Loblaw's** stock, the highest was $74.75 and the lowest price, $58.85.

Source: Data from *National Post*, January 19, 2016, http://www.financialpost.com/markets/company/index.html?symbol=L&id=33668.

Table 16.4 Estimated Common Stock Price–Earnings Ratios and Dividends for Selected Companies

Ticker Symbol	Company Name	Price Per Share	Dividend Per Share	Dividend Yield	Earnings Per Share	P–E Ratio
L	Loblaw	63.43	1.00	1.53	1.86	34.10
QSR	Restaurant Brands	49.02	0.52	1.07	$-1.59	—

Source: Data from *National Post*, January 19, 2016, http://www.financialpost.com/markets/company/index.html?symbol=L&id=33668

pay out large proportions of their earnings in the form of dividends, thereby allowing their shareholders to reinvest their dividend payments in higher-growth companies. Table 16.4 presents a sample of companies and the dividend each paid on a single share of stock. As shown in the table, when the dividend is divided by the price, the result is the **dividend yield**. The dividend yield is the cash return as a percentage of the price but does not reflect the total return an investor earns on the individual stock. If the dividend yield is 1.3 percent on a company and the stock price increases by 10 percent, then the total return would be 11.3 percent. It is not clear that stocks with high dividend yields will be preferred by investors to those with little or no dividends. Most large companies pay their shareholders dividends on a quarterly basis.

dividend yield the dividend per share divided by the stock price

Investment Banking

A company that needs more money to expand or take advantage of opportunities may be able to obtain financing by issuing stock. The first-time sale of stocks and bonds directly to the public is called a *new issue*. Companies that already have stocks or bonds outstanding may offer a new issue of stock to raise additional funds for specific projects. When a company offers its stock to the public for the very first time, it is said to be "going public," and the sale is called an *initial public offering*.

primary market the market where firms raise financial capital

secondary markets stock exchanges and over-the-counter markets where investors can trade their securities with others

New issues of stocks and bonds are sold directly to the public and to institutions in what is known as the **primary market**—the market where firms raise financial capital. The primary market differs from **secondary markets**, which are stock exchanges and over-the-counter markets where investors

can trade their securities with other investors rather than the company that issued the stock or bonds. Primary market transactions actually raise cash for the issuing corporations, while secondary market transactions do not.

Investment banking, the sale of stocks and bonds for corporations, helps such companies raise funds by matching people and institutions who have money to invest with corporations in need of resources to exploit new opportunities. Corporations usually employ an investment banking firm to help sell their securities in the primary market. An investment banker helps firms establish appropriate offering prices for their securities. In addition, the investment banker takes care of the myriad details and securities regulations involved in any sale of securities to the public.

investment banking the sale of stocks and bonds for corporations

Just as large corporations such as BCE and Bombardier have a client relationship with a law firm and an accounting firm, they also have a client relationship with an investment banking firm. An investment banking firm such as CIBC World Markets can provide advice about financing plans, dividend policy, or stock repurchases, as well as advice on mergers and acquisitions. Many now offer additional banking services, making them "one-stop shopping" banking centres. When companies merge, they often use investment bankers to help them value the transaction. Each firm will want an outside opinion about what it is worth to the other. Sometimes mergers fall apart because the companies cannot agree on the price each company is worth or the structure of management after the merger. The advising investment banker, working with management, often irons out these details. Of course, investment bankers do not provide these services for free. They usually charge a fee of between 1 and 1.5 percent of the transaction. A $20 billion merger can generate between $200 and $300 million in investment banking fees. The merger mania of the late 1990s allowed top investment bankers to earn huge sums. Unfortunately, this type

DID YOU KNOW?

A single share of Coca-Cola stock purchased during its original 1919 IPO would be worth more than $5 million today.[6]

of fee income is dependent on healthy stock markets, which seem to stimulate the merger fever among corporate executives.

The Securities Markets

LO6   Describe the various securities markets in Canada.

Securities markets provide a mechanism for buying and selling securities. They make it possible for owners to sell their stocks and bonds to other investors. Thus, in the broadest sense, stocks and bonds markets may be thought of as providers of liquidity—the ability to turn security holdings into cash quickly and at minimal expense and effort. Without liquid securities markets, many potential investors would sit on the sidelines rather than invest their hard-earned savings in securities. Indeed, the ability to sell securities at well-established market prices is one of the very pillars of the capitalistic society that has developed over the years in Canada.

securities markets the mechanism for buying and selling securities

Unlike the primary market, in which corporations sell stocks directly to the public, secondary markets permit the trading of previously issued securities. There are many different secondary markets for both stocks and bonds. If you want to purchase 100 shares of Google common stock, for example, you must purchase this stock from another investor or institution. It is the active buying and selling by many thousands of investors that establishes the prices of all financial securities. Secondary market trades may take place on organized exchanges or in what is known as the over-the-counter market. Many brokerage houses exist to help investors with financial decisions, and many offer their services through the Internet. One such broker is TD Waterhouse. Its site offers a wealth of information and provides educational material to individual investors.

Stock Markets

Stock markets exist around the world in New York, Toronto, Tokyo, London, Frankfurt, Paris, and other world locations. The TMX Group operates cash and derivative markets for multiple asset classes—such as equities, fixed income, and energy—including Canada's two national stock exchanges: the Toronto Stock Exchange serving the senior equity market and the TSX Venture Exchange serving the public venture equity market. Now owned by the TMX Group, the Montreal Exchange was Canada's oldest exchange and has leadership in the financial derivatives market. The two biggest stock markets in the United States are the New York Stock Exchange (NYSE) and the NASDAQ.

Exchanges used to be divided into organized exchanges and over-the-counter markets, but during the last several years, dramatic changes have occurred. The TSX, NYSE,

and NASDAQ became publicly traded companies. They were previously not-for-profit organizations but are now for-profit companies. Additionally, exchanges have bought or merged with electronic exchanges—for example, the NYSE with Archipelago and the NASDAQ with Instinet. Electronic trading is faster and less expensive than floor trading (where brokers meet to transact business) and now accounts for most of the stock trading done worldwide.

In an attempt to expand their markets, NASDAQ acquired the OMX, a Nordic stock exchange headquartered in Sweden, and the New York Stock Exchange merged with Euronext, a large European electronic exchange that trades options and futures contracts as well as common stock. Both the NYSE and NASDAQ have expanded their reach, their product line, and their ability to trade around the world. What we are witnessing is the globalization of the world's financial markets.

Traditionally, the NASDAQ market has been an electronics market, and many of the large technology companies such as Microsoft and Apple trade on it. The NASDAQ operates through dealers who buy and sell common stock (inventory) for their own accounts. The TSX has traditionally been a floor-traded market, where brokers meet at

© Photographer's Choice/Getty Images

The Toronto Exchange is the world's tenth-biggest stock exchange in terms of market capitalization.

trading posts on the floor of the Toronto Stock Exchange to buy and sell common stock. The brokers act as agents for their clients and do not own their own inventory. This traditional division between the two markets is becoming less significant as the exchanges become electronic.

The Over-the-Counter Market

Unlike the organized exchanges, the **over-the-counter (OTC) market** is a network of dealers all over the country linked by computers, telephones, and Teletype machines. It has no central location. Today, the OTC market consists of small stocks, illiquid bank stocks, penny stocks, and companies whose stocks trade on the "pink sheets." Once NASDAQ was classified as an exchange by the SEC, it was no longer part of the OTC market. Further, because most corporate bonds and all U.S. securities are traded over the counter, the OTC market regularly accounts for the largest total dollar value of all of the secondary markets.

over-the-counter (OTC) market a network of dealers all over the country linked by computers, telephones, and Teletype machines

Measuring Market Performance

Investors, especially professional money managers, want to know how well their investments are performing relative to the market as a whole. Financial managers also need to know how their companies' securities are performing when compared with their competitors'. Thus, performance measures—averages and indexes—are very important to many different people. They not only indicate the performance of a particular securities market but also provide a measure of the overall health of the economy.

Indexes and averages are used to measure stock prices. An *index* compares current stock prices with those in a specified base period, such as 1944, 1967, or 1977. An *average* is the average of certain stock prices. The averages used are usually not simple calculations, however. Some stock market averages (such as the S&P/TSX Composite Index) are weighted averages, where the weights employed are the total market values of each stock in the index (in this case 500). The Dow Jones Industrial Average is a price-weighted average. Regardless of how constructed, all market averages of stocks move closely together over time.

Many investors follow the activity of stock indexes like the S&P/TSX or the Dow Jones Industrial Average very closely to see whether the stock market has gone up or down. Table 16.5 lists the top ten constituents that currently make up the S&P/TSX 60.

The numbers listed in an index or average that tracks the performance of a stock market are expressed not as dollars but as a number on a fixed scale. A period of large increases in stock prices is known as a *bull market*, with

---

RESPONDING TO BUSINESS CHALLENGES | Advancing Gender Diversity in Finance

While more than half of accounting majors in university undergraduate programs are women, only 9 percent of CFOs at major companies are female. This discrepancy is a concern to companies that are trying to emphasize diversity in management. Although sexual discrimination is still a problem, studies suggest that other factors contribute to this low percentage.

One theory is that women do not have as many connections with higher-level finance executives as men. According to a former portfolio consultant, because female employees do not often connect as well with male supervisors, they may inadvertently be passed up for future management opportunities. The support of senior executives is often essential for career advancement because these executives can more successfully advocate on behalf of the employee.

A solution that some companies have implemented is formal mentorship programs for women, but even these efforts have not seemed very successful. Instead, certain businesses have created programs to encourage female executives to form long-lasting relationships with female finance employees. In one such program, female finance executives agree to spend a year mentoring employees who have been recommended by their managers. It is believed that this longer time period will enable the executive and the employee to form a closer relationship; this in turn could result in more female employees being sponsored for financial leadership positions. Another example is a program at the financial institution Goldman Sachs, which has created a six-month Women's Career Strategies Initiative. The initiative pairs potentials with sponsors and seeks to help women form contacts by introducing them to executives throughout the organization.[7]

DISCUSSION QUESTIONS

1. Why do you think there are so few female CFOs?

2. Describe some ways that companies are trying to promote management positions to female finance employees.

3. Do you feel that a mentorship program will help close the gap?

Table 16.5 Top Ten Constituents by Index Weight on the S&P/TSX 60 (as of December 31, 2015)

Constituent	Symbol	GICS® Sector
Royal Bank of Canada	RY	Financials
Toronto-Dominion Bank	TD	Financials
Bank of Nova Scotia	BNS	Financials
Canadian National Railways	CNR	Industrials
Suncor Energy Inc.	SU	Energy
Bank of Montreal	BMO	Financials
BCE Inc.	BCE	Telecommunication Services
Valeant Pharmaceuticals International Inc.	VRX	Health Care
Manulife Financial Corp.	MFC	Financials
Enbridge Inc.	ENB	Energy

Source: Based on data from S&P Dow Jones Indices, http://www.spindices.com/indices/equity/sp-tsx-60-index (accessed January 19, 2016).

the bull symbolizing an aggressive, charging market and rising stock prices. A declining stock market is known as a *bear market*, with the bear symbolizing sluggish, retreating activity. When stock prices decline very rapidly, the market is said to *crash*. Figure 16.2 graphically displays the long-term performance of the Canadian stock market.

For investors to make sound financial decisions, it is important that they stay in touch with business news, markets, and indexes. Of course, business and investment magazines, such as the *Financial Post*, the *Report on Business*, and *Money*, offer this type of information. Many Internet sites—including the *CNN/Money*, *Globe Investor*, and other online newspapers, as well as *PR Newswire*—offer this information as well. Many sites offer searchable databases of information by topic, company, or keyword. However investors choose to receive and review business news, doing so is a necessity in today's market.

"Many investors follow the activity of the S&P/TSX to see whether the stock market has gone up or down."

Figure 16.2 Long-Term Performance of the Canadian Stock Market

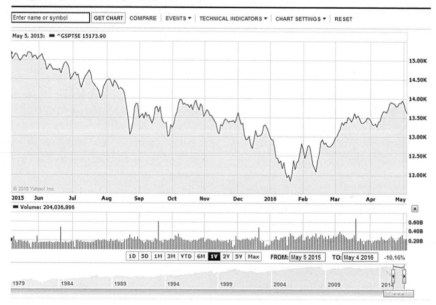

S&P/TSX Composite index (^GSPTSE) - Toronto

13,632.00 ↓75.68(0.55%) May 4, 4:20PM EDT

TEAM EXERCISE

Compare and contrast financing with long-term liabilities such as bonds versus financing with owners' equity, typically retained earnings, common stock, and preferred stock. Form groups and suggest a good mix of long-term liabilities and owners' equity for a new firm that makes wind turbines for generating alternative energy and that would like to grow quickly.

LO1 Describe some common methods of managing current assets.

Current assets are short-term resources such as cash, investments, accounts receivable, and inventory, which can be converted to cash within a year. Financial managers focus on minimizing the amount of cash kept on hand and increasing the speed of collections through lockboxes and electronic funds transfer and investing in marketable securities. Marketable securities include Treasury bills, certificates of deposit, commercial paper, and money market funds. Managing accounts receivable requires judging customer creditworthiness and creating credit terms that encourage prompt payment. Inventory management focuses on determining optimum inventory levels that minimize the cost of storing and ordering inventory without sacrificing too many lost sales due to stockouts.

LO2 Identify some sources of short-term financing (current liabilities).

Current liabilities are short-term debt obligations that must be repaid within one year, such as accounts payable, taxes payable, and notes (loans) payable. Trade credit is extended by suppliers for the purchase of their goods and services. A line of credit is an arrangement by which a bank agrees to lend a specified amount of money to a business whenever the business needs it. Secured loans are backed by collateral; unsecured loans are backed only by the borrower's good reputation.

LO3 Summarize the importance of long-term assets and capital budgeting.

Long-term, or fixed, assets are expected to last for many years, such as production facilities (plants), offices, and equipment. Businesses need modern, up-to-date equipment to succeed in today's competitive environment. Capital budgeting is the process of analyzing company needs and selecting the assets that will maximize its value; a capital budget is the amount of money budgeted for the

purchase of fixed assets. Every investment in fixed assets carries some risk.

LO4 Specify how companies finance their operations and manage fixed assets with long-term liabilities, particularly bonds.

Two common choices for financing are equity financing (attracting new owners) and debt financing (taking on long-term liabilities). Long-term liabilities are debts that will be repaid over a number of years, such as long-term bank loans and bond issues. A bond is a long-term debt security that an organization sells to raise money. The bond indenture specifies the provisions of the bond contract—maturity date, coupon rate, repayment methods, and others.

LO5 Discuss how corporations can use equity financing by issuing stock through an investment banker.

Owners' equity represents what owners have contributed to the company and includes common stock, preferred stock, and retained earnings (profits that have been reinvested in the assets of the firm). To finance operations, companies can issue new common and preferred stock through an investment banker that sells stocks and bonds for corporations.

LO6 Describe the various securities markets in Canada.

Securities markets provide the mechanism for buying and selling stocks and bonds. Primary markets allow companies to raise capital by selling new stock directly to investors through investment bankers. Secondary markets allow the buyers of previously issued shares of stock to sell them to other owners. The major secondary market is the S&P/TSX Composite Index in Canada. Investors measure stock market performance by watching stock market averages and indexes such as the S&P/TSX Composite Index and the Dow Jones Industrial Average.

bonds
capital budgeting
commercial certificates of deposit (CDs)
commercial paper
dividend yield
eurodollar market
factor
floating-rate bonds
investment banking
junk bonds
line of credit
lockbox
long-term (fixed) assets
long-term liabilities
marketable securities

over-the-counter (OTC) market
primary market
prime rate
retained earnings
secondary markets
secured bonds
secured loans
securities markets
serial bonds
trade credit
transaction balances
Treasury bills (T-bills)
unsecured bonds
unsecured loans
working capital management

DESTINATION CEO DISCUSSION QUESTIONS

1. What led to Watsa's success?

2. What is the relative size of Fairfax as a company?

3. Discuss the growth of Fairfax.

SO YOU WANT TO WORK *in Financial Management or Securities*

Taking classes in financial and securities management can provide many career options, from managing a small firm's accounts receivable to handling charitable giving for a multinational to investment banking to stock brokerage. We have entered into a less certain period for finance and securities jobs, however. In the world of investment banking, the past few years have been especially challenging. Tens of thousands of employees around the world have lost their jobs. This type of phenomenon is not isolated to the finance sector. In the early 2000s, the tech sector experienced a similar downturn, from which it has subsequently largely recovered. Undoubtedly, markets will bounce back and job creation in finance and securities will increase again—but until that happens, the atmosphere across finance and securities will be more competitive than it has been in the past. However, this does not mean that there are no jobs. All firms need financial analysts to determine whether a project should be implemented, when to issue stocks or bonds, or when to initiate loans. These and other forward-looking questions such as how to invest excess cash must be addressed by financial managers. Economic uncertainty in the financial and securities market has made for more difficulty in finding the most desirable jobs.

Why this sudden downturn in financial industry prospects? A lot of these job cuts came in response to the financial crises. All of these people who lost their jobs will be looking for new jobs in new organizations, increasing the competitive level in a lot of different employment areas. For young job seekers with relatively little experience, this may result in a great deal of frustration. On the other hand, by the time you graduate, the job market for finance majors could be in recovery and rebuilding with new employees. Uncertainty results in hiring freezes and layoffs, but leaves firms lean and ready to grow when the cycle turns around, resulting in hiring from the bottom up.

Many different industries require people with finance skills. So do not despair if you have a difficult time finding a job in exactly the right firm. Most students switch companies a number of times over the course of their careers. Many organizations require individuals trained in forecasting, statistics, economics, and finance. Even unlikely places like museums, aquariums, and zoos need people who are good at numbers. It may require some creativity, but if you are committed to a career in finance, look to less obvious sources—not just the large financial firms.[8]

Financial Management and Securities Markets

This chapter helps you realize that once you are making money, you need to be careful in determining how to invest it. Meanwhile, your team should consider the pros and cons of establishing a line of credit at the bank.

Remember that the key to building your business plan is to be realistic!

CASE | Hershey Foods: Melts in Your Mouth and May Melt Your Heart

Hershey Foods is the leading North American producer of quality chocolate and candy products, including much-loved brands such as Hershey's milk chocolate bar, Hershey's syrup, Hershey's cocoa, Almond Joy, Mr. Goodbar, Hershey's Kisses, Kit Kat, and Reese's peanut butter cups. A century after its founding, the company continues to operate by the values of its founder. Milton Hershey was born in 1857 and was of Pennsylvania Dutch descent. He became an apprentice to a candy maker in 1872, at age 15. By age 30, he had founded the Lancaster Caramel Company. After visiting the Chicago Exhibition in 1893, he became interested in a new chocolate-making machine. He sold his caramel factory and built a large chocolate factory in Derry Church, Pennsylvania, in 1905; the city was renamed Hershey in 1906. Hershey pioneered modern confectionery mass-production techniques by developing much of the machinery for making and packaging his milk chocolate products. The Hershey Foods Corporation as it exists today was organized under the laws of the state of Delaware on October 24, 1927, as a successor to the original business founded in 1894 by Milton Hershey. The company's stock was first publicly traded on December 1, 1927, and investors can still purchase shares today.

Milton Hershey was not only interested in innovative candy making; he also wanted to help the members of his community. An example of his concern for the community was the founding of a home and school for orphan children, the Hershey Industrial School (now called the Milton Hershey School) in 1909. Many of the children who attended the school became Hershey employees, including former Hershey chairman William Dearden (1976–1984). Today, the 10,000-acre campus houses and provides education for nearly 1,300 financially and socially disadvantaged children. Although Hershey remains a public corporation, the Milton Hershey School Trust, which financially supports the school, owns about 30 percent of Hershey Foods' total equity. The Milton Hershey School Trust also owns 100 percent of the Hershey Entertainment and Resort Company, which operates a number of Hershey's non-chocolate properties, including the Hersheypark theme park, the Dutch Wonderland theme park for younger children, the Hershey Hotel, the Hershey Lodge and Convention Center, the Hershey Bears minor league hockey team, Hershey's zoo, a four-course golf club, an outdoor sports stadium, and an indoor sports arena. Because of Milton Hershey's original funding and the wise investment management by the trust managers, the assets of the Milton Hershey School Trust have grown to a value of more than $7 billion. Milton Hershey was a visionary in terms of using a public corporation to support his philanthropic dreams.[9]

DISCUSSION QUESTIONS

1. Do you think that Milton Hershey made the right decision in leaving his foundation the controlling voting interest in the Hershey Foods Corporation?

2. Is Hershey Foods' example of founders willing stock for philanthropic purposes something that you believe that companies could do today? Why or why not?

3. Knowing that a large share of Hershey's profits support philanthropic causes, would you be more likely to purchase the company's stock?

ENDNOTES

Chapter I

1. Alexandra Bosanac, "CEO Sylvain Toutant on how he plans to grow DavidsTea in the U.S.," *Canadian Business*, September 15, 2015, **http://www.canadianbusiness.com/leadership/interview-sylvain-toutant-ceo-davidstea/** (accessed November 17, 2015); and Hollie Shaw, "DavidsTea specialty chain turns to coffee veteran for top job," *Financial Post*, May 29, 2014, **http://business.financialpost.com/news/retail-marketing/davidstea-specialty-chain-turns-to-coffee-veteran-for-top-job** (accessed November 17, 2015).

2. Victor Ferriera, "Starbucks Canada targets youth unemployment with program to hire at-risk young people," *Financial Post*, November 12, 2015, **http://business.financialpost.com/news/retail-marketing/starbucks-canada-targets-youth-unemployment-with-program-to-hire-at-risk-young-people** (accessed November 17, 2015).

3. Karl Moore, "Geoff Molson: 'I pinch myself once in a while and think about how lucky I am,'" *Financial Post*, October 16, 2015, **http://business.financialpost.com/executive/geoff-molson-i-pinch-myself-once-in-a-while-and-think-about-how-lucky-i-am** (accessed November 17, 2015).

4. Craig Torres and Anthony Field, "Campbell's Quest for Productivity," *Bloomberg Businessweek*, November 2–December 5, 2010, pp. 15–16.

5. Tahman Bradley, "Michelle Obama and Walmart Join Forces Promoting Healthy Food," ABC News, January 20, 2011, **http://abcnews.go.com/Politics/WorldNews/michelle-obama-walmart-join-forces-promote-healthy-eating/story?id=12723177** (accessed January 25, 2012).

6. Martinne Geller, "PepsiCo Lineup to Look Healthier in 10 Years: CEO," Reuters, October 17, 2011, **www.reuters.com/article/2011/10/17/us-pepsico-ceo-idUSTRE79G4ZO20111017** (accessed January 25, 2012).

7. Ron Joyce, *The Untold Story of Tim Hortons by the Man Who Created a Canadian Empire*, (Toronto: Harper Collins Publisher's Ltd., 2006), p. 180; Adam Lauzon, "Can I get a Large Double-Double, Please?", accessed July 17, 2010, **http://adamlauzon.wordpress.com/**.

8. Issuu. Retrieved 17 November, 2015, from **http://issuu.com/c40cities/docs/powering_climate_action_full_report**; "Greening the Concrete Jungle," *The Economist*, September 3, 2011, pp. 29–32; Wendy Koch, "Localities Push Own Bans on Plastic Bags," *USA Today*, October 6, 2010, p. 3A; C40org. (2015). C40. Retrieved 17 November, 2015, from **http://www.c40.org/blog_posts/toronto-s-lower-don-lands-climate-positive-project-to-transform-the-city-s-waterfront**.

9. "RBC—Corporate Responsibility," RBC, accessed July 17, 2010, **http://www.rbc.com/responsibility/community/index.html**; "Canada's biggest charitable donations," CBC News online, October 30, 2006, **www.cbc.ca/news/background/wealth/charitable-donations.html**; "Vibrant Communities: RBC 2011 Donations Report," **http://www.rbc.com/community-sustainability/_assets-custom/pdf/RBC-Donation-List-2011.pdf**.

10. "Special Report: The Visible Hand," *The Economist*, January 21, 2012, pp. 3–5.

11. "Special Report: The Visible Hand."

12. "Special Report: The World in Their Hands," *The Economist*, January 21, 2012, p. 15–17.

13. "The Dragons," CBC website, n.d., **http://www.cbc.ca/dragonsden/dragons/** (accessed November 17, 2015).

14. John D. Sutter and Doug Gross, "Apple Unveils the 'Magical' iPad," CNN Tech, January 28, 2010, **www.cnn.com/2010/TECH/01/27/apple.tablet/index.html?section=cnn_latest** (accessed February 3, 2010).

15. Solid State Technology, "China Patent Filings Could Overtake US, Japan in 2011," ELECTROIQ, October 11, 2010, **www.electroiq.com/index/display/semiconductors-article-display/1436725261/articles/solid-state-technology/semiconductors/industry-news/business-news/2010/october/china-patent_filings.html** (accessed January 3, 2011).

16. "Zimbabwe," *CIA—The World Factbook*, **https://www.cia.gov/library/publications/the-world-factbook/geos/zi.html#** (accessed February 3, 2010).

17. Status of Women Canada. Retrieved 17 November, 2015, from **http://www.swc-cfc.gc.ca/initiatives/wesp-sepf/fs-fi/es-se-eng.html**.

18. "Canada's debt to jump to $630B in 5 years: TD Bank," *CBC News* online, June 2, 2009, **http://www.cbc.ca/money/story/2009/06/02/td-forecast-canada-fiscal.html#ixzz11OXjv7zN**.

19. Terry Long, "The History of New France: The First European Settlers in Canada," Suite101.com, May 31, 2009, **http://www.suite101.com/content/the-history-of-new-france-a121662**.

20. John E. Foster, "Merger of the North West and Hudson's Bay Companies," *The Canadian Encyclopedia*, accessed July 17, 2010, **http://www.thecanadianencyclopedia.com/index.cfm?PgNm=TCE&Params=a1ARTA0003112**.

21. Josh Dehaas, "East Coast Lifestyle earns an A+ in Marketing 101," *Maclean's*, February 19, 2014, **http://www.macleans.ca/work/entrepreneur/east-coast-lifestyle-earns-an-a-in-marketing-101/** (accessed November 17, 2015); "About Us," East Coast Lifestyle website, n.d., **https://www.eastcoastlifestyle.com/pages/about-us** (accessed November 17, 2015).

22. "About Us: We are more than a social media company," Hootsuite website, n.d., **https://hootsuite.com/about** (accessed November 17, 2015).

23. Ian M. Drummond, "Economic History," *The Canadian Encyclopedia*, accessed July 17, 2010, **http://www.thecanadianencyclopedia.com/index.cfm?PgNm=TCE&Params=A1ARTA0002512**.

24. Peter J. Nicholson, "The Growth Story: Canada's Long-run Economic Performance and Prospects," *International Productivity Monitor, 2003*, **www.csls.ca/ipm/7/nicholson-e.pdf**, pp. 3–23.

25. Felicity Barringer, "U.S. Declines to Protect the Overfished Bluefin Tuna," *New York Times*, May 27, 2011, **www.nytimes.com/2011/05/28/science/earth/28tuna.html** (accessed June 15, 2011); David Helvarg, "Oil, Terror, Tuna and You," *Huffington Post*, May 9, 2011, **www.huffingtonpost.com/david-helvarg/oil-terror-tuna-and-you_b_859106.html** (accessed June 15, 2011); "Endangered Species Listing for Atlantic Bluefin Tuna Not

Warranted," NOAA, May 27, 2011, **www.noaanews.noaa.gov/stories2011/20110527_bluefintuna.html** (accessed June 18, 2011); David Jolly, "Many Mediterranean Fish Species Threatened With Extinction, Report Says," *New York Times*, April 19, 2011, **http://green.blogs.nytimes.com/2011/04/19/mediterranean-fish-species-threatened-with-extinction/** (accessed June 18, 2011); "Giant Bluefin Tuna Sells for Record Breaking Price: Big Pic," Discovery News, January 5, 2011, **http://news.discovery.com/animals/bluefin-tuna-record-auction-110105.html** (accessed June 18, 2011); "The King of Sushi," CBS—*60 Minutes*, **www.youtube.com/watch?v=dsbx6dQuRhQ** (accessed June 18, 2011).

26. "Stopping SOPA," *The Economist*, January 21, 2012, p. 33.

27. "The 2011 World's Most Ethical Companies," Ethisphere, 2011, Q1, pp. 37–43.

28. Isabelle Maignon, Tracy L. Gonzalez-Padron, G. Tomas M. Hult, and O.C. Ferrell, "Stakeholder Orientation: Development and Testing of a Framework for Socially Responsible Marketing," *Journal of Strategic Marketing* 19, no. 4 (July 2011), pp. 313–338.

29. "Key Small Business Statistics - August 2013," Industry Canada, August 2013, **http://www.ic.gc.ca/eic/site/061.nsf/eng/h_02800.html** (accessed November 17, 2015).

30. Scott Martin, "How Apple Rewrote the Rules of Retailing," *USA Today*, May 19, 2011, p. 1B; Steve Denning, "Apple's Retail Success Is More Than Magic," *Forbes*, June 17, 2011, **www.forbes.com/sites/stevedenning/2011/06/17/apples-retail-stores-more-than-magic/3/** (accessed August 22, 2011); Jefferson Graham, "At Apple Stores, iPads at Your Service," *USA Today*, May 23, 2011, p. 1B; "Apple Becomes World's Most Valuable Brand, Ending Google's Four-Year Term at the Top, says WPP's BrandZ," Millward Brown, May 8, 2011, **www.millwardbrown.com/Global/News/PressReleases/PressReleaseDetails/11-05-08/Apple_Becomes_World_s_Most_Valuable_Brand_Ending_Google_s_Four_Year_Term_at_the_Top_says_WPP_S_BrandZ.aspx** (accessed September 20, 2011).

Chapter 2

1. "Most Wanted," Global Exchange website, **http://www.globalexchange.org/corporateHRviolators#TransCanada** (accessed June 18, 2013).

2. Daniela Minicucci, "Pros and cons of the Keystone XL pipeline project," Communications, Energy and Paperworkers Union of Canada website, September 26, 2011, **http://www.cep.ca/en/news/in-the-news/pros-and-cons-keystone-xl-pipeline-project** (accessed June 17, 2013).

3. Sheldon Alberts, "An Interview with TransCanada CEO Russell Girling on the Keystone XL Pipeline," ocanada.com, October 9, 2011, **http://o.canada.com/2011/10/09/an-interview-with-transcanada-ceo-russ-girling-on-the-keystone-xl-pipeline/** (accessed June 17, 2013).

4. Ibid.

5. Paul Koring, "Obama rejects TransCanada's Keystone XL pipeline," *Globe and Mail*, November 6, 2015, **http://www.theglobeandmail.com/report-on-business/industry-news/energy-and-resources/obama-to-reject-transcanadas-keystone-xl-pipeline-source-says/article27144973/** (accessed November 7, 2015).

6. Canadian Press, "Some quotes on the US decision to reject the Keystone XL pipeline project," *Canadian Business*, November 6, 2015, **http://www.canadianbusiness.com/business-news/some-quotes-on-the-us-decision-to-reject-the-keystone-xl-pipeline-project/** (accessed November 07, 2015).

7. Tracey Johnson, "Is Keystone XL dead? Or just resting?" CBC News, November 7, 2015, **http://www.cbc.ca/news/business/keystone-xl-transcanada-nextsteps-1.3308559** (accessed November 8, 2015).

8. Jonathan Ratner, "Don't expect TransCanada Corp to take a writedown on Keystone XL just yet," *Financial Post*, November 9, 2015, **http://business.financialpost.com/news/energy/dont-expect-transcanada-corp-to-take-a-writedown-on-keystone-xl-just-yet** (accessed November 10, 2015).

9. Jane Taber, "New Brunswick, Alberta join forces to push Energy East pipeline," *Globe and Mail*, October 30, 2015, **http://www.theglobeandmail.com/news/politics/new-brunswick-alberta-join-forces-to-push-energy-east-pipeline/article27054317/** (accessed November 04, 2015).

10. Campbell Clark, "Ericsson, RIM to face off over Nortel," *Globe and Mail*, August 5, 2009, **http://www.theglobeandmail.com/news/technology/ericsson-rim-to-face-off-over-nortel/article1242512/**; "Canada Won't Intervene to Block Nortel Sale," *New York Times*, August 12, 2009, **http://dealbook.blogs.nytimes.com/2009/08/12/canada-chief-wont-block-nortel-sale-to-ericsson/**.

11. "A timeline of auto sector layoffs," CBC News, February 9, 2009, **http://www.cbc.ca/canada/story/2008/10/21/f-autolayoffs.html**.

12. "Preliminary hearing in MUHC fraud case kicks off," CTV News Montreal, March 16, 2015, **http://montreal.ctvnews.ca/preliminary-hearing-in-muhc-fraud-case-kicks-off-1.2281708** (accessed November 2, 2015).

13. Greg Farrell, "Lay, Skilling Found Guilty," *USA Today*, May 26, 2006, pp. A1, B1; *New York Times* coverage of the Enron trial, **www.nytimes.com/business/businessspecial3/index.html?adxnnl=1&adxnnlx=1147986237-z56Vd16RUkp6eHnHTTXBHw** (accessed May 18, 2006); "RCMP charge former Nortel CEO, 2 other execs," CBC News online, June 19, 2008, **http://www.cbc.ca/money/story/2008/06/19/nortel-rcmp.html#ixzz11ROltiTM**; Marguerite Reardon, "Former Nortel execs face criminal charges," cnet News, June 19, 2008, **http://news.cnet.com/8301-10784_3-9973257-7.html#ixzz11RQKFGJr**; "Enron," Wikipedia, **http://en.wikipedia.org/wiki/Enron** (accessed July 17, 2010).

14. "Firm Profile—Going Green Program," Stikeman Elliott, **http://www.stikeman.com/cps/rde/xchg/se-en/hs.xsl/11097.htm** (accessed July 17, 2010).

15. Katie Engelhart, "The Green 30: From the bottom up," *Canadian Business* magazine, May 10, 2010, **http://www.canadianbusiness.com/innovation/article.jsp?content=20100510_10024_10024**.

16. Ibid.

17. "Sarbanes-Oxley Act," Wikipedia, accessed July 17, 2010, **http://en.wikipedia.org/wiki/Sarbanes%E2%80%93Oxley_Act**.

18. Simon Houpt, "Telus sues Rogers over ad claims," *Globe and Mail*, November 18, 2009, **http://www.theglobeandmail.com/news/technology/telus-sues-rogers-over-ad-claims/article1368486/**; "Rogers stands behind its Internet advertising as fastest and most reliable," *Cape Breton Post*, February 17, 2010, **http://www.capebretonpost.com/Living/Technologies/2010-02-17/article-837486/Rogers-stands-behind-its-Internet-advertising-as-fastest-and-most-reliable/1**.

19. Russell Hotten, "Volkswagen: The scandal explained," BBC News, December 10, 2015, **http://www.bbc.com/news/business-34324772** (accessed November 07, 2015).

20. O. C. Ferrell, John Fraedrich, Linda Ferrell, *Business Ethics: Ethical Decision Making and Cases*, 6th ed. (Boston: Houghton Mifflin, 2005), p. 7.

21. Doug Alexander and Eric Lam "Valeant passes RBC as Canada's largest company by market value," *Globe and Mail*, July 23, 2015, **http://www.theglobeandmail.com/globe-investor/valeant-passes-rbc-as-canadas-largest-company-by-market-value/article25642880/** (accessed November 3, 2015).

22. Ranjit Thomas, "Is Valeant An Ethical Company?," Seeking Alpha, November 2, 2015, **http://seekingalpha.com/article/3633866-is-valeant-an-ethical-company** (accessed November 2, 2015).

23. "Valeant's High-Price Drug Strategy," *New York Times*, October 2, 2015, **http://www.nytimes.com/2015/10/04/business/valeants-high-price-drug-strategy.html?_r=0** (accessed November 5, 2015).

24. Bertrand Morotte, "Valeant revenue not fuelled by drug-price increases, CEO says," *Globe and Mail*, October 15, 2015, **www.theglobeandmail.com/report-on-business/valeant-probed-by-us-prosecutors-over-drug-pricing-concerns/article26819873/** (accessed November 9, 2015).

25. David Callahan, as quoted in Archie Carroll, "Carroll: Do We Live in a Cheating Culture?", *Athens Banner-Herald*, February 21, 2004, **www.onlineathens.com/stores/022204/bus_200402220 28.shtml**.

26. Devon Leonard, "The Curse of Pooh," *Fortune*, January 20, 2003, pp. 85–92; "Pooh Suit against Disney Dismissed," CNN online, March 29, 2004, **www.cnn.com**.

27. "Auditor General investigating MLA expense irregularities," CBC News online, February 12, 2010, **http://www.cbc.ca/canada/nova-scotia/story/2010/02/12/auditor-general-forensic-investigation-spending.html#ixzz11RZCX6Kt**.

28. Tina Comeau, "Yarmouth MLA Richard Hurlburt resigns," NovaNewsNow.com, February 9, 2010, **http://www.novanews-now.com/Natural-resources/2010-02-09/article-809272/Yarmouth-MLA-Richard-Hurlburt-resigns/1**.

29. John Lyman, "Who Is Scooter Libby?", Center for American Progress, October 28, 2005, **http://www.americanprogress.org/issues/2005/10/b109719.html**.

30. "Hwang Woo-suk," Wikipedia, accessed May 23, 2006, **http://en.wikipedia.org/wiki/Hwang_Woo-suk**.

31. "Colorado Places Barnett on Administrative Leave," SI.com, February 19, 2004, **http://sportsillustrated.cnn.com/**.

32. David Ebner, "Anti-doping agency calls for ban on Russian track-and-field athletes" *Globe and Mail*, November 10, 2015, **http://www.theglobeandmail.com/sports/anti-doping-agency-accuses-russia-of-coverup-calls-for-ban-on-athletes/article 27172282/** (accessed November 10, 2015).

33. Adrian Humphreys, "Canada's organic food certification system 'little more than an extortion racket' report says," *National Post*, November 24, 2012, **http://news.nationalpost.com/2012/11/24/canadas-organic-food-certification-system-little-more-than-an-extortion-racket-report-says/**; Mischa Popoff and Patrick Moore, "Canada's Organic Nightmare," Frontier Centre Policy Series, **http://mobi.fcpp.org/publication.php/4361**; Mischa Popoff, "Opinions and Editorials," Is It Organic? website, **http://isitorganic.ca/opinions_and_editorials** (accessed June 19, 2013).

34. Douglas Macmillan and Telus Demos, "Uber Valued at More Than $50 Billion," *Wall Street Journal*, July 31, 2015, **http://www.wsj.com/articles/uber-valued-at-more-than-50-billion-1438367457**.

35. Eugene Kim, "Uber has grown faster in its first five years than Facebook did," *Business Insider*, June 1, 2015, **http://www.businessinsider.com/uber-vs-facebook-valuation-in-years-one-through-five-2015-6** (accessed November 4, 2015).

36. Giuseppe Valiante, "Uber pushes Canadian cities to re-evaluate taxi industry," CBC News, July 19, 2015, **http://www.cbc.ca/news/canada/montreal/uber-pushes-canadian-cities-to-re-evaluate-taxi-industry-1.3159212** (accessed November 2, 2015).

37. Ibid.

38. Ibid.

39. "Uber drivers and passengers face serious legal and insurance consequences," Kennedy Insurance Brokers Inc., n.d., **http://www.kennedyinsurance.ca/uber-drivers-passengers-face-serious-legal-insurance-consequences/** (accessed November 16, 2015).

40. Ann Hui, "Uber to continue 'outside the law' in Toronto," *Globe and Mail*, October 1, 2015, **http://www.theglobeandmail.com/news/toronto/uber-to-continue-outside-the-law-in-toronto/article26628483/** (accessed November 12, 2015).

41. Ann Hui, "Ontario taxi owner files $410-million class-action suit against Uber Canada," *Globe and Mail*, July 23, 2015, **http://www.theglobeandmail.com/news/national/ontario-taxi-files-400-million-class-action-suit-against-uber-canada/article25643753/** (accessed November 13, 2015).

42. Sean Silcoff and Jacqueline Nelson, "Insurance Bureau of Canada pushing to get Uber drivers covered," *Globe and Mail*, October 13, 2015, **http://www.theglobeandmail.com/report-on-business/insurance-bureau-of-canada-pushing-to-get-uber-drivers-covered/article26792745/** (accessed November 1, 2015).

43. "National Business Ethics Survey 2005," "Survey Documents State of Ethics in the Workplace," and "Misconduct" (n.d.), Ethics Resource Center, accessed April 11, 2006, **www.ethics.org/nbes/2005/release.html**.

44. "40% of Canadians bullied at work, experts say," CBC News, December 6, 2011, **http://www.cbc.ca/news/canada/windsor/40-of-canadians-bullied-at-work-expert-says-1.987450** (accessed November 9, 2015).

45. Karen MacGregor, "Acres International convicted in African bribery case," Probe International, September 18, 2002, **http://www.probeinternational.org/odious-debts/acres-intl-convicted-african-bribery-case**.

46. Greg McArthur, "NIKO Resources: Ottawa's corruption test case," *Report on Business*, August 25, 2011, **http://www.theglobeandmail.com/report-on-business/rob-magazine/niko-resources-ottawas-corruption-test-case/article542842/** (accessed June 18, 2013).

47. Canadian Competition Bureau, June 13, 2003, **http://www.competitionbureau.gc.ca/eic/site/cb-bc.nsf/eng/01863.html**, and July 6, 2004, **http://www.competitionbureau.gc.ca/eic/site/cb-bc.nsf/eng/01863.html**.

48. "Pens and Post-Its Among Most Pilfered Office Supplies, Says New Vault Survey," Vault, November 16, 2005, **www.vault.**

com/nr/newsmain.jsp?nr_page=3&ch_id=420&article_
id=25720773 (accessed June 2, 2006).

49. David Whelan, "Only the Paranoid Resurge," *Forbes*, April 10, 2006, **http://www.forbes.com/forbes/2006/0410/042.html** (accessed June 19, 2013).

50. "Maple Leaf Foods plant linked to Listeria outbreak," CTV News, August 23, 2008, **http://www.ctv.ca/CTVNews/ EdmontonHome/20080823/recall_listeria_080823/**; Sarah Schmidt and Mike De Souza, "Maple Leaf CEO says food industry must improve safety regime," *National Post*, April 20, 2009, **http://www.nationalpost.com/news/canada/story. html?id=1516299**; Our Journey to Safe Leadership (Maple Leaf blog), accessed July 17, 2010, **http://blog.mapleleaf.com/**.

51. "6 automakers part of massive recall of 3.4 million airbags," CBC News, April 11, 2013, **http://www.cbc.ca/news/business/ story/2013/04/11/vehicle-airbag-recall-honda-nissan- toyota.html** (accessed June 18, 2013); Tim Shufelt, "Toyota moves fast on recall," *Financial Post*, August 26, 2010, **http:// www.financialpost.com/news/Toyota+moves+fast+rec all/3445963/story.html**.

52. Renata D'Aliesio, "XL owners giants in the beef business," *Globe and Mail*, October 13, 2012, **http://www.theglobeandmail. com/news/national/xl-owners-giants-in-the-beef-business/ article4611119/** (accessed June 18, 2013), "XL Foods E. coli recall preventable, probe finds," CBC News, June 5, 2013, **http://www.cbc.ca/news/politics/story/2013/06/05/pol- e-coli-xl-foods-report.html** (accessed June 18, 2013); Todd Zaun, "Mitsubishi Motors seeks damages from ex-officials," *New York Times*, March 31, 2005, **http://www.nytimes. com/2005/03/31/business/worldbusiness/31mitsubishi. html?ref=katsuhiko_kawasoe**; Yuri Kageyama, "Mitsubishi Motors Says Massive Defect Cover-ups Were Intentional," *Boston Globe*, August 22, 2000, **www.boston.com**; "Mitsubishi Cover-up May Bring Charges," *Detroit News*, August 23, 2000, **www.det-news.com/2000/autos/0008/23/b03-109584.htm**.

53. Transparency International, **http://www.transparency.org/** (accessed July 17, 2010).

54. "Music sales in Canada fall 4 percent in 2005," CRIA, March 2, 2006, **http://www.cria.ca/news/020306a_n.php**.

55. "RIAA Releases 2003 Consumer Profile: Online Music Purchasing Expands," April 30, 2004, **http://www.riaa.com/ newsitem.php?news_month_filter=&news_year_filter= &resultpage=49&id=1D5364BF-B187-A206-C3B8- 94B7424E50F4** (accessed July 27, 2010).

56. Gary Fung, "There is no way you can shut file-sharing down," periodicfitness website, **http://www.periodfitness.com/tag/ gary-fung/** (accessed June 19, 2013); Ernesto, "BitTorrent Behind the Scenes: isoHunt," TorrentFreak website, **http://torrentfreak.com/bittorrent-behind-the-scenes- isohunt-090729/** (accessed June 19, 2013); and "isoHunt," Wikipedia website, **http://en.wikipedia.org/wiki/IsoHunt** (accessed June 19, 2013).

57. Alex Gillis, "Cheating themselves," University Affairs online, March 12, 2007, **http://www.universityaffairs.ca/cheating- themselves.aspx**.

58. "Teens Respect Good Business Ethics," *USA Today*, Snapshots, December 12, 2005, p. 13-1.

59. Marianne Jennings, "An Ethical Breach by Any Other Name," College of Business Master Teacher Initiative, Colorado State University, January/February 2006 **http://www.biz.colostate.edu/ MTI/TeachingTips/Academic_Integrity/EthicalBreach.aspx**.

60. Matthew McClearn, "Probiotics: Yogurt's secret ingredient," *Canadian Business*, November 1, 2012, **http://www.canadianbusiness. com/lifestyle/probiotics-yogurts-secret-ingredient/** (accessed June 19, 2013).

61. Erica Johnson, "Questioning the Magic at Herbal Magic," CBC.ca *Marketplace* blog, February 5, 2010, **http://www.cbc. ca/marketplace/blog/2010/02/questioning-the-magic-at- herbal-magic.html**.

62. "Tracking a diet scam," CTV News, February 22, 2002, **http://www.ctv.ca/CTVNews/SpecialEvent1/20020222/ ctvnews836330/**.

63. "Mexico, United States, Canada Combat Weight Loss Fraud," U.S. Food and Drug Administration, October 24, 2005, **http:// www.fda.gov/NewsEvents/Newsroom/PressAnnouncements/2005/ucm108504.htm**.

64. "Campaign Warns about Drugs from Canada," CNN, February 5, 2004, **www.cnn.com**; Gardiner Harris and Monica Davey, "FDA Begins Push to End Drug Imports," *New York Times*, January 23, 2004, p. C1.

65. "Briefing: Tobacco Packaging and Labelling," Information Resource Center, accessed July 31, 2006, **http://infolink. cancerresearchuk.org/publicpolicy/briefings/prevention/ tobacco**.

66. Food and Consumer Products of Canada, Consumer Products Safety, **http://www.fcpc.ca/issues/safety/index.html** (accessed July 18, 2010).

67. Nestor E. Arellano. "Toronto firm fined for unlicensed software use," *IT World Canada*, October 4, 2006, **http://www.itworldcanada. com/news/toronto-firm-fined-for-unlicensed-software- use/100124** (accessed July 17, 2010).

68. "WestJet to sue Air Canada for corporate spying," CTV News, June 30, 2004, **http://www.ctv.ca/CTVNews/Canada/20040630/westjet_ suesaircanada_20040629/**; "WestJet apologizes to Air Canada for snooping," *National Post*, May 30, 2006, **http://www.canada.com/ topics/technology/story.html?p=1&k=30762&id=6138fbd4- c3db-44ca-83a7-bfb6bcc0cbdb**; "Air Canada, WestJet settle spying lawsuit," CBC News, May 30, 2006, **http://www.cbc.ca/ money/story/2006/05/29/westjet-aircansettle.html**.

69. Susan Pullman, "Ordered to Commit Fraud, A Staffer Balked, Then Caved," *Wall Street Journal*, June 23, 2003, **http://online. wsj.com**.

70. CTVNews.ca staff, "Corporate espionage costing billions each year," CTV News, November 29, 2011, **http://www.ctvnews.ca/ corporate-espionage-costing-billions-each-year-1.732885** (accessed June 19, 2013).

71. Blake Morrison, "Ex-USA Today Reporter Faked Major Stories," *USA Today*, March 19, 2004, **www.usatoday.com/**.

72. Thomas M. Jones, "Ethical Decision Making by Individuals in Organizations: An Issue-Contingent Model," *Academy of Management Review* 2 (April 1991), pp. 371–73.

73. Sir Adrian Cadbury, "Ethical Managers Make Their Own Rules," *Harvard Business Review* 65 (September–October 1987), p. 72.

74. Josh Constine, "Facebook beats in Q2 with $4.04B Revenue, User Growth Slows to 3.47% QOQ to Hit 1.49B," Tech Crunch, **http://techcrunch.com/2015/07/29/facebook-earnings- q2-2015/** (accessed November 15, 2015).

75. Stephen Fidler, "Facebook Policies Taken to task in Report for Data-Privacy Issues," *Wall Street Journal*, February 23, 2015, **http://www.wsj.com/articles/facebook-policies-taken-to-task-in-report-for-data-privacy-issues-1424725902** (accessed November 9, 2015).

76. Olivia Campbell, "Facebook will now track your browsing history on external sites & mobile apps," Abine, June 13, 2014, **https://www.abine.com/blog/2014/facebook-tracking-browsing/** (accessed November 6, 2015); Drew Guarini, "Hold your gasps, Facebook is under fire for its privacy policy again," *Huffington Post*, September 5, 2013, **http://www.huffingtonpost.com/2013/09/05/facebook-privacy-ftc_n_3873764.html** (accessed November 08, 2015).

77. Ferrell, Fraedrich, and Ferrell, *Business Ethics*, pp. 174–75.

78. Ethics Resource Center, "Misconduct" (n.d.), accessed April 11, 2006, **www.ethics.org/nbes/2005/release.html**.

79. Ethics Resource Center, "2005 National Business Ethics Survey: Executive Summary" (n.d.), accessed July 17, 2010, **www.ethic.org/nbes2005/2005nbes_summary.html**, p. 29.

80. "Whistleblower legislation: Bill C-25, Disclosure Protection," CBC News, April 28, 2004, **http://www.cbc.ca/news/background/whistleblower/** (accessed July 27, 2010).

81. Ferrell, Fraedrich, and Ferrell, *Business Ethics*, p. 13.

82. John Galvin, "The New Business Ethics," SmartBusinessMag.com, June 2000, p. 99.

83. Archie B. Carroll, "The Pyramid of Corporate Social Responsibility: Toward the Moral Management of Organizational Stakeholders," *Business Horizons* 34 (July/August 1991), p. 42.

84. Steve Brearton, "50 Best Employers in Canada," *ROB Magazine, Globe and Mail*, December 29, 2009, **http://www.theglobeandmail.com/report-on-business/rob-magazine/50-best-employers-in-canada/article1413413/**.

85. "About Us," Nexen Inc., **http://www.nexeninc.com/en/About Us.aspx** (accessed July 17, 2010).

86. Corporate Knights, **http://www.corporateknights.ca/** (accessed July 17, 2010).

87. Ferrell, Fraedrich, and Ferrell, *Business Ethics*, pp. 13–19.

88. "Canadian Auto Workers," Wikipedia, **http://en.wikipedia.org/wiki/Canadian_Auto_Workers** (accessed July 17, 2010); "Deadline passes with no deal between CAW, GM," CBC News, May 16, 2009, **http://www.cbc.ca/canada/story/2009/05/15/gm-canada-caw-talks497.html**.

89. "WestJet Airlines Ltd.—Company Profile, Information, Business Description, History, Background Information on WestJet Airlines Ltd.," **http://www.referenceforbusiness.com/history2/70/WestJet-Airlines-Ltd.html** (accessed July 17, 2010); Richard Yerema and R. Caballero, "Employer Review: Royal Bank of Canada," Mediacorp Canada Inc., November 2, 2009, **http://www.eluta.ca/top-employer-rbc**.

90. Wendy Zellner, "No Way to Treat a Lady?" *BusinessWeek*, March 3, 2003, pp. 63–66.

91. "Nestlé Boss Starts an African Crusade," *Sunday Times*, March 13, 2005, **www.timesonline.co.uk/article/0,,2095-1522290,00.html**; "The Nestlé Coffee Report," Faces of Coffee, Nestlé S.A., Public Affairs, March 2004, **www.nestle.com/NR/rdonlyres/4F893E04-4129-4E4C-92F1-91AF4C8C4738/0/2003_Coffee_Report.pdf**; "The Nestlé Commitment to Africa," Africa Report, Nestlé, **www.nestle.com/Our_Responsibility/Africa+Report/Overview/Africa+Report.htm** (all accessed November 7, 2005).

92. Chad Terhune, "Jury Says Home Depot Must Pay Customer Hurt by Falling Merchandise $1.5 Million," *Wall Street Journal*, July 16, 2001, p. A14.

93. "About Us," Office of Consumer Affairs, **http://www.ic.gc.ca/eic/site/oca-bc.nsf/eng/ca00038.html** (accessed June 28, 2010).

94. Loren Drummond, "EU representative condemns seal hunt after Canada visit," The Humane Society of the United States, March 28, 2007, **http://www.hsus.org/marine_mammals/marine_mammals_news/eu_representative_condemns_hunt.html**; "Seal hunting," Wikipedia, **http://en.wikipedia.org/wiki/Seal_hunting** (accessed July 17, 2010); "Bring on the seal war, fisheries minister tells activists," CBC News, September 7, 2006, **http://www.cbc.ca/canada/newfoundland-labrador/story/2006/09/07/seal-war.html**; "FAQs: The Atlantic seal hunt," CBC News, July 27, 2009, **http://www.cbc.ca/canada/story/2009/05/05/f-seal-hunt.html**.

95. "FAQs: The Atlantic seal hunt," CBC News, July 27, 2009, **http://www.cbc.ca/canada/story/2009/05/05/f-seal-hunt.html** (accessed July 27, 2010).

96. Campbell Robertson and Clifford Krauss, "Gulf Spill Is the Largest of Its Kind, Scientists Say," *New York Times*, August 2, 2010, **http://www.nytimes.com/2010/08/03/us/03spill.html?_r=1&fta=y** (accessed September 3, 2010); "Deepwater Horizon oil spill," Wikipedia, **http://en.wikipedia.org/wiki/Deepwater_Horizon_oil_spill** (accessed July 17, 2010).

97. Anne Hayden, "Will One Gulf's Tragedy Affect Drilling in Another?" *Gulf of Maine Times*, June 30, 2010, **http://www.gulfofmaine.org/gomt/?p=392**; Kevin Jess, "Oil drilling moratorium on Georges Bank extended," *Digital Journal*, May 18, 2010, **http://www.digitaljournal.com/article/292182**; Jean Laroche, "Georges Bank moratorium extended by Nova Scotia government," CBC News, November 26, 2015, **http://www.cbc.ca/news/canada/nova-scotia/georges-bank-moratorium-extended-1.3338283**.

98. "Drinking Water Legislation," Ministry of the Environment: Drinking Water Ontario, July 27, 2010, **http://www.ontario.ca/ONT/portal61/drinkingwater/General?docId=STEL01_046858&breadcrumbLevel=1&lang=en** (accessed Sept 16, 2010); "Safe Drinking Water Act, 2002" Government of Ontario, **http://www.e-laws.gov.on.ca/html/statutes/english/elaws_statutes_02s32_e.htm** (accessed July 16, 2010).

99. "China's Energy Crunch," Asia Economic Institute, **http://www.asiaecon.org/exclusives/ex_read/9** (accessed July 17, 2010); Bradsher, K., 2009, "China Outpaces U.S. in Cleaner Coal-Fired Plants," *New York Times*, May 10, 2009, **http://www.nytimes.com/2009/05/11/world/asia/11coal.html** (accessed June 13, 2010).

100. Dell Inc., "WEEE recycling," **http://www1.euro.dell.com/content/topics/topic.aspx/emea/topics/services/weee_directive?c=eu&l=en** (accessed July 18, 2010).

101. Cahal Milmo "The biggest environmental crime in history," *The Independent Close*, **http://www.independent.co.uk/environment/the-biggest-environmental-crime-in-history-764102.html** (accessed July 18, 2010).

102. Laura Judy, "Green from the Ground Up," *Atlanta Home Improvement*, January 2006, **www.homeimprovementmag.com/**

Articles/2006/06Jan_ground_up.html (accessed June 15, 2007); Earthcraft House, **www.earthcrafthouse.com** (accessed October 5, 2007); "Earthcraft House Program," "Green Fast Facts: Did You Know...," **www.atlantahomebuilders.com/education/earthcraft.cfm** (accessed October 5, 2007); Melanie Lindner, "Living Green" EarthCraft House," Atlanta Intown Newspaper, January 2007, **www.atlantaintownpaper.com/features/EarthCraft HouseJAN07.php** (accessed October 5, 2007).

103. Alan K. Reichert, Marion S. Webb, and Edward G. Thomas, "Corporate Support for Ethical and Environmental Policies: A Financial Management Perspective," *Journal of Business Ethics* 25 (2000), pp. 53–64.

104. "Trend Watch," *Business Ethics*, March/April 2001, p. 8.

105. David J. Lynch, "Corporate America Warms to Fight Against Global Warming," *USA Today*, June 1, 2006, p. B1.

106. Laurie Goldstein, "Marriott Meetings Go Green," *Marriott News*, July 22, 2008, **http://www.marriott.com/news/detail. mi?marrArticle=347592** (accessed July 16, 2010).

107. Lush Fresh Handmade Cosmetics, accessed July 27, 2010, **http://www.lush.ca/shop/about-lush/articles/our-green-initiatives/packaging.html**.

108. Quentin Casey, "In the Hot Seat," *Progress* magazine, April 2015, **http://www.progressmedia.ca/article/2015/04/hot-seat**.

109. David Leonhardt, "Spillonomics: Underestimating Risk," *New York Times*, May 31, 2010, **www.nytimes.com/2010/06/06/magazine/06fob-wwln-t.html** (accessed June 22, 2010); Robert Mackey, "Rig Worker Says BP Was Told of Leak in Emergency System Before Explosion," *New York Times*, June 21, 2010, **http://thelede.blogs.nytimes.com/2010/06/21/rig-worker-claims-bp-knew-of-leak-in-emergency-system-before-explosion/?scp=5&sq=BP&st=cse** (accessed June 22, 2010); "BP and the Gulf of Mexico Alliance Announce Implementation of BP's $500 Million Independent Research Initiative," BP, September 29, 2010, **www.bp.com/genericarticle.do?categoryId=20 12968&contentId=7065262** (accessed October 27, 2010); "BP Pledges Collateral for Gulf of Mexico Oil Spill Trust," BP, October 1, 2010, **www.bp.com/genericarticle.do?categoryId=2012 968&contentId=7065280** (accessed October 27, 2010); Russell Gold and Tom McGinty, "BP Relied on Cheaper Wells," *Wall Street Journal*, June 19, 2010, **http://online.wsj.com/article/NA_WSJ_PUB:SB10001424052748704289504575313010283981200. html** (accessed October 27, 2010); Joel K. Bourne, Jr., "The Deep Dilemma," *National Geographic*, October 2010, pp. 40–53.

110. "Certification" (n.d.), Home Depot, accessed April 6, 2004, **www.homedepot.com/HDUS/EN_US/corporate/corp_respon/certification.shtml**.

111. "Yes, We Have No Bananas: Rainforest Alliance Certifies Chiquita Bananas" (n.d.), *Ag Journal*, **www.agjournal.com/story.cfm?story_id_1047** (accessed April 6, 2004).

112. "Federal government, Ontario agree on $3.3B auto bailout package," CBC News, December 12, 2008, **http://www.cbc.ca/canada/story/2008/12/12/flaherty-deficit.html**; Greg Keenan, Steven Chase, Karen Howlett, and Shawn McCarthy, "Auto bailout costs soar," *Globe and Mail*, May 28, 2009, **http://www.theglobeandmail.com/report-on-business/auto-bailout-costs-soar/article1156756/**; "No bailout for Nortel, industry minister says," CTV News, June 18, 2009, **http://www.ctv.ca/CTVNews/TopStories/20090618/Nortel_CEO_090618/**.

113. Nelson Smith, "Is Bombardier Inc. on a Fast Track to Bankruptcy?" The Motley Fook, July 24, 2015, **http://www.fool.ca/2015/07/24/is-bombardier-inc-on-a-fast-track-to-bankruptcy/**.

114. "Bombardier loses $4.9B US in 3rd Quarter, Quebec to invest $1B in CSeries Program," CBC News, **http://www.cbc.ca/news/business/bombardier-quebec-cseries-investment-1.3293716** (accessed November 14, 2015).

115. "Delta Hotels and Resorts Wraps Up Cross-Canada Tour to Build Stronger Communities," Habitat for Humanity Canada, accessed Nov. 3, 2010, **http://habitat.ca/deltap4088.php**; MADD Canada, accessed Nov 3. 2010, **http://www.madd.ca/english/donating/sponsors_complete.html**; "CMHA Corporate Donors," Canadian Mental Health Association, accessed November 3, 2010, **http://www.cmha.ca/bins/content_page.asp?cid=7-19**.

116. "Who Really Pays for CSR Initiatives," *Environmental Leader*, February 15, 2008, **www.environmentalleader.com/2008/02/15/who-really-paysfor-csr-initiatives/** (accessed February 25, 2010); "Global Fund," **www.joinred.com/globalfund** (accessed February 25, 2010); Reena Jana, "The Business of Going Green," *BusinessWeek*, June 22, 2007, **www.businessweek.com/innovate/content/jun2007/id20070622_491833.htm?chan=search** (accessed June 19, 2008).

117. Mark Zuckerberg, "Six years of making connections," February 4, 2010, **http://blog.facebook.com/blog.php?post=2875 42162130**; Personal interview with Dr. Amy Thurlow, professor, Mount Saint Vincent University, May 2009.

Chapter 3

1. Canada's Most Admired CEO, n.d., **http://www.canadasmost admired.com/most-admired-ceo.html** (accessed January 10, 2016); Free The Children, n.d., **http://www.freethechildren.com/marc-and-craig/free-the-children-takes-flight/** (accessed January 10, 2016); National Speakers Bureau, n.d., **http://nsb.com/speakers/marc-kielburger/** (accessed January 11, 2016); Andrew Duffy, "Free the Children at 20: An unlikely Canadian success story," *Ottawa Citizen*, April 25, 2015, **http://ottawacitizen.com/news/national/free-the-children-at-20-an-unlikely-canadian-success-story** (accessed January 11, 2016).

2. "Top 100 Global Franchises - Rankings (2016)," Franchise Direct, 2016, **http://www.franchisedirect.com/top100global franchises/rankings/** (accessed July 29, 2016).

3. Starbucks Coffee International, **www.starbucks.com/business/international-stores** (accessed January 20, 2012).

4. Elisabeth Sullivan, "Choose Your Words Wisely," *Marketing News*, February 15, 2008, p. 22.

5. Ellen Byron, "Febreze Joins P&G's $1 Billion Club," *Wall Street Journal*, March 9, 2011, **http://online.wsj.com/article/SB10 001424052748704076804576180683371307932.html** (accessed January 7, 2013).

6. Sullivan, "Choose Your Words Wisely."

7. Michelle Yun and Kathy Chu, "Philippines May Answer Call," *USA Today*, January 10, 2011, pp. 1B-2B.

8. Adapted from Statistics Canada, "Imports, exports and trade balance of goods on a balance-of-payments basis, by country or country grouping," **http://www.statcan.gc.ca/tables-tableaux/sum-som/l01/cst01/gblec02a-eng.htm** (accessed January 6, 2016).

9. Adapted from Statistics Canada, "Imports, exports and trade balance of goods on a balance-of-payments basis, by country or country grouping," **http://www.statcan.gc.ca/tables-tableaux/sum-som/l01/cst01/gblec02a-eng.htm** (accessed January 6, 2016).

10. Adapted from Statistics Canada, "Canadian international merchandise trade: Annual review, 2014," **http://www.statcan.gc.ca/daily-quotidien/150402/dq150402b-eng.htm** (accessed January 7, 2016).

11. Adapted from Statistics Canada, "Canadian international merchandise trade," *The Daily*, February 11, 2009, **http://www.statcan.gc.ca/daily-quotidien/090211/dq090211a-eng.htm** (accessed August 17, 2009).

12. Keith Bradsher, "G.M. Plans to Develop Electric Cars With China," *New York Times*, September 20, 2011, **www.nytimes.com/2011/09/21/business/global/gm-plans-to-develop-electric-cars-with-chinese-automaker.html** (accessed December 2, 2011).

13. Calum MacLeod, "Pollution Fogs China's Future," *USA Today*, September 13, 2011, 6A; Keith Bradsher, "China Fears Consumer Impact on Global Warming," *New York Times*, July 4, 2010, **www.nytimes.com/2010/07/05/business/global/05warm.html?pagewanted=all** (accessed October 6, 2011); "China Leading Global Race to Make Clean Energy," *New York Times*, January 30, 2010, **www.nytimes.com/2010/01/31/business/energy-environment/31renew.html** (accessed October 6, 2011); Michael Scherer, "The Solyndra Syndrome," *Time*, October 10, 2011, 42–45; "Taxing Times Ahead," *The Economist*, October 29, 2011, p. 77.

14. Amol Sharma and Prasanta Sahu, *Wall Street Journal*, January 11, 2012, **http://online.wsj.com/article/SB10001424052970204257504577152342214405180.html** (accessed January 27, 2012); Indranil Bose, Shilpi Banerjee, Edo de Vries Robbe, "Wal-Mart and Bharti: Transforming Retail in India," *Harvard Business Review*, August 27, 2009, **http://hbr.org/product/walmart-and-bharti-transforming-retail-in-india/an/HKU845-PDF-ENG** (accessed January 27, 2012).

15. "Goods from Canada: A Handy Guide for Exporters. Why you have to report your exports," **www.cbsa-asfc.gc.ca/publications/pub/bsf5081-eng.html** (accessed August 17, 2009).

16. "The Restricted Zone in Mexico," Penner & Associates—Mexico Law Firm and Business Consulting for Mexico, **www.mexicolaw.com/LawInfo17.htm** (accessed January 10, 2011).

17. "Sixth Annual BSA and IDC Global Software Piracy Study," Business Software Alliance, May 2009, **http://global.bsa.org/globalpiracy2008/index.html** (accessed February 20, 2010).

18. "Loonie Hits Lowest Level Since 2003 Amid 'Identity Crisis,'" *Huffington Post*, January 6, 2016, **http://www.huffingtonpost.ca/2016/01/06/canadian-dollar-lowest-since-2003_n_8922268.html** (accessed January 7, 2016); Peter Henderson, "Loonie closes at 71 cents, lowest since 2003," CTV News, January 6, 2016, **http://www.ctvnews.ca/business/loonie-closes-at-71-cents-lowest-since-2003-1.2725376** (accessed January 7, 2016); Jason Markusoff, "The death of the Alberta dream, *Maclean's*, January 6, 2016, **http://www.macleans.ca/news/canada/the-death-of-the-alberta-dream/**.

19. Steven Chase, "New Zealand disputes Harper's stand on tariff walls," *Globe and Mail*, September 6, 2012, **http://m.theglobeandmail.com/news/politics/new-zealand-disputes-harpers-stand-on-tariff-walls/article4184159/?service=mobile** (accessed January 7, 2013).

20. Foreign Affairs and International Trade Canada website, **www.international.gc.ca/controls-controles/about-a_propos/impor/importing-importation.aspx** (accessed August 17, 2009).

21. Kitty Bean Yancey and Laura Bly, "Door May Be Inching Open for Tourism," *USA Today*, February 20, 2008, p. A5; Sue Kirchhoff and Chris Woodyard, "Cuba Trade Gets 'New Opportunity,'" *USA Today*, February 20, 2008, p. B1.

22. Keith Bradsher, "China Files W.T.O. Case Against Europe," *New York Times*, November 5, 2012, **http://www.nytimes.com/2012/11/06/business/global/china-retaliates-in-trade-dispute-with-europe.html?_r=0** (accessed January 7, 2013).

23. Julie Bennett, "Product Pitfalls Proliferate in Global Cultural Maze," *Wall Street Journal*, May 14, 2001, p. B11.

24. Greg Botelho, "2003 Global Influentials: Selling to the World," CNN, December 9, 2003, **www.cnn.com**.

25. Slogans Gone Bad, **www.joe-ks.com/archives_apr2004/slogans_gone_bad.htm** (accessed June 6, 2006).

26. David Ricks, *Blunders in International Business*, 4th ed. (Malden, MA: Blackwell Publishing, 2006), p. 70. Downloaded from Google Books, **http://books.google.com/books?id=S4L3ntwgs-8C&pg=PA68&lpg=PA68&dq=Mountain+Bell+company,+Saudi+advertisement&source=bl&ots=9apNX6s3hy&sig=Z5BEVaLe4-2p39kNYMlBd5sOX-GA&hl=en&ei=XJGFS6rfNpPKsAODk5zEDw&sa=X&oi=book_result&ct=result&resnum=5&ved=0CBcQ6AEwBA#v=onepage&q=airline&f=false** (accessed February 24, 2010).

27. J. Bonasia, "For Web, Global Reach Is Beauty—and Challenge," *Investor's Business Daily*, June 13, 2001, p. A6.

28. Matthew Wilkins, "Dell Retakes Second Rank in Global PC Market as Acer Stumbles," iSuppli, September 2, 2010, **www.isuppli.com/Home-and-Consumer-Electronics/News/Pages/Dell-Retakes-Second-Rank-in-Global-PC-Market-as-Acer-Stumbles.aspx** (accessed January 10, 2011).

29. "Our Approach, Sanergy, **http://saner.gy/ourapproach/** (accessed October 20, 2011); Patrick Clark, "Innovator: Cleaning Up," *BusinessWeek*, October 12, 2011, **www.businessweek.com/magazine/cleaning-up-david-auerbachs-sanergy-10132011.html** (accessed October 20, 2011); Jennifer Chu, "Waste-Conversion Startup Sanergy Bowls over Competition," *MITNews* online, May 12, 2011, **http://web.mit.edu/newsoffice/2011/100k-competition-0512.html** (accessed October 20, 2011).

30. "World trade talks end in collapse," BBC News, July 29, 2008, **http://news.bbc.co.uk/go/pr/fr/-/2/hi/business/7531099.stm**.

31. "What Is the WTO," World Trade Organization (n.d.), **www.wto.org** (accessed February 25, 2004).

32. Matthew Dalton, "Beijing Sparks Ire of WTO over Curbs," *Wall Street Journal*, July 6, 2011, A9.

33. *CIA—The World Factbook*, **https://www.cia.gov/library/publications/the-world-factbook/geos/us.html**.

34. "Trade in Goods (Imports, Exports and Trade Balance) with Canada," U.S. Census Bureau, **www.census.gov/foreign-trade/balance/c1220.html** (accessed February 24, 2010); "North America: Canada," *CIA—World Factbook*, **https://www.cia.gov/library/publications/the-world-factbook/geos/ca.html** (accessed February 24, 2010).

35. "America's Biggest Partners," CNBC.com, **www.cnbc.com/ id/31064179?slide=11** (accessed February 24, 2010).

36. "North America: Mexico," *CIA World Factbook,* **https://www. cia.gov/library/publications/the-world-factbook/geos/ mx.html** (February 24, 2010); International Monetary Fund, **www.imf.org/external/pubs/ft/weo/2010/02/weodata/ weorept.aspx?sy=2008&ey=2015&scsm=1&ssd=1&sort=c ountry&ds=.&br=1&c=273&s=PPPGDP%2CPPPPC&grp= 0&a=&pr.x=67&pr.y=136** (accessed January 10, 2011).

37. "Country Comparison: GDP (purchasing power parity)," *CIA—World Factbook,* **https://www.cia.gov/library/ publications/the-world-factbook/rankorder/2001rank. html?countryName=United%20States&countryCode=us& regionCode=na&rank=2#us** (accessed February 3, 2010).

38. "A Tale of Two Mexicos: North and South," *The Economist,* April 26, 2008, pp. 53–54.

39. Pete Engardio and Geri Smith, "Business Is Standing Its Ground," *BusinessWeek,* April 20, 2009, pp. 34–39.

40. "Europe in 12 Lessons," the official EU website, **http://europa. eu/abc/12lessons/lesson_2/index_en.htm** (accessed June 7, 2007).

41. Herman Van Rompuy, "Europe in the New Global Game," *The Economist: The World in 2011 Special Edition,* 97; "European countries," Europa, **http://europa.eu/abc/european_countries/ candidate_countries/index_en.htm** (accessed March 18, 2011).

42. Stanley Reed, with Ariane Sains, David Fairlamb, and Carol Matlack, "The Euro: How Damaging a Hit?" *BusinessWeek,* September 29, 2003, p. 63; "The Single Currency," CNN (n.d.), **www.cnn.com/SPECIALS/2000/eurounion/story/currency/** (accessed July 3, 2001).

43. Stephen Fidler and Jacob Bunge, "NYSE Deal Nears Collapse," *Wall Street Journal,* January 11, 2012, A1, A9.

44. Abigail Moses, "Greek Contagion Concern Spurs European Sovereign Default Risk to Record," *Bloomberg,* April 26, 2010, **www.bloomberg.com/news/2010-04-26/greek-contagion- concern-spurs-european-sovereign-default-risk-to-record. html** (accessed March 18, 2011).

45. James G. Neuger and Joe Brennan, "Ireland Weighs Aid as EU Spars Over Debt-Crisis Remedy," *Bloomberg,* **www.bloomberg. com/news/2010-11-16/ireland-discusses-financial-bailout- as-eu-struggles-to-defuse-debt-crisis.html** (accessed March 18, 2011).

46. Charles Forelle and Marcus Walker, "Dithering at the Top Turned EU Crisis to Global Threat," *Wall Street Journal,* December 29, 2011 A1; Jeff Cox, "US, Europe Face More Ratings Cuts in Coming Years," CNBC, January 20, 2012, **www.cnbc.com/ id/46072354?source=google%7Ceditorspicks%7C&par= google** (accessed January 20, 2012); Charles Forelle, "Greece Defaults and Tries to Move On," *Wall Street Journal,* March 10, 2012, **http://online.wsj.com/article/SB10001424052970204 6030045772705426250535960.html** (accessed July 19, 2012).

47. David Gauthier-Villars, "Europe Hit by Downgrades," *Wall Street Journal,* January 14, 2012, **http://online.wsj.com/article/ SB10001424052970204542404577158561838264378.html** (accessed February 1, 2012).

48. "Powerhouse Deutschland," *Bloomberg Businessweek,* January 3, 2011, 93; Alan S. Blinder, "The Euro Zone's German Crisis," *Wall Street Journal,* **http://online.wsj.com/article/SB100014**

24052970203430404577094313707190708.html (accessed January 20, 2012).

49. Gauthier-Villars, "Europe Hit by Downgrades."

50. "About APEC," Asia-Pacific Economic Cooperation, **www.apec. org/apec/about_apec.html** (accessed February 25, 2010).

51. Smith and Lindblad, "Mexico: Was NAFTA Worth It?"

52. "China Economic Growth Accelerates," BBC News, October 22, 2009, **http://news.bbc.co.uk/2/hi/business/8319706.stm** (accessed February 25, 2010).

53. James T. Areddy, James Hookway, John Lyons, and Marcus Walker, "U.S. Slump Takes Toll Across Globe," *Wall Street Journal,* April 3, 2008, p. A1; Pam Woodall, "The New Champions," *The Economist,* November 15, 2008, p. 55; Matt Jenkins, "A Really Inconvenient Truth," *Miller-McCune,* April/May 2008, p. 42.

54. "The Rise of Capitalism," *The Economist,* January 21, 2012, 11.

55. Elizabeth Holmes, "U.S. Apparel Retailers Turn Their Gaze Beyond China," *Wall Street Journal,* June 16, 2010, B1.

56. "Overview," Association of Southeast Asian Nations, **www. aseansec.org/64.htm** (accessed January 23, 2012).

57. Wang Yan, "ASEAN Works to 'Act as Unison' on Global Stage," *China Daily,* November 19, 2011, **www.chinadaily.com.cn/ cndy/2011-11/19/** content_14122972.htm (accessed January 27, 2012).

58. ASEAN website, **www.aseansec.org/** (accessed January 23, 2012)

59. "Common Effective Preferential Tariff (CEPT)," The Malaysia Government's Official Portal, **www.malaysia.gov.my/EN/Rele vant%20Topics/IndustryInMalaysia/Business/Business AndEBusiness/BusinessAndAgreement/CEPT/Pages/ CEPT.aspx** (accessed January 23, 2012).

60. R.C., "No Brussels Sprouts in Bali," The Economist, November 18, 2011, **www.economist.com/blogs/banyan/2011/11/asean- summits** (accessed January 23, 2012).

61. Kathy Quiano, "ASEAN Summit Starts amid Cloud of Thai- Cambodia Border Row," CNN, May 7, 2011, **http://articles. cnn.com/2011-05-07/world/asia.asean.summit_1_asean- leaders-asean-summit-southeast-asian-nations?_ s=PM:WORLD** (accessed January 23, 2012).

62. Eric Bellman, "Asia Seeks Integration Despite EU's Woes," *Wall Street Journal,* July 22, 2011, A9

63. Lauren Pollock, "Starbucks Adds Division Focused on Asia," *Wall Street Journal,* July 11, 2011, **http://online.wsj.com/ article/SB100014240527023036787045764402927124816 16.html** (accessed July 15, 2011); Matt Hodges, "Schultz Brews Up Major Push in China," *China Daily,* June 10–11, 2011, 5; "Starbucks Company Profile," **http://assets.starbucks.com/ assets/aboutuscompanyprofileq12011final13111.pdf** (accessed July 15, 2011); Mariko Sanchanta, "Starbucks Plans Big Expansion in China," *Wall Street Journal,* April 14, 2010, B10; "Asia Pacific," Starbucks Newsroom, **http://news.starbucks. com/about+starbucks/starbucks+coffee+international/ asia+pacific/** (accessed July 19, 2011); David Teather, "Starbucks Legend Delivers Recovery by Thinking Smaller," *The Guardian,* January 21, 2010, **www.guardian.co.uk/business/2010/jan/21/ starbucks-howard-schultz** (accessed July 19, 2011); "How Starbucks Colonised the World," *Sunday Times,* February 17, 2008, **http://business.timesonline.co.uk/tol/business/industry_ sectors/leisure/article3381092.ece** (accessed July 19, 2011);

"Greater China," Starbucks Newsroom, **http://news.starbucks. com/about+starbucks/starbucks+coffee+international/ greater+china** (accessed July 19, 2011); Laurie burkitt. (2016). WSJ. Retrieved 29 July, 2016, from http://www.wsj.com/articles/ starbucks-plans-thousands-of-new-stores-in-china-1452580905 In-text citation: (Laurie burkitt, 2016).

64. David J. Lynch, "The IMF Is . . . Tired Fund Struggles to Reinvent Itself," *USA Today*, April 19, 2006. p. B1.

67. Ilan Brat and Paul Kiernan, "Heinz Seeks to Tap Mexico's Taste for Ketchup," *The Wall Street Journal*, November 24, 2009, pp. B1–B2.

68. Canadian Commercial Corporation (n.d) **www.ccc.ca/eng/ home.cfm**.

69. Export Development Canada (n.d.), **www.edc.ca/english/ corporate.htm**.

70. Ben Worthen, "The Crazy World of Outsourcing," *WSJ.com*, February 25, 2008. **http://blogs.wsj.com/biztech/2008/02/25/ the-crazy-world-ofoutsourcing/?mod=relevancy** (accessed May 6, 2008).

71. Nick Heath, "Banks: Offshoring, Not Outsourcing," *BusinessWeek*, March 10, 2009, **www.businessweek.com/globalbiz/content/ mar2009/gb20090310_619247.htm** (accessed February 25, 2010); Coomi Kapoor, "What Now after the Satyam Fraud?" *Asia News Network*, December 1, 2009, **www.asianewsnet.net/news. php?id=3368&sec=3&t=** (accessed February 25, 2010).

72. Barclays Wealth, **www.census.gov/hhes/www/cpstables/ 032009/hhinc/new01_009.htm** (accessed March 3, 2010); Heath, "Banks: Offshoring, Not Outsourcing."

73. Kejal Vyas, "Venezuela's PdVSA Forms Joint Venture With Brazil's Odebrecht," *Wall Street Journal*, September 29, 2011, **http://online.wsj.com/article/BT-CO-20110929-710025. html** (accessed January 24, 2012).

74. Matt O'Sullivan, "Virgin Blue mines fly-in, fly-out boom," *The Sydney Morning Herald*, January 10, 2011, **www.smh. com.au/business/virgin-blue-mines-flyin-flyout-boom- 20110110-19kb3.html** (accessed January 10, 2011); Matt O'Sullivan, "Virgin Blue hooks up with regional Skywest," *The Sydney Morning Herald*, January 11, 2011, **www.smh.com. au/business/virgin-blue-hooks-up-with-regional-skywest- 20110110-19l7d.html** (accessed January 11, 2011).

75. Sharon Silk Carty, "Ford Plans to Park Jaguar, Land Rover with Tata Motors," *USA Today*, March 26, 2008, p. B1.

76. O. C. Ferrell, John Fraedrich, and Linda Ferrell, *Business Ethics*, 6th ed. (Boston: Houghton Mifflin, 2005), pp. 227–30.

77. Canadian Trade Commissioner (n.d.), **http://www.tradecom- missioner.gc.ca/eng/services.jsp**.

78. Bruce Horovitz, "Consumer Products Giant Looks beyond U.S. Borders," *USA Today*, March 18, 2010, pp. B1–B2; Jon Newberry, "Aisles of Opportunity," portfolio.com, April 7, 2010, **www. portfolio.com/companies-executives/2010/04/07/proctor- and-gamble-is-aiming-to-expand-its-marketshare-in-india** (accessed June 12, 2010); Dyan Machan, "Q&A: Procter & Gamble CEO Bob McDonald," *SmartMoney*, May 26, 2010, **www.smartmoney.com/investing/stocks/interview-with- procter-gamble-ceo-bob-mcdonald** (accessed June 12, 2010); Anjali Cordeiro, "P&G Targets India for Expansion Push," *Wall Street Journal*, June 23, 2010, **http://online.wsj.com/article/ NA_WSJ_PUB:SB200014240527487041236045753227519 34618996.html** (accessed August 16, 2010); Lauren Coleman

-Lochner, "Why Procter & Gamble Needs to Shave More Indi- ans," *Bloomberg Businessweek*, June 9, 2011, **www.business- week.com/magazine/content/11_25/b4233021703857.htm** (accessed June 15, 2011).

Chapter 4

1. Jason Freure, "The Long Decline of the Downtown Chap- ters," *The Town Crier*, April 20, 2015, **http://town-crier.ca/ ephemera/the-decline-of-chapters/**.

2. Melissa Dunn, "Are Canadian Bookstores Headed Toward Extinction?" *Metro News*, May 9, 2014, **http://www.metronews. ca/news/canada/2014/05/09/are-we-witnessing-the-death- of-the-canadian-bookstore.html**.

3. Gerrit De Vynck and Stefanie Batcho-Lino, "Indigo CEO Heather Reisman, Sets Sights on U.S Market," *Globe and Mail*, June 29, 2015, **http://www.theglobeandmail.com/report-on- business/indigo-ceo-heather-reisman-sets-sights-on-us- market/article24254756/**.

4. Ibid.

5. "Stride Rite buys Robeez Footwear," *Boston Business Jour- nal*, September 6, 2006, **http://www.bizjournals.com/boston/ stories/2006/09/04/daily12.html**.

6. Maggie Overfelt, "Start-Me-Up: The California Garage," *Fortune Small Business*, July/Aug. 2003, **www.fortune.com/fortune/ smallbusiness/articles/0,15114,475872,00.html**.

7. "1: Digital Artists Agency," *Business 2.0*, April 2004, p. 90.

8. Kiva, "About us," **https://www.kiva.org/about/stats** (accessed February 8, 2016).

9. "Facts & History," Kiva, **www.kiva.org/about/facts** (accessed March 18, 2011); David M. Ewalt, "Low-Dose Capitalism," *Forbes*, November 2, 2009, p. 40; Leena Rao, "Kiva Brings Micro- lending Home to U.S. Entrepreneurs in Need," *TechCrunch*, June 10, 2009, **www.techcrunch.com/2009/06/10/kiva-brings- microlending-home-tous-entrepreneurs-in-need** (accessed December 19, 2009); Peter Greer and Phil Smith, *The Poor Will Be Glad* (Grand Rapids, MI: Zondervan, 2009), pp. 99, 107.

10. "5 Smart Strategies of Super Startups," Kim Shiffman, *PROFIT: Your Guide to Business Success*, July 12, 2007, **http://www.profit guide.com/search?q=Dekalam%20Hire%20Learning%2C**.

11. Frank Condron, "Canada's Young Entrepreneur of the Year, 2012," December 5, 2012, **www.profitguide.com/manage- grow/innovation/canadas-young-entrepreneur-of-the- year-2012-44540**.

12. Josh O'Kane, "As game market gets crowded, Toronto's Uken may have found the sweet spot," *Globe and Mail*, December 10, 2014, **http://www.theglobeandmail.com/report-on-business/ economy/growth/going-up-against-candy-crush/article 22011000/** (accessed April 9, 2015).

13. Daryl-Lynn Carlson, "QuickSnap Invention Clicks . . . ," *Finan- cial Post*, December 11, 2008, **http://www.financialpost.com/ story.html?id=1067682** (accessed September 13, 2010).

14. Linda Tischles, "Join the Circus," *Fast Company*, July 2005, pp. 53–58.

15. "Mike Lazaridis," *PROFIT guide* online, September 1, 2009, **http://www.profitguide.com/article/4359--mike-lazaridis**.

16. Tracey Bochner, "The Case for Having a Partner," *PROFIT Guide*, September 18, 2014, **http://www.profitguide.com/manage-grow/ strategy-operations/the-case-for-having-a-partner-69106**.

17. Rick Spence, "Dragons' Den: The Magic Touch," *PROFITguide*, October 1, 2008, **http://www.profitguide.com/article/4487--dragons-146-den-the-magic-touch**.

18. Alexis Muellner, "Marlins Partners in Dispute, Still Want Rings," *South Florida Business Journal*, February 27, 2004, **www.bizjournals.com/southflorida/stories/2004/03/01/story5.html**.

19. Sissi Wang, "Why You Should Treat Your Business Partnership like a Marriage," *PROFIT Guide*, June 30, 2015, **http://www.profitguide.com/manage-grow/leadership/why-you-should-treat-your-business-partnership-like-a-marriage-84545**.

20. Sabrina Tavernise, "Harrison McCain, 76, King Of the Frozen French Fry," *New York Times*, March 21, 2004, **http://www.nytimes.com/2004/03/21/world/harrison-mccain-76-king-of-the-frozen-french-fry.html**.

21. "How Tim Hortons will take over the world," Dawn Calleja, *The Globe and Mail*, September 23, 2010, **http://www.theglobeandmail.com/report-on-business/rob-magazine/how-tim-hortons-will-take-over-the-world/article1718843/singlepage/**.

22. Chris Griffiths, "When it's time to incorporate your business," *Globe and Mail*, June 12, 2012, **http://www.theglobeandmail.com/report-on-business/small-business/sb-money/when-its-time-to-incorporate-your-business/article4242051/**.

23. The Upside, "Stocks by Market Capitalization – Toronto Stock Exchange", March 6, 2015, **http://www.theupside.ca/list-tsx-stocks-market-capitalization/**.

24. Kevin J. Delaney and Robin Sidel, "Google IPO Aims to Change the Rules," *Wall Street Journal*, April 30, 2004, **http://online.wsj.com**.

25. Lee Spears and Sarah Frier, "Facebook Set for Public Debut After IPO Seals $104 Billion Value," *Bloomberg* online, May 18, 2012, **http://www.bloomberg.com/news/2012-05-18/facebook-set-for-public-debut-after-ipo-seals-104-billion-value.html**; Dave Copeland, "The Only Facebook Number That Matters: $104.2 Billion," *readwrite* online, May 18, 2012, **http://readwrite.com/2012/05/18/the-only-facebook-number-that-matters-1042-billion#awesm=~obB2JI6oRQ7zht**; Natasha Chandel, "Mark Zuckerberg's Big Week: $19 Billion and a Wedding," *MTV News*, **http://www.mtv.com/news/articles/1685452/facebook-mark-zuckerberg-married.jhtml** (all accessed July 14, 2013).

26. Canadian Press, "Spin Master Corp Shares Rise in First Day as a Public Company," *Financial Post*, July 30, 2015, **http://business.financialpost.com/investing/spin-master-corp-shares-rise-in-first-day-as-a-public-company**.

27. Jeff Lagerquist, "Getting in on the Ground Floor: Canada's IPO Winners and Losers," *Business News Network*, June 3, 2015, **http://www.bnn.ca/News/2015/6/3/Getting-in-on-the-ground-floor-Canadas-IPO-winners-and-losers.aspx**.

28. Merissa Marr, "Video Chain CEO to Take Company Private in Buyout," *Wall Street Journal*, March 30, 2004, **http://online.wsj.com**.

29. O. C. Ferrell, John Fraedrich, and Linda Ferrell, *Business Ethics: Ethical Decision Making and Cases*, 6th ed. (Boston: Houghton Mifflin, 2005), p. 84.

30. *"Report to the Congress*: Increased Penalties under the Sarbanes-Oxley Act of 2002," **http://www.ussc.gov/r_congress/s-oreport.pdf**.

31. Matt Krantz, "Web of Board Members Ties Together Corporate America," *USA Today*, November 23, 2002, pp. 1B, 3B.

32. Emily Thornton and Aaron Pressman, "Phil Purcell's Credibility Crisis," *BusinessWeek*, March 21, 2005.

33. Krantz, "Web of Board Members."

34. Thomas Watson, "His way or the highway: Frank Stronach is God's gift to shareholders. Don't believe it? Just ask him," *Canadian Business*, May 23, 2005, **http://www.canadianbusiness.com/managing/strategy/article.jsp?content=20060109_103241_4508**.

35. Sarah Efron, "RBC, Canada's biggest company, has revenue equal to the GDP of Latvia," *FP Magazine Daily*, June 02, 2009, **http://network.nationalpost.com/np/blogs/fpmagazine-daily/archive/2009/06/02/rbc-canada-s-biggest-company-has-revenue-equal-to-the-gdp-of-latvia.aspx**.

36. Eleanor Beaton, "The lure of ESOPs," *PROFITguide*, May 31, 2007, **http://www.profitguide.com/manage-grow/strategy-operations/the-lure-of-esops-29171** (accessed June 20, 2013).

37. Ron Ruggless, "Cold Stone, Tim Hortons expand co-branding," *Nation's Restaurant News*, February 6, 2009; Robin Hilmantel, "Tim Hortons and Cold Stone Will Team Up in 100 Stores," QSR online, **http://www2.qsrmagazine.com/articles/exclusives/0209/timhortons-1.phtml** (accessed July 15, 2013).

38. Francine Kopun, "Tim Hortons Gives Up on Ice Cream", *The Star*, February 20, 2014, **http://www.thestar.com/business/2014/02/20/tim_hortons_gives_up_on_ice_cream.html**.

39. Marina Strauss, "Loblaw's Joe Fresh Hooks Up with J.C. Penney," *Globe and Mail*, July 25, 2012, **http://www.theglobeandmail.com/globe-investor/loblaws-joe-fresh-hooks-up-with-jc-penney/article4439978/** (accessed July 15, 2013).

40. Eric J. Savitz, "Movie Madness," *Barron's*, February 23, 2004, **http://online.wsj.com/barrons/**.

41. Cooperatives in Canada, February 9, 2016 **http://www.cooperativedifference.coop/co-operatives-in-canada/**

42. "What Is Community Supported Agriculture and How Does It Work?" Local Harvest, **www.localharvest.org/csa.jsp** (accessed February 18, 2008); "Community Supported Agriculture at Indian Line Farm," Indian Line Farm, **http://www.indianlinefarm.com/csa.html** (accessed February 25, 2008).

43. "Farmers Offering up Beef in a Can," CNN, March 22, 2004, **www.cnn.com/2004/US/Midwest/03/22/canned.beef.asp**; Him Suhr, "Farmers Form Canned-Beef Co-op," *Courier-Journal*, March 28, 2004, **www.courier-journal.com/business/news2004/03/28/E7-beefcan28-4323.html**; Jim Suhr, "Livestock Farmer Hopes Canned Beef Will Catch On," *The Fort Collins Coloradoan*, March 28, 2004, p. E2; Erica Coble, "Trading on Tradition," March 2005, **www.rurdev.usda.gov/rbs/pub/mar05/value.htm** (accessed March 1, 2006); **www.heartlandfarmfoods.com;www.heartlandfarmfoods.com/Company.htm**; **www.heartlandfarmfoods.com/Catalog_Page%201.htm**; **www.heartlandfarmfoods.com/Producers.htm** (all accessed March 1, 2006).

44. Jamie Sturgeon, "It's Official, Tim Hortons, Burger King Become One," Global News, December 12, 2014, **http://globalnews.ca/news/1724238/its-official-tim-hortons-burger-king-become-one/**.

45. Devin Leonard, "How Disney Bought Lucasfilm—and Its Plans for 'Star Wars,'" *Bloomberg Businessweek*, March 7, 2013, **http://www.businessweek.com/articles/2013-03-07/how-disney-bought-lucasfilm-and-its-plans-for-star-wars** (accessed July 15, 2013).

46. Dirk Libby, "How Often Disney Is Planning to Release Star Wars Movies".*CinemaBLEND*, December 12, 2015, **http://www.cinemablend.com/new/How-Often-Disney-Planning-Release-Star-Wars-Movies-94987.html**

47. Grant Robertson, "With Ally Assets, RBC Becomes Top Player in Auto Financing," *Globe and Mail*, February 20, 2013, **http://www.theglobeandmail.com/globe-investor/with-ally-assets-rbc-becomes-top-player-in-auto-financing/article4630654/?service=mobile** (accessed July 15, 2013).

48. "TD Pays $6B for Target's Retail Credit Card Unit," CBC News, October 23, 2012, **http://www.cbc.ca/news/business/story/2012/10/23/td-target.html** (accessed July 15, 2013).

49. "Scotiabank Completes the Acquisition of ING Direct Canada," Scotiabank website, **http://www.scotiabank.com/ca/en/0,,5504,00.html** (accessed July 15, 2013).

50. "CRTC Rejects Bell-Astral Merger," *The Canadia Business Journal* online, October 18, 2012, **http://www.cbj.ca/business_news/canadian_business_news/crtc_rejects_bell-astral_merger.html** (accessed July 15, 2013).

51. Derek DeCloet, "Canadians should stop worrying about foreign takeovers," *Globe and Mail*, August 29, 2012, **http://www.theglobeandmail.com/report-on-business/rob-magazine/canadians-should-stop-worrying-about-foreign-takeovers/article4507568/** (accessed June 20, 2013).

52. Phil Wahba, "Lowe's $2.3 Billion Bid for Rona Sets off Political Firestorm in Canada," *Fortune*, February 3, 2016, **http://fortune.com/2016/02/03/lowes-rona-quebec/**.

53. Peter Bright, "Microsoft Buys Skype for 8.5 Billion. Why, Exactly?" *Wired*, May 10, 2011, **http://www.wired.com/2011/05/microsoft-buys-skype-2/all/1**.

54. "Will Your PC Kill the Video Store?: Blockbuster sizes up online movie rentals and adopts the advantages for its own service," Liane Cassavoy, *PCWorld*, Mar 10, 2004, **http://www.pcworld.com/article/115160/will_your_pc_kill_the_video_store.html**.

55. "Aventis Accepts Higher, Friendly Sanofi Bid," Dow Jones Newswire, April 26, 2004, via *The Wall Street Journal*, **http://online.wsj.com**.

56. J. Connelly, "Premier Brad Wall Warns of Potash Hostile Takeover," *Business Review Canada* online, October 25, 2010, **http://www.businessreviewcanada.ca/sectors/premier-brad-wall-warns-potash-hostile-takeover** (accessed July 15, 2013).

57. Shawn McCarthy and Steven Chase, "Ottawa Approves Nexen, Progress Foreign Takeovers," *Globe and Mail*, December 7, 2012, http://www.theglobeandmail.com/globe-investor/ottawa-approves-nexen-progress-foreign-takeovers/article6107548/ (accessed July 15, 2013).

58. David Aiken, "Feds Wrestle with China's Oilsands Takeover," *Toronto Sun*, August 8, 2012, **http://www.torontosun.com/2012/08/08/feds-wrestle-with-chinas-oilsands-takeover**; Aaron Wherry, "Harper Government Approves CNOOC and Petronas Deals," *Maclean's*, December 7, 2012, **http://www2.macleans.ca/2012/12/07/harper-government-approves-cnooc-and-petronas-deals/** (accessed July 15, 2013).

Chapter 5

1. Brainy Quote website, **http://www.brainyquote.com/quotes/authors/k/kevin_oleary_2.html#CSEhoaluBliJ8UOU.99** (accessed June 24, 2013).

2. Brainy Quote website, **http://www.brainyquote.com/quotes/authors/k/kevin_oleary.html#2MjRIMbVCJPyESK8.99** (accessed June 24, 2013).

3. "Speaking Points—The Honourable Tony Clement, PC, MP, Minister of Industry—Business Development Bank of Canada Funding Announcement," Industry Canada website, June 15, 2009, **http://www.ic.gc.ca/eic/site/ic1.nsf/eng/04758.html**.

4. Ian Portsmouth (Ed.), *Profit*, March 2013, **http://www.pdfmagazines.org/magazines/business/44338-profit-march-2013.html**.

5. "The Power of Innovation," *Inc. State of Small Business*, 23, no. 7 (2001), p. 103.

6. Scott Allen, "Entrepreneur Success Story: Brian Scudamore of 1-800-GOT-JUNK?", **About.com***: Entrepreneurs*, **http://entrepreneurs.about.com/od/casestudies/a/1800gotjunk.htm** (accessed July 17, 2010).

7. Robert D. Hisrich, Michael P. Peters, Dean A. Shepherd, and Peter Mombourquette, *Entrepreneurship* (2nd Canadian edition), (Toronto: McGraw-Hill Ryerson Ltd., 2009), p. 75.

8. "U of T student named 2010 Student Entrepreneur Ontario Champion," ACE, February 17, 2010, **http://www.acecanada.ca/news/newsItem.cfm?cms_news_id=372**.

9. Tony Martin, "Profit Hot 50: Simple ways to sell more," *PROFITguide*, September 1, 2009, **http://www.profitguide.com/article/4360--profit-hot-50-simple-ways-to-sell-more**.

10. "Survey on Financing of Small and Medium Enterprises," Statistics Canada, March 11, 2009, **http://www.statcan.gc.ca/cgi-bin/imdb/p2SV.pl?Function=getSurvey&SDDS=2941&lang=en&id=imdb&adm=8&dis=2**.

11. Canadian Federation of Independent Business, **www.cfib.ca/** (accessed July 17, 2010).

12. "Key Small Business Statistics," Industry Canada: Small Business and Tourism Branch, July 2009, **https://www.safec.ca/userfiles/file/%C3%89tudes%20indicateurs%20%C3%A9conomiques/%C3%89tudes%202009%20AN/Key%20Small%20Business%20Statistics%20-%20July%202009.pdf**.

13. Exportsavvy International Projects Development for Medium and Small Business, Export Development, **http://www.exportsavvy.com/** (accessed July 17, 2010).

14. Yves Robichaud, Jean-Charles Cachon, and Rana Haq, "Motives, Success Factors, and Barriers among Canadian Female Entrepreneurs: The Case of Greater Sudbury," *Entrepreneurial Practice Review* 1(2), winter 2010, **http://www.entryerson.com/epr/index.php/jep/article/viewFile/49/27**.

15. "Sleep Country Canada gets $356M takeover offer," *Toronto Star*, August 14, 2008, **http://www.thestar.com/article/478312**.

16. "FAQs: Frequently Asked Questions," U.S. Small Business Administration, **http://web.sba.gov/faqs/faqIndexAll.cfm?areaid=24** (accessed June 1, 2006).

17. Row House Publishing Services, **http://rhps.ca/** (accessed July 17, 2010).

18. "Innovation in Large and Small Firms," Zoltan J. Acs and David B. Andretsch, *The American Economic Review* © 1988 **http://www.jstor.org/action/showPublisher?publisherCode=aea%**, p. 678.

19. Murad Hemmadi, "Why Canada's Fastest-Growing Company Keeps Innovating in Tough Times," *Profit Guide*, September 17, 2015, **http://www.profitguide.com/manage-grow/innovation/**

why-canadas-fastest-growing-company-keeps-innovating-in-tough-times-90295.

20. Hisrich, Peters, Shepherd, Mombourquette, *Entrepreneurship*, pp. 57–58; Margot Hornblower, "In a Hurry to Prove the 'Pistonheads' Wrong," *TIME* magazine, March 8, 1999, **www.time.com/time/reports/environment/heroes/heroesgallery/0,2967,ballard,00.html**; and Leonard Brody and David Raffa, *Everything I Needed to Know about Business...I Learned from a Canadian* (Toronto: John Wiley & Sons Canada Ltd., 2005), p. 14.

21. Diane Disse, "The Birth of IMAX," **http://www.ieee.ca/millennium/imax/imax_birth.html** (accessed July 17, 2010).

22. Trevor Melanson, "Is HootSuite Canada's Next Billion-Dollar Tech Titan?", *Canadian Business*, Winter 2012/13, **http://www.canadianbusiness.com/technology-news/is-hootsuite-canadas-next-tech-titan/**.

23. Ron Joyce, *Always Fresh: The Untold Story of Tim Hortons by the Man Who Created a Canadian Empire* (Toronto: Harper Collins Publishers Ltd., 2006).

24. Beth Carney, "Dyson Magic Carpet Ride," *BusinessWeek*, April 1, 2005, **www.businessweek.com/bwdaily/dnflash/apr2005/nf2005041_8000_db016.htm?campaign_id=search** (accessed June 3, 2006); Dyson Official Site, **www.dyson.com/** and **www.dyson.com/nav/inpageframe.asp?id=DYSON/HIST/MUSEUMS** (accessed June 3, 2006).

25. eBay, "2015 Entrepreneur of the year award, WINNERS, 2015," **https://eoy.ebaypromotion.ca/winners.html**.

26. Jerry Langton, "Canine couture," *Toronto Star*, November 17, 2008, **http://www.thestar.com/Business/SmallBusiness/article/538014**.

27. Douglas Quenqua, "To Create Its Hits, a Company Takes Its Toys on Tour," *New York Times*, June 9, 2008, **http://www.nytimes.com/2008/06/09/business/media/09spin.html**.

28. Ibid.

29. Peter Svensson, "U.S. Economy Grows at a Slower Pace," *Washington Post*, June 5, 2006, **www.washingtonpost.com/wp-dyn/content/article/2006/06/05/AR2006060500376.html** (accessed June 5, 2006).

30. Jim McElgunn, "Canada's Fastest-Growing Companies," *PROFITguide*, June 1, 2011, **http://www.profitguide.com/opportunity/canadas-fastest-growing-companies-3-30175** (accessed July 15, 2013).

31. "22nd Annual Profit 100: Canada's Fastest-Growing Companies," *PROFITguide*, **http://www.profitguide.com/awards/profit100** (accessed July 17, 2010); "Profit Hot 50," *Canadian Business*, 2009, **http://list.canadianbusiness.com/rankings/hot50/2009/include/PROFIT_HOT_50_2009.xls** (accessed July 17, 2010).

32. Jerry Langton, "Saving people drowning in debt," *Toronto Star*, January 19, 2009, **http://www.thestar.com/business/smallbusiness/article/573203**.

33. "Profit Hot 50," *Canadian Business*, 2009, **http://list.canadianbusiness.com/rankings/hot50/2009/include/PROFIT_HOT_50_2009.xls** (accessed July 17, 2010).

34. "21st Annual Profit 100: Canada's Fastest-Growing Companies," *Canadian Business*, **http://list.canadianbusiness.com/rankings/profit100/2009/Default.aspx?sc1=1&d1=a&sp2=1&ech=ch** (accessed July 17, 2010).

35. XMG website, "About," **http://www.xmg.com/about/** (accessed June 24, 2013).

36. "Dell at a Glance" (n.d.), Dell, **www1.us.dell.com/content/topics/global.aspx/corp/background/en/facts?c=us&l=en&s=corp&section=000&ck=mn** (accessed May 4, 2004); **www.hoouess.com/dell/--ID_13193-/free-co-factsheet.xhtml** (accessed June 5, 2006).

37. "The Evolution of Apple...," October 10, 1995, **http://www2.cs.uregina.ca/~rbm/cs100/timeline.html**.

38. Robin Wauters, "Disney Online Buys Kaboose Assets for $18.4 Million," *TechCrunch*, April 2009, **http://techcrunch.com/2009/04/01/disney-online-buys-kaboose-assets-for-184-million/** (accessed September 20, 2010).

39. "Small Business Statistics" (n.d.), Small Business Administration, **www.sba.gov/aboutsba/sbastats.html** (accessed March 16, 2004).

40. "Skoll Foundation," *Wikipedia* website, **http://en.wikipedia.org/wiki/Skoll_Foundation** (accessed July 18, 2013).

41. Elisa Birnbaum, "Investing in the Non-Profit Sector: The Social Impact Bond Makes Its Canadian Debut," *Charity Village*, November 5, 2014, **https://charityvillage.com/Content.aspx?topic=Investing_in_the_nonprofit_sector_The_Social_Impact_Bond_makes_its_Canadian_debut**.

42. Ontario, "Social Impact Bonds", February 8, 2016, **https://www.ontario.ca/page/social-impact-bonds#section-0**

43. **http://www.avisonyoung.com/Our_Professionals/Halifax/Bio/MacDonald~Kenzie/**.

44. Andrea Gordon, "Mompreneurs boom," *Toronto Star*, April 4, 2008, **http://www.thestar.com/article/409934**.

45. Colin MacDonald, guest speaker, Mount Saint Vincent University's 35th Annual Business and Tourism Conference, October 2009, Halifax, NS.

46. "Entrepreneur Success Story," Canadian Youth Business Foundation, September 2009, **http://www.cybf.ca/story-gallery/success-stories/bc/Rocky%20Point%20Kayak.pdf**.

47. Andy Holloway, "Problem Solvers: To boldly grow ..., carefully, that is," *Profit*, **http://list.canadianbusiness.com/rankings/profit100/2009/growth/article.aspx?id=20090601_30010_30010** (accessed July 18, 2010).

48. Kym Wolfe, "The Sound of Success," *Alumni Gazette* (University of Western Ontario), September 7, 2010, **http://communications.uwo.ca/com/alumni_gazette/alumni_gazetteprofiles/the_sound_of_success_20100907446732/**.

49. Laura Pratt, "PROFIT HOT 50: Safer Passage," *PROFIT*, October 2009, p. 36.

50. Ibid.

51. Dana Knight, "Big Headed Guy Gets a Big Idea for Sunglasses Business," *USA Today*, March 21, 2006, p. 4B; Fatheadz Eyewear, **www.fatheadz.com** (accessed June 5, 2006).

52. "CEO Michael Gokturk interviewed on BNN," VersaPay, January 27, 2010, **http://www.versapay.com/video/ceo-mike-gokturk-interviewed-on-bnn/**; Jennifer Myers, "The Little Shop with a Big Friend," *PROFIT*, October 2009, pp. 28–30.

53. "Burpee Seeds and Plants," **http://www.burpee.com/** (accessed July 17, 2010).

54. RBC Study, as reported in *Business Research Newsletter*, February 2005, p. 5.

55. *Small Business Quarterly*, Statistics Canada, August 2010.

56. Brandon Turner, "Why I quit my own business to work with someone else," *Globe and Mail*, February 27, 2015, **http://www.theglobeandmail.com/report-on-business/small-business/sb-tools/sb-how-to/why-i-quit-my-own-busines-to-work-for-someone-else/article23210898/** (accessed March 17, 2015).

57. Ambareen Musa, "Six things they don't tell you when you start your own business," *Globe and Mail*, January 30, 2015, **http://www.theglobeandmail.com/report-on-business/small-business/sb-tools/sb-how-to/six-things-they-dont-tell-you-when-you-leave-the-corporate-world-to-start-your-own-business/article22829151/** (accessed April 2, 2015).

58. Interview with entrepreneur Chris Neville, December 24th, 2015.

59. "You're Not the Boss of Me Now," *Weekend Today*, October 21, 2005, **www.msnbc.msn.com/id/9762771/** (accessed June 5, 2006).

60. "Small Business Resource," **www.2-small-business.com** (accessed June 5, 2006).

61. Peter Mombourquette, May 2010, interview with Dan Young.

62. Hisrich, Peters, Shepherd, Mombourquette, *Entrepreneurship*, p. 542.

63. Hisrich, Peters, Shepherd, Mombourquette, *Entrepreneurship*, p. 543; Jennifer Myers, "To Boldly Grow," *PROFITguide*, October/November 2003, **www.profitguide.com/w100/2003/article.asp?ID=1276&p.=1**.

64. "The man with the Midas touch," Jennifer Myers, *Profit*, April 2005, **http://www.canadianbusiness.com/entrepreneur/managing/article.jsp?content=20050407_004729_4968&page=3** (accessed July 18, 2010).

65. Rodney Tanake, "Clothier a Favorite of Vegans, PETA Honors Pasadena 'Animal-Friendly' Firm," *Pasadena Star-News*, **www.pasadenastarnews.com/** (accessed January 14, 2006); "About Us," Alternative Outfitters, **www.alternativeoutfitters.com/index.asp?PageAction=COMPANY**; "Alternative Outfitters News," **www.alternativeoutfitters.com/index.asp?PageAction=Custom&ID=10**; "Pasadena-based Alternative Outfitters Wins Second Straight National PETA Award," **www.alternativeoutfitters.com/index.asp?PageAction=Custom&ID=45**; "The 2005 Veggie Awards," **www.vegnews.com/veggieawards_2005.html** (all accessed January 12, 2006).

66. Centre for Entrepreneurship, Education & Development, **http://www.ceed.ca/default.asp?id=190&pagesize=1&sfield=content.id&search=919&mn=1.212.256.305** (accessed July 18, 2010).

67. Wency Leung, "Kimchi on Wheels: Food Truck Trend Gears Up In Canada," *The Globe and Mail*, June 14, 2011, **http://www.theglobeandmail.com/life/food-and-wine/food-trends/kimchi-on-wheels-food-truck-trend-gears-up-in-canada/article4261217/** (accessed June 24, 2013).

68. Kim Hart Macneill, "An Apple for the Tutor," *PROFITguide*, February 11, 2013, **http://www.profitguide.com/opportunity/an-apple-for-the-tutor-48089** (accessed June 24, 2013).

69. Nova Scotia Business Inc., **http://www.nsbi.ca/next/kiru.shtml** (accessed July 18, 2010).

70. "Parsel.Me", *Crunch Base Inc.*, 2016 **https://www.crunchbase.com/organization/parsel#/entity**

71. Jason Tchir, "Toronto startup helps YouTube and Instagram stars make money," *Globe and Mail*, January 21, 2016, **http://www.theglobeandmail.com/report-on-business/small-business/startups/toronto-startup-helps-youtube-and-instagram-stars-make-money/article27921680/**.

72. Parsel, "About Me," 2014, **http://creators.parsel.me/about**.

73. Tchir, "Toronto startup helps YouTube and Instagram stars make money."

74. Adapted from Carol Kinsey Gorman, *Creativity in Business: A Practical Guide for Creative Thinking*, Crisp Publications Inc., 1989, pp. 5–6. © Crisp Publications Inc., 1200 Hamilton Court, Menlo Park, CA 94025.

75. Nitasha Tiku, "Making the Most of a Brush with Fame," *Inc.*, August 2007, p. 19; Recycline, **http://www.recycline.com/** (accessed May 4, 2008); "Recycline: Sitting on Mainstream's Doorstep," Sustainable Is Good, **http://www.sustainableisgood.com/blog/2007/03/recycline_produ.html** (accessed May 4, 2008).

76. Kasey Wehrum, "How EcoScraps Turns Trash into Treasure," *Inc.*, May 2011, p. 93; Jennifer Alsever, "EcoScraps' $1 Million Business Built on Trash," CNNMoney, September 27, 2011, **http://money.cnn.com/2011/09/23/smallbusiness/ecoscraps/index.htm** (accessed October 11, 2011); EcoScraps website, **http://ecoscraps.net/** (accessed October 11, 2011).

77. Patrick Maloney, "Make your banker say yes," *PROFITguide*, November 7, 2001, **www.profitguide.com/maximize/article.jsp?content=694**.

78. **http://www.bostonpizza.com/en/about/PressKit.aspx** (accessed July 18, 2010).

79. Hisrich, Peters, Shepherd, Mombourquette, *Entrepreneurship*, p. 381; "Ask the Legends," *PROFIT*, March 2008, p. 72.

80. Rebecca Gardiner, "PROFIT 100 Fundraising Secrets," *Canadian Business*, May 12, 2005, **http://www.canadianbusiness.com/entrepreneur/financing/article.jsp?content=20050511_120413_4152**.

81. Ibid.

82. Rick Spence, "Sweetpea Baby Food: Stuck in the middle," *Profit*, October 2007, **http://www.canadianbusiness.com/entrepreneur/sales_marketing/article.jsp?content=20071002_12233_122337**.

83. Hisrich, Peters, Shepherd, Mombourquette, *Entrepreneurship*, pp. 397–398.

84. Alex Halperin, "A Virtual World Targets Teens," *BusinessWeek*, May 15, 2006, **www.businessweek.com/technology/content/may2006/tc20060515_945235.htm?campaign_id=search** (accessed June 5, 2006).

85. "The Success of Crowdfunding," The Brooklyn Warehouse website, February 26, 2013, **http://brooklynwarehouse.ca/theblog/2013/2/26/the-success-of-crowdfunding** (accessed July 15, 2013).

86. "Stats," Kickstarter, February 4, 2016, **https://www.kickstarter.com/help/stats**.

87. Massolutions "2015 CF The Crowdfunding Industry Report," *Crowdsourcing*, 2015, **http://www.crowdsourcing.org/editorial/global-crowdfunding-market-to-reach-344b-in-2015-predicts-massolutions-2015cf-industry-report/45376**.

88. Paul Hayward, "New 'Start-up' Crowdfunding Exemptions Adopted in Some Canadian Jurisdictions," National Crowdfunding

Association of Canada, June 5, 2015, **http://ncfacanada.org/new-start-up-crowdfunding-exemptions-adopted-in-some-canadian-jurisdictions/**.

89. Kerry Gold, "Dragons' Den success stories," MSN, December 7, 2009, **http://money.ca.msn.com/small-business/gallery/gallery.aspx?cp-documentid=22789615&page=1**; Rick Spence, "Dragons' Den: The magic touch," *PROFITguide* online, October 1, 2008, **http://www.profitguide.com/article/4487--dragons-146-den-the-magic-touch**.

90. Hisrich, Peters, Shepherd, Mombourquette, *Entrepreneurship*, pp. 397–398; Outpost, **www.outpostmagazine.com**; W.S. Good, *Building a Dream* (6th ed.) (Toronto: McGraw-Hill Ryerson Ltd., 2005), p. 277.

91. Hisrich, Peters, Shepherd, Mombourquette, *Entrepreneurship*, p. 372.

92. Douglas How and Ralph Costello, *K.C.: The Biography of K.C. Irving* (Toronto: Key Porter Books Ltd., 1993).

93. Hisrich, Peters, Shepherd, Mombourquette, *Entrepreneurship*, pp. 589, 592; Susanne Ruder, "A Tale of Two Brothers," *PROFIT*, March 2007.

94. Hayward, "New 'Start-up' Crowdfunding Exemptions Adopted in Some Canadian Jurisdictions."

95. Jessica Galang, "Today in Funding: Snug Vest, Milestone Pharmaceuticals, Lending Loop," Betakit, June 15, 2015, **http://betakit.com/today-in-funding-snug-vest-milestone-pharmaceuticals-lending-loop/**.

96. Thomas W. Zimmerer and Norman M. Scarborough, *Essentials of Entrepreneurship and Small Business Management* (4th ed.) (Upper Saddle River, NJ: Pearson Prentice Hall, 2005), pp. 118–24.

97. Ibid.

98. Peter Mombourquette, March 2010, in-class interview.

99. Adapted from "Tomorrow's Entrepreneur," *Inc. State of Small Business*, 23, no. 7 (2001), pp. 80–104.

100. David K. Foot, *Boom, Bust & Echo: How to profit from the coming demographic shift* (Toronto: Macfarlane Walter & Ross, 1996).

101. Comfort Life, Masterpiece Retirement Communities, **http://www.comfortlife.ca/masterpiece-retirement-communities.php** (accessed July 18, 2010).

102. Melissa Campeau, "Companies Anticipate Business Growth and Skills Shortage," *PROFITguide*, January 10, 2013, **http://www.profitguide.com/news/companies-anticipate-business-growth-and-skills-shortages-in-2013-46839** (accessed July 15, 2013).

103. Foot, *Boom, Bust & Echo*.

104. "Facts about Canada," Business Immigration, **http://www.businessimmigrationtocanada.ca/businessimmigrationcanadaquebecinvestorimmigrationvisa.htm** (accessed July 17, 2010).

105. **http://www.careerbuilder.com/Jobs/Company/C8C0SC719RSDTDZTZP6/Walmart-Field-Operations/** (accessed July 18, 2010).

106. Kevin Swayze, "Cost-cutting ideas shrinking Cambridge hospital's deficit still mostly secret," *Cambridge Reporter*, August 21, 2009, **http://cambridgereporter.com/news/article/185850**.

107. Gifford Pinchott III, *Intrapreneuring* (New York: Harper & Row, 1985), p. 34.

108. Paul Brown, "How to Cope With Hard Times," *New York Times*, June 10, 2008.

109. Hisrich, Peters, Shepherd, Mombourquette, *Entrepreneurship*, pp. 130, 217, 522; "Lija puts a new spin on golfwear," *PROFITguide*, July 28, 2005, **http://www.profitguide.com/article/4406--lija-puts-a-new-spin-on-golfwear**; "Lija by Linda Hipp Named One of British Columbia's 50 Fastest Growing Companies," press release (2004), **www.lijastyle.com/press.html**; Karen VanKampen, "Golfers looking hip, stylish and colourful, too," CanWest News Services, June 21, 2005; Kim Shiffman, "Canada's Fastest Growing Companies," *PROFIT*, June 2005, p. 38; A. Holloway, "The Right Way to Tee Off," *PROFIT* (December/January 2007), p. 69; Hal Quinn, "Lady of Lija," *Canadian Business*, April 25, 2005, **http://www.canadianbusiness.com/managing/article.jsp?content=20050425_66971_66971**.

Chapter 6

1. Brad Stone, "Everybody Needs a Sheryl Sandberg," *Bloomberg Businessweek*, May 16–22, 2011, pp. 50–58; Ken Auletta, "A Woman's Place," *The New Yorker*, July 11, 2011, **www.newyorker.com/reporting/2011/07/11/110711fa_fact_auletta?currentPage51** (accessed August 3, 2011); "Mark E. Zuckerberg," *New York Times*, updated January 3, 2011, **http://topics.nytimes.com/topics/reference/timestopics/people/z/mark_e_zuckerberg/index.html** (accessed August 4, 2011).

2. John Lorinc, "The Golden Goose," *PROFITguide*, October 17, 2012, **http://www.profitguide.com/manage-grow/strategy-operations/the-golden-goose-42172/2**.

3. "Our Mission," Seventh Generation, **www.seventhgeneration.com/seventh-generation-mission** (accessed March 5, 2012).

4. G. Tomas, M. Hult, David W. Cravens, and Jagdish Sheth, "Competitive Advantage in the Global Marketplace: A Focus on Marketing Strategy," *Journal of Business Research* 51 (January 2001), p. 1.

5. "Tim Hortons vows faster service to fend off rivals," UBC Blogs, October 7, 2013, **https://blogs.ubc.ca/melodylin/2013/10/07/tim-hortons-vows-faster-service-to-fend-off-rivals/** (accessed January 10, 2016).

6. Adapted from "Outside in business unit strategy: Summary of the Five Forces Model by Porter," ValueBasedManagement.net, January 6, 2016, **http://www.valuebasedmanagement.net/methods_porter_five_forces.html** (accessed January 10, 2016).

7. "Strategic Planning Tools," Chartered Global Management Accountant website, n.d., **http://www.cgma.org/Resources/Tools/essential-tools/Pages/strategic-planning-tools.aspx** (accessed January 10, 2016).

8. **http://www.quickmba.com/strategy/strategic-planning/**

9. "Strategic Management," *Wikipedia*, **http://en.wikipedia.org/wiki/Strategic_management** (accessed June 25, 2013).

10. Henry Dewing, "Cisco Strategy Evolves and Tactics Mature," *Forrester Blogs*, July 15, 2011, **http://blogs.forrester.com/henry_dewing/11-07-15-cisco_strategy_evolves_and_tactics_mature** (accessed February 17, 2012); Rosabeth Moss Kanter, "Cisco and a Cautionary Tale about Teams," *Harvard Business Review*, May 9, 2011, **http://blogs.hbr.org/kanter/2011/05/cisco-and-a-cautionary-tale-ab.html** (accessed February 17, 2012); Tom Foremski, "Is It Time for Cisco to Ditch Its Councils?" ZD Net, April 14, 2011, **www.**

zdnet.com/blog/foremski/is-it-time-for-cisco-to-ditch-its-councils/1755 (accessed February 17, 2012).

11. Bryan Walsh, "The End of the Line," *Time*, July 18, 2011, pp. 28–34; Marc Gunther, "Barramundi Fulfills Elusive Promise of Sustainable Seafood," *GreenBiz.com*, April 13, 2011, **www.greenbiz.com/blog/2011/04/13/barramundi-fulfills-elusive-promise-sustainable-seafood** (accessed July 27, 2011); "Australis Barramundi—The Sustainable Sea Bass™," *Australis*, **www.thebetterfish.com/about-us** (accessed July 27, 2011).

12. Mariko Yasu, "Panasonic Plans to Eliminate 17,000 Jobs in Reorganization," *Bloomberg Businessweek*, April 28, 2011, **www.businessweek.com/news/2011-04-28/panasonic-plans-to-eliminate-17-000-jobs-in-reorganization.html** (accessed March 5, 2012).

13. "Adecco Listed as Largest Staffing Firm in Canada by Staffing Industry Analysts," news release, August 12, 2013, **http://www.newswire.ca/news-releases/adecco-listed-as-largest-staffing-firm-in-canada-by-staffing-industry-analysts-512793531.html** (accessed January 10, 2016).

14. C. O. Trevor, and A. J. Nyberg. "Keeping Your Headcount When All About You Are Losing Theirs: Downsizing, Voluntary Turnover Rates, and the Moderating Role of HR Practices," *Academy of Management Journal* 51 (2008), pp. 259–76.

15. Jennifer Wang, "Patagonia, from the Ground Up," *Entrepreneur*, June 2010, pp. 24–32; "A Little Enlightened Self- Interest," Inc., June 2010, pp. 56–60; **www.patagonia.com** (accessed August 1, 2010); Jennifer Wang, "Patagonia Founder Yvon Chouinard on His Latest Social Venture," *Entrepreneur*, May 2011, **www.entrepreneur.com/article/219457** (accessed June 18, 2011).

16. **www.conferenceboard.ca/CPO/membership.asp** (accessed August 25, 2009).

17. "CEOs power lunch on average Canadian wage: study," Canadian Centre for Policy Alternatives, January 4, 2016, **https://www.policyalternatives.ca/newsroom/news-releases/ceos-power-lunch-average-canadian-wage-study** (accessed January 10, 2016).

18. "No. 9: Kraft Foods the DiversityInc Top 50 Companies for Diversity®," *DiversityInc*, **http://diversityinc.com/the-2011-diversityinc-top-50/no-9-kraft-foods/** (accessed March 6, 2012).

19. "Women now hold 8.5% of Canada's top jobs," CBC News, March 19, 2015, **http://www.cbc.ca/news/business/women-now-hold-8-5-of-canada-s-top-jobs-1.3001744** (accessed January 10, 2016).

20. Christine Birkner with Seth Farbman, "Back to Basics," *Marketing News*, November 30, 2011, pp. 14–20; Shirley Brady, "*Gap's New Global Brand Story: Denim, Design, Food Trucks and a Dog Named Louie*," *BrandChannel*, August 1, 2011, **www.brandchannel.com/home/post/Gap-Global-Branding-Campaign-Fall-2011.aspx** (November 18, 2011).

21. Google Management," **www.google.com/intl/en/corporate/execs.html** (accessed March 4, 2010); "The Engineer's Life at Google," **www.google.com/intl/en/jobs/lifeatgoogle/englife** (accessed March 4, 2010). Google, "Google Announces Fourth Quarter and Fiscal Year 2011 Results," *Investor Relations*, January 19, 2012, **http://investor.google.com/earnings/2011/Q4_google_earnings.html** (accessed February 17, 2012).

22. Del Jones, "Autocratic Leadership Works—Until It Fails," *USA Today*, June 5, 2003, **www.usatoday.com/news/nation/2003-06-05-raines-usat_x.htm** (accessed March 6, 2012).

23. Hayley Peterson, "Lululemon hit with its first major recall since the sheer-pants disaster," *Business Insider*, June 25, 2015, **http://www.businessinsider.com/lululemon-hit-with-another-clothing-recall-2015-6** (accessed January 10, 2016).

24. Sophie Cousineau, "At Rona, a hands-on CEO grapples with turnaround," *Globe and Mail*, January 5, 2014, **http://www.theglobeandmail.com/report-on-business/careers/careers-leadership/at-rona-a-hands-on-ceo-grapples-with-turn-around/article16200686/** (accessed January 10, 2016); Mark Brown, "Top Turnaround CEO of the Year: Robert Sawyer, Rona," *Canadian Business*, October 19, 2015, **http://www.canadian-business.com/leadership/ceo-of-the-year/top-turnaround-ceo-robert-sawyer-rona/** (accessed January 10, 2016); Paul Delean, "Rona rebuilds for turnaround," *Montreal Gazette*, May 13, 2014, **http://montrealgazette.com/business/rona-rebuilds-for-turnaround?__lsa=6049-954e** (accessed January 10, 2016); Rona.ca, n.d., **https://www.rona.ca/corporate/management-team-robert-sawyer** (accessed January 10, 2016).

25. Mark Colgate, "How to crack the code of great customer service, *Globe and Mail*, September 25, 2014, **http://www.theglobeandmail.com/report-on-business/careers/leadership-lab/how-to-crack-the-code-of-great-customer-service/article20786869/** (accessed January 10, 2016).

26. Dov Seidman, "Upgrade to the Human Operating System," *Bloomberg Businessweek*, November 9, 2010, **www.businessweek.com/managing/content/nov2010/ca2010118_005704.htm** (accessed October 24, 2011); "The View from the Top, and Bottom," *The Economist*, September 24, 2011, **www.economist.com/node/21530171** (accessed October 24, 2011); "The HOW Report SM : Rethinking the Source of Resiliency, Innovation and Sustainable Growth," *LRN*, **www.lrn.com/form/43-how-report-form.html** (accessed October 24, 2011).

27. Kerrie Unsworth, "Unpacking Creativity," *Academy of Management Review*, 26 (April 2001), pp. 289–97.

28. *Harvard Business Review* 60 (November–December 1982), p. 160.

29. Dan Schwabel, "5 Reasons Why Your Online Presence Will Replace Your Resume in 10 Years," *Forbes*, February 21, 2012, **www.forbes.com/sites/danschawbel/2011/02/21/5-reasons-why-your-online-presence-will-replace-your-resume-in-10-years/** (accessed March 6, 2012).

30. Mae Anderson, "Lululemon says no need for downward dog demo for yoga pants refund," *Financial Post*, March 27, 2013, **http://business.financialpost.com/2013/03/27/lululemon-says-no-need-for-downward-dog-demo-for-yoga-pants-refund/**; Lululemon Addict blog, March 19, 2013, **http://www.lululemon.com/media/index.php?id=225** (both accessed June 24, 2013).

31. Scott Simpson, "Lululemon grabs headlines with pants recall,"*Vancouver Sun*, March 20, 2013, **http://www.vancouversun.com/business/Lululemon+grabs+headlines+with+pants+recall/8124248/story.html** (accessed June 24, 2013).

chapter 7

1. W. Nickels et al., *Understanding Canadian Business*, 8th ed. (Toronto: McGraw-Hill Ryerson, 2013); Mark Brown, "How Loblaws stays on the cutting edge after 96 years," *Canadian Business*, March 23, 2015, **http://www.canadianbusiness.**

com/innovation/most-innovative-companies-2015-loblaw/ (accessed January 11, 2016); Tara Perkins, "Galen G. Weston's plan to grow his family's legacy," *Globe and Mail*, July 15, 2013, http://www.theglobeandmail.com/report-on-business/galen-gs-big-gamble/article13237442/ (accessed January 11, 2016).

2. Mina Kimes, "What Admired Firms Don't Have in Common," **CNNMoney.com**, March 6, 2009, http://money.cnn.com/2009/03/06/news/companies/hay.survey.fortune/index.htm (accessed March 22, 2011).

3. "A New Future for Toms Shoes, Tweed Shire and Room to Read," Reputation Report, August 7, 2009, www.reputationreport.com.au/2009/07/a-new-future-by-toms-shoes-tweed-shire-and-room-to-read/ (accessed March 22, 2011); "Our Movement," TOMS Shoes, www.tomsshoes.com/content.asp?tid=271 (accessed March 22, 2011).

4. "Best Companies to Work For: Happy Campers," *CNNMoney*, http://money.cnn.com/galleries/2011/news/companies/1104/gallery.best_companies_happy_campers.fortune/2.html (accessed February 17, 2012); Christopher Palmeri, "Zappos Retails Its Culture," *Bloomberg Businessweek*, December 30, 2009, www.businessweek.com/magazine/content/10_02/b4162057120453.htm (accessed February 17, 2012).

5. Kasey Wehrum, "An Office of Rock Stars," *Inc.*, November 2010, pp. 115–116.

6. Adapted from "Best Buy Fights Against Electronic Waste," in O.C. Ferrell, John Fraedrich, and Linda Ferrell, Business Ethics: Ethical Decision Making and Cases, 9th ed. (Mason, OH: South-Western Cengage Learning, 2013), pp. 505–15; Aman Singh, "Best Buy Releases 2011 Sustainability Report: Responsibility in a Recession," Forbes, July 15, 2011, www.forbes.com/sites/csr/2011/07/15/best-buy-releases-2011-sustainability-report-responsibility-in-a-recession/ (accessed April 9, 2012).

7. Telis Demos, "Cirque du Balancing Act," *Fortune*, June 12, 2006, p. 114.

8. Adam Smith, *Wealth of Nations* (New York: Modern Library, 1937; originally published in 1776).

9. Jyoti Thottam, "When Execs Go Temp," *Time*, April 26, 2004, pp. 40–41.

10. Malcolm Moore, "What Has Triggered the Suicide Cluster at Foxconn?" *The Telegraph*, May 16, 2010, http://blogs.telegraph.co.uk/news/malcolmmoore/100039883/what-has-triggered-the-suicide-cluster-at-foxconn/ (accessed April 9, 2012).

11. Chris Perttila, "Keep It Simple," *Entrepreneur*, February 2006, pp. 60–64.

12. "Our Businesses," Campbell's (n.d.), http://www.campbellsoupcompany.com/about-campbell/our-businesses/ (accessed January 11, 2016).

13. "The 15 Most Innovative Canadian Companies of 2015," *Canadian Business*, March 19, 2015, http://www.canadianbusiness.com/innovation/most-innovative-companies-2015-slideshow/ (accessed January 11, 2016); Sarah Barmak, "How the 'Netflix of education' is using big data in the classroom," *Canadian Business*, March 19, 2015, http://www.canadianbusiness.com/innovation/most-innovative-2015-d2l-brightspace/ (accessed January 11, 2016); "About Us," D2L, n.d., http://www.d2l.com/about (accessed January 11, 2016).

14. McDonald's India, www.mcdonaldsindia.com/ (accessed February 17, 2012).

15. "Why Work Here?" www.wholefoodsmarket.com/careers/workhere.php (accessed March 3, 2010).

16. "PepsiCo Unveils New Organizational Structure, Names CEOs of Three Principal Operating Units," PepsiCo Media, November 5, 2007, www.pepsico.com/PressRelease/PepsiCo-Unveils-New-Organizational-Structure-Names.html (accessed March 22, 2011); "The PepsiCo Family," PepsiCo, www.pepsico.com/Company/The-Pepsico-Family/PepsiCo-Americas-Beverages.html (accessed January 12, 2011).

17. Jon R. Katzenbach and Douglas K. Smith, "The Discipline of Teams," *Harvard Business Review* 71 (March–April 1993), pp. 111–20.

18. Ibid.

19. "The Secret to Team Collaboration: Individuality," *Inc.*, January 18, 2012, www.inc.com/john-baldoni/the-secret-to-team-collaboration-is-individuality.html (accessed February 17, 2012).

20. Darryl Haralson and Adrienne Lewis, "USA Today Snapshots," *USA Today*, April 26, 2001, p. B1.

21. Esther Shein, "Making the Virtual Team Real," *The Network*, April 2, 2008, http://newsroom.cisco.com/dlls/2008/ts_040208.html (accessed April 8, 2012).

22. Jerry Useem, "What's That Spell? TEAMWORK," *Fortune*, June 12, 2006, p. 66.

23. "Toyota Motor Corporation President Akio Toyoda Announces Global Quality Task Force," Toyota Newsroom, February 5, 2010, http://pressroom.toyota.com/pr/tms/toyota-motor-corporation-president-153566.aspx (accessed March 22, 2011).

24. Jia Lynnyang, "The Power of Number 4.6," *Fortune*, June 12, 2006, p. 122.

25. Richard S. Wellins, William C. Byham, and Jeanne M. Wilson, *Empowered Teams: Creating Self-Directed Work Groups That Improve Quality, Productivity, and Participation* (San Francisco: Jossey-Bass Publishers, 1991), p. 5.

26. Matt Krumrie, "Are Meetings a Waste of Time? Survey Says Yes," *Minneapolis Workplace Examiner*, May 12, 2009, www.examiner.com/workplace-in-minneapolis/are-meetings-a-waste-of-time-survey-says-yes (accessed March 21, 2011).

27. Peter Mell and Timothy Grance, "The NIST Definition of Cloud Computing," National Institute of Standards and Technology, Special Publication 800-145, September 2011, http://csrc.nist.gov/publications/nistpubs/800-145/SP800-145.pdf (accessed April 9, 2012).

28. Ashlee Vance, "Trouble at the Virtual Water Cooler," *Bloomberg Businessweek*, May 2–8, 2011, pp. 31–32; Chris Brogan, "How to Foster Company Culture with Remote Employees," Entrepreneur, May 2011, www.entrepreneur.com/article/219471 (accessed August 4, 2011); www.yammer.com (accessed August 4, 2011); "Yammer Guidelines," http://blogxero.com/2011/01/yammer-guidelines (accessed August 5, 2011).

29. "Top 10 Ideas: Making the Most of Your Corporate Intranet," www.claromentis.com/blog/2009/04/top-10-ideas-making-the-most-of-yourcorporate-intranet (accessed March 22, 2011).

30. "Corporate America vs. Workers: Companies Do More with Fewer Employees," *NY Daily News*, November 5, 2009, www.nydailynews.com/money/2009/11/05/2009-11-05_corporate_america_vs_workers_companies_do_more_with_fewer_employees.html (accessed March 4, 2010).

31. Kim Komando, "Why You Need a Company Policy on Internet Use," **www.microsoft.com/business/en-us/resources/management/ employee-relations/why-you-need-a-company-policy-on-internet-use.aspx?fbid=abWQUsC20hw#Whyyounee dacompanypolicyonInternetuse** (accessed March 22, 2011).

32. PBSNewsHour, "Apple Supplier Foxconn Pledges Better Working Conditions, but Will It Deliver?" *YouTube*, **www.youtube. com/watch?v5ZduorbCkSBQ** (accessed April 9, 2012).

33. Green Mountain Coffee Roasters website, **www.gmcr. com/** (accessed October 20, 2011); "Green Mountain Coffee Roasters," Hoovers Online, **www.hoovers.com/company/ Green_Mountain_Coffee_Roasters_Inc/chktri-1.html** (accessed October 20, 2011); "Green Mountain Coffee Roasters Brews Formula for Success," in O.C. Ferrell, Geoffrey Hirt, and Linda Ferrell, *Business: A Changing World*, 6th ed. (New York: McGraw-Hill Irwin, 2008), pp. 233–34; Leslie Patton and Nikolaj Gammeltoft, "Green Mountain Drops as David Einhorn Says Market 'Limited,' " *Bloomberg Businessweek*, October 17, 2011, **www.businessweek.com/news/2011-10-17/green-mountain-drops-as-david-einhorn-says-market-limited-.html** (accessed October 20, 2011); Christopher Faille, "Green Mountain Coffee's Trouble with Bean Counting," *Forbes*, June 23, 2011, **www.forbes.com/sites/greatspeculations/ 2011/06/23/green-mountain-coffees-trouble-with-bean-counting/** (accessed October 20, 2011); GMCR Fiscal 2010 Annual Report, **http://files.shareholder.com/downloads/ GMCR/1458238937x0x436353/9E2D 04D9-79DE-4C08-A7C6-7B161E23E586/gmcr_2010_annual_report_lo.pdf**(accessed October 20, 2011); "Green Mountain Coffee: Starbucks Bursts Its Bubble,"*SeekingAlpha*,March9,2012,**http://seekingalpha.com/ article/422241- green-mountain-coffee-starbucks-bursts- its-bubble** (accessed May 31, 2012).

Chapter 8

1. Graham F. Scott, "Canada's Top 100 highest paid CEOs," *Canadian Business*, January 20, 2015, **http://www.canadianbusiness. com/lists-and-rankings/richest-people/top-100-highest-paid-ceos-2015**; Kimberley Noble, "Gerry Schwartz (Profile)," *Maclean's*, May 11, 2003, retrieved from The Canadian Encyclopedia, last edited December 16, 2013, **http://www.thecanadi anencyclopedia.ca/en/article/gerry-schwartz-profile/**; "The World's Billionaires: Gerald Schwartz," *Forbes*, n.d., **http://www. forbes.com/profile/gerald-schwartz/**; "Gerald Schwartz," Onex.com, n.d., **http://www.onex.com/gerald_w_schwartz. aspx**; "The Power 25," *Globe and Mail*, October 27, 2005, **http://www.theglobeandmail.com/report-on-business/the-power-25/article20429456/?page=all**; "The success secrets of Gerry Schwartz," *Profit*, May 16, 2011, **http://www.profitguide. com/manage-grow/success-stories/the-success-secrets-of-gerry-schwartz-29394** (all accessed January 11, 2016).

2. Leonard L. Berry, *Discovering the Soul of Service* (New York: The Free Press, 1999), pp. 86–96.

3. Zeithaml and Bitner, *Services Marketing*, pp. 3, 22.

4. Andreas Cremer and Tim Higgins, "Volkswagen Rediscovers America," *Bloomberg Businessweek*, May 23–29, 2011, pp. 11–12; Paul A. Eisenstein, "VW Is Back in the USA and Aiming High with New Plant," MSNBC, May 26, 2011, **www.msnbc.msn.com/id/43159310/ ns/business-autos/t/vw-back-usa-aiming-high-new-plant/** (accessed July 29, 2011); Deepa Seetharaman, "Volkswagen Sees U.S. Plant as Key to Topping Toyota," Reuters, May 24, 2011, **www.reuters.com/article/2011/05/24/us-volkswagen-idUS TRE74N6RA20110524** (accessed July 29, 2011); "Germany: VW PC Brand Sales Rise 17.2% in July," Automotive World, August 16, 2011, **www.automotiveworld.com/news/oems-and-markets/88694-germany-vw-pc-brand-sales-rise-17-2-in-july** (accessed August 16, 2011); Tom Mutchler, "First Look Video: 2012 Volkswagen Passat," *Consumer Reports*, August 5, 2011, **http://news.consumerreports. org/cars/2011/08/first-look-video-2012-volkswagen-passat. html** (accessed August 16, 2011).

5. Leonard L. Berry, *Discovering the Soul of Service* (New York: The Free Press, 1999), pp. 86–96.

6. Faith Keenan, "Opening the Spigot," *BusinessWeek e.biz*, June 4, 2001, **www.businessweek.com/magazine/content/01_23/ b3735616.htm**.

7. "Dell Laptop Parts," Partspeople, **www.parts-people.com/** (accessed March 23, 2012).

8. Lonely Planet, **www.lonelyplanet.com/about/** (accessed July 2, 2010).

9. **www.orcahouseboats.com**.

10. "Making Chocolate," Hershey's, **www.hersheys.com/discover/ tour_printv.htm** (accessed January 12, 2011).

11. "Green Factories/Green Building," Honda, **www.honda.com/ newsandviews/report.aspx?id54056-en** (accessed March 23, 2012); "ISO 14000 essentials," ISO, **www.iso.org/iso/ iso_14000_essentials** (accessed March 23, 2012).

12. "Why Leading Executives Choose Canada," **www.locationcan-ada.com/art_5.htm**.

13. Stacy Perman, "Automate or Die," *eCompany*, July 2001, p. 62.

14. David Noonan, "The Ultimate Remote Control," *Newsweek*, via **www.msnbc.com/news/588560.asp** (accessed July 18, 2001).

15. Johnson Controls, *2011 Business and Sustainability Report: Growth in Every Dimension* (Milwaukee, WI: Johnson Controls, Inc., 2011).

16. "Best in Class: Top 50 Socially Responsible Companies 2013," *Maclean's*, **http://www.macleans.ca/canada-top-50-socially-responsible-corporations-2013/** (accessed January 11, 2016).

17. Bryan Walsh, "Why Green Is the New Red, White and Blue," *Time*, April 28, 2008, p. 53.

18. "BestinClass,"*Maclean's*,**http://www.macleans.ca/canada-top-50-socially-responsible-corporations-2013/** (accessed January 11, 2016).

19. O. C. Ferrell and Michael D. Hartline, *Marketing Strategy* (Mason, OH: South-Western, 2005), p. 215.

20. John Edwards, "Orange Seeks Agent," *Inband Logistics*, January 2006, pp. 239–242.

21. Ferrell and Hartline, *Marketing Strategy*, p. 215.

22. John O'Mahony, "The Future Is Now," Special Advertising Section, *Bloomberg Businessweek*, pp. S1–S11; "Recycling &Conservation," UPS, **http://responsibility.ups.com/Environment/ Recycling** 1 and 1 Conservation (accessed October 18, 2011); Rebecca Treacy-Lenda, "Sustainability Is…" UPS, July 28, 2011, **http://blog.ups.com/2011/07/28/sustainability-is/** (accessed October 18, 2011); Heather Clancy, "Sustainability Update: UPS Squeezes Out More Fuel Consumption," SmartPlanet, July 28, 2011, **www.smartplanet.com/blog/ business-brains/sustainability-update-ups-squeezes-**

out-more-fuel-consumption/17597 (accessed October 18, 2011).

23. Ari Lavaux, "Chocolate's Dark Side," *The Weekly Alibi*, February 9–15, 2012, p. 22.

24. Bruce Nussbaum, "Where Are the Jobs?" *BusinessWeek*, March 22, 2004, pp. 36–37.

25. Lisa H. Harington, "Balancing on the Rim," *Inband Logistics*, January 2006, pp. 168–170.

26. Susan Carey, "Airlines Play Up Improvements in On-Time Performance," *Wall Street Journal*, February 10, 2010, p. B6.

27. Roger Yu, "Kia Looks to Buff Image with Value, New Designs," *USA Today*, June 29, 2011, **www.usatoday.com/money/autos/2011-06-27-kia-rising_n.htm** (accessed February 22, 2012).

28. Philip B. Crosby, *Quality Is Free: The Art of Making Quality Certain* (New York: McGraw-Hill, 1979), pp. 9–10.

29. Nigel F. Piercy, *Market-Led Strategic Change* (Newton, MA: Butterworth-Heinemann, 1992), pp. 374–385.

30. "Compuware Gomez Introduces Free Web Performance Benchmarking Tool," Gomez, February 16, 2010, **www.gomez.com/compuware-gomez-introduces-free-web-performance-benchmarking-tool/** (accessed March 22, 2011).

31. K.W., "The Dog Lover," *Inc.*, October 2010, pp. 68–70; Rebecca Konya, "Marie Moody: Women of Influence 2010," *The Business Journal*, 2010, **www2.bizjournals.com/milwaukee/events/2010/women_of_influence/marie_moody_women_of_influence_2010.html** (accessed October 19, 2010); **www.stellaandchewys.com** (accessed October 19, 2010).

32. Hershey, "Hershey's Chocolate Kisses."

33. "Mouthing Off By the Numbers," *Ethisphere*, 2011, Q3, p. 9.

34. Charles Duhigg and David Barboza, "Apple's iPad and the Human Costs for Workers in China," *New York Times*, January 25, 2012, **www.nytimes.com/2012/01/26/business/ieconomy-apples-ipad-and-the-human-costs-for-workers-in-china.html?pagewanted5all** (accessed February 8, 2012).

35. "Employment Opportunities," Careers in Supply Chain Management, **www.careersinsupplychain.org/career-outlook/empopp.asp** (accessed March 5, 2010).

Chapter 9

1. "Executive Staff: Deborah Gillis," Catalyst.org, n.d., **http://www.catalyst.org/who-we-are/our-people/executive-staff/deborah-gillis** (accessed January 12, 2016); Carol Toller, "Canada's Most Powerful Business People 2016: #10 — Deborah Gillis," *Canadian Business*, November 17, 2015, **http://www.canadianbusiness.com/lists-and-rankings/most-powerful-people/10-2015-deborah-gillis-catalyst-inc/** (accessed January 12, 2016).

2. Nicole Stewart, *Missing in Action: Absentee Trends in Canadian Organizations* (Ottawa: The Conference Board of Canada, 2013), retrieved January 12, 2016, from **http://www.sunlife.ca/static/canada/Sponsor/About%20Group%20Benefits/Focus%20Update/2013/Special%20Edition%20-%20Sept.%2023%20-%20%20Sun%20Life%20co-sponsors%20major%20new%20Conference%20Board%20of%20MissinginAction_SUN%20LIFE_EN.pdf**.

3. Dan Heath and Chip Heath, "Business Advice from Van Halen," *Fast Company*, March 1, 2010, **www.fastcompany.com/magazine/**

143/made-to-stick-thetelltale-brown-mampm.html (accessed March 11, 2010).

4. "100 Best Companies to Work For 2010," *Fortune*, **http://money.cnn.com/magazines/fortune/bestcompanies/2010/snapshots/4.html** (accessed February 18, 2010); "Benefits," Google Jobs, **www.google.com/support/jobs/bin/static.py?page=benefits.html** (accessed February 18, 2010).

5. "Careers," Nikebiz.com, **www.nikebiz.com/careers/benefits/other/whq_campus.html** (accessed February 9, 2010).

6. Diane Jermyn, "Canada's Top 100 Employers make their workplaces exceptional," *Globe and Mail*, November 4, 2014, **http://www.theglobeandmail.com/report-on-business/careers/top-employers/canadas-top-100-employers-make-their-workplaces-exceptional/article21427767/** (accessed January 12, 2016).

7. Graham F. Scott, "Canada's Top 100 highest-paid CEOs," *Canadian Business*, January 20, 2015, **http://www.canadianbusiness.com/lists-and-rankings/richest-people/top-100-highest-paid-ceos-2015/** (accessed January 12, 2016).

8. Medtronic, **http://www.medtronic.com/** (accessed July 17, 2010).

9. "Why Work Here," **www.wholefoodsmarket.com/careers/workhere.php** (accessed November 9, 2011); "Best Companies to Work For Rankings," **www.wholefoodsmarket.com/careers/fortune100.php** (accessed November 9, 2011); "Whole Food Market's Core Values," **www.wholefoodsmarket.com/values/corevalues.php#supporting** (accessed November 9, 2011); "100 Best Companies to Work For: Whole Foods Market," CNNMoney, **http://money.cnn.com/magazines/fortune/bestcompanies/2011/snapshots/24.html** (accessed November 9, 2011); Kerry A. Dolan, "America's Greenest Companies 2011," Forbes, April 18, 2011, **www.forbes.com/2011/04/18/americas-greenest-companies.html** (accessed November 9, 2011); Joseph Brownstein, "Is Whole Foods' Get Healthy Plan Fair?" ABC News, January 29, 2010, **http://abcnews.go.com/Health/w_DietAndFitnessNews/foods-incentives-make-employees-healthier/story?id59680047** (accessed November 9, 2011); Deborah Dunham, "At Whole Foods Thinner Employees Get Fatter Discounts," *That's Fit*, January 27, 2010, **www.thatsfit.com/2010/01/27/whole-foods-thin-employees-get-discounts/** (accessed November 9, 2011).

10. Jermyn, "Canada's Top 100 Employers make their workplaces exceptional," **http://www.theglobeandmail.com/report-on-business/careers/top-employers/canadas-top-100-employers-make-their-workplaces-exceptional/article21427767/**.

11. Charisse Jones, "Great Work. Now Hit the Road—on Us," *USA Today*, May 12, 2010, pp. 1B–2B; V. Dion Haynes," Washington-Baltimore Benefits Survey: Part-Timers Getting More Perks," *The Washington Post*, June 8, 2010, **www.washingtonpost.com/wp-dyn/content/article/2010/06/07/AR2010060704513.html** (accessed June 10, 2010); Kim Covert, "Travel Perks One Way to Keep Employees Engaged," *The Vancouver Sun*, April 27, 2010, **www.vancouversun.com/life/Travel+perks+keep+employees+engaged/2956071/story.html** (accessed June 10, 2010); **www.pointsoflight.org** (accessed May 2, 2010); "Best Places to Work 2009," crain's, **www.crainsnewyork.com/apps/pbcs.dll/gallery?Site=CN&Date=20091207&Category=GALLERIES&ArtNo=120209998&Ref=PH&Params=Itemnr=31** (accessed May 2, 2010); **www.patagonia.com** (accessed July 10, 2010).

12. Jessica McDiarmid, "Best Employers 2016: How they hang on to their best employees," *Canadian Business*, November 5, 2015, **http://www.canadianbusiness.com/lists-and-rankings/best-jobs/best-employers-2016-employee-retention/** (accessed January 12, 2016).

13. Douglas McGregor, *The Human Side of Enterprise* (New York: McGraw-Hill, 1960), pp. 33–34.

14. McGregor, *The Human Side of Enterprise.*

15. Bharat Mediratta, "The Google Way: Give Engineers Room," *New York Times*, October 21, 2007, **www.nytimes.com/2007/10/21/jobs/21pre.html** (accessed April 16, 2012).

16. John Lorinc, "Mass market, custom display: Toronto's Nulogy solves the puzzle," *Globe and Mail*, November 26, 2015, **http://www.theglobeandmail.com/report-on-business/rob-magazine/nuology/article27322383/** (accessed January 12, 2016); Mai Nguyen, "Best Employers 2016: How small companies provide big perks," *Canadian Business*, November 5, 2015, **http://www.canadianbusiness.com/lists-and-rankings/best-jobs/best-employers-2016-perks/** (accessed January 12, 2016).

17. Jon L. Pierce, Tatiana Kostova, and Kurt T. Kirks, "Toward a Theory of Psychological Ownership in Organizations," *Academy of Management Review* 26, no. 2 (2001), p. 298.

18. Liz Rappaport, "Goldman Cuts Blankfein's Bonus," *Wall Street Journal*, February 4, 2012, **http://online.wsj.com/article/SB10001424052970204662204577201483347787346.html** (accessed April 17, 2012).

19. Ethics Resource Center, *2011 National Business Ethics Survey®: Ethics in Transition* (Arlington, VA: Ethics Resource Center, 2012), p. 16.

20. Archie Carroll, "Carroll: Do We Live in a Cheating Culture?" *Athens Banner-Herald*, February 21, 2004, **www.onlineathens.com/stories/022204/bus_20040222028.shtml**, accessed March 12, 2010.

21. Jermyn, "Canada's Top 100 Employers make their workplaces exceptional," **http://www.theglobeandmail.com/report-on-business/careers/top-employers/canadas-top-100-employers-make-their-workplaces-exceptional/article21427767/**.

22. PricewaterhouseCoopers, **www.pwcglobal.com/ie/eng/ins-sol/spec-int/globalhr/steeprise.html** (accessed July 11, 2010).

23. Geoff Colvin, "How Top Companies Breed Stars," September 20, 2007, **http://money.cnn.com/magazines/fortune/fortune_archive/2007/10/01/100351829/index.htm** (accessed March 12, 2010).

24. Amy Wrzesniewski and Jen E. Dutton, "Crafting a Job: Revisioning Employees as Active Crafters of Their Work," *Academy of Management Review* 26, no. 2 (2001), p. 179.

25. **http://www.careerbuilder.com/Jobs/Company/C8D7BN6GV5F6ZYT9WDZ/Hyatt-Hotels/**; **http://www.general mills.com/en/Responsibility/Community_Engagement/Grants/Minneapolis_area/Communities_of_color/grant_recipients_2006.aspx**; "Seminar on Human Resources and Training Session I," Conference of European Statisticians, United Nations Economic and Social Council, June 2006, **http://www.unescap.org/stat/apex/2/APEX2_S.1_Human_Resources&Training_Canada.pdf**

26. MyGuides, **USA.com**, "Which Jobs Offer Flexible Work Schedules?" **http://jobs.myguidesusa.com/answers-to-myquestions/which-jobs-offer-flexiblework-schedules?/** (accessed March 12, 2010).

27. Robert Preidt, "Workplace Flexibility Can Boost Healthy Behaviors," Wake Forest University Baptist Medical Center, news release, December 10, 2007, via **http://yourtotalhealth.ivillage.com/workplaceflexibility-can-boost-healthy-behaviors.html** (accessed March 12, 2010).

28. Jermyn, "Canada's Top 100 Employers make their workplaces exceptional," **http://www.theglobeandmail.com/report-on-business/careers/top-employers/canadas-top-100-employers-make-their-workplaces-exceptional/article21427767/**.

29. Jordana Sacks, Sharonie Valin, R. Ian Casson, & C. Ruth Wilson, "Are 2 heads better than 1? Perspectives on job sharing in academic family medicine," *Canadian Family Physician*, January 2015, vol. 61, no. 1, **http://www.cfp.ca/content/61/1/11** (accessed January 12, 2016).

30. Statistics Canada, "Working at home: An update," December 7, 2010, **http://www.statcan.gc.ca/pub/11-008-x/2011001/article/11366-eng.htm#a13** (accessed January 16, 2013).

31. "Telecommuting Benefits," **http://www.telecommutect.com/employees/benefits.php**, Telecommute Connecticut! (accessed June 21, 2006); Nicole Demerath, "Telecommuting in the 21st century: Benefits, issues, and leadership model which will work," **AllBusiness.com**, April 1, 2002, **http://www.allbusiness.com/buying_exiting_businesses/3503510-1.html**; Fran Irwin, "Gaining the Air Quality and Climate Benefit from Telework," January 2004, **http://pdf.wri.org/teleworkguide.pdf**; "The State of California Telecommuting Pilot Project: Final Report Executive Summary," JALA Associates Inc., June 1990, **http://www.jala.com/caexecsumm.pdf**.

32. "HR Executives Split on Telecommuting," *USA Today*, March 1, 2006, p. B1.

33. Stephanie Armour, "Telecommuting Gets Stuck in the Slow Lane," *USA Today*, June 25, 2001, pp. 1A, 2A.

34. Nancy Rothbard, "Put on a Happy Face. Seriously." *The Wall Street Journal*, October 24, 2011, p. R2; "How 3M Gave Everyone Days Off and Created an Innovation Dynamo," February 1, 2011, **www.fastcodesign.com/1663137/how-3m-gave-everyone-days-off-and-created-aninnovation-dynamo** (accessed October 31, 2011); "Americans Increasingly Unhappy at Work," *BusinessNewsDaily*, March 10, 2011, **www.businessnewsdaily.com/work-wellness-index-1073/** (accessed October 31, 2011); "Employee Mood Impacts Bottom Line," *BusinessNewsDaily* April 5, 2011, **www.businessnewsdaily.com/employee-mood-customer-service-1152/** (accessed October 31, 2011).

35. "Employers Reap Awards and Rewards for Psychologically Healthy Workplaces," *Employee Benefit News*, April 15, 2004, **www.benefitnews.com/pfv.cfm?id=5832**; Susan McCullough, "Pets Go to the Office," *HR Magazine* 43 (June 1998), pp. 162–68; "Pets Provide Relief to Workplace Stress," *BenefitNews Connect*, July 1, 2003, **www.benefitnews.com/detail.cfm?id=4736**; "Taking Your Best Friend to Work," *Toronto Star*, December 13, 2004, p. C11; "Working Like a Dog—Survey of Owners Reveals They Would Work More Hours or for Less Pay if They Could Bring Their Pooch to Work," **CNNMoney.com**, January 24, 2006, **http://money.cnn.com/2006/01/24/news/funny/dog_work/index.htm?cnn=yes** (accessed January 27, 2006); "Every Day Is 'Take Your Dog to Work Day' at Planet Dog," Press Releases, **www.planetdog.com/Press.asp?id=6** (accessed January 27, 2006); Best Friends Survey taken March 27, and 30, 2006, of 1,000 registered voters, "All in the Family," *USA Today Snapshots*, June 21, 2006.

Chapter 10

1. Jack Welch, *Winning*, (New York: Harper Business, 2005).

2. "Labour Market Information," Service Canada website, n.d., **http://www.servicecanada.gc.ca/eng/sc/lminfo//index.shtml** (accessed January 12, 2016).

3. Procter & Gamble, "U.S. Recruiting process," **www.pg.com/jobs/jobs_us/recruitblue/recprocess.jhtml** (accessed July 5, 2006); "The Recruitment Process," Procter & Gamble, **http://www.pg.com/en_CA/careers/view_jobs/index.shtml** (accessed June 4, 2010).

4. "Job Opportunities," *Borders*, **https://wss6a.unicru.com/hirepro/C406/applicant.jsp?Eurl54%2Fhirepro%2FC406%2Fapplicant.jsp%3FSite%3D-3%26C%3D406%26k%3Dno%26content%3Dsearch%26Lang%3Den&Site5100585&C5406&k5no&content5start&Lang5en** (accessed March 9, 2010).

5. "Canadian Human Rights Commission Policy on Alcohol and Drug Testing," Canadian Human Rights Commission, **http://www.chrc-ccdp.ca/pdf/poldrgalceng.pdf** (accessed May 17, 2010).

6. Associated Press, "Food Network Chef Fired After Resume Fraud," *USA Today*, March 3, 2008, **www.usatoday.com/news/nation/2008-03-03-chef-fired_N.htm** (accessed April 14, 2011).

7. Christopher T. Marquet and Lisa J.B. Peterson, "Résumé Fraud: The Top Ten Lies," Marquet International, Ltd., **www.marquetinternational.com/pdf/Resume%20Fraud-Top%20Ten%20Lies.pdf** (accessed April 14, 2011).

8. The Canadian Charter of Rights and Freedoms, Canadian Heritage, **http://dsp-psd.pwgsc.gc.ca/Collection/CH37-4-3-2002E.pdf** (accessed July 17, 2010).

9. Canadian Human Rights Act, **http://www.efc.ca/pages/law/canada/canada.H-6.head.html** (accessed July 17, 2010).

10. "Overview," Canadian Human Rights Commission (n.d.), **http://www.chrc-ccdp.ca/about/icm_page2_gci-eng.aspx** (accessed July 17, 2010).

11. George Waggott and Lang Michener, "Mandatory Retirement: 65 or Not?", Supreme Court Law, **http://www.supremecourtlaw.ca/default_e.asp?id=68** (accessed July 17, 2010).

12. "Our Curriculum," Hamburger University, **www.aboutmcdonalds.com/mcd/careers/hamburger_university/our_curriculum.html** (accessed April 14, 2011).

13. Doug Stewart, "Employee-Appraisal Software," *Inc.*, **www.inc.com/magazine/19940615/3288_pagen_2.html** (accessed April 14, 2011).

14. Maury A. Peiperl, "Getting 360-Degree Feedback Right," *Harvard Business Review*, January 2001, pp. 142–48.

15. Chris Musselwhite, "Self Awareness and the Effective Leader," **Inc.com**, October 1, 2007, **www.inc.com/resources/leadership/articles/20071001/musselwhite.html** (accessed April 14, 2011).

16. O.C. Ferrell, Geoffrey Hirt, Rick Bates, Elliott Currie, *Business: A Changing World*, Second Canadian Edition, p. 258.

17. Rick Nauert, "Flexible Work Place Improves Family Life, Reduces Turnover," PsychCentral, April 7, 2011, **http://psychcentral.com/news/2011/04/07/flexible-workplace-improves-family-life-reduces-turnover/25094.html** (accessed April 5, 2012).

18. Marcia Zidle, "Employee Turnover: Seven Reasons Why People Quit Their Jobs," **http://ezinearticles.com/?Employee-Turnover:-Seven-Reasons-Why-People-Quit-Their-Jobs&id=42531** (accessed April 14, 2011).

19. Angela Mulholland, "Target leaving Canada: 'Losing money every day,'" CTV News, January 15, 2015, **http://www.ctvnews.ca/business/target-leaving-canada-losing-money-every-day-1.2189973** (accessed January 12, 2016).

20. Tavia Grant, "Canada's job market in deep freeze," *The Globe and Mail* online, November 6, 2009, **http://www.theglobeandmail.com/report-on-business/economy/canadas-job-market-in-deep-freeze/article1354678/** (accessed November 3, 2010).

21. "Current And Forthcoming Minimum Hourly Wage Rates For Experienced Adult Workers in Canada," Government of Canada, **http://srv116.services.gc.ca/dimt-wid/sm-mw/rpt1.aspx** (accessed October 20, 2016).

22. John Daly, "Bulking up: How GoodLife became Canada's dominant gym," *Globe and Mail*, March 27, 2014, **http://www.theglobeandmail.com/report-on-business/rob-magazine/the-secret-of-goodlifes-success/article17673987/?page=4** (accessed January 13, 2016).

23. Robert Lachowiez, presenter, Business & Tourism Conference 2009, Mount Saint Vincent University, Halifax, Nova Scotia.

24. "WestJet Airlines' winning strategy for engagement," *Internal Comms* Hub, 1(8), December/January 2008, **http://www.bridgesconsultancy.com/newsroom/articles/youve_got_the%20strategy.pdf**, pp. 10–11.

25. Marjo Johne, "Why you should give your employees a piece of the company," *Globe and Mail*, March 22, 2012, **http://www.theglobeandmail.com/report-on-business/careers/business-education/why-you-should-give-your-employees-a-piece-of-the-company/article535271/** (accessed January 13, 2016).

26. Alison van Diggelen, "Working@Google: Green Carrots & Pogo Sticks," Fresh Dialogues, **www.freshdialogues.com/** (accessed November 9, 2011); "Can We Commute Carbon-Free," GoogleGreen, **www.google.com/green/operations/commuting-carbon-free.html** (accessed November 9, 2011); Tiffany Hsu, "Google Creates $280-Million Solar Power Fund," *Los Angeles Times*, June 14, 2011, **http://articles.latimes.com/2011/jun/14/business/la-fi-google-solar-20110614** (accessed November 9, 2011).

27. Perspectives on Labour and Income, The Online Edition, "Benefits of the Job," Katherine Marshall, May 2003, Vol. 4, No. 5, **http://www.statcan.gc.ca/pub/75-001-x/00503/6515-eng.html** (accessed July 17, 2010).

28. Stephan Miller, "Employee Loyalty Hits 7-Year Low; Benefits Promote Retention," *Society for Human Resource Management*, March 22, 2012, **www.shrm.org/hrdisciplines/benefits/Articles/Pages/LoyaltyLow.aspx** (accessed April 5, 2012).

29. "Union Coverage in Canada - 2014," Government of Canada, November 30, 2015, **http://www.labour.gc.ca/eng/resources/info/publications/union_coverage/union_coverage.shtml** (accessed January 13, 2016).

30. Severin Carrell, Dan Milmo, Alan Travis and Nick Hopkins, "Day of Strikes as Millions Heed Unions' Call to Fight Pension Cuts," *The Guardian*, November 29, 2011, **www.guardian.co.uk/society/**

31. James R. Hagerty, "Caterpillar Closes Plant in Canada after Lockout," *Wall Street Journal*, February 3, 2012, **http://online.wsj.com/article/SB10001424052970203889904577200953014575964.html** (accessed April 5, 2012).

32. **http://www.rbc.com/diversity/research.html** (accessed November 3, 2010).

33. Pat Wechsler, "And You Thought Cigarettes Were Pricey," *Bloomberg BusinessWeek*, July 4–10, 2011; pp. 24–26; A.G. Sulzberger, "Hospitals Shift Smoking Ban to Smokers Ban," *The New York Times*, February 10, 2011, **www.nytimes.com/2011/02/11/us/11smoking.html?pagewanted5all** (accessed August 12, 2011); Ken Alltucker, "Humana Won't Hire Smokers in Arizona," *USA Today*, July 1, 2011, **www.usatoday.com/money/industries/health/2011-06-30-smokers-jobs-humana_n.htm** (accessed August 16, 2011)

34. Taylor H. Cox, Jr., "The Multicultural Organization," *Academy of Management Executives* 5 (May 1991), pp. 34–47; Marilyn Loden and Judy B. Rosener, *Workforce America! Managing Employee Diversity as a Vital Resource* (Homewood, IL: Business One Irwin, 1991).

35. Paul Davidson, "Overworked and Underpaid?" *USA Today*, April 16, 2012, pp. 1A–2A.

36. Ethics Resource Center, 2011 *National Business Ethics Survey®: Ethics in Transition* (Arlington, VA: Ethics Resource Center, 2012), pp. 39–40.

37. Melanie Trottman, "For Angry Employees, Legal Cover for Rants," *The Wall Street Journal*, December 2, 2011, **http://online.wsj.com/article/SB10001424052970203710704577049822809710332.html** (accessed April 23, 2012).

38. Martin Crutsinger, "Hiring Grows as Companies Hit Limits with Workers," *MPR News*, March 7, 2012, **http://minnesota.publicradio.org/display/web/2012/03/07/hiring-grows-as-companies-hit-limit/** (accessed April 23, 2012).

39. George Anders, "The Rare Find," *Bloomberg Businessweek*, October 17–October 23, 2011, pp. 106–12; Philip Delves Broughton, "Spotting the Exceptionally Talented," *Financial Times*, October 13, 2011, **www.ft.com/intl/cms/s/0/25dc1872-f4ba-11e0-a286-00144feab49a.html#axzz1birOQlih** (accessed October 24, 2011); Joe Light, "Recruiters Rethink Online Playbook," *The Wall Street Journal*, January 18, 2011,

chapter II

1. Dawn Calleja, "How Spin Master got its mojo back," *The Globe and Mail*, January 28, 2015, **http://www.theglobeandmail.com/report-on-business/rob-magazine/how-spin-master-got-its-mojo-back/article22639332/** (accessed December 7, 2015).

2. "Spin Master Enterprise Value," yCharts website, **https://ycharts.com/companies/TOY.TO/enterprise_value** (accessed December 7, 2016).

3. Calleja, "How Spin Master got its mojo back," **http://www.theglobeandmail.com/report-on-business/rob-magazine/how-spin-master-got-its-mojo-back/article22639332/**.

4. Steve Baron, "Paw Patrol' Renewed for Season 3 by Nickelodeon," zap2it website, June 9, 2015, **http://tvbythenumbers.zap2it.com/2015/06/09/paw-patrol-renewed-for-season-3-by-nickelodeon/414804/**

5. "McDonald's Adult Happy Meal Arrives," *CNN/Money*, May 11, 2004, **http://money.cnn.com/** (accessed June 6, 2006).

6. "Wireless," EastLink website, **http://www.eastlink.ca/Wireless.aspx** (accessed July 9, 2013).

7. "In Our Restaurant: Breakfast," Tim Hortons website, **http://www.timhortons.com/ca/en/menu/breakfast-sandwich.html** (accessed July 9, 2013).

8. Tony Martin, "Ask the Legends: Walter Hachborn," *CBOnline*, March 2009, **http://www.canadianbusiness.com/article.jsp?content=20090201_30016_30017** (accessed July 7, 2010)

9. Jennifer Kwan, "Quebec's Simons Eyes Toronto Sears Locations," *Yahoo! Finance* online, June 17, 2013, **http://ca.finance.yahoo.com/blogs/insight/quebec-simons-eyes-toronto-sears-locations-180217911.html** (accessed July 9, 2013).

10. "McDonald's Adult Happy Meal Arrives."

11. Marguerite Higgins, "McDonald's Labels Nutrition," *Washington Times*, October 26, 2005, **www.washingtontimes.com/business/20051025-102731-2213r.htm** (accessed June 16, 2006).

12. "Ten Trees Are Planted," *Tentree.com*, **http://www.tentree.com/ca/treecode/map/** (accessed December 9, 2015).

13. Mary Teresa Bitti, "Dragons See the Seeds of a Good Company in Ten Tree International," Financial Post.com, October 15, 2012, **http://business.financialpost.com/entrepreneur/dragons-see-the-seeds-of-a-good-company-in-ten-tree-international** (accessed December 10, 2015).

14. "Sowing the Seeds of Business Success," *Globe and Mail*, September 30, 2015, **http://www.pressreader.com/canada/the-globe-and-mail-metro-ontario-edition/20150930/282054800845019/TextView** (accessed December 10, 2015).

15. Jamie Beliveau, "Does Size Matter When You Want to Hire a Construction Company?", Kerr Construction, **http://www.kerrconstruction.ca/articles.html** (accessed July 7, 2010).

16. "Success of Herbal Magic Franchise," The Franchise Mall, June 18, 2008, **http://www.thefranchisemall.com/news/articles/21579-0.htm** (accessed July 7, 2010)

17. Avi Dan, "When It Comes to Social Media Consumers Tell Brands to Speak Only When Spoken To," *Forbes* online, March 31, 2013, **http://www.forbes.com/sites/avidan/2013/03/31/when-it-comes-to-social-media-consumers-tell-brands-to-speak-only-when-spoken-to/** (accessed July 9, 2013).

18. Michael Treacy and Fred Wiersema, *The Discipline of Market Leaders* (Reading, MA: Addison Wesley, 1995), p. 176.

19. "Print Audit," ASTech Awards, **http://www.printaudit.com/downloads/pdf/ASTech_Profile.pdf** (accessed July 6, 2010).

20. Apple Annual Report 10-k, 2005.

21. Ipsos-Reid, **http://www.ipsos-na.com/news-polls/searchresults.aspx?search=negativek** (accessed July 7, 2010).

22. "Customer Is King—Says Who," *Advertising Age*, April 15, 2006, p. 4.

23. Venky Shankar, "Multiple Touch Point Marketing," American Marketing Association Faculty Consortium on Electronic Commerce, Texas A&M University, July 14–17, 2001.

24. Trevor Melanson, "Is HootSuite Canada's Next Billion-Dollar Titan?", *Canadian Business* online, January 9, 2013, **http://www.canadianbusiness.com/technology-news/is-hootsuite-canadas-next-tech-titan/** (accessed August 5, 2013).

25. Stephanie Kang, "The Swoosh Finds Its Swing, Targeting Weekend Golfers," *The Wall Street Journal*, April 8, 2004, p. B1.

26. "About the Company," Reitmans, **http://www.reitmans.com/en/company/** (accessed September 1, 2010).

27. Hollie Shaw, "Hudson's Bay CEO Lost in Space," *Financial Post*, **http://www.nationalpost.com/life/health/Hudson+lost+space/857928/story.html** (accessed July 7, 2010).

28. Joe Castaldo, "The Kid Stays in the Picture," *Canadian Business* online, **http://site.canadianbusiness.com/longform/asper-fntsy/** (accessed December 15, 2015).

29. Gordon Pitts, "Leonard Asper gets off the mat," *The Globe and Mail* online, May 24, 2011, **http://www.theglobeandmail.com/report-on-business/leonard-asper-gets-off-the-mat/article585972/?page=2** (accessed December 15, 2015).

30. Joe Castaldo, "The Kid Stays in the Picture," *Canadian Business* online, **http://site.canadianbusiness.com/longform/asper-fntsy/** (accessed December 15, 2015).

31. Steve Ladurantaye, "Leonard Asper places big bet on fantasy sports," *The Globe and Mail* online, January 28, 2013, **http://www.theglobeandmail.com/report-on-business/leonard-asper-places-big-bet-on-fantasy-sports/article7900233/** (accessed December 15, 2015).

32. Morgan Campbell, "Fantasy Sports: Can new TV network find an audience among poolies?," *thestar.com*, **http://www.thestar.com/business/2013/03/11/fantasy_sports_can_new_tv_network_find_an_audience_among_poolies.html** (accessed December 15, 2015).

33. Allison Marr, "Household-Level Research Gives Clearer Picture," *Marketing News*, April 15, 2006, p. 18.

34. Kara Aaserud, "How to Really Listen to Your Customers," *PROFIT guide* online, September 13, 2010, **http://www.profitguide.com/manage-grow/sales-marketing/how-to-really-listen-to-your-customers-29921** (accessed August 5, 2013).

35. Mya Frazier, "Staples Gains Footing in Hispanic Market," *Advertising Age*, April 3, 2006, p. 58.

36. Charles Passy, "Your Scoop Is in the Mail," *The Wall Street Journal*, May 25, 2001, pp. W1, W6; Allysa Bikowski, Sam Bryant, Sarah Crossin et. al., "Research In Motion: Case Study Report," October 22, 2009, **http://zenportfolios.com/theresa/files/2009/11/mktg-RIM-case.pdf**.

37. Bryan Borzykowski, "Business Plan: Can a Canadian Company Make the Next Bugatti?," *PROFITguide* online, June 2, 2010, **http://www.profitguide.com/manage-grow/success-stories/business-plan-can-a-canadian-company-make-the-next-bugatti-29744** (accessed August 5, 2013).

38. David Foot, *Boom Bust & Echo* (Toronto: Macfarlane Walter & Ross, 1998).

39. Philip Bump, "Here is When Each Generation Begins and Ends, According to Facts," *The Atlantic online*, March 25, 2014, **http://www.theatlantic.com/national/archive/2014/03/here-is-when-each-generation-begins-and-ends-according-to-facts/359589/** (accessed December 16, 2015).

40. Meng Jing, "China Gushes over High-End Bottled Water," *China Daily*, October 7–13, 2011, p. 17; "$HK1.6bn Public Offer by Tibet 5100 to Fuel Tilt at Evian Market Share," *The Australian*, June 22, 2011, **www.theaustralian.com.au/business/markets/hk16bn-public-offer-by-tibet-5100-to-fuel-tiltat-evian-market-share/story-e6frg91o-1226079779794** (accessed November 1, 2011); Tibet 5100 website, **http://hk.5100.net/** (accessed November 1, 2011); "IPO Fact Sheet: Tibet 5100 Water Resources Holdings Limited (1115.HK)," VC Group, June 20, 2011, **www.vcgroup.com.hk/CM_v2/Document/tc/IPO%20Factsheet%20--%20Tibet%205100.pdf** (accessed November 1, 2011).

41. "Our Legacy of Support," RBC website, **http://www.rbc.com/community-sustainability/community/olympic-sponsors/legacy-of-support.html** (accessed December 17, 2015).

42. RBC Financial Group Sponsorship, **http://www.rbc.com/sponsorship/ownthepodium.html** (accessed July 7, 2010).

43. Nurse Next Door, **http://www.nursenextdoor.com/index.php** (accessed September 1, 2010); Medicard Finance Inc., **http://www.medicard.com/** (accessed September 1, 2010).

44. "Under Attack, Jim Flaherty Defends Mortgage Meddling," CTVNews online, March 20, 2013, **http://www.ctvnews.ca/canada/under-attack-jim-flaherty-defends-mortgage-meddling-1.1203361** (accessed August 5, 2013).

45. "CIBC becomes first major Canadian bank to offer a Mobile Banking App for iPhone," *CNW*, February 2, 2010, **http://www.newswire.ca/en/releases/archive/February2010/02/c6153.html** (accessed September 1, 2010).

46. "Growth is in the Bag," Canada Export Achievement Awards, **http://www.exportawards.ca/exportawards/quebec.html** (accessed September 1, 2010).

47. Kim Shiffman, "Overview: Role models for the recovery," *PROFITguide* online, May 28, 2010, **http://www.profitguide.com/article/4686--overview-role-models-for-the-recovery** (accessed September 28, 2010).

48. Marina Strauss, "Rona's Big Bet on Small Stores," *The Globe and Mail* online, September 21, 2012, **http://www.theglobeandmail.com/globe-investor/ronas-big-bet-on-small-stores/article4560618/**; Sarah Barmak, "Retailers Bring E-Shopping In-Store," *Canadian Business* online, December 8, 2012, **http://www.canadianbusiness.com/companies-and-industries/retailers-bring-e-shopping-in-store/** (both accessed August 5, 2013).

49. "McDonald's Franchisee's Jobs," CareerBuilder.com, **http://www.careerbuilder.com/Jobs/Company/C8E5975ZLC66B4JB4D4/McDonalds-Franchisees/** (accessed July 7, 2010); "AboutMcDonalds," **http://www.mcdonalds.com/corp/about.html** (accessed June 17, 2007).

50. Dr. Abdullah Kirumira, BioMedical Diagnostic Inc., in a personal interview with Peter Mombourquette, 2010. Information reconfirmed 2013.

51. Eleanor Beaton, "Gabrielle Chevalier, COO and grandmother, has turned Solutions 2 Go Inc. into the market leader," *PROFIT guide* online, October 13, 2010, **http://www.profitguide.com/article/6520--gabrielle-chevalier-coo-and-grandmother-has-turned-solutions-2-go-inc-into-the-market-leader**; Solutions 2 Go Inc., **http://www.solutions2go.ca/** (accessed September 1, 2010).

52. "Lululemon: Building the Brand From the Ground—Yoga Mat—Up," Strategyonline.ca, January 13, 2003, **http://strategyonline.ca/2003/01/13/lululemon-20030113/** (accessed August 5, 2013).

53. Ellen Roseman, "Blockbuster of Books," thestar.com, **http://www.thestar.com/article/269013** (accessed July 7, 2010).

54. Lee Oliver, "Appetite for resurrection," *CBOnline*, October 2003, **http://www.canadianbusiness.com/profit_magazine/article.jsp?content=20031020_142029_3976&page=1**.

55. Wency Leung, "Tim Hortons' Extra-Large Coffee to Get Even Larger," *The Globe and Mail* online, January 16, 2012, **http://www.theglobeandmail.com/life/food-and-wine/food-trends/tim-hortons-extra-large-coffee-to-get-even-larger/article1358604/** (accessed August 5, 2013).

56. Michael J. Weiss, "To Be About to Be," *American Demographics* 25 (September 2003), pp. 29–36.

57. "Ask the Legends: Les Mandelbaum," *CBOnline*, December 2009, **http://www.canadianbusiness.com/entrepreneur/managing/article.jsp?content=20091130_145811_9872**.

58. Rasha Mourtada, "Tour business," *The Globe and Mail* online, August 29, 2007, **http://www.theglobeandmail.com/report-on-business/tourbusiness/article778331/singlepage/#articlecontent**.

59. Rick Spence, "Sweetpea Baby Food: Stuck in the Middle," *CBOnline*, October 2007, **http://www.canadianbusiness.com/entrepreneur/sales_marketing/article.jsp?content=2007 1002_12233_12233&page=1**.

60. "Online Research Spending Predicted to Grow to $4 Billion," GMI, June 14, 2005, **www.gmi-mr.com/press/release.php?p= 2005-06-14** (accessed June 16, 2006).

61. Look-Look, **www.look-look.com** (accessed June 16, 2006).

62. Faith Keenan, "Friendly Spies on the Net," *BW Online*, July 9, 2001, **http://www.businessweek.com/magazine/content/01_28/b3740624.htm**.

63. Diane Brady, "Pets Are People, Too, You Know," *BusinessWeek*, November 28, 2005, p. 114.

64. Allison Fass, "Collective Opinion, Forget the Up-Close Focus Group. Newfangled Software Lets Lego, Procter & Gamble and Others Mine Ideas from Tens of Thousands of Opinionated Customers," *Forbes*, November 28, 2005, pp. 76–79; "About Us," **www.informative.com/aboutUs.html**; "Solutions and Services," **www.informative.com/solutionsServices.html**; "Customer Communities," **www.communispace.com/customer_c.htm**; "The Communispace Difference," **www.communispace.com/difference.htm**; "Technology and Services," **www.communispace.com/technology.htm** (all accessed December 10, 2005).

65. Chris Griffiths, "A Pro's Guide to Managing Your Reputation Online," *The Globe and Mail* online, November 6, 2012, **http://www.theglobeandmail.com/report-on-business/small-business/sb-digital/biz-categories-technology/a-pros-guide-to-managing-your-reputation-online/article4887679/**; and Harvey Schacter, "What's the Real Impact of Online Reviews?", *The Globe and Mail* online, October 10, 2011, **http://www.theglobeandmail.com/report-on-business/careers/management/whats-the-real-impact-of-online-reviews/article618142/** (both accessed July 9, 2013); Yelp website, **www.yelp.com** (accessed August 10, 2010); "Yelp Adds a Tiny Bit of Transparency...And Inches Away from Pay for Placement," The Entrepreneur's Corner, TechDirt, ww.techdirt.com/blog/entrepreneurs/articles/20100330/1539268795.shtml (accessed August 20, 2010); Peter Burrows & Joseph Galante, "Yelp: Advertise or Else?," *Bloomberg Businessweek*, March 3, 2010, **www.businessweek.com/magazine/content/10_11/b41 70027355708.htm** (accessed August 10, 2010); Jeremy, YELP CEO, "Additional Thoughts on Last Week's Lawsuit, or How a Conspiracy Theory Is Born," Yelp Web Log, **http://official blog.yelp.com/2010/03/additional-thoughts-on-last-weeks-lawsuit-or-how-a-conspiracy-theory-is-born-.html** (accessed August 10, 2010); Kermit Pattison, "Talking to the Chief of Yelp, the Site That Businesses Love to Hate," *The New York Times*, March 24, 2010, **www.nytimes.com/2010/03/25/business/smallbusiness/25sbiz.html** (accessed August 10, 2010); Bill Chappell, "Yelp Goes Unfiltered. Let the Arguments Begin," all tech CONSIDERED, NPR, April 6, 2010, **www.npr.org/blogs/alltechconsidered/2010/04/06/125631274/yelp-goes-unfiltered-let-the-arguments-begin** (accessed August 10, 2010); Jessica Guynn, "Restaurant Review Site Yelp and Reservation Booking Site OpenTable Team Up," *The Los Angeles Times*, June 3, 2010, **http://latimesblogs.latimes.com/technology/2010/06/restaurant-review-site-yelp-and-reservationbooking-site-opentable-team-up.html** (accessed August 10, 2010).

66. Emily Nelson, "P&G Checks Out Real Life," *The Wall Street Journal*, May 17, 2001, p. B1.

67. Normandy Madden, "'Rolling Stone' Smacks into Great Wall of China," *Advertising Age*, April 3, 2006, p. 8.

68. Jack Kaskey, "The Superweek Strikes Back," *Bloomberg Businessweek*, September 12–18, 2011, pp. 21–22; Andrew Pollack, "Widely Used Crop Herbicide Is Losing Weed Resistance," *New York Times*, January 14, 2003, **www.nytimes.com/2003/01/14/business/widely-used-crop-herbicide-islosing-weed-resistance.html** (accessed September 26, 2011).

69. Karen Valby, "The Man Who Ate Too Much," *Entertainment Weekly*, May 21, 2004, p. 45.

70. Anjali Cordeiro, "Kelloggs Retreats on Ads to Kids," June 14, 2007, **http://online.wsj.com/article/SB118177043343134415-search.html?KEYWORDS=obesity&COLLECTION=wsjie/6 month** (accessed June 17, 2007).

71. Bruce Horovitz, "Wendy's Will Be 1st Foodie with Healthier Oil," *USA Today*, June 8, 2006, p. 1A.

72. "Blue Nile, Inc.," Yahoo! Finance, **https://finance.yahoo.com/q/is?s=NILE** (accessed December 19, 2015).

73. "NEW STUDY: Americans Overpaying by as Much as 72% for an Engagement Ring," December 9, 2014, **http://investor.bluenile.com/releasedetail.cfm?releaseid=886831** (accessed December 19, 2015).

74. "Blue Nile, Inc.," *Wikipedia*, **http://en.wikipedia.org/wiki/Blue_Nile_Inc**. (accessed August 5, 2013).

Chapter 12

1. Douglas Soltys, "Shopify Is Now Worth 1.9 Billion USD," **Betakit.com**, May 21, 2015, **http://betakit.com/shopify-is-now-worth-1-9-billion-usd/** (accessed January 11, 2016).

2. Knowlton Thomas, "Shares in Shopify Jump 23% Following Integration with Amazon," **TechVibes.com**, September 18, 2015, **http://www.techvibes.com/blog/shopify-amazon-2015-09-18** (accessed January 11, 2016).

3. Trevor Cole, "Our Canadian CEO of the year you've probably never heard of," *Globe and Mail*, November 27, 2014, **http://www.theglobeandmail.com/report-on-business/rob-magazine/meet-our-ceo-of-the-year/article21734931/** (accessed January 11, 2016).

4. "Shopify Announces Third-Quarter 2015 Financial Results," Shopify website, November 4, 2015, **https://investors.shopify.com/Investor-News-Details/2015/Shopify-Announces-Third-Quarter-2015-Financial-Results/default.aspx** (accessed December 7, 2015).

5. Cole, "Our Canadian CEO of the year you've probably never heard of," **http://www.theglobeandmail.com/report-on-business/rob-magazine/meet-our-ceo-of-the-year/article 21734931/**.

6. Mark Anderson, "Canada's Smartest Company: Shopify," *ProfitGuide*, November 28, 2012, **www.profitguide.com/industry-focus/-technology/canadas-smartest-company-44283** (accessed January 10, 2016).

7. Ibid.

8. Website Builder Expert, **http://www.websitebuilderexpert.com** (accessed January 10, 2016).

9. Zack Guzman, "Shopify CEO discusses shares surging 69% in trading debut," CNBC, May 21, 2015, **http://www.cnbc.com/2015/05/21/shopify-ceo-discusses-shares-surging-69-in-trading-debut.html** (accessed January 10, 2016).

10. Sunny Freeman, "Tobias Lutke made Shopify a Canadian tech darling," *Toronto Star*, December 28, 2015, **http://www.thestar.com/news/insight/2015/12/28/tobias-lutke-made-shopify-a-canadian-tech-darling.html** (accessed January 11, 2016).

11. Charles Arthur, "PlayBook writeoff means RIM's tablet has been a $1.5bn mistake," *The Guardian*, December 5, 2011, **http://www.guardian.co.uk/technology/blog/2011/dec/05/playbook-writeoff-rim-tablet-mistake** (accessed July 11, 2013).

12. Umbra, **http://www.umbra.com/**; "Ask the Legends: Les Mandelbaum," *Canadian Business*, December 2009, **http://www.canadianbusiness.com/entrepreneur/managing/article.jsp?content=20091130_145811_9872** (accessed September 1, 2010).

13. Galen Gruman, "Rotten Apple: Apple's 12 Biggest Failures," *CIO*, **http://www.cio.com/article/507483/Rotten_Apple_Apple_s_12_Biggest_Failures?page=13#slideshow** (accessed July 11, 2013).

14. "Nortel," *Wikipedia* website, **http://en.wikipedia.org/wiki/Nortel** (accessed July 11, 2013).

15. "New Products," The Coca Cola Company, **www.thecoca-colacompany.com/presscenter/newproducts.html** (accessed June 17, 2007).

16. Steve Rosenbush, "At GM, Tech Is Steering," *BusinessWeek*, May 27, 2004, **www.businessweek.com/**.

17. Sam Oliver, "Apple's R&D spending shoots up 42% year-over-year, hit new 19B record in Q1," AppleInsider.com, January 28, 2015, **http://appleinsider.com/articles/15/01/28/apples-rd-spending-shoots-up-42-year-over-year-hit-new-19b-record-in-q1** (accessed January 11, 2016).

18. "About Microsoft Research," Microsoft Research, **http://research.microsoft.com/en-us/about/default.aspx** (accessed September 1, 2010).

19. "Karen Crouse, "A Fashion Statement Designed to Grab Gold," NYTimes.com, February 11, 2010, **http://www.nytimes.com/2010/02/12/sports/olympics/12speedsuits.html**.

20. "About Us," Spindle, Stairs and Railings, **http://www.greatstairs.com/aboutus.cfm** (accessed June 17, 2010).

21. Joe Castaldo, "The Case for Stealing Your Success," *ProfitGuide*, June 12, 2014, **http://www.profitguide.com/manage-grow/innovation/steal-your-success-66165** (accessed January 12, 2016).

22. "Best Inventions of the Year 2012: Self-Inflating Tires," *TIME*, October 31, 2012, **http://techland.time.com/2012/11/01/best-inventions-of-the-year-2012/slide/self-inflating-tires/** (accessed July 11, 2013).

23. "*Dragons' Den*—Pitches," CBC Television, **http://www.cbc.ca/dragonsden/s5.html#ep2** (accessed June 17, 2010).

24. Brett Shevack, "Open Up to a New Way to Develop Better Ideas," *Point*, June 2006, p. 8.

25. Judann Pollack, "The Endurance Test, Heinz Ketchup," *Advertising Age*, November 14, 2005, p. 39.

26. Oliver Burkman, "Happiness is a Glass Half-Empty," *The Guardian* online, June 15, 2012, **http://www.guardian.co.uk/lifeandstyle/2012/jun/15/happiness-is-being-a-loser-burkeman**; Dan Gould, "The Museum of Product Failures," *PSFK* online, August 12, 2008, **http://techland.time.com/2012/11/01/best-inventions-of-the-year-2012/slide/self-inflating-tires/** (both accessed July 11, 2013).

27. "Digital Payment Technologies Named to Deloitte's 2010 Technology Fast 500™" in North America," Digital Payment Technologies, October 25, 2010, **http://www.digitalpaytech.com/news/press_releases/2010/101025_Fast_500.pdf** (accessed November 17, 2010).

28. Faith Keenan, "Friendly Spies on the Net," *BW Online*, July 9, 2001, **http://www.businessweek.com/magazine/content/01_28/b3740624.htm**.

29. James Cowan, "Tim Hortons' New Coffee Cup: Why the Supersize?", *Canadian Business*, February 14, 2012, **http://www.canadianbusiness.com/business-strategy/tim-hortons-new-coffee-cup-why-the-supersize/** (accessed July 11, 2013); "Tim Horton's tempest in a tea cup," CBC News, November 26, 2001, **http://www.cbc.ca/news/story/2001/11/23/TimmysTea_011123.html** (accessed June 15, 2006).

30. "Jan 24—Imperial Tobacco Canada Expands Harm Reduction program with start of a Snus market in Ottawa," Imperial Tobacco Canada, January 24, 2008, **http://www.imperialtobaccocanada.com/groupca/sites/IMP_7VSH6J.nsf/vwPagesWebLive/DO7WNJHL?opendocument&SKN=1** (accessed November 17, 2010).

31. Seasons 52, **www.seasons52.com** (accessed June 15, 2006).

32. William C. Symonds, "Gillette's New Edge: P&G Is Helping Pump Up the Fusion Razor," *BusinessWeek*, February 6, 2006, p. 44.

33. "Best Inventions of the Year 2012: Techpet," *TIME* online, October 31, 2012, **http://techland.time.com/2012/11/01/best-inventions-of-the-year-2012/slide/techpet**; "Best Inventions of the Year 2012: Google Glass," *TIME* online, October 31, 2012, **http://techland.time.com/2012/11/01/best-inventions-of-the-year-2012/slide/google-glass** (accessed July 11, 2013).

34. Reena Jana, "Green Threads for the Eco Chic," *BusinessWeek*, September 27, 2006, **www.businessweek.com/print/innovate/content/sep2006/id20060927_111136.htm** (accessed June 20, 2007); Laura Petrecca and Theresa Howard, "Eco-marketing a Hot Topic for Advertisers at Cannes," *USA Today*, June 22, 2007, **www.usatoday.com/money/advertising/2007-06-22-cannes-green-usat_N.htm?csp=34** (accessed June 23, 2007); Laura McClure, "Green Jeans," *Reader's Digest*, June 2007, p. 213; "Levi's Brand Launches 100% Organic Cotton Jeans," **www.levistrauss.com**, July 5, 2006, **http://www.levistrauss.com/News/PressReleaseDetail.aspx?pid=784** (accessed June 20, 2007).

35. "Tide Unveils Milestone in Fabric Care with New Tide Stainbrush," Procter & Gamble, press release, February 13, 2004, **www.pg.com/news/**.

36. Allison Enright, "The Urge to Merge," *Marketing News*, March 15, 2006, pp. 9–10.

37. T. L. Stanley, "Barbie Hits the Skids," *Advertising Age*, October 31, 2005, pp. 1, 33.

36. Allison Enright, "The Urge to Merge," *Marketing News*, March 15, 2006, pp. 9–10.

38. Eric Wellweg, "Test Time for TiVo," *Business2.0*, May 24, 2004, **www.business2.com/**.

39. "Glenora Distillers," *Wikipedia website*, **http://en.wikipedia.org/wiki/Glenora_Distillers**; The Glenora Inn & Distillery website, **http://www.glenoradistillery.com/glen.html** (accessed July 11, 2013).

40. David Goldman and Julianne Pepitone, "Lady Gaga is the new face of Polaroid," *CNN Money*, January 8, 2010, **http://money.cnn.com/2010/01/06/news/companies/lady_gaga_polaroid/** (accessed June 17, 2010); Jason Kirby, "Polaroid goes Gaga," *CBOnline*, February 15, 2010, **http://www.canadianbusiness.com/managing/strategy/article.jsp?content=20100113_10010_10010** (accessed June 17, 2010).

41. "Rankings," Interbrand.com, **http://interbrand.com/best-brands/best-global-brands/2015/ranking/** (accessed January 12, 2016).

42. "Best Canadian Brands 2014," Interbrand, **http://interbrand.com/wp-content/uploads/2015/08/Interbrand-Best-Canadian-Brands-2014.pdf** (accessed January 13, 2016).

43. "Loblaw Companies," **http://en.wikipedia.org/wiki/Loblaw_Companies** (accessed June 17, 2010); "Sobey's," **http://en.wikipedia.org/wiki/Sobeys** (accessed June 17, 2010).

44. Alessandra Galloni, "Advertising," *The Wall Street Journal*, June 1, 2001, p. B6.

45. Madhuri Katti, "Coke Displays Aboriginal Art on Bottles at Vancouver Winter Olympics 2010," Trends Updates, February 18, 2010, **http://trendsupdates.com/coke-displays-aboriginal-art-on-bottles-at-vancouver-winter-olympics-2010/** (accessed June 17, 2010).

46. Dagmar Mussey, "Coke Bottle Shape-Shifts for World Cup in Germany," *Advertising Age*, May 29, 2006, p. 12.

47. Pallavi Gogoi, "McDonald's New Wrap," *BusinessWeek*, February 17, 2006, **www.businessweek.com/print/bwdaily/dnflash/feb2006/nf20060217_8329_db016.htm?chan=db** (accessed February 2006).

48. Stephanie Miles, "Consumer Groups Want to Rate the Web," *The Wall Street Journal*, June 21, 2001, p. B13.

49. Rajneesh Suri and Kent B. Monroe, "The Effects of Time Constraints on Consumers' Judgments of Prices and Products," *Journal of Consumer Research* 30 (June 2003), pp. 92 +.

50. Steven Gray, "McDonald's Menu Upgrade Boosts Meal Prices and Results," *The Wall Street Journal*, February 18, 2006, p. A1.

51. Craig Sutherland, in a personal interview with Peter Mombourquette, August 4, 2010. Information reconfirmed 2016.

53. David Luhnow and Chad Terhune, "Latin Pop: A Low-Budget Cola Shakes Up Markets South of the Border," *The Wall Street Journal*, October 27, 2003, pp. A1, A18.

54. Stephanie Thompson, "Polo Jeans Thrown in the Hamper," *Advertising Age*, June 5, 2006, p. 3.

55. "Tim Hortons Changing Cup Sizes Across the Country," CTV, January 16, 2012, **http://www.ctvnews.ca/tim-hortons-changing-cup-sizes-across-the-country-1.75466**; Wency Leung, "Tim Hortons' Extra-Large Coffee to Get Even Larger," *Globe and Mail*, January 16, 2012, **http://www.theglobeandmail.com/life/food-and-wine/food-trends/tim-hortons-extra-large-coffee-to-get-even-larger/article1358604**; Emily Jackson, "Tim Hortons Supersizes Its Coffee Cups," *Toronto Star*, January 16, 2012, **http://www.thestar.com/business/2012/01/16/tim_hortons_supersizes_its_coffee_cups.html**; James Cowan, "Tim Hortons' New Coffee Cup: Why the Supersize?" *Canadian Business*, February 14, 2012, **http://www.canadianbusiness.com/business-strategy/tim-hortons-new-coffee-cup-why-the-supersize/** (all accessed July 11, 2013).

56. "In Canada, Retail Ecommerce Sales to Rise by Double Digits Through 2019," EMarketer.com, July 24, 2015, **http://www.emarketer.com/Article/Canada-Retail-Ecommerce-Sales-Rise-by-Double-Digits-Through-2019/1012771** (accessed January 13, 2016).

57. O. C. Ferrell and Michael D. Hartline, *Marketing Strategy* (Mason, OH: South-Western, 2005), p. 215.

58. "Top Threats to Revenue," *USA Today*, February 1, 2006, p. A1.

59. Todd Wasserman, "Kodak Rages in Favor of the Machines," *BrandWeek*, February 26, 2001, p. 6.

60. Tony Martin, "Ask the Legends: Walter Hachborn," *Canadian Business*, March 2009, **http://www.canadianbusiness.com/article.jsp?content=20090201_30016_30017** (accessed June 17, 2010).

61. Brad Stone, "A Virtual Garage Sale Takes On Craigslist," *Bloomberg Businessweek*, April 2, 2015, **http://www.bloomberg.com/news/articles/2015-04-02/varagesale-takes-on-craigslist-via-mobile-app** (accessed January 13, 2016).

62. "Meet Tami, Chief Mom at VarageSale," VarageSale.com, September 24, 2014, **https://www.varagesale.com/blog/meet-tami-chief-mom-at-varagesale/** (accessed January 13, 2016).

63. Stone, "A Virtual Garage Sale Takes On Craigslist," **http://www.bloomberg.com/news/articles/2015-04-02/varagesale-takes-on-craigslist-via-mobile-app**.

64. Amber MacArthur, "PEI's (million dollar) Google juice," *Globe and Mail*, July 14, 2010, **http://www.theglobeandmail.com/news/technology/trending-tech/peis-million-dollar-google-juice/article1639896/** (accessed August 3, 2010).

65. "Where advertisers are spending their money in Canada," *Globe and Mail*, September 30, 2015, **http://www.theglobeandmail.com/report-on-business/industry-news/marketing/where-advertisers-are-spending-their-money-in-canada/article26597480/** (accessed November 14, 2016).

66. "22nd Annual Profit 100: Canada's Fastest Growing Companies," *Canadian Business* online, 2010, **http://list.canadianbusiness.com/rankings/profit100/2010/include/Profit-100-Next-100-downloadable.xls** (accessed June 17, 2010).

67. "Canadians Lead in Time Spent Online," CBC News website, March 2, 2012, **http://www.cbc.ca/news/canada/story/2012/03/02/canadians-more-time-online.html** (accessed July 14, 2013).

68. Julia Alexander, "Canadians spend the most time online: Study," *Toronto Sun*, March 27, 2015, **http://www.torontosun.com/2015/03/27/canadians-spend-the-most-time-online-study** (accessed January 14, 2016).

69. Andrew Willis, "How the torch lit the way for RBC," *The Globe and Mail* online, February 9, 2010, **http://www.theglobeandmail.com/globe-investor/investment-ideas/streetwise/**

how-the-torch-lit-the-way-for-rbc/article1460954/ (accessed June 17, 2010); Marina Strauss, "HBC tries to build on Olympic momentum," *The Globe and Mail* online, February 26, 2010, **http://www.theglobeandmail.com/report-on-business/ hbc-tries-to-build-on-olympic-momentum/article1483478/** (accessed June 17, 2010); Michael Brush, "Less gold for Olympic sponsors?" *MSN Money*, February 9, 2010, **http://articles. moneycentral.msn.com/Investing/CompanyFocus/less- gold-for-olympic-sponsors.aspx** (accessed June 17, 2010).

70. Heidi Cohen, "2016 Mobile Marketing Trends Every Marketer Needs," January 11, 2016, HeidiCohen.com, **http://heidicohen. com/2016-mobile-marketing-trends/** (accessed January 14, 2016).

71. Eleanor Beaton, "Sales & Marketing: How to sell more, more, more," *PROFITguide* online, May 28, 2010, **http://www. profitguide.com/article/4689--sales-marketing-how-to- sell-more-more-more** (accessed June 17, 2010).

72. "The Top 20 Valuable Facebook Statistics," *Zephoria Digital Marketing* online, updated December 2015, **https://zephoria. com/top-15-valuable-facebook-statistics/** (accessed January 14, 2016).

73. Craig Smith, "By The Numbers: 200+ Amazing Facebook Statistics" DMR Digital Stats/Gadgets, January 2016, **http:// expandedramblings.com/index.php/by-the-numbers- 17-amazing-facebook-stats/** (accessed January 16, 2016).

74. Derek Thompson, "The Profit Network: Facebook and Its 835-Million Man Workforce," *The Atlantic* online, February 2, 2012, **http://www.theatlantic.com/business/archive/2012/02/ the-profit-network-facebook-and-its-835-million-man- workforce/252473/** (accessed July 30, 2013).

75. "Terre Bleu Lavender Farm," Facebook.com, Success Stories, **https://www.facebook.com/business/success/terre-bleu- lavender-farm** (accessed January 16, 2016).

76. "Top Sites in Canada," Alexa website, **http://www.alexa.com/ topsites/countries/CA** (both accessed July 30, 2013).

77. Tony Martin, "They blog, therefore they are … better CEOs," March 15, 2008, *GlobeAdvisor.com*, **http://www.globeadvisor. com/servlet/ArticleNews/story/gam/20080315/RWORK OUT15** (accessed June 17, 2010); Grant Robertson, "CEO blogs: The new company 'water cooler,'" *The Globe and Mail* online, February 6, 2006, **http://www.theglobeandmail.com/news/ technology/ceo-blogs-the-new-company-water-cooler/ article810687/singlepage/** (accessed June 17, 2010).

78. Kara Aaserud, "Bonding by Blogging," Provident Security Press, October 1, 2006, **http://www.providentsecurity.ca/press/31** (accessed June 17, 2010).

79. Beaton, "Sales & Marketing: How to sell more, more, more."

80. "Direct Mail," Answers.com, **http://www.answers.com/topic/ direct-marketing** (accessed June 17, 2010).

81. Jefferson Graham, "Web Pitches, That's 'Advertainment'," *USA Today*, June 26, 2001, p. 3D.

82. "Meet eBay Canada's Entrepreneur of the Year," *TechVibes* online, October 4, 2012, **http://www.techvibes.com/blog/ meet-ebay-canadas-entrepreneur-of-the-year-2012-10-04** (accessed July 14, 2013).

83. "Top Sites in Canada," Alexa website.

84. Chris Neville, in a personal interview with Peter Mombour- quette, February 14, 2013.

85. Ritesh Bhavnani, "Top Ten Mobile Marketing Trends for 2016," LuxuryDaily.com, January 5, 2016, **http://www.luxurydaily. com/top-10-mobile-marketing-trends-for-2016/** (accessed January 15, 2016).

86. Christine Dobby, "Checkout 51 App Lets You Shop Anywhere, Snap Pics of Receipt for Savings, *Financial Post*, December 14, 2012, **http://business.financialpost.com/entrepreneur/ fp-startups/checkout-51-app-lets-you-shop-anywhere- snap-pics-of-receipt-for-savings?_lsa=6930-d566** (accessed January 15, 2016).

87. Paul Skeldon, "14 Million Americans Scanned QR and Barcodes with Their Mobiles in June 2011," *Internet Retail- ing* online, August 16, 2011, **http://www.internetretailing. net/2011/08/14m-americans-scanned-qr-and-bar-codes- with-their-mobiles-in-june-2011** (accessed July 14, 2013).

88. Derek Johnson, "10 Amazing Retail Mobile Marketing Exam- ples" *Tatango*, February 18, 2014, **http://www.tatango.com/ blog/10-amazing-retail-mobile-marketing-examples/**

89. Chris Atchison, "Entrepreneurial success: Masters of one," *Canadian Business*, May 2009, **http://www.canadianbusiness. com/entrepreneur/sales_marketing/article.jsp?cont ent=20090501_30008_30008.**

90. Jim McElgunn and Kim Shiffman, "Canada's Entrepreneurs of the Decade," *CBOnline*, December 2009, **http://www.canadian business.com/entrepreneur/managing/article.jsp?cont ent=20091201_30044_30044;** Just Energy Income Fund, **http://www.je-un.ca/SiteResources/ViewContent.asp?Doc ID=3&v1ID=&RevID=730&lang=1** (accessed July 17, 2010).

91. Zach Bulygo, "How Mint Grew to 1.5M Users, and Sold for over $170M in just 2 Years", *Kissmetrics*, January 22, 2016, **https:// blog.kissmetrics.com/how-mint-grew/**

92. James Obrien, "How Red Bull Takes Content Market- ing to the Extreme", December 19, 2012, **http://mashable. com/2012/12/19/red-bull-content-marketing/#. X5vmj0F75qu** (accessed February 14, 2016)

93. Beaton, "Sales & Marketing: How to sell more, more, more."

94. Susanne Baillie and Kim Shiffman, "How to get on Oprah," *Canadian Business* online, February 2004, **http://www.canadianbusiness. com/entrepreneur/sales_marketing/article.jsp?cont ent=20040213_155625_4316** (accessed June 17, 2010).

95. Andy Holloway, "The right way to tee off," *Canadian Busi- ness* online, December 2006, **http://www.canadianbusiness. com/entrepreneur/sales_marketing/article.jsp?cont ent=20061201_152142_5592.**

96. "Lululemon Canada's Fastest Growing Brand, as TD, RIM Still Top List: Study," *Financial Post*, June 7, 2012, **http://business.financial post.com/2012/06/07/lululemon-canadas-fastest-growing- brand-as-td-rim-still-top-list-study** (accessed July 14, 2013).

97. Disruptive Dave, "Meeting Customers Where They Are At," My Disruption Blog, October 2, 2012, **http://mydisruption.wordpress. com/2012/10/02/meeting-customers-where-they-are-at** (accessed July 14, 2013).

98. "VANOC accuses Lululemon of bad sportsmanship," *Marketing*, December 16, 2009, **http://www.marketingmag.ca/english/ news/marketer/article.jsp?content=20091216_150310_ 9752** (accessed June 17, 2010); "Lululemon Athletica," **http:// en.wikipedia.org/wiki/Lululemon_Athletica**, (accessed June 17, 2010).

99. Donna Montaldo, "2005 Coupon Usage and Trends," About.com, **http://couponing.about.com/od/groceryzone/a/2005cp_usage.htm** (accessed June 17, 2010).

100. Kate MacArthur, "Sierra Mist: Cie Nicholson," *Advertising Age*, November 17, 2003, p. S-2.

101. "A tale of two customers," Canada Export Achievement Awards, **http://www.exportawards.ca/exportawards/atlantic.html** (accessed June 17, 2010).

102. Michelle Maynard, "Amid the Turmoil, A Rare Success at DaimlerChrysler," *Fortune*, January 22, 2001, p. 112.

103. "Coca-Cola North America Announces the Launch of VAULT," February 17, 2006, **www2.coca-cola.com/presscenter/newproducts_vault.html** (accessed June 16, 2006).

104. "Don't Be Fooled by Greenwashing," *The Vancouver Province* online, February 24, 2008, **http://www.canada.com/story.html?id=92a3d1cc-596c-4c10-9f69-f89c879768fa**; "Questions and Answers about Fur," **http://www.furisgreen.com/questions_about_fur.aspx** and "Fur, a Renewable Resource," Fur Is Green website, **http://www.furisgreen.com/renewable.aspx**; Shannon Kornelsen, "The Only Thing Green About Fur is Profit," *The Huffington Post; The Blog*, February 25, 2013, **http://www.huffingtonpost.ca/shannon-kornelsen/fur-isnt-green_b_2755972.html** (all accessed July 14, 2013); **http://www.canadianlawyermag.com/Watch-out-for-green-washing.html**; Laura Petrecca and Christine Dugas, "Going Truly Green Might Require Detective Work," *USA Today*, April 22, 2010, pp. 1B–2B; Laura Petrecca and Christina Dugas, "Groups Help Consumers Find 'Real' Green Products," *USA Today*, April 22, 2010, p. 2B; Julie Deardorff, "How to Spot Greenwashing," *Chicago Tribune*, May 7, 2010, **http://featuresblogs.chicagotribune.com/features_julieshealthclub/2010/05/how-to-spot-greenwashing.html** (accessed June 13, 2010); Sarah Mahoney, "H&M Introduces Its First Organic Skincare," MarketingDaily, March 3, 2010, **www.mediapost.com/publications/?fa=Articles.showArticle&art_aid=123424** (accessed June 13, 2010); Leslie Berkman, "Efforts Spread to Verify Claims of Businesses Who Market Themselves as Environmentally Friendly," *The Press-Enterprise*, January 31, 2010, **www.pe.com/business/local/stories/PE_New_Local_W_green01.46c7f14.html** (accessed June 13, 2010); **www.greenwashingindex.com** (accessed June 13, 2010); Julie Deardorff, "Eco-friendly Claims: When Is 'Green' Really Green?," *Chicago Tribune*, May 7, 2010, **http://featuresblogs.chicagotribune.com/features_julieshealthclub/2010/05/ecofriendly-claims-when-is-green-really-green.html** (accessed December 12, 2010).

Chapter 13

1. "Bio," Arlene Dickinson website, **http://arlenedickinson.com/bio/**; Angus Gillespie, "Power of Persuasion-The Inspirational Life Story of Arlene Dickinson," *The Canadian Business Journal* online, **http://www.cbj.ca/features/may_12_features/power_of_persuasion_the_inspirational_life_story_of_arlene_dicki.html** (both accessed July 16, 2013).

2. The material in this chapter is reserved for use in the authors' other textbooks and teaching materials.

3. Brad Stone and Bruce Einhorn, "Baidu China," *Bloomberg Businessweek*, November 15–21, 2010, pp. 60–67; Loretta Chao, "China's Baidu Brings App Craze to Web," *The Wall Street Journal*, September 3, 2010, p. B8.

4. Steve Ladurantaye, "Canada Tops Globe in Internet Usage," *Globe and Mail*, March 1, 2012, **http://www.theglobeandmail.com/technology/tech-news/canada-tops-globe-in-internet-usage/article551593/** (accessed July 16, 2013).

5. Ken Tencer, "What's Better than a Great Communication Strategy? Conversation," *Globe and Mail*, March 13, 2013, **http://www.theglobeandmail.com/report-on-business/small-business/sb-digital/innovation/whats-better-than-a-great-communication-strategy-conversation/article9600803/** (accessed July 16, 2013).

6. "Fortune 500," *Fortune*, **http://fortune.com/fortune500/** (accessed March 2, 2016).

7. "Fortune 500: **Amazon.com**," *Fortune*, 2009, **http://money.cnn.com/magazines/fortune/fortune500/2009/snapshots/10810.html** (accessed April 13, 2011); Josh Quitter, "How Jeff Bezos Rules the Retail Space," *Fortune*, May 5, 2008, pp. 127–132.

8. "Media Info," Hulu, **www.hulu.com/about** (accessed April 13, 2011).

9. Bobby White, "The New Workplace Rules: No Video-Watching," *The Wall Street Journal*, March 4, 2008, p. B1.

10. Melody McKinnon, "2015 Canadian Social Media Usage Statistics," CanadiansInternet.com, January 12, 2015, **http://canadiansinternet.com/2015-canadian-social-media-usage-statistics/**.

11. "A World of Connections," *The Economist*, January 28, 2010, **www.economist.com/node/15351002** (accessed January 27, 2011).

12. "Internet Users," *Internet Live Stats*, 2014, **http://www.internetlivestats.com/internet-users/** (accessed February 23, 2016).

13. Michael V. Copeland. "Tapping Tech's Beautiful Mind," *Fortune*, October 12, 2009, pp. 35–36.

14. Jacqueline Nelson, "Business without Borders: Coastal Contacts," *Canadian Business* online, March 13, 2012, **http://www.canadianbusiness.com/business-news/industries/consumer-goods/business-without-borders-coastal-contacts/** (accessed July 30, 2013).

15. "By the Numbers: 17 Amazing Etsy Statistics", *DMR Digitial Stats/Gadgets*, December 2, 2015, **http://expandedramblings.com/index.php/etsy-statistics/** (accessed January 4, 2016)

16. Miguel Bustillo and Geoffrey A. Fowler, "Walmart Uses Its Stores to Get an Edge Online," *The Wall Street Journal*, December 15, 2009, p. B1.

17. Aaron Back, "China's Big Brands Tackle Web Sales," *The Wall Street Journal*, December 1, 2009, p. B2.

18. "2009 Digital Handbook," *Marketing News*, April 30, 2009, p. 13.

19. "About Us," Mobovivo website, **http://www.mobovivo.com/about-us/team.html** (accessed July 16, 2013).

20. Cameron Chapman, "The History and Evolution of Social Media." *WebDesigner Depot*, October 7, 2009, **www.webdesignerdepot.com/2009/10/the-history-and-evolution-of-social-media/** (accessed April 19, 2011).

21. Danah M. Boyd and Nicole B. Ellison, "Social Network Sites: Definition, History, and Scholarship," *Journal of Computer-Mediated Education*, 2007, **http://jcmc.indiana.edu/vol13/issue1/boyd.ellison.html** (accessed April 19, 2011).

22. Emily Schmall, "Growing Pains," *Forbes*, August 11, 2008, pp. 60–63.

23. Zachary Karabell, "To Tweet or Not to Tweet," April 12, 2011, *Time*, p. 24.

24. "2009 Digital Handbook," p. 11.

25. Charlene Li and Josh Bernoff, *Groundswell* (Boston: Harvard Business Press, 2008), p. 43.

26. A.C. Nielsen, "Global Faces and Networked Places: A Nielsen Report on Social Networking's New Global Footprint," March 2009, **http://blog.nielsen.com/nielsenwire/wp-content/uploads/2009/03/nielsen_globalfaces_mar09.pdf** (accessed April 19, 2011).

27. "Couldn't Stop the Spread of the Conversation in Reactions from Other Bloggers," from Hyejin Kim's May 4, 2007, blog post "Korea: Bloggers and Donuts" on the blog Global Voices at **http://groundswell.forrester.com/site1-16** (accessed April 19, 2011).

28. Mia Pearson, "Why corporate blogging is on the rebound," *Globe and Mail*, March 21, 2013, **http://www.theglobeandmail.com/report-on-business/small-business/sb-digital/biz-categories-technology/why-corporate-blogging-is-on-the-rebound/article10003057/** (accessed July 17, 2013).

29. Drake Bennett, "Assessing Wikipedia, Wiki-Style, on Its 10th Anniversary," *Bloomberg Businessweek*, January 10–16, 2011, pp. 57–61.

30. Li and Bernoff, *Groundswell*, pp. 25–26.

31. "2009 Digital Handbook," p. 11.

32. Jeff Bullas, "30 Mind-Numbing YouTube Facts, Figures, and Statistics," **jeffbullas.com**, **http://www.jeffbullas.com/2012/05/23/35-mind-numbing-youtube-facts-figures-and-statistics-infographic/** (accessed July 30, 2013).

33. "Statistics", *YouTube, January 23, 2016*, **https://www.youtube.com/yt/press/statistics.html**

34. Susan Krashinsky, "YouTube unveils list of most-watched ads in Canada this year," *Globe and Mail*, December 9, 2015, **http://www.theglobeandmail.com/report-on-business/industry-news/marketing/which-ads-did-canadians-watch-most-this-year-youtube-unveils-list/article27652445/** (accessed December 18, 2016).

35. "WestJet Introduces Child-Free Cabins," WestJet website, **http://www.westjet.com/guest/en/deals/promo-code/april-fools.shtml**; "Lululemon's April Fool's Prank: Introducing Lulu Leather," *The Huffington Post* online, April 1, 2013, **http://www.huffingtonpost.ca/2013/04/01/lululemon-lululeather_n_2994378.html**; "April Fool's 'lululeather' prank disgusts some yoga fans," CBC News online, **http://www.cbc.ca/news/canada/british-columbia/story/2013/04/01/bc-lululemon-companies-april-fools.html** (both accessed July 17, 2013).

36. David Meerman Scott, *The New Rules of Marketing & PR* (Hoboken, NJ: John Wiley & Sons, Inc., 2009), p. 224; "Mainframe: The Art of the Sales, Lesson One," YouTube, **www.youtube.com/watch?v=MSqXKp-00Hm**; Ryan Rhodes, "The Mainframe: It's Like a Barn," IBM Systems, March–April 2007, **www.ibmsystemsmag.com/mainframe/marchapril07/stoprun/11984p1.aspx** (both accessed April 13, 2011).

37. "It's Your Job Video Contest," Ontario Ministry of Labour, **http://www.labour.gov.on.ca/english/contest/index.php** (accessed July 30, 2013).

38. "Crash the Superbowl Winners and Finalists," Frito Lay Facebook page, **https://apps.facebook.com/crashthesuperbowl/**;

"Crash the Superbowl," *Wikipedia*, **http://en.wikipedia.org/wiki/Crash_the_Super_Bowl** (both accessed July 30, 2013).

39. "Search Giant Google to Buy YouTube for $1.65B," FoxNews.com, October 10, 2006, **www.foxnews.com/story/0,2933,218921,00.html** (accessed April 13, 2011).

40. Zeke Camusio, "Flickr Marketing—6 Awesome Tactics to Promote Your Website on Flickr," The Outsourcing Company, February 19, 2009, **www.theoutsourcingcompany.com/blog/social-media-marketing/flickr-marketing-6-awesome-tactics-to-promote-your-website-on-flickr/** (accessed April 19, 2011).

41. Bianca Male, "How to Promote Your Business on Flickr," *The Business Insider*, December 1, 2009, **www.businessinsider.com/how-to-promote-your-business-on-flickr-2009-12?utm_source=feedburner&utm_medium=feed&utm_campaign=Feed%3A+businessinsider+(The+Business+Insider)** (accessed on April 13, 2011).

42. "How to Market on Flickr," Small Business Search Marketing, **www.smallbusinesssem.com/articles/marketing-on-flickr/#ixzz0cLIpJUTW** (accessed April 13, 2011).

43. Sage Lewis, "Using Flickr for Marketing," YouTube, uploaded February 13, 2007, **www.youtube.com/watch?v=u2Xyzkfzlug** (accessed January 11, 2010).

44. Ryan Caligiuri, "Can small businesses harness that Old Spice magic?", *The Globe and Mail* online, August 20, 2010, **http://www.theglobeandmail.com/report-on-business/your-business/grow/ryan-caligiuri/can-small-businesses-harness-that-old-spice-magic/article1679081/**; TeamSave, **www.teamsave.com/**; Becky Reuber, "Startup picks fight with social-buying giant Groupon," *The Globe and Mail* online, September 17, 2010, **http://www.theglobeandmail.com/report-on-business/your-business/grow/customer-experience/startup-picks-fight-with-social-buying-giant-groupon/article1710446/** (both accessed July 17, 2010).

45. "Audio: NPR Podcasts Downloads", *Pew Research Centre*, **http://www.journalism.org/media-indicators/audio-npr-podcast-downloads/** (accessed April 09, 2015)

46. "2009 Digital Handbook," p. 14.

47. Melody McKinnon, "2015 Canadian Social Media Usage Statistics," CanadiansInternet.com, January 12, 2015, **http://canadiansinternet.com/2015-canadian-social-media-usage-statistics/**.

48. "2009 Digital Handbook," p. 13.

49. Li and Bernoff, *Groundswell*, p. 22.

50. Charlotte Henry, "Pinterest vs. Flickr: the Battle for Photo Dominance," *The Wall* website, March 6, 2013, **http://wallblog.co.uk/2013/03/06/pinterest-vs-flickr-the-battle-for-photo-dominance/** (accessed July 17, 2013).

51. "Facebook: Largest, Fastest Growing Social Network," *Tech Tree*, August 13, 2008, **www.techtree.com/India/News/Facebook_Largest_Fastest_Growing_Social_Network/551-92134-643.html** (accessed April 13, 2011).

52. McKinnon, "2015 Canadian Social Media Usage Statistics."

53. Nick Summers, "Heated Rivalries:#9 Facebook vs. MySpace," *Newsweek*, **www.2010.newsweek.com/top-10/heated-rivalries/facebook-vs-myspace.html** (accessed April 13, 2011).

54. "2009 Digital Handbook," p. 13.

55. "Hockey Night in Canada theme contest opens," CBC News online, June 19, 2008, **http://www.cbc.ca/sports/hockey/**

story/2008/06/19/hockey-song-contest.html (accessed July 17, 2013).

56. "Measure for Measure Facebook Ads Deliver," Facebook, **https://www.facebook.com/business/success/stratford-festival** (accessed February 11, 2016).

57. "Canada Facebook Statistics," Socialbakers website, **http://www.socialbakers.com/facebook-statistics/canada** (accessed July 17, 2013).

58. Melody McKinnon, "Marketers Reveal Their Most Effective Social Marketing Tactics," CanadiansInternet.com, March 11, 2014, **http://canadiansinternet.com/marketers-reveal-effective-social-marketing-tactics/**.

59. "Pepsi Refresh Project," **www.refresheverything.com/index** (accessed April 13, 2011); Stuart Elliot, "Pepsi Invites the Public to Do Good," *The New York Times*, January 31, 2010, **www.nytimes.com/2010/02/01/business/media/01adco.html** (accessed April 13, 2011).

60. "Facebook Needs to Be a Marketing Destination, Not Just a Conduit," *Marketing News*, March 15, 2011, p. 12.

61. "2009 Digital Handbook," p. 13; "Top 15 Most Popular Social Networking Websites," *eBizMBA*, April 2011, **www.ebizmba.com/articles/social-networking-websites** (accessed April 13, 2011).

62. McKinnon, "2015 Canadian Social Media Usage Statistics."

63. Alison Doyle, "LinkedIn and Your Job Search," **About.com**, **http://jobsearch.about.com/od/networking/a/linkedin.htm** (accessed April 13, 2011).

64. Laura Petrecca, "More Grads Use Social Media to Job Hunt," *USA Today*, April 5, 2011, p. 3B.

65. "LinkedIn's Newest Features Allow for Corporate Networking and Business Promotion," *Marketing News*, March 15, 2011, p. 12.

66. Jefferson Graham, "Cake Decorator Finds Twitter a Tweet Recipe for Success," *USA Today*, April 1, 2009, p. 5B.

67. Craig Smith, "By the Numbers: 170+ Amazing Twitter Statistics," *DMR Digital Stats/Gadgets*, February 26, 2016, **http://expandedramblings.com/index.php/march-2013-by-the-numbers-a-few-amazing-twitter-stats/**.

68. McKinnon, "2015 Canadian Social Media Usage Statistics."

69. Gregory L. White, "Medvedev Sets Kremlin Atwitter," *The Wall Street Journal*, September 1, 2010, p. A12.

70. Claire Cain Miller, "Twitter Loses Its Scrappy Start-Up Status," *The New York Times*, April 15, 2010, **www.nytimes.com/2010/04/16/technology/16twitter.html** (accessed April 13, 2011).

71. **https://twitter.com/@StarbucksCanada** and **https://twitter.com/Starbucks/status/304274571845054465** (accessed July 17, 2013).

72. Josh Tyrangiel, "Bing vs. Google: The Conquest of Twitter," *Time*, October 22, 2009, **www.time.com/time/business/article/0,8599,1931532,00.html** (accessed April 13, 2011).

73. "As Twitter Grows and Evolves, More Manpower Is Needed," *Marketing News*, March 15, 2011, p. 13.

74. "Neil Patel (entrepreneur)," *Wikipedia*, **http://en.wikipedia.org/wiki/Neil_Patel_%28entrepreneur%29** (accessed July 17, 2013).

75. Daniel Zeevi, "10 Best Social Media Management Tools," Dashburst website, April 8, 2013, **http://dashburst.com/best-social-media-management-tools/** (accessed July 17, 2013).

76. "Real Cars Drive into Second Life," **CNNMoney.com**, November 18, 2006, **http://money.cnn.com/2006/11/17/autos/2nd_life_cars/index.htm** (accessed April 13, 2011)

77. Alice Truong, "Q&A: A Real Study of Virtual Worlds," *Wall Street Journal*, May 4, 2010, **http://blogs.wsj.com/digits/2010/05/04/qa-a-real-study-ofvirtual-worlds/** (accessed May 6, 2010).

78. "CNN Enters the Virtual World of Second Life," November 12, 2007, **CNN.com**, **www.cnn.com/2007/TECH/11/12/second.life.irpt/index.html** (accessed April 13, 2011).

79. Roger Yu, "Smartphones Help Make Bon Voyages," *USA Today*, March 5, 2010, p. B1.

80. Mickey Alam Khan, "Jiffy Lube Mobile Coupons Bring 50 Percent New Households," *Mobile Marketer*, January 30, 2009, **www.mobilemarketer.com/cms/news/commerce/2551.html** (accessed April 13, 2011).

81. Umika Pidaparthy, "Marketers Embracing QR Codes, for Better or Worse," *CNN Tech*, March 28, 2011, **http://articles.cnn.com/2011-03-28/tech/qr.codes.marketing_1_qr-smartphone-users-symbian?_s=PM:TECH** (accessed April 11, 2011).

82. Brad Stone and Olga Kharif, "Pay As You Go," *Bloomberg Businessweek*, July 18–24, 2011, pp. 66–71.

83. "Google Wallet," **www.google.com/wallet/what-is-google-wallet.html** (accessed May 29, 2014).

84. Miriam Gottfried, "Mobile Banking Gets Riskier," *Wall Street Journal*, July 10, 2011, p. B7.

85. "All About Widgets," *Webopedia™*, September 14, 2007, **www.webopedia.com/DidYouKnow/Hardware_Software/widgets.asp** (accessed May 29, 2014).

86. Rachael King, "Building a Brand with Widgets," *Bloomberg Businessweek*, March 3, 2008, **www.businessweek.com/technology/content/feb2008/tc20080303_000743.htm** (accessed May 29, 2014).

87. "Barkley Develops Krispy Kreme ® 'Hot Light' App and Widget," *Wall Street Journal*, December 23, 2011, **http://online.wsj.com/article/PR-CO-20111223-904499.html** (accessed February 28, 2012).

88. Mark Milian, "Why Text Messages Are Limited to 160 Characters," *Los Angeles Times*, May 3, 2009, **http://latimesblogs.latimes.com/technology/2009/05/invented-text-messaging.html** (accessed May 29, 2014); "Eight Reasons Why Your Business Should Use SMS Marketing," Mobile Marketing Ratings, **www.mobilemarketingratings.com/eight-reasons-sms-marketing.html** (accessed May 29, 2014).

89. Lauren Folino and Michelle V. Rafter, "How to Use Multimedia for Business Marketing," *Inc.*, January 25, 2010, **www.inc.com/guides/multimedia-for-business-marketing.html** (accessed February 28, 2012); "Motorola Powers House of Blues(R)," PR Newswire, **www.prnewswire.com/news-releases/motorola-powers-house-of-bluesr-54990822.html** (accessed February 28, 2012).

90. Lauren Johnson, "Orville Redenbacher Promotes Healthy Snacks with Mobile Banner Ads," *Mobile Marketer*, October 26, 2011, **www.mobilemarketer.com/cms/news/advertising/11321.html** (accessed February 28, 2012).

91. Amy Dusto, "Mobile Devices Account For Nearly A Third of Web Traffic," *Internet Retailer*, February 6, 2014, **https://www.internetretailer.com/2014/02/06/mobile-devices-account-nearly-third-web-traffic** (accessed May 7, 2014).

92. Foursquare website, **https://foursquare.com/** (accessed February 16, 2012).

93. Anita Campbell, "What the Heck Is an App?" Small Business Trends, March 7, 2011, **http://smallbiztrends.com/2011/03/what-is-an-app.html** (accessed March 29, 2014).

94. Jefferson Graham, "Mobile Apps Make It Easier to Go Green," *USA Today*, May 12, 2011, **www.usatoday.com/tech/products/2011-05-12-green-tech_n.htm** (accessed October 6, 2011); "Green Apps That Can Save You Money," Reuters, February 18, 2011, **http://blogs.reuters.com/environment/2011/02/18/green-apps-that-can-save-you-money/** (accessed October 6, 2011); Jefferson Graham, "GoodGuide App Helps Navigate Green Products," *USA Today*, May 13, 2011, **www.usatoday.com/tech/products/2011-05-12-GoodGuideapp_n.htm** (accessed October 6, 2011).

95. Li and Bernoff, *Groundswell*, p. 41.

96. Ibid., pp. 41–42.

97. Ibid., p. 44.

98. Ibid., pp. 44–45.

99. Rebecca MacLary, "New Canadian User Friendly Crowdfunding and Crowdsourcing Apps," Daily Crowdsource website, **http://dailycrowdsource.com/crowdsourcing/company-reviews/341-new-canadian-user-friendly-crowdfunding-and-crowdsourcing-apps** (accessed July 17, 2013).

100. Mya Frazier, "CrowdSourcing," *Delta Sky Mag*, February 2010, p. 70.

101. Li and Bernoff, *Groundswell*, pp. 26–27.

102. "Why Social Media Marketing?", Digital Visitor website, **http://www.digitalvisitor.com/why-social-media-marketing/** (accessed July 30, 2013).

103. Sarah Nassauer, "'I Hate My Room,' The Traveler Tweeted. Ka-Boom! An Upgrade!" *Wall Street Journal*, June 24, 2010, p. D1.

104. John W. Miller, "Yahoo Cookie Plan in Place," *Wall Street Journal*, March 19, 2011, **http://online.wsj.com/article/SB10001424052748703512404576208700813815570.html** (accessed April 11, 2011).

105. Melissa Harris, "Viewpoints Network Snags Client, Enhances Its Long-Term Outlook," *Chicago Tribune*, May 23, 2010, **http://articles.chicagotribune.com/2010-05-23/business/ct-biz-0523-confidential-viewpoints-20100523_1_autistic-adults-business-plan-venture-capitalists** (accessed April 13, 2011); Michael Krauss, "Moog Synthesizes Social Media," *Marketing News*, September 30, 2010, p. 10.

106. Jon Swartz, "Facebook Changes Its Status in Washington," *USA Today*, January 13, 2011, pp. 1B–2B; "Details of 100 Million Facebook Users Published Online," MSNBC.com, July 29, 2010, **www.msnbc.msn.com/id/38463013/ns/technology_and_science/?GT1=43001** (accessed July 29, 2010); Julia Angwin and Steve Stecklow, "'Scrapers' Dig Deep for Data on Web," *Wall Street Journal*, October 12, 2010, pp. A1, A18.

107. Quentin Hardy, "In Mark We Trust," *Forbes*, October 11, 2010, pp. 81–86; Swartz, "Facebook Changes Its Status in Washington," pp. 1B–2B.

108. Jennifer Valentino-DeVries, "Ad Industry Takes Another Look At 'Do-Not-Track' in Browsers," *Wall Street Journal*, March 31, 2011, p. B5.

109. "About TRUSTe," TRUSTe website, **www.truste.com/about_TRUSTe/index.html** (accessed April 13, 2011).

110. Better Business Bureau Online, **www.bbbonline.org/** (accessed April 13, 2011).

111. Larry Barrett, "Data Breach Costs Surge in 2009: Study," *eSecurityPlanet*, January 26, 2010, **www.esecurityplanet.com/features/article.php/3860811/Data-Breach-Costs-Surgein-2009-Study.htm** (accessed April 13, 2011).

112. Steve Rennie, "Government Faces Class-Action Lawsuits Over Student Loan Borrowers' Lost Data," *Globe and Mail*, January 17, 2013, **http://www.theglobeandmail.com/news/politics/government-faces-class-action-lawsuits-over-student-loan-borrowers-lost-data/article7492261/** (accessed July 30, 2013).

113. Sarah E. Needleman, "Social-Media Con Game," *Wall Street Journal*, October 12, 2009, p. R4.

114. "Facebook Takes Strong Stance Against Haiti Fraud," *Media Street*, January 19, 2010, **www.www.media-street.co.uk/blog/facebook-takes-strong-stance-against-haiti-fraud** (accessed April 19, 2011).

115. Brad Stone and Bruce Einhorn, "Baidu China," *Bloomberg Businessweek*, November 15–21, 2010, pp. 60–67.

116. Abigail Field, "Viacom v. YouTube/Google: A Piracy Case in Their Own Words," *Daily Finance*, March 21, 2010, **www.dailyfinance.com/story/company-news/viacom-v-youtubegoogle-a-piracy-case-in-their-ownwords/19407896/** (accessed April 13, 2011).

117. Kevin Shanahan and Mike Hyman "Motivators and Enablers of SCOURing," *Journal of Business Research* 63 (September–October 2010), pp. 1095–1102.

118. "Seventh Annual BSA and IDC Global Software Piracy Study," BSA, **http://portal.bsa.org/globalpiracy2009/index.html** (accessed April 13, 2011).

119. Max Chafkin, "The Case, and the Plan, for the Virtual Company," *Inc.*, April 2010, p. 68.

Chapter 14

1. Michael Lev-Ram, "A Twitter Guy Takes on Banks," *Fortune*, February 7, 2014, pp. 37–42; Jason Tanz, "Twitter Cofounder Shakes Up the Credit Card Biz," *Wired*, May 17, 2014, **www.wired.com/magazine/2014/05/mf_qadorsey/all/1**; Dan Fletcher, "The 50 Best Inventions of 2013," *Time*, November 11, 2013, **www.time.com/time/specials/packages/article/0,28804,2029497_2030652_2029712,00.html** (both accessed November 2, 2014); Karsten Strauss, "The New Billionaire Behind Twitter And Square: Jack Dorsey," *Forbes* online, July 25, 2012, **www.forbes.com/sites/karstenstrauss/2012/07/25/the-new-billionaire-behind-twitter-and-square-jack-dorsey/** (accessed July 18, 2013); **http://en.wikipedia.org/wiki/Jack_Dorsey** (accessed January 21, 2012); Fortune.com. (2014). *Fortune*. Retrieved 17 January, 2016, from **http://fortune.com/2014/06/02/jack-dorsey-the-man-with-two-brains/**.

2. "About the AcSB," Financial Reporting & Assurance Standards Canada, n.d., **http://www.frascanada.ca/accounting-standards-board/what-we-do/about-the-acsb/index.aspx** (accessed January 14, 2016).

3. Adapted from Financial Reporting & Assurance Standards Canada, **http://www.frascanada.ca/index.aspx** (accessed January 22, 2013).

4. *Overcoming Compliance Fatigue: Reinforcing the Commitment to Ethical Growth*, Ernst & Young (2014), **https://webforms.ey.com/Publication/vwLUAssets/EY-13th-Global-Fraud-Survey/$FILE/EY-13th-Global-Fraud-Survey.pdf** (accessed January 17, 2016).

5. See, for example, Tara Gray, "Canadian Response to the U.S. Sarbanes-Oxley Act of 2002: New Directions for Corporate Governance," Library of Parliament Economics Division, October 4, 2005, **http://www.parl.gc.ca/content/lop/research publications/prb0537-e.htm** (accessed January 14, 2016).

6. "Issue Brief: Global Banking Regulations and Banks in Canada," Canadian Bankers Association, last updated May 2016, **http://www.cba.ca/global-banking-regulations-and-banks-in-canada**.

7. "About the ACFE," ACFE website, **www.acfe.com/about-the-acfe.aspx** (accessed September 28, 2016).

8. "Sustainability," Chartered Accountants of Canada website, **http://www.cica.ca/focus-on-practice-areas/sustain ability/item61279.aspx**; "CIMA, AICPA and CICA release global survey findings on accounting for sustainability practices" Chartered Institute of Management Accountants," December 16, 2013, **http://www.cimaglobal.com/About-us/Press-office/Press-releases/2013/December-2013/CIMA-AICPA-and-CICA-release-global-survey-findings-on-accounting-for-sustainability-practices/**; "Sustainability, Reporting and Assurance," American Institute of CPAs (AICPA) website, **http://www.aicpa.org/INTERESTAREAS/BUSINESS INDUSTRYANDGOVERNMENT/RESOURCES/SUSTAIN ABILITY/Pages/Sustainability%20Accounting,%20 Reporting,%20Assurance%20and%20Other%20Services. aspx** (all accessed July 18, 2013).

9. Mary Williams Walsh, "State Woes Grow Too Big to Camouflage," *New York Times*, March 29, 2010, **www.nytimes.com/2010/03/30/business/economy/30states.html** (accessed March 31, 2010).

10. Sarah Johnson, "Averting Revenue-Recognition Angst," *CFO*, April 2012, p. 21.

11. Evelyn M. Rusli and Peter Eavis, "Facebook Raises $16 Billion in I.P.O.,"*New York Times*, May 17, 2012, **http://dealbook.nytimes.com/2012/05/17/facebook-raises-16-billion-in-i-p-o/?hp** (accessed May 25, 2012); Brad Stone and Douglas MacMillan, "How Zuck Hacked the Valley," *Bloomberg Businessweek*, May 21–May 27, 2012, pp. 60–67; Facebook Newsroom, **http://newsroom.fb.com/content/default.aspx?NewsAreaId=22** (accessed May 25, 2012); "Facebook IPO Fallout Continues," *Washington Post*, May 24, 2012, **www.washingtonpost.com/business/economy/facebook-ipo-fallout-continues/2012/05/24/gJQAJcTxnU_story.html** (accessed May 25, 2012); Brett Philbin and David Benoit, "Morgan Stanley Revisits Facebook Trades; Investors File Suit," *Wall Street Journal*, **http://online.wsj.com/article/SB10001424052702304707604577422063685311108.html? KEYWORDS=Investors+File+Suit+Against+Facebook** (accessed May 25, 2012).

12. "IFRS FAQS," AICPA IFRS Resources, **www.ifrs.com/ifrs_faqs. html#q3** (accessed September 19, 2011); Michael Rapoport, "Accounting Move Pits Big vs. Small," *Wall Street Journal*, July 6, 2011, pp. C1–C2; David Bogoslaw, "Global Accounting Standards? Not So Fast," *Bloomberg Businessweek*, November 13, 2008, **www.businessweek.com/investor/content/nov2008/pi20081112_143039.htm** (accessed September 19, 2011); Marie Leone, "Comparability: Still Up in the Air?" *CFO*,

September 1, 2011, **www3.cfo.com/article/2011/9/gaap-ifrs_gaap-ifrs-migration** (accessed September 19, 2011).

13. Bureau of Labor Statistics, "Accountants and Auditors," Occupational Outlook Handbook 2013–2014, **www.bls.gov/oco/ocos001.htm** (accessed April 26, 2014).

14. Adapted from: **www.icao.on.ca/CA/CompensationSurvey/page4862.aspx** (accessed August 20, 2009).

15. "EBay sellers warned to pay taxes," CBC News, July 30, 2009, **http://www.cbc.ca/news/ebay-sellers-warned-to-pay-taxes-1.839480**; James Bradshaw, "Tax crackdown on Netflix, Apple could sting consumers," *Globe and Mail*, January 9, 2015, **http://www.theglobeandmail.com/report-on-business/international-business/digital-tax-crackdown-against-industry-giants-could-sting-consumers/article 22371670/** (accessed January 14, 2016).

Chapter 15

1. "Stephen S. Poloz," Bank of Canada website, n.d., **http://www.bankofcanada.ca/profile/stephen-s-poloz/**; Elton Hobson, "Who is Stephen Poloz?" Global News, May 2, 2013, **http://globalnews.ca/news/530931/who-is-stephen-poloz/** (both accessed January 19, 2016).

2. Paul Krugman, "Why Is Deflation Bad?" *New York Times*, August 2, 2010, **http://krugman.blogs.nytimes.com/2010/08/02/why-is-deflation-bad/** (accessed May 29, 2012).

3. "First Annual Negative Inflation in 49 Years," *RTE News*, February 12, 2009, **www.rte.ie/news/2009/0212/inflation.html** (accessed May 29, 2012).

4. Phillip Inman, "Ireland Back in Recession as Global Slowdown Hits Exports," **guardian.co.uk**, March 22, 2012, **www.guardian.co.uk/business/2012/mar/22/ireland-recession-global-slowdown-exports** (accessed May 29, 2012).

5. "Currency in Circulation (WCURCIR)," Economic Research: Federal Reserve of Saint Louis, **http://research.stlouisfed.org/fred2/series/WCURCIR** (accessed May 24, 2012).

6. Bank of Canada, "Polymer Series (2011)," **www.bankofcanada.ca/banknotes/bank-note-series/polymer/** (accessed January 21, 2012).

7. Royal Canadian Mint, "Phasing out the Penny," **www.mint.ca/store/mint/learn/phasing-out-the-penny-6900002**, (accessed January 21, 2012).

8. "Should We Stop Using the Penny," Desjardins Economic Studies, February 15, 2007, **www.desjardins.com/en/a_propos/etudes_economiques/actualites/point_vue_economique/pve70215.pdf** (accessed August 20, 2009).

9. "The Economic Impact of Counterfeiting," Bank of Canada, February 2016, **http://www.bankofcanada.ca/wp-content/uploads/2012/07/economic_impact_counterfeiting_feb2016.pdf**.

10. "Yuan Will Be Fully Convertible by 2015, Chinese Officials Tell EU Chamber," *Bloomberg Businessweek*, September 8, 2011, **www.bloomberg.com/news/2011-09-08/yuan-to-be-fully-convertible-by-2015-eu-chamber.html** (accessed November 1, 2011); Kersi Jilla, "Global Common Currency—Part 1—Understanding Convertible Currency," *Forex Metrics Blog*, **www.forexmetrics.com/blog/?p=1114** (accessed November 1, 2011); "Foreign Reserve," *Business Dictionary*, **www.businessdictionary.com/definition/foreign-reserve.html**

(accessed November 1, 2011); Wang Xiaotian, "Experts: China's Yuan Will Go Global," *China Daily*, June 27, 2011, **www.chinadaily.com.cn/china/2011-06/27/content_12780327.htm** (accessed November 1, 2011); "New Move to Make Yuan a Global Currency," *The Wall Street Journal*, January 12, 2011, **http://online.wsj.com/article/SB10001424052748703791904576076082178393532.html** (accessed November 1, 2011); Stephen Elliot, "Yuan Has Potential to Become 'International Currency,'?" *China Daily*, August 5, 2011, **www.chinadailyapac.com/article/yuan-has-potential-become-international-currency** (accessed November 1, 2011).

11. Financial Consumer Agency of Canada, "New Credit Card Rules," **www.fcac-acfc.gc.ca/eng/partners/campaign/rulescc/index-eng.asp** (accessed January 21, 2012).

12. **www.bankofcanada.ca/en/about/currency.html** (accessed August 20, 2009).

13. **www.bankofcanada.ca/en/financial/financial_system.html** (accessed August 20, 2009).

14. **www.bankofcanada.ca/en/about/funds.html** (accessed August 20, 2009).

15. **www.cba.ca/en/section.asp?fl=2&sl=204&tl=&docid** (accessed August 20, 2009).

16. **http://www.fin.gc.ca/toc/2005/fact-cfss-eng.asp** (accessed August 9, 2010).

17. "C40 and World Bank Form Groundbreaking Climate Change Action Partnership," The World Bank, June 1, 2011, **http://web.worldbank.org/WBSITE/EXTERNAL/TOPICS/EXTSDNET/0,,pagePK:64885161~contentMDK:22928707~piPK:5929285~theSitePK:5929282,00.html** (accessed November 9, 2011); World Bank Confronts Sustainability Criticism," *Business Ethics*, March 19, 2011, **http://business-ethics.com/2011/03/19/1900-world-bank-confronts-sustainability-criticism/** (accessed November 9, 2011); "Benefits," Support **Narmadadam.org**, **www.supportnarmadadam.org/sardar-sarovar-benefits.htm** (accessed November 9, 2011); "About Us," The World Bank, **http://web.worldbank.org/WBSITE/EXTERNAL/EXTABOUTUS/0,,pagePK:50004410~piPK:36602~theSitePK:29708,00.html** (accessed November 9, 2011); "Renewables Almost a Quarter of World Bank's Energy Lending," The World Bank, **http://climatechange.worldbank.org/content/world-bank-renewable-energy-lending-rises** (accessed November 9, 2011).

18. **http://www.fin.gc.ca/toc/2005/fact-cfss-eng.asp** (accessed August 9, 2010).

19. **www.cdic.ca/1/2/1/8/index1.shtml** (accessed August 20, 2009).

20. Michael Lev-Ram, "A Twitter Guy Takes on Banks," *Fortune*, February 7, 2011, pp. 37–42; Jason Tanz, "Twitter Cofounder Shakes Up the Credit Card Biz," *Wired*, May 17, 2011, **www.wired.com/magazine/2011/05/mf_qadorsey/all/1** (accessed November 2, 2011); Dan Fletcher, "The 50 Best Inventions of 2010," *Time*, November 11, 2010, **www.time.com/time/specials/packages/article/0,28804,2029497_2030652_2029712,00.html** (accessed November 2, 2011).

21. Harry Maurer and Alexander Ragir, "Brazil's New Middle Class Goes on a Spree," *Bloomberg Businessweek*, May 12, 2011, **www.businessweek.com/magazine/content/11_21/b4229010792956.htm** (accessed October 12, 2011); Kenneth Rapoza, "No Major Slowdown as Brazil Consumers Still Happily Spending," *Forbes*, August 12, 2011, **www.forbes.com/sites/kenrapoza/2011/08/12/no-major-slowdown-as-brazil-consumers-still-happily-spending/** (accessed October 12, 2011); "FACTBOX-Bright and Troubled Spots in Brazil's Economy," *Reuters*, August 18, 2011, **www.reuters.com/article/2011/08/18/brazil-economy-idUSN1E77E1EZ20110818** (accessed October 12, 2011).

22. **www.fin.gc.ca/toce/1999/banke.html** (accessed August 20, 2009).

23. Laura Kane, "Why Credit Unions Could Gain from Shrinking Direct Banking Market," *Toronto Star* online, March 24, 2013, **http://www.thestar.com/business/personal_finance/2013/03/24/why_credit_unions_could_gain_from_shrinking_direct_banking_market.html** (accessed July 18, 2013); Jane J. Kim, "Credit Unions: A Better Bet Than Banks?" *The Wall Street Journal*, June 5–6, 2010, p. B8; **Bankrate.com**, "Are Credit Unions Better Than Banks?" **Bankrate.com**, **www.bankrate.com/finance/savings/are-credit-unions-better-than-banks.aspx**; Mark Maremont and Victoria McGrane, "Credit Unions Bailed Out," *The Wall Street Journal*, September 25, 2010, **http://online.wsj.com/article/SB10001424052748703499604575511225406368236.html** (both accessed November 15, 2010).

Chapter 16

1. Peter Kuitenbrouwer, "Fairfax Financial Ltd chief Prem Watsa tells his 'Horatio Alger' story," *Financial Post*, May 22, 2015, **http://business.financialpost.com/news/fp-street/fairfax-financial-holdings-ltd-chief-executive-prem-watsa-tells-his-horatio-alger-story**; "Company Profile," Fairfax website, n.d., **http://www.fairfax.ca/Corporate/company-profile/default.aspx**; Guru Focus.com, n.d., **http://www.gurufocus.com/StockBuy.php?GuruName=PremWatsa**; "Fairfax Financial," Wikipedia, n.d., **https://en.wikipedia.org/wiki/Fairfax_Financial**; (all accessed January 17, 2016).

2. Kate O'Sullivan, "Going for the Other Green," *CFO*, September 2011, pp. 52–57; Carlye Adler, "Thinking Big," *Time*, May 3, 2011, **http://bx.businessweek.com/carbon-markets/view?url5http%3A%2F%2Fc.moreover.com%2Fclick%2Fhere.pl%3Fr4627673218%26f%3D9791** (accessed September 26, 2011); Canadian Press, "25 years later, Loblaw still pushes going green to shoppers," CTV News, July 26, 2014, **http://www.ctvnews.ca/business/25-years-later-loblaw-still-pushes-going-green-to-shoppers-1.1933078** (accessed January 19, 2016).

3. **http://ycombinator.com** (accessed September 15, 2010); Ira Sager, Kimberly Weisul, and Spencer Ante, "Tech Investing: How Smart Is the Smart Money?" *Bloomberg Businessweek*, February 2010, **http://images.businessweek.com/ss/10/02/0225_angel_investors/12.htm** (accessed October 7, 2010); Om Malik, "Notes From a Conversation With Y Combinator's Paul Graham," *Gigaom*, February 1, 2010, **http://gigaom.com/2010/02/01/ycombinator-paul-graham/** (accessed September 20, 2010); Paul Graham, "A New Venture Animal," March 2008, **www.paulgraham.com/ycombinator.html** (accessed June 20, 2009); Sean Ellis, "Y Combinator Hatches Brilliant Entrepreneurs," Start Up Marketing Blog by Sean Ellis," December 2, 2008, **http://startup-marketing.com/y-combinator-hatches-brilliant-entrepreneurs/** (accessed June 20, 2009); Andy Louis-Charles, "Ignore Y Combinator at Your Own Risk," *The Motley Fool*, April 28, 2009, **www.fool.com/investing/general/2009/04/28/ignore-y-combinator-at-your-own-risk.aspx** (accessed June 20, 2009); Josh Quittner, "The New Internet Start-Up Boom: Get Rich Slow," *Time*, April 9, 2009, **www.time.com/time/magazine/article/0,9171,1890387-1,00.html** (accessed June 20, 2009).

4. Calculated by Geoff Hirt from Apple's annual reports and website on June 16, 2014.

5. "About Relativity Media," **www.relativitymediallc.com/about. asp** (accessed November 2, 2011); Ben Fritz, "Relativity Media Deal Opens Film Door to China," *Los Angeles Times*, August 4, 2011, **http://articles.latimes.com/2011/aug/14/business/la-fi-ct-china-studio-20110814** (accessed November 2, 2011); Ronald Grover, "Ryan Kavanaugh Is Ready for His Close-Up," *Bloomberg Businessweek*, February 17, 2011, **www.businessweek.com/magazine/ content/11_09/b4217024893975.htm** (accessed November 2, 2011); Ron Grover, "Ryan Kavanaugh May Make Believers Out of Hollywood Yet," *Bloomberg Businessweek*, February 7, 2010, **www. businessweek.com/innovate/FineOnMedia/archives/2010/02/ ryan_kavanaugh_may_make_believers_out_of_hollywood_ yet.html#more** (accessed November 2, 2011).

6. Joshua Kennon, "Should You Invest in an IPO?" **About.com, http:// beginnersinvest.about.com/od/investmentbanking/a/ aa073106a.htm** (accessed May 30, 2012).

7. Marielle Segarra, "Taking the Next Step," *CFO*, July 15, 2011, **www. cfo.com/article.cfm/14586563?f5singlepage** (accessed November 3, 2011); Dan Fitzpatrick and Lisa Rappaport, "Financial Firms' Ceiling," *The Wall Street Journal*, September 8, 2011, **http://online. wsj.com/article/SB1000142405311190410340457655571003 84026220.html?KEYWORDS5Financial1Firms%275Ceiling** (accessed November 3, 2011); Kyle Stock, "Ranks of Women on Wall Street Thin," *The Wall Street Journal*, September 20, 2010, **http://online.wsj.com/article/SB10001424052748704858304575498071732136704.html** (accessed November 3, 2011).

8. Vincent Ryan, "From Wall Street to Main Street," *CFO Magazine*, June 2008, pp. 85–86.

9. Hershey Trust, "About Hershey Trust Company" (n.d.), **www. hersheytrust.com/cornerstones/about.shtml** (accessed March 26, 2006); O. C. Ferrell, "Hershey Foods' Ethics and Social Responsibility," case developed for classroom use, Colorado State University, revised edition, 2004; Hershey Foods, "Frequently Asked Questions," (n.d.), **www.hersheyinvestorrelations.com/ireye/ ir_site.zhtml?ticker5HSY&script51801** (accessed June 10, 2004), "Company History," **www.hersheys.com/discover/history/ company.asp** (accessed March 27, 2006); William C. Smith, "Seeing to the Business of Fun: Franklin A. Miles Jr., Hershey Entertainment & Resorts Co.," *National Law Journal*, December 22, 2003, p. 8; "Funding the School Trust," **www.hersheys.com/discover/milton/ fund_school_trust.asp** (accessed March 27, 2006).

Appendix B

1. Dana Matiolli, "At Kodak, Patents Hold the Key to the Future," *Wall Street Journal*, April 20, 2010, p. B8; Grant Gross, "ITC to Investigate Apple's Patent Complaint Against Kodak," *ComputerWorld*, May 14, 2010, **www.computerworld.com/s/ article/9176792/ITC_to_investigate_Apple_s_patent_ complaint_against_Kodak** (accessed June 15, 2010); Franklin Paul, "UPDATE3-Kodak Growth Concerns Overshadow Patent Riches," *Reuters*, April 29, 2010, **www.reuters.com/ article/idUSN2923844820100429** (accessed June 15, 2010), United States Patent and Trademark Office, **www.uspto.gov** (accessed October 15, 2010); Geoff Duncan, "Samsung and Kodak Reach Patent Settlement," *Digital Trends*, December 23, 2009, **www.digitaltrends.com/mobile/samsung-and-kodak-reach-patent-settlement/** (accessed October 16, 2010).

GLOSSARY

absolute advantage a monopoly that exists when a country is the only source of an item, the only producer of an item, or the most efficient producer of an item

accessibility allows consumers to find information about competing products, prices, and reviews and become more informed about a firm and the relative value of its products

accountability the principle that employees who accept an assignment and the authority to carry it out are answerable to a superior for the outcome

accountant a professional employed by large corporations, government agencies, and other organizations to prepare and analyze their financial statements

accounting the recording, measurement, and interpretation of financial information

accounting cycle the four-step procedure of an accounting system: examining source documents, recording transactions in an accounting journal, posting recorded transactions, and preparing financial statements

accounting equation assets equal liabilities plus owners' equity

accounts payable the amount a company owes to suppliers for goods and services purchased with credit

accounts receivable money owed a company by its clients or customers who have promised to pay for the products at a later date

accrued expenses an account representing all unpaid financial obligations incurred by the organization

acquisition the purchase of one company by another, usually by buying its shares

addressability the ability of a business to identify customers before they make purchases

administrative managers those who manage an entire business or a major segment of a business; they are not specialists but coordinate the activities of specialized managers

advertising a paid form of non-personal communication transmitted through a mass medium, such as television commercials or magazine advertisements

advertising campaign designing a series of advertisements and placing them in various media to reach a particular target market

agency a common business relationship created when one person acts on behalf of another and under that person's control

agenda a calendar, containing both specific and vague items, that covers short-term goals and long-term objectives

agent in an agency relationship, the one who acts on behalf of the principal to accomplish the task

analytical skills the ability to identify relevant issues, recognize their importance, understand the relationships between them, and perceive the underlying causes of a situation

angel investors private investors who supply equity financing for businesses

annual report summary of a firm's financial information, products, and growth plans for owners and potential investors

arbitration settlement of a labour/management dispute by a third party whose solution is legally binding and enforceable

Asia-Pacific Economic Cooperation (APEC) community established in 1989 to promote international trade and facilitate business; as of 2013, has 21 member countries

asset utilization ratios ratios that measure how well a firm uses its assets to generate each $1 of sales

assets a firm's economic resources, or items of value that it owns, such as cash, inventory, land, equipment, buildings, and other tangible and intangible things

Association of Southeast Asian Nations (ASEAN) trade alliance that promotes trade and economic integration among member nations in Southeast Asia

attitude knowledge and positive or negative feelings about something

automated banking machine (ABM) the most familiar form of electronic banking, which dispenses cash, accepts deposits, and allows balance inquiries and cash transfers from one account to another

balance of payments the difference between the flow of money into and out of a country

balance of trade the difference in value between a nation's exports and its imports

balance sheet a "snapshot" of an organization's financial position at a given moment

Bank of Canada an independent agency of the federal government established in 1934 to regulate the nation's banking and financial industry

bank rate the rate of interest the Bank of Canada charges to loan money to any banking institution to meet reserve requirements

behaviour modification changing behaviour and encouraging appropriate actions by relating the consequences of behaviour to the behaviour itself

benefits non-financial forms of compensation provided to employees, such as pension plans, health insurance, paid vacation and holidays, and the like

blog a Web-based journal in which a writer can editorialize and interact with other Internet users

board of directors a group of individuals, elected by the shareholders to oversee the general operation of the corporation, who set the corporation's long-range objectives

bonds debt instruments that larger companies sell to raise long-term funds

bonuses monetary rewards offered by companies for exceptional performance as incentives to further increase productivity

boycott an attempt to keep people from purchasing the products of a company

branding the process of naming and identifying products

breach of contract the failure or refusal of a party to a contract to live up to his or her promises

bribes payments, gifts, or special favours intended to influence the outcome of a decision

brokerage firms firms that buy and sell stocks, bonds, and other securities for their customers and provide other financial services

budget an internal financial plan that forecasts expenses and income over a set period of time

budget deficit the condition in which a nation spends more than it takes in from taxes

budget surplus the condition in which a nation spends less than it takes in from taxes

business individuals or organizations who try to earn a profit by providing products that satisfy people's needs

business ethics principles and standards that determine acceptable conduct in business

business plan a precise statement of the rationale for a business and a step-by-step explanation of how it will achieve its goals

business products products that are used directly or indirectly in the operation or manufacturing processes of businesses

buying behaviour the decision processes and actions of people who purchase and use products

Canada Deposit Insurance Corporation (CDIC) a federal Crown corporation that insures bank accounts

capacity the maximum load that an organizational unit can carry or operate

capital budgeting the process of analyzing the needs of the business and selecting the assets that will maximize its value

capitalism, or free enterprise an economic system in which individuals own and operate the majority of businesses that provide goods and services

cartel a group of firms or nations that agree to act as a monopoly and not compete with each other, in order to generate a competitive advantage in world markets

cash flow the movement of money through an organization over a daily, weekly, monthly, or yearly basis

centralized organization a structure in which authority is concentrated at the top, and very little decision-making authority is delegated to lower levels

certificate of incorporation a legal document that the provincial or federal government issues to a company based on information the company provides in the articles of incorporation

certificates of deposit (CDs) savings accounts that guarantee a depositor a set interest rate over a specified interval as long as the funds are not withdrawn before the end of the period—six months or one year, for example

chartered banks the largest and oldest of all financial institutions, relying mainly on chequing and savings accounts as sources of funds for loans to businesses and individuals

chequing account money stored in an account at a bank or other financial institution that can be withdrawn without advance notice; also called a *demand deposit*

classical theory of motivation theory suggesting that money is the sole motivator for workers

codes of ethics formalized rules and standards that describe what a company expects of its employees

collective bargaining the negotiation process through which management and unions reach an agreement about compensation, working hours, and working conditions for the bargaining unit

commercial certificates of deposit (CDs) certificates of deposit issued by commercial banks and brokerage companies, available in minimum amounts of $100,000, which may be traded prior to maturity

commercial paper a written promise from one company to another to pay a specific amount of money

commercialization the full introduction of a complete marketing strategy and the launch of the product for commercial success

commission an incentive system that pays a fixed amount or a percentage of the employee's sales

committee a permanent, formal group that performs a specific task

common shares shares whose owners have voting rights in the corporation, yet do not receive preferential treatment regarding dividends

communism first described by Karl Marx as a society in which the people, without regard to class, own all the nation's resources

comparative advantage the basis of most international trade, when a country specializes in products that it can supply more efficiently or at a lower cost than it can produce other items

competition the rivalry among businesses for consumers' dollars

compressed workweek a four-day (or shorter) period during which an employee works 40 hours

computer-assisted design (CAD) the design of components, products, and processes on computers instead of on paper

computer-assisted manufacturing (CAM) manufacturing that employs specialized computer systems to actually guide and control the transformation processes

computer-integrated manufacturing (CIM) a complete system that designs products, manages machines and materials, and controls the operations function

concentration approach a market segmentation approach whereby a company develops one marketing strategy for a single market segment

conceptual skills the ability to think in abstract terms and to see how parts fit together to form the whole

conciliation a method of outside resolution of labour and management differences in which a third party is brought in to keep the two sides talking

connectivity the use of digital networks to provide linkages between information providers and users

consumer products products intended for household or family use

consumerism the activities that independent individuals, groups, and organizations undertake to protect their rights as consumers

continuous manufacturing organizations companies that use continuously running assembly lines, creating products with many similar characteristics

contract a mutual agreement between two or more parties that can be enforced by law

contract manufacturing the hiring of a foreign company to produce a specified volume of the initiating company's product to specification; the final product carries the domestic firm's name

control consumers' ability to regulate the information they receive via the Internet, and the rate and sequence of their exposure to that information

controlling the process of evaluating and correcting activities to keep the organization on course

cooperative or co-op an organization composed of individuals or small businesses that have banded together to reap the benefits of belonging to a larger organization

corporate citizenship the extent to which businesses meet the legal, ethical, economic, and voluntary responsibilities placed on them by their stakeholders

corporation a legal entity, whose assets and liabilities are separate from its owners'

cost of goods sold the amount of money a firm spent to buy or produce the products it sold during the period to which the income statement applies

countertrade agreements foreign trade agreements that involve bartering products for other products instead of for currency

credit cards means of access to preapproved lines of credit granted by a bank or finance company

credit controls the authority to establish and enforce credit rules for financial institutions and some private investors

credit union/caisse populaire a financial institution owned and controlled by its depositors, who usually have a common employer, profession, trade group, or religion

crisis management or contingency planning an element in planning that deals with potential disasters such as product tampering, oil spills, fires, earthquakes, computer viruses, or airplane crashes

Crown corporations corporations owned and operated by government (federal or provincial)

culture the integrated, accepted pattern of human behaviour, including thought, speech, beliefs, actions, and artifacts

current assets assets that are used or converted into cash within the course of a calendar year

current liabilities a firm's financial obligations to short-term creditors, which must be repaid within one year

current ratio current assets divided by current liabilities

customer departmentalization the arrangement of jobs around the needs of various types of customers

customization making products to meet a particular customer's needs or wants

debit card a card that looks like a credit card but works like a cheque; using it results in a direct, immediate, electronic payment from the cardholder's chequing account to a merchant or third party

debt to total assets ratio a ratio indicating how much of the firm is financed by debt and how much by owners' equity

debt utilization ratios ratios that measure how much debt an organization is using relative to other sources of capital, such as owners' equity

decentralized organization an organization in which decision-making authority is delegated as far down the chain of command as possible

delegation of authority giving employees not only tasks, but also the power to make commitments, use resources, and take whatever actions are necessary to carry out those tasks

demand the number of goods and services that consumers are willing to buy at different prices at a specific time

departmentalization the grouping of jobs into working units usually called departments, units, groups, or divisions

depreciation the process of spreading the costs of long-lived assets such as buildings and equipment over the total number of accounting periods in which they are expected to be used

depression a condition of the economy in which unemployment is very high, consumer spending is low, and business output is sharply reduced

desired reserves the percentage of deposits that banking institutions hold in reserve

development training that augments the skills and knowledge of managers and professionals

digital marketing uses all digital media, including the Internet and mobile and interactive channels, to develop communication and exchanges with customers

digital media electronic media that function using digital codes via computers, cellular phones, smartphones, and other digital devices that have been released in recent years

direct investment the ownership of overseas facilities

directing motivating and leading employees to achieve organizational objectives

discounts temporary price reductions, often employed to boost sales

diversity the participation of different ages, genders, races, ethnicities, nationalities, and abilities in the workplace

dividend yield the dividend per share divided by the stock price

dividends profits of a corporation that are distributed in the form of cash payments to shareholders

dividends per share the actual cash received for each share owned

double-entry bookkeeping a system of recording and classifying business transactions that maintains the balance of the accounting equation

downsizing the elimination of a significant number of employees from an organization

dumping the act of a country or business selling products at less than what it costs to produce them

e-business carrying out the goals of business through utilization of the Internet

earnings per share net income or profit divided by the number of stock shares outstanding

economic contraction a slowdown of the economy characterized by a decline in spending and during which businesses cut back on production and lay off workers

economic expansion the situation that occurs when an economy is growing and people are spending more money; their purchases stimulate the production of goods and services, which in turn stimulates employment

economic order quantity (EOQ) model a model that identifies the optimum number of items to order to minimize the costs of managing (ordering, storing, and using) them

economic system a description of how a particular society distributes its resources to produce goods and services

economics the study of how resources are distributed for the production of goods and services within a social system

electronic funds transfer (EFT) any movement of funds by means of an electronic terminal, telephone, computer, or magnetic tape

embargo a prohibition on trade in a particular product

entrepreneur an individual who risks his or her wealth, time, and effort to develop for profit an innovative product or way of doing something

entrepreneurship the process of creating and managing a business to achieve desired objectives

equilibrium price the price at which the number of products that businesses are willing to supply equals the amount of products that consumers are willing to buy at a specific point in time

equity theory an assumption that how much people are willing to contribute to an organization depends on their assessment of the fairness, or equity, of the rewards they will receive in exchange

esteem needs needs for respect—both self-respect and respect from others

ethical issue an identifiable problem, situation, or opportunity that requires a person to choose from among several actions that may be evaluated as right or wrong, ethical or unethical

eurodollar market a market for trading U.S. dollars in foreign countries

European Union (EU) community established in 1958 to promote trade within Europe; as of 2013, has 27 member countries

exchange the act of giving up one thing (money, credit, labour, goods) in return for something else (goods, services, or ideas)

exchange controls regulations that restrict the amount of currency that can be bought or sold

exchange rate the ratio at which one nation's currency can be exchanged for another nation's currency

exclusive distribution the awarding by a manufacturer to an intermediary of the sole right to sell a product in a defined geographic territory

expectancy theory the assumption that motivation depends not only on how much a person wants something but also on how likely he or she is to get it

expenses the costs incurred in the day-to-day operations of an organization

exporting the sale of goods and services to foreign markets

express warranty warranty that stipulates the specific terms a seller will honour

external shocks unanticipated events that occur in a firm's external environment that hurt the company's business

extrinsic reward a benefit and/or recognition received from someone else

factor a finance company to which businesses sell their accounts receivable—usually for a percentage of the total face value

finance the study of money; how it's made, how it's lost, and how it's managed

finance companies businesses that offer short-term loans at substantially higher rates of interest than banks

financial managers those who focus on obtaining needed funds for the successful operation of an organization and using those funds to further organizational goals

financial resources the funds used to acquire the natural and human resources needed to provide products; also called capital

first-line managers those who supervise both workers and the daily operations of an organization

fixed-position layout a layout that brings all resources required to create the product to a central location

flexible manufacturing the direction of machinery by computers to adapt to different versions of similar operations

flextime a program that allows employees to choose their starting and ending times, provided that they are at work during a specified core period

floating-rate bonds bonds with interest rates that change with current interest rates otherwise available in the economy

franchise a licence to sell another's products or to use another's name in business, or both

franchisee the purchaser of a franchise

franchiser the company that sells a franchise

franchising a form of licensing in which a company—the franchiser—agrees to provide a franchisee a name, logo, methods of operation, advertising, products, and other elements associated with a franchiser's business, in return for a financial commitment and the agreement to conduct business in accordance with the franchiser's standard of operations

fraud a purposeful unlawful act to deceive or manipulate in order to damage others

free-market system pure capitalism, in which all economic decisions are made without government intervention

functional departmentalization the grouping of jobs that perform similar functional activities, such as finance, manufacturing, marketing, and human resources

General Agreement on Tariffs and Trade (GATT) a trade agreement, originally signed by 23 nations in 1947, that provided a forum for tariff negotiations and a place where international trade problems could be discussed and resolved

general partnership a partnership that involves a complete sharing in both the management and the liability of the business

generic products products with no brand name that often come in simple packages and carry only their generic name

geographical departmentalization the grouping of jobs according to geographic location, such as state or province, region, country, or continent

global strategy (globalization) a strategy that involves standardizing products (and, as much as possible, their promotion and distribution) for the whole world, as if it were a single entity

grapevine an informal channel of communication, separate from management's formal, official communication channels

gross domestic product (GDP) the sum of all goods and services produced in a country during a year

gross income (or profit) revenues minus the cost of goods sold required to generate the revenues

group two or more individuals who communicate with one another, share a common identity, and have a common goal

human relations the study of the behaviour of individuals and groups in organizational settings

human relations skills the ability to deal with people, both inside and outside the organization

human resources the physical and mental abilities that people use to produce goods and services; also called labour

human resources management (HRM) all the activities involved in determining an organization's human resources needs, as well as acquiring, training, and compensating people to fill those needs

human resources managers those who handle the staffing function and deal with employees in a formalized manner

hygiene factors aspects of Herzberg's theory of motivation that focus on the work setting and not the content of the work; these aspects include adequate wages, comfortable and safe working conditions, fair company policies, and job security

identity theft when criminals obtain personal information that allows them to impersonate someone else in order to use their credit to access financial accounts and make purchases

implied warranty warranty that is imposed on the producer or seller by law

import tariff a tax levied by a nation on goods imported into the country

importing the purchase of goods and services from foreign sources

income statement a financial report that shows an organization's profitability over a period of time—month, quarter, or year

inflation a condition characterized by a continuing rise in prices

information technology (IT) managers those who are responsible for implementing, maintaining, and controlling technology applications in business, such as computer networks

infrastructure the physical facilities that support a country's economic activities, such as railroads, highways, ports, airfields, utilities and power plants, schools, hospitals, communication systems, and commercial distribution systems

initial public offering (IPO) selling a corporation's shares on public markets for the first time

inputs the resources—such as labour, money, materials, and energy—that are converted into outputs

insurance companies businesses that protect their clients against financial losses from certain specified risks (death, accident, and theft, for example)

integrated marketing communications coordinating the promotion mix elements and synchronizing promotion as a unified effort

intellectual property property, such as musical works, artwork, books, and computer software, that is generated by a person's creative activities

intensive distribution a form of market coverage whereby a product is made available in as many outlets as possible

interactivity allows customers to express their needs and wants directly to the firm in response to its communications

intermittent organizations organizations that deal with products of a lesser magnitude than do project organizations; their products are not necessarily unique but possess a significant number of differences

international business the buying, selling, and trading of goods and services across national boundaries

International Monetary Fund (IMF) organization established in 1947 to promote trade among member nations by eliminating trade barriers and fostering financial cooperation

intrapreneurs individuals in large firms who take responsibility for the development of innovations within the organizations

intrinsic reward the personal satisfaction and enjoyment felt from attaining a goal

inventory all raw materials, components, completed or partially completed products, and pieces of equipment a firm uses

inventory control the process of determining how many supplies and goods are needed and keeping track of quantities on hand, where each item is, and who is responsible for it

inventory turnover sales divided by total inventory

investment banking the sale of stocks and bonds for corporations

ISO 14000 a comprehensive set of environmental management standards determined by the ISO that help companies attain and measure improvements in their environmental performance

ISO 9000 a series of quality assurance standards designed by the International Organization for Standardization (ISO) to ensure consistent product quality under many conditions

job analysis the determination, through observation and study, of pertinent information about a job—including specific tasks and necessary abilities, knowledge, and skills

job description a formal, written explanation of a specific job, usually including job title, tasks, relationship with other jobs, physical and mental skills required, duties, responsibilities, and working conditions

job enlargement the addition of more tasks to a job instead of treating each task as separate

job enrichment the incorporation of motivational factors, such as opportunity for achievement, recognition, responsibility, and advancement, into a job

job promotion advancement to a higher-level position with increased authority, responsibility, and pay

job rotation movement of employees from one job to another in an effort to relieve the boredom often associated with job specialization

job sharing performance of one full-time job by two people on part-time hours

job specification a description of the qualifications necessary for a specific job, in terms of education, experience, and personal and physical characteristics

joint venture a partnership established for a specific project or for a limited time involving the sharing of the costs and operation of a business, often between a foreign company and a local partner

journal a time-ordered list of account transactions

junk bonds a special type of high interest–rate bond that carries higher inherent risks

just-in-time (JIT) inventory management a technique using smaller quantities of materials that arrive "just in time" for use in the transformation process and therefore require less storage space and other inventory management expense

labelling the presentation of important information on a package

labour contract the formal, written document that spells out the relationship between the union and management for a specified period of time—usually two or three years

labour unions employee organizations formed to deal with employers for achieving better pay, hours, and working conditions

leadership the ability to influence employees to work toward organizational goals

learning changes in a person's behaviour based on information and experience

ledger a book or computer file with separate sections for each account

leveraged buyout (LBO) a purchase in which a group of investors borrows money from banks and other institutions to acquire a company (or a division of one), using the assets of the purchased company to guarantee repayment of the loan

liabilities debts that a firm owes to others

licensing a trade agreement in which one company—the licensor—allows another company—the licensee—to use its company name, products, patents, brands, trademarks, raw materials, and/or production processes in exchange for a fee or royalty

limited liability partnership (LLP) a partnership agreement where partners are not responsible for losses created by other partners

limited partnership a business organization that has at least one general partner, who assumes unlimited liability, and at least one limited partner, whose liability is limited to his or her investment in the business

line of credit an arrangement by which a bank agrees to lend a specified amount of money to an organization upon request

line structure the simplest organizational structure in which direct lines of authority extend from the top manager to the lowest level of the organization

line-and-staff structure a structure having a traditional line relationship between superiors and subordinates and also specialized managers—called staff managers—who are available to assist line managers

liquidity ratios ratios that measure the speed with which a company can turn its assets into cash to meet short-term debt

lockbox an address, usually a commercial bank, at which a company receives payments in order to speed collections from customers

lockout management's version of a strike, wherein a worksite is closed so that employees cannot go to work

long-term (fixed) assets production facilities (plants), offices, and equipment—all of which are expected to last for many years

long-term liabilities debts that will be repaid over a number of years, such as long-term loans and bond issues

management a process designed to achieve an organization's objectives by using its resources effectively and efficiently in a changing environment

managerial accounting the internal use of accounting statements by managers in planning and directing the organization's activities

managers those individuals in organizations who make decisions about the use of resources and who are concerned with planning, organizing, staffing, directing, and controlling the organization's activities to reach its objectives

manufacturer brands brands initiated and owned by the manufacturer to identify products from the point of production to the point of purchase

manufacturing the activities and processes used in making tangible products; also called production

market a group of people who have a need, purchasing power, and the desire and authority to spend money on goods, services, and ideas

market segment a collection of individuals, groups, or organizations who share one or more characteristics and thus have relatively similar product needs and desires

market segmentation a strategy whereby a firm divides the total market into groups of people who have relatively similar product needs

marketable securities temporary investment of "extra" cash by organizations for up to one year in Treasury bills, certificates of deposit, commercial paper, or eurodollar loans

marketing a group of activities designed to expedite transactions by creating, distributing, pricing, and promoting goods, services, and ideas

marketing channel a group of organizations that moves products from their producer to customers; also called a channel of distribution

marketing concept the idea that an organization should try to satisfy customers' needs through coordinated activities that also allow it to achieve its own goals

marketing managers those who are responsible for planning, pricing, and promoting products and making them available to customers

marketing mix the four marketing activities—product, price, promotion, and distribution—that the firm can control to achieve specific goals within a dynamic marketing environment

marketing orientation an approach requiring organizations to gather information about customer needs, share that information throughout the firm, and use that information to help build long-term relationships with customers

marketing research a systematic, objective process of getting information about potential customers to guide marketing decisions

marketing strategy a plan of action for developing, pricing, distributing, and promoting products that meet the needs of specific customers

Maslow's hierarchy a theory that arranges the five basic needs of people—physiological, security, social, esteem, and self-actualization—into the order in which people strive to satisfy them

material-requirements planning (MRP) a planning system that schedules the precise quantity of materials needed to make the product

materials handling the physical handling and movement of products in warehousing and transportation

matrix structure a structure that sets up teams from different departments, thereby creating two or more intersecting lines of authority; also called a project-management structure

mediation a method of outside resolution of labour and management differences in which the third party's role is to suggest or propose a solution to the problem

merger the combination of two companies (usually corporations) to form a new company

middle managers those members of an organization responsible for the tactical planning that implements the general guidelines established by top management

mission the statement of an organization's fundamental purpose and basic philosophy

mixed economies economies made up of elements from more than one economic system

mobile marketing using a mobile device to communicate marketing messages

modular design the creation of an item in self-contained units, or modules, that can be combined or interchanged to create different products

monetary policy means by which the Bank of Canada controls the amount of money available in the economy

money anything generally accepted in exchange for goods and services

money market accounts accounts that offer higher interest rates than standard bank rates but with greater restrictions

monopolistic competition the market structure that exists when there are fewer businesses than in a pure-competition environment and the differences among the goods they sell are small

monopoly the market structure that exists when there is only one business providing a product in a given market

morale an employee's attitude toward his or her job, employer, and colleagues

motivation an inner drive that directs a person's behaviour toward goals

motivational factors aspects of Herzberg's theory of motivation that relate to the content of the work itself, include achievement, recognition, involvement, responsibility, and advancement

multi-segment approach a market segmentation approach whereby the marketer aims its efforts at two or more segments, developing a marketing strategy for each

multidivisional structure a structure that organizes departments into larger groups called divisions

multinational corporation (MNC) a corporation that operates on a worldwide scale, without significant ties to any one nation or region

multinational strategy a plan, used by international companies, that involves customizing products, promotion, and distribution according to cultural, technological, regional, and national differences

mutual fund an investment company that pools individual investor dollars and invests them in large numbers of well-diversified securities

natural resources land, forests, minerals, water, and other things that are not made by people

net income (or net earnings) the total profit (or loss) after all expenses including taxes have been deducted from revenue

networking the building of relationships and sharing of information with colleagues who can help managers achieve the items on their agendas

non-profit corporations corporations that focus on providing a service rather than earning a profit but are not owned by a government entity

non-profit organizations organizations that may provide goods or services but do not have the fundamental purpose of earning profits

North American Free Trade Agreement (NAFTA) agreement that eliminates most tariffs and trade restrictions on agricultural and manufactured products to encourage trade among Canada, the United States, and Mexico

offshoring the relocation of business processes by a company or subsidiary to another country; it differs from outsourcing because the company retains control of the offshored processes

oligopoly the market structure that exists when there are very few businesses selling a product

online fraud any attempt to conduct fraudulent activities online

open market operations decisions to buy or sell Treasury bills (short-term debt issued by the government) and other investments in the open market

operational plans very short-term plans that specify what actions individuals, work groups, or departments need to accomplish in order to achieve the tactical plan and ultimately the strategic plan

operations the activities and processes used in making both tangible and intangible products

operations management (OM) the development and administration of the activities involved in transforming resources into goods and services

organizational charts visual displays of the organizational structure, lines of authority (chain of command), staff relationships, permanent committee arrangements, and lines of communication

organizational culture a firm's shared values, beliefs, traditions, philosophies, rules, and role models for behaviour

organizational layers the levels of management in an organization.

organizing the structuring of resources and activities to accomplish objectives in an efficient and effective manner

orientation familiarizing newly hired employees with fellow workers, company procedures, and the physical properties of the company

outputs the goods, services, and ideas that result from the conversion of inputs

outsourcing the transferring of manufacturing or other tasks—such as data processing—to countries where labour and supplies are less expensive

over-the-counter (OTC) market a network of dealers all over the country linked by computers, telephones, and Teletype machines

owners' equity equals assets minus liabilities and reflects historical values

packaging the external container that holds and describes the product

partnership a form of business organization defined as an association of two or more persons who carry on as co-owners of a business for profit

partnership agreement document that sets forth the basic agreement between partners

penetration price a low price designed to help a product enter the market and gain market share rapidly

pension funds managed investment pools set aside by individuals, corporations, unions, and some non-profit organizations to provide retirement income for members

per share data data used by investors to compare the performance of one company with another on an equal, per share basis

perception the process by which a person selects, organizes, and interprets information received from his or her senses

personal property property that consists of basically everything else; can be subdivided into tangible and intangible property

personal selling direct, two-way communication with buyers and potential buyers

personality the organization of an individual's distinguishing character traits, attitudes, or habits

physical distribution all the activities necessary to move products from producers to customers—inventory control, transportation, warehousing, and materials handling

physiological needs the most basic human needs to be satisfied—water, food, shelter, and clothing

picketing a public protest against management practices that involves union members marching and carrying anti-management signs at the employer's plant

place/distribution making products available to customers in the quantities desired

plagiarism the act of taking someone else's work and presenting it as your own without mentioning the source

planning the process of determining the organization's objectives and deciding how to accomplish them; the first function of management

podcast an audio or video file that can be downloaded from the Internet with a subscription and automatically deliver new content to listening devices or personal computers

preferred shares a special type of share whose owners, though not generally having a say in running the company, have a claim to profits before other shareholders do

price a value placed on an object exchanged between a buyer and a seller

price skimming charging the highest possible price that buyers who want the product will pay

primary data marketing information that is observed, recorded, or collected directly from respondents

primary market the market where firms raise financial capital

prime rate the interest rate that commercial banks charge their best customers (usually large corporations) for short-term loans

principal in an agency relationship, the one who wishes to have a specific task accomplished

private corporation a corporation owned by just one or a few people who are closely involved in managing the business

private distributor brands brands, which may cost less than manufacturer brands, that are owned and controlled by a wholesaler or retailer

process layout a layout that organizes the transformation process into departments that group related processes

product departmentalization the organization of jobs in relation to the products of the firm

product layout a layout requiring that production be broken down into relatively simple tasks assigned to workers, who are usually positioned along an assembly line

product liability a business's legal responsibility for any negligence in the design, production, sale, and consumption of products

product line a group of closely related products that are treated as a unit because of similar marketing strategy, production, or end-use considerations

product mix all the products offered by an organization

product-development teams a specific type of project team formed to devise, design, and implement a new product

production the activities and processes used in making tangible products; also called manufacturing

production and operations managers those who develop and administer the activities involved in transforming resources into goods, services, and ideas ready for the marketplace

products goods or services with tangible and intangible characteristics that provide satisfaction and benefits

profit the difference between what it costs to make and sell a product and what a customer pays for it

profit margin net income divided by sales

profit sharing a form of compensation whereby a percentage of company profits is distributed to the employees whose work helped to generate them

profitability ratios ratios that measure the amount of operating income or net income an organization is able to generate relative to its assets, owners' equity, and sales

project organization a company using a fixed-position layout because it is typically involved in large, complex projects such as construction or exploration

project teams groups similar to task forces that normally run their operation and have total control of a specific work project

promotion a persuasive form of communication that attempts to expedite a marketing exchange by influencing individuals, groups, and organizations to accept goods, services, and ideas

promotional positioning the use of promotion to create and maintain an image of a product in buyers' minds

psychological pricing encouraging purchases based on emotional rather than rational responses to the price

public corporation a corporation whose shares anyone may buy, sell, or trade

publicity non-personal communication transmitted through the mass media but not paid for directly by the firm

pull strategy the use of promotion to create consumer demand for a product so that consumers exert pressure on marketing channel members to make it available

purchasing the buying of all the materials needed by the organization; also called procurement

pure competition the market structure that exists when there are many small businesses selling one standardized product

push strategy an attempt to motivate intermediaries to push the product down to their customers

quality the degree to which a good, service, or idea meets the demands and requirements of customers

quality control the processes an organization uses to maintain its established quality standards

quality-assurance teams (or quality circles) small groups of workers brought together from throughout the organization to solve specific quality, productivity, or service problems

quick ratio (acid test) a stringent measure of liquidity that eliminates inventory

quota a restriction on the number of units of a particular product that can be imported into a country

ratio analysis calculations that measure an organization's financial health

real property property consisting of real estate and everything permanently attached to it

receivables turnover sales divided by accounts receivable

recession a decline in production, employment, and income

recruiting forming a pool of qualified applicants from which management can select employees

reference groups groups with whom buyers identify and whose values or attitudes they adopt

responsibility the obligation, placed on employees through delegation, to perform assigned tasks satisfactorily and be held accountable for the proper execution of work

retailers intermediaries who buy products from manufacturers (or other intermediaries) and sell them to consumers for home and household use rather than for resale or for use in producing other products

retained earnings earnings after expenses and taxes that are reinvested in the assets of the firm and belong to the owners in the form of equity

return on assets net income divided by assets

return on equity net income divided by owners' equity; also called return on investment (ROI)

revenue the total amount of money received from the sale of goods or services, as well as from related business activities

routing the sequence of operations through which the product must pass

salary a financial reward calculated on a weekly, monthly, or annual basis

sales promotion direct inducements offering added value or some other incentive for buyers to enter into an exchange

savings accounts accounts with funds that usually cannot be withdrawn without advance notice; also known as time deposits

scheduling the assignment of required tasks to departments or even specific machines, workers, or teams

secondary data information that is compiled inside or outside an organization for some purpose other than changing the current situation

secondary markets stock exchanges and over-the-counter markets where investors can trade their securities with others

secured bonds bonds that are backed by specific collateral that must be forfeited in the event that the issuing firm defaults

secured loans loans backed by collateral that the bank can claim if the borrowers do not repay them

securities markets the mechanism for buying and selling securities

security needs needs to protect oneself from physical and economic harm

selection the process of collecting information about applicants and using that information to make hiring decisions

selective distribution a form of market coverage whereby only a small number of all available outlets are used to expose products

self-actualization needs needs to be the best one can be; at the top of Maslow's hierarchy

self-directed work team (SDWT) a group of employees responsible for an entire work process or segment that delivers a product to an internal or external customer

separations employment changes involving resignation, retirement, termination, or layoff

serial bonds a sequence of small bond issues of progressively longer maturity

shares shares of a corporation that may be bought or sold

small business any independently owned and operated business that is not dominant in its competitive area and does not employ more than 500 people

social classes a ranking of people into higher or lower positions of respect

social needs needs for love, companionship, and friendship—the desire for acceptance by others

social network a Web-based meeting place for friends, family, coworkers, and peers that lets users create a profile and connect with other users for a wide range of purposes

social responsibility a business's obligation to maximize its positive impact and minimize its negative impact on society

social roles a set of expectations for individuals based on some position they occupy

socialism an economic system in which the government owns and operates basic industries but individuals own most businesses

sole proprietorships businesses owned and operated by one individual; the most common form of business organization in Canada

span of management the number of subordinates who report to a particular manager

specialization the division of labour into small, specific tasks and the assignment of employees to do a single task

staffing the hiring of people to carry out the work of the organization

stakeholders groups that have a stake in the success and outcomes of a business

standardization the making of identical interchangeable components or products

statement of cash flows explains how the company's cash changed from the beginning of the accounting period to the end

statistical process control a system in which management collects and analyzes information about the production process to pinpoint quality problems in the production system

strategic alliance a partnership formed to create competitive advantage on a worldwide basis

strategic plans those plans that establish the long-range objectives and overall strategy or course of action by which a firm fulfills its mission

strikebreakers people hired by management to replace striking employees; called "scabs" by striking union members

strikes employee walkouts; one of the most effective weapons labour has

structure the arrangement or relationship of positions within an organization

supply the number of products—goods and services—that businesses are willing to sell at different prices at a specific time

supply chain management connecting and integrating all parties or members of the distribution system in order to satisfy customers

tactical plans short-range plans designed to implement the activities and objectives specified in the strategic plan

target market a specific group of consumers on whose needs and wants a company focuses its marketing efforts

task force a temporary group of employees responsible for bringing about a particular change

team a small group whose members have complementary skills; have a common purpose, goal, and approach; and hold themselves mutually accountable

technical expertise the specialized knowledge and training needed to perform jobs that are related to particular areas of management

test marketing a trial mini-launch of a product in limited areas that represent the potential market

Theory X McGregor's traditional view of management whereby it is assumed that workers generally dislike work and must be forced to do their jobs

Theory Y McGregor's humanistic view of management whereby it is assumed that workers like to work and that under proper conditions employees will seek out responsibility in an attempt to satisfy their social, esteem, and self-actualization needs

Theory Z a management philosophy that stresses employee participation in all aspects of company decision making

times interest earned ratio operating income divided by interest expense

top managers the president and other top executives of a business, such as the chief executive officer (CEO), chief financial officer (CFO), chief operations officer (COO), and, more recently, chief privacy officer (CPO), who have overall responsibility for the organization

tort a noncriminal act other than breach of contract

total asset turnover sales divided by total assets

total quality management (TQM) a philosophy that uniform commitment to quality in all areas of an organization will promote a culture that meets customers' perceptions of quality

total-market approach an approach whereby a firm tries to appeal to everyone and assumes that all buyers have similar needs

trade credit credit extended by suppliers for the purchase of their goods and services

trade deficit a nation's negative balance of trade, which exists when that country imports more products than it exports

trademark a brand that is registered with the Canadian Intellectual Property Office and is thus legally protected from use by any other firm

trading company a firm that buys goods in one country and sells them to buyers in another country

training teaching employees to do specific job tasks through either classroom development or on-the-job experience

transaction balances cash kept on hand by a firm to pay normal daily expenses, such as employee wages and bills for supplies and utilities

transfer a move to another job within the company at essentially the same level and wage

transportation the shipment of products to buyers

Treasury bills (T-bills) short-term debt obligations the Canadian government sells to raise money

trust companies corporations that act as a trustee and usually also provide banking services

turnover occurs when employees quit, or are fired, promoted, or transferred, and must be replaced by new employees

undercapitalization the lack of funds to operate a business normally

unemployment the condition in which a percentage of the population wants to work but is unable to find jobs

unsecured bonds debentures, or bonds that are not backed by specific collateral

unsecured loans loans backed only by the borrowers' good reputation and previous credit rating

venture capitalists persons or organizations that agree to provide some funds for a new business in exchange for an ownership interest or stock

viral marketing a marketing tool that uses the Internet, particularly social networking and video-sharing sites, to spread a message and create brand awareness

wage/salary survey a study that tells a company how much compensation comparable firms are paying for specific jobs that the firms have in common

wages financial rewards based on the number of hours the employee works or the level of output achieved

warehousing the design and operation of facilities to receive, store, and ship products

whistleblowing the act of an employee exposing an employer's wrongdoing to outsiders, such as the media or government regulatory agencies

wholesalers intermediaries who buy from producers or from other wholesalers and sell to retailers

wiki software that creates an interface that enables users to add or edit the content of some types of websites

working capital management the managing of short-term assets and liabilities

World Bank an organization established by the industrialized nations in 1946 to loan money to underdeveloped and developing countries; formally known as the International Bank for Reconstruction and Development

World Trade Organization (WTO) international organization dealing with the rules of trade between nations

INDEX

A

Aaron's, 27, 335
Abbas, Hamid, 124
Abbott, Jason, 268
absolute advantage, 60
abusive behaviour, 33–34.
    See also bullying
academic dishonesty, 38
accessibility, 317
accessory equipment, 284
accountability, 172
Accountability Act, 29
accountant, 344, 366
accounting
    accountant, 344
    accounting cycle, 348–349
    accounting information uses,
        345–347
    audited accounting information, 347
    bookkeeping vs., 345
    defined, 344–347
    equivalent terms in, 351
    financial statements, 347, 349–359
    industry analysis, 363
    integrity, importance of, 363–364
    nature of, 344
    process, 347–349
    ratio analysis, 359–363
    sustainability and, 346
accounting cycle, 348–349
accounting equation, 348, 349, 354
accounting firms, 344
accounting information
    external uses, 346–347
    internal uses, 345–346
accounting information uses
    annual report, 346–347
    budget, 346
    cash flow, 345
    equivalent terms in, 351
    external uses, 346–347
    internal uses, 345–346
    managerial accounting, 345
accounting process
    accounting cycle, 348–349
    accounting equation, 347–348
    double-entry bookkeeping, 348
Accounting Standards Board
    (AcSB), 344
accounting standards for not-
    for-profit organizations
    (ASNPO), 344

accounting standards for private
    enterprises (ASPE), 344
accounts payable, 357, 391
accounts receivable, 357, 390
accrued expenses, 357
ACNielsen, 282, 283
acquisition, 101, 107
Acres International, 34
Across Asia on the Cheap, 193
Action Plagiarius, 63
ad valorem tariff, 64
addressability, 317
Adecco Employment Services
    Limited, 147
administrative managers, 152–153
Adolph Coors Inc., 94
Advanced Micro Devices (AMD),
    36–37
advertainments, 302
advertising, 297–298
advertising campaign, 298
Advil, 12
agenda, 159
Agriculture Canada, 99
AIG, 212
Air Canada, 12, 40, 266, 292, 308
Airbus, 53
Alcan, 107
Alcoa, 49
Alien Workshop, 133
allowance for bad debts, 357
Ally, 102
Alsbridge, 200
Amazon, 12, 60, 111, 178, 279,
    288, 293, 318
AMC Theaters, 301
American Express, 373
American Institute of CPAs
    (AICPA), 346
American Psychological
    Association, 229
American Solar Energy Society, 55
analytical skills, 156
Anders, George, 251
angel investors, 127, 128–129
Angel Network, 59
Angel One Investor Network, 127
Ann Taylor, 277
annual report, 346
Anthem Media Group, 262
anti-tobacco legislation, 39
Apple, 12, 16, 21, 37, 117, 194, 205, 258,
    280–281, 286, 288, 395

application, 233–234
applications (apps), 302–303
April Fool's Day, 324
arbitration, 246
Arthur Andersen, 26
Articles of Incorporation, 92
Aryzta AG, 91
ASEAN Economic Community
    (AEC), 71
Asia-Pacific Economic Cooperation
    (APEC), 70–71
Ask O'Leary, 109
Asper, Izzy, 187
Asper, Leonard, 262–263
asset utilization ratios, 360–361
assets
    accounts receivable, 357
    balance sheet, 357
    current assets, 357
    defined, 347
Association of Certified Fraud
    Examiners, 345
Association of Southeast Asian
    Nations (ASEAN), 71
Astral Media, 102
Athlon Energy, 101
Atlantic Canada Opportunities
    Agency, 297
Atlantic Tours, 133
Atlas Cold Storage, 26
Atomic Tea, 88, 128–129
attest, 349
attitude, buying behaviour, 270
audited accounting information, 347
Auerbach, David, 68
Australia, 9
Australis Aquaculture, 145
autocratic leaders, 153
AutoDesk, 229
automated banking machine
    (ABM), 380–381
avatar, 330
Aventis, 103
average, 401

B

Baby boomers
    legal issues, 236
    market segment, 263, 266
Backpage, 302
bad-debt adjustment, 357
bad moods and productivity, 226

M

MacDonald, Colin, 119
MacDonald, Kenzie, 117
MacDonald, Rebecca, 122, 303
MacInnes, John, 258
MacLean, Alex, 16
MacLean, Lauchie, 287
Magee, Christine, 113, 114
Magna International, 82, 93, 95, 97, 150
Maguire, Chris, 320
major equipment, 284
Malcolm Baldrige National Quality Award, 202
Mallette, 344
management
  activities, 159
  agenda, 159
  analytical skills, 156
  business plan, 162
  conceptual skills, 155
  controlling, 142, 148
  decision making, 157–159
  defined, 142
  directing, 142, 147
  functions, 142, 150
  hiring, 156–157
  human relations skills, 156
  leadership, 153–154
  nature of, 142
  networking, 159
  organizing, 142, 146
  overview, 5
  planning, 142–146
  roles, 153
  skills, 153–156
  small business, 119
  staffing, 142, 146–147
  styles, 219–220
  tactic, 245–246
  technical expertise, 154–155
  training, 157
  types of management. See management types
management styles
  comparison, 220
  employee involvement, 221
  participative management, 220–221
  quality circles, 220
  self-directed work teams, 221
  Theory X/Theory Y, 219
  Theory Z, 219–220
management tactics, 245–246
management types
  administrative managers, 152–153

financial managers, 151
first-line managers, 149, 151
human resources managers, 152
IT managers, 152
levels, 149
management functions, importance of, 150
marketing managers, 152
middle managers, 149, 151
production and operations managers, 151–152
top managers, 148–150
managerial accounting, 345–346
managers, 142, 162. See also management
Mandelbaum, Les, 268, 280
Mandelstam, David, 301
manufacturer brands, 288
manufacturing, 117, 188
manufacturing business, 188, 189–192
manufacturing economy, 15
Manulife Financial Corp., 91, 97, 150, 402
Maple Leaf Foods, 17, 37, 89
maquiladoras, 69
Maritime Travel, 242
market, 260
market segment, 261
market segmentation
  bases for, 263–264
  concentration approach, 261
  defined, 261
  multi-segment approach, 261
  niche marketing, 262
  requirements, 262–263
market value, 398
marketable securities, 388
marketing
  buying behaviour, 270–272
  careers, 276
  channel, 292–295
  concept, 256–258
  defined, 254
  digital media, impact of, 338
  environment, 272–274
  exchange relationship, 255
  functions of, 255–256
  mixed. See marketing mix
  nature of, 254–259
  orientation, 258–259
  overview, 6
  research, 256, 267–269
  social media, 259
  strategy, 260–264
marketing channel
  business product, 295

consumer products, 294–295
defined, 292
general merchandise retailers, 293
Internet retailers, 293
retailers, 292–293, 294
supply chain management, 294
wholesalers, 293, 294
marketing concept. See also marketing
  buying behaviour, 270–272
  communication, 257–258
  customer relationship, 256
  customer satisfaction, 256
  defined, 256
  evolution, 258–259
  implementation, 257
  marketing orientation, 259
  production orientation, 258
  productivity, 256–257
  sales orientation, 258–259
  social media, 259
marketing economy, 15
marketing environment
  changes in forces, 273–274
  competitive and economic forces, 273
  marketing mix, 264, 274
  political, legal, and regulatory forces, 273
  social forces, 273
  technological forces, 273
marketing functions, 255–256
marketing information system (MIS), 269
marketing managers, 152, 310–311
marketing mix
  defined, 264
  digital marketing, 319–322
  distribution, 266–267. See also distribution
  marketing environment, 264, 274
  marketing strategy, 280
  place/distribution, 266–267. See also place/distribution
  price, 265–266. See also price
  product, 264–265. See also product
  promotion, 267. See also promotion
  social media, 321–322
marketing orientation, 259
marketing research, 256
  buying behaviour, 270–272
  defined, 267
  marketing information system (MIS), 269
  mystery shoppers, 268
  primary data, 268
  secondary data, 268

mutual fund, 379
Mycoskie, Blake, 166
Myers-Briggs Type Indicator, 234, 235
MySpace, 324, 327, 330
mystery shoppers, 268

N

NASDAQ, 400–401
National Angel Capital Corporation, 127
National Business Ethics Survey (NBES), 31, 37, 42, 341
National Post, 26, 111
natural resources, 7
Naturalab, 39
near money, 373
NearlyNewlywed.com, 277
Nepal earthquake, 5
Nestlé, 46, 76
net income, 353
Netflix, 99, 320
networking, 159
Neville, Chris, 82, 121, 302
Neville, Sean, 268
new digital economy, 15
new idea screening, 281–282
new issue, 399
New York Stock Exchange (NYSE), 400
The New York Times, 23
Nexen Inc., 44, 107
Ng, Cheryl, 116
Ngo, Minh, 258
niche marketing, 262
Nichol, Dave, 288
Nielsen Marketing Research, 319
Nike, 63, 213, 260
Niko Resources, 34
Nixon, Gord, 302
Nokia, 223
non-bank liabilities, 393
non-banking institutions
    brokerage firms, 379–380
    diversified firms, 378
    finance companies, 380
    future, 381–382
    insurance companies, 378
    mutual funds, 379
    pension funds, 378
non-profit corporations, 94–95
non-profit organizations, 4
non-traditional marketing, 253, 267
Nooyi, Indira, 6, 175
Nortel Networks, 25, 26, 52, 281
North American Free Trade Agreement (NAFTA), 69

North American management style, 220
North West Trading Company, 15
Notable.com, 124, 126
Notice of Directors, 92
Notice of Officers, 92
Novartis, 103
NS Power, 10
Nucleus Research, 341
Nulogy, 220
Nurse Next Door, 130, 133, 266

O

Obama, Barack, 24
objective assessment, 238
objectives, 143
Occupy Movement, 27, 109
Odebrecht, 75
offshoring, 75
Old Port of Montreal, 29
Old Spice, 326
O'Leary, Kevin, 95, 109–110, 128–129
O'Leary Fine Wines, 110
O'Leary Funds, 110
O'Leary Mortgages, 110
oligopoly, 12
Olympics, 29
OnceWed.com, 277
1-800-GOT-JUNK?, 82, 111
Onex Corporation, 93, 103, 111, 127, 150, 187, 214
online banking, 381
online classified advertising, 302
online fraud, 336–337
online games, 302
online marketing, 298–302
Ontario Public Service, 218
Ontario Safe Drinking Water Act, 49
on-the-job training, 237
open market operations, 374–375
operational plans, 146
operations, 188. *See also* operations management (OM)
operations and production managers, 151–152
operations management (OM). *See also* operations system design
    careers, 208
    communication, 178–180
    defined, 188
    designing operations systems, 192–197
    inputs/outputs, 188–189
    integrating with supply chain management, 205

manufacturing vs., 188
nature of, 188–189
operations, 188
planning operations systems, 192–197
process of, 188–189
production vs., 188
quality, 201–205
service businesses, 189–192
supply chain, 197–201
tangibility, 188
transformation process, 188–189
operations system design. *See also* operations management (OM)
    capacity, 194
    capacity planning, 194
    customization, 193–194
    facilities, 194–196
    modular design, 193
    process design, 192–194
    product, 192
    product planning, 192
    standardization, 192–193
    sustainability, 196–197
opportunity identification and assessment, 123–124
Orca Houseboats, 193
Oreck Canada, 298
organic food, 31
Organic Trade Association, 285
Organization of Petroleum Exporting Countries (OPEC), 66
organizational charts, 168, 171
organizational culture, 166–167. *See also* ethical issues
organizational layers, 174
organizational tasks
    customer departmentalization, 171
    functional departmentalization, 170
    geographical departmentalization, 170–171
    product departmentalization, 170
    specialization, 169
organizations
    communication, 178–181
    culture, 166–167
    group/team roles, 176–178
    responsibilities, 171–174
    structure, 167–168, 174–176
    tasks, 168–171
organizing, 146
orientation, 236–237
Orkut, 317, 322
Orville Redenbacher, 332
Ouchi, William, 219
Outpost magazine, 129

KERENSA CLARKE.